A LIFE FOR DEER

A LIFE FOR DEER

A DEER VET TELLS
HIS STORY AND THEIRS

John Fletcher

with vignettes by Maggy Lenert

VICTOR GOLLANCZ
in association with
PETER CRAWLEY

Copyright © John Fletcher 2000

First published in Great Britain 2000
by Victor Gollancz
in association with Peter Crawley
An imprint of Orion Books Ltd,
Orion House, 5 Upper St Martin's Lane,
London WC2H 9EA

A CIP catalogue record for this book is
available from the British Library

ISBN 0 575 07090 0

Typeset by Selwood Systems, Midsomer Norton

Printed and bound in Great Britain by
Butler & Tanner Ltd, Frome and London

CONTENTS

ILLUSTRATIONS

(Unless otherwise noted, all photographs are by the author)

1a   Summer, and stags in full velvet box
1b   Aristotle in the laundry at Kilmory (Fiona Guinness)
2a   The dead stag on Rannoch Moor that started it all
2b   Warble fly larvae in the partially skinned carcass
2c   Fiona Guinness filming on Rum
3a   The wild hind, Crottal, by the Mathieson family grave, Kilmory, Isle of Rum
3b   Scott, the hummel from Mar Lodge, wallows
3c   Friction and Manfred fight for hinds
4   Reediehill in 1974 (top) and 1999
5   The antler cycle
6a   A boatload of sleeping deer
6b   Sandy and her twins Bonnie and Clyde immediately after the birth
7a   Nickie feeding a stag at Reediehill
7b   Antlers for sale in a Chinese medicine shop, Hong Kong
8a   The author pours a bucket of water over Ferox at the Royal Show
8b   A red deer stag is helicoptered out of the New Zealand bush (Rex Forrester)
8c   A herd of deer is driven along a public road in New Zealand, confounding the experts (Peter Fraser)

Propose to any Englishman any principle ... however admirable, and you will observe that the whole effort of the English mind is directed to find a difficulty, a defect, or an impossibility in it. If you speak to him of a machine for peeling a potato, he will pronounce it impossible. If you peel a potato with it before his eyes, he will declare it useless, because it will not slice a pineapple.

Charles Babbage (1792–1871)
often credited with the invention of the computer

To Nickie

INTRODUCTION

Beneath our clothes we are all hunter-gatherers. The species to which we belong, *Homo sapiens*, with brains and bodies almost identical to our own, evolved in Africa about 130,000 years ago. Thus during some five thousand generations as *Homo sapiens*, to say nothing of the three hundred thousand generations before that, our bodies became exquisitely adapted to eating and metabolising a diet of wild food: plants provided fruits, berries and nuts as well as roots, but animal protein, often fish, was also crucial.

Then, about ten thousand years ago, humans in several parts of the world began to cultivate certain plants and animals. The animals provided dung for the plants as well as a means of drawing ploughs and carts, and with careful selection they came to yield more and more milk and wool as well as a valuable carcase. From the huge array of animals available only a very few were selected; so that today, for example, of the hundred or so grazing species worldwide, only sheep, goats, cows and pigs are domesticated as food animals on any scale. In ten millennia there have been virtually no additions to that short list of domesticants, although each of the species domesticated has changed significantly.

One of the most remarkable changes has been the development of fatter and fatter carcases. Our grandparents wanted fat to sustain their physically demanding lifestyle as well as to help them keep warm. But in particular they needed tallow, to provide candles with which they could penetrate the darkness and shorten the long nights. Now, of course, we have electricity. Despite strenuous efforts to breed leaner carcases we find that existing domestic animals have a carcase composition which is damaging our health. Our bodies over those many thousands of generations evolved to cope well with game meat, but cannot yet perfectly metabolise the products of domesticated animals, to which we have only been exposed in volume for ten or twelve generations. The answer seemed clear to me when I started to work with deer thirty years ago, but I had underestimated the modern tabus that were to face us.

During the mediaeval period there are thought to have been nearly two thousand deer parks in England and Wales. Those parks were for meat production. Venison was a vital commodity for those who could afford meat, and until the industrial revolution deer were evidently an important part of our life in Europe. Not surprisingly there is a wealth of myth ascribing strange attributes to deer. They even appear in the symbolic pavement in Westminster Abbey on which British monarchs are anointed.

Almost universally, as human populations grow and before rural depopulation intervenes, game animals become threatened. Deer were close to extinction in many parts of Britain in the eighteenth and nineteenth centuries. It was this that deflected the attention of the stag hunts to the inedible fox.

Now, however, the numbers of deer are increasing dramatically throughout the developed world. Britain has over one million, more than at any time since at least Roman times. We cannot ignore them. In many areas they prevent the regeneration of woodland; in England they have destroyed habitats vital for nightingales and orchids, in Sweden they are the major cause of motor accidents, and, fairly or otherwise, they are incriminated in the spread of Lyme disease. The perception of deer as rare and precious creatures to be glimpsed at dawn and dusk is, sadly, under threat.

Yet deer are deservedly objects of wonder: their antlers, for example, can grow two or three centimetres in a day to hold the record as the fastest-growing mammalian tissue, and the spectacular way in which the antlers are annually renewed could hold the key to our understanding of wound healing and regeneration. We need to know more about these animals that are becoming so numerous. This book is an effort to encourage a realisation of the growing part that deer will play in industrialised and urbanised societies and the potential value of that role.

ACKNOWLEDGEMENTS

In carrying out the work that is the basis for this story I have accumulated many debts of gratitude and I welcome the opportunity to acknowledge some of these.

First of all I wish to thank my mother and my late father who always encouraged me to write, and especially my mother who has endlessly but invaluably badgered me to finish the job.

I am writing in a small cottage above Elgol on Skye, and as I do so I can see through the window the Isle of Rum floating in the mist. This is very fitting because it was on that island that my story really began. I was very privileged to work there with Roger Short, Fiona Guinness, Gerald Lincoln and Tim Clutton-Brock who each in their own way inspired me. So, a few years later, did the late Sir Kenneth Blaxter who never failed to provide encouragement.

After that came the farm at Auchtermuchty, to which enterprise a great many have contributed help over the years. In particular Alfie Barnard, the son and husband of vets, arrived early on and shared our ups and downs before ill health forced him to leave us. The young Richard Pirie was a committed and enthusiastic colleague who, had he lived, would still have been with us at Reediehill. Heather and Magnus Doull have been great friends for many years, and now Magnus, with patient common sense, trims my most extravagant flights of fancy while helping me to realise those that are possible. Gillian Winterborn likewise has been an invaluable confidante and adviser for many years; she typed the early chapters of this book and encouraged me to believe it had worth. Barry Burns has been a loyal friend and skilled butcher.

We have been very fortunate in our neighbours, especially Clare du Boulay, who have among other things had to put up with traffic to the farm shop and occasional wandering deer.

In Sussex Carl Wheeler has been a wonderful and generous friend whilst Janice and Adrian Gumbley have never failed to provide friendly help. Amongst vets, those at the Moredun Research Institute and the members of the Veterinary Deer Society have been especially good friends, whilst within the deer-stalking fraternity Sandy Masson and Donald Ewan Darroch are particularly supportive.

I wish to thank Damaris Fletcher who read an early draft and was perceptive and generous, Susie Lendrum and Paul Broda who provided bolt-holes, Anthony Turner for his interest and diplomacy in editing, and especially Peter Crawley who radiated enthusiasm about the book from the very beginning.

A particular debt of gratitude is due to my dear friend Maggy Lenert for her entertaining and inspired embellishments in the form of vignettes at every chapter head.

Fiona Guinness has allowed me to use several photographs of deer on the Isle of Rum; these pictures are the distillation of a lifetime's photographic work and for her to give me free access to those is a touching act of great generosity. Rex Forrester kindly allowed me to use his photograph of deer being lifted by helicopter. If I have used any photographs without attributing the source, I can only apologise most sincerely; it is simply because I do not know whence they came.

I wish to thank Luath Press in Edinburgh for their generous per-mission to use material from *Rum: Nature's Island* by Magnus Magnusson.

Most of all there are Nickie, Stella and Martha who have always been encouraging, and without too much opposition from me have often suggested that the occasional extra day trucking through France was permissible if it yielded another few thousand words.

Over the years deer farming has brought me many friends in Britain and overseas, too many to name, but the subject attracts individualists and all of them in their own way have helped to make my life, and Nickie's, entertaining, exciting, occasionally exasperating, but always fun. I am grateful to them all.

Finally the deer must be thanked for all the pleasure they have given me.

1   HIJACKED ON THE ROAD
TO THE ISLES

Late and dark, pitch black and rain sluicing down. Also I am hungry and drive the ageing little lorry round Tarbert harbour twice, looking for somewhere to eat. But no hostelry quite lives up to the anticipation. Tired, restless and indecisive, I roll on towards the ferry pier at Kennacraig. On into the country again another few miles, until, under trees, the rain seems less and a widening of the road lets me pull in for the night.

Grabbing my bag I jump down from the cab and climb through one of the side doors into the back. I light a candle, spread a bale of straw, arrange a pillow, set an alarm clock for 5 a.m., take all my clothes off and slip into the old down sleeping bag. Liberated feathers float in candlelight but are extinguished with one breath. Now it's really crow black.

Contentment spreads through my stiff muscles and I actually savour the hard bed and the loud twangs of rain on the metal roof. Like millions of campers in Scotland I ponder why raindrops from trees seem bigger than raindrops from the sky.

It was 1980 and relaxation under such circumstances was easier then.

Hailed, with justification or not, as the pioneer of British deer farming, I was caught up in a movement which was already threatening to revolutionise agriculture in the Scottish Highlands and had the potential to transform livestock farming worldwide. We were creating perhaps the first new domesticated animal for five thousand years. History was in the making. There was the sudden realisation that red deer were the ideal animal for converting grass into a magnificent almost fat-free meat to which man was uniquely adapted. No problems stood in our way. The present difficulty in locating breeding stock was just a stepping stone on the road to an established 'industry'.

Successive politicians had assured us that subsidies for sheep, and indeed all sectors of farming, had the skids under them. A host of agricultural journalists had passed the message on loud and clear. That was just what we wanted; we were doing the right thing.

With a warm glow I think of how the deer I hope to catch next day on the island of Jura will, after a period of acclimatisation, soon be speeding to Denmark where, I know, they thrive as they never could on the impoverished grazings of our Scottish hills. Many wild Highland deer never make it through the winter, perishing in the spring.

The survivors remain, stunted, not calving until three or four years old, whereas on the farm, their sleek relatives usually calve at two years, and the cosseted youngsters which they produce reach the weight of an adult wild deer at eighteen months, and grow for another year still. Wild Scottish hinds, if they're lucky enough to reach maturity, may produce in their lifetime seven or eight calves, of which perhaps only four or five may reach breeding age. Satisfied, I lie back and contrast this with my farmed red deer. Of those, more than nine out of ten will themselves come to motherhood, and can be expected to achieve families of fourteen in their average sixteen years of life. And all of that without once becoming thin.

I relish being able to supply an alternative and superior venison to that from the Highland estates and the game dealers. Wild venison is always a by-product of the sporting business, its quality varying from the very best to a fifteen-year-old stag that would tax the teeth of a lion. Though the properties of wealthy men, Highland estates are invariably loss-making now and if they continue to suffer losses I fear for their employees, several of whom I am proud to call friends. The supply of wild hinds for breeding stock to deer farmers is already proving a valuable new source of income to those estates.

Ironic that it was Danes in their longships a thousand years ago who had called Jura 'the Island of Deer'. Perhaps they too had taken Jura deer back to Jutland.

My heart warms at the prospect of these stout wee animals which, I have found, when accustomed to life on the farm, once lifted from the rain- and wind-lashed romantic isle to the lush grasslands of Jutland, are temperamentally ideal for farming. Only a few weeks previously on a trip to Denmark I had seen Jura deer transformed in twelve months to docile contented beings with their calves, conceived in Scotland, already enormously larger than their stay-at-home contemporaries, and almost as big as their authentic Scots mothers.

Transplanting often seems to have this effect – so many people from the same Highlands and Islands, uprooted 150 years ago, had, within one or two generations, surpassed in material wealth the wildest dreams of their ancestors. Now, visiting Scotland, the descendants of those émigrés, hunting out their roots, were usually of a markedly rounder physique, testifying to a change of diet from oats, potatoes and occasional herring to hamburgers and French fries.

> A single violet transplant,
> The strength, the colour, and the size,
> (All which before was poore, and scant,)
> Redoubles still, and multiplies.

A strange irony that here am I lying in the Highlands dreaming of the English poet, John Donne, who had worked in London under the Scots King James. That same James VI had transplanted himself and his court to England leaving the creation of fine Scots culture rudderless in the absence of a court. Perhaps, I drowsily muse, Donne's reference to the benefits of transplanting was intended to flatter his new patron?

Anyway, like John Donne's violets overcrowded in their bed, the benign effects of transplanting deer are clear. But how had the Scottish deer come to their present predicament? Was it really overcrowding, stretching a limited supply of food? Or an environment so bleak that it could never yield a population of deer as well fed and productive as my farm animals?

It is common knowledge that the present Highland red deer herd, from near-extinction in the late eighteenth and early nineteenth centuries, has grown to a number not previously known in Scotland since the last glaciation, if even then. From only a few thousand in the 1790s, red deer have thrived on the depopulated pastures. The human clearances that came with the collapse of the clan system were made in the name of sheep but the rise of Australasian flocks with their superior wool, coupled later on with the advent of refrigeration and the arrival of New Zealand lamb, had soon turned those large 'sheep walks' into treeless deer forests. Ironic that those faraway flocks and their masters had so often grown from livestock and shepherds transported from Scotland.

The thoughts flow round me like ripples in still water which continue even after the boat which caused them has ceased to move.

Then with Balmoral, and Albert's Teutonic love of hunting red deer, came royal patronage of the sport of deer stalking; and the sort of obsequious adulation that allowed Landseer to paint *The Monarch of the Glen* as a commission for the House of Lords Refreshment Room.

Thus began 150 years of protection from poaching and, throughout that time, arguably never quite sufficient deer were killed by the sportsmen. Even as recently as the early 1970s the Red Deer Commission assessed deer numbers at less than 200,000, and by 1990 they had risen to around 300,000. Was the diminutive size of the Scottish red deer due to this rapid build-up of numbers? The grazing pressure was also exacerbated by rising sheep numbers: Malthus' 'perpetual struggle for room and food'? Or was it the absence of woodland shelter from predators and the wind? No doubt my erstwhile colleague Tim Clutton-Brock with his team working on the Isle of Rum and elsewhere would answer these questions in his indefatigably energetic way.

Trees have been in a decline ever since the advent of man with his slash-and-burn tactics, and later his more sophisticated needs for shipbuilding and for charcoal for smelting iron ore, and all the time his livestock nibbling at the seedling trees.

Undoubtedly those modern deer that successfully sneak into the commercial woodlands, when the fences are covered in snow or flattened by fallen trees, are astonishingly more productive than their luckless colleagues excluded from shelter. And then those shut out may have lost their best grazing to trees. In winter, belts of fenced woodlands can prevent access to the shelter of the glens. The size and prolificacy of those woodland wild deer are often comparable with the best farmed deer. There are even rumours of calves conceiving at four months of age in the very best woodlands.

And that is the last coherent thought dredged up. The very prospect of Tim's enthusiastic delvings must have been too much for I am asleep and know no more.

Zzzzzzzzzzzzzzzzzzzzzzzzzz.

Suddenly I am galvanised into activity. Someone is starting the engine. Visions of being driven south to Glasgow incarcerated in my own beloved vehicle are enough. Like a Greek god, with winged heels, I leap naked from my sleeping bag, out of the rear of the truck, a few yards down the road, and hurl myself into the cab through the passenger door even as we begin to move. Desperation refreshes my jaded muscles. Taking advantage of what I hope is my new-found chauffeur's terror, in one smooth movement I lean over, grab the steering wheel, open the driver's door and push him out, simultaneously wrestling the vehicle to a standstill. Immediately the mood of action leaves me. I wind down the window and look back. A drunken West Highlander is resignedly walking along after me.

'So where were you going anyway?' I shout.

'Och and wasn't I only looking for a lift tae the bloody ferry.'

Either that soft West Coast accent softens me or my Christian education triumphs and a deeply instilled reflex to reconcile and forgive at all costs takes over, for I find myself saying, 'Well just get in, that's where I'm going too.' So my would-be villain hoists himself up, into the passenger's seat this time. Conscious of an enviable odour of alcohol, and of my nudity uncomfortably illuminated by the glow from the panel lights, I drive silently the last mile or so to the hideous yellow mercury-vapour illuminations, reflected in the wet road, that mark the ferry terminal ahead.

2   INITIATION

In the late 1970s and early 1980s those late-night drives north to catch early ferries were welcome interludes in an increasingly frenetic pursuit of breeding stock for the steady growth of deer farms in Britain and overseas.

For several years I was responsible for capturing and rehabilitating some thousand hinds per annum and probably, all told, the rest of the deer-farming industry was taking another thousand. Feeding hungry deer into a deer-fenced enclosure in the bottom of a Highland glen is not too difficult. The owners of the deer, the lairds of the sporting estates, who had their stalkers catch these deer for sale to myself and other deer farmers, found this a welcome new source of income to sustain those financially precarious tracts of hill. The only other way to prevent deer starving to death is to shoot them, and the price we paid for those hinds we took away live was much greater than would have been realised from the sale of venison to the game dealer.

How had I come to this? How had I found myself so embroiled in this new agricultural project?

So far as I can remember, my interest in deer began very young when I was ill in bed and my mother read me *The Story of a Red Deer* by

Fortescue. But that was sentimental; I wanted to get closer to these animals, beneath their skin and *know* them, not just remain a distant admirer. When I joined with three young friends and, as a twelve-year-old, cycled round the Isle of Arran, my principal objective had been to see the wild red deer. I browbeat my best friend, Sam, to come with me on a day of lashing rain. We two climbed from the youth hostel at Lochranza up and south, through the rain into thick mist, until we knew that Glen Iorsa was somewhere below us. Dispirited we sat down with our backs to a peat bank and had something to eat whilst we planned our next move.

In the literary world such moments are known as epiphanies: the mist rolled back and Sam and I were surrounded by more deer than I could have dreamt of. We lay quite still and they came around us. We could hear them grazing, the calves squeaking and the hinds' low bleats back. Then at once they left us and the clouds descended again. I was satisfied. I knew what I wanted. I needed to find out more about these animals. How did such large wild animals survive in such a hostile environment?

It wasn't good enough just sentimentally to admire their graceful movements and beauty. Even then I knew that the deer did not have an easy ride in the Scottish Highlands. Sam and I had seen enough corpses on our walk to make me understand that.

Deer, unknowing, are constantly burdened with the epithet of nobility. I came to understand that whatever fine names we give them you can be sure they would rather have shelter and good food. Deer are flesh and blood, unlikely to be impressed by the admiration of sportsmen and naturalists who revere them as 'noble'. They would, I believe, exchange it all for a life of good grass. This is what I have spent my life trying to give them.

I completed my veterinary course at Glasgow University in 1970. I have no especially strong memories of the course. From the seclusion of a home in the country and a boarding school, the excitements of Glasgow came very welcome. Though I do remember some problems with buses. I remember queuing on Great Western Road and getting on. Was it going to Bearsden I asked the conductor. 'No,' it was not. 'Y'd better ger off.' I did, but by then the bus was going at about thirty miles an hour. I hung on to the shiny steel pole on the back for a while, feet flying and body horizontal. Then I let go and slid along the road for a few yards before limping back to the shocked queue and wondering whether I should go to the end or rejoin the front. My clothes were torn and I was bleeding.

Later there were rounds of boozy parties, generally revolving around Glasgow University Mountaineering Club, the 'Gum Club'; initiations into heart-breaking young love, and ... in the manner of Tristram Shandy, there is a digression which I should like to make that concerns my student days but has nothing whatsoever to do with my general tale.

There was a quiet and retiring Singhalese student on the veterinary course called Candiah. He lived at the Catholic Centre. I became quite friendly with Candiah. One day he came into lectures looking rather nervous and confided in me the following. (Did I dream all this or was it reality?) Candiah said: 'I am living this last few days by myself at the Catholic Centre because the priest who normally resides there is away for a few days. Yesterday I was working at home when there was a knock at the door. I opened it and there was a man, quite well dressed, who said: "I have come from the Metropolitan Museum in New York. I am trying to trace a plaster model which we believe Michelangelo used as a study for his marble *pietà* that is now in St Peter's in Rome. We believe it is here. Can we come and look?" I didn't know what to do but he seemed sincere and I let him in. We walked around the building and sure enough, on the window of the staircase, was a plaster sculpture of a *pietà*. So this man says: "Yes undoubtedly that is it. You should look after it very carefully. I have done my work and will make a report." And then he left.'

I was staggered by Candiah's story. I had read *The Agony and the Ecstasy* so I was an authority. 'What did you do, Candiah?' 'I was terrified,' he said. 'I hid it under the bed and that is where it is now. I do not know whether I dare come to lectures today. You must come and see it this evening.' And so I did. Candiah pulled out a white plaster model about two feet tall which looked for all the world like the *pietà* in St Peter's. I turned it over and there in the unfinished plaster of the base were fingerprints. Were they Michelangelo's? The priest came back in a few days and Candiah was able to hand it over and sleep more soundly. We never saw the *pietà* again. The establishment had taken its own.

But above all I remember and have cause to be thankful for the days I spent on the rocks and hills with the Gum Club. They nurtured in me a fascination for the red deer which eke out their existence in that inhospitable terrain. There remain memories of descending from the tops in the gloaming, eyes still dazzled by the snow, and all around the bleached, parched brown vegetation, its colour, after the whiteness, unnaturally vivid. And there would be the deer in groups steadily grazing away on this impoverished herbage. Whilst we went into the shelter of a bothy for the night they would remain outside, in their element.

One pivotal day I remember well. I had conceived a bold solo expedition that was to draw me still closer to the red deer. I planned to use skins tied to the bottom of skis. These cunning devices are nowadays synthetic, but were originally made from real sealskin and, by virtue of their pile, slide easily forward but only reluctantly backwards, so that skiing uphill becomes possible. Eager to try them, I took advantage of a spell of Arctic cold and sunshine. Catching a train one afternoon from Glasgow to Corrour railway station, inaccessible by road, I skied off the end of the platform. My plan was to go the ten or so miles to Ben Alder cottage, an unmanned bothy offering shelter to all, and then ski back. Progress was simple until, about half-way there, the binding of one of my skins broke.

Time was of the essence and dusk was looming. And, since the snow was in good condition, I decided to make myself an igloo. Construction proceeded apace until I realised I had made a fundamental error. I couldn't reach to put the top block on and was too lacking in confidence in my building skills to risk climbing up the outside. So I lay there in my sleeping bag relishing the views of the constellations but not able to recapture the true Inuit atmosphere. I slept adequately but in the morning felt quite pleased to have an excuse – the broken skin – to abandon the project and head back to

Corrour. If I had skied down to the bothy at Ben Alder that would have been fine, but the climb back up with only one skin would have been tricky. The weather was wonderful then but it wouldn't last for ever. I chose discretion.

Not having so long a journey for the next day and that mostly downhill, I was in no hurry, and when I saw a freshly dead stag thought it would be interesting, in a spirit of veterinary investigation, to skin him and open him up as an autopsy.

I still have the slides I took of that stag with his skin on first, and then half skinned, and I still use them when I lecture to vet students. It is an impressive testimony to the suffering of our wild deer. He was only a young stag of two or three years and I don't suppose he had many more warbles than his living colleagues, but it came as a shock to me in my ignorance. There must have been two to three hundred half-inch-long warble maggots waiting under the skin to emerge in the early spring.

For those who don't know this horrid parasite, its maggots drop from the back of living deer in March and April, immediately turning into pupae that rapidly develop into bee-like flies and take to the air in the Highland spring, when the nights hardly become dark, to search out red deer on which to lay their eggs. Even newly born calves are fair game. The eggs hatch and the minute larvae penetrate the hide and move through the deer to develop under the skin of the back during the winter before they again bore their way out to leave a running sore as they fall to the ground to complete their sordid cycle. They do not seem to me worthy of their godly name, *Hypoderma diana* (illustration 2b).

Similar parasites used to be commonplace in cattle but it is one of the less publicised, yet most humanitarian, successes of the veterinary profession to have eliminated the cattle warble from Britain. It was fortunate for that eradication programme that the deer warble can distinguish deer from cattle and prefers venison.

The poor old red deer has also to carry the burden of nostril bots. If I had split open the head of that dead animal it would have revealed a score or so of three-centimetre-long maggots, well equipped with bristles, at the base of his nostrils.

The dead stag left a deep impression on me. The suffering of wild deer due to warbles, the death of so many from starvation and the attrition of weeks of winter weather, climaxes in the spring when most sportsmen are away. Only a few of those who come to the hills to shoot deer will ever skin one and see the full horror.

As we in the Gum Club participated in mountain rescues and lost our own club members at a shameful rate, comparable to a wartime front line, so grew my admiration for the ability of the deer to resist exposure and still multiply. Voraciously I read Lea McNally's books about deer and then Frank Fraser Darling's *Herd of Red Deer*. Listening to his Reith Lectures and climbing the hills as a student at Glasgow Vet School, I learnt my vocation.

I therefore cast around for an opportunity to work with Scottish red deer and was offered a chance to join a team based at the Cambridge University Veterinary School investigating the deer on the Isle of Rum in the Inner Hebrides. I don't think I realised at the time just how lucky I was.

Roger Short, the vet from Cambridge who supervised me for my Ph.D., was and still is a brilliantly innovative scientist whose forte is an ability to coalesce the research results of other scientists, as well as his own, into the general scheme of things and then communicate them to a wide audience. Would that there were more like him. His interest in unravelling the mysteries of reproductive behaviour in man and beast had led him to red deer as a subject for research. That may seem a rather odd choice but, as I came to realise, the reason is that red deer are extraordinarily seasonal in their breeding pattern. In effect the stag experiences an annual puberty. Why are they so seasonal? The answer was soon to become clear to me. Also, of which more later, their antlers reflect their reproductive condition and indicate hormonal status as unmistakably as litmus paper signifies acidity.

I had to go down to Cambridge for an interview with Roger and was immediately in his, and the department's, thrall. There have been two or three occasions in my academic career when I have been the recipient of good news and each time I have been so completely overwhelmed with astonishment and delight that I have momentarily swooned. When Roger broke his news to me I was sitting on a wooden laboratory stool, and so great was the shock that I had to save myself from falling off.

Roger was keen for me to work with deer in Thetford Forest just north of Newmarket but I was able to persuade him that the red deer on Rum would be more interesting, and he agreed. My predecessor, who had started the work on Rum with the deer, was Gerald Lincoln. A tall, gaunt and brilliant scientist who was starting to write up his Ph.D. thesis as I began research for mine, he still lives near me in Fife and remains a close friend. Gerald has a formidable mind and a natural curiosity about things biological and he was then, all those years ago, a very hard act to follow, exuding tremendous physical vigour and a great sense of fun. He was also highly competitive.

Just before I joined the Cambridge team I was told that Gerald had published an anonymous paper in that most prestigious scientific journal, *Nature*. To publish anonymously in *Nature* is almost unheard of, but the editor understood that he wished to save his colleagues embarrassment. In the correct scientific spirit of measuring everything, Gerald had apparently developed the habit of weighing his electric-razor shavings each morning. This provided a crude measure of fluctuations in his levels of testosterone, the male sex hormone. On Rum, in monastic seclusion, he had noticed, no doubt with a certain amount of apprehension, that his beard growth declined but he had been fascinated, and surely equally relieved, to record a repeatable increase in beard growth associated with the infrequent visits of his lady friends.

What was important scientifically was the fact that this occurred in anticipation of the visit: as soon as notice reached Gerald of impending female companionship, his beard would start into rapid growth. This demonstrated that the higher centres of the brain could influence testosterone secretion – something that had not hitherto been appreciated. It is perhaps truly all in the mind.

The other person whom I was privileged to join on Rum was Fiona Guinness (illustration 2c). She had arrived to join the team for the first time one year before me. Her stamina and persistence in learning to recognise each animal simply by its face and body, became, over the thirty or so years she was to work on the island, legendary. Many could not believe this skill, and few could emulate it, so that we had to attach ear tags to the deer to prove her right.

After twenty-five years studying the deer on Rum her feet have now worn a path in the peat; but in her first year it was bare feet she wore. By walking the same route every day she was eventually able to touch some of the deer. Fiona was recently awarded an honorary degree by Edinburgh University and must be a contender for the distinction of being the first honorary graduate to wear jeans for the occasion.

It seems astonishing now, but in the late sixties no one even knew the precise length of pregnancy in the red deer hind, let alone such simple matters as when they come into heat, for how long, and so on. Gerald, Roger and Fiona had managed to unravel these basic facts just prior to my arrival and soon published the results; but there was plenty more left to find out.

3 DOMINANCE, PHEROMONES AND HUMILITY ON RUM

Like, I fancy, most visitors to that island, I remember my first arrival on Rum in September 1970 very clearly. The *Loch Arkaig*, the Mac-Brayne's steamer, comes into the shelter of Loch Scresort, suddenly calm after the swell, and there is the red sandstone excrescence of Kinloch Castle at the head of the loch, an Edwardian pile. The ship cannot come alongside on Rum and so a tender is employed. It is early morning, overcast and drizzling, but Fiona is there on the pier head with a Land Rover and drives us the few hundred yards to the castle for porridge which she has specially made for the occasion.

The *Loch Arkaig* was a converted minesweeper that had been designed with a wooden hull so as to avoid detonating magnetic mines, and yet – with what seemed to me a fundamental flaw in marine architecture – she had been given a substantial metal superstructure. Consequently she rolled. She rolled so alarmingly that I would always plot out my escape route ready for a quick dash in case she never did come back up. Another consequence was that I did not eat Fiona's porridge with much conviction. I cannot recall she ever offered them* to me again.

---

* It is customary in Scotland to refer to porridge in the plural, as, I suppose, in oats. They should also be eaten whilst standing or slowly walking, presumably to allow more to be packed in.

That first day was long. Skoots, one of the tame deer kept in the enclosure behind the castle, had managed to enter the disused squash court where we kept the bags of feed and had gorged herself. The ruminant's digestive system is complicated and delicate. Even as an eager, newly qualified vet, keen to be a hero, there was not much I could do. Fiona must have had great hopes awaiting the arrival of this tyro vet but Skoots died late the next night and we were both despondent. Such deaths were extremely unusual in our tame deer on Rum; indeed I believe that was the only one of those hinds that we ever lost. Over the years since, I have come to learn just how susceptible deer are to overeating grain and how difficult it is to save them.

In the afternoon, abandoning the sick Skoots for a few hours, we found time for a hasty visit up to the north of the island, beautiful Kilmory, reached by twelve miles of very rough Land Rover track. The builders of Kinloch Castle, the Bullough family, had used that road to enable their washing to be done well away from the castle. The wooden building, clad with corrugated iron, remains, now in tatters, at Kilmory and is still called the Laundry. And there I saw for the first time the wild deer Fiona was working with. She had already decided to make the hinds her especial study; Gerald had worked with the stags, and so this was logical. It is much more difficult to work with wild deer, of course. Even after Gerald's painstaking efforts to make the stags accessible by enticing them with maize, they were still wild animals, and, at that time, Fiona's hinds could only be approached to a few hundred yards.

It was fortunate, from my point of view, even if less romantic, that it wasn't only the wild deer we worked with. I was lucky in being able to study a group of eleven deer that had been taken from the hill as young calves and bottle-fed by Dick Youngson who later became a stalker for the Red Deer Commission. These hinds had names often taken from their places of discovery such as Cnap an Breaca – a Gaelic name meaning the speckled hill – and Shellesder who had been born in Glen Shellesder; or less beguilingly, Moke because she looked like a donkey, and Sandy for her colour – or was it because she had been found in Sandy Coire? These were to become my future, and not just during the Rum years.

Dick had, aided I think by the Nature Conservancy stalkers, caught these deer during their first few days of life when they lie prone and can be picked up and reared on the bottle. This may seem heartless but one has to remember that a sizeable proportion of the calves born in the wild will die owing to predation from eagles, lack of adequate mothering skills in their dams, or just insufficient milk; or they may drown in a bog, or be born too small to survive their first winter. By taking a calf from a hind at least she is saved the great nutritional stresses of lactation and may yield a more viable calf the next year. Indeed the hind herself may survive a winter that might otherwise have carried her off. Certainly the calf, pampered with a bottle, will stand a better chance of survival than if it were to be left with its mother on the hill.

Homo sapiens and the pygmy chimpanzee or bonobo are probably unique amongst mammals in enjoying copulation at any or all stages of the female cycle. As Roger Short and Malcolm Potts recently explained in their enlightening book *Ever since Adam and Eve*, this is to strengthen family bonds and ensure the prolonged parental care which large-brained animals require. No wonder we need Viagra. In all other species the female will accept, or is attractive to, the male, only at certain times when the chances of conception are at their highest. This period is known as 'oestrus' or 'heat'. Within seasonal limitations, imposed by changing day-length, red deer hinds in Britain will come into heat every eighteen days, starting around 1 October and continuing until February or March in the unlikely event of their not becoming pregnant; they are thus known as seasonally poly-oestrous short-day breeders.

When I first went to Rum no one had accurately reported this; no one knew whether the hinds came into heat more than once, or for how long, or even how long pregnancy lasted. We already had a pretty good idea that roe deer females, or does, needed to be vigorously chased by the bucks in order to induce their ovulation and oestrus, but this didn't seem likely in the red deer hinds. We wanted to find out.

Accordingly Gerald, Roger and Fiona had run Dick Youngson's bottle-fed hinds with a vasectomised stag, Ed, so that we could record his ineffective matings and thus define the hinds' heat periods. We knew these would begin in the autumn but we didn't know whether – or for how long – the periods would recur and the hinds continue to cycle.

Dick's hinds were running in the enclosure at the back of the castle and in the old walled garden. Feeding them every day and recording their interactions it was surprising to me that their 'peck order' or dominance hierarchy was almost completely linear. That is to say that Moke would be dominant to Mini, and Mini to Shellesder, and Shellesder to Kilmory, whilst triangular relationships – for example, had Shellesder been dominant to Moke, or Kilmory to Mini – were very unusual. Of course, this was a highly artificial group, all brought up together and all of the same age, but it was nevertheless interesting.

Each morning Fiona and I would feed the deer from a long line of troughs and sit and watch them for a set period of time. This is a most fascinating exercise and I was very privileged to have the opportunity. I came to see things which I would never, from the elevated stance of a newly qualified vet, have previously believed. First of all it soon became obvious that it is not difficult, given time, to recognise each animal by its face. This soon became so clear that it was simpler to use the face than the individual identification tags for recognition. Much more remarkable were the family resemblances. It was easy to confuse daughters with dams, or sisters with each other; but no other confusion was really possible when you had become familiar with the animals. These resemblances seemed to me more pronounced than those between people and I put this down to the highly mobile faces of humans. The outward appearance of people must come to reflect their temperament, or the facial expressions they use most. I often think that the sensual pouting of the lips of French girls is due to their vowel pronunciation, though my theory does not explain why French men do not have equally seductive lips. But then I am not an objective observer in this matter.

There were other interesting things to be learnt from the chance to become intimate with a group of deer. For example, grooming behaviour, in which one animal spends minutes standing, evidently entranced, whilst another individual uses her teeth to comb the other's coat, was a regular activity, which anthropomorphically we might consider to be subservient activity. But it was only ever carried out by Beauty, who was the most dominant hind. Shades, perhaps, of the Maundy ceremony in which British monarchs symbolically bathe the feet of the poor. In any event I removed Beauty for a month with her daughter and one or two other deer and watched what happened. In the main group there were many times when one hind would approach another and wait expectantly to be groomed but each time they were disappointed: on no occasion did grooming take place. On the day when Beauty was returned to be with her friends again she groomed six other hinds in the first hour.

The stalkers had implausible stories to tell us about the deer and we were, as confident young scientists, highly sceptical. After all, was not the following strange Gaelic proverb discussing the age of the stag believed into the nineteenth century?

> Thrice the age of a dog, the age of a horse;
> Thrice the age of a horse, the age of a man;
> Thrice the age of a man, the age of a deer;
> Thrice the age of a deer, the age of an eagle;
> Thrice the age of an eagle, the age of an oak tree.

I have since learnt that this myth of the long-lived stag exists not only in Celtlc folklore but also dates back to the *Precepts of Chiron*, ascribed to the Greek poet Hesiod. It forms the basis for the mediaeval pavement in front of the high altar at Westminster, in the centre of which English monarchs were anointed and crowned.

But back to Rum ... one tale that was often presented to us by the stalkers definitely tested our credulity; were they having us on? We were told that stags with an injury such as a broken leg would 'ae grow a twisted horn', usually on the opposite side. Over the years we came, to our bemusement, to see that this phenomenon is unquestionably real. Deer show an extraordinary capacity for repairing fractures spontaneously, but where the pain of a healing limb – or other wound – was present when the antler was growing, an asymmetrical antler with distorted growth, normally very rare, was the almost inevitable accompaniment. Perhaps, we reasoned, this might have an explanation in common with acupuncture? By stimulating nature's own painkillers, the endorphins, could this affect the nervous outflow from the brain and disturb the growth of the antler? It is the biologist's duty to benefit from these unexplained natural experiments and make deductions; we must be voyeurs seeking deep insights when, for a moment nature lets her dress slip.

Pheromones were very much in the wind, as you might say, at Cambridge in those days. These are scents which animals use to transmit messages, usually sexual. It is, for example, presumed that pheromones are the means by which young women in dormitories are often found to have unconsciously synchronised their menstrual cycles. Roger suggested that I investigate the vaginal odours and secretions from the hinds to see if we could identify the scents which the stag uses to detect heat. While Roger had thought that we might train a dog to do this, Fiona and I decided to start off using our own noses. We found it difficult enough to get close to the rear end of the hinds ourselves, and we felt that the deer would take a very long time to become accustomed to being sniffed by dogs. So it was, that for many months, each morning would find us notebook in hand, sniffing the backsides of the deer as they took their daily feed; an unlikely sight and one which found its way into the pages of *The Scotsman*.

Actually, the scent of hinds on heat had already been described by Henry Evans, the great nineteenth-century deer researcher, who wrote of the red deer on the Isle of Jura: 'The beds of bands of hinds through October have a strong odour, quite different from the rut odour of stags.'

I was given special dispensation to work for my doctorate outwith the prescribed normal limit of five miles from the church of St Mary's, Cambridge and commuted every few weeks between flat Cambridge and mountainous Rum. There were four boats a week to the island from the fishing port of Mallaig. It used to take me about eleven hours of hard driving in my Mini Moke. I remember one evening at around 6 p.m., after work in the lab at Cambridge, making a decision, on a whim, to dash up for the 6 a.m. boat. I stopped for a good supper at Wetherby and then blazed on, going well, in winter darkness but with deserted, dry roads and no frost, until at Appleby, then with no bypass, the law caught up with me. They were understanding when I explained that no, there was no fire, but I did have a ferry to catch at Mallaig in five hours' time. They would press no charges, but perhaps I could join them for a chat in their squad car for a while until I had cooled down a little? They talked to me for half an hour, which they judged would just be about enough to remove any possibility of my catching the boat.

They were probably right but my blood was up. Eschewing comfort stops, I tore on north, hurtling through Glasgow in the wee small hours and then beside the black water of Loch Lomond and through the immensity of familiar Glencoe. On the long, tortuous single-track road between Fort William and Mallaig there was a steady stream of articulated trucks carrying herring south to the continent. And by now there was a rising wind and squalls of rain. Each lorry entailed a few moments' frustration and I knew that when I reached the pier it would be neck and neck. I was right. The *Loch Arkaig* was just six feet away from me, separated by a rapidly growing strip of black, oily water. I was so angry that I tore hair out as I sat on the breakwater and watched her diminishing lights.

As she turned south to round Sleat Point I could see her port light glowing red and becoming fainter. And then . . . what was happening . . . surely that was green? And wasn't it growing brighter?

She had decided the weather was too bad and put back into harbour. I was forced to spend two days in Mallaig waiting for the gales to abate. As so often, divine providence seemed to be asking me to revise my philosophy. A young, arrogant scientist with a determined disbelief in things that cannot be proven, I found it hard to believe in a power trying to tell me to slow down. I didn't listen.

4   RED DEER RULED BY SEX

The fruitless copulations of our vasectomised stag, Ed, had shown us that hinds not becoming pregnant will keep on coming into heat from early October until February or March. Naturally the hind on the hill, exposed every few minutes to the violently competitive and turbulent stag in his frenzied checking, is unlikely to pass through an oestrous cycle unnoticed and so will normally conceive early in the season. Nevertheless tales of very late calves are common in Scotland, presumably because the often poor nutrition of the hinds prevents their coming into heat until late. I remember seeing a wild hind on Rum being mated in December. Even as late as that, the stags were vigilant to the slender chances of perpetuating more of their genes and a local, short-lived Yuletide rut resulted.

The intensity of the hind's heat grows with each successive cycle, so that in October the oestrus is almost imperceptible to the human observer but come December she is rampant with the overt urge to be mated and solicits the stag shamelessly. By spring some of her ardour is abating.

Fiona found that the hinds came into oestrus every eighteen days, plus or minus two days, and that on each occasion the stags would mate them once, twice and occasionally, late in the year, three or four times during a heat that might last twenty-four hours. No mean achievement when you consider that a stag on a farm may successfully cover seventy or eighty hinds in a three- or four-week period! No wonder the stag finishes the rut as a thin, haggard vestige of his sleek, late summer self; he has lost maybe a fifth of his body weight and has to feed hard to recover some condition before the winter closes in.

We removed Ed and replaced him with a fertile stag to allow some of Dick Youngson's hinds to conceive in the early spring when the oestrous cycles were declining. It was from this that Fiona, Gerald and Roger were able to establish that the pregnancy of a red deer hind lasts on average 231 days, plus or minus four or five days; that is, about seven and a half months. Later Fiona and others were able to show that the less well-fed hinds on the hill had a very slightly shorter gestation.

The inevitable consequence of this was that we had a number of autumn-born calves which we ended up bottle-rearing, otherwise they would surely have perished. The mothers would have been unlikely to have had sufficient milk in the depths of the winter just when the calves would have been at their hungriest. This meant that we had a nursery of several calves to feed at all hours of day and night. Their beauty was bewitching and strengthened my continuing obsession.

I remember vividly the patter of hard little deer calves' hooves on the brown lino in our kitchen at the back of the castle that winter, and the only slightly softer rattle of deer droppings descending on the same surface. The regular pools of urine were even more silent and inconvenient. One morning Roger awoke to find his slippers, left warming by the Raeburn stove, awash with the yellow liquid. That solved the naming problem for that particular calf and it was curious, years later, to see Slipper, standing huge and black, roaring belligerence on the hill.

One of those late-conceived births was epoch-making. Gerald, Fiona and I had by some wonderful coincidence gathered to watch Sandy give birth. Strangely, although wild hinds will make off into the hills for miles to find solitude for their births, bottle-fed hinds remain apparently oblivious to onlookers, seeming completely absorbed in the business of creating a new life. So we watched, festooned with cameras, and fascinated and privileged to witness that magical process.

Sure enough, on to the autumn leaves, like a fish out of water, flopped a spluttering and sneezing calf. 'It's a bit small,' I ventured.

The others agreed. Sandy was our biggest hind; this was a disappointment. But while we were expecting her to get on with the business of expelling her afterbirth, and then of eating those hormonally valuable tissues, it became clear that she was showing no sign at all of having completed her labour.

The feet of deer calves, like other hoofed species, are encased in bright yellow cartilage; these soft 'golden slippers' protect the mother and allow the embryo to carry out its very necessary muscle-strengthening kicking exercises in the womb without any risk of the feet tearing it. The golden slippers were of interest to us because they wear off in the first day or two of life as the calf makes its first ungainly gambols on the abrasive heather and we didn't often have a chance to examine them. Gerald as usual was the first to notice anything unusual. 'She's having another,' he whispered excitedly and at the same time we could all see the two golden slippers of a second calf being forcefully squeezed out. The enthusiasm was understandable; twins carried to full term in red deer were at that time unrecorded, at least in Scottish deer (illustration 6b).

Sandy, doing what was probably the most sensible thing for a Scottish hind, abandoned those calves. It was too close to winter, they would certainly not have survived, and her job was to get back into condition so that she could stand the best chance of conceiving and rearing a calf at the right time next year. So we had to raise those two on a bottle, and Bonnie and Clyde became quite celebrated. The late Lea McNally, deerstalker and chronicler of Highland natural history, was so surprised – and perhaps a little sceptical – that he came over to Rum especially to see what was happening and wrote it all up in an enthusiastic article.

It is pretty clear now that if given adequate feeding, as on a deer farm, about one in a hundred hinds will give birth to twins. In the wild on the Scottish hills the figure is about one in a thousand, reflecting their straitened circumstances.

All this, while fascinating, and indeed thrilling for me, was secondary to the main object of our interest. Red deer, like all herbivores in a temperate climate, are intensely seasonal, for their survival depends on the birth of the calves coinciding with the flush of spring vegetation. I had noted in my mountaineering expeditions with the Gum Club just how desperate was their struggle to survive the miserable Highland winter. All those deer which may look so relaxed and well fed in the late summer are actually on a knife-edge. Unconsciously their whole life, every pattern of behaviour and every movement, is directed towards their own survival, and ultimately to bringing as many as possible of their progeny to breeding condition.

Perhaps there is a parallel in educated man when, for example, we see the determined sacrifice of career prospects made by British politicians to find what they perceive to be the best possible schooling for their family, even when it may be contrary to their avowed political policy and so, presumably, what they judge to be the common good! Extrapolation of points of animal behaviour to humans is unwise and rightly frowned on by scientists. Nevertheless this is far from being a scientific treatise, and it is fascinating to think how we all strive so energetically 'to do the best' for our families. It is only during the last few decades in our own affluent society that material prosperity has come to be dissociated from our ability to rear large families. Does our collective subconscious still tell us that a 'good start' will increase the chances of our progeny rearing a family and perpetuating our genes?

For the stag, anyway, all efforts are directed into maximising his success in the rut, the mating season. His weight, his vigour in fighting other males, in remaining vigilant against other stags encroaching on his harem, his ability to deter other stags by roaring strongly and frequently, perhaps the strength of his rutting odour, the thickness of his neck, the length of his neck mane, the depth of his colour achieved by wallowing in peat hags, as well as the size of his antlers and no doubt many more subtle features will determine his success. And underlying all that is the size of his energy store, the fat deposits which he has achieved during the summer to enable him to conduct a successful rut and still survive the rigours of the winter, so that he can live to fight again the next year and sire yet more progeny.

Gerald had written of the importance of all this in the stag and shown much of the way in which the sex hormone, testosterone, is the chemical messenger responsible for these life-and-death affairs. But who sends the messenger?

We wanted to find out more about the ways in which the seasonal cue, which we knew was day-length, acts on the animal and is translated into the hormonal changes which bring about the rise in testosterone in the male and of other hormones in the female. For the crucial point is that the stag ruts so dramatically each autumn in order not to miss the short hours during which the female will accept the male, as well as to stimulate her to come into heat. The period is brief because in our very seasonal climate it is of vital importance that the young are born at such a time as to allow the hind to lactate during the short season when the pasture is at its best. Farmers, and mothers themselves, know just how much of a strain is lactation. Many, usually men, comment on the enormous strain on the stag's metabolism of growing antlers; this is insignificant compared to the resources demanded of the lactating female. How often do breast-feeding ladies start to lose their hair? Even with abundant good feeding lactation is a burden. Accurate synchronisation of birth, and consequently lactation, is fundamental to the survival of any grazing species in our temperate climate. The few weeks of good grass are crucial to the chances of a deer calf making it through its first winter. The only way in which this accuracy can be achieved is by using the changes of day-length as a cue.

The lactation of the hind, when she may daily yield up to two kilogrammes (nearly five pounds) of very concentrated milk, is a huge nutritional demand and she will certainly lose weight for a period. This is especially important in Scotland where the rain and wind of winter are so extreme, and the quality of winter feed so poor, and the summer so short, that the number of calves succumbing in their first year is terribly high. Between February and April an average of one in four calves will die and in some particularly harsh winters on the most exposed deer forests the figure is much higher. And the wild deer calves most likely to die are those born either early or late in the calving season, especially the latter. Over the years the successful deer is the one who synchronises his mating in such a way as to ensure that his progeny are born in mid-season.

This principle is of the utmost importance also to the farmer, of course. During the northern European summer the grass is only at its best during a brief few weeks between awakening from the winter cold and reaching the flowering stage, because once flowered, most of the protein in the herbage is lost. In our Scottish spring the day-length is very long, so that the light-dependent growth of the vegetation is impressive for just those few weeks before flowering. Cattle and sheep, originating far from our temperate climate, will, left to their own devices, drop their young at times inappropriate to our spring grass flush in the Scottish hills.

On Rum I watched with horrified fascination the feral goats whose ancestors nibbled the sparse vegetation of the arid desert edge, as now they dropped their kids in February on the storm-lashed sea cliffs. For the first time, I thought how much more natural to farm deer.

As a young vet I soon found that although my all-round education in the way mammals work was the best possible, I had much to learn about the survival strategy of the wild animals. It is easy enough to comprehend the principles of Darwin's theory of evolution but only by observing wild animals, and the intensity of their struggle, does its relevance become really clear. Unless an individual leaves at least one offspring which in its turn successfully procreates, then in biological terms that individual might as well have never lived. Every facet of an animal's behaviour has been honed by natural selection to achieve that end with ruthless efficiency.

To accomplish this all-important spring calving it is clear that, since the duration of pregnancy is a near-constant, synchrony of mating is pivotal. To watch the simultaneous efforts of hundreds of red deer stags each striving to secure as large a group of hinds as he can immediately prior to their coming into heat is spectacular. In their life-and-death struggle to mate as many hinds as possible, they create what is probably the most impressive wildlife phenomenon in Europe. Because of the severity of the conditions and the high level of mortality among the calves, there is a dreadful urgency for the deer; they must impregnate all hinds they can in that narrow window of time to allow the fruits of their couplings the best chance of surviving until they too in their turn can mate. Red deer are the largest European land mammal – saving the few surviving bears and the moose – and when stags cease eating to devote all their resources of fat, painstakingly accumulated in the lazy days of summer, into a pent-up orgy of courtship and mating, it is awe-inspiring.

Turbervile, in his book *The Noble Art of Venerie*, written in 1576 but owing much to earlier French authors, gives a good account of the rut in a chapter entitled 'The Vault of Hartes':

> Harts do beginne to Vault about the middlest of September, and their Rut doth continue about two monethes, and the older that they be, the hottere they are, and the better beloved of the Hyndes. The old harts go sooner to vault than the yong, and they are so fierce and so proude, that until they have accomplyshed their lust, the yong harts dare not come neare them, for if they do, they beate them and dryve them away. The yong Deere have a marvellous craft and malice, for when they perceive that the olde Hartes are wearie of the Rut and weakened in force, they runne uppon them, and eyther hurt or kill them, causing them to abandon the Rut and they remayne maisters in their places.
>
> Hartes do much sooner kyll each other when there is scarcitie of Hyndes, for if there be Hyndes plentie, then they separate themselves in one place or other. It is a pleasure, to beholde them when they goe to Rutte and make their vaulte. For when they smell the Hynde, they rayse their nose up into the ayre, and look aloft as thou they gave thankes to nature which gave them so great delight.

That argues for a good deal of time spent watching the deer, since mating, especially amongst woodland red deer, is not often witnessed. The raising of their noses in the air is the act of 'flehmen' by which we believe the stags are testing the urine of the hinds to check whether they are on heat.

From time to time during the rut we would come across stags so exhausted as to lie asleep, eyes closed. I remember being able to walk up to one such sated wild monarch, normally unapproachable, and touch him before he leapt up and away. Cameron in his *Wild Red Deer of Scotland* notes this too, of the rutting stag: 'his slumbers are deep, for twice in a single season did the Grand Duke Sergius Michaelovitch surprise sleeping stags which never woke.' Hardly sporting, I should have thought.

It is not just the effort of the rut that makes rutting stags sleep, I think. It is well known that ruminants do not sleep in the normal way but stay awake with glazed eyes chewing their cud. Analysis of their brain's electrical activity at that time shows a great resemblance to the sleep patterns seen in other animals during conventional sleep. Yet in the rut stags do not eat. Over those few days they lose perhaps a fifth of their body weight. Could the absence of periods of cudding compel them to take naps just as do those animals that do not ruminate?

In the larger open glens of Rum, such as Guiridil or Glen Shellesder; or on the flat top of Fionchra, as elsewhere in the Highlands, each autumn one can watch stags roaring from the steep sides of the hills; weighing up their opponents: who can roar largest and loudest and most often? Who looks biggest and blackest? Who smells strongest? Who carries the largest antlers and who the heaviest body? And then perhaps, at the end of a long day of challenging, two mighty stags may come to combat. A slow, stiff-legged approach leads into the famous parallel walk. The two combatants march side by side, only a few metres apart, in a highly ritualised display, stopping frequently to roar, thrash the peat with their antlers and jerk their penises and spray urine. (And perhaps even sperm. Gerald, ever the scientist, had found spermatozoa on vegetation doused by a stag at the climax of his ecstasy. 'Was he masturbating?' asked Gerald. If so, what could be the evolutionary value of that?) From a few seconds to half an hour or more the appraisal continues with two possible outcomes. One stag's nerve may break and he runs for his life or else the fight is really on. Then with frightening speed antlers are locked and, flattening themselves to maximise pushing power, the stags struggle. On the steep hillsides the uppermost has the advantage.

And while the battles rage there is often a lone wandering dis-possessed stag eyeing up his chances before sneaking quietly in on a hind.

These contests exact a price. On Rum, broken antlers are almost the norm, as are broken ribs, whilst lost eyes and fractures of the limbs are often seen. Gerald one autumn saw our revered Kilmory patriarch,

Aristotle, thrown by an opponent clean off his feet and rolled twice, head to tail, right over on the steep slopes of the Bloodstone Hill.

Watching such duels with even a glimmer of understanding of the reason behind their actions, it is difficult not to extrapolate to man and, like Jung, search for reasons for his tribal, religious and nationalist struggles. Animals have more excuse; we should be able to understand the value of co-operative effort. Our evolution is now, one hopes, on a psychosocial level and our progress intellectual, capable of being passed from generation to generation by book and example. Could that be the basis of our urge to 'make a name for ourselves' or 'to be remembered after our time'? Yet how frequently apparently educated societies are pulled down not only to the animal level of courtship rivalry, but beyond, even into the mire of 'ethnic cleansing'. We have to believe that man will progress beyond that mindless aggression otherwise it is difficult not to despair.

Of course, the rut is not just about roaring, though that is what the word rut means, or even fighting; it is about siring calves. A stag expends much of his energy at this time in trying to herd his hinds together into a tight harem and then in chasing them to see if at last they will stand and accept his advances. This very chasing, and the roaring and the stink of the stags, must all serve to bring hinds into heat. Eventually, late in the rut, the hinds will stand, and after some nervous clumsy attempts the stag will rapidly come to ejaculation, and presumably orgasm, and with one colossal thrust lift all his four legs off the ground and push the hind forwards. As Turbervile put it: he 'will begin to vault, and to bellow, casting him selfe with a full leape upon the Hynde to cover hir, and that quickly'.

I worked on and off Rum for four years, overlapping at the end with Tim Clutton-Brock who built up a team of behaviourists at Cambridge and who was able to work with Fiona to monitor the life histories of the wild deer at Kilmory to good effect. Tim was a very highly motivated evolutionary behaviourist. We had shared a house together in Cambridge and I came to know him very well. To Gerald and myself, red-blooded physiologists, interested in the mechanisms, what made animals tick etc., the study of behaviour always seemed perhaps a little effete, rather nebulous. Nevertheless Tim's work was pursued with ferocious intensity, but, more importantly, with highly professional analysis, at a time when evolutionary behaviour was just becoming fashionable. Desmond Morris's *The Naked Ape* had appeared, and Robert Ardrey's *Territorial Imperative*, but *The Selfish Gene* and *The Blind Watchmaker* by Richard Dawkins only became bestsellers years later. Tim, capitalising on Fiona's ability to recognise the deer as individuals, was able to examine just how successful each one of a significant number of individual deer had been in achieving progeny during their lives. Such longitudinal studies of large mammals are, for good reason, very rare. With wild red deer stags living as long as twelve years and hinds up to fifteen or more, vertical studies of this species ideally need to last about twenty years.

An interest in what Tim was trying to do was borne in on me when he asked in his bantering way why I thought it was that hinds bark and stags don't. What he was referring to is the alarm bark that one of a group of hinds will often make when she is being approached and she becomes suspicious. It is a noise that is the bane of stalkers, or even of field biologists, trying to approach a group of hinds without disturbing them. Stags on the other hand rarely make this noise. The question was why not?

Of course I hadn't thought about it very much and hadn't a clue, although the answer provided by Tim seems very clear to me now, and like all good theories makes you wonder why you hadn't thought of it sooner. Hinds generally spend their lives with close relatives: a mature hind is normally accompanied by her daughters of successive years and by her sisters. (In fact Roger and Fiona had shown that stags castrated as calves will associate even more closely with their dams than do the hinds.) Stags on the other hand tend to disperse quite widely as one- and two-year-olds, and so are much less likely to associate with close relatives. Now, as readers of *The Selfish Gene* know only too well, an animal has a strong interest in doing everything it can to protect and procreate its own genes, whilst the more distantly related another animal is, the less advantage there is in assisting its chances of survival. Indeed quite the reverse; this distant relative represents competition and there may be advantage in hindering its chances of reproducing.

Thus will a lion taking up with a new lioness often kill the cubs she has borne to his predecessor and the Hanuman langur, an Indian monkey, makes infanticide of his spouse's babies a way of life. By killing the suckling baby he causes lactation to halt abruptly and oestrus and ovulation to resume, making an early fertile copulation possible. More disquietingly, Potts and Short point out that human stepfathers are up to sixty times more likely than the biological father to kill a baby. But back to the deer: obviously then the hind barking will, by alarming her family, improve their chances of survival even at some small risk to herself, whereas the stag, surrounded by much less closely related individuals, does not find the risk worth while and keeps quiet, looking after number one. Tim's explanation as to why hinds give the alarm bark and stags don't seemed plausible to me. At the same time in a complementary way we physiologists could probably explain many other things.

Thus I suggested, contentiously, a reason why hinds often roar like stags in the few days prior to calving but at no other time: during late pregnancy, oestrogen levels rise but we know that until a few days before giving birth the hormone of pregnancy, progesterone, is also present at high levels and that this hormone seems to neutralise the effects of oestrogens on the brain. When progesterone levels fall in those last few days of gestation then the brain is exposed to the full behavioural effects of oestrogen and, as I had been able to demonstrate in the work I had done for my Ph.D., oestrogen mimics the male hormone testosterone in acting to stimulate roaring in either sex. So, probably, if my conjecture was correct, the occasional roar prior to calving had no significant survival value one way or the other. If it had then it would either have disappeared or become more common. The hind's roar was, I argued, merely a hormonal accident.

Tim, by careful statistical analysis of all the data collected by himself, his students and especially Fiona, was able to unravel all sorts of fascinating points. One of the most interesting was his identification of the fact that the hinds most dominant in competing with other hinds had a more than average chance of producing a male offspring. This is real grist to the mill of the evolutionary biologist, who may argue that because stag calves are likely to be larger and drink more milk than hind calves they are more 'expensive' to produce but that equally, if they survive, they may have better prospects of promulgating their genes.

Not quite biological determinism, but perhaps enough to make you question your own motives and always look for the mechanistic solution.

5 THE HISTORY OF A SCOTTISH ISLAND – HOW STRANGE A CYCLE

From the first day, together with the incessant rain, the island's past soaked in. Fiona and I were lodged in Kinloch Castle, albeit in the servants' quarters, and we worked every morning in the remains of the walled garden behind the castle. Sometimes our stags rutted and hinds calved within ruined glasshouses where once, in living memory, turtles and humming-birds had revelled in heated luxury. What a monument to the vanity and impermanence of material achievement.

Conversely during much of the day, and especially in the evenings, we were walking through the remains of the abandoned village at Kilmory with the graveyard beside it, raised high over several centuries by the accumulation of mortal remains. The only legible gravestone there told of the shepherd, Murdo Mathieson, losing five of his family in three days to diphtheria in 1873 (illustration 3). That had been enough for him, poor man, he had upped sticks and transplanted himself to New Zealand where his family, like John Donne's violet, prospered: his son gave his name to Lake Mathieson.

I suppose most folk who have come to spend some of their lives on the Isle of Rum become haunted by the history of the place. Like the landscape, its story is very stark and I soon became immersed in the subject, researching and eventually writing some of it into my thesis. Although my particular interest was, of course, the deer, it would not be possible to remain unmoved by the vicissitudes of the human population on such a largely inhospitable piece of land.

I want to describe the history of Rum, its people and its deer in a little detail now. My task has been made easier by *Rum: Nature's Island*, written by Magnus Magnusson and published in 1998 by Luath Press to aid Scottish Natural Heritage in their work on the island now in their care.

The story of the islanders and the deer seems to me a perfect microcosm of man's struggle to develop in disparate environments worldwide, and his influence on the environment and on game, and so may reveal some universal patterns applicable elsewhere in the world. More modestly, it is undeniable that many parts of the west and north of Scotland have a very similar story to tell, and I believe that man's interactions with deer on Rum represent, at the very least, a pattern for our involvement with grazing and browsing wild animals, certainly in the temperate regions populated by deer.

As on Rum, so elsewhere, it appears that from its beginnings the rural human population grows, slowly at first and then all too quickly, and as it does so, it eliminates or reduces the large wild game whilst usually removing most of the woodlands. These two go together, since in all societies, with the advent of food production, that is farming, there is a need to destroy forest, and this tends to expose animals to hunting pressures which also increase with the density of the human population.

During the next phase, urbanisation, there is a progressive depopulation of the countryside associated with the move into cities and towns, and game numbers rebound. Throughout the developed world, deer populations, for example, are with few exceptions now increasing very rapidly, and efforts to control them are not always proving successful. In Scotland between 1970 and 1992 deer numbers, despite pressure from the Deer Commission on the sporting estates to kill more, increased from around 190,000 to over 300,000, although strenuous efforts to increase the cull have now perhaps recently stabilised numbers. In France the roe deer population is thought to be doubling every twenty years, and in England the muntjac population is increasing by 10 per cent per annum. But it is in the United States that deer numbers are most impressive. Thus the American white-tailed deer numbered less than half a million at the beginning of the twentieth century, but around twenty million by the 1980s. The deer hunters of the United States were, in 1976, killing some two and a half million deer per annum and spending as an industry 2,600 million dollars in doing it. Now they are killing over six million deer per annum.

In Sweden, Linnaeus, the eighteenth-century biologist, is thought never to have seen a moose, yet now there are more than 300,000 in his country, of which 100,000 are shot annually. Moose in Sweden also represent the major cause of car accidents.

On Rum the relationship between man and deer showed the same cycle and it is remarkably well documented. We know, for instance, that the island was visited very early in Scotland's history since recent excavations have shown, in a field behind Kinloch Castle, the earliest known evidence of human habitation in Scotland, dating back almost nine thousand years. Unfortunately these sites have not yet revealed much of what was being eaten except for some hazelnut shells and, much more recent, about five thousand years old, a brew identified (from pollen analysis of material found attached to a piece of pot) as oats and barley flavoured with meadowsweet, heather honey and bog myrtle. This sounds to me suspiciously like the Athole brose well known in nineteenth-century Scotland.

Deer bones do appear elsewhere, in the midden of a cave site which may date to the Mesolithic, and it seems likely that deer were present in large numbers on Rum from soon after the last ice age. It is logical to assume that those early visitors found the deer on Rum a valuable addition to their diet as well as a source of antler and leather.

There are quite abundant early references to Rum, reflecting the relative ease of movement by water as against land transport, and consequently the value of islands. Yet as islands go it was always a particularly inhospitable, infertile place – for example, in 1549 when Donald Monro, Dean of the Isles, wrote one of the first descriptions of Rum, a permanent human population had still probably not been established or was at least very small. Monro wrote: '. . . ane forrest of heigh mountains, and abundance of little deir in it, which deir will never be slain downwith, but the principal settis must be in the height of the hills, because the deer will be called upwards always by the tinchel, or without the tinchel they will pass up . . . also many wild nests upon the plaine mure as men pleasis to gadder, and yet by reason the fowls has few to start them except deire'.

The 'settis' or setts to which Dean Monro refers would be traps or funnels, often known as 'elricks', designed to allow a large body of people – a 'tainchell' or 'tinchell' – to drive a number of deer through a narrow defile in which they could be slaughtered by waiting armed men.

In 1796 the Old Statistical Account of Scotland describes how these were thought to have functioned on Rum: 'Before the use of firearms, their method of killing deer was as follows: on each side of a glen, formed by two mountains, stone dykes were begun pretty high in the mountains, and carried to the lower part of the valley, always drawing nearer, till within three or four feet of each other. From this narrow pass, a circular space was inclosed by a stone wall, of a height sufficient to confine the deer; to this place they were pursued and destroyed. The vestige of one of these inclosures is still to be seen in Rum.'

Such setts or elricks on Rum can still be just about made out and two have been described high up on the south slopes of Orval by John Love, while in 1995 Historic Scotland reported a further three possible setts on Rum.

Shortly after Dean Monro's account, in about 1580, the king commissioned a description of the islands which reported that Rum could only be relied on to muster six or seven fighting men compared to sixty from Eigg. The same report described Rum as 'an ile of small profit . . . the hills and waist glennis are commodious only for the hunting of deir'.

In 1703 Martin Martin published his *Description of the Western Isles*, a volume that was taken with them and much used by Boswell and Johnson on their tour of the Hebrides seventy years later. Martin describes some hundreds of deer on Rum at the time of his writing and he also, interestingly, recounts a tradition among the resident Macleans of not shooting at them in one specific area, the slopes of Fionchra, for to do so 'they say proves fatal to the posterity of Lachlin, a cadet of Maclean of Coll's family'. Yet despite this early and far-sighted piece of nature conservation, reinforced by superstition, deer numbers continued to fall. In his *Report of the Hebrides* of 1764 and 1771, Walker wrote, 'although the wood is now gone, a herd of red deer still remains'. At that time the human population was, he said, 304 in fifty-seven families; hardly surprising that so many people on such an inhospitable island, together with their livestock, should have eliminated the trees.

Boswell and Johnson were blown past Rum in 1773 in a storm and although Boswell 'became very sick' he was able to report that there were still deer in the hills of Rum. When next year Thomas Pennant managed to land he was told there were just eighty deer left. The setts, aided latterly by firearms, had almost finished their work.

Finally the Old Statistical Account of 1796 reported not only the loss of the trees but also the end of the deer: 'In Rum there were formerly great numbers of deer; there was also a copse of wood, that afforded cover to their fawns from birds of prey, particularly from the eagle: while the wood throve, the deer also throve; now that the wood is totally destroyed, the deer are extirpated.'

Thus it is pretty clear that by about 1790 the deer had gone and it is hard not to believe that the human population was as important a predator of the deer as the eagles. By then they had access to firearms. Is it too fanciful to imagine that the collapse of the clan system, due to the ravages of the Duke of Cumberland's forces after Culloden and other economic factors, meant that such pieces of clan lore and restraint as that of the Macleans described by Martin had fallen into decay? Might this have just saved the deer from extinction?

It seems unlikely. All the accounts suggest a very small human population on Rum until the mid-seventeenth or early eighteenth century. But from 1728, when a census carried out by the Society for the Propagation of Christian Knowledge recorded 152 persons over the age of five years, to around 1770 when Walker's census revealed 304 inhabitants, and to the figure of 443 in 1796 when the Old

Statistical Account was compiled, it is very clear that population growth was massive. A consequent growing demand for firewood would be likely to reduce any woodland and that, together with the obvious requirement for food, must have put tremendous pressure on the deer. Their extinction was inevitable, and reflected a similar pattern throughout the Highlands and Islands where deer numbers had become very low by the end of the eighteenth century. In southern Britain comparable reasons led to the decline of stag hunting to be followed by the new fad for chasing the 'uneatable' fox, though the use of carted deer allowed many through the eighteenth century and later to go on hunting deer in areas where they had become rare or extinct.

The astonishing rise in the human population is typical of much of Scotland in that period and its causes remain conjectural: possibly the introduction of the potato, improved systems of cultivation of grain, smallpox vaccination, or just a more stable life following the disruption of the clan system; or a combination of all three factors.

After his first and last military victory at Culloden in 1746, the fat Duke of Cumberland, his reputation preserved by Handel who commemorated his achievement by writing 'See the Conquering Hero Comes', had behaved with terrible brutality, encouraging his soldiers to kill and mutilate the wounded. And thereafter he had his men lay waste much of the Highlands, killing men, women and children alike.

The clan system, already fatally damaged, then broke down quickly as chieftains began to exact their dues in cash instead of fealty, to provide for, among other things, their education in Paris at the Sorbonne as well as elsewhere in Europe. Nevertheless, as the old order collapsed there came a new period of calm which may have contributed to the population build-up.

There was also a rapid change from a grain-based diet to one dangerously dependent on the potato. In fact, there is evidence that few of the islanders on Rum were even making cultivations for grain production until the early eighteenth century. John Walker in 1764 reports the recent death of an inhabitant of Rum aged one hundred and three. This man was described as having been fifty years old before having ever tasted bread: 'I was even told, that this old man used frequently to remind the younger People, of the simple and hardy Fare of former times, used to upbraid them with their Indulgence in the Article of Bread, and judged it unmanly in them to toil like Slaves with their Spades, for the production of such an unnecessary Piece of Luxury.' This account must be typical of legions of comments made over many millennia wherever food-production systems overtook those of the hunter-gatherer.

The potato came much later than grain, of course. It hadn't made its appearance in the islands before the early to mid-eighteenth century. Did this vegetable allow such an improved diet that the fertility of the people could improve? In fact it would seem that, on Rum at least, the expansion of the human population preceded the arrival of the potato. Nevertheless, dependence on the potato exposed people to risks of crop failure due to blight, and the resulting potato famines and associated cholera epidemics which visited Scotland and Ireland between 1846 and 1856.

A more important consideration was the introduction of smallpox vaccination. In 1764 John Walker had noted of Rum: 'the island was then accounted populous, as it had not been visited by the Small Pox for 29 years; for by this Disease upon former Occasions, it had been almost depopulate.' And Samuel Johnson describes the laird of the Isle of Muck arranging vaccination of his islanders when he visited in 1773.

Whatever the answer the conclusion was inevitable. Pennant had described 'famine in the aspect' of the Rum islanders as early as 1772, and in 1812 and again in 1817 Maclean of Coll had been forced to provide grain shipments for his starving clansmen. But by 1825 personal economic pressures compelled him to take drastic action and he leased Rum to Dr Lachlan Maclean of Gallanach on Coll, a kinsman by marriage. At Whitsun 1825 the islanders were all given twelve months to quit in order to make way for eight thousand blackface sheep.

On 11 July 1826, three hundred islanders of all ages were cleared into two ships, the *Dove of Harmony* and the *Highland Lad* bound for Port Hawkesbury in Nova Scotia. Fifty years later the scene was recalled by John McMaister, a shepherd on Rum at the time, as 'of such stressful description that he would never be able to forget it till his dying day ... the wild outcries of the men and the heart-breaking wails of the women and their children filled all the air between the mountainous shores of the bay.'

That left only around fifty people on Rum and these were shipped off two years later in the *Saint Lawrence*, together with 150 from the Isle of Muck. Only one family of native islanders remained, eleventh-generation Macleans, though Dr Maclean was then obliged to import a dozen families from Skye and Mull to look after his sheep.

In the event the wool and mutton industry soon collapsed, ironically owing to imports from Australia and New Zealand, destinations for so many emigrants. Throughout the Scottish Highlands and Islands famine ensued, though never reaching the severity of the great Irish hunger.

In 1838 two members of the Statistical Society of Glasgow published a report entitled *Remarks on the Evils at present Affecting the Highlands and Islands of Scotland* in which they referred to Rum as: '... one of the most rugged, bleak and barren of the Hebrides ... so peculiarly liable to violent storms of wind and rain, as, with the exception of a few hundred acres of low lying land, to afford no encouragement to the raising of crops on any part of its surface. It is occupied as a sheep farm by Dr Maclean, who, with his family and shepherds and a few cotiers, forms its only inhabitants.'

Hugh Miller, born in 1802 in Cromarty, a small village on the north-east coast of Scotland, was one of those towering intellects of the nineteenth century whose nonconformist example inspires wonder and humility in those of us who look back from a world full of all advantages. A wild and intractable boy, he left school young and became a stonemason. His experiences with the rocks led him to become an internationally renowned geologist and palaeontologist, corresponding with Darwin and Agassiz. Despite this he remained a creationist and became editor of the Free Church journal, *The Witness*. He wrote prolifically and his writings are highly readable and well worth exploring today. I find his prose compelling and inserted the following stomach-churningly melancholic account from his book *The*

Cruise of the Betsy into my thesis. He is describing Rum as he found it in 1846, that is twenty years after the clearance.

> The armies of the insect world were sporting in the light this evening by millions; a brown stream that runs through the valley yielded an incessant poppling sound; ... along a distant hillside there ran what seemed the ruins of a gray stone fence, erected, says tradition, in a remote age, to facilitate the hunting of the deer; there were fields on which the heath and moss of the surrounding moorlands were fast encroaching, that had borne many a successive harvest; and prostrate cottages, that had been the scenes of christenings, and bridals, and blythe new-year's days; ... but in the entire prospect not a man nor a man's dwelling could the eye command. I do not much like extermination carried out so thoroughly and on a system; ... and I cannot quite see on what principle the ominous increase which is taking place among us in the worse class, is to form our solace or apology for the wholesale expatriation of the better ... It did not seem as if the depopulation of Rum had tended much to any one's advantage. The single sheep farmer had been unfortunate in his speculations, and had left the island, and the proprietor, his landlord, seemed to have been as little fortunate as the tenant, for the island itself was in the market; and a report went current at the time that it was on the eve of being purchased by some wealthy Englishman, who purposed converting it into a deer forest. How strange a cycle!

Indeed, as Hugh Miller indicated, the next phase of the cycle, as for so many other parts of the Highlands and Islands of Scotland, was transformation into a deer forest or sporting estate.

Though materially often destitute, the islanders had been culturally rich and well able to mount a ceilidh in honour of visitors. Thus the geologist John MacCulloch, visiting the very remote glen of Guiridil on the north-west of Rum six years prior to the evictions, wrote: 'There was an old fiddle hanging up in a corner, very crazy in the pegs and in the intestines, but still practicable ... A ball here requires no great preparations. The lassies had no shoes and marvellous little petticoat; but to compensate for these deficiencies they had an abundance of activity and good will. Where shall I go into such a house in England, find such manners and such conversation ... and see such smoky shelves covered not only with the books of the ancients, but of the moderns . . . well thumbed and well talked of?'

The material life these people lived was not so very different from that of the Neolithic, yet it is a bizarre fact, typical of so many Highland communities, that no sooner had the indigenous peoples been removed, in a process not unlike ethnic cleansing, than they were replaced by Victorian and Edwardian magnates at the cutting edge of global industrialisation.

Despite their poverty, the strong culture and civility of the Hebridean islanders had also been commented on by Boswell, fifty years earlier. Of his time on the Isle of Raasay in 1773 he wrote: 'More gentleness of manners, or a more pleasing appearance of domestick society, is not found in the most polished countries.'

In the case of Rum the wealthy Englishman alluded to by Hugh Miller was the second Marquis of Salisbury, whose son came to be prime minister. He bought the island in 1845. His object was clearly and simply the creation of a sporting estate and he set about this with a will. In an effort to improve the fishing he employed three hundred workmen for two years cutting a channel through rock and constructing a dam. Unfortunately the dam was built back to front, that is concave instead of convex, and burst two days after completion. This £11,000 folly is still clearly visible and known to all on Rum as 'Salisbury's Dam'.

Of much greater interest to me, however, is Salisbury's role in reintroducing deer to Rum. As well as making an ill-judged attempt to establish the softer fallow deer on the island, he also imported red deer from Scottish estates and English parks and by the time he sold the island in 1860 there are thought to have been about six hundred red deer on the island. The period of their absence must have only been some seventy years.

After one more change of hands the island was purchased by John Bullough, a Lancastrian industrialist, whose improvements to the weaving loom brought him and his family great wealth. His son, Sir George Bullough, was responsible for Kinloch Castle where Fiona, Gerald and I were originally billeted, on the east side of Rum. It took three hundred men from Eigg and Lancashire almost three years to build, and history relates that they were paid a shilling a week extra to wear the new Rum tartan kilts, while smokers received twopence per week extra as an incentive to deter the midges. How strange a cycle, indeed!

The castle at Kinloch was supplied by a hydroelectric system and was only the second place in Scotland to be lit by electricity – the first being Glasgow. The walled garden in which Fiona and I worked with our tame deer was in total decay by 1970, but in its heyday it had been home to six domed palm houses with humming-birds, turtles and alligators.

The castle, it has been argued, remains the most intact example of an Edwardian country house in Britain. It has been much described and always fascinates but it is peripheral to the present story. Suffice it to say that Sir George died in 1939 whilst playing golf in Boulogne-sur-Mer and he now lies in the huge Doric temple of a mausoleum which he had erected for his father at Harris on the south-west coast of Rum. His wife, the celebrated beauty, Lady Monica, sold Rum to the Nature Conservancy in 1957 for the very modest price of £23,000. She lived on, in Newmarket, until 1967 and now too lies beside Sir George.

Before we finally leave the Bulloughs to rest in their mausoleum beside the storm-lashed beach of Harris there are two little coincidences which serve to bring this recent history into perspective.

In 1970 my grandfather, who had spent his life in the Yorkshire textile industry, came to visit me in Kinloch Castle. He was then well into his eighties and was able to recount how he had regularly done business with Howard and Bullough Ltd in Accrington. And secondly, Roger Short had been filling his car with petrol near Cambridge in 1967, prior to making a trip north to Rum, when he fell into conversation with the garage proprietor who also ran a fleet of taxis and hearses. When Roger mentioned he was bound for Scotland the garage keeper remarked that he had only the previous month visited Scotland with a hearse on a most curious mission. He had been accompanying Lady Monica to her last resting place, the final few miles of which they had had to accomplish with the coffin in a Nature Conservancy Land-Rover. No longer were the roads maintained by fourteen full-time roadmen; the journey to Harris had become a bottom-gear job.

Returning now to the broader picture; from the point of view of the deer, what happened on Rum is, as I have pointed out earlier, a microcosm of what occurred elsewhere in the Scottish islands and through the Highlands. Deer numbers were high at the beginning of the historical epoch but as the human population swelled, the deer declined. By the late eighteenth century Scottish deer numbers had become very low. Samuel Johnson describes firearms as being so prevalent at the time of his visit in 1773 that he believed that deer on the islands must soon become extinct. And then, finally, with the clearance of the people there were few mouths left to eat venison and at the same time the deer were protected. Consequently their numbers rose almost without interruption to the present levels which, in conjunction with the hill sheep, have become ecologically damaging and arguably responsible for creating what Frank Fraser Darling called the 'wet desert' which covers much of the Highlands today. Recently I played host to a party of deer farmers from the north of Sweden and even they commented that the Highlands of Scotland seemed a desert.

A rather similar story may be told over much of the world: growth in human populations leads to the diminution, and in some cases extinction, of wild grazing mammals, and a decline in biological diversity. The diet changes from wild foods to the products of farms and a much higher intake of animal fats. There then often follows a period of urbanisation with a resulting decline in the human rural population. Pressure on land use is alleviated as still more specialised crop-production systems are introduced to feed the urban population, and, in many areas those wild grazing animals become once more numerous. There are more deer in Britain now than at any time since at least Roman times. Could this give us hope for the grazing animals of Africa? Rural depopulation tragically accelerated by the AIDS epidemic is already occurring locally, but the rocketing human population of Africa makes the destruction of natural grazing, and especially browsing, systems seem inevitable. Potts and Short have pointed out that 'there were 255 million people in the whole of Africa in 1960. By the year 2000 there will be 780 million and the population will be set to double in another twenty-six years.' It is hard to imagine any ecosystems surviving that pressure. A similar fate awaits many other developing parts of the world.

6 FISHING NETS, ANTLERS AND HORNS, AND TRANQUILLISERS

The days on Rum rushed by for me. Working at such close quarters with the deer continued to be an adventure; something unpredictable was always happening.

Man's thoughtlessness had then, in 1970, and probably still does have, an implication for the stags on Rum and other sea-coast deer forests in a very practical way that no one could have anticipated: surprisingly often, stags entangle themselves in fishing nets which trawlers have discarded to litter the beaches. Thrashing their antlers is a normal activity for stags and if they succeed in decorating themselves with vegetation then, during the rut especially, this is a bonus making them more intimidating to other stags.

One late summer evening shortly after I had arrived on Rum I was scoring down specific behaviour patterns in a group of stags at Kilmory against the amazing backdrop of the Skye Cuillins. Chief amongst those stags was one of Gerald's old stalwarts called Crusader; aged perhaps ten years, he was our most mature and impressive stag. During my half-hour observation session Crusader wandered the few hundred yards to the beach and once I had finished I strolled off in his wake.

When I caught up with him his peaceful economy of movement had changed; he had found the great nylon cod-end of a fishing trawl washed up on the beach and must have playfully worked his newly cleaned antlers into it. Inevitably they had become entangled and now the old stag had panicked. He was thrashing his antlers in earnest and desperately trying to rid himself of the burden.

I realised there was no hope of my catching him and even the sharpest knife would make heavy weather of the thick twisted nylon. I rushed up to the Land-Rover for the tranquilliser darting equipment. By the time I had got back to the beach with the loaded dart, perhaps five minutes later, the scene had changed. Now, following a common panic reaction, Crusader had swum out a few yards into the rocky bay until the net was pulling him under. Red deer are very strong swimmers, normally thinking little of swimming a mile across a loch to sweeter grazing on the other side, but this heavy net was too much for poor old Crusader. I tore off my boots and jumped in, covering the few yards easily, but I was too late. Fiona had arrived and she also ploughed into the freezing water, but it was no good. We dragged Crusader's body ashore.

Once our teeth had stopped chattering and we were in dry clothes again, my enthusiasm for venison overcame my reluctance to eat old friends even in those days. I persuaded Fiona to come with me that evening to help take his corpse back for our freezer. This must seem pretty heartless but I think that a reluctance to see waste, inculcated during my Yorkshire Methodist upbringing, has something to do with it.

Also perhaps, studying and grappling with the mysteries of physiology, respect grows for the beauty and complexity of a living system which makes one reluctant to just let it all rot away. I often wonder if vegetarians have considered the fate of all the animals that would either require killing to protect crops, or which would die as a result of populations of herbivores overgrazing their habitats. I for one would find it very difficult to kill animals and then leave them to rot; that connection between hunting, food preparation and eating seems to have permeated at least my own and I believe other people's subconscious.

Anyway, Crusader was desperately tough eating and for the first time I came to understand the importance of age in the quality of meat! Or perhaps it was the stress of his final moments that had rendered the meat all but uneatable.

Other stags entangled in fishing nets lasted longer. Some were found secured by the nets to rocks where they had eventually starved to death. And, in at least one harrowing instance, a stag dragging a length of net, no doubt fancying his new-found headgear, picked a fight, or perhaps just a friendly spar, with another stag. The result was horribly predictable: the two stags were occasionally seen during the winter, grazing together for weeks or months in unnaturally close proximity until death should intervene or, if they were lucky, eventually one, and then the other, should cast his antlers in the spring. I could not get near enough to try a dart. Even the stalkers, employed by the Nature Conservancy to take the annual cull on the island in an effort to keep the deer population in bounds, tried unsuccessfully to free these stags by shooting through their antlers. Ultimately it was deemed merciful to shoot both dead.

When Roger Short had been asked to come up from Cambridge University Veterinary School to use the new-fangled darting and tranquillising systems to catch and mark the deer on Rum in 1965, that had been real pioneering work. And Roger, ever curious, had taken the opportunity to develop the deer connexion further and investigate their breeding behaviour. As such pronounced seasonal breeders, and with that perennial yet deciduous curiosity, antlers, as well, deer were of great interest to the reproductive physiologist. Roger's worldwide reputation had been made in the study of hormones at a time when the research which culminated in the development of birth-control pills was getting under way. He was able to see how understanding the way in which deer breed might contribute to our knowledge of the role and action of hormones, with the ever-present chance of making advances in human and veterinary areas. Science would have made little progress had it not been for the role of serendipity. As Charles Darwin's grandfather, Erasmus Darwin, wrote: 'a fool ... is a man who never tried an experiment in his life.'

It is hard to realise just how little was known about the life of deer in the 1960s, and just how lowly was rated the study of wild animals in relation to their environment. An Englishman called Henry Evans had devoted many years of his life to an investigation of red deer on the island of Jura, which he published in about 1890 as *Some Account of Jura Red Deer*, a study many years ahead of its time. He had got his stalkers to ear-tag newly born calves and to make systematic counts of dead deer in such a way as to unravel much of the demographics of that population. But it was left to Frank Fraser Darling to describe in detail the behaviour of wild Scottish deer in his *Herd of Red Deer*. This wonderfully readable account, published in 1937, had no follow-up until the work on Rum began in the sixties. Like so many others I had been taught by him to believe in the gravity and inevitability of the ecological crisis. When Fraser Darling died it always seemed to me that the obsequies were inadequate for a Scot of such genius and foresight.

The excitement of the rut and its meaning had stimulated Gerald to investigate the changes in the stag which precede the mating season. For example, the neck muscles of an adult stag, stimulated by the same testosterone that bodybuilders abuse, will double in girth in preparation for the rut and the fighting that will accompany it. With these colossal neck muscles a rutting stag could, I suppose, very easily turn over a small car. And then, of course, there is the yearly antler cycle. Very few people seem to understand this; and, even if they know that the antlers fall off and regrow each year, then many do not understand why.

The fact is that deer are distinguished from grazing species all over the world by, amongst other things, their antlers. Cattle, sheep, antelope, gazelle, goats, all possess *horns* and are called *bovids*; deer on the other hand grow *antlers* and are quite distinct, being called *cervids*. There is thus, you could argue, as close a relationship between, say, cows and goats as there is between, for example, fallow and roe deer; and in any case, it is quite clear that gazelle or antelope are more closely related to sheep or cows than they are to deer. It was for this reason that it came as no surprise to any zoologist that BSE, bovine spongiform encephalopathy, 'Mad Cow Disease', which had originated in cattle fed 'meat and bonemeal' derived from sheep infected with scrapie, also appeared in antelope in zoos but never in the deer.

Incidentally, while we're on that subject, 'meat and bonemeal' has been fed to livestock in Britain since at least the nineteenth century, and scrapie has been a recognised sheep disease for around 250 years. Thus, although we would all, especially journalists, like to allocate blame to greedy 'agribusinessmen' or feckless politicians, it may be a little unfair to pinpoint modern intensive farming practices as the cause of the BSE epidemic. So often we are told how unnatural it is to feed meat and bonemeal to herbivores, yet nothing is ever quite so black and white in biology. Herbivores have developed a strategy of eating vegetation which, especially grass, is highly indigestible, even if usually available in quantity. Cows have therefore only rudimentary skills in hunting other animals for the pot! Yet most grazing animals will, given a chance, chew up dead animals, or even live ones. I have seen deer knock over rabbits diseased with myxomatosis and chew them up, and an interesting paper was published by a scientist on Rum, which described deer waiting on the tops of the mountains for Manx shear-waters to make their nocturnal return to feed their chicks in burrows; the deer killed shearwaters by blows of the foreleg and then ate them. Deer on the impoverished grazings of Rum regularly chew cast antlers and will quite quickly reduce them to a stump – in fact they can sometimes be seen chewing on the antlers of their colleagues while they're still attached to their heads!

Now, I hear you, get back to the point: what is the difference between a horn and an antler? The answer is that the horn is permanent. It does not fall off each year like an antler, but instead is, in the middle, a live, growing thing. The outside is covered by a dead protective layer of keratin, like hooves or fingernails. Because horns grow all through an animal's life but at different rates depending on season and nutrition, the horns of a goat, for instance, have ridges which indicate the seasonal growth surges. In this way you can see the age of a goat by counting the ridges on its horns. The antler, in contrast, falls off each year and is replaced by another antler similar in shape. The antlers of a stag will in successive years tend to become larger, especially in his early years, but after about seven or eight they show little increase and will from about ten years start to become smaller again. It is clear then that stags do not produce a new point each year and there is no truth in the suggestion, dating back to Pliny, that you can age a stag by counting his antler points.

When a stag is growing his antlers, which for the red deer takes place during the summer, they are completely alive with lots of blood coursing through them and grow very rapidly, faster indeed than any other mammalian tissue (illustrations 1a, 5). Thus an adult red deer stag may grow a centimetre a day and its larger relative the Canadian elk up to an inch a day. At this time the antler is covered with fur, has nerves and can feel, as well as having veins and arteries, skin, hair and grease glands, and somehow, the innate ability to regrow in a shape similar to that of previous years. The regeneration of the antler is one of the mysteries of biology which, if we could fully understand it, might even open the door to allowing us to enable amputees to regenerate limbs.

Why do antlers drop off every year? As I have already mentioned, many stags break their antlers in fighting during the rut. On Rum I remember that the stag Cecil broke both his antlers off right at the base one year; but, by being able to make good that damage, the next year he was able to compete, unhandicapped, once more for access to the hinds. Thus a broken antler is not a total disaster for the individual. This means that he can afford to grow much more fancy headgear than the horned animal; for if a horn is broken, the bovid is almost certainly doomed to death and is in any case unlikely to be successful in breeding again. The fracture of an antler is but a temporary inconvenience.

And, while we are at it, why do they have antlers anyway? The answer is plainly and simply that the hard dead antler of deer is present for the rut; it is a weapon and a shield for competing with other stags for the favours of the females. The cleaning of the velvet and the appearance of the hard burnished antler coincides, as Gerald had shown, with the time of rapidly growing male sex hormone levels and it is thus very obviously ready for use in the rut. This comes as no surprise because it is quite clear from watching deer that they grow their antlers as secondary sexual characters. Antlers are deterrents and, since deterrents cannot work if no one dares to test them in earnest, they are also used in fighting off other stags with designs on the same group of hinds. These fights frequently result in injury. Stags may damage their eyes, break bones and, most commonly, their antlers, but usually by the next autumn those wounds have healed and the fight to perpetuate their genes is on again.

Evolutionarily we believe that antlers originated in something rather like the bumps on the heads of giraffes. We can imagine primordial deer fighting with their heads, then developing bony outgrowths which made them more effective in fighting. In a temperate climate only those young born in the spring would survive, so that successful matings could only take place over a short period. Thus the bony knobs would only be needed for a few weeks during which we can imagine them becoming damaged and a scabby growth forming. This scab would bring about healing ready for the next mating season. The larger the resulting bony structure the more intimidating it is and the more likely to be effective in a fight. Evidence for this theory comes from the fact that the velvet antler is seen when examined under the microscope to have much in common with a healing wound. This must all go to strengthen the possibility that a study of velvet antlers could do much to help an understanding of wound healing with possible human and veterinary benefits.

Gerald had gradually enticed a few stags into regular attendance at Kilmory by feeding them outside the Laundry with maize, and eventually this grew into a substantial number. A lot of my time was to be spent capturing these in order to mark them with either ear tags or neck collars. Indeed it had been to catch the deer that Roger had first come to Rum in the early sixties, shortly after the island had been sold to the Nature Conservancy. Sir Frank Fraser Darling had at that time made the memorable remark that Rum should be seen as a 'natural laboratory'. Work on the deer in this natural lab would be seriously impeded if it was not possible to identify them or if they were shot during the annual cull.

Roger, freshly returned from Africa where he had used the revolutionary new drug M99 to capture antelope, was the best man to help the Nature Conservancy. His first efforts involved the use of carrots.

A solution of the highly potent M99 was mixed with DMSO (dimethyl sulphoxide) and sealed into ampoules. DMSO has the fascinating property of being able to 'carry' other drugs through the skin. It used to be a popular trick for students to mix it with oil of peppermint. Dabbing a little on the finger has the remarkable effect of allowing the peppermint to taste in the mouth. The idea with the carrots was that if a phial were concealed in a carrot, a stag would greedily munch up the vegetable and then find himself transported into stupefaction. In practice the idea was not a great success, mostly because the stags had an uncanny facility for picking up a carrot, chewing it and then astonishingly spitting out the fragile ampoules intact.

After this, Roger developed a system using a crossbow, bought at a London toy shop, with metal darts designed by him and made up by the university engineering labs at Cambridge. Pressurised by a spring, the drug was sealed with a plastic tube which broke on impact. Sometimes, if the dart was in the bow for a time before a shot could be made, the plastic would rupture and release a fine spray of the drug. This unpredictable element lent an added dimension to the frisson of excitement as one waited to see if the chosen stag would wander into range.

At the time we were helping the manufacturers to evaluate M99, and had been given a substantial supply of the dry powder which had to be weighed and dissolved for use. This drug was the major breakthrough in the search for a potent tranquilliser for wild animals, as Roger had shown in Africa, where it was now being eagerly taken up for conservation and research work. However, evaluation was still under way and it was not yet available commercially. Before M99 came on to the market the most effective drug had been succinyl choline which had the horrific effect of paralysing the animal rather than rendering it unconscious. It has thankfully been superseded by M99 which seems to act perfectly humanely.

Although much discussion still centres around the means of firing a dart, the real high technology is the drug. It is now, looking back those thirty years, just amazing how effectively M99 and its chemical relatives have stood the test of time. There are still few – if any – drugs as effective. It can be reliably reversed to bring the animal back to consciousness: KO–OK as the manufacturers used to say in their promotional literature. It has allowed scientists to find out much more about large mammals, and one of the first applications was, for example, in the capture and evacuation of rhinos from the area to be flooded by the Kariba dam.

Its one drawback is the susceptibility of man to its effects. We didn't fully appreciate this in the early days, and I remember receiving a substantial dose squirted from a dart into my eye when I was alone and several miles from the nearest possible assistance. I washed it out in a burn and seemed none the worse. But since then some vets have recounted strange sensations from handling the drug and there have even been fatalities.

M99, now marketed as a constituent of the commercially available Immobilon, is also effective in sheep although I have never had occasion to use it for that purpose. A Cambridge research team needing to catch some of the wild Soay sheep on St Kilda once asked me to supply them with the drug, and after taking advice from the Royal College of Veterinary Surgeons, this I agreed to do.

The island of St Kilda is very remote. Its declining population was, sadly but inevitably, and by broad agreement amongst themselves, evacuated in 1930. By the time of their departure the St Kildans and their lifestyle, dependent on the capture of wild seabirds by climbing the huge sea cliffs, had become an anachronism for the amusement of passing tourist ships.

Over one hundred miles off the Scottish mainland, the island has served for years as an army outpost as well as a place for scientists to investigate its unique wild life. The garrison is served by air from Benbecula in the Outer Hebrides about sixty miles away, although there are occasional boat landings as well. By courtesy of the army, regular mail is dropped from aircraft because there is no landing strip. Since the Immobilon was wanted in a hurry it was despatched on the weekly mail drop by air, and because of the dangerous and urgent nature of the package of drugs, it was privileged to be given a mailbag to itself. Along with the other heavier bags, this one was flung out when the aircraft made its low-level pass but, being so light, it was whisked up by the slipstream and became firmly clamped to the tailplane whence it was retrieved after the aircraft had come to a standstill back in Benbecula. Ever helpful, the crew put a brick in the bag, flew back to St Kilda, and this time made an uneventful drop.

7 HUNTING, COOKING AND WILD FOOD

I came to quite enjoy darting deer with tranquillisers. It had all the excitement of hunting, I suppose, without the *coup de grâce*. Man in those five or six million years before he learnt to domesticate animals must have developed a taste for hunting which was essential to his survival, and became fixed in his genetic make-up. The urge to hunt, now made redundant by farming, is still there, and this compulsion is evidenced by the hordes of modern hunters in North America or Europe and elsewhere, who take to the fields and forest each year, dwarfing even the Allied mobilisation of the Second World War.

The Spanish philosopher Ortega y Gasset wrote: 'Only the hunter, imitating the perpetual alertness of the wild animal, sees everything.' This seems to be the essence of why people enjoy hunting. The poet Ted Hughes was an avid hunter, and of fishing he wrote: 'Any kind of fishing provides that connection with the whole living world. It gives you the opportunity of being totally immersed, turning back into yourself in a good way. A form of meditation, communion with levels of yourself that are deeper then the ordinary self.' And 'hunting and fishing ... reconnect you in a gentle, natural way without going into artificial situations or altered consciousness. You just seem to go into a more natural mode. And people who don't fish and hunt are finding difficulty making that reconnection with the whole cycle.'

The same must be true, I imagine, of gardening. Why else do we have this urge to dabble in the mud every spring? And what about cooking? Upon the practice of these arts to occupy every waking moment depended the survival of our forebears. Isn't it reasonable to suppose that these ingrained survival skills have not left us in the few years since they have been made superfluous by industrial technology? Would you not expect them to have been incorporated into our genetic constitution? They remain the most popular of pastimes even if they are often sublimated in television. Probably more enjoy vicariously the preparation of food on the screen than in the kitchen now. Maybe the sight of others cooking is sufficient to satisfy that inherited urge to cook.

I am not particularly attracted to hunting – perhaps the primeval urge is sated by my work in darting animals – but I do understand the requirement, paradoxically on welfare and environmental grounds, in Scotland at least, both to reduce the deer population and keep it at such a level as to allow trees to regenerate and to prevent huge die-offs in bad winters. We vets are well versed in the practice of euthanasia, 'putting animals to sleep' when they are suffering, and the idea of allowing the wild deer population to increase to starvation point is anathema to most of us, let alone the ensuing environmental damage.

Talking about cooking, we naturally had to cook for ourselves on Rum. This pleased me greatly. Much of my time that should perhaps have been spent on more academic pursuits was spent cooking. Fiona knew about wine, something that Glasgow University had not pre-pared me for, and, with her knowledgeable participation, we gradually tasted. When she left for a year's overland travels with Gerald in search of the largest surviving reptile, the Komodo dragon, she left behind wine that we had jointly bought and which I shamefully consumed. The guilt remains, and perhaps still adds a certain piquancy to my interest in and enjoyment of wine.

But it was really in an appreciation of food that I passed the long evenings on the island. You might think the scope would have been fairly limited, but the island at that time still possessed a minute dairy herd to supply the inhabitants with fresh milk and cream. And there was a grocery delivery so that telephoned orders would be packed into cardboard boxes for the next day's ferry. And there was always the fish. Most of the daylight hours were sacrosanct – we were just too busy working; but occasionally we would fish for mackerel, and at the right time there were saithe that could be lured on to a hook with the clumsiest of baits – a hooked feather on a piece of twine on a long bamboo. The bay at Kilmory was quite frequently netted by a very respectable poacher in the summer nights, but I never got round to that and the best I achieved was, with Fiona's help, one or two sea-trout on a spinner.

One dark evening, Roger and I were walking back to the bothy. It was high tide and the sea was only a few feet from the post office door. We could not avoid noticing that the water was seething unnaturally. Whitebait were being driven ashore by, we supposed, mackerel. In a trice I had my pullover off and with the sleeves knotted had entangled several suppers' worth. The resulting glut has made me ambivalent to whitebait to this day.

The older folk on the island could recall when herring had been so plentiful that they too were sometimes driven on to the beach so families could fill their buckets, but by the 1970s those days were long gone. Mallaig had become the biggest herring-fishing port in Europe. Decrepit ships, some of which had evidently once depended on sail, were anchored offshore, and loaded herring from the fishing boats to take back to Scandinavia and Russia; they were known as klondikers. With the cured herrings in barrels piled high on their decks they didn't always seem the most seaworthy vessels, and we often found those barrels washed up on the beaches. And there was their modern counterpart, articulated juggernauts loading herring for a dash back to Holland and Germany. As the trucks were being loaded from the boats the herring spilled out on to the quay in great piles and, when in Mallaig, I used to shovel up a few bagfuls for pickling. It was no wonder that herring were less commonly driven ashore on Rum. We were witnessing the death throes of a time-honoured industry.

Once we found piles of labels on the beach at Kilmory. They were in Russian and must have belonged on tins of fish; frugally we used the backs of them for writing notes. Even more exciting was the discovery of an encoded ship's logbook, still clearly legible despite its immersion in the sea. Provocatively I sent a few sample pages up to the Foreign Office in London asking them to name their price for the rest of it; I never expected to hear any more. One evening though, George MacNaughton, the warden of the island and the only survivor of pre-Nature Conservancy days, came and knocked on the door. 'What is it, George?' I asked without the least thought of the logbook. 'Come on in.' George, amongst his many official duties on the small island such as lifeboatman, coastguard, mountain rescuer, etc., was also policeman. He looked unnaturally grave and came uncharacteristically straight to the point. 'Did you find some papers on the beach and send some of them up to London?' There was no denying it. 'They want the rest now and you are legally charged to hand them over.' And off they went, evidently a Russian submarine's log.

For shellfish on Rum we ate crabs and mussels, but the mussels, though extra-delicious, were very small and laborious to prepare. Later, Tim Clutton Brock had a rubber dinghy and lobster pots but it was mostly crabs he caught. I grew some herbs in the garden but the one I remember best was the wild thyme from the hills; perfect with cream and fried mushrooms and puff-balls, gathered on the closely deer-grazed greens above the dunes. I also developed a taste for puddings. Fiona would painstakingly beat egg whites into a meringue with a fork and then we would create queen of puddings, lemon meringue pie and so on.

But above all there was the venison. At that time the culling required to keep the deer population in bounds was carried out by Geordie Stirton, a man from East Scotland. Small in stature but formidable in talent, he was assisted by one or two other stalkers who often tried Geordie's patience. One played the pipes and, encouraged by a little whisky, once waded the Kinloch river in his kilt with pipes in full skirl.

Geordie was an excellent butcher and each household would, in season, receive a weekly venison allowance, magically left on the kitchen table. This was usually from adult deer and as often as not would have a layer of fat around the outside; years later I came to understand that younger deer, up to about two years old, would have no fat. We ate our venison in fairly conservative ways. Braising was a favourite because the rolled and boned shoulder, or whatever it was, could, after a quick browning in the frying pan, be placed in a covered pot with a few onions and put in the Raeburn oven in the morning as we set off to the hill. By the time we returned, often past midnight in the spring, we would be greeted by an exquisite aroma and a magnificent feast. Nothing could be easier; convenience food indeed.

Apart from the slow braising we would sometimes roast a piece of haunch. The Raeburn would be carefully stoked with coal, riddled and have its ash-pit door opened to raise the fire to a good heat, then in with the joint. I learnt that the fat on a mature stag's haunch is almost inedible. It has a very high melting point; certainly it has a distinct and pleasant flavour, but a mouthful taken even quite hot can congeal rapidly in the mouth, especially if inadvertently cooled by a draught of wine, truly rendering the inexperienced venison eater speechless. A similar effect, though less instantaneous, could probably be achieved by chewing candles. Indeed, the use of deer tallow for candles must be almost as old a practice as fire itself. There exist antique serving dishes with a base designed to take hot water so as to keep the meat warm, and these were designed specifically for venison. Now I learnt why.

Geordie, I discovered, took most of the fat off the carcases and turned it into a leather soap for the stalking saddles the ponies wore to carry the carcases down from the hill. And that is one very great advantage of the venison carcase, for the fat is carried, most conveniently for the consumer, around the kidneys and over the haunches; it can be very simply removed to leave the flesh virtually fat-free. Unlike beef and lamb, venison has no fat insidiously lurking in the muscles. That is partly why the meat from the deer is so dark red. This lean meat is, I found, wonderful. I know now that it has less fat even than the skinless flesh of chicken. The market for such a 'designer meat' – one that can be safely recommended for those on low-fat diets and yet which tastes superb and is so tender that it melts in the mouth – had to be assured.

It also crossed my mind that mankind had been eating venison for most of his time and that it was only on the last stroke of midnight, so to speak, that he had resorted to eating 'improved' domestic animals. His system must be better adapted to venison consumption than to the fattier beef and lamb. Later I found that others had pursued this theory in depth, and shown that not only is venison healthier in containing less fat, but that what fats there are, as well as the other constituents such as iron, are present in healthier forms in venison. This meat could, with a willing minister of agriculture, be a valuable weapon in fighting the epidemic of heart disease and obesity.

All my time at veterinary school in Glasgow I had been conscious of the pressure on the meat industry to reduce fat levels, yet here in Scotland, in abundance, was a meat leaner by far than anything that could be produced by cattle, sheep, pigs or even chicken. Like many other students we had eaten wild venison steaks bought at the game dealers in Byres Road; it had been not only good eating then, but also cheap. And, for me, an added attraction was the way in which venison could be obtained so humanely. A quick shot and then oblivion; there was no need for the horrors of the abattoir. An idea began to formulate itself.

I could see the difficulties that even such a perfectionist as Geordie had in achieving really good carcases. Stalking was time-consuming; three or four in a day was good going and required two men. Unless very close to the beast, a head or neck shot was impossible and the chest or heart shot was the objective. That destroyed a lot of the shoulder meat. And then there was the question of age.

Rum is an exception but on all other estates the stags are shot to produce trophies for the paying sportsmen. This means that stag venison is from deer that might be mere 'knobbers' but could be up to ten or even twelve years old. And ageing the hinds, however carefully stalkers try, is never foolproof so that with them too the age at death is very variable. When the hinds are shot it is customary to shoot their calves at foot as well to avoid leaving orphans, so that a proportion of the venison is immature. And after the shot, there is the practical difficulty of retrieving the carcases in good condition from very remote locations. On Rum there are ponies but most estates use 'all-terrain vehicles' of one sort or another.

As a student at Glasgow I had visited a large venison dealer and seen something of the game trade from his side. His difficulties, he had explained, were the very seasonal nature of the business, with something like 60 per cent of the red deer coming into his premises during only a month to six weeks of the year. This meant that the best he could do was freeze everything or hope to get some of it away as quickly as possible to his main market in Germany. He had to arrange collection from remote deer forests, often during the depths of winter, entailing journeys of hundreds of miles for perhaps only two or three carcases. Stalkers, he said, were under great pressure to shoot large numbers of hinds in an effort to control the population and consequently the bullets did not always go where they should, so that there was much damaged meat. Sometimes carcases were left overnight on the hill so that putrefaction developed. In the spring, carcases were often emaciated, whilst in the rut they stank, and in the late summer were too fat. I had already seen the warble damage so I knew that many carcases needed extensive trimming to remove those as well, and the hides were virtually worthless owing to the warble holes.

Ironically, because you could never tell where the deer had been grazing – they might have spent the night on some recently sprayed arable crop, for example – wild venison could not even qualify for organic status.

It became very clear to me that, with the best will in the world, no game dealer could possibly supply venison of the quality that Geordie gave us on Rum, consistently, day in, day out. By the hygiene standards of the beef and lamb trade, game venison would have been almost completely condemned.

Of course that was many years ago and there have been many improvements made, but I could see the intrinsic difficulties then and it encouraged me to ponder the advantages of embarking on a project to produce modern-day park venison from a 'deer farm'. Here quality venison would be the objective and the meat would not be a by-product of the sporting industry.

8 VENISON, THE FOOD OF OUR ANCESTORS

About this time, in 1970 or 1971, word had begun to drift back from the mainland that Kenneth, later to become Sir Kenneth, Blaxter, Director of the Rowett Research Institute, had managed, despite scepticism from an entrenched establishment, to get a scheme off the ground to investigate the feasibility of farming deer. Roger had attended a meeting to discuss the idea in Aberdeen in 1969 and from this had sprung a pilot project.

It says a very great deal for the far-sightedness of Blaxter that he saw this through against heavy odds. His motivation was to provide an alternative for the vast area of marginal land in the Scottish Highlands for which the only choice was then – and is still – hill sheep or trees. This marginal land makes up three-quarters of Scotland and over more than half of this, wild red deer roam.

Blaxter had observed, of hill-sheep farming, how, during the late sixties 'any meagre profit was entirely due to the amount of subsidy support. Indeed it was estimated, on the basis of careful costing, that 130–190 per cent of the net profit of these farms was accounted for by the subsidy payments they received.' The most remarkable thing about this is that the general picture and even the figures remain almost unchanged today, thirty years later: very few hill-sheep farmers, if indeed any, are not wholly dependent on subsidy, even if that subsidy is now passed through the Common Agricultural Policy.

As a result farmers have increasingly reduced their inputs and hill shepherds have become more and more thin on the ground. Yet because the subsidies are paid on a headage basis the flock is undiminished. The sheep are less frequently gathered and have almost become wild animals. Grazing alongside those sheep are the wholly wild red deer which breed so successfully in the Highlands that it is not always easy to keep their population in bounds.

A few preliminary investigations were undertaken at the Rowett Research Institute and proved very encouraging. They showed that deer ate and digested more heather than sheep did on similar grazings, suggesting that they might be dietarily better adapted to the rough hill land. 'Furthermore, the experience gained in handling captive deer ... showed how very tame they could become.'

Blaxter pointed out that venison prices, reflecting demand from Europe, were so strong in the late sixties and early seventies that 'the monetary return from a red deer carcase had ... become about double that from a hill ewe'.

The extensive hill grazing land in the Highlands produces around two to three kilograms of sheep meat per hectare whilst some deer forests achieve over one kilo of venison per hectare. On the face of it this makes the sheep sound more productive than the deer, but it has to be remembered that the sheep are managed to maximise meat production with only a small number of adult males; the overwhelming proportion of the flock is productive ewes and, furthermore, the young stock are removed before winter. The deer herd is, on the contrary, managed with the sole object of yielding more adult males with antler trophies. Consequently a very large proportion of the deer population is made up of unproductive males.

Blaxter continued: 'It seemed possible that meat production from this poor land might well be similar under some type of deer husbandry system to what it was under a subsistence hill farming economy. It also seemed possible that a wild animal, which for many hundreds of years had survived under these poor conditions on the hills, might be better adapted to them than the domesticated sheep.' Blaxter did not say so – perhaps he was too much of a diplomat – but he must also have been thinking that the Middle Eastern origin of sheep hardly encourages us to imagine that they would be at their most efficient in the Scottish Highlands. Developed by man largely for wool production, the fleece of hill sheep now scarcely repays the costs of shearing. The wool of British sheep is ideal for the manufacture of carpets; those woolly pullovers for which Scotland is famous are today often made from wool from Australian sheep and, sadly, are sometimes even manufactured in the Far East.

Eventually Blaxter's ideas led to a meeting, the Rowett Deer Conference of January 1969. When you read the report of that 1969 meeting the sense of dull, entrenched opposition to anything so radical still jumps out of the polite enough text. Almost all the delegates were civil servants or academics and most were very negative.

The eminent Professor Wynne-Edwards, summarising the meeting, stated that: 'Intensive deer farming would, in practice, be fraught with difficulty and almost certainly unprofitable financially.' The Highlands and Islands Development Board representative said: 'Every new development is a process of experimentation which, like marriage, should be entered into with caution and circumspection.' Echoes of the manse there, and Blaxter remarked that it 'appeared that such was the caution and circumspection that the whole concept might never attain a consummation!'

But Blaxter stuck to his guns. He was assisted by the ineluctable fact that venison prices, from animals with non-existent rearing costs, compared very favourably with the price of heavily subsidised lamb. Finally a research project was sanctioned. Funding was offered by the Department of Agriculture, and the Rowett Research Institute and the Hill Farming Research Organisation entered into a joint research programme.

An area of over two hundred hectares mostly lying around one thousand feet above sea level and consisting largely of heather grazings was chosen for the project. The farm is known as Glensaugh and lies above Fettercairn immediately east of the Cairn o' Mount road to

Banchory. It is reached by a long forestry road through pine woods.

The initial breeding stock were collected, as Dick Youngson's had been, by watching hinds to see where they had lain their calves. We used to do the same on Rum in order to ear-tag, weigh and sex wild calves. For the first few days of life a deer calf will rest immobile and can be approached, handled and, for the Glensaugh project, picked up and reared on a bottle. Hinds will leave their calves and travel up to a mile off, returning only two or three times a day to suckle, so this is feasible though testing work. It requires great determination to watch a hind a mile or more away for hours at a time, through a telescope, when midges are feeding. At times even wearing a pair of tights over the head was not enough, and that in any case made using binoculars or a telescope almost impossible.

The calves for Glensaugh were gathered by a dedicated band of enthusiasts and gently loaded into rucksacks for the journey down the hill. Usually within twenty-four hours they were eagerly awaiting their bottle and bidding fair to pull the teat off. The success rate in rearing these calves was good and, of course, it guaranteed friendly breeding stock. Two or three of Dick's Rum deer were contributed to the Glensaugh project as a gesture of goodwill and year by year Kenneth Blaxter's project grew.

Not, it must be said, without opposition. On the first open day Bill Hamilton, the manager, was approached by a titled landowner who confided to him: 'I might as well let you know that I personally hope this project proves completely unsuccessful.' Bill later told me with a twinkle in his eye what he thought of such prejudice. Not all land-owners were like that and Bill was later roped in to present progress reports on the Glensaugh project to the Duke of Edinburgh and other influential Highland landlords.

It was always interesting that the estate deerstalkers, that is to say the men employed as full-time professionals, who guide visiting sportsmen to the stag in the autumn, and then later in the depths of winter shoot hinds, in my experience almost invariably welcomed the deer-farming concept. These stalkers spend their lives working with deer at arm's length, or more accurately rifle's and telescope's length. Yet many do not have the chance to see the deer year round, since the fishing or the grouse may intervene, and in any case the deer are always wild and distant. Avid for real knowledge of their charges, most working stalkers embrace the notion of domesticating the deer with enthusiasm.

These professional stalkers are the ones who know the reality that is the lot of wild red deer: challenged by the weather, often short of feed in the winter and spring, and host to a horrible burden of parasites. Many stalkers have also had direct experience of bottle-feeding orphan calves for one reason or another. With most stalkers, Blaxter's idea of 'farming the red deer' struck a chord: by careful winter feeding and by treatment of the deer to get rid of the warbles and other parasites, they knew the farmed deer would be the lucky ones.

Yet the lairds, often absent endeavouring to earn sufficient to keep their Highland estates, were, like most amateur hunters in Europe and North America, often vigorously and instinctively opposed to the idea of farming deer. Perhaps they felt threatened, or maybe it was their reluctance to lose a dream. They had been brought up in the wonderful tradition of Buchan's John McNab, flavoured with all the Victorian and Edwardian sporting literature of the Scottish Highlands. To these romantics deer are noble and mysterious, leading a life quite independent of man except when prey to the rifle. Any attempt to interfere with their freedom by putting up a fence to contain them, for instance, is an abomination. The fact that each spring several thousand Scottish deer might die of starvation was often overlooked; the laird was not usually about the deer forest then, and the stalker was perhaps not always too keen to let his employer know the scale of deaths on the hill.

Heavy losses of deer and a reluctance to admit to them have perhaps become a thing of the past, largely as a result of the Red Deer Commission (now with responsibility for all deer species and renamed the Deer Commission for Scotland) and the formation of adjoining deer forests into local deer management groups. Over the years many landowners have become sympathetic to deer farming and some have joined our ranks.

It is as well to remember too that the taxpayer actually benefits from the sporting estates which were, until recently at least, compelled to pay rates. The sporting estate may not represent the most popular sector in the public eye, but it is still about the only form of land use in Britain – apart of course from deer farming – that is independent of state handouts. And the incoming sportsmen and women, whether from southern Scotland, England, the Low Countries or the USA, do much to sustain the Highland economy.

Anyway, there was no doubt that the deer at Glensaugh appeared very content. Bottle-fed, they had early come to associate the farmer with the good things in life, and most of those working with deer were delighted how readily even the second generation, that had been suckled naturally by their mothers, were evidently relaxed and approachable. It was those animals themselves that converted some of the sceptics, for who could fail to be charmed by deer that, far from showing any signs of stress, were very obviously more at home in human company than most hill sheep and cattle. I had already been struck by the ease with which the tame deer I had been using for my experimentation on Rum could be managed; the Glensaugh project seemed to me certain to succeed.

And there was another angle to this. As a vet student compelled to rise early to do my dark winter stint at the Glasgow municipal abattoir, the horrors of trucking animals to a massive central killing point had left a forcible impression on me. Slaughter on such a scale is almost inevitably stressful for the livestock and also brutalising for the men paid to do it. My occasional sorties with the deerstalker had seemed less demeaning for man and beast. And if the deer were farmed and approachable to close quarters then their despatch by rifle could be completely instantaneous. A modern deer park or farm, it seemed to me, might be able to provide meat not only of healthier composition but also more humanely than other systems, even if not on a very large scale.

In fact Kenneth Blaxter had understood from the outset that the farmed deer would have to be killed in a slaughtering facility located either on the farm or at a neighbouring abattoir. Years later when I saw those deer passing through a commercial abattoir my worries were largely quieted.

Underwriting the whole concept was my faith in the quality of the meat: demand seemed assured. From the days when as Glasgow students my flatmate Anthony, another embryo vet, and I had vied with each other to produce the most economical and impressive spreads for our girlfriends, the value of good food had been clear to me. Although occasionally, like Ernest Hemingway, I resorted to street pigeons snatched untimely from the claws of our landlords' Burmese cat, Pico, most guests fared rather better. No matter that the girls' ideas of pushing out the boat were limited to spaghetti bolognese; when they came to eat with us it was jugged hare, or, inspired by Elizabeth David, venison cutlets in the Ardennes style. I suppose that I already felt that food, especially flesh, was something sacred which demanded care in its preparation.

Which brings me back to perhaps the most important reason for attempting to farm deer. Kenneth Blaxter's institute, the Rowett, is avowedly concerned with the nutrition of both man and beast and he was anxious to investigate an animal which could not only survive and breed successfully on the impoverished Highlands, when sheep required substantial mollycoddling, but would also yield a carcase with a proportion of prime-grade lean meat that should have been the envy of the cattle and sheep farmers. At that time cattle farmers were still using implants of steroid hormones to make their carcases grow quicker and leaner.

But Sir Kenneth never seems to have made much play of the leanness of venison. Perhaps it was less topical in those days or conceivably he was such a diplomat that he did not want to inflame the cattle and sheep farmers. Instead of the low fat levels of venison, Blaxter and his colleagues concentrated on the conformation of the carcase, pointing out that the proportion of high-value cuts suitable for quick cooking – frying and roasting – was very much higher in deer than in cattle and sheep.

In my eyes it was above all the absence of fat that made the meat, already recognised by me as supremely delicious, also highly marketable. This endowed the deer-farming concept with an ethical basis in that deer farmers would be producing a food that would save lives. We had the basis for a moral crusade.

At that time I didn't know the actual figures or I might have been even more enthusiastic. But I know them now. As the officially accepted figures from the most recent edition of the standard McCance and Widdowson's Composition of Foods show, 100 grams of venison contain only 103 kilocalories compared to beef with 198, lamb with 187, pork with 213, whole chicken 201, or skinned 108. And of course venison has more protein, and is also much higher than other meats in many other nutritional goodies. For example, 100 grams of venison contain 3.3 grams of iron in comparison to beef with 1.7, lamb 1.4, and chicken and pork 0.7. The published levels of fat show venison with 1.6 grams per 100 grams, whole chicken 13.8, skinned chicken 2.1, beef 12.9, lamb 12.3 and pork 15.2. In cholesterol content venison has much less than other meats and only around one-third that of skinned chicken. Venison also comes top of the list in its content of that emblem of the healthy eater, the celebrated omega-3 and omega-6 fatty acids, a much-vaunted panacea for heart disease.

These figures mean that those dieting for reasons of cardiac care, or diabetics reducing their fat intake, or even just those eager to lose weight, can now eat a red meat confident that it is doing them much less harm than even skinned chicken. And of course for athletes and bodybuilders, venison is the ideal food.

On Rum, Geordie's venison had allowed us to taste the meat in all its guises; I had soon become a complete convert to the innocent delights of good food. We rarely ate lunch but thought we had deserved a good dinner. How wonderful is an appetite when you can readily satisfy it; however much abused, it always, in good health and with exercise, returns. If we are lucky enough to have food when so many are hungry then a lack of interest or care in the cooking seems to me akin to blasphemy or sacrilege. In the words of Burns:

> Some ha'e meat and canna eat,
> Some would eat that want it:
> But we ha'e meat and we can eat,
> Sae let the Lord be thankit.

And so it was that ideas for farming deer once my time on Rum was over grew stronger.

9 BASKING SHARKS AND 'SELF-SUFFICIENCY'

Looking back now it is clear that in spite of a healthy, youthful confidence in my own originality I was inevitably a child of the times. As a student I had hitch-hiked all over Europe, North Africa, and Central and North America; the hippie movement with its apocalyptic vision of a future redeemable only by renunciation of material extravagance no doubt influenced me. I have already mentioned the Reith lectures given by Fraser Darling; equally relevant was the publication of *The Blueprint for Survival* by Edward Goldsmith. To me as a biologist the scenarios depicted rang very true. At school I had read Rachel Carson's *Silent Spring*, and at Glasgow Anthony and I had had 'Ban DDT' stickers printed and distributed. This was despite forthright opposition from some of the staff who reasonably pointed out that DDT had probably saved more lives than any other chemical man had ever produced. That argument still goes on, as malaria continues to rank as one of the world's biggest killers and DDT as its most effective opponent.

There was a sense of being part of a 'back to the countryside' movement. John Seymour had had a great success with a series of books on what he called self-sufficiency. It is hard to recall now just how insecure the future seemed then but in 1973, with Mr Heath's three-day week and the Arabs' success in raising oil prices, times were exciting and any outcome seemed possible.

Another consideration was getting married. I had admired Nickie from afar as the schoolgirl daughter of my landlords for a year at Glasgow, but we only really got to know each other on a sailing weekend on Loch Fyne.

It is strange how often there are decisive periods of just a few years or months when everything in one's life can be epoch-making, vivid and important. Looking back on such times we know that nothing can ever again be so momentous.

For me such a time was the spring and summer of 1970 and it reached its exquisite pinnacle on one particular weekend. My place at Cambridge was secure; we had had our final veterinary exam results that Friday afternoon. Anthony had had a legacy a few months earlier, £500 I think, and he had, against my sober and boring advice, purchased a decrepit sports car which he figured would enhance his success with the girls. Within weeks of yielding to the blandishments of the dubious Great Western Road car salesman, Anthony had found himself one moment sitting behind the wheel of his superb racing machine and the next resting his bottom on that same Great Western Road. Rust had triumphed. A skilled welder was enlisted and so it was that Anthony was able to give me a lift up to Loch Fyne so that we could celebrate our exam results.

I have entertaining memories of that drive. It was a peerless night. At an early stage in the journey the exhaust system began to part company with the engine but as we roared, hood down, up the twisty road beside Loch Lomond, we revelled in the sporty sound. Midnight in June in the west of Scotland is a magic twilit time even when you are being deafened and gassed. Then quite suddenly the engine began to falter. Anthony managed to coast in under a street lamp beside a small and ancient roadside pub, and we raised the bonnet. Underneath, a very pretty sight met our eyes. The engine was suffused with a deep orange glow whilst from one of the electrical connections, a plug lead, long white sparks arced across to any piece of metal they could find. By deft poking with a bit of stick whilst Anthony sat in the cockpit, I managed to push the offending plug lead into a position where the arcing abated. Just to check the success of my 'repair' I shouted to Anthony, 'Rev her up a bit.' This he did to good effect and the countryside reverberated gratifyingly to the ear-splitting roar. It was at this moment that about eighteen inches behind and above my ear I became aware of a soft and patient voice: 'Will ye be long?' it was asking. Looking up I could see it came from a 'benightied' female form leaning out of her bedroom window, pale-faced, polite and patient. But certainly not beckoning.

Surprisingly the journey was thereafter more or less uneventful. A pause, as the name of the infamous Rest and Be Thankful Pass demands, showed that the climb had added to the brilliance of the orange glow, but still the car ran.

On arrival at the cottage Anthony went in to his lady so I, alone, taking a bottle of whisky, rowed out into the middle of the flat calm loch and lay down in the bottom of the boat. What a wonderful thing it is to have achieved something long worked for and so clear and simple as a happy exam result. There seemed no worries. For the young person privileged and optimistic there are no shadows of the difficulties that adulthood may bring, just a sublime confidence. It grew darker. I became aware of a gentle unexpected movement of the boat and a hissing as the surface of the water was broken. Reluctantly I forced myself into a sitting position and put my head over the gunwale. What I saw tested my powers of credulity, for only three or four yards away were several enormous black triangular dorsal fins each protruding one or two feet from the water and cruising around me in a good imitation of a cartoon drawing in the newspaper. Of course, as a newly qualified veterinary, I knew these were only harmless plankton-filtering basking sharks incapable of eating me even if they had had an urge in that direction; but as it was, alone in the middle of the loch in the middle of the night armed only with a half empty-bottle of whisky . . .

I rowed as hard as I could for the shore.

And it was the next day that I met Nickie. Setting off in a little flotilla, she impressed me no end by jumping into my dinghy and abandoning her boyfriend of the previous two years. Are women prey to an evolutionary strategy which inclines them to choose men who are innovators and unorthodox? I flatter myself they are. On one of the happiest days of my life, we became becalmed and entangled on a perfect June afternoon off Inveraray. The basking sharks, much less threatening in the sunshine and with Nickie to bolster my courage, were still cruising around the loch. In the distance they occasionally leaped quite clear of the water, plainly audible a mile or more away as they crashed back in again. Or sometimes they inspected us so closely we could touch them with an oar. That didn't deter Nickie from suggesting that we swim off the boat despite the absence of bathing clothes. Then a few weeks later she hitch-hiked down to Cambridge and I was very definitely impressed. Perhaps to a scientist an art student seems especially beguiling; in any event I had no doubts that life with Nickie would be fun.

We were married on 8 July 1972 in Glasgow University Chapel while I was still working on Rum and while Nickie was still studying at Edinburgh Art College to be a jeweller, with a group of crafts-men and -women friends. Indeed so talented a jeweller was she that the college encouraged her to stay on for a post-graduate year and rewarded her with a scholarship.

Meanwhile, the idea of a rural retreat and an attempt to be 'self-sufficient' became more and more attractive. Not only to Nickie and myself but to many of our friends. Tim Stead, the sculptor of wood and creator of furniture; David Kaplan and Annica Sandstrom, the glass-blowers; and Mike de Haan, the potter, all settled down in the Scottish countryside that year. And they are all there still except for the South African, Mike, who was always restless, hankering for warmer weather. He finally settled in New Zealand. We were all of a time, and establishing bases in the country was important to us all. The die was cast. Those makers, as craftsmen are now apparently called, were the cream of the art colleges, each highly talented; and while once it annoyed me, now it only amuses that the unimaginative, hidebound structure of the 'arts' establishment almost completely ignores them. Only painters, writers, musicians, film-makers, occasional sculptors and, strangely, potters seem to gain a mention, in the arts radio broadcasts at any rate.

Was it just the sixties that enthused us with an idealism? Or are all young people like that? I often encourage myself in dark moments by thinking that every time a new baby is born mankind has a reprieve, because that person is a clean canvas on which we can all start again. I suppose we felt in the sixties and seventies that rural labour was in some way liberating. It has been said that in youth we should all be socialists.

> Is there for honest poverty
> That hings his head, an' a' that?
>
> Then let us pray that come it may –
> As come it will, for a' that –
> That sense and worth, o'er a' the earth
> Shall bear the gree, an' a' that;
> For a' that, an' a' that,
> Its comin yet for a' that,
> That man to man the world o'er,
> Shall brothers be for a' that.

Even if, as we mature, and boring responsibility and the need to support our progeny and prepare for our own decrepitude intrude, and our liberal notions wane, we were once idealists, weren't we?

Meantime Nickie was developing her skills at Edinburgh as well as being given two prestigious travel bursaries. These she decided to use on a visit to Czechoslovakia to see a jewellery exhibition at Jablonec near the Polish border and I was to be allowed to go along too. It was only three years after the Russian invasion following the Prague spring and our impressions were of a country desperately subdued. We saw a Russian soldier rudely treating an elderly and tearful lady on the streets, they searched under the train and under the seats at the border. This was oppression and nothing to do with our socialist ideals. We should have known. The world is full of paradoxes: churches which preach love can create the Inquisition, or the Irish problem, or ban contraception, and now here was a socialist 'democracy' running a despotic nightmare.

With the clarity of vision of unquestioning youth, we had no doubt but that a small farm was what we wanted to occupy for the rest of our lives. For some reason that Czech trip confirmed us in our plans.

Back in Cambridge I wrote to the accomplished botanist and eminent classics don at King's College, John Raven, because I knew that he had a Highland estate at Ardtornish; perhaps he would have somewhere we could try out my deer farming ideas. He generously asked us both to spend a day or two at Ardtornish so that we could talk it over. John was tremendously welcoming and keen to help but somehow neither Nickie nor I felt that the situation was quite right either for us, or for marketing the venison, and the estate factor at that time was clearly unenthusiastic too. Reluctantly we decided to keep on looking.

While we were at Ardtornish I asked John Raven about the Heslop Harrison affair. In the 1940s a Professor of Botany at Newcastle called John Heslop Harrison had stretched the credulity of the scientific establishment by making a series of remarkable reports of plants and insects that he claimed to have found on the Isle of Rum. These all gave support to his theory that Rum had not been covered by ice during the last glaciation. John Raven, then a young research fellow at King's, had followed Heslop Harrison to Rum in 1948 in an effort to find out whether these claims could be true. John told us in minute detail what he had seen and how he had stalked the Professor. Clearly he was in no doubt that many of those discoveries had indeed been 'plants' introduced with a trowel and were fraudulent.

Later I asked the warden on Rum, Peter Wormell, what he thought of it all. Peter said that he was frequently surprised just how many of Heslop Harrison's finds had subsequently been vindicated. Nevertheless many were truly incredible. He also told the strange tale of how in 1961 the Professor, by then a very old man, had visited Rum for the last time. He had wanted to return to the site of his finding of *Carex bicolor*, the obscure sedge which had proved to be his most controversial claim. Peter had taken him part of the way and had instructed some of the children on the island not to let him out of their sight. Unfortunately the cloud had descended and the Professor was lost and made his own way down. When Peter caught up with him in the evening sure enough he had a fresh sample of *Carex bicolor* in a plastic bag. It was a very romantic story.

After Ardtornish I returned to Rum, and Nickie was charged with attempting to locate a suitable small farm and I promised to come off Rum to look at the fruits of her searching as soon as there was something to look at. My brother Paul generously offered to contribute and, because my father had passed on some of my inheritance on my marriage, we were able to hope for a very small farm. That all sounds so easy to say now and in fact it was. Land prices and house prices were still low and we were, of course, very lucky to be able to do what we did.

Deprived of her new husband, it took Nickie only two weeks to find our farm. Immediately she wrote in one of her enthusiastically illustrated letters: 'and there is a small farm advertised at Auchtermuchty ... the particulars say: "Reediehill is situated about two miles northwest of Auchtermuchty on the Mournipea Road leading to Pitmedden Forest. The farm extends to about 48 acres and it is considered that up to 40 suckler cows could be carried. The farmhouse faces south and could be developed into an attractive home." '

'Where's Auchtermuchty?' I wrote back.

10 THE DEER MOVE IN – AND OUT

We went to look at Reediehill on a wet autumn day in 1973. Two miles up a steep hill out of the royal burgh of 'Muchty we drove before the road turned and led us down to the bottom of the farm track. Five hundred yards of unmetalled rock and gravel track clinging to the side of a wooded ghyll above the little burn and we were there. Though it didn't occur to me then, that road was Reediehill's umbilicus and upon its continued existence depended the survival of the farm; there was no other way to get there. The fields were north-facing and sodden but the little house, two up, two down, was bright and dry and, as it had said, looked south. There was no garden but a fenced enclosure in front of the cottage in which a cow had just slipped a dead calf. I did not take this as a portent although I guessed that the cause was brucellosis.

We had arranged to meet the vendor who arrived in the pouring rain, got out of his car and then stood silent and stationary for two minutes. I had forgotten it was Remembrance Sunday.

We both felt there was no need to look further. Strangely without any feeling of undue moment, we placed our bids by sealed tender, in the way these things happen in Scotland. And a week later we became the owners of Reediehill Farm, forty-eight acres of north-facing grassland seven hundred feet above sea level at a latitude that puts us closer to the Arctic Circle than is Moscow. As they say, lock (the house), stock (the aborting cows) and barrel (perhaps the 'unexpired manurial residues' detailed in the sales particulars) (illustration 4).

Later, of course, we learnt much about Reediehill and its situation. Not only that Jimmy Shand, the celebrated accordionist and band-leader, and now Sir Jimmy Shand, with many gold discs and a gold heart too, was our illustrious neighbour, but that the road was a long-established drove road by which cattle had been driven between the fertile Howe of Fife on the east and Perth, Strathearn, Strathtay and the Highlands to the north and west. From the hill above us you can see from Ben Lomond on the west to Dundee's tower blocks and the coast in the east and the Highlands – Schiehallion, Lochnagar and the Angus hills – in the north, whilst to the south is Loch Leven and its island castle whence Mary, Queen of Scots escaped by night.

Nickie and I, and later Stella and Martha, have come to love that small farm with a ferocious passion, almost like a parent's for a child. When, much later, we feared that we might not be able to go on living there, the bottom really did seem to fall out of our lives. But neither Nickie nor I believed for a minute that we should spend more than a few years at Reediehill. It was, we thought then, almost inconceivable that we should still be living there thirty years on.

More important than the views from the hill were the people of Auchtermuchty. Apart from transient school and university life I had never before really been part of a community. We have always been made welcome, and considering that we came as complete foreigners, erected six-foot-high deer fences around the place and 'Venison for Sale' signs, and then when invited to give talks I sometimes forgot to go, I think we have been lucky.

My brother Paul agreed to buy half the land, which amounted to a third share of the value then, and I was to pay him a fair agricultural rent for this. It must have been the worst investment that he ever made but without his enthusiasm we should not have been able to proceed. With the land secure we could now deal with the deer.

I had become very involved with the tame deer on Rum, and as they had naturally multiplied during the years, there had arisen the question of what to do with the surplus. Someone had to pay for their daily feeding. Turning them out of the enclosure on to the island would not have worked; they would have hung around the fence and the houses making a nuisance of themselves. They were far too tame ever to integrate with the wild population. For a while their fate hung in the balance. I knew, of course, what I wanted to happen to the animals. I wanted my old friends to become the nucleus of a breeding herd. They were to be the subjects of a grand experiment. I wanted to take them off to Auchtermuchty where I would watch what became of them and let them realise their full productive potential, but first it would have to be cleared with the Nature Conservancy, as it was then, who owned the island and the deer. Fortunately, with generosity and a minimum of bureaucracy, they agreed.

The next problem was how to get the deer off the island. In the past, occasional deer such as those sent to Glensaugh had been shipped by putting them in a crate and manhandling the crate from the landing stage into the boat and then out of the boat on to the ferry and finally from ferry to lorry or even train.

I tried this once with two tame yearling hinds. The crates would not, of course, fit in the Mini Moke so I put them on the train at Mallaig. My recollection is that they came, by some quite complicated routing, direct to Edinburgh Waverley and there under the shadows of the castle I loaded them into a friend's borrowed trailer for the last stage of their journey to Auchtermuchty. How strange that idea seems now when we cannot, I think, put any livestock on trains.

Anyway, it is very clear that this experience was not very nice for man or beast. Yet this time-honoured system of individual crating had been the one used for centuries, most recently for the restocking of the Highlands in the Victorian era and onwards till at least the Second World War. During that hundred years or so countless deer had been sent up north by train in crates from English deer parks. I have spoken to an old man who recalls going with his father in a horse and cart to a rural rail halt in Yorkshire, now a tearoom; there he collected two crates of English park deer and took them back to his farm where for thirty years or so those deer and their descendants remained, occasionally jumping stone walls for a brief 'donder' around.

What a nasty shock for big English beasts, spoilt with soft life on lowland pasture, to suffer the stresses of a probably rather primitive capture, and a lengthy journey, before the sudden arrival and turning-out on to a Highland hill! There is an axiom amongst livestock farmers in Britain that you should always buy breeding stock in the north and bring it south rather than the other way round. Certainly many of those English stags must have perished without ever spawning any progeny.

Yet elderly Highland estate workers have stories of how the English park stags were turned out each autumn for the rut. They were allowed to spend a heady few weeks having their way with the Scots lassies, and no doubt struggling to fend off their smaller, fitter, less heavily antlered rivals, before making a strategic retreat to the shelter and feed of the park for the rest of the winter. Even wapiti from the United States and Canada, and perhaps deer from other far-flung parts of the Empire, were used in this way in a misguided effort to 'improve' the indigenous Scottish stock, displaying a touching faith in the value of 'blood' and breeding which I sometimes think reflects on the mentality, and perhaps even the degree of inbreeding, of those lairds of an earlier era. For undoubtedly the limiting factor in the productivity of Highland red deer is very rarely the genetics of the deer but rather the environment: food and shelter. The lesson is clear: transplants need nurturing and only if the conditions are right can they prosper.

Anyway, we didn't have enough crates; so, I reasoned, why not simply anaesthetise the deer in the bottom of the open boat? Nice dreams for the deer and, provided they didn't wake up and jump out, all would be fine. Stretchers made out of sacks and galvanised roofing struts from the old hothouse round the back of the castle, where the Bulloughs had once kept turtles, would make lifting the sleeping deer in and out relatively easy.

Nickie was bound to be a little sceptical. Just a few weeks previously I had been attempting to find a different drug cocktail for darting the stags on Rum and she had been enlisted to help. The darting went well and the inebriated stag gently subsided. I took hold of his antlers and all seemed safe so I left Nickie with the usual directions: 'Just stand astride him holding his head up by his antlers and if he starts to struggle apply a little gentle weight with your knees to his shoulders.'

I walked back up to the Land-Rover to fetch some equipment, but before I got there I was surprised to hear the rumbling of hooves from behind me. Against the blue sea and the Cuillins, Nickie was hurtling, astride a stag in full flight, towards the cliffs. Clasping his antlers like a latter-day Peer Gynt, she looked magnificent. The reality when she eventually fell off was different. As I too rolled helpless in the turf I came to understand that it hadn't been a pleasure trip; I was in disgrace and that particular drug combination was not tried again.

The deer finally came over from Rum uneventfully (illustration 6a). Gerald himself was there to help and we certainly needed him because, as we came into Mallaig harbour in the little *Sioras* from Rum, we saw firstly that it was low tide with a twenty-foot lift. And secondly, that what seemed several bus-loads of bemused tourists were gazing down from the pier on to our cargo of peacefully sleeping deer. I had rented a van: little did the hirers know what its unorthodox load was to be. In the event the tourists actually rallied round and helped us with the stretchers. I wonder if they would do the same today.

After that unorthodox sea crossing the deer seemed to settle in at Reediehill very well. For the first time in at least two hundred years red deer grazed above Auchtermuchty. They clearly relished the improved pasture and showed little inclination to pace the fences.

However, a few months after the successful installation of our deer herd our neighbour's tractorman came up to see us. After a good deal of beating about the bush and nervous shuffling from one foot to another, he sheepishly confessed the reason for his visit. Apparently, sometimes whilst walking home in the dark, he had heard a large animal following him. We said that we knew all our animals were in and so it couldn't possibly be one of our deer. Then he said, 'It made a noise like a half-dead chain saw,' and proceeded, mouth closed, to make a series of guttural sounds somewhere between a subdued roar and a moan. Now that is a perfect description of the bleating call that a tame red deer, looking for feed, makes and we knew he was right. The puzzle was: where had the animal come from? There were no wild red deer about us and we were sure that all our deer were there.

The answer came a few days later when, looking out of the bedroom window early one morning, I caught sight of our hand-reared hind

Bonnie, one of the twins, trotting back up the farm road and, scarcely slowing down or breaking step, worming her way under the gate, back home in time for her morning feed. And so I learned that a space of twelve inches under a gate is too much for a deer farm.

11   THE LAST RESTOCKING OF A HEBRIDEAN ISLAND?

There were nowhere near enough deer for the forty fenced acres but, feeling that understocking was better than overstocking, we did not initially make very strenuous efforts to find more. In any case, where could we hope to purchase them? We decided to see how the deer did, whether any problems arose, and to develop a system of deer farming suitable for Reediehill before we went out to try and increase the herd.

Nickie was soon hammering and soldering her jewellery and silver-ware in a shed across the farmyard whence emerged treasures for exhibition and commission. Soon her work was in the permanent collections of the Royal Museum of Scotland and the Victoria and Albert Museum in London, as well as Bing Crosby's private collection! Meanwhile, I was busy writing up my thesis and, though growing, the need to make money did not yet seem pressing; we naively believed we could live more or less off the land with our income bolstered by occasional veterinary locums and the sale of jewellery and eventually venison. It was an idyll.

The deer farm attracted, from the start, disproportionate publicity. I forget which publication was the first but I know that the strangely unchanging *Scots Magazine*, with a big circulation amongst the

Scottish diaspora, was early on the scene, and the *Scotsman* newspaper did something too at the beginning. There followed pieces the same year in the *Telegraph* and the *Sunday Telegraph*, the *Dundee Courier* and even *Reveille*.

Not all publicity was friendly. Two years after we started, the *Scottish Daily News*, functioning terminally as a workers' co-operative, was frankly hostile. 'Bred for the Bullet' was the headline for our centrefold piece. A simulated rifle sight was superimposed over one of the few precious Rum-born bottle-fed calves, intended for our breeding hind group. Surprisingly this did us no harm at all. In fact the only response was from a nearby local authority which asked me to help them establish a deer farm. That farm, funded entirely from the public purse, is still going strong.

There was even an exchange in the *Daily Telegraph* in which a well-known journalist, J. Wentworth Day, whose view epitomised that of the countryside establishment, expressed his disapproval of what we were trying to do. However, a riposte from Nickie's aunt, unsolicited by us, abruptly ended the correspondence to our great satisfaction. It was this and other little triumphs that taught me how, in a challenge between the small and struggling deer farmer and the pompous, powerful, self-opinionated establishment figure, we usually win in the public relations stakes. And I learnt of the pleasure such trivial triumphs may bring.

In a few years' time we were to learn just how valuable the friendship of the press could be to us in exposing injustices to unsympathetic politicians.

My thesis was now sent off and to my delight accepted, and I began to think of farming deer a little more seriously. We were already getting approaches for venison but had nothing to sell, and soon we should need to find more deer. In the meantime we had cause to be thankful to the news media for creating the publicity which gave us our first, and one of the most rewarding, deer-related jobs that I ever had to do. Although it depleted our little herd of deer, it did bring in cash and it was a challenge.

A consortium of landowners, of the enlightened category, approached me with a request to establish a population of deer on the island of South Uist. I actually viewed this political hot potato with a good deal of trepidation, and would probably consider it even more carefully now. Deer can be very destructive, and the crofters on the western side of the island, on the fertile, low-lying, cultivated *machair*, would be unlikely to welcome the depredations of deer. And, deer in the Highlands were then at least still seen as symbols of the sporting estate, absentee landlords and all those other institutions folk love to hate.

However, a walk over the area showed us that there really did seem to be a substantial part of the eastern side of the island now uninhabited by man, where few sheep lived and those that did seemed to be rarely gathered. Furthermore it was clear that wild deer would in any case eventually encroach from the north, where their numbers were high, even if we did not hasten the colonisation with a few immigrants from Fife. The problem was to ensure that any deer introduced would stay in this area.

We left it to the estate to carry out appropriate public relations by having meetings in community halls. These seemed to go well despite an aggressive editorial stance taken by the *West Highland Free Press* who, to my amusement, placed all the blame for the forthcoming introduction on the Nature Conservancy.

We persuaded the estate to construct a release pen close to the beach and of only about an acre. Into this pen it was planned to introduce the cervine boarding party and to keep them there for a week or two until, we hoped, they had come to regard it as their secure home. It was obviously absolutely crucial to the success of the reintroduction that those deer did not wander over to the west, and I believed that this release strategy would work.

There was great concern on the part of the estate that once confined to their enclosure the deer would be sitting ducks for seaborne poachers. We needed a watchman to keep an eye on the deer in their remote outpost, ten miles from the nearest house, and we cast in our minds as to who should be allotted this task since I would have to get back to Reediehill to look after things there.

By good fortune it so happened that one day we had been talking to our postie at Reediehill, and he had confided to us that he was worried about his young brother Jim who had been getting a bit bored with life in nearby Glenrothes. There had been some trouble that had landed Jim with a fine. Big brother reckoned that life at Reediehill would be therapeutic and we were happy to oblige.

Actually, as an aside, Jim's time at Reediehill was not always uneventful and, if therapeutic, perhaps not always quite in the manner anticipated. One day, while Nickie and I were away, a small group of people, interested in deer and deer farming, arrived, and Jim sensibly took it upon himself to do the showing-around. It was winter, the ground was a quagmire, and Jim, strictly against the rules, decided to give a solo feeding performance, shovelling potatoes off the back of the moving tractor, to encourage the deer to come nice and close to the visitors.

In even more flagrant disregard of all safety, he put the tractor into its lowest gear and walked along behind it. We don't know exactly how it happened, but when Jim ran round to steer the tractor as it approached a fence the inevitable happened. His foot went under the rear wheel which, of course, continued to turn whilst the little tractor was prevented from moving any further forward by the fence. Jim couldn't move either but was saved from serious physical injury by the soft mud. To the horror of the onlookers on the other side of the fence this wasn't the end of his woes, because the electric fence was switched on and every few seconds he received a pulse of several thousand volts. Springing into action, one of the more agriculturally knowledgeable visitors ran round the fence, in through the gate, and pulled the stop button on the old grey Fergie. Thankfully, apart from a little bruising, only Jim's pride was seriously damaged, and it was years before we came to hear of his narrow escape, from one of the spectators who told us it beat anything he had ever seen at the circus.

When the question of poachers on South Uist was broached, all minds immediately turned to Jim, and it was duly planned that he be stationed by the release pen in a tent about five miles from the nearest road. The idea was for Jim to stay there two weeks then release the deer and move out.

The deer were loaded at Reediehill into the South Uist estates lorry and driven through Skye to meet the ferry to Lochmaddy at Uig. On the boat I talked at length with one of the islanders. He had a dreamy eye which, cynically, I could have put down to that very real spirit of the isles, whisky. But at the time he had an other-worldliness about him which left a lasting impression on me. He told me how the deer were the cattle of the fairies and how the hinds' milk sustained the tribe of elfin, and of how their cervine steeds flew so magically they would not dash the dew from the cup of a harebell. He also told me that one day I would surely come to live in the Outer Isles. That has not happened yet but I have not forgotten; I can certainly think of no more beautiful a place. Nickie has always said I am a changeling.

Following our by now well-tested technique, the deer were anaes-thetised in the lorry and carried by stretcher – still the Rum turtle-house frames with sacks – from lorry to boat and then after a short sea crossing from boat to release pen. All went smoothly with no loss or injury.

The landscape of the Outer Isles exudes melancholia. One of the boatmen told us he had been born there at our release point, yet now all that remained were a few tumbled stone shapes to indicate where the village had been. Like so much of the West Highlands the beguiling beauty of the place was sharpened with nostalgia. Hugh Miller's poignant description of the recently cleared Rum tantalised me as I wandered around the abandoned homes of Uist: 'there were fields on which the heath and moss of the surrounding moorlands were fast encroaching, that had borne many a successive harvest; and prostrate cottages, that had been the scenes of christenings, and bridals, and blythe new-year's days . . .'

Jim held out for only a very short while. Unaccustomed solitude after the bright lights of Glenrothes, together with rain and gales, probably played as much a part as those ghosts of 'christenings, and bridals, and blythe new-year's days'.

Despite his early retreat, which meant that the deer were only fed within their release pen for three or four days, the experiment was a great success. Jim tied the gate open and the deer were free to come and go as they wished yet, when Gerald and I went back there with Jim almost twelve months later, to our great delight two animals were actually in the open enclosure and the rest within a mile or two of it and calves had, of course, been born. I gather that, by and large, after an initial exploratory phase during which almost the whole little party came wandering curiously over to the west, the deer have continued to stay in the right place. In any case the crofters are entitled, I suppose, to shoot any marauding animals and put them in their freezers.

And so we had played our part in what must have been one of the last red deer restocking exercises in the Highlands and Islands following the great human depopulation of rural Scotland that had lasted from the late eighteenth to the mid-twentieth century, and which is now slowly being reversed.

12 HUMANE MEAT PRODUCTION AND A CAT'S CONSCIOUSNESS

Back at Reediehill, life was not all a bed of roses but Nickie and I were very happy.

My memories of those early days are of the cold, and strangely also of the sun. After Rum I suppose the brightness and cold would strike me. Fife has an enviable record for hours of sunshine – I believe St Andrews has as many hours of sun as London – whereas on Rum I remember it once rained every day for three months. Fife can also be very cold. My brother Nicholas, then a young doctor with a still undulled spirit of scientific enquiry, came to stay one winter and expressed his surprise after a bath. 'I didn't think it was physiologically possible to lie in hot water and whilst being warm below water level have goose pimples above.' We had no central heating of course, but there was ample firewood and the rooms were small and the ceilings low.

The deer had to start to pay their way. From the outset, of course, we had understood that they would have to be killed. I knew there would be a surplus of stags. We used only one stag to thirty or forty hinds. And we had to remove the extra stags before they became too aggressive and whilst they were at their best for eating. So at the beginning we killed at about two years of age and whenever, regardless of season, we had anyone wanting to buy. Even had the idea been remotely feasible, I had no intention of taking deer to abattoirs and, benefiting for once from the novelty of our situation, we had no legal need to do so. For unlike cattle and sheep which must be killed in an abattoir if the meat is to be sold, and which cannot legally be killed on the farm, deer can legitimately be slaughtered in the field. This has always been a key attraction of the whole deer-farming experiment. It means that a farmer can, if he wishes, create a completely self-contained and 'vertically integrated' meat-production system.

I had become accustomed to seeing deer shot on Rum, and indeed had been impressed by how humane is the effect of a large rifle at close quarters, and that had been a strong factor in deciding me to start a venison farm. Nevertheless it goes without saying that killing the deer is not a favourite job. Ortega y Gasset confesses that 'every good hunter is uneasy in the depths of his conscience when faced with the death he is about to inflict on the enchanting animal'. That is as it should be. Most societies have a token rite by which they beg forgiveness of the animal for what they have to do. It is only when we kill on an industrial scale that the procedure brutalises the slaughterman and impedes humane treatment of the animal.

As a vet the blood and gore didn't upset me, but the taking of a healthy life was an unpleasant novelty. I have learnt to rationalise it. If I don't kill the young stock then obviously I couldn't afford to keep those breeding hinds and stags which we had come to know over many years. Another option, sending the deer off for someone else to kill, was not what I wanted. The deer would need to be gathered and loaded and transported, which was stressful, and then we would need to buy the carcases back so that financially it was not sensible either. In a rather righteous way I felt that I should participate in the killing. Mankind has for the last ten thousand years or so accepted that he will eventually have to kill the animals which have been raised as a part of his household; why shouldn't I? And I have always believed that those who eat meat should understand that by so doing they are contributing to the life and death of those animals. Finally, this field slaughter had been a planned part of the enterprise from the outset.

Reediehill can produce only grass, for, being north-facing and so high up and so rocky and hilly, it is not well suited to cropping. The potatoes that we grew at the beginning are a greedy crop and need to be part of an arable rotation; at our altitude and with our rocky 'knowe heads', routine arable cropping would be madness. Like so much, if not all, of the hills and uplands of Britain we can produce only meat or give up and plant trees which would not afford us a living. If I could show that deer farming was technically feasible and then, later, that it was financially viable, I would have an alternative enterprise which beleaguered upland sheep and cattle farmers could adopt with few changes to their own grassland farms. These farmers have few options, and yet here was one which was unsubsidised and would yield a meat much healthier than lamb or beef. I therefore bought a rifle and soon discovered a surprising fact which has kept us in good stead ever since.

Feeding out the deer was a daily winter task that entailed either walking in a long line pouring feed out of a bag or sometimes, if there were two of us available, my driving the wee grey Fergie tractor while Jim or someone shovelled potatoes off the back. When it came to shooting the deer it was a simple matter to walk or drive back past the line of feeding deer, select the victim and then, at very close range – perhaps only four or five yards – shoot him (for it was always stags in those days) in the head or neck. The surprise was that, despite the very large calibre of rifle I used, and the loud explosion, the deer startled only momentarily before returning within seconds to eat within a few feet of their fallen comrade. This meant that it was simple, if needed, to shoot several deer at a time without causing any panic or distress. And as the deer were shot weekly from a large group, it was curious how the survivors, over the months, became inured to this and startled progressively less.

I have often thought that this behaviour is similar to that of the speeding motorist who sees a fatal motorway accident yet resumes speeding seconds later. Another's misfortune carries no lessons. I should not really have been surprised. I am more and more convinced that although they will avoid eating a potato 'contaminated' with blood, deer have no conception of death and mortality. The same is, I believe, almost certainly true of other animals, always excepting the primates and perhaps elephants and whales, with their large brains.

At that time legislation on animal welfare in abattoirs made a big issue of preventing any possibility of one animal witnessing the slaughter of another. This remains good practice, but for a very gregarious species the stress of isolation prior to slaughter may contribute more to their misery than seeing another animal fall. For those of us brought up with Peter Rabbit running around our dishes, anthropomorphism – attributing human consciousness to animals – dies hard.

However, no sooner have I delivered myself of this arrogant and contentious view than I call to mind a very strange story which Nickie told me about our two cats, spayed female litter mates, Tiger and Hester, one day when I returned home after a trip away. 'There are more things in heaven and earth, Horatio, than are dreamt of in your philosophy.' If it had not been Nickie telling me I should not have found it very easy to believe.

'It was Sunday morning,' she said, 'and I had planned an extra hour in bed. At about 6 a.m. I gradually came to and there was a cat wailing outside the window. It went on and on. I looked out and there was Tiger sitting looking up at the window and howling. On and on. I thought she'd been shut out, the cat flap had jammed or something, though she's never done this before. So eventually I put on my dressing gown and went down. It was a beautiful sunny morning. As soon as Tiger saw me she headed off down the drive looking back and howling. I had no choice but to follow. Whenever I stopped or made to go back she sat down and wailed at me again. So I followed. We went all the way down to a dip in the road outside Clare's garden.' (That's about half a mile.) 'And I began to feel a bit silly on the road in a dressing gown. Anyway when we got there Tiger just sat down, stopped howling and looked at me as much as to say, "There, I've done my bit, now it's up to you." I looked around and couldn't see anything untoward. But then Tiger bounded up the bank and scrambled up a tree. I followed as best I could, and as soon as I was out of the hollow and on to the bank, I could hear another cat mewing on the other side of the road in Clare's garden. And then I realised – at the bottom of the tree was Clare's dog, Yoyo, staring up the tree, grinning and panting, whilst half-way up the tree was Hester. It didn't take a minute to rescue Hester and the two cats ran off up the drive together.'

This story fascinates me. I can think of no rational explanation except that Tiger showed an actual ability to plan a rescue. The cats have never ever shown similar behaviour since, and it takes some stamina for a small cat to wake a sleeping person through an upstairs window. Eventually Tiger developed mammary tumours and I had to end her suffering; Hester seemed not in the least affected by the loss of her sibling, saviour and lifelong companion.

Nickie and I soon realised that with our practice of shooting deer in the field we were incidentally blazing a trail towards what many, apart from us, saw as a more humane means of meat production. That had always been at the back of our minds but we gradually came to understand just how important this was. We had a visit from Ruth Harrison, a member of the newly formed Farm Animal Welfare Council (FAWC) who was an animal welfarist specialising in humane slaughter.

Ruth was tremendously encouraging about what we were doing and saw us as creating a precedent that would allow small farmers to kill conventional livestock on farms. This would obviously avoid the stresses of transporting animals to the strange surroundings of an often distant abattoir. She believed fervently that this was a more humane option and Nickie and I were inclined to agree with her. Our experience of shooting the deer at Reediehill in the field to achieve an immediate death with no possible pre-slaughter stress had been very encouraging, and we had become quite evangelistic about the system.

In due course FAWC was assigned the task of investigating the welfare of farmed deer, and when it came to the matter of slaughter it was decided that they should all come up to Reediehill to see how it was done. I drove the tractor into the field and shot two deer for them, they concluded this as a humane way to kill deer and we were permitted to continue.

At Reediehill the venison in those days was hardly a volume trade. In the beginning I would shoot an occasional deer and hang it up in one of the outhouses before cutting it up on the well-scrubbed kitchen table. Then, if it was for immediate despatch, I would stitch the venison up in muslin and pack it in a cardboard box with hay to allow ventilation. Any cut bones or other likely sites of putrefaction were rubbed with ground ginger. The parcel was then committed to the care of the GPO. It was strictly a winter-time activity! But it has to be said that some of the venison we despatched south in those days I still remember as very fine.

The freezer for home sales was situated in Nickie's jewellery workshop, an outhouse on the other side of the farmyard, where it helped her to keep warm as she worked and where customers could easily be served. Actually it is a wonder we had any customers at all, but the trickle of publicity kept flowing and I suppose that brought in the curious. Some of those trailblazing customers are still with us more than twenty years later.

We had, however, to think of a way of encouraging more sales. Funnily enough, because we certainly didn't think of ourselves as Country Gentlemen, we were nevertheless members of their Association. We had found that membership of the CGA supplied us with a useful discount on woodworm treatment of our house and we had stayed loyal ever since. In the back of the CGA magazine was a section of classified advertisements, free for members, and so it was here we first advertised.

This stimulated a stream of customers of a very friendly but fairly predictable pattern. There was one retired colonel who asked if he could have some more venison because he found it 'excellent for shooting sandwiches'. Images of a new sort of clay pigeon and a new sort of ammunition floated in front of our eyes. Then there was another delighted customer in the Channel Islands who was quite unconcerned about the delay in delivery and eventually sent us a postcard saying, 'Venison arrived today, stinking and delicious.' Not quite what we had planned.

We certainly attracted loyal and dedicated customers; they had to be to get up our track. One winter the road froze, as so often was the case then, and became completely impassable just as the venison buyers started coming to collect their Christmas joints. An intrepid consumer, John MacGillivray, after struggling up through the snow, excited by the novelty, accepted Nickie's offer of a large plastic sack filled with straw and hurtled off down the track and into the dusk, clutching his Christmas joint on this makeshift toboggan.

13 THE FIRST SKIRMISH WITH POLITICIANS

One of the best and most important things to be done at Reediehill was to start a family. Nickie seems to be very adept, I hesitate to say lucky since I am sure that there must be skill involved, in being able to pass through a very speedy and trouble-free labour. Stella, our first-born, came on the last day of February. The doctor had threatened to induce her if nothing happened within a day or two, and as there was a beautiful snowy spell Nickie decided to go tobogganing. This did the trick evidently because a hectic car dash to hospital was only just in time.

Some twenty-two months later Martha was due and Nickie was determined to have a home delivery. The doctor, after a prudent cautioning, was all-supportive. I remember sneaking a look at the notes he had written and reading with a surprised sense of self-importance: 'Husband a vet – should be OK.'

Nickie's parents and younger brother and sister came for Christmas, and just as the festive supper reached the table Martha heralded her arrival. Nickie's family wisely fled. Stella was commendably asleep and Nickie was couched in front of the fire in our little parlour. I summoned the midwife who, on account of the seasonal ice, could not get her car up the road without a push, and by the time that I had finished my pushing, Nickie had finished hers.

Stella woke to find her new sister and all was story-book perfect.

But that road continued to be a serious headache. If we were to develop a business it had to be passable at all times. We needed people to visit our shop and many were unaccustomed to off-road driving. Following our experiences with a flood in 1974, when the farm track came to resemble a white-water rafting experience, I realised something must be done to secure our road and I applied for a grant.

There existed in 1973, and for many years afterwards, grants payable to all farmers at up to 70 per cent for capital works. At that time almost all farm 'improvements' came under this heading, even such environmentally damaging ones as grubbing up hedges and orchards. The scope of these grants has been substantially reduced over the years, but in 1973 road improvements as well as fencing were certainly included.

To my genuine surprise, as we were a registered agricultural holding with a 'holding number' and received regular census forms and so on, the application was rejected. This represented a major setback. What is more, I considered it very unfair: no 'level playing field' here. My sense of justice was outraged. I had not expected assistance for our deer fences. But the roads . . .?

For the first time I understood how, by opting to farm a new species, I was placing us outside the security net which protects conventional farmers from the rigours of the market place. Agricultural support was set up, for the main part, after the war in order to ensure that the nation should always be able to provide sufficient cheap food far all, and never again be in danger of starvation in time of war. A whole host of grants and subsidies were then, and are still, provided for those who farm cattle and sheep. But now like a cold douche came the realisation that I was putting us outside the system. As a deer farm, Reediehill, it had been decided by the bureaucrats and politicians, should never share in this bounty. Any improvements that we wished to make would have to be paid for entirely out of our own pockets. That in itself I would have found entirely reasonable, but my neighbours were for the same work receiving government handouts of half or three-quarters of the cost. That was unjust. Were we not both producing meat from grass? For the time being I had no choice but to sit, think and fume.

Meanwhile the road continued to provide intermittent entertainment for many years. One winter's night I returned home with a lorry, Stella and Martha securely strapped in place, and found that, as so often, the running water on the track had frozen. Two columns of ice filled the parallel ruts like two miniature Cresta bobsleigh courses. By 'taking a run at it' I managed to complete all but the last hundred yards; lifting out Martha, I set out to carry her up to the house leaving the first-born in control of the truck. I returned a few moments later and to my horror, even with the benefit of a torch, could find no sign of the vehicle or Stella. Had she rolled over the edge? I walked and slid down the ice keeping a firm hold on those dark thoughts, and some fifty yards back down the road there it was – Stella still strapped in place and stoically sucking her thumb, oblivious of the pleasure her slide might have given had she been a few years older. Secure with its wheels in the ruts, the lorry had merely glissaded down the track.

Following my disappointment over the grants for capital improvements to the road I embarked on a campaign of letter-writing through my MP, Sir John Gilmour, a grand old knight of the shires who was extremely supportive, and also to the press. I felt that I had an undeniable case; I was not looking at that time for all the multifarious forms of production support that cattle and sheep farmers seemed to assume as their right. Even then a hill-sheep farmer's income from sales was often only half as much as the subsidy he received. But if they were receiving assistance for such items as road improvement, I could see no justice in our being denied it. We were as much a bona fide agricultural enterprise as any other. Furthermore there were already public mutterings about 'grain and beef mountains' and the like. There seemed to be no such surplus of venison. In 1976 the game dealers were offering 85 pence per pound (£1.87 per kilo) for wild venison, a price substantially greater than that of lamb, and one which probably equates to a price today of over £3 per pound (£6.60 per kilo).

At that time there was a great resurgence of support for the Scottish National Party which culminated in the referendum of 1979. I suppose my little campaign struck a chord with the Nationalists. Red deer are often seen as an emblem of Scotland and also, more importantly, it was genuinely and justifiably felt that deer farming could contribute to the Highland economy. Consequently one snowy day we were hosts to the entire SNP parliamentary party. On account of the snow several cars got stuck on our road, amply demonstrating the need for improvement. As good as their word, those SNP MPs tabled a large number of written parliamentary questions on the recognition of deer farming as a regular agricultural activity worthy of the same support for capital improvements as conventional farming systems. This undoubtedly helped to bring my campaign much-needed publicity at a time when Westminster was feeling it politic to keep those north of the border happy and quiet.

Notice of success came in a surprising way. One evening Barry Wilson, an agricultural journalist, phoned me to say that a large new deer park in the Home Counties had just been set up (by someone who, it subsequently transpired, is one of the wealthiest men in the world as a result of patents on waxed paper cartons), and the owner had been awarded support for the long deer fence around his property. I immediately phoned his farm manager and he confirmed the truth of the story.

I wrote letters to the broadsheet newspapers and got, as usual, friendly support from the journalists. Given that this had happened in England it was only a matter of time before justice prevailed in Scotland, and in the years to come we were lucky indeed to receive grants of 15–50 per cent for all improvements including, when the time came, the renewal of deer fencing (for we were obviously too late for the initial deer fence). And finally, wonder of wonders, we learnt that even our road would be eligible for grant aid. But by then we had learnt to live with, if not exactly relish, its potholes and reluctantly we decided that we could not really afford our part of the expenditure: road improvements would have to wait a while yet. But at least the principle was won.

14 PARKS AND DARTS

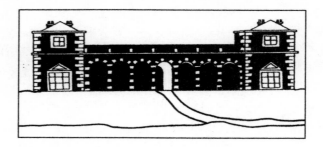

The press coverage meant that we soon found ourselves being approached by a growing band of farmers wanting to start deer farming. They believed, like us, that the writing was on the wall for subsidies for sheep, cattle and grains. Unfortunately, after the South Uist adventure, our deer herd was depleted and the choice of replacements was very limited. Thus began the long period of searching all over Britain for any deer whether wild or tame.

Soon I learnt that throughout England, in particular, there remain a great many long-established and traditionally managed deer parks. These places, of great beauty and environmental importance, are but relics of what were once a vital part of the rural scene. They were at the height of their economic importance in the mediaeval period, though in 1577 Harrison could still state in Holinshed's Chronicles: 'In everye shyre of Englaunde there is great plentye of Parkes ... in Kent and Essex only are to the number of a hundred wherein great plenty of deere is cherished and kept.' And a few years later, in 1617, Morison wrote: 'every gentleman of five hundreth or a thousand pounds rent by the yeare hath a Parke for them [i.e. deer] inclosed with pales of wood.'

We could, I discovered, procure a few deer from some parks for only about £30 and in so doing, of course, prevent them from being killed. The problem was to catch them humanely and in good condition. This is where I reckoned my veterinary experience and my time on Rum would come in handy.

About the first effort I made was at Studley Royal Deer Park beside Fountains Abbey near Ripon in Yorkshire. This became a happy hunting ground of mine and over some twenty years I must have taken about five hundred deer from Studley. But on this first occasion I arrived inadequately equipped with the toy crossbow and spring-loaded darts pioneered on Rum. I was met by Ernest Kemp, a very wonderful and experienced deerkeeper who had a deep understanding of and affection for his charges, as well as a dry sense of humour that kept me from becoming too pompous. Ernest is one of those who might sit quietly in the corner of a crowded room but will always command interest and respect.

The first thing I learnt was how much bigger were the English park deer than their poor deprived relatives on the northern hills. Our darts, cunningly designed by Roger Short specifically for work on Rum, took only half a millilitre of drug and this was generally enough for our island stags, especially if we used our home-made double-strength cocktail. Now I found to my chagrin that English park stags were fully twice as big, and also that the drug now being marketed by the manufacturers was slightly less potent.

It is among the first discoveries that one makes in working with deer that they are more easily approached by vehicle than on foot, and for darting deer this is always the first tactic to employ, especially if the animals can be coaxed into range with some feed. In those days West Riding Council were economical in their deer management, restricting Ernest's mobility to a very small, very noisy and very slow dumper truck. I lay concealed among the mangolds and turnips in this motorised wheelbarrow whilst Ernest swung the crank handle, and we then 'put-put-putted' around the beautiful Capability Brown landscape at little more than walking speed.

I soon found that the English deer were less enthusiastic about coming to close quarters than the hungry Scots hill animals, presumably because of their high living in the lush grass parkland, or because their good condition led to increased fecundity and a consequent need to cull more frequently with a rifle. Or could it be that after hundreds of years during which generations of overworked deerkeepers have been given short notice to find some venison for dinner, there has been a genuine genetic shift towards animals of a more wary nature? I often think so, for truly wild red deer usually produce quieter stock than those of park origin.

My crossbow had an effective range of only about fifteen metres. We selected the tamest stag, and by aiming about six feet over his back I managed to hit him with one shot, and then another, and another; yet it was clear that the dart's payload of drug was too small. At about 2 p.m. I encouraged Ernest to go and have lunch, and by lucky stalking through the trees I finally managed to bring that first stag to a drug-induced slumber. There he lay like Saint Sebastian pierced with many darts. When Ernest came back I was able to feel a little happier, and in his inimitable style he ignored all the problems and we set about loading the sleeping animal into my car trailer.

This may sound fairly amusing and innocuous but I was far from content. The stag had not suffered after the first injection of drug had rendered him, I imagine, 'high'. But although I was always able to reassure myself that I was saving him from death, because his useful days in the park were over and there would be the danger of him mating his daughters if he was left there any longer, nevertheless the experience had been unnerving for me and undignified for the poor old stag, and it had to be admitted that I had benefited from a good deal of luck. I resolved then and there to dart no more deer until I had thoroughly investigated some of the modern dart guns that were just beginning to become available.

By the mid-1970s the techniques of wild animal capture had progressed. The availability of M99, later to be known as Immobilon, and its antidote Revivon had meant that dart guns could be designed with purpose, and several manufacturers were now marketing weapons. I chose the American Cap Chur gun produced by a Mr Red Palmer in Atlanta, Georgia, and it has served me very well ever since. This does not mean that the system is trouble-free. A great deal of care and attention is needed to keep the barrel clean and free of grit and it requires stern resolve to renew darts which you feel might just manage another shot. I have keen sympathy with tribal hunting and fishing societies, which attach such importance to superstition. Darting is a truly hit-and-miss affair. Even after my purchase of state-of-the-art darting equipment, things could still be a little unpredictable. Two later incidents at Studley stand out.

In the first I was asked to dart and transport a sika stag to another park. Sika is the Japanese word for deer, but it has come to be used for any one of about thirty different sub-species of a family whose natural range is from the far north to the south of east Asia. Now I had never darted sika before and was unable to find any published reports of dose rates, so on the basis of sika being close relatives of red deer I simply adjusted the dose to take account of the lower body weight of sika, and off we went. In those days we had graduated from the small dumper truck and were using a tractor and trailer, with me in the trailer. This was all right except that it was so noisy that communication between the driver and his passengers was not easy. In fact, unless the driver was interested and receptive, rather than lost in his own daydreams, it was impossible. After rattling around the park for about half an hour I managed to dart the sika and in a worryingly short time he had slid quietly to the ground. Instead of ten minutes he had taken only four. We headed over to him on the tractor. 'Speed up a bit,' I shouted, to no avail. We eventually arrived, hoisted him on to the trailer and set off back to my lorry, with me sitting anxiously supporting the sleepy stag's head. Shout and wave as hard as I might, the driver, lost in blissful reverie, kept on steadily across the park. The stag seemed to be getting sleepier and sleepier and finally I could stand it no longer. He would, I felt sure, die if I didn't do something. So out with the syringe and in with the antidote. It would in any case be unlikely for the stag to respond before we reached the lorry, I reasoned. Within seconds, or so it seemed, the stag I had thought so near to death began to stir. As the lorry hove in sight, surrounded by a little party of curious visitors armed with cameras, he began to do more than this: he began to wake up. Hastily I stripped my pullover off and put it on his head as a makeshift blindfold. By now we were nearing the truck and the excited tourists, and I was spreadeagled on the poor stag who was struggling to stand up. He had got his hind legs clear now and, almost purposefully engaging a hind hoof in the belt of my trousers, kicked with all his might. In one instant my trousers opened like the proverbial sardine tin from belt to ankle. Yet still I hung on, and with Ernest's encouragement we not so much lifted him into the lorry as aimed him like a cork from a champagne bottle. The visitors, embarrassed by my undress, melted away. After that the sika stag settled happily into his new home and the only loss was my trousers and dignity.

The second misadventure I remember at Studley was potentially more serious. Ernest and I were on the trailer with a sedated stag and all was well. It had been raining and the ground was greasy, and when the driver attempted a short cut up a steep incline we became a little uneasy. Sure enough, just before the top the tractor's wheels started spinning and we began to move backwards at an increasing speed. The trailer rapidly jackknifed into the tractor and I thought it inevitable that Ernest, the stag and I would be catapulted out. Our hour had come. But instead it was the tractor that rolled over and we were left upright. Ernest made some laconic remark and we climbed off with our darted deer, none the worse, to release the shaken driver, who emerged through the horizontal cab door like an astronaut through a hatchway.

In the late 1960s and early 1970s there had been several winters when there were substantial die-offs in many parks throughout England, although thankfully, owing to Ernest's efforts, not at Studley. I remember a picture on the back page of the *Manchester Guardian* in, I think, the long, hard winter of 1962–3, of a tractor pulling a trailer piled high with dead deer from one English park. In that year Woburn Deer Park, for example, had, by dint of hard feeding, managed to contain its losses to 150, which compares with the 670 they lost in the hard winter of 1947 when feeding was not practised so con-scientiously, and when in the immediate aftermath of the war less feed was available. There is no doubt that as demand for breeding stock for the farms developed in the late 1970s and 1980s most parks benefited financially and some of this was passed on to help the deer. Winter feeding standards rose and numbers of deer were kept at a sustainable level. Some diseases prevalent in parks vanished with the improved management. The same was true to some extent with the capture of Scottish wild deer; the ones we took live directly reduced the number needing to be shot, and in some cases encouraged the estates to feed the deer better.

Sadly, since those days the National Trust, no doubt nervous of any controversy, has decided to forbid the tranquillising of any deer in its parks. The consequence is that that illustrious body, of which I have been a member for many years, is deprived of a source of income, and its surplus deer must all be shot dead instead of having the opportunity to live and breed happily for many more years on farms or other deer parks. Since the removal of deer by darting is in my view a humane procedure I do not understand their rationale.

Urban man does not want to see blood shed. If there are to be parks the deer must not be allowed to breed, he says, and much effort is being expended on researching fertility control measures. I have now been approached to see if I will get involved in vasectomising stags or administering contraceptives. This I should be reluctant to do on welfare grounds. It does not seem right to me to deprive the deer of their ability to breed, and in any case there would be deleterious effects on the animals. Vasectomised males would continue to serve the females all winter with possible ill effects in prolonged rutting activity and consequent loss of condition. There would also of course be a gradual attrition of the older animals; would these be left to become progressively more emaciated until the winter took them away? Would new stock be introduced to maintain the stock numbers? Or is an attempt being made to phase out the deer herds? There would also, in all but the largest herds, be a serious logistical problem in administering the contraceptives or in capturing every single male to carry out the vasectomies. I would not much fancy the sight of a deer herd artificially manipulated so that it had no young.

Sometimes it seems as though the activists pressing for these rather bizarre measures are less concerned about the welfare of the animals than their own nice feelings.

The welfare of the deer after I had captured them was dependent on the establishment of good management techniques, but the value of deer on farms soon became so high that this was usually not a problem. We always aimed to let the wild incoming deer mix with tame animals, which I felt was important, and yet we also had to be on the lookout for bullying. Red deer are among the most gregarious of deer species and it was astonishing how quickly newcomers settled in. On balance, then, I felt that we were doing the right thing in prolonging the life of those red deer we took on to farms.

Contrarily, I find the rehabilitation of many species of wild deer after injury, usually as a result of colliding with cars, much more difficult ethically. The scale of the deer problem is surprisingly large and growing. One English rehabilitation centre already handles over two hundred muntjac per year, and in Sweden more than half the traffic accidents and a significant number of human fatalities relate to collisions with moose. Muntjac deer, introduced from south-east Asia to Woburn in Bedfordshire early this century, are thought to be increasing by about 10 per cent per annum and have been incriminated in the disappearance of orchids from one nature reserve and the decimation of bluebells in wide areas of England, as well as in the destruction of nightingale nesting habitat.

Many of these animals are subjected to heroic surgery by my talented colleagues and given all possible tender loving care by devoted and well-meaning rehabilitators, yet I wonder if in numerous cases the stresses are not more than this prolongation of life can justify. The animals' injuries necessitate frequent close contact with their carers and to mix them with other deer is not usually feasible – nor with the less sociable species would it be desirable anyway. These issues become still more complex when the background of a rapidly growing wild deer population, throughout Britain and the developed world, is taken into account. The more solitary species of deer such as the roe, and now the muntjac, which comprise the bulk of these cases have a highly complex social structure. Once removed, even if subsequently reintroduced at the same place as the accident occurred, they may find it difficult or impossible to re-enter that society. If they are placed in a new locality their problems are likely to be worse. This disappointing conclusion has been substantiated by studies of the success of rehabilitating a variety of species, in particular of birds, such as the barn owl, which have been given all possible care yet still show very poor success in readjusting to life in the wild. Hedgehogs, however, I am pleased to be able to report, apparently do well after rehabilitation and release. We urgently need more follow-up studies to establish the survival rates of more species.

The story of the enthusiastic deerstalker crawling carefully and painstakingly through the undergrowth to shoot a poor, thin specimen of a deer only to find, when he walks up to the dead beast, that it was wearing a plaster cast, is, I hope, apocryphal; but it has a point.

I have explained how, following industrialisation, deer numbers in a variety of different nations increase. In England there are now estimated to be over one million deer of all species with numbers rising strongly for most species. Increasingly people are seeing deer in their gardens, on their fields and dead beside the roads. There is no sign of this trend being reduced. In the USA in 1997 12.4 million hunters each spent an average of 860 dollars killing 6.25 million deer, yet still numbers rise. I believe that unless serious efforts are made to control deer numbers, we shall find that what we value now as a beautiful and infrequent sight will come to be viewed increasingly as a pest. The damage deer do to gardens, crops, nature reserves and woodlands is growing.

It is significant that Lyme disease, a bacterial infection transmitted by ticks and which can cause disease in people, is earning deer a bad name because that is where many ticks feed. Yet those ticks can just as easily feed on birds, mice, dogs or any other warm-blooded animal.

15 THE 'TAINCHELL' – PART OF A LONG TRADITION

Encouraged by early successes in the deer parks, but always limited by the numbers available, we took on a new challenge by attempting to recruit the much more numerous adult hinds from the Scottish hills. If catching deer in the deer parks had been problematic, then taking wild deer by darting was almost impossible unless they could be tempted in to feed. It took only one memorable, bright, snowy day to prove this point.

I am to be guided by a highly experienced stalker. We start at dawn and toil two thousand feet up from the hill road, until we are able, very carefully, to come to a suitable hind within the thirty- to forty-yard range of my dart gun. I take my time, still my heaving breast, aim as accurately as my open sights permit and press the trigger. I would have done as well with my eyes closed, for the dart, lifted by a gust of wind, misses by miles and the deer move off at a trot.

We have a brief discussion. The stalker is doubtful if such a good opportunity can come again but I have to try to prove the system works. Finally he agrees. He will attempt to outflank the group of hinds and drift them past me, through a narrow gully much higher up, at a very slow walking speed. It will take time. I climb slowly up to the appointed ambush point and flatten myself stomach down into the wet turf. There is a timeless, clean, acid, earthy smell as I press my body close to the peat. It is almost a sexual communion but Mother Earth does not move for me as she did for Hemingway. She lies cold, inert and, through overgrazing and inclement weather, sterile. Between perishing snow squalls driven by a snell wind come periods of calm when the sun lights even the deep recesses of the glen beneath. I can see the Land-Rover, a speck on the road, and I know that within it, warm and perhaps with the wise precaution of a flask, wait the stretcher party, radios alert.

Through this glen, or one very close, must have passed, in Robert Louis Stevenson's imagination, Davie Balfour and Alan Breck on their run back to the Forth with the redcoats in pursuit. Not much in this landscape has changed since those days. Perhaps there had been a few trees then; now there are none.

Time passes. My head aches with cold and I worm deeper into the heather. As the snow flurries rush by, they leave me and the ground white. I am a part of that environment. This place is the perfect natural ambush point. Are those few stones an old sheiling or perhaps the remnant of a 'sett', placed there to direct deer up to this defile? A thousand or maybe ten thousand years ago had other men lain just here feeling the earth solid beneath them, waiting for the deer?

I have been reading recently how deer had been, if not actually 'farmed' or domesticated, then at least systematically culled, as far back as the late Palaeolithic and Mesolithic. Analysis of the refuse middens of these people, throughout Europe from the middle of Italy to Jutland, shows a most remarkable preponderance of red deer bones. In fact their remains were found at 95 per cent of 165 sites examined. This indicates that for between five thousand years in the north and fifty thousand years in southern Europe, red deer were the predominant source of meat. This venison-eating belt even seems to have extended as far east and as early as Pekin man, of whose diet, according to some sources, deer meat formed 70 per cent. It was clear that venison, especially that from red deer, had been the staple diet of at least the European for far longer than anything else.

And antler had been vitally important too. Had its use not spanned so many eras we might have had an antler age to compare with the stone, bronze and iron ages. I found in my researches the story of Grime's Graves. Here in the middle of East Anglia is a most astonishing network of neolithic flint mines. For many centuries man quarried flint here to export throughout at least England if not further afield. My interest was drawn by the fact that the tool he used for all this quarrying was the red deer antler. So many antlers were used for picks in those flint mines that it is supposed that each of the dozens of mineshafts may have required between one hundred and four hundred antlers per year. They are so well preserved that some still show the 3000-year-old finger- and handprints of the miners. Juliet Clutton-Brock has reported that the majority of a sample of 283 antler picks which she examined were from fully mature stags. Four out of five antlers had been shed and several were clearly successive antlers from the same individual stags. Her explanation of this, which seems the only feasible one, is that care was being taken to avoid these adult stags being killed so that their antlers could be collected each spring. It occurred to me that for a large group of mature stags to be retained in one area of woodland, so that their antlers could readily be retrieved, would be extremely difficult without regular feeding. Since these mines predate the growing of crops, what could they have been fed?

Why had those people over countless generations not done what I was now seeking to do: domesticate the red deer? Was there some insurmountable obstacle that I had still to encounter?

And it was not only European red deer either. Frank, my Danish friend, had recently sent me some photographs taken by early aviators in the 1920s of curious kite-like shapes in the desert. These had now been recognised as massive setts constructed for the capture and slaughter of entire herds of migrating gazelles. Bones in middle eastern middens revealed that gazelle had been the staple diet there for millennia. And the same story can be told the world over, of bison in America, for example, or caribou in the Canadian Arctic. Systematic culling of the dominant game species seemed to be the rule.

But even more exciting was the evidence unearthed by some of the archaeologists which indicated that, in the case of the European red deer at least, a surprising majority of those bones were from young males. Could this have been a deliberate culling policy? Some of those archaeologists had even argued that there must have been a degree of husbandry to allow for this selective culling. Many are critical of that theory, yet it is rather hard to see how even the most expert hunter, armed with nothing more sophisticated than spear, or bow and arrow, could accomplish such a methodical cull unless the deer had been rendered approachable to some degree.

Hard evidence for that very early husbandry is missing, but something much closer to domestication, and well documented, took place centuries later in the 'classical' period when deer parks seem to have become almost commonplace. For example, writing in about AD 65, the Roman author Columella describes how 'wild creatures, such as ... deer ... sometimes serve to enhance the splendour and pleasure of their owners, and sometimes to bring profit and revenue'. How true! He then goes on to describe how '... if the cheapness of stone and labour make it advisable ... a wall built with unhewn stone and lime is put round it; otherwise it is made with unburnt bricks and clay or they may be shut up with a post fence; for this is the name given to a certain kind of lattice made of oak or cork-wood ... in this manner you can even enclose very wide regions and tracts of mountains' and, in relation to feeding the animals in the park, 'the careful head of a household ought not to be content with the foods which the earth produces by its own nature, but, at the seasons of the year when the woods do not provide food, he ought to come to the help of the animals which he has confined with the fruits of the harvest which he has stored up, and feed them on barley or wheat-meal and beans ... in a word he should give them whatever costs the least.'

Coming forward another thousand years to the England of the Domesday Survey, only thirty-six deer parks are described, but more than seventy deer 'hayes'. The French word for a hedge is *haie* and these 'hayes' of Norman England were probably hedges or fences designed to capture deer or to allow an ambush and battue, rather like the setts and elricks of the Highlands. Such a system of driving deer towards archers or into nets was known in mediaeval French as *chace a la haie*.

I had communicated eagerly with Professor Leonard Cantor at Loughborough who claims to have identified around two thousand deer parks in mediaeval England and Wales, though not all of these were in use at the same time. This is an astonishing number given that the human population at that time was only about four million. Imagine two thousand – or even one thousand – deer parks in modern Scotland with its population of five million! Professor Cantor confirmed his findings and sent me a fistful of publications which detailed his research.

Then, nearer to home, I came across the book *Hunting and Hunting Reserves in Mediaeval Scotland* by John Gilbert. I met and corresponded with John and his minutely reported findings gave me great encouragement. It was clear that a substantial economy in Scotland had revolved around deer parks. These parks were certainly used as sources of meat, together with the dovecot for pigeons, the warren for rabbits and the stews for fish. Thus in 1503 a stalker and two men had worked in Falkland Park, only five miles from Reediehill, for twelve days to provide venison for the king's wedding.

These parks were regularly replenished, often after royal visits and the associated banquets had emptied them, by bringing in wild deer, or by taking deer from one park to another. In Scotland we find, for example, that an Englishman, Master Levisay, was employed in Falkland Park, in 1502 and again in 1505, to use nets to catch deer without harming them, perhaps for transport by horse-drawn litter to restock Stirling deer park – a journey which, even if everything went well, took a minimum of three days. Management within the parks was also quite sophisticated: hay and grain must have been fed regularly and we have records from Stirling park of payments for hay in 1288, and for oats fed at Falkland from 1504 to 1507. In 1479 two cows were purchased to supply milk for rearing deer calves at Falkland – there must have been quite a few calves to rear.

Keeping the deer in was obviously one of the biggest tasks and must have entailed substantial labour. Only the largest parks such as Linlithgow in Scotland could boast stone walls; much more usual were ditches with a bank surmounted by a wattle or wooden post-and-rail palisade, or a hedge. Deer did escape, as for instance from Stirling in

1504, although on that occasion the king was lucky since the escapee was chased back in by a 'wif'.

In England and Wales the parks seem to have flourished during the early Middle Ages, from 1066 until about 1350, after which they experienced a rapid decline. Probably this was due to the depletion of the available labour force by successive visitations of the plague and as the general movement into cities continued and even accelerated. But the economic revival of the late fifteenth century saw a growth of parks once more, though these were increasingly associated with large houses and were probably established for pleasure rather than as sources of meat.

In 1532 Henry VIII established St James's Park in London, and in 1536 Hyde Park, both as hunting parks. Henry loved hunting but still one imagines he preferred the more challenging chases outwith the parks. He sent an intimate and perhaps rather risqué note to Anne Boleyn accompanying a gift of red deer venison: 'Seyng my darlyng is absent I can no less do than to sende her summe flesche, representyng my name, whyche is hart flesche for Henry, prognosticating that here after, God Wyllyng, you must injoye summe of mine whyche he pleased I wolde were now ... I wolde we were to gyder an evenning.'

Prior to the Tudors one gains the impression that it would not have been considered quite the thing to hunt in a park for sport, that is using hounds and horseborne followers, or hunting *par force* as it was known. In his review of Scottish mediaeval deer parks, John Gilbert could only find one account of deer being killed in a park by royalty and that was of James IV in 1508 going with a certain John Methven into Falkland Park 'to stalk ane deir with the culveryn'. This also is the first record of anyone stalking deer with a firearm. In any case nearly all of these parks were far too small for anyone to hunt *par force* within them. The idea is truly ludicrous to anyone familiar with deer in parks: the effect would soon have been to drive the animals out over the inevitably rather insubstantial ditches, palings and hedges that kept them in. Probably the Tudors were obliged to hunt in parks because already around London free-ranging wild red deer were becoming rather scarce.

As in Scotland so in England there is a rich store of well-documented anecdotes describing the ways in which park deer were managed. One of the most incredible techniques used was that of driving deer from one park to another. Thus as late as 1830, Stonor Park at Henley-on-Thames was stocked by the expedient of driving all the deer from Watlington Park five miles along the roads to Stonor. Even more remarkable was the feat of Joseph Watson, park keeper at Lyme Park in Cheshire, who for a wager of £500 drove twelve brace of red deer stags from Lyme Park to Windsor, perhaps two hundred miles. Watson died in 1753 at the age of one hundred and four, having been keeper at Lyme for sixty-four years. Shirley, writing in his valuable *Deer and Deer Parks* in 1867, cites another, undated, account from Playford's *Introduction to Music*: 'Travelling some years since, I met on the road near Royston a herd of about twenty bucks following a bagpipe and violin, which, while the music played, went forward, when it ceased they all stood still; and in this manner they were brought out of Yorkshire to Hampton Court.' Those of us who have trained deer to come to call for feeding will find such accounts believable, but only just.

In any event, the numbers of English deer parks grew dramatically in the late sixteenth century and by 1577 William Harrison wrote of England, 'The twentieth part of the realm is employed upon Deer and Conies already ... the owners still desirous to enlarge those grounds do not let daily to take in more.' Yet only twenty-five years later in 1602, Carew in his *Survey of Cornwall* describes how a great many parks 'within the memory of man have been disparked, the owners making their deer leap over the pale to give the bullocks place.' And Morison, in his Itinerary of 1616, wrote: 'every gentleman of five hundreth or a thousand pounds rent by the yeere hath a Parke for them inclosed with pales of wood for two or three miles compasse. Yet this prodigall age hath so forced Gentlemen to improve their revenewes, as many of these grounds are by them disparked, and converted to feede Cattell.'

This decline in the number of deer parks was further accelerated by the Civil War and the Commonwealth of Oliver Cromwell. Come the Restoration there was some revival of interest in parks as witnessed by Johannes Kip's famous engravings of country houses (1709), almost all of which show deer in the foreground. There were indeed several importations of deer from mainland Europe to make good the losses of the Civil War and the Commonwealth. With the advent of the parks of William Kent, 'Capability' Brown and Humphry Repton, deer became part of a carefully contrived landscape and this notion has persisted, through the Victorian love of the decorative, to the present. During those years deer came and went in the parks, but reached an all-time nadir during the twentieth century when the depredations of the world wars and the requisitioning of so many stately homes took their toll.

Why, I muse, as I lie stiffening with cold, did domestication not progress any further? Why was a species that was of such crucial importance as a food source for many thousands of years abandoned when cattle and sheep came along? Why did all those deer parks decline? If it is accepted that deer were at least available for domestication, and already emparked on a considerable scale a few hundred years ago, why were they later 'overtaken' by cattle and sheep? In historical terms that was a very recent development.

I grow numb and my thinking becomes ponderous.

Just five miles from where I lie, with the cold now really penetrating, Mary, Queen of Scots had been present in 1563 at a deer drive organised by the Duke of Atholl. No doubt on his mettle to impress, the duke had gathered two thousand red deer as well as fallow and roe. The bulk of the deer broke back, killing two or three of the beaters, but 360 deer and five wolves were slaughtered. And long before that, before the Normans and into prehistory, huge tainchells were organised to drive deer into the elricks. The early twelfth-century Gaelic poem 'The Enchanted Stag' describes how one thousand men, one hundred women and one thousand dogs killed two hundred deer. Later Gaelic poems describe the deeds of Finn and his dog Bran, with the numbers swollen to three thousand men, each with two dogs, killing six thousand deer.

Even allowing for exaggeration, such drives required powerful leaders and it was probably small groups of hunters with coursing dogs who claimed the most deer over succeeding centuries, aided later by firearms. Deer numbers dwindled; but long before that had come the cattle, with centuries of raiding between feuding clans and then the trade in cattle born in the Highlands and Islands, slowly swum across the narrows and lochs, and driven along the broad drove roads to the trysts at Crieff, Falkirk, Dumfries and ... and thence eventually, after fattening in Norfolk, as far as Smithfield. Reediehill was once on a drove road, I muse, and the ruins of a drovers' halt still remain. The cattle had been shod with metal shoes for those long journeys; skills and trades proudly developed and now all gone.

While I lie there dreaming and musing I watch and listen, with senses taut as a hunter's bowstring. I concentrate on the point at which the deer must surely soon emerge. I struggle to keep my hands warm and the dart gun's mechanism dry. How could those stone-age bowmen have been so effective in restricting their cull to young males?

And then suddenly there they are. A group of hinds with well-grown calves slowly grazing upwards. I have to discipline myself to wait until one hind is standing stationary across my line of fire so that the dart doesn't bounce off. The range seems tremendous after the relatively easy shots in grassy parks.

The stalker's patience after my first effort had been commendable but frustration at the miss was inevitable; set alongside the incredible accuracy of the modern high-velocity rifle normally used at between one hundred and three hundred metres, the blundering failure of my weapon is bound to make him doubt my competence. My reputation is on the line and it is now or never.

I am forced to risk a wild shot from a very long range. I aim a good twelve feet over the hind and the gamble pays off. The dart describes a parabola to end up perfectly placed on her shoulder. A great fluke. She runs off until at the top of the ridge, silhouetted, she pauses, stands and then quite gracefully lies down in the snow. I am jubilant and when we reach her, thankfully warmed by the climb, I take a momentous photograph. In the snow we are able to slide her carefully down to the burn; there the rest of the party meet us with a stretcher and eventually, as the shadows lengthen, I can drive my prize home to food and shelter. But never again: I could not expect that much luck to strike twice.

16 DARTING BY APPOINTMENT

The realisation came that, unlike deer which have been fed into range, ambushed or stalked deer will run when darted, and that in any case it is extremely difficult, given the limitations of the dart gun and dart, actually to stalk close enough, say thirty metres, to place a dart at all precisely. This is a difficult message to convey to anyone used to rifles, but for a dart to fly in a straight line, horizontally, without dropping, it has to go quite quickly; and yet if it is not to bruise or injure an animal, it must not strike too fast.

The quick-witted fallow deer, alerted by the report of the gun, sometimes spots approaching darts and dodges them! It requires fine judgement and regular practice for the marksman to judge his range so that the dart neither falls short nor hits the animal too hard. An alternative, now much used, is to employ a light plastic dart but, in Scottish conditions at least, these usually blow around too much in the wind. The need to avoid injuring the deer is not a problem shared by bow hunters who can be effective at much greater ranges. Sir Ralph Payne-Gallwey, the nineteenth-century toxophilist, reckoned that 'a skilful archer with his longbow might quite possibly pierce a galloping stag with an arrow at a distance of seventy yards'.

I suppose that to the uninitiated the idea of firing a dart at an unsuspecting deer sounds barbaric, but it has to be said that in very many cases the deer do not even notice that anything has happened until they feel an uncontrollable urge to lie down. Nevertheless it does require practice to dart deer successfully. I must have darted some five thousand over many years, yet still I learn.

In the early days of darting, Roger Short and I were the object of a BBC *Tomorrow's World* programme. The film crew came all the way to Rum, braving seasickness, and then embarked on the very rough twelve-mile Land-Rover trip to reach Kilmory. All I had to do was dart one of the stags. Everything that could go wrong did, but the crew were patient and when I saw the edited piece I realised why it is that everyone imagines darting to be so quick and straightforward. All my misses, underdosings, darts bouncing off and so on had been skilfully erased.

Not all producers are so kind. When I darted a stag more recently for another programme, the entire sequence was left intact as a sort of *cinéma-vérité* with my suppressed oaths and ignominious searches for lost darts and all. Given the problems of tranquilliser rifles and darts, to call the guy with the gun a marksman is a bit of a misnomer; he can only use his experience to minimise the variables, aim and hope.

As the demand for deer grew we had to look at ways other than stalking with a dart gun and we soon found that, as on Rum, many landowners feed their deer during the winter and darting these was much easier. On some of these estates, such as that on the Isle of Jura, cattle were being fed the famous 'draff', which is the waste from the whisky distillery once the alcohol has been washed off the fermented barley. The deer were just interlopers snatching a snack from the cattle. On other estates winter feeding was thought to help the stags stay on the property and keep them in better condition so they would produce larger antlers for the sportsman the following autumn. Certainly stags are usually greedier and more aggressive than hinds. So the females, which we wanted, often did not come into range; but if all went well and if a number of feeding sites were employed we would usually get between three and ten 'feeder hinds' in a day.

It was about this time, in 1979, that I received a request from

Balmoral to see if we could help them by darting hinds to send down to Windsor. Windsor Great Park had had deer in it from the early thirteenth century until the Second World War, when the herd was dispersed. Now the Queen had proposed that it would be interesting to restock. It was suggested that it would be a good idea to use solely Scottish deer, and although not everybody was entirely supportive it was nevertheless agreed. From my viewpoint it was a thoroughly good plan. I had always been fascinated to know how well Scottish deer would perform in good lowland conditions, and this was the ideal testing ground.

Years later we found that in body weight they compared favourably with 'indigenous' English deer, and though the Scottish stags' antlers never matched those of the English, their temperament and body conformation for meat production were better. Anyway, I had a number of enjoyable days at Balmoral, starting with sighting the gun in on the front lawn and then working with the head stalker, Sandy Masson, and his cheerful crew. Sandy had started his time as a rabbit trapper and keeper around the coal mines of industrial Fife and this, combined with his army experiences, made him an ideal head stalker who always commanded respect and set an example. Sandy was invariably forthright and, I imagine, happy to trade curses with Prince Philip. He loved life at the top and would tackle any job if it provided a challenge. His fund of stories never ran dry. It was Sandy who, perhaps as much as any, changed Prince Charles's attitude from one of reluctance to shoot any deer to a more realistic appreciation that the numbers must be reduced to prevent serious environmental damage and to reduce spring mortality among the deer themselves.

It so happened that in those days our bank manager in Auchtermuchty was Sandy's cousin, and he suggested coming with me on a deer-catching expedition. It was a glorious sunny day but there was quite a depth of snow at the end of Loch Muick, and we had to drive up between a track cut through the drifts by the snowplough. There were two or three Land-Rovers, my little van, and a Snowmobile or two which were ideal for retrieving the anaesthetised deer. We got on famously because the snow had brought the deer down nicely and they were hungry enough to feed very well. Old John Robertson lived there and he had an ancient tractor with an adapted fertiliser spreader which spewed out pellets of feed to the impatient masses of deer. I sat precariously on the back of the tractor attempting to dart the hinds. We had one or two battues, and about fifteen or twenty deer were lying comfortably asleep for collection by the Snowmobiles when the wind began to get up very stormy. The loose snow started to drift and it was soon clear that the track home would be impassable.

Sandy phoned up for a snowplough and in due course late in the afternoon there arrived in succession two snowploughs and a snowblower. Unfortunately the depth of snow was now such that these stuck too, and we were all obliged to pass the night in John's cottage. The deer were by this time all ensconced in deep straw in my truck enjoying better shelter than their friends on the open hill. In the cottage, despite the hospitality, there was a substantial shortage of beds and floor space, and for a while I thought I might be sharing a bed with my bank manager.

When the first lot of deer got down to Windsor they were turned out into the park outwith my control and without anyone thinking to treat them for warbles. Needless to say, deer on farms are easily cleaned of warbles by treatment on arrival and subsequent restriction of access to wild deer and their warbles. The obvious concern at Windsor was that we might create a pool of Scottish warbles in the Scottish deer but fortunately it hasn't happened like that. Perhaps jackdaws came and gobbled up the larvae, delighted at the strange feast.

Having established the hinds we needed a stag of independent breeding. Lord Dulverton, President of the British Deer Society, decided it would be a fine idea to contribute a really good stag from his Scottish estate at Glen Feshie as a gift from the society to Prince Charles, and he asked me to come and dart it.

The stag Lord Dulverton had in mind was a particularly handsome chap by Scottish trophy standards. It would have been completely impossible to approach him close enough except by attracting him in to feed, but unfortunately he could only be lured in to feed in the bottom of the glen at dusk. The idea was that, since it was early autumn and quite dry, we would use His Lordship's Jaguar car as our approach vehicle. We waited impatiently all afternoon. I made up my dart as dusk approached and we waited on. Finally in virtual darkness the beast arrived. The laird, who had previously been rather on tenter-hooks, swiftly became the man of action and we swept down the glen at a terrific rate, leaving some paint and gaining a dent as we crossed the bridge over the burn. Across the rocky boulder field towards the stag we sped. The poor car crashed and bounced along and I slithered from side to side on the slippery leather of the back seat. 'Where is he? Where's he gone?' Astonishingly the stag stood his ground while I fired a hasty dart. It missed. I commanded a strategic retreat in order to load another dart in the darkness with deadly syringe needles all about me.

Conscious that Lord Dulverton had run the Army Sniping School during the war, I was on my mettle now. It was so dark that the gun flashed and the foresight was quite invisible. For five agonising minutes we waited unaware of whether the dart had gone home; and then to my immense relief the stag lurched a couple of times and lay quietly down.

Darting should in my opinion be recognised as a veterinary pro-cedure; after all, we are administering a general anaesthetic by remote injection. But it is rarely if ever included in the overcrowded veterinary curriculum at our six British veterinary schools and vets have shown little interest in becoming involved. Instead there are a number of laymen equipped with dart guns who must obtain their drugs from the vets, and who carry out most of the darting.

I find myself called upon to dart a variety of runaway animals but most often cattle. Almost invariably this is very straightforward, humane and quick. It is generally a simple matter to approach the animal close enough to place a dart. Also the massive haunch and thick hide of a cattle beast can absorb darts more safely, so that one doesn't need to be quite so careful about firing the dart a bit more powerfully. Usually the poor animal has been pursued by the anxious farmer assisted by the police with attendant blue flashing lights, and by the time I arrive has found sanctuary in somebody's garden. Urgency sometimes dictates that I too should arrive escorted by more flashing blue lights. Often it is dark and the scene is illuminated by spotlights, making the whole enterprise rather surreal. I make my approach stealthily through the neighbour's vegetables and carefully take my shot over the garden fence, watched from a number of windows. As the drug takes effect the animal will normally begin an uncoordinated shamble which on one occasion I remember flattened a greenhouse. In any case it all seems preferable to the use of a heavy rifle, which is the usual alternative where busy roads or railway lines are concerned.

Darting deer is more difficult since they are quicker to scent someone and their visual acuity is better. Also we are often asked to dart several animals at the same time, which makes the job much more demanding. Surprisingly, though, if one hides up a tree deer will pass below and rarely notice the unusual sight: this must have been a very common ruse for early hunters, along with stalking-horses and other tricks.

In any event, the Glen Feshie stag settled in well and sired many calves in the unaccustomed lush pasture of Windsor.

17 HOW NEW ZEALAND BEAT US TO IT

The Glensaugh project had started in 1970, and in 1974 the first report of what was grandly called the Strathfinella Improvement Group was published. The first chapter was, even more grandly, called 'Genesis and Its Accompanying Vicissitudes', and I think that encapsulates the feeling of all us early deer farmers that we were engaged in something epoch-making. The members of the group were those who had played a part in setting up the pilot deer farm. Because it had been established as a joint endeavour between the two institutes, Sir Kenneth Blaxter, Director of the Rowett Research Institute, and Ian Cunningham, Director of the Hill Farming Research Organisation, headed the list of authors. Years on, its optimism reads refreshingly; it made a lasting contribution to our understanding of red deer. A second report was also eventually published in 1988; by then the project was not so shining new, but what the second report lacks in novelty it makes up for in scientific content.

In, I think, 1978, Ian Cunningham went to New Zealand and on his return I listened to a lecture of his about New Zealand deer farming. What particularly struck me were his stocking-density figures; that is the numbers of deer carried per hectare of New Zealand farmland. Perhaps over the years my memory plays me false, for it is a terrible thing to suggest that such an eminent agriculturist, who has always been a good friend to me, could possibly have made an error. Nevertheless I believe that Ian actually did make a mistake in converting acres to hectares, and the figure he gave in response to a question from the audience increased the stocking density by a factor of two and a half when it should have been *reduced* by that factor! In any case Ian's talk whetted my appetite – those stocking-density figures were truly amazing – and I went to a bucket shop and bought a ticket to Fiordland at the southern extremity of New Zealand, where at Te Anau in 1979 the New Zealand Deer Farmers' Association were having their annual get together.

As soon as I got off the flight in Auckland I realised the New Zealand advantage. The climate was perfect. The stags had just finished their rut and our hinds were about to start calving; it was May, and when I phoned home Nickie said she had six inches of snow. Such a late snowfall is a rarity with us but in New Zealand much more so. On my farm we have to feed the deer for two hundred days at least. Few New Zealanders need to feed for more than one hundred days. Their advantage is the grass; it grows almost all year on very productive volcanic soils that have been cropped for only a century. Perhaps Ian had not made a mistake about stocking density after all.

It was a very exciting meeting. Far more delegates attended than had been anticipated and we were bussed around the conference in a convoy of fifteen charabancs. They even managed to show us helicopters emerging from the bush with drugged deer slung underneath them in nets ready for release on to deer farms. At that time the helicopters were catching about ten thousand deer a year for the new farming industry. Deer farming, it seemed, had really come of age in New Zealand. Whilst, like most British, I was shocked to see the way in which these wild deer were being shot or darted from helicopter – so very different from the meticulously careful individual rifle shooting which is supposed to be practised in Britain – I soon learnt the reasons.

The story of New Zealand's deer industry makes a fascinating tale. When the Europeans arrived in New Zealand there were no mammal species except, I believe, seals and perhaps a bat. Because of its isolation from the largest land masses the evolutionary breakthrough that the mammals represented had still not reached New Zealand. However, in naive simplicity, for sport or conceivably meat, but mostly perhaps for plain nostalgia, red deer, along with a terrible list of other animals and plants, were taken out from Europe to exact their toll on the delicate native flora and fauna. Red deer probably throve better than just about any species except rabbits, or the opossums introduced from Australia. The deer also did just about as much damage as the others. It is difficult to grasp what a huge environmental impact these grazing animals inflicted on a uniquely rich ecosystem which had evolved with no need for protection against herbivores.

In other ecosystems worldwide, plants have developed a whole battery of defence mechanisms against browsing: they synthesise chemicals to make themselves poisonous or indigestible or simply to taste unpleasant, they have learnt to coppice, that is to sprout up again with several shoots when they have been grazed down to ground level so that bark stripping is less likely to kill them, and they have spines to provide mechanical protection. But such mechanisms were less developed in the New Zealand bush. There were many species of birds unique to that habitat, some of them, like the kiwi itself, being flightless; they had no need to fly in the absence of predators. Many, owing to destruction of habitat and the introduction of mammalian predators, have now become extinct or desperately endangered. The deer thrived and the population exploded and colonised more and more of the bush. Soon deer were even being blamed for erosion as the forest was reduced. Something had to be done.

Within twenty years of the last introductions of red deer to New Zealand, the State Forest Service had realised the awful mistake and strenuous efforts were soon being made to control the animals' spread. Stalkers were provided with free ammunition and paid a bounty on deers' tails. For a period around the war the skins made good prices which encouraged many hunters, and the tally of deer killed rose, but not enough; still the population increased. And then, with the post-war growth of the German economy forcing venison prices up world-wide, came a change. In the 1960s, when the same set of economic factors prevailed globally as those which were eventually to lead to Glensaugh's establishment in Scotland in 1970, namely high venison and low lamb prices, Kiwis started thinking of new ways to extract the venison. Inevitably their minds turned to helicopters, and in April 1963 Tim Wallis and a few friends hired a helicopter and made the first effort to use it for venison shooting and recovery. Soon the use of helicopters from which to shoot the deer and retrieve the carcases became widespread. In the very rough terrain of much of New Zealand it was the only practicable solution.

To sporting deerstalkers in Britain this seems heresy but, as in all such issues, one must look at the options. In this case the alternatives were particularly stark: it was death by rifle and not always a perfect shot, given a moving deer and a helicopter, or it was sit back and watch the destruction of the ecosystem. Reducing deer by traditional stalking had proved ineffective, and poisoning was barely feasible, as well as being inhumane and wasteful. For let no one misunderstand the ecological imperative – if deer numbers had not been reduced in New Zealand the native bush would have vanished, leaving only a few vestiges of a wonderfully rich flora and fauna on offshore islands. Loss of that unique habitat would have meant the end of many species of plant, bird and animal, including ultimately most of the deer too.

Only the New Zealanders could turn a potential ecological catas-trophe into a valuable new agricultural industry, but that is what happened; New Zealand's deer farming can be looked on as a by-product of saving the ecosystem, I suppose. A substantial industry grew around the sale of wild venison to Germany: requirements included helicopters, fixed-wing aircraft, jet boats, ships, factories and chillers. Wild deer numbers began to fall and thoughts turned to the farming of deer. In 1968 the first deer-farming trials were set up at Lincoln College and proved successful. And then in 1975 the German auth-orities imposed much more stringent sanitary regulations, and consequently the costs of procuring wild venison rose dramatically. The trickle of new deer farms became a flood and in 1977 the first auction of live deer was held. The New Zealand Deer Farmers' Association was founded in 1975.

One of the factors accelerating the development of the New Zealand deer-farming industry was the presence of eager investors called, after Auckland's business quarter, 'Queen Street farmers'. Encouraged by favourable taxation regulations, these businessmen entered into 'share-farming' arrangements with the farmers and dramatically speeded up the industry's growth.

The price of deer for breeding shot up and more and more helicopters were enlisted to catch live deer. Within six months ten million dollars' worth of helicopters were imported into New Zealand with the sole object of capturing live deer. This was achieved first by the simple if ruthless expedient of jumping out and wrestling the animals into submission, then putting them in a net and hauling them out. Later came the less exciting but much more humane technique of shooting them with a dart gun, then finally – and this is the technique that has stood the test of time – shooting a net over them with the so-called 'Gotcha Gun'.

The ethics of capturing wild deer in the manner favoured in New Zealand in those days, and even of shooting them from helicopters, are bound to be controversial, especially in more urbanised societies such as England. For the animals it must certainly have been a profoundly shocking experience made only slightly more acceptable by the use of tranquillisers. Nowadays the 'live capture industry' has all but vanished and very few deer are caught by helicopter. In its heyday, perhaps twenty thousand deer were caught in a single year and for several years the annual catch remained around ten thousand.

New Zealand has close ties to the Far East, and Korean buyers had for many years been visiting to purchase antler from the shot deer. The importance of 'velvet' as a by-product of deer farming was clear to New Zealanders from the beginning.

The velvet antler as consumed by the traditional Chinese medicine taker is the whole growing antler. During the period of regrowth the antlers are said to be 'in velvet' and are soft, covered in fur and full of blood, nerves and cartilage. As the velvet antler reaches full size, after about four months in red deer, it starts to harden and the furry skin or velvet peels off to leave the antler as 'hard horn', actually bone.

It is this velvet antler which has, for at least two thousand years (since we have a silk scroll from a Han tomb dated to 165 BC testifying to the use of velvet antler), been credited by the Chinese with pharmaceutical powers. Second in importance only to ginseng in the traditional Chinese pharmacopoeia, it is used particularly as a tonic for invalids and children and for old men with declining potency. Velvet is thought to strengthen the 'yang' aspects of the consumer, that is the masculine, active, ascending elements. As providers of velvet, deer have actually been 'farmed' for at least a few hundred years in eastern Russia, China and parts of southeast Asia. The international trade in velvet is large and centres mostly on Korea, but also on Hong Kong and Singapore, where frozen antler is sent for drying, and Taiwan, where fresh velvet is especially prized. Dried velvet is traded in China and other markets. It is a multi-million pound industry worldwide, as New Zealand was not slow to realise. In the 1980s one of the most successful entrepreneurs in this business even flew the world in his own jet, buying velvet antler from reindeer in Alaska, elk in Mongolia, Manchuria and Canada, and even red deer in Scotland (illustration 7b).

New Zealand deer farmers found Koreans beating a path to their door, and the farming of deer for velvet as well as meat soon came to be an accepted practice in New Zealand. Incredibly, in a country with a human population not much more than half that of Scotland, by 1983 there were nearly two and a half thousand deer farms, and between 1991 and 1997 New Zealand exported annually between about 150 and 200 tonnes of dried velvet antler, worth over \$US30 million per annum, a sum usually equal to about a third of their venison exports.

The financial crisis in the Asian economies which began in 1998 damaged velvet production but within twelve months recovery was well under way, demonstrating the resilience of the trade. There is some indication from New Zealand scientists that velvet antler has genuine pharmacological activity, and the New Zealanders are endeavouring to expand their markets by selling velvet products through health-food outlets to occidental customers in the United States and elsewhere.

My visit in 1979 coincided with a boom time for deer farmers and especially velvet producers, and it was exhilarating to be there. Even if, the New Zealanders reckoned, velvet prices fell, there was an ongoing demand for venison; indeed it is probably fair to say that most Kiwis always looked to the venison trade as the ultimate reason for keeping deer.

It was a time for heroes and one such was Tim, now Sir Tim, Wallis, who was the man with enough conviction to start using aircraft first to cull deer and then to catch them live for the fledgling deer-farming industry. As the helicopter cull began to reduce deer numbers, Tim bought an old tramp steamer, put in a refrigeration plant and a helicopter landing pad, and was then able to work in the difficult terrain of Fiordland. The *Ranginui* could carry six hundred carcases in her refrigerated hold and it took two helicopters only three days to fill her up. When the live capture business took off the *Ranginui* was fitted up with stalls and used to accommodate newly captured live deer.

Tim Wallis has been an inspiration to deer farmers everywhere. His personal courage is an example to us all. Like many of the helicopter pilots operating in the New Zealand deer business he has had several flying accidents. Until recently the worst took place in 1968 when he was taking hay up to sheep in very heavy snowfall and poor visibility and he contacted high-tension power lines. He broke his back and was paralysed from the waist down. Told he would never be able to walk again, after months of recuperation not only did he learn to walk unaided but incredibly he managed to get back into helicopters once more and take up from where he had left off.

Travelling the world to keep his various businesses in good shape, Tim is known to almost all deer farmers and universally admired. He has developed the most successful and humane capturing systems and has used his helicopters to catch animals worldwide to assist conservationists.

Tim's hobby has been the collection and restoration of Second World War aircraft, and it was while flying a Spitfire that he had an accident in 1996 which put him in a coma for many weeks. No one expected him to survive, but at the World Deer Conference in Ireland in summer 1998 there he was, being promenaded in a wheelchair by that other deer-farming pioneer and knight of New Zealand, Sir Peter Elworthy. Interesting that Sir Peter, the first Chairman of the New Zealand Deer Farmers' Association, had also been President of the nearest equivalent to our National Farmers' Union; imagine our British NFU headed by a prominent agricultural diversifier! It could not happen. Tim's mind is as acute and perceptive as ever and rumour had it that he was swimming thirty lengths every morning in the hotel swimming pool.

Helicopter capture is fast and efficient. It has to be because of the costs, and because, if overstressed, deer will not make good farmstock. Just how fast and efficient I found out when I was taken up by a pilot. Strapped in the back of the minute machine, unable to see much through the crazed perspex, I soon threw up. Fortunately I had a small bag of films with me and was able to put it to good use and avoid disgracing myself. After that I felt much better. Within the first ten minutes of hectic searching we had located a hind, swerved in, and a minute later shot a net over her. The shooter leapt out to secure the animal and give her an injection to quieten her while we flew off to land and prepare the strop, then back again for a hazardous hover about a metre above a tree top for two or three minutes to secure the netted, sedated creature and re-embark the shooter, who was able to scramble aboard from the top of the tree, and off again to the farm where the hind was lowered into a darkened shed. So within less than fifteen minutes of being sighted, that hind was in rehabilitation.

The skills accumulated by these capture teams were awe-inspiring. A number of crews were killed, and at times competition for deer-rich areas was fierce. A hangar was thought to have been burnt by a competing company and several farmers strung cables across narrow valleys to deter the choppers. Poaching of farmed deer by helicopters became for a period almost common.

As a naive, well-brought-up boy from another country I dropped into this frontiers world in 1979 and rubbed my eyes. The first night I was asked to give a brief talk to the meeting about United Kingdom deer farming, and got a good response when I told them they didn't have much to worry about in the way of competition from the UK in the foreseeable future. I was right. Only two or three British farmers had followed me at that stage. I was treated with such courtesy and welcomed with such open hearts wherever I went, that it was all very humbling.

One thing I did on that first trip was to stop in Hong Kong on my way back and chase up some of the velvet buyers. When I came home I found that many Scottish stags are shot in late summer during the early part of the stalking season when they are in full velvet. This velvet I was able to buy and freeze. I then invited my Hong Kong friends over and they paid me enough to cover my trip with some besides. I still have the photo of three smiling Chinese posing outside Reediehill after they had examined the contents of our little chest freezer. 'I go home now and immediately open LC for you.' This was my first encounter with the 'confirmed irrevocable letter of credit', opened this time on the Hong Kong and Shanghai Bank: the romance of trade!

Back in staid old Britain I began to think about the velvet business. Two things seemed clear. Firstly the ethics: I was not too keen on the idea of keeping deer simply for the purposes of amputating a piece of live tissue each year, and I was equally sure the British public would not look kindly on it either, even if it was done under anaesthetic with veterinary supervision. If it had been crocodiles or rats it might have been acceptable, but the Bambi syndrome is well developed in Britain. And as I was soon to find out, those susceptible to the Bambi syndrome had strange but powerful bedfellows in the landowning, deerstalking lobby. I had come into deer farming to promote lean meat, not to deal in a substance whose merits, or production ethics, seemed unlikely to withstand close scrutiny.

Secondly, I thought that velvet prices would not be sustainable. The market would soon be saturated, and westernisation of the velvet-eating peoples would lead to a gradual decline in consumption. But now, twenty years on, I wonder if perhaps I was wrong; time will tell.

So when I was asked to speak to the British Deer Society shortly after my return from New Zealand, I aired the subject of velvet production quite thoroughly. I made no value judgements but I remember saying that it was to be expected that someone would take my comments to heart, and that is just what happened. Within a year velvet production in Britain was declared illegal on welfare grounds.

18 HUSBANDRY BEFORE DOMESTICATION

As the newspapers and television continued to show an interest in deer farming, and as we became more of a feature at agricultural shows and in the media, I was asked to give more talks. These were usually to farmers in one guise or another, but included the usual round of Rotary and Probus clubs. I also had a short innings with the Scottish Women's Rural Institute, but was only asked once for the simple reason that I forgot to go on the appointed night.

I remember Nickie and I were enjoying a peaceful supper by ourselves, or more accurately were about to enjoy one, when the phone rang. 'Are you coming'? they said. 'We're all ready.' Seized with terror, I leapt into the car and drove like Ben-Hur thinking the whiles about what I should say. No chance to select slides, they would have to look at me for forty minutes while I tried to entertain them. On arrival, there was the village hall with the upturned, expectant, and by now actually rather angry, faces. I hastily judged the 'Dressed Coathanger' competition, which no doubt further alienated all except the winner, and then I was off on a long rambling discourse. Without the benefit of slides, which require the lights to be doused so that those who have had a busy day can at least slumber unnoticed, a speaker becomes all too clearly aware of the impact, or lack of it, that he is making. The poor speaker who, in my case, had himself fallen under the influence of Lethe earlier that evening can but envy the sleepers and try hard to shock them out of their reveries.

Shamefully I have to say that this experience was but the first of several. Usually preceded by a series of verbal requests for the talk, and notwithstanding my efficient entry of the date, time and place in the diary, for some reason that awful plaintive phone call – 'Doctor Fletcher? We're all sitting here waiting, Doctor' – still happens. It isn't, so far, the talks at distant conferences or the teaching appointments at universities that have been forgotten, but always the local organisations. Why is this? It must reflect some flaw in my psyche, and those good people, whom I especially wish to be nice to, must think very badly of me.

The last time this happened was mid-morning on 1 April. The phone rang and, since the venue was actually in Auchtermuchty, they generously allowed me ten minutes to put some slides together whilst they concluded their own business. That, and by now accumulated years of experience in giving these talks, coupled with the surge of adrenaline associated with the element of guilt and surprise, meant that I actually gave an adequate performance. The generous voter of thanks even managed to gloss over my rude delayed appearance by convincing some of the audience that it was all a carefully contrived April Fool's joke.

On the more normal occasions I can generally be relied on to stimulate some questions, and one of the commonest – usually emanating from a cocky, complacent and well-heeled sceptical farmer who probably banks a subsidy cheque of at least £50,000 each year – is: 'If it's such a good idea to farm deer, why wasn't it done before?' Yes; just the same question that continued to bother me.

I felt duty-bound to try and answer this conundrum to my own satisfaction. If I couldn't, then perhaps I should be asking myself what I was doing farming deer in the first place. I devoted quite a lot of time into researching and thinking out an answer to this really very obvious question, and eventually I developed a thesis that satisfies me.

I had already established that, to a surprising extent, deer had been husbanded in parks over the last thousand years. Long before that, we had the unexplained fact that mesolithic man had somehow learned to selectively cull the young male deer, thus maximising the production of their local deer population. How could they do this without some degree of husbandry? Yet in turn, how could a society with no crops possibly even tame the deer, let alone 'domesticate' them?

Suddenly, to my great delight, I came across a possible explanation. Excavations and pollen analysis of mesolithic dwelling sites showed puzzlingly high levels of pollen from ivy. The only explanation was that substantial quantities of ivy were being hoarded. Why on earth was ivy being collected in such quantity? The archaeologists proposed that it was being harvested as a winter food for deer.

I remained sceptical of this interpretation until my father-in-law showed me a passage from the diary of Celia Fiennes. This redoubtable lady, born in 1662, rode around England recording things which interested her, in 'a spirit of pure curiosity', as she declared. And one of the sights which spurred her to take up her quill was foresters using browse to tempt deer into a park on a winter's day in the New Forest in southern England

... what is peculiar to the New Forrest and known no where else are these Brouce Deare; at these severall Lodges the Keepers gather Brouce and at certaine tymes in the day by a call gathers all the Dear in within the railes which belongs to each Lodge and so they come up and feed upon this Brouce and are by that meanes very fatt and very tame so as to come quite to eate out of your hand; all the day besides they range about and if they meete any body, if it be their own keeper, without the pail of the Lodge will run from him as wild as can be; these Lodges are about 4 miles asunder and its a great priviledge and advantage to be a Cheefe Keeper of any of these Lodges, they have venison as much as they please and can easily shoote it when the troop comes up with in the paile ...

Celia Fiennes' observations had bridged the gap between the Mesolithic and our own experiences at Reediehill; a way in which these prehistoric hunters could selectively cull out the young males had been staring me in the face. For, at feeding time, it is a simple matter to select an individual animal and despatch it instantaneously without upsetting even its friends. This could certainly have been the way in which the people of the Mesolithic managed to cull their deer selectively. I believe that with a bow and arrow, or even conceivably a spear, it would have been eminently feasible. Was it farming? It seemed rather similar to what Nickie and I were attempting.

This brought me face to face with those who have for centuries been debating what exactly constitutes domestication. I found that first of all, for archaeologists, the index of domestication has to be the first point at which they can see definite change in the size or shape of the bones of a species. This is not surprising, since the skeleton is almost the only material the archaeologist has had to work with, at least until very recently. Consequently the accepted definition of domestication amongst archaeologists is the point at which a species has its breeding under the control of man and no longer has access to breed with its wild relatives, for under those conditions it will soon change its physical form.

This definition seems to me unsatisfactory. For example, it excludes elephants which have been used from the earliest historical times as fighting machines, for transport, for work and for ceremony. Those elephants are surely, in the eyes of most of us, domesticated. And yet they are always mated by wild bulls since the bull elephant is too dangerous to handle in *musth*. Similarly, camels have by most common-sense definitions been domesticated for many centuries; and yet, because they still interbreed with wild camels, there is virtually no physical difference between the wild and domesticated populations. And what about reindeer? May they not be mated by wild reindeer or caribou over much of their range? As a result, the reindeer, the elephant and the camel closely resemble their wild relatives and are usually classed as undomesticated by archaeologists.

'Isn't this all rather academic?' you must be thinking. I suppose you are right, except that the crucial importance of the process of domestication is not often realised except by the specialists. In his book *Guns, Germs and Steel*, the American physiologist and biologist Jared Diamond recently reviewed the literature on this subject and drew some fascinating conclusions.

It has long been recognised that in the slow, painful, halting, progress of mankind from the stone age to modern technology, one of the first steps, and perhaps the most crucial of all, has been the domestication of crops and livestock for food. Through the development of systems of food production, it is estimated that an acre of land could be made to yield between ten and one hundred times more food than in its uncultivated state. The story goes that this allowed our ancestors to abandon a nomadic way of life, for the most part, and to settle down. Anyone who has been on a camping holiday will know the advantages that brings.

The domestication of livestock allowed the production of manures so vital to crop yields and health, and the animals could be used to till the ground and produce milk, tallow for candles, and wool and leather for clothing. Meat must have been of secondary importance. By being able to anticipate annual harvests and gluts and times of shortage, and relieved of the necessity of hauling food around, early farmers were able to develop systems of food storage; and although they probably worked even longer hours than their hunter-gatherer ancestors, their patterns of work became predictable and a hierarchy was established which did not simply give all accolades to the most successful hunter. Associated with the hierarchy was the creation of a leisured class: writing, philosophy, politics, religion and so on could all become much more sophisticated, and so bands became tribes, tribes clans and clans nations whilst villages became towns and towns cities. No longer were the daily and weekly rounds of societies dependent on the vagaries of wild animals, but feasts and festivals could be precisely timed around the harvests and the sowing of crops. Settlement created possessions. Even wives became chattels to be jealously guarded, since with them and their progeny passed ownership.

Expansionist ideas took hold, and wherever peoples that had successfully domesticated plants and animals encountered hunter-gatherers they prospered at the expense of the more traditional societies. Jared Diamond points out that this was due not only to their often more advanced technologies (writing, the use of livestock for haulage and in war, food storage, etc.) but also, crucially, to the support of an unseen ally: disease. Unlike the hunter-gatherer way of life in which infectious diseases were probably non-existent, aggregation of the population in settled villages opened the door to epidemics. These diseases, like most if not all infections, have their basis in the livestock. Peoples living in close proximity to their animals, often sharing the same houses, soon developed resistance to these bacteria and viruses but, as Diamond explains, when they came into contact with peoples that had never previously encountered those infectious agents the results were devastating. When Cortés conquered Mexico with only six hundred Spaniards, the population of some twenty million Aztecs had already been nearly halved by smallpox which had arrived a few years earlier, borne by an infected slave from Spanish Cuba. Similarly Pizarro, reaching Peru in 1531, found that the Incas had already been decimated by smallpox which had arrived overland around 1526.

Is it stretching the point too far to say that, conversely, as modern man loses contact with livestock and becomes thoroughly sanitised and urbanised he becomes more susceptible to animal-borne disease such as Escherichia coli 0157? We know that increasing levels of asthma, for example, are associated with diminishing exposure to bacteria in early life. Certainly many scientists would agree that the way forward is not through progressively more sterile food, but that some more realistic alternative must be found to protect us against pathogens.

The questioning farmer has by now either lost track of my argument or is looking just a little more respectful.

19 HOW OUR TABUS PREVENT PROGRESS

Archaeologists have been puzzled for a long time by just how few species of animals have been domesticated compared to the very large number of potential domesticates. Thus, of the herbivorous animals over an arbitrary one hundred pounds' body weight, Diamond lists only fourteen which have been domesticated. Why were so few used? It was Francis Galton, that extraordinary mid-nineteenth-century polymath and cousin of Charles Darwin, whose musings led to a list of criteria which he considered rendered an animal suitable for domestication. (Incidentally it was the same Galton who wrote so enthusiastically about selective breeding that he was deemed to have strayed into eugenics. It has been argued that his work provided the Nazi party with a spurious scientific basis for their crimes.) Writing in 1865, Galton listed

> . . . those conditions under which wild animals may become domesticated:
> 1. They should be hardy
> 2. They should have an inborn liking for man
> 3. They should be comfort loving
> 4. They should be found useful to the savages
> 5. They should breed freely

6. They should be easy to tend

It would appear that every wild animal has had its chance of being domesticated, that those few which fulfilled the above conditions were domesticated long ago, but that the large remainder, who fail sometimes in only one small particular, are destined to perpetual wildness so long as their race continues. As civilisation extends they are doomed to be gradually destroyed off the face of the earth as useless consumers of cultivated produce.

In other words Galton states that every species not yet domesticated must by now have been tested countless times and been found wanting. This argument has been accepted by all subsequent writers on the subject up to the present. Diamond even points out that the latest evidence suggests that cattle were domesticated independently on three separate occasions – in south-west Asia, in India and in north Africa. That seems to strengthen the argument that cattle were particularly suitable for domestication and that any species remaining undomesticated must have been left alone for good reason.

Thus Diamond cites and agrees with the archaeologist Juliet Clutton-Brock and the behaviourist Valerius Geist in saying that red deer, simply because they have not previously been domesticated, are not susceptible of domestication. This seems astonishing given that around two million red deer are on farms within New Zealand alone, and that, even using the archaeologists' own strict definition of domestication, these deer are absolutely domesticated or at least well down that road. Not only are the deer used for breeding selected as carefully as are sheep and cattle, but there is widespread use of artificial insemination and even embryo transplantation. No longer is there any interbreeding with wild deer, and indeed some degree of change is already apparent in the body shape of farmed deer compared with their wild relations: after all, even in English parks the antlers of red deer stags are quite different from any seen elsewhere in the world. In fact red deer appear to be the perfect candidates for domestication: they are gregarious and they eat grass; two vital prerequisites for a new pastoral domesticant.

If Galton and his successors are wrong in suggesting that all species as yet undomesticated are intrinsically incapable of domestication, we are still left to produce some alternative hypotheses as to why so few species were ever domesticated. As someone who has spent his life attempting to sell the idea of husbanding red deer to a conventional farming community, I feel that I have some of the answers. I believe that the stability of societies is ensured by rituals, tabus and traditions whose strength may often be underestimated by biologists. The connections which a society makes with its principal sources of food are deep. Opposition from a powerful lobby of established livestock breeders and hunters, invariably supported by politicians, in modern societies is, I believe, an expression of that tradition – and one with which modern deer farmers worldwide have become very familiar!

After all, why should a society well supplied with existing domestic animals such as cattle and sheep wish to domesticate any new grazing species for meat production? Until very recently it would have been highly expensive in time and resources, and the speed of genetic improvement would have been such that nothing as productive as cattle and sheep could ever have been produced without long selection. Deer, for example, could never in less than several hundred years yield the milk, fleeces, traction, fat or other products of existing domesticates already selected by man. Crucially, I suspect, cattle were also favoured by the relative ease with which the new tame strains could be genetically isolated from their increasingly rare wild relatives, forcing inbreeding and speeding up selective breeding.

Deer, on the other hand, offered principally meat, leather and antlers – items for which no selection was required. If culling could be achieved by the simple expedient of supplying browse, such as ivy, during the winter there would have been no pressure to carry the procedure further.

One day I was reading about the seventeenth-century 'naive' paintings of English sheep, pigs and cattle. To my eye the paintings illustrated seemed not only naive but absurd. Huge rounded bodies on minute thin legs. Reading on, I came to understand that these 'naive' painters travelled the country taking commissions from farmers who expected their stock to be represented as they wished them to appear. In other words the stockmen wished their animals to be fatter than we can possibly imagine. The fat was very desirable. And, with selection, cattle and sheep soon came to provide prodigious quantities of fat. Tallow was not so much a by-product as a co-product valued as highly by most people as the meat, since in the form of candles it allowed the day's work to be prolonged by light. And of course dietary fat would always be popular in a society with no heated houses and most of its work manual. Even the deer were especially valued if they were fat, as Jane Austen makes clear in *Pride and Prejudice*: '... venison roasted to a turn; everyone said they had never seen so fat a haunch.'

Now, although much progress has recently been made by breeding for leanness, our conventional domestic animals remain very fatty. Not only that, but the constitution of those fats is particularly injurious to human health. This fat is now identified as a major source of disease. We need to look at healthier meats. Our needs have changed and we need to broaden our search, beyond cattle and sheep. The time is ripe for a new grassland domesticant.

While it may be correct for Juliet Clutton-Brock to suggest as she did, as late as 1981, in describing the progeny of the hand-reared first generation of the Glensaugh deer, that they 'cannot really be counted as successful domestic animals', it is surprising that at a time when the New Zealanders were already farming several hundred thousand red deer, she should have made so much of the difficulties of sawing off the antlers – 'a difficult task and not practical for a large herd' – and felt impelled to state that 'the hinds can also be untrustworthy and aggressive'. The same can still be said of cattle despite their ten thousand years or so of domestication!

Diamond also ignored the New Zealand farmed deer herd, which was over one and a half million strong by the time he wrote the following in 1997: 'modern efforts have achieved only very limited successes' and 'one never sees ... tame deer ... driven in herds like sheep' (but see illustration 8c).

Clutton-Brock also cites the Canadian behaviourist Valerius Geist as saying 'that man can associate with wild sheep and goats in a way that is not possible with red deer ... the reasons for this are that the deer are territorial animals which although they live in groups or herds do not have a social structure that is based on dominance hierarchies'.

These comments perhaps demonstrate the tabus and prejudices associated with one of our society's deepest-rooted traditions. It is extremely interesting that the strongest reaction to farming deer always arises among hunting communities, with the established livestock-breeding bodies following close behind. There often seems no rational basis to their complaints. Their voices make it more difficult for any far-sighted bureaucrat or politician to extend the scope of agricultural support beyond the traditional. The hunting lobby in Denmark, for example, has successfully pressurised the government to make it illegal to house even the introduced Mediterranean fallow deer during the winter, thereby creating an inevitable threat to the animals' welfare!

But to be fair, the hunter may also feel something else. I return to Ortega y Gasset: 'the domesticated animal is a degenerate one, as is man himself ... domestication partially de-animalizes and partially humanizes the beast. The domestic animal is an intermediate reality between the pure animal and man.' The hunter wants to glimpse the wild animal from afar: alert, and ready for flight with its senses perfectly acute, a challenge to the stalker. I was not blind to the beauty of the deer but wanted to get closer, to help it, to let it relax and to admire and understand its physiology.

The availability of readily domesticated cattle and sheep must, for centuries, have removed the incentive for anyone to domesticate further grazing species. Also, the development of rituals and traditions in a society serves to fix a pattern and create a culture. This inhibits innovation. In every generation the elderly decry the modernism of the young. It is the role of tradition and ritual to stay the rebellious. Domestic animals are a crucial part of the culture of farming societies, and to challenge the status quo is bound to create controversy. We have seen how some of the Scottish landowners greeted the Glensaugh experiment. Each society has its own ways of ritualising practices, often through established religions; in the late twentieth and early twenty-first centuries bureaucracy is perhaps the establishment that deters new ideas.

In Britain the National Farmers' Union has a near-monopoly of input into the government's agricultural policy and has, at least until very recently, shown itself quite hostile to grazing animals other than cattle and sheep. This has been a perfect instance of bureaucratic enforcement of tabus and rejection of new ideas.

It is not just in Britain that powerful forces of conservatism encourage cattle farming in situations where game animals would seem to offer greater benefits. Over very large areas of Africa the tsetse fly spreads disease, *ngana*, to cattle making many areas impossible to farm. Cattle were introduced into Africa south of the Sahara quite recently by the Bantu as they migrated south between AD 500 and 1000, and they have still not developed resistance to *ngana*. The many different species of game animal, however, remain unaffected and can safely colonise those areas. Nevertheless cattle occupy so vital a position in the culture that massive programmes to eliminate wild game in an effort to remove the tsetse fly's hosts and so control the fly have been undertaken by government hunters. In what was then Southern Rhodesia, around 700,000 wild animals were shot during the first half of the twentieth century. Nothing was gained, many rare species were damaged and millions of pounds' worth of meat was destroyed. Were it not for cultural considerations it would have been vastly more logical to crop the game in a sustainable way and leave the cattle behind.

Nickie and I found that students, journalists and so on relished our deer-farming ideas whilst the older more sedate conventional farmers often either mocked or felt threatened. But the real obstacles to our plans were set by the bureaucracy – subsidies were restricted to cattle, sheep and conventional crops. This was a strong disincentive for anyone to invest in deer farming. Furthermore, legislation took no account of farmed deer and required rewriting in many details, and this was often controversial.

It has become a cliché to say that the English are good at ideas but that the establishment is frightened of innovation. Babbage, who created a mechanical device that is often considered to be the forerunner of the computer, had similar trying experiences. 'Propose to any Englishman any principle ... however admirable, and you will observe that the whole effort of the English mind is directed to find a difficulty, a defect, or an impossibility in it. If you speak to him of a machine for peeling a potato, he will pronounce it impossible. If you

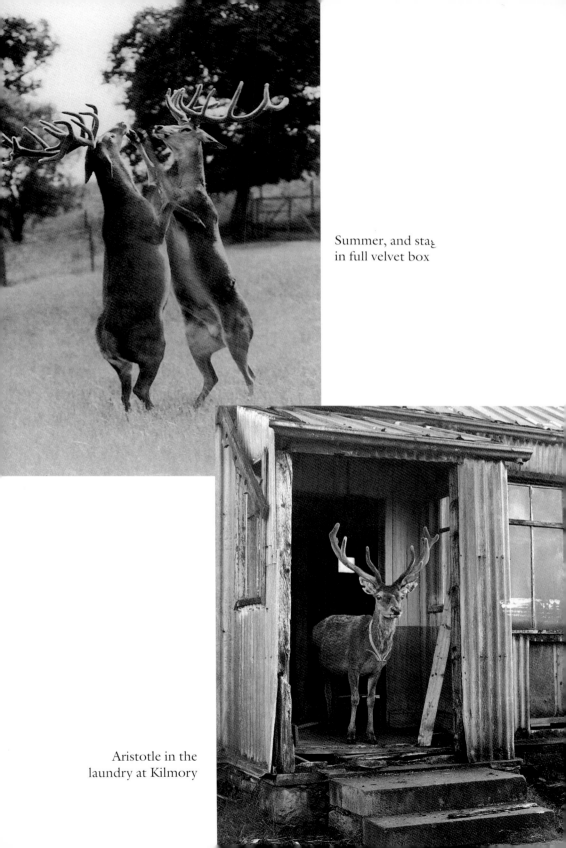

Summer, and stag
in full velvet box

Aristotle in the
laundry at Kilmory

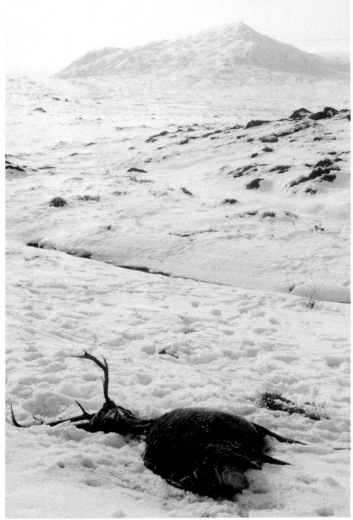

The dead stag on
Rannoch Moor
that started it all

Warble fly larvae
in the partially
skinned carcass

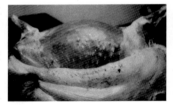

Fiona Guinness
filming on Rum

Above The wild
hind, Crottal, by
the Mathieson family
grave, Kilmory, Isle
of Rum

Right Scott, the
hummel from Mar
Lodge, wallows

Below Friction and
Manfred fight for
hinds

Reediehill in 1974

. . . and in 1999

Top left Five minutes after antler casting the wound bleeds

Top right Ten days later the new antler is in full growth with the healing wound still visible

Centre Early summer and the velvet antler is forty days old

Right Late summer and the fully grown and hardened antler is cleaned of its velvet ready for the rut

A boatload of sleeping deer

Sandy and her twins Bonnie and Clyde immediately after the birth

Nickie feeding a stag at Reediehill

Antlers for sale in a Chinese medicine shop, Hong Kong

Above The author pours a bucket of water over Ferox at the Royal Show

Right A red deer stag is helicoptered out of the New Zealand bush

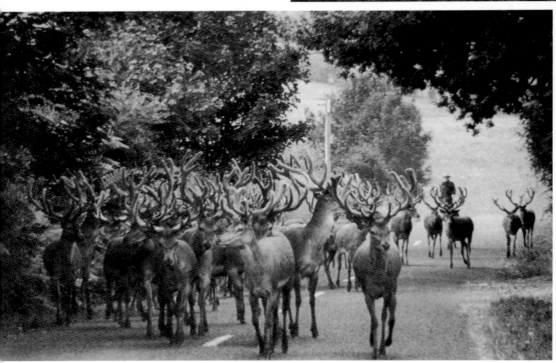

A herd of deer is driven to market along a public road in New Zealand, confounding the experts

peel a potato with it before his eyes, he will declare it useless, because it will not slice a pineapple.'

Only in New Zealand, where the country is so young that change is itself a part of the culture, could deer farming really take hold. There, agriculture is still the nation's major industry and attracts innovators who in more industrialised nations might gravitate to cities, commerce and manufacturing. Or is it that those new countries, such as New Zealand, Australia, Canada and the USA, took all the most radical thinkers, the most innovative and entrepreneurial of our society, and that two or three generations on we still feel the loss? Watching the All Blacks rugby team, recruited from a population half the size of Scotland's, one might be forgiven for thinking so! Did the talents of those settlers behave like John Donne's violet transplant: 'The strength, the colour and the size, all of which before was poore and scant, redoubles still, and multiplies'?

New Zealand remains an agricultural economy. The thrusting entre-preneurs of Auckland, with business interests often rooted in the very different cultures of south-east Asia, are keen to retain a link with their rural background and seek a stake in new farm enterprises. The arrangement works well. The successes of the kiwi-fruit industry, the wine and deer-farming businesses, say something. A young British entrepreneur is unlikely to invest in an agricultural enterprise, or, if he does, he soon finds that subsidies discourage diversification into new schemes and that the dice are heavily loaded in favour of cattle and sheep where grazing options are concerned. In New Zealand, on the other hand, deer farming has risen in twenty years to be an industry adding $NZ200 million per annum to the country's balance of trade and with a farmed deer population of over one and a half million.

As well as cultural traditions that discouraged innovation there were obvious practical constraints. For the earliest people who contemplated domesticating deer, perhaps five thousand years ago, they must first of all have been difficult to enclose. Even much later, when deer parks were established and represented a vital part of the mediaeval rural economy as I have described, keeping up the pale must have been onerous. And when the Black Death killed a quarter of Europe's population between 1346 and 1352, and as the feudal system declined, and with growing urbanisation, the mediaeval park surrounds, mostly a ditch and hedge or wooden paling, could no longer be kept in repair. Merely containing the animals must have become a problem. And deer, unlike cattle which no longer had wild relatives to slow up their selective breeding, were still wholly subject to seasonal factors. Once deer have lost their fear of man and have become tame the stags can be dangerous, especially during the autumn rut. It would have taken a very determined and long-term strategist to domesticate deer in historic times when cattle and sheep were already yielding milk, wool, leather and tallow from grass.

But times have changed now. Saturated fats, ideal for candles, are modern man's biggest killer: if he is to eat meat it must be lean. Our physically active ancestors needed a lot of fat in their diet to keep warm, and as tallow for lighting; now our needs are different. Few of us live a very energetic life and we use fossil fuels to provide warmth and light and locomotion. Consequently we are becoming very fat, and heart disease is without question the epidemic of our time and society.

The modern western diet is lethal. Soon the British will be as fat as the Americans. Dominated by dairy produce, our diet seems to be associated not only with heart disease but also breast and colonic cancer, multiple sclerosis, diabetes and arthritis. One in four men will have a heart attack or stroke before retirement age in many western societies. Colonic cancer and a host of other conditions have been linked with obesity, and are becoming more common as we grow more overweight. Nor is obesity solely a disease of the developed world; it is rapidly becoming a problem in the urban centres of developing nations, too.

There is another point which I think is of vital importance. Scratch the skin and we are all hunter-gatherers, with the behaviour and physiology of our forebears. All the evidence indicates that our brains, and presumably much else besides, have remained unchanged for hundreds of thousands of years. Domestication of both animal and plant food sources only took place around twelve thousand years ago, so that the consumption of these foods is a novelty. As for the fatty meats taken from animals bred for fat, they have formed a significant part of our diet for only a few centuries. It is reasonable therefore to argue that we have not yet made the necessary physiological adaptations to that fatty diet and may be suffering the consequences.

The nutritionist Professor Michael Crawford has pointed out that because man has, for nearly all his existence as a species, eaten more wild meats, especially venison, than any other meat, his body is best adapted to that meat. He argues that '99.8 per cent of man's life has been spent eating wild food' and that 'man is still a wild animal not yet adapted to eating other than wild foods'. In other words, he argues, we have still not become habituated to the meat of cattle and sheep which we have, in the biological scale of things, only been eating for a very short time. This may seem a little far-fetched, but the fats of domesticated animals are not only more substantial in quantity – in Britain we now eat enough animal fat to power all our light bulbs – but also very different in structure from those of the game species.

There are many fatty acids, the constituents of fats, which are vital parts of our diet: the essential fatty acids (EFAs). They are, for example, essential in building the brain. These structural fatty acids are the polyunsaturates, notably the omega-3 fatty acids. Along with fish, game animals such as venison are rich in these acids. It may be relevant that for long before cattle and sheep began to be domesticated, fish was a key element of man's diet; indeed, worldwide, we still derive as much of our protein from fish as from meat. On the other hand, the fat of the domesticated animals we eat is rich in the injurious saturates.

Crawford points out that in game meat the fat is predominantly structural and intracellular, high in polyunsaturates and made up for the most part of essential fatty acids (EFAs) which are vital, as their name suggests, to the proper functioning of the body. Among these are the larger-molecule EFAs, the omega-3 and omega-6 fatty acids. Dairy products, like the meat of the animals from which they come, are deficient in such acids. Crawford notes that cows' milk contains more protein than human milk but far fewer EFAs; this makes it better suited to sustaining body development, whilst the milk of women, being abundantly supplied with essential fatty acids, is adapted to nourishing the growth of neural tissue: brain versus brawn.

I reason, therefore, that instead of trying to breed cattle and sheep to be thinner, we should widen our horizon and look at the species which are already lean. Venison is, after all, dark red because it has less fat, and more iron, than the paler beef, lamb, pork and chicken.

There remains, of course, the danger that by domesticating our deer, selecting unwisely and feeding cereal-based rations, we breed too much, and more saturated, fat into the deer. Certainly that is a risk but, alerted to it, the modern farmer can surely avoid making the mistakes of our ancestors who were, after all, eager for fats.

And by this time that well-heeled farmer has assuredly taken himself off to the bar.

20 HUMMELS, POLITICIANS AND ABATTOIRS

On 30 November 1978, The British Deer Farmers' Association (BDFA) was founded. The first issue to be handled was the legality of velvet harvesting. The Farm Animal Welfare Council (FAWC) had just been set up by the government to examine various procedures involving livestock, and in a move not unrelated, I think, to my talk to the British Deer Society on my return from New Zealand, the very first topic they addressed was 'velveting', as it came to be known. In 1980 they found against it; legislation was quickly pushed through and I was relieved: now we could concentrate on producing venison.

In fact it is not quite so simple. Most British deer farmers still remove the hard dead antlers from their stags in the late summer, and although the deer cannot feel this it does involve handling them. It would be extremely satisfactory, for both the farmed deer and the deer farmers (although not for the trophy hunters), if we could breed 'hummels'. These are antlerless stags which occur quite commonly in the wild in Scotland, probably as a result of a period of poor nutrition at a critical phase of their development. Congenitally polled cattle used to be called hummels, as Samuel Johnson noted in 1773: '... some are without horns, called by the Scots "humble" cows, as we call a bee an "humble" bee, that wants a sting.'

There is a myth amongst Scottish deerstalkers firstly that hummels are abnormally well grown, secondly that they are particularly effective during the rut in defeating antlered rivals, and thirdly that hummels beget hummels. On Rum, with Roger Short's help, Gerald had set about attempting to breed hummels, and when we came to Reediehill the programme continued. In fact those deer which went to South Uist had a considerable amount of hummel blood in them. The first hummel we used was captured by Roger at Mar Lodge and named Scott after the head keeper at Mar (illustration 3). He behaved impeccably in the enclosure behind the castle and sired many progeny including Bonnie and Clyde, all the males of which in due course became antlered. Even breeding him back to his daughters yielded antlered staggies. Although an impressive beast, Scott was never successful in competition with antlered stags – but of course the conditions in our enclosure were very different from those on the wild hill.

At about this time one of the Nature Conservancy scientists did a check on all the hummels whose weights had been recorded in the game books of sporting estates. He could find no significant heavyweights amongst them. It was a little disappointing. Perhaps when we see hummels on the hill they seem larger because we are unconsciously comparing them with the similarly antlerless hinds. And maybe in the hurly-burly of the rut the antlered stags make the same error and fail to chase the hummels away from their harems because they think they are females to be courted. This is all very speculative. We concluded that hummels remain without antlers because they are, for a crucial phase of their development, exposed to particularly straitened circumstances; they are in fact stunted. It is no coincidence that we rarely see hummels anywhere except on the most impoverished of Scottish deer forests.

I became Chairman of the BDFA in 1980 and was almost immediately thrust up against the fact that legislation continued to be drafted without taking any account of deer farming. In this case it was a new Scottish Deer Bill. If enacted as it stood, this would prevent Nickie and me and the other small band of Scottish deer farmers from killing deer except during the three-and-a-half-month hunting season. It all hinged on a slight change of wording which had, I suspect, been inserted by someone who specifically opposed deer farming and who was, as we were now accustomed to finding in our most implacable opponents, a hardened deer hunter. By good fortune someone noticed this threat the day before the bill was to go through its critical third reading. I decided that we had to make a stand.

My MP was still Sir John Gilmour who continued to show helpful interest in our unusual enterprise, and when I phoned him he immediately put me on to Sir Hector Munro whose bill it was. He suggested we meet. I flew straight down to Westminster and after twenty minutes of friendly and businesslike discussion it was agreed he would include an exemption for farmed deer. A clause, 'Clause 7', was introduced, and despite entrenched opposition from John Farr, MP, and Lord Northfield it was incorporated into the legislation. For the first time the words 'farmed deer' appeared in British law. Under the heading 'Deer Farming' it reads: 'This section does not apply to the killing of deer by any person who keeps those deer by way of business on land enclosed by a deer-proof barrier for the production of meat or foodstuffs, or skins or other by-products, or as breeding stock ... provided that the deer are conspicuously marked to demonstrate that they are so kept ...' In this way we found ourselves with a legal definition of a deer farm, and in the absence of anything better this has stood the test of time. The bill received royal assent on the 28 June 1982.

Following our success in having close-season regulations relaxed in Scotland, the legislation in England eventually caught up and at last deer farmers throughout Britain were no longer constrained by close seasons that had been designed for hunters.

Meanwhile a growing number of deer farmers were showing interest in having their animals killed in abattoirs. In New Zealand this had been done for years. Specialised abattoirs, known as 'deer slaughter premises', were constructed so that venison could be exported from New Zealand into Europe as game meat and to avoid the stranglehold that the unions had on sheep abattoirs. All New Zealand farmed deer are killed on such premises, and this entitles the New Zealanders to pay a game-meat tariff of only 3 per cent on the farmed venison they export to Europe instead of the much higher tariff of 14 per cent payable for lamb, beef and even, astonishingly, domesticated reindeer imported into Europe. We European deer farmers have campaigned for years to have this anomaly removed for the benefit of the European economy. Such a move would be of tremendous value to Europeans selling game venison as well as to us farming deer. Strangely the EU bureaucracy seems reluctant to act.

Many deer farmers felt quite reasonably that deer farming could only grow to what they considered a worthwhile-sized venture if their beasts were sent off to an abattoir. After all, most farmers in Britain, whether producers of grain, meat or whatever, have for years simply concentrated on farming to a very high standard; they have left the marketing, promotion and processing to other specialists. Few farmers in the conventional meaning of the word want to become involved in meat processing; far from it! The last thing most farmers want to engage in is the slaughter of their stock on farm. I have always felt differently, at least from the ethical viewpoint, since in principle I think farmers, like consumers, should understand that what they do, whether producing meat or eating it, has its downside of slaughter.

As chairman of the deer farmers at the time, however, it was my job to do what we could to ensure that legislation would allow deer farmers to use abattoirs, as well as to continue to kill deer in the field. In fact, because in England the legislation listed those animals which cannot be killed in slaughterhouses and in Scotland it listed those that can, and since neither list included deer, the anomaly existed by which deer could be taken off for slaughter in English abattoirs but not in Scottish! By this stage I had come to understand that deer can be transported easily and in suitable vehicles with plenty of space and bedding, and that perhaps abattoirs had improved since my student days.

FAWC had decided in 1982, following the Scottish exemption of farmed deer from the close-season legislation, that they should consider the general welfare of farmed deer including their transport and slaughter. They immediately undertook to prepare a report. We in the BDFA co-operated as best we could. So FAWC came up to Scotland to witness deer being killed in an abattoir, and were for the most part content with the way it had gone. I had actually been present on that occasion, and one notable and intelligent animal welfarist subsequently wrote to me saying he had been very impressed, and that the deer had appeared less stressed than many sheep he had seen being slaughtered.

Since many sheep, especially off the hills, are handled much less than farmed deer this was perhaps not too surprising; but one must remember that deer have not had any significant amount of breeding for docility and tractability whereas for some ten thousand years, albeit rather haphazardly, sheep and cattle have.

Anyway, FAWC could not make up its mind unanimously on this hot potato; although the majority found no fault with the idea of deer going into abattoirs, a minority, including Ruth Harrison, found the concept repugnant. Along with the rest of the council she had been to Reediehill to watch me shoot deer in the field with a rifle, and evidently preferred this in-field slaughter to the abattoir alternative.

Since that time deer have regularly been slaughtered in specially adapted abattoirs in England, Scotland and Wales, as well as in Ireland, and legislation has been amended where necessary to make this procedure legal. No particular problems have emerged, and although Nickie and I still prefer to kill the deer at Reediehill in the field we accept that for other farmers abattoir slaughter is the only way to kill significant numbers of deer, and that it can be carried out in a well-controlled and humane way.

My two-year stint as BDFA Chairman was over. There were inevitable schisms and factions among such a disparate group of individuals and I was happy to pass the baton to Alan Drescher, a cheerful but tenacious pig farmer from East Yorkshire who had diversified into deer. Alan was typical of the best new entrants into deer farming, who had been moved by endless discussion in the media and encouragement from politicians to believe that agricultural support would decline and that 'diversification' was the thing. Many of these new deer farmers were large arable farmers who were interested in deer and were also highly competent stockmen, with abundant assets in the way of arable by-products such as straw, and fodder beet for winter feeding, and also very often in possession of redundant farm buildings that made good winter housing. These people were invaluable assets to the embryo deer-farming industry. They had joined us in response to the blandishments of successive governments to diversify into market-led industries in readiness for the removal of subsidies. They were to remain disappointed.

21 EXPORTS, SWISS CHALETS AND VEAL

I suppose that eventually an order from overseas was inevitable, and when it came it was very welcome. Our early unexpected successes in attracting publicity had been gratifying, and naturally a lot of the magazines and broadcasting snippets went abroad. Soon foreign agricultural journalists came specifically to interview and photograph us and we became quite blasé about seeing ourselves in Dutch, Swiss and Italian magazines. But you don't necessarily grow wealthy from seeing your picture in the papers. The few sales of deer to embryo British deer farmers helped and the venison sales were growing, albeit from a very low base. Nevertheless the need to make a living at Reediehill was becoming more insistent.

It was as a result of one of these features that we received an unannounced visit one afternoon from a young Swiss farmer. Max Bürgi was everything a man from the mountains should be. His very voice made me nostalgic for my old Gum Club holidays climbing in the Alps. He moved and spoke with the quiet deliberation that comes of pacing your way up the mountain and planning every footfall. His accent had a beautifully soft and measured rise and fall; his posture and gestures were redolent of snow, sun and rock. Of course, we asked him to stay the night and next morning came the proposition. Max had, it seemed, successfully inspired the government in his local canton – the Jura – to try an experiment. 'I am looking for a way to make those small farms in the Alps survive. We all have cows and that's OK, but we need a new local enterprise if we are to continue without being so dependent on grants. Venison is very popular in Switzerland; we could produce it like you do here.' How often I was to hear that story. 'Great,' I said, 'but where can you get your animals from?' 'I have persuaded the authorities in Basle to help ten farmers set up deer-farming operations using in some cases fallow and in others red deer. I want to buy the deer from you. This spring you bring some red deer?'

Although livestock transport was not, in the late 1970s, the emotive procedure that riots twenty years later were to make it, this business nevertheless already gave me much food for thought. For me it was important firstly that the deer were for breeding and that their higher value meant that they could be allowed a lot of space and ample bedding, secondly that I could go with them and ensure tender loving care throughout, and thirdly that I should be happy that Max would treat them well in Switzerland.

I had never transported deer anything like so far before, but I reasoned that when I did move them they always seemed to travel well enough and that if I gave them plenty of space and fed them well on the journey they should do fine. And so it was decided that Nickie and I would set out together with the deer as soon as Max phoned to tell us that the road was clear of snow. We wanted to move quickly so as to give the hinds plenty of time to settle in before calving.

Impatiently Nickie and I sat in Scotland as the days rolled by. April passed and we couldn't believe there was still snow. We phoned Max for a progress report. 'There is still two metres on some parts of the road but I will dig it away with the tractor. I think you can come next week.'

The sun beat down as we spun through the north of England and then greyed as we entered the grime of the Midlands and southern England. There was no M25 then, and by the time we finally pitched up in Dover it was dark and about midnight.

I commented to Nickie, 'Wonderful. No queues, we should get on the first ferry.' Yet as we followed the signs to 'Freight Departures' I began to realise, green though I was at this game, that something was a little odd. Everything was closed. The docks were all but deserted. Eventually I found someone and asked what was happening. He looked at me as if I had come from another planet. 'Don't mean to tell me you haven't heard about the customs strike? Don't you have television up there?' Well, I suppose he wouldn't have believed me if I told him that we didn't. I had actually heard about the strike but had not imagined, in my blithe innocence, that it would pose any problems. Evidently the boats were sailing, but they would not carry me unless I had the appropriate pieces of paper. Nickie and I retreated to the lorry cab for a council of war. It certainly seemed desperate. To find local accommodation for the deer in Dover while we awaited an end to the strike was unthinkable. What were we to do?

Ever the man of action, I strode off to the shipping office and delivered an ultimatum. 'Tell whoever is in charge of the strike that unless we get our papers now I shall telephone all the national papers and tell them that it was his absence that caused the death of twenty red deer.' It worked like magic: the power of the press. Within an hour the Chief Customs Officer was out of his bed and, with perhaps justified ill grace was stamping our papers. 'Where do you want to clear customs?' he asked. 'I haven't the faintest idea,' I said, 'but I suppose at the end of the autobahn at Basle.' 'OK,' and he wrote: 'Basle Bahn.'

We were soon aboard and slept well on an empty boat, waking refreshed. The journey through Germany was uneventful. I remember picking branches from some trees, which down in the south were in full leaf, and feeding them to our passengers. The first green leaves they had eaten for six months. The deer did wonderfully. They lay down on their straw beds and almost seemed to enjoy the journey, looking out inquisitively or lying quietly cudding as we swept along.

In due course we arrived at the end of the autobahn at Basle and the frontier. We showed our documents to the uninterested customs officer who waved us through and told us that since our papers were marked 'Basle Bahn' we couldn't clear customs with him but must go to the railway station. This seemed rather unusual but we did as requested and made our way to the station. Here the deer attracted some attention from curious passers-by. Eventually a very helpful railway official arrived and when I showed him the papers he set off determinedly with me in his wake. For a good half-hour we went from office to office, nobody showing the slightest interest in my papers. Reluctantly, with his goodwill a little tarnished, the helpful rail worker turned to me: 'I think it is hopeless. You must continue.' Jubilant, I hurried back to Nickie and the admiring crowd and off we zoomed.

Once more the sun shone; never have the Alps looked more exhilarating. As we drove, I instructed Nickie to tear up our redundant papers in very small pieces and throw them out of the window. It was a catharsis.

Within two hours of leaving Basle railway station, we had crawled up precipitous narrow lanes between walls of melting snow, turned the deer out to look around them in wonderment at the mountains and the pristine green grass, and then, with our knees under the Bürgi family dining table, were downing spätzli, that delicious fried-noodle/pancake/pasta product, prepared and cooked by Max's wife Helena.

It was during this memorable meal that I came to realise one of the more unusual perils of life in the Alps. Their chalets are constructed on steep hillsides, and good use is made of the incline so that hay can be loaded for the long winter at the rear of the house at ground level directly into the loft which extends over the entire cowshed and human dwelling space below. It can then be easily forked down to the beasts. The resulting dung is then wheelbarrowed out at the front of the building, along an elevated plank, and built into a midden downhill from the chalet. Between mouthfuls of spätzli, Nickie and I both noticed, in the kitchen ceiling above us, an irregularly shaped area where Max had evidently replaced some of the pine boards recently. 'What happened there?' I asked. There was an embarrassed silence as the Bürgis looked at each other a trifle abashed. Finally Max came out with: 'It was a cow.'

'A cow?'

'Yes, in the middle of the night, it wandered into the loft above and down it came through the ceiling.'

Apparently unharmed, Max had been able to lead it out of the kitchen, but Helena had not been as amused as we were.

We stayed on a few more days trying to understand the economics of the Swiss alpine farmer. Twice a day Max would take his single-legged milking stool, strap it around his waist and proceed to hand-milk some ten cows. Infinitely precious is traditional alpine dairy farming to the Swiss culture, and through tourism, to its economy. An alp must either be pasture grazed through the summer or a meadow with the grass cut for hay; without grazing or mowing, it slowly reverts to scrub and eventually woodland. Without cows no one would cut hay: ergo no cows, no alps, no skiing, no tourists. And so rich is the Swiss nation or so keenly does it treasure the alps, that the subsidies are sufficient to allow each farmer to survive with only a handful of cattle. This system ensures that the grass is cut for hay as neatly as ever, using specialised tractors and mowers that can operate on grassy slopes that would be difficult to walk up but which were previously scythed. In Max's tractor was a glass-covered saucer with a ball to indicate the level of tilt and warn the driver if he is being over-ambitious.

One evening Max took us to see his neighbours. We walked through the spring grass and wild flowers for a mile or so. He wanted, he said, to show us a truly traditional alpine farm. I remember in particular the solitary veal calf. Proudly reared to yield the truly finest veal, this animal was tethered in the depths of a huge, beautiful and very ancient wooden chalet. In almost complete darkness he had drunk his milk copiously all winter and was now substantial. In order to satisfy his craving for fibre he had also gnawed through some bulky timbers. Here, I thought, light years away from a 'factory farm', exists this miserable creature with all around him the most exquisite rural idyll. Yet you cannot eat the scenery, and life was hard for these people and even harder for their veal calf. Of course, having never known any other way of doing things, and because of the demand for white veal,

Max's neighbours were doing as their forebears had for centuries and any accusations of discomfort, let alone cruelty, would have shocked and hurt them. It was in an effort to change all this that Max was seeking to establish a new pastoral industry and we were being enlisted to help.

With a great sense of relief after the rather stressful delivery, we took off for a few days' break to enjoy the Swiss lakes and mountains in springtime. We hired a rowing boat in one of the lakes and swam from it. It was a perfect day and we were very happy. We drifted past a landing stage belonging to a rather smart hotel, in fact a veritable *schloss*. I have always had a weakness for opulent hotels beyond my means, and on impulse I ran up the steps to the imposing, brilliantly painted white edifice and into the hall. I stood at the reception desk dripping wet in my swimming trunks, and booked us a room. That evening we ate on a terrace to the accompaniment of a piano, and the next morning took a chairlift up from behind the hotel.

We ascended slowly and silently through the green forest canopy. As we climbed we looked back over our shoulders. 'Look, there's the hotel.' Sure enough it was easy to see its showy whiteness dominating the pristine Swiss landscape. 'Which is our room?' 'There it is and . . .' Nickie's voice trailed off in horror. Her new blue jeans, washed for the first time and left to dry on the balcony, had made their mark. Descending for two floors was a broad blue stripe on the hotel's newly painted wall. Sheepishly and guiltily, but quickly, we descended and checked out.

That wasn't quite the end of our Swiss adventure. Several months later an official-looking letter written in German arrived for me from Basle. I was comfortably home again by then, it was winter and all our reports from Max indicated that the deer were revelling in their Swiss sunshine and alpine hay despite the deep snow. In fact the snow was so deep that the fences were completely submerged and the deer were free to come and go as they wished, but the lure of Max's sweet, herb-rich hay was enough to keep them. It all seemed a far cry from the rain of Scotland and the daily pressures of running the farm at Auchtermuchty; I was not inclined to take a long tract of German from a distant bureaucrat very seriously. It lay quietly and accusingly on my desk. Christmas passed and Hogmanay arrived. Our dear polyglot Luxembourgeoise friend Maggy Stead came to stay and I thought of the letter.

'Oh, Johnny, you are in deep trouble!' said Maggy. 'You are due to appear in court in Basle on 20 January and it says that unless you respond and put up a good defence for the illicit introduction of livestock to Switzerland you will never be able to visit Switzerland again without being arrested.'

I thought of the green pastures and snowy alps and knew that I did want to go back some day. So I wrote a long letter explaining the whole saga, how we'd done our best at the railway station, and pleaded ignorance of all the regulations – after all I was only a vet not a professional lorry driver. Maggy laughed and said my letter was very British, by which I suppose she meant unashamedly amateurish and incompetent. Anyway she nobly translated it and we posted it off. Again the months passed and finally, finally, I was officially exonerated.

And so much for my European exports. I could write of the frustrations of being delayed by ships whose skippers would not take my deer in anything more than a stiff breeze, of my early ignorance of paper requirements so that the French customs told me that I should have to kill all my deer and throw them in the docks, of delays due to absurd and unnecessary veterinary requirements which can do more to compromise the welfare of the animals than to control disease, of my delaying ships by failing to wake on arrival, so precipitating a full-scale search of the whole ferry, of stowaways, of fires on ship and much more besides. Of deer formally released, in the full glare of the media, on to a Dutch polder in front of their Minister of Drains to help transform that reclaimed seabed into a national nature reserve. Or of Scottish deer taken to French agricultural research colleges to pioneer new enterprises in the Massif Central. Through it all there have been kind, helpful people who have enabled me to treat my deer with patience and care.

I am as keen as the next man to condemn the export of live animals for slaughter; indeed I have for many years been a paid-up member of Compassion in World Farming, and why else would we go to such lengths to kill our deer on the farm here rather than have them hauled off to an abattoir? I believe that my deer, on beds of straw with plenty of space, deserve the chance to live longer lives as breeding stock in good conditions overseas. And, of course, I do go back to visit them and find them happily established.

With the benefit of hindsight, I can enjoy all these adventures now. There can be few experiences so abidingly pleasurable as the release of the deer from their long incarceration into the mild European spring after the cold privations of a Scottish winter. Fresh grass weeks early, and the silence and sweet smells, as the deer walk slowly away into the woodlands: those are the best memories.

22 VENIBURGERS, VENISON AND CHEFS

Right from the start, venison sales had been the objective. Nickie and I were united in the knowledge that deer meat was tasty and healthy and that we must get this message across so that more people would try it. I had modestly planned at one stroke to reduce the excessive and fast-growing Highland deer population, develop a new Scottish industry in *farmed* venison and improve the nation's health. And so far it seemed we were on track.

The demand for breeding stock was gratifying and certainly necessary to create a new agricultural industry, but perhaps it sidetracked us from our main goal of increasing venison consumption. Though growing, venison sales remained small; we needed to encourage venison eating on a grander scale.

What was needed was a way of broadening the market. There would always be a small nucleus of venison eaters who had been obliged as children on summer holidays in shooting lodges to gnaw their way stoically through old stags and had eventually developed a taste for it. But in fact many others had in this way been put off venison for life; after all, who grills steak from old bulls? Only the young lamb, heifer or steer is good enough for the dining table; the cull or cast breeding animal should end up in a sausage or pie. What surprised us was not so much that people came all the way up to the farm to tell us their dismal experiences, but that they were prepared to give it a second chance. This was encouraging. Over the years, Nickie's books, firstly *Venison, the Monarch of the Table*, devoted entirely to venison, and then *Game for All*, dealing with other types of game as well, created a following and were successful in disseminating simple and foolproof rules for the cooking of venison. We began to see new-style eaters coming to the shop and could see the scope for growth.

Somehow we had to extend this small group, to seduce potential new venison consumers with the meat of young deer. We knew how good it could be. To do this we needed a simple product which anyone could cook, and that we could grill and sell direct to the consumer, allowing us to talk to them at the same time so that we could tell them what venison actually was, and, crucially, how to cook it. When we stood at agricultural shows most people had not the foggiest idea what we were trying to sell. 'Venison? Wha's that?' They even confused it with veal.

Then along came a whirlwind of youthful energy and chaos, brimming with bright ideas, in the form of Alasdair Darroch. Studying agriculture at Edinburgh University, Alasdair, like so many students, became seized with the idea of farming deer. Alighting on us at Reediehill, he immediately started some trials for his Honours thesis, helped us while we extended the farmhouse, and brought his friends for jovial weekends when Nickie, Stella, Martha and I basked in their goodfellowship. As Alasdair's time at Edinburgh came to an end everyone became enthused with venison promotion. We plotted; we schemed.

The answer we came up with was a venison burger. This could be made easily and sold cheaply. It had, if not actually a downmarket image, an air of being generally available, faintly trendy and, of course, undemanding of culinary skills. What is more we could sell it at shows for people to eat immediately. Nickie went to work on the development and the 'Veniburger' was born. The name was obvious, and though the *Guardian* was later to quip that they should have been called 'Bambiburgers', we were happy.

We reasoned that those agricultural shows would be an appropriate testbed and the Royal Highland Show in Edinburgh was chosen as the place for the launch. The Deer Farmers' Association had secured a site suitable for exhibiting two or three tame deer and we judged that these animals could make our message even more emphatically. No doubt a few squeamish souls would cavil at the idea but we knew that the deer wouldn't mind; I have never been one to resist the temptation of rumpling a few stuffed shirts, and we would have a chance to explain things to the squeamish.

We embarked for Edinburgh and the Royal Highland Show in June 1983 and set up a small marquee with some trestle tables, a kitchen area and a small domestic gas barbecue. Some signs reading '*Quarter Pound Veniburger in a Sesame Seed Bun with Salad and your choice of Dressings, 80p*' were produced and off we went. The response was phenomenal. We had not realised how deprived the poor Highland Show-goer must have been. By lunchtime on the first day, queues were twenty yards long and they never diminished all day. As the show went on, word got around and demand grew.

We had a cheerful write up in the *Financial Times*, Veniburgers' first publicity, and then a live studio broadcast for BBC and so it went on. Each day our noble gang of workers became more and more exhausted. Around lunchtime when we were going flat out, the fat from the burgers would regularly ignite and send flames rushing up into the branches of a sycamore, adding to the brio of the occasion. Eyes reddened and eyelashes melted. We became regulars at the First Aid tent. St John's Ambulance stalwarts were rewarded with well-grilled burgers.

On our return we held a council of war. How to capitalise on our success? It was clear that the first thing we needed was a small team of helpers to make the burgers. We advertised, and in this way we found Barry Burns who, nineteen years on, is still here. Sharing many of the attributes of his famous-namesake Rabbie, Barry is redoubtable. His intelligence and quickwittedness have not been blunted by too much education and he retains a great capacity for organising and remembering things, but, above all, he remains a highly skilled and very fast butcher; what we would have done without Barry it is hard to say. He knows everyone, and now that his reputation as the stud of Newburgh is becoming a memory and the prospect of his settling down no longer seems laughable, he keeps regular hours and we are very happy. It was not ever thus. I got distinctly fed up with having to haul him out of his bed in the mornings, being obliged on one occasion to climb a ladder to rouse him through the window only to find that he was generously sharing his bed with two ladies. And there was the night when the police rang to tell me that I had better come to Newburgh to collect my tractor. Barry had put a large round bale of straw on the foreloader at the front and driven it up the High Street before, in parking it outside the pub, he had removed their rainwater guttering, or as we say here, rhones.

Flushed with the Veniburger's success at the Highland 'launch', we set off to shows all over Britain. Especially successful, five hundred miles away, was the Kent Show where, in amongst the cherry and apple tents, stood our deer. The Duchess of Kent politely told us she didn't like venison and I immediately classed her as one of those who'd been obliged to eat an overcooked old stag once too often.

As we became more professional we had to employ a bigger and bigger group of folk and our sales speeded up. We reached an all-time high at the national Game Fair at Romsey near Southampton in July 1984 when we sold nearly four thousand Veniburgers a day for three days. Our teamwork was phenomenal: one person slit the rolls, another stuffed them with sliced-up salad and wrapped them in a napkin, a third took the napkin and held the roll open to receive the cooked burger and hand the ensemble to the customer, and the fourth took the money. Once a rhythm had been built up we could go at a great rate and the queue would shuffle past at a walk. On one occasion Barry was taking the money so fast that he had people's change ready before they had even ordered. He was holding out a roll with burger and salad packed into it when one unassuming country gentleman said:

'Do you mind awfully if I don't have any cucumber? It doesn't agree with me.' Quick as a flash Barry said, 'Nae cucumber? Nae problem,' and, whipping the cucumber out of the bun and into his mouth, handed over the roll, burger and change. The customer was past and we had probably served another ten before he knew what had happened.

Eventually the principal caterer must have decided we were becoming too popular, to the detriment of his pocket. We were pushed to the side and he surrounded us with what we considered downmarket hot-dog stands, candyfloss sellers and so on. Sadly we had to reduce our presence each year until it was no longer sense for us to go. The shows are the poorer, because 'charcoal-grilled Veniburgers' were what the showgoers wanted. Also, for many years, even at game fairs, our venison was the only game visitors could buy.

After our successes at the shows we naturally wanted to expand into other sales outlets. Pubs and shops were singled out. We purchased, second-hand, a little van and had it painted with the Veniburger logo (antlers on the letter V) and '*They're not just any burgers they're ...* *Veniburgers*', and set to work delivering. Our full-time salesman Dougie, his technique honed by the high-pressure selling of American vacuum cleaners for which he had won prizes, worked as hard as he could driving the van all hours.

As a result of the publicity from the shows we were astonished to find ourselves the subject of a full twenty-minute film made by BBC Northern Ireland. Television cameras followed our van and filmed Dougie as he delivered into a shop in Auchtermuchty. Finally there was a sequence of Nickie and myself having a candlelit dinner of roast venison with a glass of red wine, actually filmed mid-morning but with the curtains drawn, while the presenter gravely asked us questions of great pith and moment. We were being depicted as the ideal farm diversification, taking no public money yet employing four or five people on a very small farm: it was all very flattering and gratifying.

Alasdair's optimism was unquenchable, and as month succeeded month he remained resolutely cheerful. But things were not going well. Our original idea with the Veniburgers had been that by choosing a 'downmarket' type of product we would explode the myth that venison was a habit pursued only by the ruddy-cheeked port-drinking classes. In this way we would introduce a wider eating public to the delights of this healthiest of all meats. Instead of 'Wa's tha' then, eh? Nae thanks' we looked for 'Oh, aye, venison, aye, Ah like tha'. Gie's a bi' o' tha'.' We were really quite successful at that, but when we came to try and increase sales by venturing away from our captive show market to compete in the real world of commercial burgers, we found things a little more tricky. Our main difficulty lay in the catering trade.

Despite the entreaties of salesmen wishing to get us hooked on coloured hamburger fillers and extenders, we naively yet honourably used proper red meat whilst 'the trade' generally used a mixture of fat and 'mechanically recovered meat'. It was the case then, and probably still is, that you could sell a sausage or a burger into the catering trade without putting any 'meat', as we know meat, into it at all. At least the products sold in shops must have a declared minimum meat content. As you might expect, we had designed our Veniburger to have lots of meat and taste good, something indeed that would not shame us. Not for nothing did we call them 'the honest burgers of Auchtermuchty'.

However, when Dougie took them along to a fish and chip shop, for example, the proprietor would frequently show great interest and might even occasionally risk tasting one, but as soon as the price was discussed he would fall about laughing. We were looking to sell our burgers for about 20p each and they were buying their 'beefburgers' for about 2p! The other quality demanded by the discerning fryer was elasticity. 'Och, nae use that, gie it a wee waggle and it's a' in pieces.' By which they meant that the process of dipping the burger in batter was traditionally followed by a brisk shake to remove surplus batter before immersion in the deep fryer. Our Veniburger lacked the necessary measure of elasticity. In fact I doubt whether any burger with a normal complement of red meat could pass the waggle test without the incorporation of some high proportion of latex or similar binding material.

Dougie would not give up, though, and soldiered valiantly on; but eventually there were days when the van returned without a single sale. The time finally came when I had to go with Alasdair to the bank and say enough was enough, would they please lend us no more money. Dougie was laid off. Alasdair was devastated and we had a series of stormy meetings, sometimes with accountants officiating, but usually just the three of us, until eventually we reached an amicable agreement and have remained friends to this day. We were chastened, a lot poorer, and our first failure was behind us.

Nevertheless lessons had been learned, and one of them was that the catering trade was not for us. All but the few elite restaurants will buy whatever is cheapest; virtually none say where their ingredients come from and thus there is no premium paid for good quality or local products.

Fortunately, all this time sales of live deer for breeding were holding up well and indeed growing. I was kept increasingly busy at home and abroad with sales and some consultancy work. Prices were fine and we were not dependent on venison sales. And just in case there was any danger of our becoming too modest, it was about this time that BBC Radio Four with Sonia Beasley chose to devote a full length *Enterprise* programme to me. It is everybody's dream to be able to talk about oneself with a friendly presenter on the radio or television and I cannot deny how much I enjoyed the experience. Once more everything was going our way, and the Veniburgers had become merely a necessary episode on the road to what we still never doubted would be eventual success, fame and glory.

Over the years, Nickie continued to promote venison in a whole variety of ways. Apart from her own two books, she compiled another for the Deer Farmers' Association; she gave venison- and game-cooking demonstrations, lectured at conferences, featured on television and radio programmes, encouraged school and student projects and talked tirelessly to our customers, both on the telephone and in the little shop. We were both touched and delighted when she was chosen to be the recipient of the very first Scottish Food Awards lifetime achievement award.

Of all these activities, the most crucial was liaison with journalists, since they could spread our message for us. Those broadcasting from Reediehill on the subject of venison have included Derek Cooper,

Sophie Grigson, Loyd Grossman, Marguerite Patten, Jancis Robinson, Oliver Walston and, of course, the Two Fat Ladies. Even the late brilliant Jeremy Round visited and wrote of us. Our pile of newspaper and magazine clippings is a deep one.

We had two main messages for the journalists. One was the lean and healthy aspect of venison. It never ceases to astonish me how often chicken is recommended for those on low-fat diets. Is there a hidden agenda here? After all, environmentally, chicken production has to be more damaging than a grass-fed product, nor do we feed our deer antibiotics. A growing number of people on low-fat diets who become bored by chicken and fish are delighted to realise that they can eat venison as a red meat since it has even less fat than skinless chicken. And as for cholesterol, venison has about one-third the cholesterol of skinned chicken.

The other message we had to convey was that, contrary to what many believed, good venison needn't be dry or tough. You could cook it gently for a few hours in a low oven as a pot roast like we used to do in the Raeburn on Rum, in which case the liquids kept it moist. Or you could cook it very quickly at a high temperature and serve it rare. No marinading, no larding necessary. A short period of resting will leave the meat pink and moist throughout. It is physically impossible for pink meat to be dry.

This was perhaps a forgotten message; it was hardly new. Over a hundred years ago, the celebrated chef, Alexis Soyer, who did so much to improve military catering during the Crimean War, knew all about cooking venison. In the *Gastronomic Regenerator* of 1846 he wrote: 'Venison must be underdone, red in the middle, and full of gravy.' And again: '... even after all that nature has done in point of flavour, should it fall into the hands of some inexperienced person to dress, and be too much done, its appearance and flavour would be entirely spoilt, its delicious and delicate fat melted, and the gravy lost.'

At last some understanding is beginning to take root; this simple secret is becoming recognised more widely with the improved availability of farmed venison of a known and guaranteed youth. Wild venison responds well to this treatment as long as it is from a young animal, but it is extremely difficult if not impossible for the cook to know what she has when she buys wild venison over the counter. Sadly, game 'venison' could be anything from African antelope to locally shot roe deer or even kangaroo. This is arguably correct, since historically the word venison merely means the meat of a hunted animal. Nevertheless it does not make life easy for the would-be gourmet. After all, the antelope is more closely related to cows or sheep than to deer, and there is as little connexion between red and roe as between cows and sheep.

Most cookery books, with very few exceptions, do not assist in resolving this confused situation. It is usually clear that the authors themselves know next to nothing about the seven or eight different species of deer that can provide the British cook with wild venison, or about the seasonal difficulties created by the differing rutting seasons or the legal close seasons. Roe deer, for example, are only distantly related to red deer; they are also only about one quarter the size, and are in season at very different times of the year. To further irritate the aficionado, most cookery writers get the nomenclature quite wrong as well, hopelessly muddling red deer (stags, hinds and calves), roe (bucks, does and kids) and fallow (bucks, does and fawns). All very trivial maybe, but for those who know deer, as important as not calling lambs kids and so on.

However, there have been some notable conversions. Quite early on, the late Jane Grigson wrote an article about venison for the *Observer*, and sent Nickie the draft to read through. It contained many of the old chestnuts and Nickie agonised for days. How could we presume to correct someone whose integrity and writings we admired so much? Eventually Nickie sent in her corrections, all backed up by evidence, and, with professional grace, Jane Grigson completely rewrote the piece.

As for chefs, for an example of just how successful we have been in explaining what we are trying to do, and that farmed venison is a safer bet than wild, I can quote Raymond Blanc. In *Cooking for Friends* in 1991 he wrote: 'Try to avoid farmed game which is much cheaper, but not worth buying, with the exception of venison'; and again in the same book: 'I rarely recommend game that has been farmed, but farmed deer is one of the exceptions.'

Although Nickie's efforts were crucial to the development of a taste for venison we were also undoubtedly benefiting from the vogue for new food products that has come with increased wealth and affluence. Awareness of the product has changed dramatically in the few years we have been taking trade stands. The comments are generally informed and enthusiastic; a far cry from the Veniburger launch. It has required a great deal of hard work but the results have been rewarding.

There was always the danger when we started promoting farmed venison that people would think of it as inferior to wild when in fact, of course, the reverse is more likely to be the truth. Even now there are still a few dinosaurs of journalism trotting out this unfounded prejudice, usually without having tried both types of meat. There is a romantic appeal about the wild which is wholly understandable, and if there is a complaint about farmed venison, it is invariably that it will be bland. This is often heard from people who have always eaten marinated venison. We were able to demonstrate through blind tasting trials that it is not possible to tell the difference between wild and farmed venison – you can have bland, or well-flavoured, or marinated, or over-strong versions of either. It is merely that farmed is more consistently good, more reliable.

After a great deal of trial and error at Reediehill we found that maturing our venison for two to three weeks gave the best balance of flavour, and this is what we have done here ever since. The meat is hung as a whole carcase, without its skin, in a refrigerator. Some people are surprised that we hang it for so long, but Nickie and I believe that one reason for the general decline in meat-eating is the complete tastelessness and watery texture of much meat exposed for sale. The old butchers used to hang their beef for a very long time and we believe that, although it is expensive to do so, it is worthwhile. For many years we milked a cow at Reediehill and once reared one of the calves for beef. We hung that huge fatty carcase for five *months*, after which time it had grown a rind like a Stilton cheese; but once trimmed, the meat inside was quite extraordinarily delicious.

Large meat companies supplying supermarkets, who now take 70 per cent or more of the retail meat trade, cannot normally afford to hang whole carcases for long. They would lose up to 10 per cent of the carcase weight through drying-out, there would be a loss of cash flow, and it would require large, expensive conditioning rooms. This is one reason why our venison is more expensive than that available from other suppliers. The New Zealand venison processors, who use an electric current to tenderise their meat, obviously think we are completely unhinged to mature our meat in this old-fashioned and wasteful way. But fortunately our discerning customers appreciate the service.

It is not easy for anyone new to the farmed/wild venison debate to understand fully the complex issues, and I often refer to our product as being simply that of the deer park. After all, what we produce is only the same as the mediaeval park was attempting. The plethora of deer parks at that time cannot possibly have all existed to provide hunting grounds. Most were too small anyway. They were, in my view, like the hundreds of doocots which are liberally sprinkled over Fife, intended for meat production, and so were respectable forerunners of the twentieth-century deer farm. I should be very surprised if the mediaeval parker did not aim to concentrate his cull on two-year-olds in order to maximise his production – after all, the mesolithic hunters had.

23 AN ARABIAN INTERLUDE WITH ENDANGERED ORYX

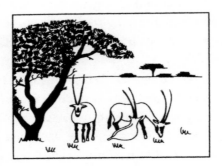

While Veniburgers rolled on, I was making frequent deliveries of hinds to people, mostly in France, who were starting to farm deer. Over the next few years I calculate that I assisted in the establishment of around thirty new deer herds in France alone. And there were beginning to be more glamorous but less frequent trips outwith Europe, lecturing and doing some consultancy work. It seemed as though everything was on the up; we could do no wrong; whatever we touched came right. We didn't see the demise of Veniburgers as anything more than a temporary setback.

One winter evening as Nickie and I settled down to supper with the wild rain lashing down, the curtains shifting in the draught through the ill-fitting sash window and the cat flap hovering at the horizontal, the telephone rang. 'Ees that Dr Fletcher?' It was a foreign voice loaded with drama. 'Yes,' I replied. 'This ees the household of Sheikh Zayed, Ruler of Abu Dhabi. His Royal Highness wishes to discuss with you a problem with his deer. He would like to see you in London tomorrow.'

By remarkable good fortune I had to go to London the next day, so this arrangement suited perfectly. It was agreed that I should go to the upper floor of a private hospital. This hospital belonged to Sheikh Zayed and he had taken over the top floor for a period in which to hold court while his teeth underwent some work. After a short wait I was escorted in.

There were, I remember, double doors held open for me, and as I entered I was confronted with the raised buttocks of the previous appointment leaving backwards on hands and knees. Nevertheless my welcome was cordial and I was bade sit next to His Highness on a couch and share some fresh dates with him. Even with the limited language resources that we shared it was fairly obvious that the 'deer' were actually antelope. Now antelope, if I may remind the reader, are actually bovids related to sheep and cattle; they have horns which grow continuously and they are not at all closely related to deer with their antlers which fall off and regrow each year. Anyway, evidently the antelope were in his private park and were lame. But there seemed to be something else too. After a good deal of prevarication and embarrassed gesturing on his part and equally embarrassed guessing on mine, it became clear that the animals were further afflicted by a swelling of the testicles. Since the lameness was also apparently accompanied by a swelling of the joints the likely diagnosis was simple – brucellosis. This, I explained, would need to be confirmed by laboratory tests of suitable samples and appropriate treatment of the outbreak instituted.

'Good,' he said. 'Go there now and see to it. You may take your wife and family.' The interview was obviously over. I explained to his secretary outside that I would need to collect some things from Scotland, in particular my dart gun, as well as rearrange my diary. But they were adamant we move quickly, and I agreed to fly up to Scotland that night and thence from Edinburgh to the Middle East the next day. I would not be taking my wife and family.

The prospect of this trip at such short notice was exhilarating, as I had only just started winning overseas consultancies. I was easily impressed. The tickets were of course, first class, and as I sat in the first class lounge at Schiphol Airport, Amsterdam, not only the champagne but everything else went to my head. With the unaccustomed leisure I was avidly devouring the daily papers and thinking of

Nickie back home shovelling potatoes to the deer off the back of the tractor. An item caught my attention and I was soon scribbling a letter to the *Telegraph* and another to the *Guardian* and thinking myself a great swell. It was only when I got back that I saw both had been published. Since then I have found it easier to understand how the supposed makers and breakers of our society find time to write and read in a busy schedule. There is nothing more conducive to constructive thought than sitting in a half-empty aeroplane being plied with food and wine.

On my arrival in Abu Dhabi there was a flurry of excitement as my suitcase was opened to reveal that I was carrying both firearms and drugs; that is my tranquilliser gun, ammunition, syringes and tranquillisers. They were all confiscated. I was booked into a magnificent hotel and left there. The next day I made every effort to retrieve the darting equipment and by judicious use of Sheikh Zayed's name succeeded, but still nothing happened to indicate when my pleasant, though sober (it being Ramadan), interlude at the hotel should end. Daily I phoned the palace explaining that I had been told that I was on a matter of great urgency and that I had greatly inconvenienced myself by coming out at the drop of a hat. Each afternoon I swam, sunbathed and wrote by the pool, occasionally windsurfed on the sea and generally carried on as I thought befitted a consultant. There was nothing else I could do; I had no idea where the antelope were.

Finally word came. A car would collect me the next morning. And so I was driven south into the desert. Like most young boys I had been captivated by the romance of the desert. I had read *The Seven Pillars of Wisdom*, seen the film *Lawrence of Arabia*, and read Thesiger and others about the Empty Quarter. To be there now myself and comprehend the extraordinary revolution which had, within a decade or two, turned the races that had lived the most austere existence on our planet into the most affluent people on earth was a great privilege.

After a few hours' drive across the desert we came to the huge oasis of Al Ain. I was reinstalled in another air-conditioned palace of a hotel to await developments. All around I could see the most astonishing pieces of modern architecture that I have ever come across. The owners of these lavish palaces were for the most part sitting outside in the sand on rugs, eating from low tables. We joined one such group and were given camel to eat. Many parties had huge television screens erected in front of them. What a strange concatenation of the old and the new, I thought. Most of those of more than middle age, now living in these vast, extravagantly designed concrete palaces would have been brought up in tents in the desert. No matter if many might not be able to read or write, they must have a huge wealth of inherited desert lore and it would soon vanish for ever.

I was privileged to be taken to the royal falconry mews, where rows of falcons were perching on their blocks awaiting hunting expeditions. Each hawk and falcon was kept in precise condition to ensure maximum performance on the appointed day. It was explained to me that the sheiks would travel into the desert on motorised hawking and hunting safaris several times each year. This, I reflected, was a continuation of the regime that had brought extinction to the free-living Arabian oryx, of all grazing mammals the best adapted to survive in extremely arid conditions. In the nineteenth century it ranged through most of the interior of peninsular Arabia, but hunting progressively eroded the population until in 1972, around 18 October, the last six wild Arabian oryx were killed. Now no oryx survive in that region except for the few still preserved in zoos and private collections, and for those being reintroduced into Oman in a project funded by His Majesty Sultan Qaboos bin Said of Oman and his government.

As soon as I arrived in Al Ain, I realised that I was only some fifty miles away across the desert and mountains from a great friend of ours, Mark Stanley Price, who, with his wife Karen, was living in the desert in Oman actually carrying out this reintroduction of the Arabian oryx, mostly from San Diego Zoo. Mark and Karen spent seven years there and he published an excellent book about it all when he left. The main strategy was to encourage the local tribe of *bedu* to view the oryx with pride as a part of their heritage, and to follow each animal day after day so that its habits became known and any risk of poaching or predation was minimised.

Mark and Karen had been to stay with us at Reediehill during breaks from Oman and we had followed accounts of their project with fascination. So well adapted is this magnificent animal to its arid habitat that it can even lactate without drinking, using only its fat reserves and scant dew as sources of moisture. The loss of these beautiful white animals through extinction would indeed be grievous; there is so much more that we have still to learn from them. It is therefore thoroughly satisfactory to be able to report that the Oman oryx project has been a resounding success and a brilliant example of how such reintroductions can work if the habitat is intact and if the people living in that habitat are sympathetic to the ends of the scheme. There are, sadly, not too many other examples in place as yet.

Still, I remain optimistic. The Arabian oryx had declined to virtual extinction as the human population rose, firearms and vehicles became available and technology developed. Now the oryx are gradually increasing again following their well-planned reintroduction. This story mirrors the red deer model I had observed on Rum and the Scottish mainland. There must be some hope in this for other endangered wildlife.

Back at Al Ain, the next day I was taken a few miles further to see the affected animals. The Ruler had certainly been accurate in his description: the antelope were in dire straits, but even more of a surprise to me was the fact that these poor creatures were not, as I had expected, just the normal gazelles of the region or even imported African animals – they were the highly endangered Arabian oryx. They were sharing their enclosure with a large number of gazelle but it seemed to be the oryx that were most seriously affected. They were in pain, their testicles enormously distended and their limb joints swollen so that walking was difficult, and it was simple to catch two or three of them to take blood samples and administer some antibiotics.

The pattern of disease was absolutely typical of brucellosis. I asked the driver to drive me round the enclosure and I was interested to see a large flock of fat-tailed sheep and goats penned in on the other side of the fence on a piece of ground slightly raised above the oryx and gazelle.

I collected what samples I could and went away to think about it. On the way back to the hotel, I fell into conversation with the driver, who was from India. I had just seen the film *Gandhi* and asked him if he had seen it. 'Oh, yes, sir. We thought it was a little unfair to the English.' I was very surprised to hear this but suitably gratified, and we talked on. He said that his father was forever bemoaning the departure of the British from India. And then he said, 'Why don't you go to see the English vet at the zoo?' This was the first that I had heard of the presence of a compatriot, let alone a co-professional, so I thought this sounded a pretty good idea and suggested we go there right away.

At the zoo, which was, of course, new and lavish, I was astonished to see some red deer sitting under a tree in the heat. It transpired that these had come out from one of the English parks and were apparently coping remarkably well in one of the hottest places on earth provided they had adequate shade and water and good feeding. And the man charged with supplying these needs to the deer and all the other animals was none other than Chris Furley. I had known Chris's partner at Cambridge and so we were able to have a very useful exchange about the 'antelope'. Chris had been to see them himself and had already confirmed the diagnosis and instituted treatment. 'It happens every time it rains,' he said. 'Whenever it rains – which doesn't happen often, like once every three or four years, but when it does it's usually pretty torrential – all the detritus from those sheep and goats gets washed down into the oryx and gazelles. We know all about the brucellosis.' What he meant was that the dirty bedding and dung from the sheep, who had probably more or less come to terms with their infection and so showed no signs of clinical disease, were washed down into the oryx enclosure to contaminate their pasture and spread the infection to these endangered animals.

We discussed the situation further. The remedy was so simple it was really hard to believe that nothing was being done to prevent a recurrence. 'Last time this happened he brought consultants from all over to have a look, and the one whose advice was taken was someone who supplied some brightly coloured powders and left instructions that these were to be sprinkled on the ground at the full moon.'

I had just one chance to speak to the Ruler's brother that night before I returned to Scotland to prepare a report. It was an anticlimax. Whilst he was very gracious to me, it was clear that, try as I might, I was not really making an impression. My admiration for Lawrence of Arabia soared.

Back in Auchtermuchty, I wrote quite a short but detailed report making the obvious suggestions. Nickie even did beautiful sketches of the Arabian oryx on every page. I also went further and indicated to him that he might wish to consider a programme for eliminating this disease from the entire country. That would be a tall order but the technology was available. The months went by and became years and I heard nothing.

24 TOKYO, CHERNOBYL, PARISIAN MICE AND THE QUEEN'S AWARD

Venison sales were growing steadily but we were still dependent on the income from setting up new deer farms. We had, by virtue of our early start, been privileged to sell deer throughout Britain and our reputation stood very high. At one time I had sold deer to every single member of the eleven-strong BDFA council. France had also been good, but we were now competing with herds in the south of England that we had ourselves established and who now in turn had stock for sale. They had a five-hundred-mile advantage over us so that competing on cost was difficult. Also, deer on the hills of Fife never grow as quickly as do deer in more favoured locations further south. Although they are certainly not genetically disadvantaged it is not always easy to convince customers of the truth of this. I therefore reasoned, encouraged by my Swiss experiences and one or two French trips, that we should, in the true entrepreneurial spirit of Thatcherite Britain, be looking further afield – outwith Europe even.

Thus when a man from the ministry came along to tell us that the Department of Trade and Industry were sponsoring a British stand at an agricultural show in Tokyo, this seemed ideal. We had had previous enquiries from Japan, and though these had come to nothing we were attracted by the prospect of our deer, in a highly suitable climate, adorning a Japanese park. Deer are the perfect complement to the carefully designed, symbolic yet informal Japanese landscape. Besides I knew that their indigenous deer, the sika, occupied a privileged place in the Shinto religion. So, impulsively, with none of the expensive and time-consuming market research which we are told should always accompany a launch into new markets, I decided we would take a stand.

Two calves, imaginatively named Jamie and Willie, were carefully bottle-fed and manicured for the publicity, and preparations put in train. Nickie, as usual, dreamed up brilliant and economical graphic design panels and these were laboriously translated into Japanese. I wrote explanatory pamphlets and these too were translated.

It was at about this time that a pleasant little bombshell landed at Reediehill. The New Zealand Deer Farmers' Association wanted me to address their annual general meeting as keynote speaker. Critically they would also pay all my costs, and the day of the AGM coincided to the hour with the opening of the Japanese trade fair. What to do? I wasn't going to throw up this chance. We racked our brains and a solution soon materialised. Frank Vigh Larsen, a previous super-student from Denmark, was infinitely adaptable. Was he available, and how much bribing would he take to accompany Nickie as my 'envoy'?

A phone call and an instant decision from Frank and our plans were laid – I would fly off to Auckland. The two calves, by now very good friends and very spoilt, would be required to spend a few days before the show in quarantine, courtesy of the Japanese Ministry of Agri-culture, so Frank would go out to Tokyo for a few days prior to the show to look after them and prepare the way. Nickie would zoom in at the last minute to create our stand (which was to be highly sophis-ticated despite being accomplished on a shoestring). Frank and Nickie would man it together. I would rendezvous with Nickie at Bangkok on the way back and we would spend a few days in Thailand relaxing before flying home. We were assured that there would be no problem in finding a buyer for Jamie and Willie together. We certainly did not want to separate them.

After several false starts we found that Jamie and Willie were to travel in style on the inaugural direct, non-stop flight from London to Tokyo. The aircraft was to be a 747 combining people and freight. Apparently many animals, especially pigs, had travelled in this way in the past. But the human passengers had had their blithe insouciance rudely shattered when the air-conditioning on one flight 'mal-functioned', pumping strong agricultural odours into the first-class cabin.

It all worked out ... eventually. There were several very nerve-racking bureaucratic hurdles to be jumped, and we had to load the two calves at Auchtermuchty on and off the lorry several times before we could finally set off down to London to put them on the plane.

The stand in Tokyo was a triumph. We established good and loyal agents, indeed the same as supply the imperial household, a number of sales resulted, and we even took on a charming Japanese stockman in Auchtermuchty for a training period.

And what, you may be asking, happened to our hand-reared Jamie and Willie, that Frank had taken out and looked after so well? They were sold to a wealthy Japanese who insisted on paying us the four million yen in cash. Now according to Japanese law such transactions must be witnessed and the money checked at the time of sale. Con-sequently Frank was required to count the yen with quite an audience of British diplomatic staff as well as the prestigious purchaser and his party. Frank was given a table and chair and set to work surrounded by the smiling faces of the onlookers. As he finished his embarrassing task, Frank looked up very gravely and said, 'I am afraid there must be some mistake.' Dismay and horror were writ large on the normally inscrutable faces of the Japanese. Then Frank with immaculate timing dropped his punchline: 'You have given us one yen too much!' After a moment's silence the Japanese rocked backwards and forwards in laughter and relief.

The deer throve in a climate not very different from that of central Europe, and when I went to see them all a few years later they had settled in excellently and were being looked after in great style.

My New Zealand trip went well and as usual was highly educational for me. Afterwards Nickie and I met up in Bangkok and travelled to Phuket Island for a week in the sun. We went on a very small boat to an idyllic little offshore island only to find we had to share our beach with a group of Americans. And did they have news for us? Yessir, they sure did. Hadn't we heard about the nuclear explosion in Europe? European details were scanty – they were clearly more worried about the possibility of fallout in California. We watched the sand crabs scuttling to and fro, ate some more lobster and agonised about our two poor little girls left behind in Scotland with Tim and Maggy Stead. It turned out that this was Chernobyl.

Amongst the less talked-about consequences of that disaster was the collapse of European venison prices due to concern in Germany about the levels of radioactivity in reindeer meat. In the event, and despite a rather unhelpful press release from the Ministry of Agriculture effectively warning everyone not to eat venison, we were able to demonstrate on our return that our venison was not contaminated and that its becquerel rating was fine. The ministry was compelled to recant and Chernobyl left our business pretty well unscathed, though the wild venison trade was seriously damaged.

Encouraged by our successes in Japan we began to look at more active promotion in France. There is, held annually in Paris, a huge agricultural show. In fact, as befits such an agricultural and gastronomic giant as France, it was Europe's largest. We knew of course just how many French farmers were looking at alternatives to cattle and sheep and it seemed a good chance.

We soon became hooked on those Paris shows and went to four in a row. How we used to enjoy them, hard work though it certainly was! One of the five or six colossal exhibition halls at the Salon d'Agriculture features regional stands, each with its own restaurant. Customers share benches at trestle tables and eat oysters on the Brittany stand maybe, or on the Toulouse stand cassoulet, or perhaps on the Savoie stand cheese fondue. All is exhausting for the servers, a non-stop four-day party, but for the consumers it is the perfect release from tramping around the show. If only we could aspire to something like that in Britain; many Parisians must attend the show solely for that treat, and come away with feelings of bonhomie towards the farmers and food producers and loyalty towards France's regional food.

One night as we returned from a jazz club to our little hotel for a few hours' sleep before the next day's session, we found ourselves admiring a display of bread in a darkened baker's shop window. It was a very smart shop in a fashionable *quartier* – all fancy breads, not your good old *baguettes* and *ficelles*. As we stared vacantly, we suddenly realised that we weren't the only things interested in the bread. In a scene redolent of Beatrix Potter's *Three Bad Mice*, and oblivious of us, many minute rodents were industriously nibbling away the inside of loaves to leave the crusts intact. It was a brilliant accomplishment. Next morning the apparently pristine bread was still on view while the mice, who were presumably sleeping off their nocturnal excesses in the loaves, were now invisible to the smartly dressed passers-by. Only a few tell-tale droppings gave the game away to us initiates. We watched them every night, and the next year they were still there; but when we came back two years later to show Stella and Martha, all had gone.

By 1990 overseas sales were going really well. Further deer farms were set up in Japan; we sold a consignment to a very friendly man in Minnesota, but above all there seemed a never-ending stream of French farmers. They were, no doubt, encouraged by seeing us at the Paris Show with all the ensuing publicity – indeed one year we won the Prix d'Innovation for our stand. They were, like us, concerned to explore new ways of making their farms work since there was widespread belief that the Common Agricultural Policy was not going to sustain them indefinitely.

Soon I found that my little lorry was not large enough, and I began to employ bigger trucks from a firm of professional hauliers whom I could trust. We would load the juggernauts at Reediehill after first bedding them with abundant straw and after that a good covering of potatoes or carrots. And then I would travel out in my small vehicle in convoy with the large one. The deer travelled extraordinarily well, thank goodness, and I had great confidence in the drivers, whom I could readily appraise from the level of fellow-feeling they expressed towards the animals as we loaded them up. My dictum remains that good bedding and plenty of space are the key ingredients for the safe transport of deer; and, of course, we must remember that all our animals are destined for breeding, so that not only can we afford to take care but it would be folly not to do so. I used to look at the other livestock trucks on the docks and ferries with a great deal of sympathy for the sheep and calves they carried. There really is no excuse for taking animals hundreds of miles just to slaughter them on their arrival. Such a system is demeaning for the drivers and stockmen and horrific for the animals; its very existence must be a bureaucratic anomaly and it should not be beyond the ingenuity of our politicians and civil servants to think of ways of making this trade unnecessary.

The pinnacle of our foreign successes was reached with the prestigious Queen's Award for Export Achievement in 1990. It was interesting in retrospect that the award came our way when it did. There seems to be some sort of pattern with these awards. It has become a cliché to say that a business award generally precedes a collapse. In many cases awards are based on turnover, and a company that is selling very strongly is often underpricing, with the inevitable consequences. Or perhaps, growing faster than it knows how, it becomes overgeared, or maybe simply manages just to develop too big an idea of its own importance. In our case it was actually none of those things. It was simply that we had been part of a little boom, and before the Queen's Award application had even been processed – let alone before the junketing had begun – I knew we were in for hard times. Winning the award was a matter of great excitement. We were the smallest company ever to win the thing, and it was a huge morale boost for our entire little team just when we needed it.

The Queen's Award for Export Achievement is given to companies which can show a sustained growth in export earnings over three years. Our figures were indeed good; we had much more than doubled our export earnings each year. This was entirely made up of my consultancy services and the exports of deer breeding stock.

We were presented with the award by Lord Elgin, the Lord Lieutenant of Fife, and we put up a marquee. I was determined that the deer should be part of the occasion, so we let them run around and into the marquee in the field during the proceedings. We had to stop the tamest from eating the food. It was a beautiful day, Nickie of course cooked a magnificent feast, and lots of friends came over. When I gave my speech of acceptance I probably cast rather a pall over the occasion when I said that I couldn't imagine this unique type of business ever being successful again, as New Zealand farmed venison imports were growing and the British government showed no sign of doing anything to help deer farming compete on the same terms as sheep and cattle.

But then a few weeks later we all went up to Buckingham Palace and, perhaps because I was wearing a kilt, we were singled out for a lengthy chat with the Queen and all was celebratory.

25 EDUCATING THE WORLD
– A VENTURE INTO TOURISM

The gradual growth in trade at our minute farm shop (only two or three can fit in at once), as well as the steady development of the mail-order venison sales, was proof of Nickie's success with her books, articles and broadcasts. The occasional customers grinding up the hill to visit us and purchase venison had become a steady trickle. Since their journey demands a two-mile detour from the main Edinburgh to St Andrews road, and that uphill all the way from Auchtermuchty on a narrow track, this remains highly gratifying. Nevertheless I pondered, as the years went by, that if we had a base down on the main road away from the farm this would allow us a good deal more peace at Reediehill and would surely increase sales. I was still apprehensive about our continuing dependence on sales of breeding stock. I did not believe that those sales would continue indefinitely, nor did I want them to.

Also, less prosaically, I had a yearning to tell people about deer. To me they were the perfect means of introducing all sorts of educational subjects, not just biology, although there was plenty of that at all levels, but also the history of our forebears and their dependence on deer, human nutrition, cooking, agriculture and many other disciplines.

For several years I had been strongly of the opinion that there was a hidden value in deer as a tourist resource. This was rooted in our experience of taking stags in full velvet antler to shows all over Britain. The attention they attracted and the pleasure I had from answering questions about them were compelling reasons for wanting to go on with this. 'No, they don't grow a new point on their antlers every year so you can't tell how old they are from the number of points.' 'Yes, it is true that their antlers fall off each spring and yes, they do grow all that again each year. Those antlers have grown in six weeks; nearly an inch a day, the fastest-growing mammalian tissue.'

I also wanted to demonstrate that deer were not mysterious and uncontrollable wild beasts, but had the same need for care and attention as cattle and sheep, and that given good husbandry they would thrive in a farm environment – and that they produced a delicious and very healthy meat which was easy to cook.

I wanted to share my own fascination, to explain that the stag's antler cycle was synchronised by day-length: the antlers growing in the spring, hardening in the summer and losing their velvet as the days draw in so that they are ready for use by the stags in their crucial competition for the hinds – that contest between the stags to sire as many calves as possible that is the autumn rut. I wanted to show that this is evolution in action. Why was it all organised by day-length? To achieve a calf drop synchronised to make best use of the short period of grass growth – didn't the hinds yield two litres of milk a day for those fast-growing Bambis? And so on ... and on ... and on.

When we took stags to shows they genuinely seemed to relish the attention. Our particular stars were dear old 'Number Eight' and 'Ferox', both of whom would walk sedately up the ramp into the lorry in anticipation of going to the show, and who would approach people so that they could be stroked through the fence. When I took groups of people into their pen they seemed to revel in being the centre of attention. Number Eight was Scottish through and through, whilst Ferox was a magnificent, blue-blooded English park stag from Normanby Park near Scunthorpe (illustration 8a). At no time did any of the stags ever threaten visitors by standing on their hind legs and boxing, which would have been their natural defence in the summer.

Once, I had arranged a bed in the back of the lorry for Nickie on our homeward run from a show. Nickie, exhausted after a series of cookery demonstrations and going down with a cold, had slept fitfully and watched how the stags would lie down, or stand up, or chew on some hay, or look out of the ventilators as much as to say, 'Only Manchester – another five hours yet.' They seemed to travel like the seasoned professionals they were.

My experience with the stags at shows confirmed in me the belief that a permanent site could work. I developed a vision of a deer farm close to a main road and centres of population, where people could come and see the deer, stroke their antlers during the summer (that was very important), and learn a little of the magic that held me in its thrall.

I envisaged school visits where, through the deer, students could learn of the biology of survival, evolution and much more besides. They might discover the importance of antler as a material for making tools, and of the mediaeval deer park; they would find out how hunting had been so much a part of our ancestors' daily lives, and how the deer had eventually been almost banished from even the Scottish hills until, with the advent of the clearances, came the sheep and then the sporting estates; and they would hear of the role of venison as a staple meat nourishing man for nearly all this time. And then the visitors could go and taste venison in the restaurant and buy it in the shop. Our enterprise would become the centre for enquiries about deer, where we could develop a library, a cookery theatre, a directory of deer herds and much more besides.

In the wildest ramifications of my scheme we would have a butchery where, through a plate-glass window, visitors could watch the skinning and evisceration of carcases and the skilled craft of meat-cutting. My theory was that the present century is the first since man came out of the trees in which he has not been a frequent witness to the slaughter, disembowelling and dismembering of his meat. I believe this unfamiliarity is a factor in the rejection of meat, and for the grass-growing regions of the world, including Scotland, a decline in meat-eating would be a catastrophe.

I knew from the many visitors to Reediehill that young children are invariably unperturbed and fascinated by this novel sight that had always been so much a part of the lives of all our ancestors. It was only their elders and the media that brainwashed them into the irrational 'ugh'. There is nothing repulsive about the sight of fresh meat, organs and viscera. On the contrary, they are, as Rembrandt and other painters of an earlier age recognised, beautiful; familiarity with such things is a good basis for a better understanding of what makes us all tick. It is only when flesh rots that it becomes disgusting; presumably a long-developed adaptation to ensure the avoidance of unhealthy food.

As a way of making this point, in my early years at Auchtermuchty I had even dreamed of hiring a room during the Edinburgh Festival in which to exhibit cases of meat and possibly even whole dead deer. From beautiful pieces of fresh meat, these would slowly decompose, aided by the summer flies, so that, between the opening and closing Festival parties, the enticing red meat would be reduced to shrivelled remnants with only the brown shells of the flies' vacated pupae to show what had happened. I wanted to confront this tabu, with its attendant shock and disgust, head-on. The display would also, of course, have symbolised the waste of deer dying in the wild each spring because they haven't enough food, and more ambitiously, the universality of death and corruption. Dream on, Damien Hirst! Your shows are but a pale imitation of what I had in mind.

I realised naturally that the commercial possibilities of these more extreme ideas were very limited, but I was sufficiently encouraged by the public's interest in deer, as demonstrated at the shows, to believe that it would be possible to create a deer-based tourist venture in Scotland. The 'add-ons' of merchandising, catering, children's play areas and so on would be fundamental to the financial success, but the principal summer attraction would be the chance for visitors to have hands-on encounters with the deer in the presence of a guide. This was to be the Scottish Deer Centre.

I painstakingly drafted a business plan. It soon became obvious that the hackneyed tenet of all retailers, hoteliers and others – that the three secrets of success were 'location, location, location' – was also true of deer-based tourist centres. In the absence of a site, in vain I touted my business plan around various investors who showed no trace of interest. And then, at a dinner party one night, we met some new neighbours who had recently purchased a property about five miles from Auchtermuchty. It had some farm buildings close to the Edinburgh–St Andrews road near Cupar which I happened to know rather well, for I had used them for several winters to house our deer from Reediehill.

When our exports of deer had been at their height and before we had constructed our own shed, we had rented farm buildings all over Fife to house deer through the winter and as quarantine premises. One site had been those roadside steadings. The new owner asked what I thought he should do with them and I told him of my plans for a Scottish Deer Centre.

Meetings were held, and having formed a partnership we rushed ahead to open for the spring. The Scottish Tourist Board helped, the buildings were renovated, the fences erected and the deer installed. My project for an on-farm butchery and viewing chamber was not incorporated! But we did install an audio-visual theatre and a walk-through exhibition. In the exhibition I chose to work backwards. Firstly the present situation of Scottish red deer with numbers still climbing, the resultant conflict with farming and forestry, deer dying in the spring, the difficult job of the professional stalker, and then the history – the sheep walks, the 'great sheep', preceded by the Highland clearances with sheep displacing man and deer forests, and before that the deer parks as exemplified by that at nearby Falkland Palace. Finally we installed a man in the mouth of a cave by the embers of his fire, dreaming of the deer he hopes to kill in the hunt as he stares up at the constellation of Orion the hunter. Nickie contributed many pieces, including some facsimiles of antler tools copied from the many in the Royal Scottish Museum of Antiquities. In the first year we had around forty thousand visitors.

The audio-visual script was also written by me, and I supplied photographic slides from my own collection and begged others from friends. It was intended to demonstrate the yearly round as exemplified by deer. Slides of Callanish, the huge stone circle on Lewis which long predates Stonehenge, began the show, accompanied by a piece of music by the contemporary Scottish composer John Maxwell Geddes entitled 'Callanish', which had been its inspiration and whose score lies buried by the circle. It is thought that Callanish was used, by aligning stones with the sun, to time events in the calendar of its constructors and my point was that the deer also timed their life by the sun. Photoperiodic control is fundamental to the success of seasonal breeders such as red deer. I wanted to convey the urgent need for the deer to drop their calves so as to make best use of the early summer grass for the hinds' lactation.

I was determined that we should use the name Scottish Deer Centre. I envisaged it, probably correctly I still believe, as being a point of contact for people interested in any aspect of Scottish deer and their husbandry. I wanted them to feel that we were the 'one-stop shop'. The word Scottish was a protected name and we had to use lawyers to overcome the opposition to its being used as a business name.

In haste we appointed a manager, but at a very early stage it became obvious that things were going wrong. A week before opening, the manager told us that our partner, who had recently broken his leg in a car accident, had attacked him with his crutch. Whether true or not, it was clear that tensions were running high.

We struggled on for two or three years and visitor numbers reached 85,000 a year, but the partnership was not a happy one. Peace of mind and such simple pleasures as a good night's sleep are worth any cost, and reluctantly Nickie and I decided to leave, abandoning our substantial investment and three years of hard work. It was a huge waste of a part of our lives and there had been much acrimony and no enjoyment. For the first time since Veniburgers, something big had gone wrong – and at least with Veniburgers there had been buckets of fun.

Nickie and I felt the loss of our involvement in the Deer Centre project very deeply, but even in such a fiasco there were benefits. We had both learnt a lot about managing deer-based tourist projects. I got a job investigating the feasibility of such a scheme in northern Spain, which was interesting and lucrative, but I was especially keen to try again in Scotland. By dint of asking landowners, we did find another site – probably the very best situation for a tourist project in

Scotland. Here the proprietor was willing at least to entertain the idea. We were commissioned to carry out a project to investigate the viability of the site. The result was encouraging and the cash-flow projections looked very promising. The proposal was put to the directors in our absence. We understood that the board was strongly in favour of progressing the scheme, but the elderly landowner vetoed it.

We had been paid a fair consultancy fee for our six months' work, and as the weeks passed by I became calmer. I felt that finally I had got the idea of deer-based visitor centres well and truly out of my system. Nickie was relieved: 'Surely we can just keep it small and at Reediehill?' And so we resolved.

That was always assuming that we could remain solvent and keep the farm. For now the financial ramifications began to tell: interest rates were rising fast and our overdraft suddenly seemed an unscalable mountain. But before we could concentrate our minds on whittling down the debt, we had to experience another blow.

26 AN EPIDEMIC AND MORE MYOPIC POLITICIANS

The origins of the calamity lay in Sussex. It had all begun when I was engaged by a company of New Zealand stock agents called Dalgety to help them locate and quarantine deer of good quality for export back to improve their bloodlines. This task was to last several years and was made pure pleasure by the buccaneering nature of the Kiwis. I remember one night driving a load of deer down Park Lane en route to Gatwick in the days before the M25 motorway. My companion was a young 'cocky', a New Zealand deer farmer, who had recently inherited a remote property and with it a huge debt. In effect there was no chance of his ever being able to trade his way into solvency. Until, that is, he started to catch the wild red deer by feeding them on to his land. So valuable had farmed deer become that after one great night's work, daylight showed that he had enough hinds to clear his debt with some to spare. He sent a card to his grandmother telling her that he had just driven some deer through London and down the famous Park Lane. When he got back and saw her she said in her strong New Zealand accent, 'Good heavens, boy, they must have fine dogs to be able to drive deer through the middle of London!'

The focus of our activity was the London airports, and when someone called Carl Wheeler expressed an interest in starting to farm deer near Gatwick I was immediately interested. The farm and house were beautiful. Though it was so close to London, Carl's father had managed to have every phone and electric cable hidden so that from the garden a view of tens of miles of Sussex countryside was uninterrupted by anything man-made. I was very keen to become involved and took to Carl straightaway. He was obviously a highly competent farmer, the land was good and above all I enjoyed his company. The conversation went something like this:

'Carl, if you go deer farming, I would like to join in.'

'OK, how about a fifty-fifty partnership?'

And I don't recall that we ever put anything in writing.

At the start the scheme was a great success. I darted hinds from the best of English parks that by now I knew so well, and delivered them in sixes and tens. We aimed to run 150 hinds on the fifty acres and in a couple of years we were there. The deer throve. We soon had sales to Italy, New Zealand, Ireland and France and all was going well.

A lot of this success was due to our stockman, Janice. I have never met such a human dynamo. Accustomed to running a dairy herd, Janice soon got to know all the deer with their foibles and eccentricities. In order to effect real improvement in a herd of animals of any sort, you need to know precisely, with no room for error, which mother produced which offspring. Without this information you cannot select the bloodlines that you want to cultivate as being nearest to your ideal. This is the sort of genetic engineering that man has been carrying out for many millennia in livestock and crops. When it came to spring and the tricky, time-consuming job of identifying the mother of each calf as it was born, and weighing, sexing and tagging the calves, Janice was peerless. She drove set routes through the field in her own Land-Rover every morning and evening feeding the deer and noting those ladies who did not rush forward to join in. Then she would slowly move about the field until the truants were noted, and like as not they would be in labour. The carefully set routes were necessary to prevent any chance of driving over young calves hidden in the grass, and the Land-

Rover itself was a wise security measure, providing a point of refuge in case hinds became over-protective.

Hinds, like some breeds of beef cattle, can be fiercely protective of their young. I had noticed years before that the most dangerous hinds were usually those that were tame enough to have lost their fear of people – but not, interestingly, the hand-reared hinds, who in my experience are always quite oblivious to human presence as they pass through labour and will tolerate their calves being handled without any sign of concern.

Meanwhile I had to work for the New Zealanders. As their deer-farming industry grew, demand developed there for different blood-stock. The genetic base of the early introductions had been very small and there was something of a rush to breed the perfect deer. We had a whale of a time touring Europe from Sweden to Yugoslavia. East European deer were all the rage on account of their being so large – many deer farmers have what I like to think of as a latent Texan syndrome.

Although I didn't much like their leggy characteristics, it did seem that Carl and I should at least give them a trial. Accordingly, when we were approached by a New Zealander with a deer farm in Essex who wanted to sell three German stags we agreed to proceed. It was a fatal mistake.

The stags arrived just in time for the rut, and when one of them failed to recover condition after his strenuous round of mating we didn't take it too seriously. We buried him on the farm. Subsequently we lost a hind. Now normally deaths in the Sussex herd were an extreme rarity, so we had an autopsy done.

Carl phoned me up: 'They think it might be TB and they've sent samples to the ministry for culture.' That meant a wait of many weeks while the lymph glands from the diseased deer were carefully treated in an attempt to grow the bacteria they contained. Smears from the glands would be made on a choice of growth media in different mixtures of gases. Then the bacterial cultures would be subjected to a variety of tests to see if they really were the mammalian strain of tuberculosis. The weeks passed, during which time we lost another deer and then came the verdict: positive.

It was only gradually that the awful significance of this dawned on us. Although I was a vet and knew all about TB in cattle, and that it was a 'notifiable disease', there were no regulations with regard to deer; perhaps through some protective instinct I didn't grasp the implications for our precious herd. In other words we did not immediately start to panic.

Nevertheless, as soon as we had had the initial report, even before the culture results came through to confirm the diagnosis, we had, fearing the worst, started to make a plan for the deer. With the last year's calves, we had about three hundred deer on the farm, and that number was set to grow to 450 by the next spring. We aimed to create three groups: one which was known to have spent a lot of time with the German stags, a second group which had had some contact, and a third which had never encountered them.

In addition, as soon as the positive diagnosis was made, we started testing. The test we used was the tuberculosis skin test designed for cattle. This has been used for seventy-five years and has been wonderfully successful in eliminating tuberculosis from cattle. Moreover, by thus reducing the contamination of milk it has also saved many hundreds of thousands of human lives. It is one of the greatest achievements of the veterinary profession, although sadly it is being eroded as the levels of TB in cattle and badgers are rising so quickly now. The test consists of injecting a non-infectious extract prepared from the bacteria into the skin. Three days later the site of the injection is re-examined, and if it has swollen up the test is considered positive. This procedure had been developed for cattle but the New Zealanders, in the face of quite high levels of tuberculosis (often spread by opossums – which they had imported rashly from Australia – in the same way that the unfortunate badger spreads TB in Britain), had found that this skin test also worked reasonably well in deer. So we set to work to use it on our herd. We were helped in this by vets and scientists from the Central Veterinary Laboratory who were keen to learn something about TB in deer. We tested and we tested and we tested . . .

It was a slow job. We got results, but it was hard work for man and beast alike. Each test required the deer to be handled once for the initial injection and then again two days later to read the test. We could only repeat the test every two months or so because there was some evidence that it lost sensitivity if the interval between tests was too short.

I have not explained in enough detail the predicament that confronted Carl and me while all this was going on. As soon as the diagnosis had been suspected the ministry had served upon us a 'Form A'. This made it illegal for us to remove any deer from the farm – as if we would have wanted to anyway – until it could be shown either that tuberculosis had not been confirmed or that the disease had been eliminated, when a Form B would be served. This legislation had been created for cattle and, as we were soon to find out, deer were treated very differently. In the case of cattle, farmers are compensated for animals presumed to have TB which are then slaughtered. We deer farmers were told we would receive nothing; there was no legislation in force. We were in a terrible limbo.

And that was not all. There had been regular movements of deer from the Sussex farm to Reediehill. Consequently there was a distinct risk that the TB had spread to the Auchtermuchty herd. The Scottish Department of Agriculture was obliged to serve a Form A on our Scottish farm; now we could move deer neither on nor off Reediehill.

For Nickie and me this was crippling. We still had a good overseas trade, and that Form A effectively prevented us using the farm for any sales. Since there is no recorded instance of tuberculosis being spread by the eating of meat from infected animals, the venison sales could continue; but coming after the blow of the Scottish Deer Centre, and with no prospect of anything but expense from Sussex, those meat sales were nowhere near enough.

I agonised for about one month and then took the decision. We would have to slaughter all our precious breeding herd built up so slowly and carefully from the Rum nucleus, with all our old friends known to us for up to twenty years. If I didn't do this, we should have had to sell the farm and still lose the herd. There was really no choice. I often think of the cattle farmers faced with compulsory slaughter of their herds and I sympathise, but at least they receive compensation. We would not get a penny for this Reediehill slaughter. But what else could I do? It seemed likely in any case that the deer might have tuberculosis. Testing would take at least a year, and probably much longer, during which time we would have little or no income. Delay would be fatal. There was no sign of any reparation forthcoming from the government.

The department was helpful and sympathetic. We carried out the grisly affair over two days with help from a game dealer friend. On the second day I made sure I was away. It was too much. Then the farm was silent and empty; all our stock had gone.

We left the farm unstocked for six months and reseeded the paddocks. It was very lonely. Two months after that desperate week the department phoned to tell me the supremely ironic and surprising fact that of all the samples taken from the slaughtered animals, none had proved positive for tuberculosis. All our deer had been healthy.

Meanwhile in Sussex our problems seemed no nearer resolution. Carl and I, with Janice's blood and sweat, had built up that deer herd as well over several years. Janice especially had made friends with many of the animals whilst Carl had spent long hours recording the herd and working out with me our breeding strategy. They were the progeny of my hand-picked English deer; we cherished those animals, and the fact that science seemed to have no solution to our problems, and that the government which had encouraged us to diversify had allowed German deer to be imported with tuberculosis, took a little getting used to. Undoubtedly the Ministry of Agriculture, it could be argued, carried some of the blame. Those deer had been imported under regulations drawn up by the ministry specifically to exclude such disease, and it bore some responsibility for ensuring that imported livestock was healthy.

It was now clear that if we bowed to the seemingly inevitable and simply had our deer shot, I at least would be bankrupt, and I would also have been responsible for getting Carl into a most unholy mess. Not that Carl even at the most desperate moments ever hinted that he felt I was to blame.

For Janice the blow might not be financial but it would be even more heart-rending. To her had fallen the crucial job of relating dam to offspring, tagging the newborn calves, and all the daily feeding. Her involvement with the deer was bound to be close. During all the testing of the deer she was the one to hold their heads as we shaved the sides of their necks. Although no case of TB being passed from deer to man had ever been reported at that time, we thought it advisable to check that everyone working with the deer was still healthy. They went off to be tested themselves and we awaited the results.

In the meantime I was trying to think of strategies to save at least our precious bloodline, and also to secure some compensation from the government such as we should have received if we had been one of the growing number of cattle herds compulsorily slaughtered after a diagnosis of TB. We had several meetings with the Chief Veterinary Officer and also with successive Ministers of Agriculture, but it was the height of Mrs Thatcher's austerity and they were implacable.

'You might as well forget any possibility of compensation. The Treasury is absolutely determined not to allow any more expenditure on livestock farming.' And, conveniently forgetting their encouragement to diversify: 'Nobody told you to go deer farming. Don't expect any assistance from us.'

There are drugs available for treating TB and, at least in man, they have been extremely effective, although now the disease is becoming increasingly resistant to most of them. Vets, especially in the livestock industry, have to control the disease rather than save the individual. Historically, serious infectious diseases in animals have always been eliminated by the identification and removal of diseased animals rather than by their treatment. In the hard world of meat production, treatment is expensive and the protection of the health of the national herd paramount, so the veterinary profession has learnt over the years to sacrifice the few to preserve the many. Thus it is only in a few valuable zoo herds that treatment of tuberculosis has been attempted. The classic approach is to treat the pregnant females and, on the assumption that they are then less infectious, 'snatch' their calves from them as soon as they are born and rear them on the bottle in isolation.

Well, I reckoned if it was good enough, and evidently successful, for zoos, why not give it a try? Carl was in agreement and we started to search for the drugs. Nothing was available in Britain in sufficiently large quantity but we eventually ran some to earth in Finland. It was flown into Gatwick. But that's as far as it got because the government, keen to prevent us treating our animals, refused us an import permit and the whole lot had to be destroyed at the airport – at our expense.

Nevertheless, even without the safeguard of treating the pregnant hinds with drugs, we determined to press on with our plans to 'snatch' the calves. We decided to collect about forty female calves from the hinds in the group we reckoned least likely to be infected. A helper was found to assist Janice in the colossal labour and Carl had some ideal pens which would allow the calves to be isolated from each other. In the event, the weaning and rearing were a tremendous success. Fed on milk from Carl's adjoining dairy herd, the calves thrived mightily. Each litre of cow's milk was enriched with an egg, a teaspoonful of cod liver oil and a tablespoonful of glucose. Of thirty-eight calves, only two failed to make it and they had been very poor things to begin with. Those thirty-six were the best hand-reared calves I have ever seen, and how Janice and her colleague did all that work for two months, never sleeping for more than a few hours a day and up several times each night, I shall never know.

In November that year came an unexpected development. Edwina Currie was reported as stating, albeit inaccurately, that most British-produced eggs carried salmonella, thus precipitating the first of the food hygiene panics that have punctuated the nineties. Egg producers went out of business and there was a huge rise in imported eggs carrying even more salmonella than the home-produced ones had. We were told not to make mayonnaise and that eggs should only be eaten 'piping hot'. Mrs Currie resigned and the government was clearly on the defensive. Excited journalists hunted around for more stories along similar lines and soon came up with one on listeria in soft cheese.

Here at last was our opportunity. As the government did not seem even remotely sympathetic to our plight, Carl and I decided that the only resort left to us was the press. It was at this juncture that Janice came back from a visit to the consultant with the disturbing news that she had evidently contracted tuberculosis from her cervine charges. She was prescribed a six-month course of antibiotics and the prognosis was good. We asked if Janice would mind if her story was given to the press. She agreed without hesitation. In the space of a few days we did several television and radio programmes and many newspaper pieces.

It wasn't many more days before the government succumbed and passed legislation which granted deer farmers 50 per cent compensation in cases where their deer herds had to be destroyed as a result of tuberculosis. That is to say that the Ministry would value the deer and pay half the agreed valuation to the farmer before having them compulsorily slaughtered. Cattle farmers at that time received 75 per cent compensation and this was increased to 100 per cent in 1998, whilst the underprivileged deer farmer still only receives 50 per cent.

It was nearly two years too late for my herd at Reediehill, but Carl and I felt that 50 per cent was as good as we could hope for. Because we had been prevented from treating the disease we were now losing deer and there was no choice. We received what in the circumstances was a generous valuation and the grisly business of disposal of our old friends began. In two days that too was all over.

So what lessons might we learn? One is that the media, whether or not they are always accurate, are an effective check on the government. This is the democracy of our children's time and perhaps it's not such a bad thing. We know no other. In the often arrogant lack of response we encountered in successive Ministers of Agriculture – Donald Thomson, John Gummer and David Curry – were the seeds of the Conservative Party's overwhelming defeat of May 1997. Governments need at least to appear sympathetic.

Those German deer had been imported with a standard of health status sanctioned by the ministry. Might we have been successful in a court of law on that issue? Who knows? A more sympathetic approach at the outset would have saved taxpayers' money and the government's face. In terms of cost–benefit analysis the government acted very stupidly.

There was one closing feature to this horror story: the hand-reared calves. In retrospect, perhaps they stood no chance. The ministry, in its bureaucratic way, could not risk taxpayers' money by offering them a reprieve. As it was, they had us skin-test the calves and imposed so stringent an interpretation that it would have been difficult to conceive of them all passing. Of the thirty-six, three were deemed inconclusive using a test that required us to measure skin changes to half a millimetre. They were all killed; our precious bloodline was lost.

After this we believed tuberculosis was bound to prove a serious problem in farmed deer, and deer farmers set to work to monitor the situation minutely. With the passing of time, however, it has become clear that our fears were largely unfounded. There have been no more serious outbreaks in farmed deer, and deer seem no more susceptible to the disease than cattle. But wild deer, especially the fallow and sika, have not been so lucky. Almost certainly related to the rapidly growing badger population, there have been dramatic breakdowns in the health of wild deer in parts of England and a steadily growing incidence in cattle.

27 A WALK OUTSIDE

By the time the Queen's Award ceremony had come round, several months after the award itself had been announced, I could see the future was not going to be easy. The notification of the award had come during the same week that we had abandoned our investment at the Deer Centre. The tuberculosis had still been running at the farm in Sussex with no end in sight except more and more meetings with intransigent ministers and civil servants. The combination of the Deer Centre debacle with the loss of two herds of deer brought our Reediehill business to its knees. The compensation eventually received had all gone into restocking Reediehill. And to make matters worse there came a collapse in the confidence of UK deer farmers.

Most had started to farm deer in anticipation of disappearing subsidies: they had been encouraged by successive governments to think that 'diversification' was the right thing to do. But European agricultural policy still showed no sign of dramatic subsidy cuts. Deer farmers became doubtful; some returned to the cushioned world of support, and hind prices fell.

Then came the introduction of sheep quota. This meant that any farmer with a given number of ewes was awarded an equivalent amount of quota, free. Quota is a tradeable commodity worth a great deal of money. A deer farmer who had given up his sheep perhaps a year or two previously missed out on this golden handshake and found his farm dramatically reduced in value as a consequence. And if that misguided deer farmer now decided he wanted to resume his sheep enterprise he could not, because the quota was all allocated. Instead he would have to *buy* quota from sheep farmers who had been *given* it. Well, nobody ever told us that life was fair!

Then Britain entered the European Exchange Rate Mechanism at an artificially high rate, and the strength of the pound suddenly made exporting very difficult. Interest rates soared. Our income was in free fall and our overdraft was growing at a fearsome speed. I felt it was only a matter of time before the bank would foreclose. All that we had worked for was at risk. The farm and the house would have to go. Our overdraft was more than the value of the deer, the house and farm and everything else we had. And all the time interest rates were rising.

Although very few deer farmers were like us in having no other enterprise to fall back on, others were feeling the pinch: by 1996 about 30 per cent of British farmed hinds had disappeared, mostly to the game dealers, and the stage was set for a big shortage of farmed venison.

I made it clear to Nickie that, while I would do the best I could on my side of the business as a vet and consultant, with occasional live sales, venison marketing must now be the absolute priority for Reediehill. We had to effect all the cost cuts we could and yet work together to build our meat sales.

We had come to Reediehill in 1973 determined to pioneer the production of a new, delicious and much healthier meat in a humane, environmentally sound way. At that time we were the only commercial deer farmers in existence and it was obvious that it was up to us to make shift to sell our production in the best way we could. We had exploited the only avenue open to us and had constructed our own venison-processing plant and farm shop and continued to kill the deer in the field with a rifle. These facts were to stand us in good stead.

The farm shop and mail-order venison sales had been growing steadily but slowly and from a very low base, and we had not worked too much to try and develop them. When a breeding hind at eighteen months can find a ready sale at £450 there is much less incentive to develop sales of the male counterpart who, as meat, is worth perhaps only £150. But soon we found that we might also have to start killing potential breeding hinds for meat. Nickie was obliged to work even longer hours and together we manned venison stands at shows like the BBC Good Food Show and the Country Living Show, as well as the usual agricultural shows. There was little time for jewellery and no time to write more cookery books, even though *Game for All* had gone into a third printing.

We settled down to several years of hard graft with Nickie working on the venison sales, talking endlessly on the phone or in the shop. It wasn't unknown for people to phone her for advice as they put the joint in the oven. And sales did grow.

Meanwhile I cut my prices to the bone and continued to search for new markets. That spring Nickie came with me to Verona where we exhibited at a trade fair. As we arrived at the show there seemed rather a lot of excitement with an even larger number of police than usual. In the evening there was a banquet at which the British Minister of Agriculture, John Gummer, was to have toasted his Italian counterpart – but we soon found out that the reason for the police presence had actually been the arrest of the guest of honour, who was imprisoned and so unable to respond to our minister! We certainly welcomed the banquet where we drank some of the finest wine I have ever tasted.

However, when we had driven back from this show we were summoned to the bank. It was the year end and the results would, I knew, be dreadful. The manager was polite but the figures were plain to be seen. If there was no improvement in the next six months we would have to sell; the level of borrowing was far too high. As we left he said, 'Do you really think that you will ever be able to trade your way out of this?'

Nickie went through the accounts with me and it was manifest that the venison side of the business was sustaining the farm. It seemed as though the obvious thing was to sell most if not all of the breeding deer and merely buy in enough to satisfy the venison sales.

I went for a walk in the forest. Clambering over the deer fence and into the trees I soon found myself in an area I did not recognise. I was above the farm and I could see it all in the sun (illustration 4): the garden, the drystone wall I had built around the garden, the road we had struggled to improve, the fences that had been the root of political argument over grant aid; the house itself, now more than doubled in size since we had arrived, the huge deer shed to protect the animals from the wind, rain and snow, and finally the deer, some of them wallowing exultantly in pools, some spreadeagled on the ground basking, and a group of calves playing. And I wept.

28 THE POUND FALLS BUT VENISON TAKES OFF

Although the prospects for our recovery seemed very slim, I did have a number of sales to France organised for the next winter. I had quoted for these in French francs, since I believed that Mrs Thatcher had entered the European Exchange Rate Mechanism with the pound fixed at an unreasonably high level. It seemed to encapsulate her delusions of British superiority, and somehow, driving around Europe, I just didn't believe it. I had taken a risk which I could not really afford to take, but I believed that small French farmers would not work so happily in pounds, and above all I had to secure the sales.

We were driving to a friend's house that Wednesday to dart some stags and remove their antlers. The news was riveting. Speculators were attacking the pound. Nickie came with me in the car because it was just too tense to do anything else. We were then paying the bank around a hundred pounds per day in interest. As the Chancellor increased interest rates almost hourly it became clear that we would not be able to survive financially. Somehow it was all quite surreal and

I no longer felt dejected. The sun was shining and it was all outside my control. I had done my best to start a new industry and it had been absurd from the start. Perhaps we would be able to rent a small cottage and settle down to a less gruelling lifestyle. Maybe I should try to return to routine veterinary practice if anyone would still employ me.

We had tea with our friends, I darted the stags and we returned home. And then we heard that Britain had decided to come out of the ERM. There was hope. Surely the pound would fall to more reasonable levels? The interest rates came down again that evening. It was looking very much better. Over the next few weeks the pound fell by around 15 per cent. All my French sales consequently yielded 15 per cent more and this effect was maintained for the next two years. We hung on.

Less lucky was a friend who chose that Wednesday afternoon to shoot himself.

There is no doubt that, like those fevers in Victorian novels, this one had reached its crisis. With the sudden deliverance from the absurdly high price at which the pound had been pegged in the ERM we had room to manoeuvre again. The bank manager granted us a stay of execution.

It was then, of course, that Mad Cow Disease chose to rear its sick head. Suddenly everything agricultural was in chaos, including the meat trade; there were no winners in the BSE drama but we came near it. In the weeks after the March declaration by Stephen Dorrell that there might be a connexion between bovine spongiform encephalopathy and Creutzfeldt-Jakob disease, our sales rose fivefold and we have maintained increased sales to this day. Our winter 1998 sales were up 30 per cent on the same period in 1997, and we managed to keep prices stable despite colossal fluctuations in the price of wild venison.

Gradually it emerged that my consultancy business had not died. A series of fascinating and highly satisfying jobs arose in Spain, Thailand and Vietnam. My exports also began to look up. I have a great customer and friend in Belgium, and he asked me for 150 breeding hinds for yet another new deer farm.

The pressure was off now, and Nickie was able to find time to write regular newsletters to those on her venison mailing list as well as to accept more jewellery and silversmithing commissions. Among these was a request for a facsimile of the exquisite and complex fifteenth-century reliquary constructed to hold the tenth-century crosier of St Fillans. Work on this sacred relic seemed especially fulfilling and relevant.

Slowly, almost imperceptibly, we began to feel a little more light-hearted.

For the deer-farming industry as a whole there has also been encouragement: the large retailers are beginning to look with renewed enthusiasm at alternative and healthier meats produced in less intensive ways. They can see for their own reasons, I imagine, the strength in being diversified. At the moment of writing, one of the biggest supermarkets has just told me that its venison Grillsteak (rather like a Veniburger, I should imagine) has outsold any other red meat products in its stores. This single fact has inspired me like no other. Could it really be that we are witnessing a change to a healthier meat? It is sad that the Grillsteak has to be made from New Zealand farmed venison, but at the moment there just isn't enough British.

Also as I write, Nickie is in London selling venison from an outdoor street market and has phoned me up to say that she has sold out the whole three days' allocation in only two days. How very satisfying that so many people now want to eat the venison that I learnt in my days on Rum was the best possible of all meats.

Many cancers are becoming more common, particularly in the developed world, and diet is often implicated. The World Cancer Research Fund and the American Institute for Cancer Research published *Food, Nutrition and the Prevention of Cancer: a global perspective* in 1997, and pointed out that 'increasing consumption of meat and fatty foods will lead to a massive increase in incidence of a large number of diseases that are expensive to treat' and that 'obesity is an increasing major public health problem not only in developed countries but also now in urban areas of developing countries. As well as increasing the risk of a number of cancers, obesity increases the risk of cardio-vascular disease, adult onset diabetes and other major chronic diseases and reduces life expectancy.' They conclude that 'if eaten at all, red meat to provide less than 10 per cent of total energy ... but consumption of meat from non-domesticated animals is preferable'. They also highlight the stupidity of a system in which 'for many years subsidies have been given ... to the most fatty foods of animal origin'.

The agricultural grant scene has not materially changed from what it was when we started our deer farm twenty-seven years ago, and indeed I have more or less given up hoping. There is talk of reducing agricultural subsidies and of 'decoupling' them, that is to say paying money regardless of the nature of the production system. Were that really to happen we should be in with a chance, but these things have been talked about for so long that I have come not to build hope. The government is not at all interested in helping anything other than the large power bases such as the cattle and sheep trade represented by the NFUs. Thus the hard-won 50 per cent compensation package for tuberculosis which we squeezed out of the Tory government as they ran scared after Edwina Currie's faux pas about eggs remains at just 50 per cent, whilst the present administration has raised the compensation payable to cattle farmers from 75 to 100 per cent. It seems a rather cynical gesture. If there were to be any increase in deer farming it would save the Exchequer large sums of money because of the displacement of the heavily subsidised cattle and sheep – not to mention savings in the Health Service.

But wait a moment; there is change in the air. Conventional farmers are beginning to squeak whilst for deer farmers the future is suddenly looking good. The supermarkets are beginning to buy British farmed venison despite its much higher price.

Nickie and I have for several years supported an enterprise called Schools Challenge. Each year we dream up a few projects for school students to carry out. One year we suggested that they examine country-of-origin labelling. We knew that one supermarket was selling New Zealand venison and labelling it 'Produce of the UK'. They imported the venison in large primal cuts and then sliced and repacked it. They could have argued that it had been 'substantially changed' in Britain, in which case the labelling would have been legal, but no court of law would sustain the case that simple cutting and packing represented 'substantial change'. We covertly directed the students to that product in the supermarket as well as to the packing plant. Of course they managed to show that it was indeed of New Zealand origin. The trading standards officer was contacted, press releases issued, the children were interviewed on local radio and a great supermarket chain had to change its labels. 'Out of the mouths of babes and sucklings ...' The school won its challenge and its project came top in the judging. The supermarket now sells British Quality Assured Farm Venison despite the fact that it could buy from New Zealand much cheaper.

There is a welcome revival of deer parks for large country houses. These parks provide the perfect setting for impressive mansions; they are beautiful, they give pleasure to many – and they produce venison of very good quality. This development thrills me.

The British Deer Farmers' Association has been working hard over the last few years to create a stringent quality assurance scheme. Each farm is examined minutely to ensure that the deer are well looked after and that standards are met. This quality assurance scheme has transformed the approach of British supermarkets, who are now seeking British farmed venison, only to find that there isn't enough for their Grillsteaks. And conventional farmers seem at last to be waking up. The British Deer Farmers' Association has increased its membership for the first time in years. Once again I have been elected Chairman. I look forward to a campaigning two-year stint just eighteen years after my last term.

What has been achieved worldwide in those thirty years since I first went to work with deer on Rum? In New Zealand there was no deer farming then, but now there is a thriving industry with nearly two million deer and export earnings of about £100 million sterling per annum. Most of those exports come to Europe where consumption of venison is steadily rising. In the United States there are now some 250,000 farmed deer valued at about £35 million, and Australia has a similar-sized industry.

In Britain and the rest of Europe, with an agriculture ossified by subsidies, deer farming has developed much less rapidly. Yet there is a realisation that we can produce more of this meat in a green and humane way to allow grassland farmers another form of livelihood.

Eventually, maybe when we're dead and gone, those subsidies will be redistributed; then deer farming can compete with other enterprises on an equal footing. We have unquestionably and by all measures achieved a new domesticant and its meat is one which mankind is supremely well adapted to eating. The public health advantages are enormous and real if we can build on this start. Even gourmets rejoice.

And what about Reediehill? After all these years, I have located a generous grant for planting hedges, and even wild flowers under the hedges. How strange a cycle ... twenty years ago, and even until much more recently, farmers were paid to uproot their hedges. Reediehill didn't have any then but it will soon. We have planted three-quarters of a mile of hedges this year. I have always wanted to do that. The deer benefit from the shelter and will trim the hedges as they grow through the fences. And now we are getting grants for ponds, so I have dug three of those too.

Stella and Martha have grown up and Nickie and I know now that we have been and still are very lucky. We may never be rich but it looks as though we and the deer should be able to afford to stay here. As the trees and the hedges grow around the deer, the view from our windows becomes more and more beautiful. Jewellery commissions trickle in, Nickie is writing another book, and we can continue to sell venison through our farm shop and the mail-order business. And as deer farming grows and the demand for healthier red meats from consumers overwhelms the inertia of bureaucrats and governments, well, we can sit back and say we were a part of that radical change in eating habits. Maybe one or two people will have lived longer. And maybe that reverie before I was stolen away in my little old lorry on the road to Jura was not rubbish after all ...

BIBLIOGRAPHY AND SOURCES

Anon., *Food, Nutrition and the Prevention of Cancer: a global perspective*, World Cancer Research Fund and American Institute for Cancer Research Washington, 1997.

Babbage, Charles, *The Works of Charles Babbage*, edited by Martin Campbell-Kelly, London and Pickering, 1989.

Bannerman, M. M., and Baxter, K. L., *The Husbanding of Red Deer* (Proceedings of a conference held at the Rowett Institute, Aberdeen in January 1969), The University Press, Aberdeen, 1969.

Bath, Michael, *The Image of the Stag* (Iconographic Themes in Western Art), Verlag Valentin Koerner, Baden-Baden, 1992.

Baxter Brown, Michael, *Richmond Park – the history of a royal deer park*, Robert Hale, London, 1985.

Blaxter, K. L., Kay, R. N. B., Sharman, G A. M., Cunningham, J. M. M., and Hamilton, W. J., *Farming the Red Deer – the first report of an investigation by the Rowett Research Institute and the Hill Farming Research Organisation*, Her Majesty's Stationery Office, Edinburgh, 1974.

Blaxter, Sir Kenneth, Kay, R. N. B, Sharman, G. A. M., Cunningham, J. M. M., Eadie, J., and Hamilton, W. J., *Farming the Red Deer – the final report of an investigation by the Rowett Research Institute and the Hill Farming Research Organisation*, Her Majesty's Stationery Office, Edinburgh, 1988.

Cameron, Allan Gordon, *The Wild Red Deer of Scotland – notes from an island forest on deer, deer stalking, and deer forests in the Scottish Highlands*, Blackwood, London, 1923.

Cameron, Archie, *Bare Feet and Tackety Boots – a boyhood on the island of Rhum*, Luath Press, Edinburgh, 1988.

Cantor, Leonard, *The Mediaeval Parks of England: a gazetteer*, Loughborough University, Loughborough, 1983.

Carew, Richard, *Survey of Cornwall 1602*, edited by F. E. Halliday, Andrew Melrose, London, 1953.

Chan, W., Brown, J., Lee, S. M., and Buss, D. H., *Meat, Poultry and Game*, fifth supplement to the fifth edition of McCance and Widdowson's *The Composition of Foods*, published by the Royal Society of Chemistry and the Ministry of Agriculture, Fisheries and Food, 1995.

Clutton-Brock, Juliet, *Domesticated Animals from Early Times*, William Heinemann and British Museum of Natural History, 1981.

Clutton-Brock, Juliet (ed.), *The Walking Larder – patterns of domestication, pastoralism and predation*, Unwin Hyman, London, 1989.

Clutton-Brock, T. H., Guinness, F. E., and Albon, S. D., *Red Deer – behavior and ecology of two sexes*, University of Chicago Press, Chicago, 1982.

Clutton-Brock, T. H., and Albon, S. D., 'Trial and Error in the Highlands', *Nature*, vol. 358 (1992), pp. 11–12.

Columella, L. Junius Moderatus, *Of Husbandry, in Twelve Books*, London, 1745.

Crawford, Michael, and Marsh, David, *The Driving Force – food in evolution and the future*, William Heinemann, London, 1989.

Cummins, John, *The Hound and the Hawk – the art of medieval hunting*, Weidenfeld and Nicolson, London, 1988.

Darling, Fraser, *A Herd of Red Deer*, Oxford University Press, 1937.

Dasmann, Raymond F., *African Game Ranching*, Pergamon, London, 1964.

Diamond, Jared, *Guns, Germs and Steel – the fates of human societies*, Jonathan Cape, London, 1997.

Evans, Henry, *Some Account of Jura Red Deer*, printed privately by Francis Carter, Derby, *c.*1890.

Farm Animal Welfare Council, *Report on the animal welfare implications of the harvesting of deer antlers in velvet*, FAWC Secretariat, Government Buildings, Hook Rise South, Tolworth, Surbiton, Surrey, KT6 7NF, 1980.

—*Report on the welfare of farmed deer*, FAWC Secretariat, Surbiton, 1985.

Fiennes, Celia, *The Journeys of Celia Fiennes* (1696), edited by Christopher Morris, The Cresset Press, London, 1947.

Fletcher, Nichola R., *Game for All – with a flavour of Scotland*, Victor Gollancz in association with Peter Crawley, London, 1987.

Fletcher, T. J., in *Management and Diseases of Deer – a handbook for the veterinary surgeon*, edited by T. L. Alexander and D. Buxton, second edition, Veterinary Deer Society, 1994.

—in *Evolution of Domesticated Animals*, edited by I. L. Mason, Longman, London, 1984.

—in *Wildlife Production Systems*, edited by R. J. Hudson, K. R. Drew and L. M. Baskin, Cambridge University Press, 1989.

Forrester, Rex, *The Chopper Boys – New Zealand's helicopter hunters*, Whitcoulls, Christchurch, 1983.

Galton, Francis, 'The first steps towards the domestication of animals', *Transactions of the Ethnological Society*, London, n.s., 3 (1865), pp. 122–38; reprinted in *Inquiries into Human Faculty*, J. M. Dent, London, 1907.

Gasset: *see* Ortega y Gasset.

Gilbert, John, *Hunting and Hunting Reserves in Medieval Scotland*, John Donald, Edinburgh, 1979.

Hackett, Frances, *Henry the Eighth*, Jonathan Cape, London, 1929.

Haigh, Jerry C., and Hudson, Robert J., *Farming Wapiti and Red Deer*, Mosby-Year Book Inc., Missouri, 1993.

Haldane, A. R. B., *The Drove Roads of Scotland*, Edinburgh University Press, 1952.

Hart-Davis, Duff, *Monarchs of the Glen – a history of deer stalking in the Scottish Highlands*, Jonathan Cape, London, 1978.

Hughes, Ted, *The Guardian Saturday Review*, 9 January 1999: interview with Thomas Pero of *Wild Steelhead and Salmon Magazine*, Seattle, USA.

Jarman, M. R., 'European deer economies and the advent of the Neolithic', in *Papers in Economic Prehistory*, edited by E. S. Higgs, Cambridge University Press, 1972.

Johnson, Samuel, and Boswell, James, *Johnson's Journey to the Western Islands of Scotland (1775) and Boswell's Journal of a Tour to the Hebrides with Samuel Johnson, LL.D. (1786)*, edited by R. W. Chapman, Oxford University Press, 1924.

Kip, Johannes, *Britannia Illustrata or Views of several of the Queen's Palaces as also of Principal Seats of the Nobility and Gentry of Great Britain*, London, 1709.

Kyle, Russell, *A Feast in the Wild*, Kudu Publishing, Kidlington, Oxford, 1987.

Legge, Anthony J., and Rowley-Conwy, Peter A., 'Gazelle killing in Stone Age Syria', *Scientific American*, vol. 257 (1987), pp. 76–83.

Love, John, *Rhum, the Natural History of an Island*, Edinburgh University Press, 1987.

MacCulloch, John, *The Highlands and Western Islands of Scotland*, 1824.

McCance and Widdowson: *see* Chan, W. et al.

McNally, Lea, *Wild Highlands*, J. M. Dent and Sons, London, 1972.

Magnus Magnusson, *Rum: Nature's Island*, Luath Press, Edinburgh, 1998.

Martin, Martin, *A Description of the Western Isles of Scotland*, London, 1703.

Miller, Hugh, *The Cruise of the* Betsey, William P. Nimmo, London and Edinburgh, eleventh edition, 1874.

Monro, Donald, in *Account of the Western Isles of Scotland* (1549), edited by D. Munro, Morrison, Glasgow, 1884.

New Zealand Deer Farming Journal, various issues from 1979, WHAM Deer Ltd., P.O. Box 11 092, Wellington, NZ.

Ortega y Gasset, José, *Meditations on Hunting* (1942), translated by Howard Wescott, Charles Scribner's Sons, New York, 1972.

Payne-Gallwey, Sir Ralph, *The Crossbow* (new edition), Bramhall House, USA, 1958.

Pennant, Thomas, *A Tour in Scotland and Voyage to the Hebrides*, Chester, 1774.

Potts, Malcolm, and Short, Roger, *Ever since Adam and Eve – the evolution of human sexuality*, Cambridge University Press, 1999.

Red Deer Commission Annual Reports, HMSO (*now* The Stationery Office), Norwich.

Shirley, Evelyn Philip, *Some Account of English Deer Parks*, John Murray, London, 1867.

Simmons, I. G., and Dimbleby, G. W., 'The possible role of ivy (Hedera helix L.) in the mesolithic economy of Western Europe', *Journal of Archaeological Science*, vol. 1 (1974), pp. 291–6.

Soyer, Alexis, *The Gastronomic Regenerator*, London, 1846.

Stanley Price, Mark R., *Animal Re-introductions: the Arabian Oryx in Oman*, Cambridge University Press, 1989.

Thiebaux, Marcelle, *The Stag of Love – the chase in medieval literature*, Cornell University Press, London, 1974.

Turbervile, George, *The Noble Arte of Venerie or Hunting* (1576), Tudor and Stuart Library reprint, Oxford, 1908.

Walker, John, *Report on the Hebrides of 1764 and 1771*, edited by M. M. Mackay, Edinburgh, 1980.

Whitehead, Kenneth, *Deer and Their Management in the Deer Parks of Great Britain and Ireland*, Country Life, London, 1950.

Whitehead, G. Kenneth, *The Deer of Great Britain and Ireland*, Routledge and Kegan Paul, London, 1964.

Yerex, David, and Speirs, Ian, *Modern Deer Farm Management*, Ampersand Publishing, Carterton, New Zealand, 1987.

Zeuner, Frederick E., *A History of Domesticated Animals*, Hutchinson, London, 1963.

INDEX

* NB There is always confusion about the nomenclature of elk, wapiti and moose. When Europeans reached North America they saw for the first time the large relatives of red deer, *Cervus elaphus cenadensis*, called by the natives, wapiti. The Europeans familiar with elk, *Alces alces*, therefore called the wapiti elk, whilst Europeans continue to call *Alces alces* elk, rather than use the North American native name of moose.

RESPONSES TO CRIME

Volume 2

Responses to Crime

VOLUME 2

Penal Policy in the Making

Lord Windlesham

CLARENDON PRESS · OXFORD
1993

Oxford University Press, Walton Street, Oxford OX2 6DP

Oxford New York Toronto
Delhi Bombay Calcutta Madras Karachi
Kuala Lumpur Singapore Hong Kong Tokyo
Nairobi Dar es Salaam Cape Town
Melbourne Auckland Madrid
and associated companies in
Berlin Ibadan

Oxford is a trade mark of Oxford University Press

Published in the United States
by Oxford University Press, New York

British Library Cataloguing in Publication Data
Data available

Library of Congress Cataloging in Publication Data
(Rev. for vol. 2)
Windlesham, David James George Hennessy, Lord, 1932–
Responses to crime.
Includes bibliographical references and index.
Contents: [1] [without special title] —
v. 2. Penal policy in the making.
1. Criminal justice, Administration of—
Great Britain. 2. Crime—Great Britain. I. Title.
HV9960.G7W56 1987 364.941 87–12297
ISBN 0–19–825583–7 (v. 1)
ISBN 0–19–825416–4 (v. 2)

1 3 5 7 9 10 8 6 4 2

Typeset by Selwood Systems, Midsomer Norton
Printed in Great Britain
on acid-free paper by
Biddles Ltd, Guildford and King's Lynn

Time present and time past
Are both perhaps present in time future
And time future contained in time past.

T. S. Eliot, *Four Quartets*

Preface

WHILE writing the first volume of *Responses to Crime* (Clarendon Press, 1987) I became curious about the way penal policy is formulated. In the course of exploring some leading issues in criminology and public policy it seemed to me that in its application to criminal justice the laborious process of law-making was less schematic than the regular cycle of legislation might suggest. From time to time ministers and civil servants entertained a larger vision, but the uncertain tenure of the former and the endemic burden of work upon the latter inhibited their ability to think strategically. Recurrent crises and political problems demanded responses by Government, and the response of the moment had then to be incorporated into a presentation of criminal justice policy as a coherent and consistent whole.

Ostensibly Government is at the heart of the policy-making process and does not share, other than on very rare occasions, its prerogative of bringing forward legislative proposals that will be enacted and become law. But where are the antecedents to be found? With ministers, Parliamentarians, judges, officials, or the operational services? With political parties, penal reform groups, or other special interests? Is there significance in the departmental structure of Whitehall? What are perceived as restraints upon governmental action such as the financial cost, the prospects of a bad press or Parliamentary opposition, relations with the higher judiciary and, as time went on, the need to comply with the case law of the European Court of Human Rights? How does public sentiment towards criminal offending, always a potent force, make itself felt?

In pursuit of answers to these questions the trail led back over several hilltops to the years immediately after the end of the Second World War. From a number of possible points of departure I chose to begin in 1947 with the legislation then before Parliament. The Criminal Justice Bill of that year was not, nor was it intended to be, a radical reforming measure, being regarded more as a workmanlike component of the Labour Government's programme of reconstruction. To the discomfort of the Cabinet, however, it instigated a great debate on capital punishment which continued with passionate intensity until the abolition of the death penalty for murder was made permanent twenty-one years after the Criminal Justice Act 1948 left it untouched. The controversy is not yet extinct, although on each of the fourteen occasions since 1969 when the House of Commons has debated motions to restore capital punishment they have been defeated by substantial majorities in votes which have not followed party lines.

After describing the political context in the opening chapter, I move on chronologically to review the principal legislative milestones of penal policy over four decades, ending with a detailed analysis of the preparatory stages and the passing of the Criminal Justice Act 1991. In doing so I have been able to draw on the public records which are now available for the earlier part of the period, and the Conservative Party Archive for the 1960s and 1970s. As a minister I had relatively little to do with criminal justice, but over the past ten years, ever since I became Chairman of the Parole Board for England and Wales in 1982 (although I no longer have this vantage point), I have been simultaneously a close observer and a participant in the events which are recounted in the later chapters. The reader must therefore allow for my own opinions in the commentary that follows, and the judgments made upon the personalities, objectives, and policies that were adopted from the mid-1980s until the present.

WINDLESHAM

Brasenose College, Oxford
August 1992

Acknowledgements

Chapters 6 and 7 incorporate parts of articles previously published in the *Criminal Law Review,* [1988] Crim. L.R. 140 and [1989] Crim. L.R. 244, and (1990) 29 *Howard Journal of Criminal Justice* 291. Permission has been given by the editor of the *Criminal Law Review* and Blackwell Publishers respectively. The documents held at the Public Record Office which are cited in Chapters 2 and 8 are Crown copyright and are reproduced with the permission of the Controller of Her Majesty's Stationery Office. The letters from Margaret Thatcher and Home Office ministers in Chapters 6, 7, and 9, and extracts from Crown and Parliamentary copyright publications, are reproduced with similar permission. The Chairman of the Conservative Party allowed me access to the Archive at the Bodleian Library, and I acknowledge the assistance received from the archivist, Dr Sarah Street, as well as the Chairman's permission to quote the documents referred to in Chapter 3. Further acknowledgements are made where appropriate in the footnotes or text.

A mass of material derives from the richest mine of all, the Home Office, and I am obliged to the many people there who provided information about legislative and policy developments. The arrangement was that a recently retired official, W. J. Bohan, who until 1989 had been Head of the Criminal Policy Department, would act as the conduit for my researches, following up enquiries with the Home Office and other official sources, eliciting facts and generally enabling me to acquire a sufficiently informed insight into the way policies had evolved to make an appraisal of them. As the book progressed I became increasingly indebted to Bill Bohan. For more than two years he kept up a steady flow of factual information, also reading and commenting in detail on the content of each chapter in draft. The work was onerous, voluntary, and time consuming, and it was carried out with scrupulous fairness and impartiality. The use I have made of the material and the conclusions reached are entirely my own responsibility.

As with the first volume, David Faulkner has been a continuing source of encouragement and stimulation. Now a Fellow of St.

John's College and Senior Research Associate at the Centre for Criminological Research at Oxford, Faulkner was a Deputy Under-Secretary of State at the Home Office before his retirement in 1992. His knowledge and experience of criminal policy, allied to the sophistication of his mind and methods, earned him an unsurpassed reputation inside and outside the public service. The idea for the frontispiece map occurred to him after reading the book in type-script, and has been realized with ingenuity by the Technical Graphics Department of the Oxford University Press.

Professor Paul Rock, who has written so well about the changing perception of victims in the process of criminal justice, gave valuable advice, commenting on the original proposal and reading the typescript. Throughout the lengthy period when I was working on the book, my secretary, Mrs Patricia Spight, maintained willing and painstaking support, and in the later stages Gerard McMeel joined us to check the accuracy of the references. The Home Office Statistical Department did the same with the figures in the Tables. To all of them I express my heartfelt gratitude. The diligence and expertise of the Library Clerks and the Legal Library Executive at the House of Lords call for special thanks, their efforts being supplemented by the staff of the Bodleian Law Library in Oxford. The Dean and Faculty of the School of Law at the University of California, Los Angeles, generously provided facilities to assist my research in America during the Summer of 1991.

In addition to those mentioned above, I wish to thank the following for information and comments: Lord Allen of Abbeydale, K. R. Ashken, Professor Andrew Ashworth, T. Baltz, Edward Bickham, Sir Louis Blom-Cooper, Martin Brandon Bravo, Anthony Brennan, Lord Callaghan, Paul Cavadino, R. Ciulik, Alastair B. Cooke, Sir Charles Cunningham, Audrey Glover, Sir Terence Higgins, Dr Roger Hood, Nicholas Hopkins, Douglas Hurd, Dr M. R. Jack, Lord Lawson of Blaby, Nicholas McBride, T. V. Mohan, Professor K. O. Morgan, Steven Norris, Christopher Nuttall, Sir Derek Oulton, John Patten, J. Michael Quinlan, Baron-ess Serota, Lord Shawcross, Sir Ian Sinclair, Dr David Thomas, Dennis Trevelyan, Dr Isolde Victory, M. J. Ward, Nigel Whiskin, Viscount Whitelaw, and Dr Bryan Wilson.

The first three lines of 'Burnt Norton' from *Four Quartets* by T. S. Eliot are reproduced by permission of Faber and Faber, Ltd and Harcourt Brace Jovanovich, Inc.

Contents

List of Tables

TRIBUTARIES TO LEGISLATION
1987–91

Research

Penalties

Parole

Sentencing

Youth Court

PENAL

REFORM

Children's Evidence

Unit Fines

Responsibilities of Parents

Inspection

Default Powers

Financial Constraints

Cash Limits

Information

Non-discrimination

EFFICIENCY

AND

EFFECTIVENESS

Curfews and Tagging

American Example

Contracting Out

POLITICAL

CONVICTION

Life Sentences

SEA OF STATUTES
(Criminal Justice Act 1991)

1

Law-Making: Politics and Structure

Between 1948 and 1991 Parliament passed eight substantive Criminal Justice Acts for England and Wales, one Criminal Law Act which was close enough in content to the specifically criminal justice legislation to be similarly classified, four Scottish Criminal Justice Acts, and several acts dealing with criminal justice administration, international co-operation, and minor matters requiring legislation. Details are shown in Tables 1 and 2. The result of this legislative output has been the creation of a statutory framework for the administration of criminal justice and the sentencing and treatment of offenders. In the main the structure is permissive; with some exceptions, setting limits on what can be done rather than laying down by law what must be done. Successive acts have altered the shape of the structure; either by adding bits on (parole, community service orders, compensation orders, contract prisons), or, less often, by taking bits off (corporal punishment, detention centres, partly suspended sentences, the remand of juveniles to prison).

Other statutes created new offences, amended penalties, reorganized the structure of the courts, reclassified the types of offence tried in them, defined the powers of the police, and set up an independent prosecution service. If the results did not always work out in the way intended, the blame for the failings of the criminal justice system cannot be attributed to any lack of zeal to legislate. Although there was no causal connection between the two trends, it became evident that as the volume of legislation increased, public confidence in the ways of bringing offenders to justice and punishing the guilty declined. Apart from the designated criminal justice legislation, the statutes discussed in the narrative of this book include: the Murder (Abolition of Death Penalty) Act 1965, the Courts Act 1971, the Bail Act 1976, the Police and Criminal Evidence Act 1984, the Prosecution of Offenders Act 1985, the

TABLE 1. *Criminal Justice: England and Wales,*[a] *substantive legislation, 1947–91*[b]

	1st Reading	No. of clauses at 1st reading	Enacted	No. of Sections
Criminal Justice Act 1948 (c. 58)	31 Oct. 1947	[Bill 9] 70 cl., 10 sch.	30 July 1948	83 secs., 10 sch.
Criminal Justice Act 1961 (c. 39)	2 Nov. 1960	[Bill 8] 42 cl., 5 sch.	19 July 1961	45 secs., 6 sch.
Criminal Justice Act 1967 (c. 80)	29 Nov. 1966	[Bill 141] 72 cl., 5 sch.	27 July 1967	106 secs., 7 sch.
Criminal Justice Act 1972 (c. 71)	10 Nov. 1971	[Bill 12] 49 cl., 3 sch.	26 Oct. 1972	66 secs., 6 sch.
Criminal Law Act 1977 (c. 45)	30 Nov. 1976	[HL 7] 46 cl., 10 sch.	29 July 1977	65 secs., 14 sch.
Criminal Justice Act 1982 (c. 48)	2 Dec. 1981	[Bill 32] 52 cl., 14 sch.	28 Oct. 1982	81 secs., 17 sch.
Criminal Justice Act 1987 (c. 38)	14 Nov. 1986	[Bill 2] 128 cl., 10 sch.	15 May 1987	18 secs., 2 sch.
Criminal Justice Act 1988 (c. 33)	29 June 1987	[HL Bill 3] 139 cl., 11 sch.	29 July 1988	173 secs., 16 sch.
Criminal Justice Act 1991 (c. 53)	8 Nov. 1990	[Bill 6] 82 cl., 10 sch.	25 July 1991	102 secs., 13 sch.

[a] The territorial designation follows the *Index to Statutes* (1989), although certain sections in each Act extend to Scotland.

[b] A further Criminal Justice Bill (HL Bill 33) had its First Reading in the House of Lords on 22 Oct. 1992. The scope was confined largely to commercial crime. Forty-eight clauses and four schedules included provisions on the jurisdiction of the courts to try cases of fraud and related offences where there is a significant foreign element; drug-trafficking offences and powers of confiscation; money laundering; the proceeds of criminal conduct; insider dealing; and regulations made under the European Communities Act 1972 implementing EC directives on the supervision of banking and credit institutions.

Source: House of Lords Library.

TABLE 2. *Criminal Justice: Scottish legislation, administration, international co-operation, and minor Acts, 1949–90*

Criminal Justice (Scotland) Act 1949 (c. 94)
Criminal Justice (Scotland) Act 1963 (c. 39)
Criminal Justice (Scotland) Act 1980 (c. 62)
Criminal Justice (Scotland) Act 1987 (c. 41)

Criminal Justice Administration Act 1956 (c. 34)
Criminal Justice Administration (Amendment) Act 1959 (c. 41)
Criminal Justice Administration Act 1962 (c. 15)

Criminal Justice (International Co-operation) Act 1990 (c. 5)

Criminal Justice Act 1965 (c. 26)[a]
Criminal Justice (Amendment) Act 1981 (c. 27)[a]

[a] Each of these Acts had only two sections.
Source: House of Lords Library.

Public Order Act 1986, and the War Crimes Act 1991. Each of these measures was confined to a single area of policy, dispute over which sometimes crossed party political lines, as with the abolition of capital punishment and the legislation to enable the prosecution of a handful of elderly men against whom there might be evidence of war crimes committed half a century earlier outside the jurisdiction of the United Kingdom courts.

Certain acts, for example the reorganization of the higher courts in which indictable offences are tried, and the Police and Criminal Evidence Act 1984, stemmed from Royal Commissions or similar forms of independent inquiry. What distinguishes the series of Criminal Justice Acts is the comprehensiveness with which they bring together a range of generally disparate proposals, originating from different sources, bearing on the content of the criminal law, the powers and procedure of the courts, and the treatment (in the widest sense) of offenders. While not necessarily dealing with the most important, nor the most contentious, matters, the criminal justice legislation, by virtue of its comprehensiveness and regularity, suggests more of a systematic approach to keeping in good repair the administration of justice and the working of the penal system than can be substantiated by events. A conclusion which emerges

clearly in the account that follows is how the addition of fresh
elements can dilute the purity of the original concept, sometimes
leading to unexpected results.

What, then, are the characteristics of the legislative process in
this context? Once introduced, always at the initiative of the
Government, Criminal Justice bills are rolling stones gathering
accretions as they travel down the Westminster hillside towards
their final destination on the statute book. Some of the clauses may
be abandoned and others amended, but much more is added than
is taken away. The very existence of a bill, invariably with a broad
scope, attracts numerous proposals for amendments and additions.[1]
Table 1 contrasts the length of the bills on introduction and at
enactment. When it obtained the Royal Assent, the Criminal Justice
Act 1988 had expanded to 173 Sections and sixteen schedules, half
as long again as the Bill which had its First Reading in November
1986, allowing for the separate provisions of the 1987 Act. The
reason why the original bill was split into two Criminal Justice
Acts is explained in Chapter 4.

Long drawn out and unpredictable as the process may be, it has
one great advantage for the policy-maker. A regular cycle of multi-
purpose bills permits adjustments in criminal law and practice to
be made without the necessity for each change to have its own bill.
An element of public accountability can also be identified in the
recurrent attentions of elected Members of Parliament. The period
of time a bill is before Parliament determines how long the window
of opportunity to legislate on criminal justice matters remains open.
Once closed, the Home Office will fall back on the well-worn refrain
that legislation is required to make a surprisingly large number of
the proposals that are put forward, and that no Parliamentary time
is available.

The forum in which the legislation is first introduced is usually
the House of Commons, although bills can be introduced in either

---

[1] Amendments to a bill must be within its scope, the extent of which is inferred
from the totality of its provisions as introduced. Most Criminal Justice bills contain
such a wide variety of clauses concerning the sentencing and treatment of offenders,
as well as other matters, that there is generally little difficulty in bringing forward
alternative or additional proposals in the form of new clauses. Proposals to alter
the substantive criminal law will be in order only if the bill as presented already
contains provisions of a similar kind.

House of Parliament.[2] It is puzzling that the House of Commons is not seen to better advantage during the passage of legislation on criminal justice. In theory it should afford a textbook instance of the Executive, in the form of the Home Secretary, bringing before Parliament a set of legislative proposals which have been painstakingly prepared by experienced officials in his Department, normally after testing opinion in advance by way of discussion documents and a White Paper. Members of Parliament then have an opportunity to discuss and amend, accepting or rejecting the proposals in the light of what they consider to be the needs and desires of their constituents. In reality, little more than the faintest outlines of such a legislative model can be detected. A blurred shape is perceptible to those who look hard enough, but the process is more amorphous than the stereotype might suggest.

Despite the fact no one doubts that popular opinions on crime and its containment are extensively and deeply held, whenever Criminal Justice bills are before the Commons the atmosphere seems detached and wary, with few MPs participating and a majority keeping the subject at arm's length. Except on the big set-piece confrontations, the death penalty above all else, the debates are seldom well attended. It is true that lengthy and detailed scrutiny takes place in a Standing Committee off the floor of the House, but even then it is typically the special interest groups, briefing Opposition spokesmen and Government back-benchers alike, which provide more of the dynamic than the representation of constituents' views.

Why this should be so is worth pondering. Constituents may be vocal in demanding what are seen as cruder and more punitive measures than their MP feels comfortable with. Few MPs are willing to risk antagonizing those upon whose electoral favour they depend, especially where there are no immediately apparent benefits to be earned by the espousal of penal policies in the way that policy changes in health, housing, social security, education, and the environment can be of direct benefit to their constituents. It is an over-simplification to say there are no votes in crime. Ministers in

---

[2] The Criminal Law Bill in 1976 and the Criminal Justice Bills of 1986 and 1992 were introduced in the Lords. Of the 199 government bills which were enacted during the Parliament of 1983–7, eighty-five were first introduced in the House of Lords. J. A. G. Griffith and M. Ryle, *Parliament: Functions, Practice and Procedures*, Sweet and Maxwell, London, 1989, p. 310.

particular are keenly aware that whereas it is uphill work to gain popular support for specific policies, it is very easy to lose public confidence in the way that crime is handled.

If we accept that public opinion broadly comes in two varieties: the popular and what can be regarded as the informed,[3] each of the two strands is clearly visible whenever Parliament addresses the topic of criminal justice. Although the House of Commons has always contained some MPs who take an informed interest in the subject,[4] they are in a small minority, irrespective of Party allegiance, being heavily outnumbered by those who are guided more by what they sense to be the prevailing expectations of the public. There is nothing wrong with this; the Commons is, after all, the nearest thing we have to a democratic assembly, but it does not make for thorough and well-informed debate. Consequently it is just as well that the injection of expert opinion is one of the functions of the contemporary House of Lords. As in the Commons, the scrutiny is provided by a relatively small number of peers, lacking in elective legitimacy, but justifying their Parliamentary role by bringing to bear special knowledge of criminal policy or the administration of justice.

By tradition, Lords of Appeal in Ordinary, current or retired, are not precluded from contributing the fruits of their judicial experience and legal expertise to debates in the Lords. The Lord Chief Justice may put forward the views of the higher judiciary on the more important issues relating to the criminal law or sentencing in the course of a bill's progress, although his ability to attend is limited by the demands of his court. Many other peers have experience as magistrates, as members of the Bar, or as solicitors. A number have had responsibility for the operation of parts of the system of criminal justice, including former Home Office ministers,

[3] For a discussion on the relationship between the two, see 'Politics, Publicists, Power' in Windlesham, *Communication and Political Power*, Cape, London, 1966, pp. 229–55. Dr R. G. Hood's report to the United Nations Committee on Crime Prevention and Control (published as *The Death Penalty: A World-Wide Perspective*, Clarendon Press, Oxford, 1989) includes a chapter at pp. 149–58 on 'Public Opinion and Knowledge' which contrasts popular opinion with the impact on policy attributable to opinions expressed by professional organizations, particularly those involved with the criminal justice system.

[4] Apart from ministers and Opposition front-bench spokesmen, names that occur in the narrative of the book include Sydney Silverman, Christopher Hollis, William Deedes, Emlyn Hooson, Leo Abse, Sam Silkin, Robert Kilroy-Silk, Mark Carlisle, Robert Maclennan, Sir Edward Gardner, and Sir John Wheeler.

retired senior civil servants and police officers, and chairmen of the Parole Board.[5]

Members and supporters of the main penal reform groups are to be found in both Houses, but their presence is most felt in the Lords where some of their officers invariably sit. Their work is supplemented by that of specialized bodies representing the interests of people such as the victims of crime and those professionally engaged in the administration of justice. In the first category of penal reform groups come the National Association for the Care and Resettlement of Offenders (NACRO), the National Council for Civil Liberties (Liberty), the Howard League for Penal Reform, JUSTICE, and the Prison Reform Trust. Examples of special interest groups are Victim Support (formerly known as the National Association of Victim Support Schemes), Parents of Murdered Children, the National Association of Prison Visitors, the National Association of Probation Officers, the National Association of Senior Probation Officers, the Association of Chief Officers of Probation, the Association of Chief Police Officers, the Superintendents' Association, the Police Federation, the Prison Governors' Association, and Prison Officers' Association. Most of the national organizations have counterparts in Scotland.

Penal reform groups have a long and honourable history and have played an important part in the development of criminal justice policy over the years. The high point was the abolition of capital punishment which, although finally decided by Parliament after free votes in both Houses in 1965 and 1969,[6] would not have been possible but for the long campaign, outside Parliament as much as inside, mounted by the penal reformers of the day. More generally in lobbying for changes in policy, by way of briefing MPs and peers and organizing publicity in the media, penal reform groups contribute to the prevailing climate of opinion which is of particular relevance in the pre-legislative stages. Home Office officials maintain contact with them by attending conferences and meetings, and periodically on a closer and more continuing basis.

[5] Five out of the six chairmen of the Parole Board for England and Wales to date have been in the House of Lords: Lord Hunt (1967–74), Lord Harris of Greenwich (1979–82), the author (1982–8), Viscount Colville of Culross QC (1988–92), and Lord Belstead (1992–).

[6] An account of the Parliamentary proceedings leading to abolition follows in Chapter 2.

A good example can be found in a discussion group of civil servants, academics and penal reformers which met regularly throughout the 1980s.

The initiative in convening meetings at intervals of every two or three months was taken by David Faulkner[7] while an Under-Secretary at the Prison Department in 1981, and continued during the eight years he was the Deputy Under-Secretary of State in charge of the Criminal and Statistical Departments and the Research and Planning Unit at the Home Office from 1982 to 1990. The focus was originally on prison subjects: a code of standards, justice in prisons, and the treatment and control of dangerous prisoners. Both the focus and the composition of the group changed in 1982 on Faulkner's promotion to the Criminal Department, being joined *inter alia* by Bill Bohan, a knowledgeable Assistant Under-Secretary who headed the Criminal Policy Department from 1979 until his retirement in 1989, and the directors of the Cambridge Institute of Criminology and the Oxford Centre for Criminological Research, Professor Anthony Bottoms and Dr Roger Hood. From then on the group concentrated on issues of sentencing, crime and the causes of criminality, and the criminal justice process. One member would be invited to introduce a subject (agreed at the previous meeting), followed by a discussion for an hour or so before more general discussion over a buffet supper.

The existence of the group was not advertised, but no secret was made of it either. Opinions were expressed openly and freely without any breach of confidence. The group ceased meeting when Faulkner left the Criminal Department to become Principal Establishment Officer at the Home Office in 1990. It was not the purpose of the meetings to produce or agree upon policy proposals; nor was there any attempt to do so. They provided a sounding board, enabling the civil servants to keep abreast of the state of reformist opinion, and for the penal reform groups and academic researchers to obtain an insight into current thinking at the Home Office.

[7] Joint Secretary to the Inter-Party Conference on House of Lords Reform, 1968; Private Secretary to the Home Secretary, 1969–70. Home Office: Assistant Secretary, 1970–6; Assistant Under-Secretary of State, 1976–8; Under-Secretary, Cabinet Office, 1978–80. Director of Operational Policy, Prison Department, 1980–2; Deputy Under-Secretary of State, in charge of the Criminal and Research and Statistics Departments, 1982–90, and Principal Establishment Officer, Home Office, 1990–2. Fellow of St. John's College and Senior Research Associate, Centre for Criminological Research, Oxford, 1992– .

In the Parliamentary setting a similar function was performed by an All-Party Penal Affairs Group. Reconstituted in 1979, with a clerk provided by NACRO[8] and administrative expenses funded by a grant from a charitable trust,[9] MPs and peers from all the main political parties met to discuss current issues of criminal justice policy and practice. Robert Kilroy-Silk, a Labour MP, was an energetic chairman until 1986, being followed by a Conservative, (Sir) John Wheeler. Political differences were minimized and a wide variety of outside speakers invited to address the group at monthly intervals when Parliament was sitting, normally in a House of Commons Committee Room. Out of a nominal membership of seventy, the attendance at meetings averaged fifteen in 1991, rising to the mid-or high twenties on occasions of particular interest. This is a larger and more active membership than most other all-party groups can claim. Four reports were published,[10] backed up by a series of duplicated papers which were circulated to interested parties.[11] Unlike Faulkner's discussion group, the Parliamentarians could and did agitate for action to be taken on certain issues for which there was all-party support. Its greatest achievement was in devising, and later revising, criteria for the custodial sentencing of young offenders which were incorporated in the Criminal Justice Acts of 1982 and 1988.[12] Another cause, finally endorsed by legis-

[8] Paul Cavadino, Senior Information Officer of NACRO. During the debates on the Criminal Justice Bill in the House of Lords in 1991 Cavadino was complimented as a 'one man Civil Service' in the briefing which he had provided for Opposition and other peers. *Parl. Debates*, HL, 529 (5th ser.), col. 631, 4 June 1991. At most stages of legislation not more than three advisers or research staff may be nominated each day by the Opposition parties for places in the Clerk's Box on the floor of the House of Lords. From there they can pass notes and be consulted by peers in the same way that ministers are able to communicate with officials in the civil servants' box opposite. During the debates on the Criminal Justice Bill in 1991 this facility was used by the Parliamentary All-Party Group for Children, as well as the Penal Affairs Group, and by the Association for Juvenile Justice and the Magistrates' Association.

[9] An annual grant from the Barrow and Geraldine S. Cadbury Trust enabled the part-time employment of Cavadino as Clerk to the Group.

[10] *Too Many Prisoners* (1980), *Young Offenders—A Strategy for the Future* (1981), *The Prevention of Crime Among Young People* (1983), and *Life Sentence Prisoners*, all published by Barry Rose (Publishers), Chichester.

[11] Duplicated reports included *Still Too Many Prisoners* (1981), *Part Time Prison* (1984), *A New Deal for Victims* (1984), *Statutory Restrictions on the Use of Custody for Young Offenders* (1985), *The Rising Prison Population* (1986), *Submission to Lord Justice Woolf's Inquiry on Prison Disturbances* (1990).

[12] See Chapter 4.

lation in the Criminal Justice Act 1991, was ending the remand of
juveniles to penal establishments.

II

The Parliamentary scrutiny to which all bills are subject enables
MPs and peers to apply political and expert opinion to legislative
proposals. As this book will show, the approval of Parliament is
no rubber-stamp. The key function none the less lies in the drawing
up of the legislation; deciding what should go into a bill and what
should be omitted, and how the proposals should be drafted. Here
the initiative rests squarely with the Government, in the person of
the Home Secretary as the minister in charge of the sponsoring
department. The promotion of legislation comes at the top of the
catalogue of his responsibilities listed below. In addition to functions
directly connected with the process of bringing alleged offenders to
justice and supervising their subsequent punishment or treatment,
the Home Secretary has responsibility for the operation of the
Criminal Injuries Compensation Scheme and other provisions for
the victims of crime, and for stimulating crime prevention measures.
His main criminal justice responsibilities are:

1. Promoting legislation to amend the criminal law, or to alter
the powers and procedure of criminal courts;

2. overseeing the administration, financing, and efficiency of the
police and probation service, with varying powers of central control
in respect of each service;

3. the provision and administration of prisons and young
offender institutions;

4. the release on licence of offenders sentenced to life imprisonment, and the grant of parole to those serving long-term sentences
(both on the recommendation of the Parole Board);[13]

5. the control of mentally disordered persons found unfit to
plead, or subject to restriction orders under the Mental Health Act
1983;

---

[13] For a description of revised statutory procedures regulating the release of
discretionary life-sentence prisoners and certain categories of determinate-sentence
prisoners which became effective on 1 Oct. 1992, see Chapter 9.

6. the exercise of the Royal Prerogative of Mercy or other powers to remedy miscarriages of justice;

7. extraditing fugitive offenders and providing mutual assistance to other states in criminal matters.

High as is the priority for promoting legislation, when the time comes the Home Secretary is not in the position of an artist free to fill the canvas with the products of his own inspiration. Even if he had the knowledge and inclination to do so, there are too many distractions. The life of a Home Secretary has been depicted by several former holders of the office as being unduly susceptible to interruption by sudden and totally unexpected incidents which require all his attention:

It is truly said that he can go to bed at night with a clear sky as far as Home Affairs are concerned and wake up the next morning with a major crisis on his hands. Worst of all, many of these particular events permit no simple solution and provide the Press with marvellous copy. The unfortunate Home Secretary then receives much advice of a totally impractical nature for the solution of the problem. At the same time he is blamed for allowing the incident to arise when it is usually inconceivable that he could have prevented it.[14]

Crisis management apart, there is the constant burden of case-work which calls for much reading of detailed dossiers before reaching decisions on individual cases. Lord Callaghan listed the following examples:

... admittance to Britain or deportation; cases where the Home Secretary has to consider an appeal in which wrongful conviction is alleged, or appeals to him from police officers, or prison officers, against disciplinary decisions; and prisoners' petitions to the Home Secretary. A Home Secretary spends many hours conscientiously reading background papers which set out the whole history of a single police officer's alleged offences, sometimes in a bundle of papers an inch thick, in order that justice and equity may be done.[15]

This quality is lacking in departments such as the Treasury or the Foreign Office which are preoccupied more with policies than with the handling of individual cases. The result is that all Home

[14] *The Whitelaw Memoirs*, Aurum Press, London, 1989, pp. 160–1. William Whitelaw was Home Secretary, 1979–83. He was created a Viscount in 1983.
[15] *The Home Office: Perspectives on Policy and Administration*, RIPA, London, 1983, p. 13. James Callaghan was Home Secretary, 1967–70.

Secretaries are grossly overworked, although most will have found their own ways of keeping their heads above water. Nor are officials immune from the narrowing of vision which comes from consistent overwork. Reputations outside the Office, however, are not built upon application to paperwork or the efficiency with which business is dispatched. No one could question the diligence of Maxwell Fyfe,[16] Soskice, or Brooke as Home Secretary, but their reputations have suffered grievously from lack of vision and flair.

A further inhibiting factor on the Home Secretary's freedom of action is the pressure on Parliamentary time available to the Government to get its legislative programme enacted. Other ministers stake out their claims, urged on by their civil servants. Even within the Home Office, one of the most heavyweight of all Whitehall Departments, the Secretary of State will have to set his own priorities between immigration and nationality, criminal justice, national security, gambling, the fire service, Sunday trading, dangerous dogs, and many other topics for legislation, some of which may be urgent, and most of which will be controversial.

The portrayal so far is of national politics painted with a broad brush, giving a picture lacking in definition and detail. To add perspective, we can visualize a Home Secretary taking office, conscious of the weight of tradition, and the reservoir of inherited expertise from which departmentally generated policies are drawn. The day-to-day routine of the Home Office in supervising prisons, the Probation Service and the police, including the handling of prisoners' petitions and applications for the Royal Prerogative of Mercy, gives it a fund of practical experience of how the law is working and what changes ought to be thought about.

Partly due to its history, and partly to temperament, the Home Office is conservative procedurally and cautious in outlook.[17] Pre-

---

[16] R. A. Butler's remark about his former Cabinet colleague, Sir David Maxwell Fyfe (later Lord Kilmuir), was made only after the latter's death: 'He may have been living proof that Carlyle was wrong to define genius as a transcendent capacity for taking trouble; but he did have a most astounding appetite for and application to paper work, which he often carried to bed with him ...' *The Art of the Possible: The Memoirs of Lord Butler*, Hamish Hamilton, London, 1971, p. 144.

[17] Although obtained from a different standpoint, my own experience largely corresponds with the impressions gained by Paul Rock. See his analysis of the Home Office as a still centre in *Helping Victims of Crime: The Home Office and the Rise of Victim Support in England and Wales*, Clarendon Press, Oxford, 1990, pp. 7–18. Paul Rock is Professor of Sociology at the London School of Economics and a former member of the Parole Board.

cedent counts for much, especially in the dreadfully slow handling
of individual cases. Caution may arise from the civil servants'
commendable desire to protect their minister from criticism or embarrassment, but it may also result from ministerial reluctance to
contemplate unpopular options. Financial restraints limit the scope
for many otherwise appealing new departures, although the down-
ward pressure on public expenditure is not confined to the Home
Office. What is peculiar, even unique compared with other departments of government, is a special brand of stuffiness. There is a
premium on thoroughness and accuracy. Every avenue must be
explored and each of the alternatives fully considered. This takes
time, and calls for contributions from different parts of the Office,
as well as elsewhere in Whitehall. In the interests of sound administration, it is claimed, all of the financial, practical, and other
consequences of a course of action must be properly worked out.
The process cannot be skimped.

Through this dense mesh, proposals for change must pass. In
attributing origins it is hard to disentangle the input of ministers
and that of officials, or the operational services, political or Parliamentary influences, or interest groups; nor does the present civil
service culture encourage any attempt to do so. Generally speaking,
most ministers rely on others for most of their ideas. Examples of
internally generated policy proposals can be seen in the formative
thinking on crime prevention, with a strong research base, in the
1970s and 1980s; the development of an alternative to the Royal
Commission on Criminal Procedure's plan for the organization of
an independent prosecution service; proposals for modifying the
'right of silence', incorporating new safeguards for the defence; and
efforts to improve the situation of ethnic minorities in the criminal
justice system. Not all of these initiatives were welcomed initially
by ministers; indeed in some instances they were greeted with
scepticism bordering on suspicion. But they were sustained and
developed, with ministerial acquiescence, eventually obtaining
varying degrees of support.

Internal generation, the energy and will to bring forward proposals for change, or to adopt them from outside, and persevering
in the face of criticism or indifference, is a crucial element in the
policy-making process. The characteristic contribution of the senior
civil servant lies not so much in the originality and imagination he
or she may display in thinking up new policies—these can be a

positive nuisance without the ability to convince and lead those, often outside the service, who will have to put them into effect— but the skills to recognize promising new ideas and the opportunities to develop them, and to exploit the opportunities when they occur.[18]

When it comes to considering legislation, as in managing his Department, the minister soon faces the first test of the statesman: the reconciliation of political ideology and opinion to the demands of sharply practical situations. Established ways of doing things are not easily changed; current policies cannot be reversed without disruption; internal and external patterns of relationship are resistant to rapid dismantling. He discovers very quickly that there are no short cuts. Only difficult decisions. Practical constraints crowd round him to limit his room for manœuvre. Wherever he turns he finds there is very little uncommitted money to fund new policies. At times he feels that the most he can hope for is to identify some fissures in the accumulating mass of proposals in their formative stages into which he can try to insert something of his own political values.

The process of fusing ministerial intentions and departmental expertise in the formulation of policy is a great deal more subtle than it appears to be at first sight. Proposals seldom spring from a single source, although it is not unknown for them to do so.[19] In parallel with the manifesto or other commitments of incoming ministers, Home Office officials will have prepared a list of such internally generated proposals as are ripe for implementation. Some of these may be of long standing, an example being an improvement in the standard of fire precautions in places of public resort. Necessary as legislation was in terms of public safety, for years it was unattractive to ministers since it required considerable expenditure whilst at the same time being unlikely to attract any votes.[20] More

---

[18] For a perceptive commentary on the relationship between Home Office officials and ministers, see David Faulkner in Home Office Papers by Senior Officers, *Continuity and Change in the Home Office*, Occasional Papers in Administrative Studies, No. 2, 1991, pp. 13–15.

[19] Baroness Wootton of Abinger's championship of the idea of community service orders as an additional sentence available to the courts is noted in Chapter 3. Another example was the first experimental bail hostel, organized by the Salvation Army at the expense of a private individual interested in penal affairs.

[20] During his tenure as Permanent Under-Secretary of State at the Home Office (1966–72), Lord Allen of Abbeydale had urged on successive Home Secretaries legislation to provide greater protection against fire risks, until Reginald Maudling

often ministers are attracted to what is novel, makes only a limited demand on financial resources, and is not already identified with someone else. Brittan on reparation, Waddington on victims, and Baker on dangerous dogs, joy riding, and offending on bail, were all examples of this dictum.

Next there is the proverbial shelf containing what one veteran bureaucrat has aptly called the harvest of the work of various advisory bodies and departmental committees.[21] Although governments do not always adopt their recommendations, specialist committees are often a necessary device to investigate the practical implications of proposals for change. In matters of law reform especially, expert reviews constitute a methodology which broadens the range and depth of enquiry, at the same time enabling the subject to be reviewed from a more independent viewpoint. In the course of a Second Reading Debate on the contentious Courts and Legal Services Bill in December 1989, Lord Hailsham spoke scathingly about the fact that the bulk of the proposals arose from within the Government machine, so disregarding 'almost every principle of the methodology... which ought to be followed in law reform'.[22]

The final element in the policy-making process is the response to events over which governments have no control. The Home Office is not alone among government departments in facing challenge from the courts. On an application for judicial review, the High Court may decide that the Secretary of State has exceeded the powers conferred on him by Parliament, or acted in a way that was irrational or procedurally unfair. If so, changes in practice or in the legislation may be required. The possibility of judicial review is constantly in the mind of ministers and officials when preparing legislation and putting it into effect. No statutory formula has been found that can make a provision judge-proof, in the sense of

---

was persuaded to introduce what became the Fire Precautions Act 1971. The Act strengthened the law relating to fire precautions in places of public entertainment and resort and certain kinds of residential premises. It did not apply to premises such as offices, shops, and railway premises which were covered by existing legislation. The main instrument of control was the fire certificate.

[21] Lord Allen of Abbeydale, 'Reflections of a Bureaucrat' in *The Home Office: Perspectives on Policy and Administration*, p. 34.

[22] Hailsham's strictures did not apply to that part of the Bill which was based on the results of a Civil Justice Review set up by himself when Lord Chancellor. *Parl. Debates*, HL, 514 (5th ser.), cols 150–1, 19 Dec. 1989.

inducing the courts to accept it as excluding all opportunity for review, not even providing that a decision 'shall not be called in question in any court of law'.[23]

At the preparatory stage in drafting legislation civil servants will try to find a way of indicating Parliament's intentions as to the sort of considerations of policy or fact that are to be treated as properly relevant to the decision, and the procedural requirements to be observed, but without tying the minister's hands too tightly in situations which cannot be foreseen. Although normally the courts will be reluctant to intervene in 'matters depending essentially on political judgment',[24] the prospect of challenge in the Divisional Court is one that any minister exercising a statutory power, or any official advising on such a decision, is bound to keep in mind. Guidance on the circumspection required in the day-to-day exercise of administrative powers is provided for civil servants in a booklet ominously entitled *The Judge over your Shoulder*. Judicial review of administrative decisions by central or local government and certain other bodies is now commonplace. In both 1989 and 1990 leave to apply for judicial review was granted by the courts in more than 900 cases, with a resulting delay of about eighteen months between the granting of leave and the hearing of the case.[25]

Coincidental with the growth of judicial review by the domestic courts has been the growth in the volume of applications by private individuals seeking redress from the European Commission and Court of Human Rights at Strasbourg. If an application is declared admissible, and a friendly settlement cannot be achieved, the sub-sequent decisions of the Court are binding on the United Kingdom. The enforcement of the Convention on Human Rights and Funda-mental Freedoms is the subject of Chapter 8. It has led to changes in the law on the continued confinement of restricted mental patients;[26] the release of discretionary life-sentence prisoners;[27] and regulations on the marriage of prisoners,[28] their correspondence,[29]

---

[23] *Anisminic Ltd* v. *Foreign Compensation Commission* [1969] 2 AC 147.
[24] *Hammersmith and Fulham London Borough Council* v. *Secretary of State for the Environment* [1990] 3 All ER 589 per Lord Bridge of Harwich at 637.
[25] *The Times*, 5 May 1992.
[26] *X* v. *The United Kingdom* (1982) 4 EHRR 188.
[27] *Thynne, Wilson and Gunnell* v. *The United Kingdom* (1991) 13 EHHR 666.
[28] *Hamer* v. *The United Kingdom* (1981) 4 EHRR 139.
[29] *Silver* v. *The United Kingdom* (1983) 5 EHRR 347.

and access to lawyers.[30] Revisions have also been made to the prison disciplinary code.[31]

The two streams may on occasion converge. As a result of challenges to the previous practice, both in the High Court and the European Court of Human Rights, telephone tapping has been subject to legislation since 1986.[32] The tapping of any telephone call now requires the authority of the Home Secretary conferred by means of a warrant which must be approved (and is normally signed) by him personally. Any information so discovered must be confined to the authority empowered by the warrant to discover it, and may not be disclosed to private persons or private bodies. In practice, information gained by interception is only used for the purpose of assisting police or Security Service investigations, and is not tendered as evidence in court.

III

These are the main tributaries from which the flood of initiatives to alter the course of criminal justice derive. Each calls for political decision, frequently more than once in the course of hammering out a policy. It is at this stage ministers must make their distinctive contribution. Officials, the party political organization, assorted advisory committees, outside commentators, and special interest groups may all be clamouring for action, but they seldom do so with one voice. A successful Home Secretary needs enough versatility and openness of mind to listen to what is said before making a choice between tinkering with the status quo and the more radical alternatives which are open to him. Indecisiveness, insufficient

[30] *Golder* v. *The United Kingdom* (1979–80) 1 EHRR 524.
[31] *Campbell and Fell* v. *The United Kingdom* (1985) 7 EHRR 165.
[32] James Malone, a Surrey antiques dealer, was charged in March 1977 with handling stolen goods, but was ultimately acquitted. It emerged at the trial that a telephone conversation between him and another person had been intercepted. In Feb. 1979 the Vice-Chancellor (Sir Robert Megarry) dismissed an action in which Mr Malone sought a declaration that the interception was unlawful; see *Malone* v. *Commissioner of Police of the Metropolis (No. 2)* [1979] 2 All ER 620. In August 1984, however, the Strasbourg Court held that there had been a violation of Article 8 of the European Convention on Human Rights (protection of privacy); see *Malone* v. *The United Kingdom* (1985) 7 EHRR 14. The Interception of Communications Act 1985, which came into force on 10 Apr. 1986, put both telephone tapping and the interception of mail on a statutory basis.

financial resources, a hostile press, the inability to count on sufficient political support, and lack of creative imagination are the negative factors which will bear on his personal decision. Moreover, any adept Home Office minister knows that continuity has to coexist with innovation. The interdependence of criminal justice, where the working of one part has an effect on what happens in the other parts, means that to set off too fast, or prematurely, in a given direction, may lead to unexpected reverses. To an incoming minister, who may owe his appointment more to adeptness in handling argument on paper or on the floor of the House of Commons, such inhibitions can come as an unwelcome surprise.

With the power to select between policy alternatives; with direct authority over his department and some, although not all, of the component parts of the system of criminal justice, but exercising strong influence over other parts; the Home Secretary still possesses unmatched opportunities for individual decision-making. To take full advantage of these positive factors he needs to deploy the accumulated knowledge of his officials, married to presentational skills, tenacity, and a sound grasp of tactics. Important though each of these qualities is for his survival in office, they are over-shadowed by that most prized of all political virtues: knowing where he wants to go.

Little that is unfathomable or startling passes through the mind of a minister preparing legislation. Personalities vary, but typically he will be guided as much by intuition and personal judgment as by precept or regulation as he surveys the political landscape he must traverse before reaching his destination. The chapters of this book recount the way in which Home Secretaries from both of the main parties handled their assignments between 1947 and 1979 and, in more detail, during the long period of Conservative Administration between 1979 and 1992. Other ministers at other times may have acted differently, but the legislative context is one that would be familiar to them all.

Four features stand out above all else. First are ministers' relations with their own party, in Parliament and the constituencies. Then there is the constant attention given to the more vociferous organs of populist opinion, in particular the tabloid and middle market press. Such awareness does not govern everything a Home Secretary does or says in public, but it will never be far from his thoughts. Less pressing, but still ubiquitous, is a sensitivity towards the reactions, actual or anticipated, of the higher judiciary. Finally the views of fellow ministers need to be heeded, most notably those of the Prime Minister.

General elections provide regular milestones in the evolution of party policies, especially on matters falling under the rubric of law and order. As they draw near the necessity to publish proposals in the form of a manifesto concentrates the minds of ministers and party leaders on the future. If success follows at the polls, legislative programmes then have to be drawn up to implement the new Government's undertakings.[33] Thereafter meetings of members of the Cabinet will be held from time to time, complemented by advisers and policy units, in order to review progress. While the public may be cynical about electoral promises, governments of whatever complexion customarily take pains to demonstrate that they have carried out the main proposals embodied in their manifesto,[34] as well as other commitments or 'pledges' given at election time. A small, but characteristic, exchange recorded in Richard Crossman's diaries reads as follows:

... as I have often noted in this diary, Harold [Wilson] is extraordinarily sensitive on the issue of Party pledges, and when I approached him privately he said, 'This is a party pledge which has to be fulfilled'.[35]

Between elections the paramount need for any Home Secretary is to maintain the support of his own party members, a task made harder in each of the major parties by the fact that local party workers often hold more extreme views on what should be done than do ministers. Even the most popular personalities, as William Whitelaw was in 1981, can run into difficulty. As he candidly admitted in his memoirs the issue of capital punishment, which resurfaced in that year at the Conservative Party Conference, and his own handling of the debate, damaged his standing as Home

[33] Civil servants customarily study the policy statements made by the main parties at elections and have detailed submissions ready for the incoming ministers suggesting how their political commitments can best be translated into legislative or administrative form.

[34] The drafting of a manifesto in such a way as to appeal to the electorate without giving too many hostages to fortune if returned to office is an arcane skill possessed by few politicians. Christopher Patten, Conservative Party Chairman, 1990–2, gained this experience while Director of the Conservative Research Department, 1974–9.

[35] *The Diaries of a Cabinet Minister* (vol. 1), Hamish Hamilton/Jonathan Cape, London, 1975, pp. 420–1.

Secretary, making it more difficult to introduce some planned reforms in sentencing policy:

I certainly both dreaded and disliked the prospect of the law and order debate, for the atmosphere was so strangely hostile and so different from that accorded to all one's colleagues ... pressure and even bullying by so-called 'hangers and floggers' served only to force Conservative MPs who were against hanging to stand up for what they believed to be right. It was therefore a diversion from some crucial issues, such as sentencing and prison overcrowding.[36]

Twenty years earlier, R. A. Butler had shared the same fate, recalling the 'blood curdling demands' made annually at the Conservative Party Conference for the restoration of corporal punishment which had 'quite clouded' his time as Chairman of the Party.[37] Capital and corporal punishment, to which majorities in the House of Commons had consistently been opposed, long remained at or near to the top of the short but touchy list of policy issues separating Conservative ministers from their party followers. More often it is a matter of tone and stance. Irrespective of party, Home Secretaries are well aware that there are occasions when they are expected to appear 'tough' and take care to adjust their vocabulary and presentation according to their audience. The effect of this imperative on successive Tory Home Secretaries when legislation was in preparation comes through clearly in later chapters.

It is not only their own party supporters, inside and outside Parliament, that ministers watch with care. While policy is in the formative stages there is a constant worry over how a particular initiative, or response to a crisis, will appear in the mass media. Although the substance of a decision may not be altered materially, it may be trimmed with the timing of its announcement, or the explanations offered, being geared to the anticipated reception by populist opinion, especially as evidenced by the press. Prediction is made hazardous because of the volatility and diversity of the press. There is an inconvenient possibility that the quality, mid-market, and tabloid papers will take contrary stances making it necessary to select which readership is more important for the purpose.

[36] *The Whitelaw Memoirs*, p. 196.
[37] *The Art of the Possible*, p. 201. Butler was Home Secretary, 1957–62 and Chairman of the Conservative Party, 1959–61.

Without being too censorious about the effects of presentational considerations on policy, the consequences can be double-edged. Short-term advantage gained at the price of keeping alive prejudices and misconceptions may make more difficult, or even preclude, later changes in the direction of policy.

The stereotype of toughness also flourishes at the grass roots in party circles. In Parliament, as on constituency platforms, Conservative ministers know they are constantly under scrutiny by some of the more outspoken of their colleagues for any signs of 'wetness'. Although in common use throughout the Thatcher years, the expression is not easy to define. In this context being 'wet' embraces what is seen as an insufficiency of robustness in outlook; a suspicion that overmuch interest is being directed towards the treatment of the convicted offender at the expense of the plight of the victim; and a distaste for the infliction of physical forms of punishment. It is a paradox that the more ministers learn about the complex and uncertain causes and circumstances of crime, the less dogmatic they become in their opinions at the very moment when, as Whitelaw found to his cost, they become most vulnerable to censure by their own supporters.

Each week when the House is sitting the Home Secretary will confer with the officers of his party's Home Affairs Committee. The discussion customarily takes place in the early evening in the Home Secretary's room at the Commons, and is intended to keep him in touch with back-bench opinion. Ministerial contacts of this kind are supplemented by the activities of the junior ministers, the Parliamentary Private Secretaries, and the Government Whips. Although less visible, these exchanges are as important to a minister as the ritual confrontations in the Chamber. Backed by a comfortable working majority, which successive Conservative Administrations enjoyed between 1979 and 1992, any competent Home Secretary has little to fear from the party opposite. The Opposition invariably will exploit opportunities to denounce the Government and all its works. Provided a minister can maintain an effective performance in the House, the Whips see to it that he will get his way. The critics he must satisfy sit behind him.

The tabloid press tries hard to make a Home Secretary's life a misery. Strident in tone, punitive in outlook, and personalizing issues in ways that can cause great distress to individuals, the tabloids are the stocks of the modern age. At the same time, exposure in the press is a powerful weapon against the abuse of authority and wrongdoing. The very fact they are bought and read daily by millions of people gives mass circulation newspapers an undeniable political role. The views expressed may or may not be shared by their readerships, but they are invested with a special status by virtue of numbers. The same is true of the mid-market press and the quality newspapers. The arguments advanced may be somewhat more refined and the ideals more lofty, but here again it is the size of the readership, rather than the merits of the editorial comment, that counts most.

In democratic societies it is inevitable that politicians will be attracted to large audiences. Readers are simultaneously voters; what appeals to them will be of compelling interest to those who need to do the appealing at election time. Stephen Koss's verdict on the political press during the twentieth century applies with equal force to its impact on the operation of criminal justice: 'At its worst, the political press had mischievously fanned passions and fed prejudices. At its best it had focused ideas and inculcated democratic values.'[38]

IV

Journalists inhabit the outer fringes of the world of politics. They meet politicians frequently inside and outside the lobby of the House of Commons. It does neither any harm to be seen to be trying to influence the other. It is all part of the job. Ministers ensure that there are well-staffed press offices to promote the most favourable reception for their policies and decisions.[39] Special relationships with chosen journalists, their editors and proprietors, are cultivated. Bribery apart, there is almost no method of persuasion which is considered to be out of bounds. The contrast with judicial contacts is pronounced. Here it is thought proper to preserve a respectful distance on both sides. Even in private encounters, judges do not discuss their cases with politicians, and in return

[38] S. Koss, *The Rise and Fall of the Political Press in Britain*, vol. 2, *The Twentieth Century*, Hamish Hamilton, London, 1984, p. 684.
[39] In February 1992 the Home Office listed twenty-one Information Officers employed in its Press Office. *News Release* 21/92, 12 Feb. 1992.

politicians should avoid embarrassing judges by involving them in what are essentially political issues.

The dividing line is not easily drawn. When a judge, particularly one with Lord Scarman's breadth of mind, is appointed to inquire into an outbreak of violence and serious disorders on the streets of Brixton and the policing of the area,[40] it is unrealistic to expect him to avoid any recommendations of a political nature as to the causes. Similarly, it can be anticipated that a judge investigating a disaster at a football ground in which ninety-five people have been crushed to death will reach out into public policy in putting forward ways of avoiding such tragedies in the future.[41] Lord Justice Woolf's inquiry into the serious disturbances that erupted at Strangeways and other prisons in the spring of 1990 extended beyond the immediate causes to an examination of such underlying factors as prison overcrowding, conditions and regimes, and policies towards remand prisoners.[42] The more serious the incident, the more likely it is that a judge's professional neutrality and independence, as well as his legal training in taking evidence and establishing the facts, will be sought so as to command public confidence. Yet it is in identifying the lessons for public policy that the more enduring value of judicial inquiries often lies.

The dissociation between the executive and the judiciary is the legacy of the independence granted to the judiciary in the Act of Settlement.[43] Judges are bound to uphold the rights of the individual against the Crown, which in this context is now virtually synonymous with the Government of the day. In the administration of criminal justice the principle of independence from the wishes of government is of supreme importance. Anyone who is accused of committing a crime is entitled to the protection of the due process of law, not enshrined in any written statute as in the

[40] *The Brixton Disorders 10–12 April 1981*, Report of an Inquiry by Lord Scarman (Cmnd. 8427), HMSO, London, 1981 (reprinted 1986).
[41] *The Hillsborough Stadium Disaster 15 April 1989*, Inquiry by Lord Justice Taylor, Final Report (Cm. 962), HMSO, London, 1990. The Report expressed 'grave doubts' about the feasibility of a national membership scheme contained in the Football Spectators Act 1989 and 'serious misgivings about its likely impact on public safety', p. 75. Lord Taylor of Gosforth succeeded Lord Lane as Lord Chief Justice in April 1992.
[42] *Prison Disturbances April 1990*, Report of an Inquiry by Lord Justice Woolf and Judge Stephen Tumim (Cm. 1456), HMSO, London, 1991.
[43] See O. Hood Phillips and P. Jackson, *Constitutional and Administrative Law* (7th edn.), Sweet and Maxwell, London, 1987, p. 387.

Constitution of the United States, but dependent upon convention and common law tradition. Ever since the thirteenth century a criminal offence, being an infringement of the King's peace, has been seen as a direct injury to the sovereign. This is why prosecutions are brought in the name of the Crown. During the last century they came to be conducted largely by the police and lawyers instructed by them, who were replaced for most purposes by the Crown Prosecution Service in 1986.

The right of a private individual or an agency other than the Crown Prosecution Service to institute and conduct criminal proceedings on their own behalf was preserved by Section 6(1) of the Prosecution of Offences Act 1985. Statutory or voluntary agencies such as HM Customs and Excise, the Inland Revenue, the Department of Social Security, the Health and Safety Executive, and the RSPCA regularly initiate prosecutions in the criminal courts.[44] Prosecutions by private individuals are much rarer, being brought mainly by aggrieved parties. In either type of case the Director of Public Prosecutions has the power to take over the proceedings at any stage, either by conducting them himself or discontinuing them. Of its own motion the court may decide to bring a private prosecution to the attention of the Crown Prosecution Service; indeed a justices' clerk is obliged to do so if a private prosecutor withdraws or fails to proceed in circumstances in which the reason given appears unsatisfactory.[45]

Since virtually all of the agencies which regularly institute criminal proceedings have acquired their own expertise, they are generally well enough equipped to conduct cases and the Crown Prosecution Service will 'neither wish nor need to intervene'.[46] Prosecutions brought by determined private individuals may present greater problems. The Director will not intervene lightly, since it was the intention of the statute to preserve the right of an individual to have some recourse. Yet awkward circumstances can arise, sometimes raising questions of abuse of process. In the case of *Turner*, a convicted defendant initiated a prosecution against his accomplice, who had obtained a prior undertaking from the Director that he

---

[44] I am grateful to K. R. Ashken, Head of Policy and Information Division, the Crown Prosecution Service, for supplying the information upon which this passage is based.

[45] Prosecution of Offences Act 1985, Section 7(4).

[46] Letter from K. R. Ashken, 4 July 1990.

would not be prosecuted for his part in the offence. The Director's action in intervening to offer no evidence, on the ground that it was not in the interests of justice or the public for the prosecution to continue, was upheld by the courts.[47] In another case, the Court of Appeal held that a prosecution had been properly discontinued when a defendant had taken out a private prosecution for perjury against a witness who had given evidence against him at committal proceedings.[48]

Some well-ventilated cases turn on conflicting interpretations of the public interest. An example was a private prosecution brought by Mrs Mary Whitehouse[49] against a National Theatre director on charges of gross indecency in the staging of a play titled *The Romans in Britain*. In this instance Mrs Whitehouse had drawn the play to the attention of the Director, and instituted proceedings only after he had declined to prosecute. Her argument was that simulated sexual acts on the stage, an attempted scene of male rape, were not only offensive but constituted a criminal offence under Section 13 of the Sexual Offences Act 1956. Eighteen months after the prosecution had been launched, and amidst much controversy over artistic expression and theatrical censorship, the case reached the Central Criminal Court in March 1982. The point of law was never decided, since leading counsel for Mrs Whitehouse withdrew the prosecution and the Attorney General then terminated the case by invoking the *nolle prosequi* procedure, leaving each side claiming victory.[50]

In 1988 Ian Brady and Myra Hindley, both serving life sentences for murder, were back in the headlines when the Greater Manchester Police reopened the Moors murders case and discovered the body

---

[47] *Turner* v. *DPP* (1979) 68 Cr. App. R. 70.

[48] *Raymond* v. *Attorney General* (1982) 75 Cr. App. R. 34.

[49] General Secretary of the National Viewers' and Listeners' Association, 1965–80, and President since 1980. In 1977 Mrs Whitehouse had initiated a private prosecution against *Gay News* and its editor for blasphemous libel. The magazine had published a poem written as if by a homosexual Roman centurion, describing his feelings towards Christ after the crucifixion. The DPP took over the prosecution and, on conviction, *Gay News* was fined £1,000. The Editor received a suspended sentence of nine months' imprisonment (quashed by the Court of Appeal) and was fined £500 (the fine was sustained). The convictions were upheld by the House of Lords in *Whitehouse* v. *Lemon* [1979] AC 617, and later by the European Commission of Human Rights in *Gay News Ltd and Lemon* v. *The United Kingdom* (1983) 5 EHRR 123.

[50] See *The Times*, 19 Mar. 1982.

of another child. A report was submitted to the Director who declined to prosecute on public interest grounds. When Oldham Magistrates granted summonses against Brady and Hindley for the murder of the child following a private application, the Director, having already decided that in all the circumstances it would not be in the public interest to institute proceedings against them, used his statutory powers under Section 6(2) of the Prosecution of Offences Act 1985 to take over the conduct of the case and to discontinue it under Section 23(3).[51]

Decisions on prosecution can also be treacherous ground for the Law Officers. The Attorney General and Solicitor General (and the Lord Advocate and Solicitor General for Scotland), are members of the Government. Despite holding political appointments, in all matters of criminal prosecution they must act independently of the interests of government. Political prosecutions and political imprisonment may be deemed so far in the past as to be without modern day relevance. But it has not always been so, and there are occasions when the perennial justification of the overriding interests of the security of the state re-emerges into public view. The continued liberty of the subject demands vigilance on the part of the judges in ensuring that no trial on a criminal charge, or appeal, bears any trace of being biased towards an outcome which the Government wants to see. Terrorist offences, which do not fit easily into systems of justice devised for other purposes, make it doubly important that this ideal is preserved. It is also vital at times of national emergency such as during the miners' strike in 1984/5.

The most sensitive boundary of all between the executive, in the shape of ministers, and the judiciary, in the shape of the Lord Chief Justice and puisne judges of the Queen's Bench Division, is the sentencing of offenders. With very few exceptions the rule is that Parliament determines the maximum penalty and it is then for the courts, having listened to the evidence, and seen the defendant in person, and heard what can be said in mitigation on his behalf, to decide upon the appropriate punishment in all the circumstances of the case. The constitutional separation does not prevent some Members of Parliament echoing the condemnation of the tabloid press in intemperately criticizing individual judges for what they may consider to be an unduly lenient sentence. It is rare, if not

[51] Letter from K. R. Ashken, 4 July 1990.

unknown, for the same voices to be heard if a sentence is too severe, although the Criminal Division of the Court of Appeal frequently reduces sentences for just that reason.

In practice the only exceptions to judicial sentencing are fixed penalties and obligatory disqualification for certain Road Traffic offences,[52] the mandatory destruction of a dog following the conviction of an offender under provisions contained in the Dangerous Dogs Act 1991, and the penalty of life imprisonment for murder. Where the conviction is murder the sentence is determined by Parliament and simply pronounced by the judge. The courts may also impose a discretionary life sentence for certain other serious crimes. Appeal against any non-mandatory sentence requires the leave of the Court of Appeal (Criminal Division), or of a single High Court judge acting on its behalf. Since 1988 the Crown has also been able to appeal in certain circumstances against lenient sentences. Under Section 36 of the Criminal Justice Act 1988, where it appears to the Attorney General that the sentencing of a person in the Crown Court has been unduly lenient he may refer the case to the Court of Appeal, with leave, for the sentence to be reviewed. On such a reference, the Court of Appeal may quash the sentence, or substitute such sentence as it thinks appropriate within the limits permitted to the court below. The legislative history of this provision is recorded in Chapter 4.

Although the actual sentence passed by the court is out of the reach of legislators and departmental officials, sentencing policy occupies a no man's land between territories claimed by government and the judiciary. Whereas there is general acceptance that the apportionment of punishment is a judicial function, the legal framework of penalties is the creation of Parliament. Maximum penalties, and occasionally fixed penalties, are set out in statutes and periodically revised. Parliament may, as it did in the Criminal Justice Act 1991, lay down criteria governing the use of custody

---

[52] Under Part III of the Road Traffic Offenders Act 1988, a person whom a police officer or authorized traffic warden believes to have committed an offence listed in Schedule 3 (ranging from speeding offences to infringements of parking regulations) may be given notice that he is liable to pay a fixed penalty. The alleged offender then has the option (exercisable within twenty-one days) of either paying the penalty or requesting a hearing by a court. Under Section 34(1) of the same Act, where a person is convicted of an offence involving obligatory disqualification, the court must order him to be disqualified for at least twelve months unless for special reasons it thinks fit to order a shorter period or not to order him to be disqualified.

and the length of custodial sentences. Earlier legislation paved the way by limiting the use of custody as a penalty for offenders under the age of twenty-one.[53] The Labour Party, backed by a sizeable body of informed opinion, wanted to go further and establish a sentencing council (with strong judicial representation) to define sentencing aims and policies and to produce guide-lines for sentencing over 'a range of cases in an interrelated structure'.[54]

Throughout the 1980s the expanding prison population caused Home Office administrators to question how long it would be possible to go on supplying an unlimited number of places, at enormous cost, for however many convicted or remand prisoners were sent to them by the courts. It was this factor more than any other which caused officials and ministers alike to adopt such defensive postures. With the exception of Douglas Hurd's Indian summer lasting for about two years after the 1987 election,[55] the prevailing mood in the Home Office was one of institutional pessimism. More positive thinking survived in one or two parts of the monolithic building in Queen Anne's Gate, but the overall impression gained by outside observers was of a dispirited department in which no one really seemed to know what could be done about crime in general and the prisons in particular. The most that could be expected of policies, it was implied, was to moderate the worst effects of criminal offending.

[53] Section 1(4) of the Criminal Justice Act 1982, as amended by Section 123 of the Criminal Justice Act 1988, provided that a custodial sentence might be passed on an offender under the age of twenty-one only if the circumstances, including the nature and the gravity of the offence, were such that, if the offender were aged twenty-one or over, the court would pass a sentence of imprisonment; and then only if at least one of three further conditions was satisfied. These were that the offender had a history of failure to respond to non-custodial penalties and was unable or unwilling to respond to them; that only a custodial sentence would be adequate to protect the public from serious harm from him; or that the offence was so serious that a non-custodial sentence for it could not be justified.

[54] *A Safer Britain: Labour's White Paper on Criminal Justice*, The Labour Party, London, 1990, p. 14. The fate of this proposal in the 1990/1 legislation is noted in Chapter 9.

[55] Hurd's attempt to create a longer-term sense of direction and purpose crystallized in the policy of punishment in the community described in Chapters 5 and 9.

V

Just as the Home Secretary is inhibited in policy-making by Parliament, his party, public opinion, the judiciary, and the courts, so is the freedom of action of the Home Office restricted within the Whitehall bureaucracy. There is constant pressure from the Treasury, and to some extent from 10 Downing Street, for limiting public expenditure, and for increased efficiency and the more effective use of resources. Few in the Treasury believed that it really was impossible to control the prison population if ministers were sufficiently determined. Nor was the Treasury convinced by the repeated arguments for the costly increases in police manpower which most Home Secretaries felt they had to secure in order to demonstrate their credibility. The open-ended commitment to a vastly expensive discretionary scheme for criminal injuries compensation, sanctioned by statute in 1988 but not yet brought into force at the time of writing, was a particular Treasury *bête noire*, leading to pressure to cut back on other things if ministers maintained that it was politically unacceptable to curtail the cost.

The hand of the Treasury is never far away. The Chancellor of the Exchequer will expect to be a member of the Cabinet Committee considering important legislation in any field, including criminal justice, although if at a particular meeting the main Treasury interest lies in resource costs the Chief Secretary to the Treasury might go in his place. Because of other demands on his time, the Chancellor will not usually be a leading participant on a regular basis. But in some cases his role will be more active. For example, Nigel Lawson chaired the sub-committee that dealt with Lord Mackay's proposals for reforming the legal system which were later embodied in the Courts and Legal Services Bill. Because of his responsibilities for taxation as well as the banking system and building societies, the Chancellor had a special interest in the subject of financial fraud. Hence Lawson also chaired an *ad hoc* group of ministers which led to the setting up of the Serious Fraud Office.

Like other ministers, Chancellors do not confine themselves solely to matters where they have a departmental interest. They may hold views on issues which derive from previous experience. As an ex-financial journalist,[56] Lawson had opinions about the limitations of trial by jury formed by what he had seen of financial scandals when working as a City editor. It was partly because of this experience that he had no hesitation in supporting whole-heartedly the Roskill recommendation to depart from the principle of jury trial in complex fraud cases,[57] against the (ultimately successful) Home Office view advocated by Hurd.

Although the issue of fraud trials was one in which Mrs Thatcher also took a personal interest, she did not normally intervene on the details of criminal policy. There is no record that the Prime Minister had ever visited a prison, but she was known to be offended by the deplorable conditions and personal indignities caused by over-crowding. Over her eleven-year premiership the only substantial issue of penal policy in which Mrs Thatcher played a decisive part was the privatization of prisons and remand centres, and the contracting out of certain criminal justice services.

The views of his ministerial colleagues, not least the Prime Minister, will be of particular relevance whenever a subject overruns departmental boundaries and the Home Office is competing for Parliamentary time. This commodity is always in short supply and it is hard fought for, especially after a general election when an order of priority has to be set in the legislative programme for fulfilling manifesto and other pledges. In the all-important matter of resources, the Prime Minister's outlook can be decisive. If law and order is seen as a key issue it will strengthen the Home Secretary's arm in his dealings with the Treasury. Once legislative proposals are sufficiently advanced to be put to ministers for endorsement they will go before the Ministerial Committee on Legislation[58] which must give its approval before a place is found in the programme. Even before that stage is reached, the Cabinet Office will have been monitoring the progress of the more significant proposals by departments in order to alert the Prime Minister or

[56] A member of the editorial staff of the *Financial Times*, 1956–60, and City editor of the *Sunday Telegraph*, 1961–3, Lawson was Chancellor of the Exchequer, 1983–9, and was created a life peer as Lord Lawson of Blaby in 1992.

[57] Letter from Nigel Lawson MP, 17 Jan. 1990.

[58] The composition of the Ministerial Committee on Legislation and its terms of reference, together with details of other Standing Ministerial Committees, were made public by John Major 'in the interests of greater openness about the machinery of Government' shortly after the 1992 General Election. *Parl. Debates*, HC, 208 (6th ser.), col. WA 114, 19 May 1992.

Lord President of the Council of any wider implications. The Prime Minister personally will authorize the inclusion of each commitment to legislate in the Queen's Speech.

Prime Ministerial power also makes itself felt in less direct, although crucial, ways. Like all ministers, the Home Secretary must maintain the Prime Minister's confidence if he is to continue in office. Dismissal on grounds of incompetence or political differences is far less common than sudden transfers of ministers to other departments as a result of events quite unconnected with their policies or performance. At the very moment when Hurd was preparing to unveil the fruits of a long period of gestation in the form of a White Paper on criminal justice, Lawson resigned as Chancellor.[59] After only three months at the Foreign Office, John Major, previously Chief Secretary, was brought back to the Treasury as Chancellor, leaving the Foreign Secretaryship unexpectedly vacant. Hurd, a former career diplomat and Foreign Office Minister of State, was the obvious choice as his successor.[60] In this way, one of the best Home Secretaries of the post-war era was abruptly removed from the Home Office at a few hours notice, leaving behind a collection of unfinished artefacts to be completed by other hands.

VI

In the absence of a Ministry of Justice the Home Office has acquired its responsibilities for criminal justice piecemeal over many years. It does not let go of them easily, and an aura of permanence and continuity is evidence of its tenacity. Over the period covered by this book new rivals have appeared on the Whitehall scene. Until comparatively recently the list of Home Office functions summarized earlier in this chapter would have been longer than it now is. It would have included responsibility for the finance, organization,

---

[59] His resignation in October 1989 was precipitated by an argument with Mrs Thatcher over the role of her personal economic adviser, Professor Sir Alan Walters.

[60] Private Secretary to Leader of the Opposition (Edward Heath), 1968–70; Political Secretary to the Prime Minister, 1970–4. Minister of State: Foreign and Commonwealth Office, 1979–83; Home Office, 1983–4. Secretary of State for Northern Ireland, 1984–5; Home Secretary, 1985–9; Secretary of State for Foreign and Commonwealth Affairs, 1989– .

and administration of the Magistrates' courts,[61] and for criminal
legal aid. Each of these functions was transferred (or lost, in the
eyes of the Home Office) to the Lord Chancellor's Department.
The transformation of what was little more than a set of lawyers'
chambers to a fully-fledged government department is a story worth
telling, with portents still to come.

As late as 1960 all of the 'officers', as the Lord Chancellor's legal
staff were known, not officials as elsewhere in the civil service, were
able to sit around a not particularly large octagonal table in the
Permanent Secretary's room at his fortnightly office meetings. There
was enough space for a retired Brigadier, who handled ecclesiastical
appointments,[62] and a higher executive officer in charge of the
Crown Office, dealing with ceremonial and the passing of documents
under the Great Seal.[63] The work was quite unstructured. A new
entrant, joining in July 1960, had devilled for all but one of the
dozen or so lawyers by Christmas. There was no hierarchical
organization in the modern sense, the work being allocated and
dealt with in what struck the newcomer, later to become the
Department's Permanent Secretary,[64] as being a delightfully hap-

---

[61] In December 1991 the Lord Chancellor in the House of Lords, and the Home
Secretary in the Commons, made similar statements by way of Written Answer on the
reorganization of the Magistrates' courts service in England and Wales. Following a
scrutiny of the service, and a study of costs by independent consultants, the
Government had decided against bringing forward proposals to reconstitute it as
an executive agency. No immediate change was envisaged in the balance between
central and local financing, but the responsibilities assigned to the Home Secretary
in relation to the finance, organization, and management of the Magistrates' courts
would be transferred to the Lord Chancellor with effect from 1 Apr. 1992. The
Home Secretary would continue to answer to Parliament for the criminal and
procedural law of the Magistrates' courts in the same way as for the Crown Court.
Parl. Debates, HL, 533 (5th ser.), cols. WA 83–4, and HC, 201 (6th ser.), cols. WA
249–50, 19 Dec. 1991.

[62] The staff handling the Lord Chancellor's ecclesiastical patronage was amalgamated with that of the Prime Minister in 1964 when the Prime Minister's Secretary
for Appointments became also the Ecclesiastical Secretary to the Lord Chancellor.

[63] Office legend averred that earlier in his career this officer had discovered in the
Crown Office store, near to Chancellor's Gate at the House of Lords, a mass of
warrants made out ready to give effect to Asquith's threat to ennoble 249 additional
Liberal peers to ensure the passage of the Parliament Bill in 1911. A list of names
was found amongst Asquith's papers and is printed as an Appendix to Roy Jenkins's
Life of Asquith, Collins, London, 1964, pp. 539–42.

[64] Sir Derek Oulton QC, Private Secretary to the Lord Chancellor, 1961–5;
Secretary, Royal Commission on Assizes and Quarter Sessions, 1966–9. Lord
Chancellor's Office (later Department): Assistant Solicitor, 1969–75, Deputy Sec-
retary, 1976–82, and Deputy Clerk of the Crown in Chancery, 1977–82; Permanent
Secretary, and Clerk of the Crown in Chancery, 1982–9. Fellow of Magdalene

hazard way. Looking back wistfully three decades later, he recalled that during the summer months the Office followed the Law Courts in observing what were called 'vacation hours'.

When the volume of work increased, as it did throughout central government, the wind of change hit the Lord Chancellor's Office with particular force because it started from such a tiny base. In a quiet period after the end of the Second World War in 1945 the Secretary of Commissions, responsible for the appointment of the lay magistracy over the country as a whole, found that days passed when no letter came into his office and no letter went out.[65] New responsibilities were added, starting with the Legal Aid and Advice Act 1949, which conferred upon the Lord Chancellor departmental responsibility for civil legal aid and advice. At first the load was trifling, annual expenditure in the 1950s running at about £1 million, rising to around £5 million annually in the mid-1960s. A big step up came when the Lord Chancellor took over criminal legal aid from the Home Secretary in 1980. The combined responsibility, and the very large increases that occurred in both civil and criminal work, coinciding with the Treasury's insistence that expenditure from public funds be kept in bounds, led to acrimonious and repeated clashes with the legal profession over fees and rates of remuneration. These culminated in unprecedented proceedings in the Divisional Court brought by the Bar and the Law Society against Lord Chancellor Hailsham by way of judicial review.[66] The controversy over the levels of remuneration for legal aid work, added to the magnitude of the task of creating a new Legal Aid Board and transferring the administration from the Law Society, caused a noticeable increase in the burdens on the Lord Chancellor's Department.

The next strand led back to the notorious case of Crichel Down

College, Cambridge, 1990– . I am grateful to Sir Derek Oulton for much of the factual information contained in this section. The inferences drawn are my own.

[65] This remark by Sir Rupert Howarth, a former Deputy Secretary to the Cabinet, was made in oral evidence to the Royal Commission on Justices of the Peace on 30 Oct. 1946. One of his successors, Sir Thomas Skyrme (Secretary of Commissions, 1948–77), has confirmed that the situation was exactly the same when he became Assistant Secretary in 1947, although it changed rapidly after the Royal Commission had reported in 1948 and legislation followed in the Justices of the Peace Act 1949. Letter from Skyrme to Oulton, contents passed on to the author, 11 May 1992.

[66] For Lord Hailsham's account of the events which were to cause him 'deep distress', see *A Sparrow's Flight*, Collins, London, 1990, pp. 442–5.

in 1954.[67] To allay the disquiet which had been caused, the Lord Chancellor of the day, Lord Kilmuir, set up a committee on administrative tribunals and inquiries under the chairmanship of Sir Oliver Franks.[68] Such tribunals, generally deriving from statutory provisions, had multiplied as the range of governmental activity spread. The report of the committee enunciated that whereas tribunals were not courts of law, neither were they appendages of government departments. Although varying in constitution, function, and procedure, tribunals typically dealt with cases in which an individual citizen was at issue with a government department, or some other public body, over his rights or obligations under a statutory scheme. A few dealt with disputes between citizens, while others had more regulatory than adjudicating functions.

The committee declined to accept the view put to them by the Joint Permanent Secretary to the Treasury that tribunals ought to be regarded as part of the machinery of public administration for which the Government should retain a close and continuing responsibility. Instead, it considered that they should more properly be regarded as machinery provided by Parliament for adjudication independent of the relevant government department.[69] To oversee this relationship Franks recommended the establishment of two standing councils, one for England and Wales, and one for Scotland, with a remit to keep the constitution and working of tribunals under continuous review. The Council on Tribunals for England and Wales should be appointed by and report to the Lord Chancellor. The recommendation was accepted and implemented in the

[67] A public inquiry into the disposal of compulsorily purchased land at Crichel Down in Dorset had strongly criticized the actions of the Agricultural Land Commission and some public servants for whose conduct the Minister of Agriculture was responsible. Although not personally implicated, the then minister, Sir Thomas Dugdale, resigned on the grounds of individual ministerial responsibility for their actions. For his resignation speech, see *Parl. Debates*, HC, 530 (5th ser.), cols. 1178–94, 20 July 1954. A list of ministerial resignations from 1903–86 is contained in G. Marshall (ed.), *Ministerial Responsibility*, Oxford University Press, 1989, pp. 102–5. The same volume contains two chapters on the Crichel Down case by D. N. Chester (pp. 106–11) and I. F. Nicolson (pp. 112–14).

[68] Later Lord Franks. Permanent Secretary, Ministry of Supply, 1945–6; Provost, Queen's College, 1946–8, and Worcester College, Oxford, 1962–76; British Ambassador to the United States, 1948–52. Veteran chairman of many public committees and inquiries.

[69] *Report of the Committee on Administrative Tribunals and Enquiries* (Cmnd. 218), HMSO, London, 1957, pp. 8–9.

Tribunals and Inquiries Act 1958.[70] Thereafter, the Lord Chancellor became responsible for the Council on Tribunals, appointing its chairman and members, staffing it, and sticking up for it when it needed help against recalcitrant departments.

Franks contended it was undesirable in principle that the appointment of so many chairmen and members of individual tribunals should rest with the departmental ministers concerned, when it was their own departments which frequently would be a party to proceedings before a tribunal.[71] Misgivings were also expressed about the practice of departments supplying clerks for tribunals from their local and regional staffs on a secondment basis. This had led to a feeling that tribunals were too dependent on, and influenced by, the departments. In future the duties of the clerk should be regulated by the Council on Tribunals being confined to secretarial work, the taking of notes of evidence, and advice on the functions of the tribunal. Unless sent for to advise, the clerk should be debarred from retiring with the tribunal.[72]

In order to stress their independence, Franks wanted the Lord Chancellor to assume full administrative responsibility for the operation of virtually all tribunals. In the late 1950s, however, his Office was still very small and not equipped to take on the extra load. The merits of the argument were accepted notwithstanding, and gradually the Lord Chancellor and his staff took over the appointments of the chairmen of most, and the members of many, tribunals. In addition, rules of procedure were framed and approved. More recently, as the size of the Department and its financial and manpower resources permitted, it was able to provide a centralized service for a growing number of tribunals.

The late 1950s and 1960s also saw the accession of one venerable institution, the Public Record Office, and the creation of a new one, the Law Commission. Until the Public Records Act 1958 the care and preservation of public records was in the hands of the Master of the Rolls, an anachronistic responsibility for a senior judge who in his modern incarnation is fully occupied in presiding over the civil work of the Court of Appeal. Important as they were

---

[70] This Act, and the Tribunals and Inquiries Act 1966 which extended it to further classes of statutory inquiries and hearings, was consolidated in the Tribunals and Inquiries Act 1971.

[71] *Report of the Committee on Administrative Tribunals and Enquiries*, p. 11.

[72] Ibid., p. 14.

for historians of the future, and as a source for scholarship generally, public records generated less political and academic controversy then than later. The principal causes were departures from the thirty-year rule for access, and the move of post-1800 government records from the familiar Public Record Office in Chancery Lane to a purpose built, high-technology, centre at Kew. Although it is the Lord Chancellor who makes orders closing records for longer than the normal thirty-year period, in practice he is bound to rely on the advice of other departments. Yet it is he, and not their minister, who has to defend closure orders in Parliament. This can leave him in an uncomfortably exposed position, while denying Parliament any effective control. Neither of the alternatives, to give the responsibility to the Prime Minister or to make departmental ministers answerable for their own decisions on closure, were pursued. As on other issues, Parliament as well as the relevant ministers, preferred to let the Lord Chancellor's gown of fairness and impartiality be thrown over what were essentially governmental decisions on where the public interest lay.

The legislative architect of the Law Commissions was Gerald Gardiner, Labour's Lord Chancellor from 1964 to 1970, and his achievement is remarked on in Chapter 3. Before then law reform had been handled sporadically. The Law Reform Committee, a standing body with a Secretary provided by the Lord Chancellor's Office, functioned on a part-time basis producing reports on those aspects of the civil law as were referred to it by ministers. A Criminal Law Revision Committee under the aegis of the Home Office periodically considered changes in the criminal law. Occasionally special committees were set up to inquire into particularly important or topical questions, the Royal Commission on Capital Punishment being a notable example in 1949–53. But there was no systematic or continuing mechanism for law reform, with frustrations caused by the difficulties in getting Parliamentary time to implement the recommendations of the Law Reform Committee or the Criminal Law Revision Committee.

Gardiner's abiding interest in law reform changed the picture dramatically. In putting through Parliament the Law Commissions Act 1965 he created separate Law Commissions for England and Wales, and for Scotland, each with a seconded High Court judge as chairman, and a staff of qualified lawyers and others with the obligation to investigate particular questions referred to it, or on its own initiative to conduct a regular programme of inquiry into the general state of the law or any particular question, civil or criminal, which they chose to select.[73] Not the least of Gardiner's successes lay in getting Parliamentary Counsel assigned full time to the Commissions. This enabled reports to be published with draft bills annexed. With much of the preliminary work already done, ministers were more amenable to finding the time to legislate. Between 1979 and 1987, including consolidation and statute law revision, eighty-one acts reforming and updating the law were passed through both Houses of Parliament.[74] Heightened legislative activity on this scale gave the Lord Chancellor and his office enhanced standing in Whitehall. Additional resources followed in train to handle the consequential work.

The final factor contributing to departmental growth was the most significant of all. The reorganization of the higher courts once again owed much to Gardiner, and it was he who initiated the appointment of a Royal Commission on Assizes and Quarter Sessions in 1966. The implementation of the recommendation to set up the Crown Court is recounted in a later chapter, but we should note here the implications for the Lord Chancellor. When Gardiner was considering the Royal Commission's Report he was asked by its Secretary if he appreciated that, for the first time, a minister would become answerable to Parliament for the working of the higher courts, including the delays and other initial setbacks that might be expected. 'I welcome it' was his answer.[75]

Although before the Courts Act 1971 in theory it could be claimed that government was ultimately responsible for the running of the courts, in practice responsibility was so diffused between local authorities, the High Sheriffs and Under Sheriffs of counties,

[73] See Hailsham, *A Sparrow's Flight*, p. 383.

[74] Ibid., p. 384. By the early 1990s a deterioration had set in. In its Annual Report for 1991, the Law Commission complained that its productivity was not being matched by the actual reform of the law. With the exception of 1983, a general election year, 1991 was the first year since the Commission had been set up in which no law reform bill based on its work had reached the statute book. While six out of the sixty-nine public general Acts receiving the Royal Assent were consolidation Acts drafted at the Law Commission, not one was a law reform measure based on the Commission's recommendations. Nor did the Government's legislative programme for 1991/2 include any Law Commission law reform measure. *Twenty Sixth Annual Report 1991* (Law Com. No. 206), HC 280, HMSO, London, 1992, p. 1.

[75] Letter from Sir Derek Oulton, 8 Apr. 1992.

and the judiciary,[76] that there was no real way in which Parliament could call anyone to account. Parliamentary Questions and Ministerial Statements were almost unknown. Today they are commonplace; the Lord Chancellor answering in the Lords, and a junior minister representing his department in the elected House. Previously, Questions had been replied to in the Commons by one of the Law Officers, although they were neither attached to the Lord Chancellor's Department nor directly subordinate to him. In the administration formed by John Major after the General Election in April 1992, a solicitor, John Taylor, was appointed as the first Parliamentary Secretary to the Lord Chancellor's Department. In addition to answering Questions and the handling of all departmental business in the Commons, the Parliamentary Secretary was given responsibility for legal aid and the development of legal services; relations with the Land Registry and Public Record Office; some budget and resource matters; and equal opportunities and women's issues outside the judicial context.

The Department falls within the purview of the Select Committee system in the Commons and also of the Parliamentary Commissioner for Administration. In organizational terms the consequences of greater accountability have been pronounced, bringing about changes in staffing, expertise, training, and accommodation to respond to the demands made.

Another feature of the courts' reorganization was that the Department was no longer located only in London. National legal administration called for regional delegation. An Under-Secretary was appointed to take charge of each Circuit, assuming all of the responsibilities which had been shared in running the assizes and quarter sessions before. With their replacement by the High Court and the Crown Court at fixed centres throughout the country, a new administrative structure had to be devised and substantial numbers of non-lawyer administrators were imported from other departments and elsewhere. By ill-fortune the period of upheaval coincided with a large increase in the volume of work of the higher

---

[76] Appendix 4 to the Royal Commission on Assizes and Quarter Sessions 1966–9, *Report* (Cmnd. 4153), HMSO, London, 1969 showed the numerous authorities responsible before the Courts Act 1971 for all the main aspects of the administration of the courts (p. 160). These arrangements were criticized in paragraphs 56–63 in the body of the Report (pp. 31–2), and the Royal Commission's recommended new structure was contained in paragraphs 299–330 (pp. 103–10).

criminal courts, resulting in problems of delay that still are not eradicated. But, had the changes introduced by the Courts Act 1971 not been in place, there would have been a real possibility that the old system would have collapsed under the strain.

The successive reorganizations have brought the Lord Chancellor's Department, with a total staff of close on 12,000,[77] and the Crown Prosecution Service, with about 2,000 lawyers and 4,000 administrative staff,[78] alongside the Home Office as public instruments for the administration of justice. The distinction between the responsibility of the Home Office for the criminal law, and the Lord Chancellor's Department for the civil law, has been preserved, but its significance has been lessened by the gloss that it is the latter which exercises control over all court administration for criminal as well as civil cases. In times of financial stringency, when almost any change in criminal justice legislation or practice is likely to affect court costs, this responsibility gives the Lord Chancellor's Department heightened influence across the penal field as a whole.

The defined responsibilities of the Lord Chancellor's Department for criminal justice are now fourfold. They are: the administration of the Crown Court and Court of Appeal (Criminal Division); the financing, organization, and management of the Magistrates' courts; legal aid, legal services, and costs from central funds (policy and provision); and the appointment, or advice on the appointment, of almost all judges, judicial officers, and magistrates in England and Wales, and in Northern Ireland. The judiciary is independent of government, although it is the Lord Chancellor who advises the Queen on the appointment of Recorders, Circuit judges, and High Court judges. He also advises the Prime Minister on appointments to the Court of Appeal and certain senior judicial appointments, including the Lord Chief Justice and the Presidents of the Divisions of the High Court.

High Court judges and above hold office during good behaviour until retirement, but the Courts Act 1971, following earlier legislation, gives to the Lord Chancellor a power, seldom used, to

---

[77] At 31 Mar. 1992, the total number of staff employed in the Lord Chancellor's Department was 11,598. The estimate of out-turn for the Department's running costs for 1991–2 was £349.8 million.

[78] At 31 Mar. 1992, the Crown Prosecution Service had 1,999 lawyers in post out of a total staff numbering 5,920. The requirement of lawyers (2,146) and total staff (6,113) was higher than the numbers in post.

remove Circuit judges for 'misbehaviour or incapacity'. For these reasons, if none other, the Lord Chancellor is more than a nominal head of the judiciary. As well as being a Cabinet Minister and Speaker of the House of Lords he sits as a judge, presiding over the Law Lords in the Appellate Committee when time allows. When acting in a judicial capacity he is thrown back on his own resources, whereas in his ministerial capacity he is assisted by the staff of a major department of state. As such, these officials are part of the executive branch of government.

VII

The word in vogue in Whitehall to describe the relationship between the Home Office, the Lord Chancellor's Department, and the Crown Prosecution Service is trilateralism. It was the arrival on the scene of the last named that precipitated a new relationship. The Permanent Secretaries at the Home Office and the Lord Chancellor's Department decided that the fledgling service had to be welcomed into the fold and helped to become an effective department. Neither the Cabinet Office, nor the three responsible ministers—the Home Secretary, the Lord Chancellor, and the Attorney General[79]—were party to the initiative, except in the sense of agreeing to the holding of regular meetings by their senior officials. Even before the advent of the Crown Prosecution Service, the Home Office had extended the hand of friendship to the Lord Chancellor's Department, recognizing that it made no sense for each of them to prepare their annual public expenditure forecasts in isolation from the other. After the Director of Public Prosecutions (DPP) had taken charge of the Crown Prosecution Service he was invited to join in their discussions, so completing the triangle.

Towards the end of 1987, ministers decided that the informal links between the three departments should be strengthened and put onto a more systematic basis. Ministerial trilateral meetings were inaugurated in order to discuss current government business, and not just litigation as had tended to be the case previously. Their contacts were underpinned by meetings between officials from

[79] The Attorney General is ministerially responsible for the Crown Prosecution Service, the Treasury Solicitor's Department, and the Serious Fraud Office.

the three departments at every level between Permanent Secretary and Grade 7. Two-day conferences of the Permanent Secretaries are now held annually, with meetings between Grade 2 officers (Deputy Secretaries) taking place at intervals of two or three months, in each case supplemented by frequent day-to-day contacts.

The basic premiss of the meetings has been that 'co-operation between the various agencies which comprise the criminal justice system is crucial to the successful operation of the system as a whole'.[80] Obvious as the proposition may sound, the aim is not always realized, or sometimes attempted, by departments with overlapping interests and markedly different histories and traditions. Moreover, departmental rivalries are endemic in the style of central government whereby competitive bids are made for limited financial resources. Trilateralism was certainly an effective antidote to isolationism, even if it did not extinguish the assertiveness shown by the Lord Chancellor's Department in securing a faster growth in the rate of expenditure on the courts and legal aid than did the Home Office on the police and prisons. The three departments did, however, discuss the figures and assumptions on which their public expenditure survey bids depended, partially in a genuine spirit of co-operation, but also as a defensive tactic against Treasury inclinations towards divide and rule. Information and opinions are now exchanged on broad questions of strategy, policy, and resources; the preparation of legislation and White and Green Papers; the gathering of statistics about the operation of the system;[81] and the uses of technology in the courts and in the preparation of cases. The efficiency of the Magistrates' courts, the tensions between the Probation Service and the Crown Court over social inquiry reports, and the need to widen opportunities for members of ethnic minorities, were examples of the kind of item which exercised officials in recent times.

There is also a Senior Liaison Committee, which includes representatives from the three departments, and from the police and the Justices' Clerks, which meets twice a year under the chairmanship of the Director of Public Prosecutions. This Committee is an oper-

---

[80] Answer by the Lord Chancellor, Lord Mackay of Clashfern, to a Parliamentary Question by the author, *Parl. Debates*, HL, 522 (5th ser.), cols. WA 1893–4, 31 Oct. 1990.

[81] A cumbrous and slow process. The annual *Criminal Statistics England and Wales 1990* were not published by the Home Office until May 1992 (Cmnd. 1935).

ational extension of trilateralism, intended originally to enable the Director to interpose himself or herself[82] more effectively on the practical interface between the CPS, the police and the courts. In the formative stages, unavoidably perhaps, relationships were tense and difficult, with a great deal at stake in terms of the resources and status of each service. As they have settled down, the Committee has concentrated on the specific delivery of services within the system.

In a newer development, which belongs in Chapter 9, the civil service Heads of the Home Office, the Lord Chancellor's Department, and the Department of Health, together with the DPP, sit on the Criminal Justice Consultative Council. With a wider membership than the committees already mentioned, the Council was established in 1992, initially under the chairmanship of the Permanent Under-Secretary at the Home Office, Sir Clive Whitmore,[83] to implement one of the recommendations of Lord Justice Woolf's Report into the prison disturbances of 1990: the creation of a national forum to promote better understanding, co-operation and co-ordination in the criminal justice system.[84]

The centralized administration of the courts, and the acquisition of new responsibilities, has given the Lord Chancellor's Department more of a leading role in the sphere of criminal justice. None of the transfers of function were consciously designed to counterbalance or diminish the authority of the Home Office, yet the stature of the new arrival has visibly grown at its expense. On the victim in court project, for instance, officials from the Lord Chancellor's Department have worked closely with Victim Support,[85] one of the existing 'clients' of the Home Office. It was symptomatic that when the judges were excluded from membership of the area consultative committees in the formative stages by a ruling by the then Lord Chief Justice, that it was the Circuit or courts administrators from the Lord Chancellor's Department who were identified as being

[82] Mrs Barbara Mills QC, previously Director of the Serious Fraud Office, was appointed Director of Public Prosecutions in April 1992 following the resignation of Sir Allan Green QC.

[83] Principal Private Secretary to the Prime Minister, 1979–82; Permanent Under-Secretary of State, Ministry of Defence, 1983–8; Permanent Under-Secretary of State, Home Office, 1988– .

[84] *Prison Disturbances April 1990*, pp. 21 and 262.

[85] See Paul Rock, *The Social World of an English Crown Court*, Clarendon Press, Oxford, 1993, Chapter 8 on 'The Politics of the Witness'.

best placed to act as chairmen, rather than Home Office officials who were unable to draw on any existing regional organization. Despite all the fence-mending that has gone on, relations have been, and remain, strained at times, leading to frequently repeated disavowals of territorial ambition by the Lord Chancellor's Department. The expansion, it is pointed out, relates solely to administration, with responsibility for the formulation of criminal policy being retained in the hands of the Home Office.

Adherence to same orthodoxy was reflected in the phrasing of the Labour Party's policy review in advance of the 1992 General Election. In a commitment to set up a Department for Legal Administration, Labour's alternative White Paper stated:

This would replace the present Lord Chancellor's Department which administers a very substantial budget, but which is not directly accountable to the House of Commons. The new department would be headed by a Minister in the House of Commons and would be responsible for the administration of justice. The Home Office would retain powers over policing, penal policy, and the criminal law. Many of the issues raised in this alternative White Paper would fall within the remit of the new department.[86]

Britain is not yet ready for a Ministry of Justice, but if such a change were to come it is unlikely that the distinction between administration and policy would endure for long. The best argument for a separate ministry, more extensive in range than a Department of Legal Administration, is that the regulatory functions of the Home Office: the maintenance of public order, the strength and standards of the police, the operation of the prisons and the penal system, immigration control and extradition create unavoidable conflicts with the promotion of justice. Many people at the Home Office would deny this, arguing that the imperatives of fairness and justice should permeate every branch of its work and cannot be hived off and left to others. The debate is a profound one and it is only just beginning to reach out to a wider audience. In its next, more public phase, it is likely to be dominated as much by events as by concepts.

The remarkable growth of the Lord Chancellor's chambers into a major Department of State has been the most telling event yet.

---

[86] *A Safer Britain*, p. 3. The undertaking was repeated in Labour's manifesto for the 1992 General Election, *It's Time to Get Britain Working Again*, p. 24.

As its rival has acquired new functions, the Home Office, so long a repository for a bewildering assortment of responsibilities, has been losing them. In April 1992, the month in which responsibility for the financing, organization, and management of the Magistrates' courts passed to the Lord Chancellor's Department, machinery of government changes made in the aftermath of the General Election transferred five existing Home Office functions to other departments. Four of them went to the new Department of National Heritage. They were: broadcasting policy; safety at sports grounds; the issues of press freedom and privacy which had been considered by a committee under the chairmanship of (Sir) David Calcutt QC in 1989–90,[87] leading to a further review of the effectiveness of newspaper self-regulation; and the proposed National Lottery. Gambling policy stayed with the Home Office, and although the Department of National Heritage would be responsible for the legislation to create the lottery, it would do so in conjunction with the Home Office. The list was completed by the transfer to the Department of Employment of responsibility for co-ordinating government policy on issues of particular concern to women and for sex equality policy. There were no inward transfers.

Although large numbers of staff are not involved, the changes will lead to a reduction in Home Office manpower. The future of the Prison Service is likely to have far greater impact. Once it achieves agency status,[88] the Lord Chancellor's Department will outnumber the Home Office. Numerical strength does not necessarily confer power, but in Whitehall it has always counted towards influence. Too many signs to ignore are now pointing towards the dawning of a new era in which the dominant hold exercised by the Home Office over the system of criminal justice, the connecting thread of this book, will be lessened if not relinquished altogether.

[87] Home Office, *Report of the Committee on Privacy and Related Matters* (Cm. 1102), HMSO, London, 1990.
[88] On 1 April 1993.

2

Ministering to a Gentler Age, 1947–65

I

Commending the Criminal Justice Bill to Parliament in 1947 the Home Secretary, Chuter Ede,[1] said that it followed closely on the lines of a Bill which had been before the House of Commons in the session 1938–9. The previous Bill had passed through Committee and was well advanced 'when international affairs so occupied the time of this House that it was impossible to carry the Measure to the Statute Book'.[2] The circumlocution obscured the compelling fact that the earlier Bill had been abandoned two months after the outbreak of war with Germany.[3]

That all thought of penal reform had not been completely shelved for the duration of hostilities was shown by a written answer to a Parliamentary Question addressed to the Home Secretary in April 1944. Asked whether he would consider reintroducing the pre-war Criminal Justice Bill, Herbert Morrison replied:

I share my hon Friend's appreciation of the value and importance of the large reforms proposed in the Bill of 1939, and when I decided, as I announced on 23rd March, to appoint an Advisory Council to assist in the preparation of a programme of reforms, I certainly had it in mind that many of the proposals in that Bill—improved it may be by further consideration and fresh ideas—might find a place in such a programme.[4]

Two days earlier the Home Secretary had sent a minute to the Prime Minister explaining that he proposed to answer on these

---

[1] J. Chuter Ede served as Home Secretary throughout the Labour Government, 1945–51, longer than anyone else since the Reform Act 1832. He became a life peer in 1964 and died in 1965.

[2] *Parl. Debates*, HC, 444 (5th ser.), col. 2129, 27 Nov. 1947.

[3] *Parl. Debates*, HC, 353 (5th ser.), cols. 532–5, 14 Nov. 1939. According to *The Times* (12 Mar. 1946) the Bill had been withdrawn reluctantly and to the general disappointment of the House. An unsuccessful attempt to get the decision reconsidered had been led by Clement Attlee, then Leader of the Opposition.

[4] *Parl. Debates*, HC, 398 (5th ser.), col. 2180, 6 Apr. 1944.

lines. Although preoccupied with planning the invasion of the continent of Europe (Operation Overlord) which came on 6 June 1944, Winston Churchill devoted his attention to a matter which must have seemed far removed from the great events by which he was surrounded. On 13 April, in the midst of a period described by his biographer as 'these trying, troubled days with "Overlord" looming',[5] the Prime Minister responded in unmistakably personal terms:

I should not advise raising this topic at the present time. So many people are having very hard things demanded of them, and our prisons have been vastly reformed in the last 30 years or so. I should have thought it was very ill-timed to feature this.

Sir Samuel Hoare was very keen, and in 1937 he insisted on leaving the Admiralty in order to make a great feature of prison reform. He was pretty well adrift from realities at that time. I should recommend waiting for a gentler age than that in which we are condemned for a while to dwell.[6]

Sticking to his guns in the face of this majestic broadside called for tenacity and skill. In a minute drafted in his own hand, with many crossings out and revisions in the original, Morrison replied:

I hope you will not think that I, too, am 'adrift from realities' if I return to the charge and stake out a claim for a Penal Reform Bill in our legislative programme of social reconstruction after the war. Indeed, I am very conscious of the desirability of avoiding 'sloppiness'.

The question at issue is not so much prison reform—although our prison buildings are now shamefully antiquated, obsolete and, for the most part, entirely unsuitable for use as penal establishments—as the provision of up-to-date and more enlightened methods of dealing with the problem of treating the offender, and in particular the juvenile offender. This is not a sentimental journey in quest of ways and means of making life easier for the offender, but a realistic attempt to tackle the economic problem of saving the community from the losses and suffering caused by the anti-social activities of criminals.

The initiative does not rest with me or with the Home Office. All the organisations interested in penal reform are disappointed that the Criminal Justice Bill did not pass into law before the outbreak of war and will immediately on the termination of hostilities in Europe bring pressure to

---

[5] Martin Gilbert, *Winston S. Churchill*, vol. 7, *Road to Victory, 1941–1945*, Heinemann, London, 1986, p. 748.

[6] Public Record Office (hereafter PRO): HO 45/21948; Prime Minister's Personal Minute M. 406/4.

bear on the Government to reintroduce that Bill, with or without amendment. Even if the Government do not propose legislation themselves, I imagine that some Private Member will introduce a Bill and I must confess that I can see no way of postponing this issue to a 'gentler age'.

In these circumstances, I hope you will feel able to concur in my view that this is not an issue which can be postponed and that the Government must face up to its responsibilities of trying to find a solution to an urgent social and economic problem, it being, of course, understood that there should be no interference with the war effort.

And, of course, I realise that when I bring forward proposals they will have to be judged on their merits.[7]

With magnanimity, perhaps mindful of his own ambitious plans for prison reforms more than thirty years earlier,[8] the Prime Minister minuted on 10 May: 'By all means mature your proposals.'[9] When finally published in 1947, the provisions of the post-war Criminal Justice Bill had a predictable, even inevitable, quality. Ede was no innovator, and the Bill was regarded as a disappointment by some of his Party colleagues, in the Cabinet as well as on the back benches.[10] The changes incorporated in the legislation represented the end-product of a gradual, and in the event protracted, evolution since the mid-1930s. Few of the proposals were contentious, leaving the debate to be sharpened by the emotive issues of corporal punishment,[11] which was included in the Bill as presented to Parliament on Second Reading, and the death penalty, which was

[7] HO 45/21948.
[8] Churchill had brought 'a questioning mind and fresh ideas' to the Home Office when he had been Home Secretary in Asquith's Liberal Government in 1910–11. See 'The Churchillian Onslaught' in L. Radzinowicz and R. Hood, *A History of English Criminal Law and its Administration from 1750*, vol. 5, Stevens, London, 1986, pp. 770–5. Another historian of the period, Martin J. Wiener, noted that soon after arriving at the Home Office, and eager to implement modern ideas, Churchill had ordered his officials to draw up plans for reorganizing the entire penal system into 'a regular series of scientifically graded institutions which would gradually and increasingly become adapted to the treatment of every variety of human weakness'. *Reconstructing the Criminal: Culture, Law, and Policy in England, 1830–1914*, Cambridge University Press, Cambridge and New York, 1990, p. 379.
[9] HO 45/21948.
[10] K. O. Morgan, *Labour in Power, 1945–1951*, Clarendon Press, Oxford, 1984, pp. 55–6.
[11] In an examination of the historical arguments advanced for and against flogging and whipping, Radzinowicz and Hood bring out the deeply seated motives for punishment which, as they remark, are often more revealing than abstract principles. *A History of English Criminal Law and its Administration from 1750*, vol. 5, pp. 699–719.

not. Under the Bill, whipping was to be abolished as a punishment ordered by the courts,[12] being retained only in prisons (but not in borstals) as a penalty for the most serious infringements of prison discipline.[13] Having defended the exclusion of capital punishment at Second Reading, the Home Secretary and his ministerial colleagues conceded a free vote on a new clause moved at Report stage by a private member, Sydney Silverman,[14] which had the effect of suspending the death penalty for murder[15] for an experimental period of five years.

The decision was an uncomfortable one which had troubled ministers over several months and caused dissension in the Labour Party.[16] Between June 1947 and July 1948 the Cabinet considered capital punishment six times. It was not simply the well-rehearsed and deeply felt arguments for and against abolition which exercised and divided its members, but the proper role of the Government on what was seen as a question of conscience. In a paper dated 2 March 1947,[17] prepared for the Lord President's Committee[18] and

[12] Since 1861 corporal punishment had been available only for a limited range of offences. For adults its use had been confined virtually to offenders convicted of robbery with violence. In each of the four years before the Criminal Justice Act became law in 1948, sentences of corporal punishment (including Juvenile Court sentences of birching on boys under sixteen) totalled: 68 in 1944, 39 in 1945, 48 in 1946, and 58 in 1947. Home Office, *Corporal Punishment*, Report of the Advisory Council on the Treatment of Offenders (Cmnd. 1213), HMSO, London, 1960, Appendix B.

[13] In England and Wales the most serious disciplinary infringements punishable by flogging were mutiny, incitement to mutiny, and gross personal violence to a prison officer. In Scotland there had never been power to order corporal punishment for any offence against discipline in local prisons or in borstal institutions. Prisoners serving sentences of penal servitude at Peterhead prison were an exception. See Home Office, Departmental Committee on Corporal Punishment, *Report* (Cmd. 5684), HMSO, London, 1938, pp. 99–100.

[14] The clause had been tabled by a carefully balanced all-Party list of sponsors. Besides Silverman (Lab.) they were: Derick Heathcoat-Amory (Con.), Christopher Hollis (Con.), Lady Megan Lloyd George (Lib.), Reginald Paget (Lab.), and John Paton (Lab.). As editor of a publication called *The Penal Reformer*, Paton had campaigned for abolition in the 1930s. See E. O. Tuttle, *The Crusade against Capital Punishment in Great Britain*, Stevens and Sons, London, and Quadrangle Books, Chicago, 1961, pp. 55–83, which contains a useful account of the Parliamentary proceedings on capital punishment during the Criminal Justice Bill in 1948.

[15] The death penalty would remain unchanged for certain other offences which are listed in n. 156 to this chapter.

[16] Morgan, *Labour in Power, 1945–1951*, pp. 62–3.

[17] HO 45/21951; LP (47) 39.

[18] Herbert Morrison, later Lord Morrison of Lambeth, was Lord President of the Council and Leader of the House of Commons for most of the period 1945–51,

later circulated to the Cabinet,[19] the Home Secretary forecast the outlines of the coming controversy:

There are two issues upon which controversy is likely to centre in connection with these proposals. The first is the abolition of the powers of courts to pass sentence of corporal punishment. This was the subject of a unanimous recommendation by the Departmental Committee on Corporal Punishment which reported in 1938 after a most careful and exhaustive enquiry into the whole subject. I propose that the new Bill, like the Bill of 1938, should contain a provision to carry out this recommendation.

The second issue is the question of the abolition or suspension of capital punishment. During the Committee Stage of the 1938 Bill an amendment was moved to suspend the death penalty for a period of five years. The Select Committee on Capital Punishment, 1929–30, recommended the abolition of capital punishment for an experimental period of five years, and an amendment in this sense is likely to be moved if a new Criminal Justice Bill is introduced. I would propose that any such amendment should be resisted on the ground that it is inappropriate that such a far-reaching change in the law should be included in a Criminal Justice Bill, and that, if any such change in the law were to be effected, it should be after full consideration in a separate Bill dealing solely with this subject.[20]

The Cabinet considered the Home Secretary's paper at a meeting on 19 June 1947. The proposal to abolish corporal punishment as a judicial penalty was approved, although the minutes record the Lord Chancellor, Lord Jowitt,[21] as saying that he was still of the opinion that it would be unwise to abolish the powers of courts to pass sentences of corporal punishment, and would have favoured

having served as Home Secretary and Minister of Home Security in the coalition government during the war years, 1940–5. His own account of the Committee's function was that 'The Lord President's Committee had referred to it questions of domestic policy not assigned to other Committees, including in the earlier period internal economic policy and the supervision of the general development of the nation's economy. It could be described as a sub-Cabinet or general purposes committee, and was, therefore, a committee of particular importance in the civil field. Its business ranged over a wide field of domestic affairs from matters of relatively small importance up to questions of considerable significance. It settled many issues of important policy and the agenda was usually heavy.' *Government and Parliament: A Survey from the Inside*, Oxford University Press, 1954, p. 20.

[19] Annexed to CP (47) 182.

[20] HO 45/21951.

[21] As Sir William Jowitt, Attorney General, 1929–32, and Solicitor General in the coalition Government, 1940–2. Jowitt held other ministerial offices between 1942–5, becoming Lord Chancellor in the Labour Government, 1945–51. Created a Baron in 1945, a Viscount in 1947, and an Earl in 1951, Jowitt was leader of the Opposition in the House of Lords, 1952–5.

the retention of the use of the birch. Nevertheless, he realized that for political reasons it would be very difficult to do less than had been proposed in the Bill introduced in 1938.[22] The minutes continued:

The Cabinet then discussed the question of the abolition of capital punishment.

It was agreed that it would be impossible to draft the title of the Bill in such a way as to exclude an amendment to abolish capital punishment, and that it would be unconvincing to argue that the inclusion in the Bill of a provision for the abolition of capital punishment would be inappropriate.

On the question whether on merits it would be desirable to abolish capital punishment Ministers were divided.

It was urged, on the one hand, that public opinion was not yet ready for the abolition of capital punishment and that it would be particularly unwise to abolish it at the present time when there was an abnormal amount of robbery with violence. The judges were convinced that the fear of capital punishment was a real deterrent, and it was difficult to see what effective alternative punishment could be inflicted on murderers. Moreover, if capital punishment were abolished in this country, it would be difficult to justify its retention in the Colonies and in the British Zone of Germany.

On the other hand, it was argued that the infliction of capital punishment was degrading to the public and that there was no real evidence of its deterrent effect. Thus, practically all the cases of murder which the Home Secretary had had to consider during the past two years had been unpremeditated. The attitude of the Bench to past proposals for the reform of the criminal law did not suggest that their judgment in such a matter was reliable, and those Government supporters in Parliament who had given most study to the matter were unanimously in favour of abolition.

In further discussion the suggestion was made that the best course would be to introduce the Bill without any provision abolishing capital punishment and to explain in the Second Reading debate that, since the question of capital punishment was one on which there were differences of opinion transcending Party lines, the Government felt that the matter should be left to a free vote. It should be made clear, however, that, since the matter was obviously one which should be considered by the House as a whole, it would have to be dealt with at the Report Stage.

THE PRIME MINISTER suggested that the Cabinet should resume their discussion of the question of the abolition of capital punishment at a further

---

[22] CM (47) 55th Conclusions.

meeting. This would not preclude the Home Secretary from completing the preparation of the rest of the Bill.[23]

A month later, on 15 July, the Cabinet had before it a further memorandum from the Home Secretary which ventilated some alternative strategies:

How should the matter be handled in Parliament? In view of the evident division of opinion among Ministers, it was suggested at the meeting of the Cabinet on 19th June that the best course would be to introduce the Criminal Justice Bill without any provision abolishing capital punishment and to explain in the Second Reading Debate that since the question of capital punishment was one on which there were differences of opinion transcending Party lines, the Government felt that the matter should be left to a free vote on the Report Stage of the Bill. There are, of course, objections to the proposal that the Government should not take the initiative in this matter. To leave it to a free vote of the House might be taken as an indication that the Government had not made up its mind and would be an invitation to the House of Lords to delete from the Bill the clause abolishing the death penalty. When the Bill came back to the Commons the question whether its reinsertion should be left again to a free vote of the House would raise some very difficult problems.

Unless, therefore, we decide to resist the proposal, however strong may be its supporters in the House of Commons, there is much to be said for taking the initiative and inserting in the Bill, as introduced, a clause for the abolition of the death penalty.

There is an alternative to either of these courses which may be worth considering and that is that the Government should take the line that they have come to the conclusion that, while some restriction ought to be made in the infliction of the death penalty, the time has not yet come for its complete abolition. On these grounds they would propose to resist the clause proposing abolition, but, in order to enable the House to consider whether there should be a more frequent recommendation for the exercise of the Royal Prerogative, the Government would propose to table a Resolution in the same sort of terms as that included in the conditional recommendations of the Select Committee [of the House of Commons on Capital Punishment, 1929–30], and that if such a Resolution were passed, the practice governing recommendations for the exercise of the Prerogative would be altered accordingly.[24]

[23] Ibid.
[24] CP (47) 200. The PRO document reference is HO 45/21959 for this file and for all later references to Cabinet Papers and Minutes between July 1947 and July 1948.

The minutes disclose continuing differences of view. The Lord Chancellor:

thought that ... in preference to the suggestion that there might be more frequent recommendations for the exercise of the Royal Prerogative, it might be possible to introduce a system similar to that adopted in some parts of the United States under which a distinction was made between murder in the first and second degree, the death penalty being reserved for cases of the former kind.

At the end of the discussion the Cabinet:

(1) Invited the Home Secretary to ascertain whether it would be possible to draft the title of the Criminal Justice Bill in such a way as to exclude any amendment for the abolition of capital punishment;

(2) Invited the Lord President to take soundings among Government supporters with a view to determining whether it would be possible to persuade those who were in favour of the abolition of capital punishment that in the interests of securing the passage of the Criminal Justice Bill in the 1947–48 Session they should refrain from pressing for this change in the law;

(3) Invited the Home Secretary to circulate a memorandum to the Cabinet on the suggestion made by the Lord Chancellor that it might be possible to distinguish between certain types of murder for which capital punishment would be retained and other types for which it would be abolished.[25]

The Home Secretary accordingly circulated another paper on 28 July.[26] It dealt with the point about the title of the Bill, concluding:

I do not see on what grounds it could be argued that an amendment on the subject of Capital Punishment is outside the scope of a comprehensive Bill amending the law relating to the methods by which the courts are empowered to deal with offenders.

The paper went on to consider the question of 'The Grading of Murders', traversing the same ground as a Royal Commission would do six years later, and reaching the same negative conclusions, except that Ede rejected the idea of giving the jury any discretion:

The fundamental principle ... of our law is that the Jury has only the function of determining the question of guilt or innocence, and is relieved

---

[25] CM (47) 61st Conclusions.
[26] CP (47) 217.

of any responsibility for the subsequent penalty. As the Select Committee of 1930 pointed out in their Report, 'the evidence before the court is restricted to what is directly relative to the proof of the charge and excludes many weighty considerations that are thrown into the balance when the Home Secretary is advising on the Prerogative of Mercy'. The Committee said grading by the Jury 'would lead to great inequality of judgment and administration'.

There is the further consideration that if after a Jury has deliberately decided that a person ought to be put to death, the Home Secretary should nevertheless find it his duty to recommend clemency, there would appear to be a conflict between the Crown and the Jury.

On 7 August the Cabinet accepted Ede's conclusions that an amendment providing for the abolition of capital punishment could not be ruled out of order on the grounds that it did not come within the scope of the Bill,[27] and that it would be impossible to grade murders into those for which capital punishment would be retained and those for which it would be abolished. The Attorney General, Sir Hartley Shawcross,[28] agreed with the Lord Chancellor that the grading of murders would be unworkable, adding that he still remained in favour of providing for the abolition of capital punishment in the Bill.[29]

II

After the summer recess the Cabinet reverted to the subject of capital punishment on 3 November, with the Lord President of the Council reporting on the results of the soundings of Government supporters which he had taken at the request of the Cabinet at its meeting on 15 July. Since then he had attended a meeting of the Parliamentary Labour Party at which he, the Lord Chancellor and

[27] This view was to prevail whenever the question arose, as it regularly did, during the consideration of later Criminal Justice Bills. After the abolition of the death penalty for murder, amendments were normally directed towards its reintroduction for certain types of homicide or terrorist offences.

[28] Sir Hartley Shawcross, Attorney General, 1945–51; President of the Board of Trade, 1951; life peer, 1959. Chairman, Royal Commission on the Press, 1961–2, and of the Press Council, 1974–8. In the Lord President's Committee Shawcross had argued a minority view that the Bill as introduced should provide for the abolition or suspension of capital punishment: HO 45/21951; LP (47), Minutes of 8th meeting, 7 Mar. 1947.

[29] CM (47) 70th Conclusions.

the Home Secretary had spoken. It was clear to Morrison, as the chief manager of Government business, that:

Government supporters would make no difficulties over the fact that the Criminal Justice Bill, as introduced, contained no provision for the abolition of capital punishment. It was equally clear, however, that an amendment to abolish capital punishment would be moved in the course of the proceedings of [sic] the Bill in the House of Commons and that it would be strongly pressed by a substantial number of Government supporters. A majority of those attending the meeting of the Parliamentary Labour Party had favoured the abolition of the death penalty; and the strength of their feeling on this issue was such that it was most unlikely that they could be persuaded to refrain from voting for the amendment.

The Cabinet agreed that in these circumstances it was inevitable that the decision on this issue should be left to a free vote.

Discussion then turned on [sic] the question whether the Government should give any guidance to the House on the merits of the issue, and whether Ministers should also be free to vote in accordance with their personal convictions. On this question opinion was divided. Some Ministers felt that this was wholly a matter for the conscience or judgment of the individual, and that Ministers who held strong views on the moral issue should not be asked to subordinate those views to a collective decision of the Cabinet. Other Ministers argued that, while the moral issue might be a matter of personal conviction, the Government as such had a duty to advise Parliament on the probable consequences of abolishing the death penalty. The Government were responsible for the preservation of law and order, and must assume the responsibility of a collective decision on the risks to law and order which the abolition of the death penalty might involve.

After an inconclusive discussion, the Cabinet agreed to return at a later meeting to the question 'whether the Government, as such, should tender advice to the House of Commons on the abolition of the death penalty'.[30] The debate resumed on 18 November, when the Cabinet had two more papers before it dealing with capital punishment and the role of government. In the first,[31] the Home Secretary proposed a fixed (i.e. mandatory) sentence of imprisonment for life as an alternative penalty for murder if the abolitionists' amendment were carried. The argument that convicted murderers should be subjected to more rigorous conditions than

[30] CM (47) 84th Conclusions.
[31] CP (47) 306.

other long-sentenced prisoners was rejected, with the implication that detention for more than ten years should be avoided whenever possible:

If the death penalty were abolished it would be possible either to substitute a fixed penalty of imprisonment for life or to give the Judge discretion to pass sentence of any term up to imprisonment for life. The Select Committee recommended the first course and said that the life sentence should be interpreted and administered in the same way as the sentence to which a reprieved murderer is subject at present. This course seems preferable. There are some reprieved murderers whom it is right to release on licence after very short periods of imprisonment (for example, a mother who kills an imbecile child from merciful motives), and it would be undesirable in such cases for a court publicly to pass a sentence of imprisonment for a few months or for a year or two, and thereby to create the impression that the taking of human life may in certain circumstances be no graver a crime than theft.

If, when the jury returns a verdict of murder, the Judge has no option but to pass a sentence of imprisonment for life, it will rest with the Home Secretary to decide when the prisoner shall be released on licence. In many cases of murder detention would no doubt be necessary for at least ten years. In some cases longer detention would be requisite, and there may from time to time be murderers who can never be released. For purposes of prison administration it is essential that the cases where the prisoner is never released should be exceptional and that there should be maintained amongst those serving life sentences a general hope of release and consequent incentive to good behaviour. Moreover, experience shows that imprisonment for more than about ten years is liable to have so deleterious an effect on the prisoner that longer detention should be avoided whenever possible.

The conditions under which murderers would serve their life sentences must be no more rigorous than those applied to other long-sentence prisoners. The longer the period of detention the greater is the need for creating in the prison conditions which will keep alive the prisoner's mental interests and social instincts.

It has been suggested that in some countries where capital punishment has been abolished the alternative is the imprisonment of murderers under more rigorous conditions than are applicable to other prisoners, but from the information collected by the Select Committee it appears that this suggestion is unfounded. The evidence given to the Select Committee showed that in Norway and Belgium it was the practice to keep in solitary confinement prisoners (whether sentenced for murder or for other crimes) who had not a criminal record, but this method was adopted for reformative purposes and for protecting such prisoners from contamination by other prisoners.

In the second paper,[32] the Secretary of State for Scotland (Arthur Woodburn) argued that it was the duty of the Government to give a lead:

On an issue so important as that of the death penalty I feel that the House is entitled to expect a lead from the Government; we fail in our duty unless we give the view of those responsible for maintaining law and security for the citizens. I have reluctantly come to the conclusion that the lead should be in favour of retaining the death penalty for the present. But I feel that the policy practised in the Scottish Courts of accepting a doctrine of diminished or impaired responsibility should be encouraged in order that murders which are clearly partly by accident, impulse or temporary madness or passion should be treated differently from those crimes which constitute a deliberate war against society. This would in effect abolish capital punishment in most cases though it would remain in reserve in case of need and to prevent fear arising from its complete abolition.

Strongly differing reactions to the two papers were recorded in the minutes:[33]

The Cabinet first considered whether it was their duty to advise Parliament that the abolition of the death penalty would involve serious risks to law and order. On this point THE HOME SECRETARY said that there was no reliable evidence that the abolition of the death penalty in foreign countries had been followed by a significant increase in the number of murders. It was true that those concerned with the enforcement of the law in this country were apprehensive that the abolition of the death penalty would be followed by an increase in crimes of violence; but their predecessors had in the past opposed for the same reason the abolition of the death penalty for offences less serious than murder and their apprehensions had not in the event proved justified. On the other hand, THE SECRETARY OF STATE FOR SCOTLAND urged that the experience of countries like Norway and Sweden did not justify the conclusion that the death penalty could safely be abolished in this country, where conditions were different. He attached special importance to the risk that the withdrawal of this penalty might lead to an increase in crimes of violence by gangsters in large centres of population like Glasgow and London.

In further discussion, it was suggested that, even though opinion was divided on the merits and on the question whether the abolition of the

[32] CP (47) 310.
[33] CM (47) 89th Conclusions.

death penalty would in normal circumstances give rise to an increase in the number of murders, the Cabinet might be able to agree that this was not an appropriate moment at which to take the risk of abolishing the death penalty. There was a substantial body of opinion which would support the view that, whatever convictions were held on the merits, it would be inopportune to introduce this experiment in the unsettled conditions following a major war, when the number of violent crimes was abnormally high and respect for the sanctity of human life had inevitably been impaired by the circumstances of war. It was difficult for the Government to judge in present circumstances whether a majority of the electors desired that capital punishment should be abolished. Would it not be preferable, therefore, if the Government, while avoiding any expression of opinion on the merits, advised Parliament that this was not an opportune moment at which to make this important change in the law?

The reference to the wishes of the electorate, although seldom recorded in the minutes of the Cabinet, was unlikely to have been far from the minds of those ministers responsible for the conduct of government business. As Shawcross later recalled:

It was of course appreciated that the public at large was in favour of retaining the death penalty and that its abolition would be likely to lose votes for the Labour Party. How far this influenced some members of the government it is difficult to say but I have no doubt it was one of the factors which led to a majority being against abolition.[34]

The measured prose of the final sentence of the Cabinet minute surely deserves a place in *The Handbook of Political Fallacies*.[35] Among the fallacies of delay, Bentham listed the Procrastinator's Argument, or 'Wait a Little, This is Not The Time':

Under this head belongs every form of words by which, in speaking of a proposed measure of relief, an intimation is given that the time at which the proposal is made, whenever it may be, is too early for the purpose.[36]

The habits and compromises of political life have not much changed since the early part of the last century. It is still true that the tactic

[34] Letter from Lord Shawcross, 19 Nov. 1991.
[35] The first English version of Jeremy Bentham's *Handbook of Political Fallacies* was published in 1824. An edition revised and edited by Professor Harold A. Larrabee for the Johns Hopkins Press, Baltimore, was published in 1952. A paperback, with a new introduction by Crane Brinton of Harvard University, followed in 1962.
[36] Harper Torchbooks, the Academic Library, Harper Bros., New York, 1962, p. 129.

of procrastination is often employed by those who are basically hostile to the purpose of a measure. Sometimes, however, they prefer not to appear to be opposed, claiming to be generally sympathetic to the proposal, differing only on the appropriate time to bring it forward. By its nature, the argument of timing is subjective; assertions can be and frequently are advanced on the scantest of evidence. The doubts and fears of the archetypal political procrastinator were aptly summed up by Bentham: 'Rest assured that whatever he finds too soon today, tomorrow he will also find too soon, if not too late.'[37]

Cabinet minutes do not reveal the numerical division of opinion for and against decisions which then become Government policy by which, in theory at least, all ministers are bound. One well-informed historian of the period believes that the Cabinet was in favour of retaining the death penalty by a majority of eleven to five, and this estimate was to be borne out in a vote in the Commons the following April.[38] Each of the ministers with his hands on the levers of Whitehall power on the issue—the Lord President (Morrison), the Lord Chancellor (Jowitt), the Home Secretary (Ede), and the Scottish Secretary (Woodburn)—was numbered among the majority. But any minority that included Sir Stafford Cripps, who had succeeded Hugh Dalton as Chancellor of the Exchequer on 13 November 1947, and Aneurin Bevan was unlikely to have gone unheard. Moreover, they could count on widespread support on the Labour benches of the House of Commons where abolition was a popular cause.[39] In such a setting, it would not have been surprising if an authentically Benthamite flavour had permeated the debates in Cabinet.

The question posed on 11 November was answered a week later when the Cabinet:

(1) Agreed that in the proceedings on the Criminal Justice Bill the Government should advise Parliament that the present was not an opportune time for abolishing capital punishment; and took note

[37] Ibid., p. 130.
[38] Morgan, *Labour in Power, 1945–51*, p. 56. Two members of the Cabinet (Jowitt and Addison) were in the House of Lords, so reducing the number eligible to vote in the Commons to fourteen.
[39] 187 MPs had signed a memorial to the Home Secretary in July 1947 asking him to include in the Criminal Justice Bill a provision for a five-year period of suspension; see T. Morris, *Crime and Criminal Justice since 1945*, Basil Blackwell, Oxford, 1989, pp. 78–9.

that the Home Secretary would define the Government's attitude towards this question when moving the Second Reading of the Bill in the House of Commons;

(2) Reaffirmed their decision of 3rd November that the decision on this issue should be left to a free vote, preferably on the Report stage of the Bill in the House of Commons; and agreed that Ministers who dissented from the advice which was to be tendered in accordance with Conclusion (1) above should be free, if they so desired, to vote for the abolition of the death penalty, though they should refrain from expressing in debate views contrary to that advice ... [40]

III

The freedom of abolitionist ministers to vote for Silverman's new clause did not survive the volatile pressures of party politics. On 9 April 1948, less than a week before the crucial debate at Report Stage in the House of Commons:

THE LORD PRESIDENT invited the Cabinet to review their decision that Ministers should be free to vote against the advice which was to be given on this issue by the responsible Minister as representing the considered view of the Government. It was undesirable in principle that Ministers who shared a collective responsibility should vote in different Lobbies, even on an issue of this kind ... [41]

The Cabinet accepted Morrison's request, agreeing that:

members of the Government (including Law Officers and junior Ministers) who felt unable, on grounds of conscience, to vote against the abolition of the death penalty should abstain from voting in the Divisions to be taken on this issue in the proceedings on the Criminal Justice Bill.[42]

At the start of the following week, James Callaghan, then a young Parliamentary Secretary,[43] was among a group of ministers outside the Cabinet who were summoned to be told of the Cabinet's

[40] CM (47) 89th Conclusions.
[41] CM (48) 27th Conclusions.
[42] Ibid.
[43] Parliamentary Secretary, Ministry of Transport, 1947–50; Parliamentary and Financial Secretary, Admiralty, 1950–1. Chancellor of the Exchequer, 1964–7; Home Secretary, 1967–70. Secretary of State for Foreign and Commonwealth Affairs, 1974–6; Prime Minister, 1976–9. Leader of the Labour Party, 1976–80. Life peer, 1987.

decision. It was a stormy meeting during which Callaghan was one of those who clashed angrily with Morrison, arguing that the abandonment of the free vote meant pressurizing them to change their convictions, or at least to keep them in cold storage.[44]

Winding up for the Government when the new clause was debated in the House of Commons on 14 April 1948, Ede faithfully followed the Cabinet's line, expounding the case for retention on the grounds that public opinion was not conducive to any change, adding as a supporting argument that the unarmed police had to contend with a 'class of gangster and armed criminal which hardly existed at all before the war'.[45] The House as a whole did not find the Home Secretary's arguments convincing, accepting the clause by 245 to 222, a majority of twenty-three. Despite the diligence of the Government Whips, an unusually large number of MPs, amounting to 173 including the Law Officers and several ministers, abstained in the division (or were absent).

The five Cabinet members who indicated their sympathy for the abolitionist cause by abstaining were: Cripps, Bevan, Arthur Creech Jones, Philip Noel-Baker, and Harold Wilson. Eight of their colleagues followed the Prime Minister, Clement Attlee,[46] into the No Lobby. They were: A. V. Alexander,[47] Ernest Bevin, Ede, George Isaacs, Morrison, George Tomlinson, Tom Williams, and Woodburn.[48] Throughout the debate it was evident that opinions were fervently held and eloquently expressed. On all sides: the abolitionists, the retentionists, and the abstainers, the vote was recog-

[44] Personal information from Lord Callaghan, confirmed in his contemporary diary (letter from K. O. Morgan, 5 Nov. 1991).

[45] *Parl. Debates*, HC, 449 (5th ser.), col. 1085, 14 Apr. 1948.

[46] Attlee was Prime Minister from 1945 to 1951, having served as Churchill's deputy in the wartime coalition. He resigned as Leader of the Labour Party in 1955, was created an earl, and died in 1967.

[47] In the week before the debate, Alexander, as Minister of Defence, had written personally to Ede saying that from the point of view of the Services 'it would be preferable that the issue should continue to be confined to the death penalty for murder and that any move to widen the scope of the amendments to include treason as well, would, from our point of view, be unfortunate.' (HO 45/21959).

[48] Apart from Attlee, who did not regard himself as 'partisan' on the subject, six of the eight Cabinet members who voted against the new clause came from working class backgrounds where the campaign against capital punishment had made least headway. The exceptions were Woodburn and Ede. In 1938–9 and again in the 1950s Ede was opposed to the continuation of the death penalty. When challenged in 1947 he replied: 'My mind is not static on any subject'. *Parl. Debates*, HC 444 (5th ser.), col. 2151, 27 Nov. 1947.

nized as a momentous one in which the consciences of Members
of Parliament were engaged with a profound issue transcending
party politics. *The Times* described an emotional scene:

Excitement had been steadily rising in the crowded chamber during the
closing stages of the debate on a new clause to be added to the Criminal
Justice Bill, but jubilation found vent in a roar of cheering when it was
evident how the vote had gone ... Excited members stood in their places
and waved their Order Papers, while others shook hands with their nearest
neighbours. It was some minutes before the hubbub died down.[49]

When it reached the more sober atmosphere of the Upper House,
the clause was decisively rejected, again on a free vote (except for
the Government front bench), by a majority of 153 (181 votes to
28),[50] despite a powerful plea in its support by Viscount Templewood, who, as Sir Samuel Hoare, had been the Home Secretary so
enthused about pre-war prison reform.[51] By one of those somersaults
that can make Parliament so perplexing, whereas ministers in the
Commons had been forbidden to vote for abolition, in the Lords
they were instructed to support the suspension of the death penalty
for five years. The reasoning was that in the interval the Home
Secretary had announced on Third Reading in the Commons that
the Government accepted the decision reached by a majority of the
House.[52] Welcome as the Cabinet's new policy must have been to
some ministers in the Lords, notably Lord Pakenham, then Minister
of Civil Aviation and an abolitionist to his fingertips,[53] voting
for suspension cannot have been an agreeable experience for the
unyielding retentionist Lord Chancellor, Jowitt.

Shorn of its new clause, the Bill returned to the Commons. Now

[49] *The Times*, 15 Apr. 1948, p. 4.
[50] *Parl. Debates*, HL, 156 (5th ser.), cols. 175–8, 2 June 1948.
[51] An attempt to abolish capital punishment for a five-year period had been
defeated in the Commons Standing Committee. Hoare, later to become an ardent
exponent of abolition, led the opposition for the Government. In his autobiography,
he wrote that as capital punishment had always been given a unique place in the
administration of justice, its abolition should be the subject of specific, and not
general, legislation. See Templewood, *Nine Troubled Years*, Collins, London, 1954,
p. 247.
[52] *Parl. Debates*, HC, 449 (5th ser.), col. 1306, 16 Apr. 1948.
[53] Chancellor of the Duchy of Lancaster, 1947–8; Minister of Civil Aviation,
1948–51; First Lord of the Admiralty, 1951. Succeeded his brother as Earl of
Longford in 1961. Leader of the House of Lords, 1964–8; Secretary of State for the
Colonies, 1965–6. Author and penal reformer, see especially *Punishment and the
Punished*, Chapmans, London, 1991.

it was the Attorney General, Shawcross, who moved an amendment
limiting capital punishment to a number of specific types of murder,
a compromise which had been canvassed by Jowitt in Cabinet on
15 July 1947, but favoured neither by Shawcross nor by a majority
of the Cabinet at that stage. His line of argument was the only
respectable one open to him: that it was historically consistent with
the way the death penalty had been restricted progressively to crimes
of murder to propose a further restriction to certain categories of
murder only.[54] After a much interrupted speech that lasted for
nearly an hour, he ended resoundingly: 'I believe that the best way
in which the State can encourage respect for human life is by
refraining from taking life itself, unless it is compelled to do so by
the direst and most certain necessity'.[55]

A heated debate followed in which Churchill, drawing on his
own experience as Home Secretary nearly forty years earlier, led
for the Opposition.[56] The outcome, however, was unchanged; the
compromise clause meeting the same fate as the amendment suspending the death penalty, being carried in the Commons but again
defeated in the Lords.[57] This time with the Parliamentary Recess
fast approaching, the Government urged the Commons not to insist
on its disagreement with the Lords. In winding up, Morrison stated
explicitly that the Whips were on, warning that if 'this House

[54] The Home Secretary told the Cabinet that in framing the clause it had been
his object to retain the death penalty for those types of murder which most stirred
the public conscience. He had tested its efficacy by applying its provisions to the 98
persons convicted of murder in the years 1944 to 1947. During that period fifty-one
persons had been executed, twenty-eight of whom would not have been sentenced
to death if the clause had been in operation. CM 47 (48).
[55] *Parl. Debates*, HC, 453 (5th ser.), col. 1430, 15 July 1948.
[56] Churchill praised the Lords for rejecting the proposal to suspend the death
penalty: 'In acting as they did in accordance with their convictions ... the Second
Chamber were only discharging the duties which fell upon them. Scarcely less
important than this, they were undoubtedly expressing the views and the wishes of
the overwhelming majority of the nation. There is no doubt whatever that they
showed themselves far more truly representative of public opinion than did the
majority of the House of Commons.' *Parl. Debates*, HC, 453, col. 1434.
[57] The House of Commons had disagreed by 332 votes to 196 with the Lords
action in deleting the new clause, and replaced it with the Government's compromise
proposal. *Parl. Debates*, HC, 453 (5th ser.), col. 1530, 15 July 1948. This was carried
on a division by 307 votes to 209. Ibid., col. 1539–40. The compromise clause,
described by the Marquess of Salisbury, Leader of the Conservative peers, as being
both illogical and unworkable, was disagreed to five days later by the House of
Lords by 99 votes to 19. *Parl. Debates*, HL, 157 (5th ser.), cols. 1066–71, 20 July
1948.

tonight proceeds to disagree with the Lords ... then the Bill is dead'.[58] With many abstentions, the Commons reluctantly followed his advice, the Government obtaining 215 votes to thirty-four in the division. On 30 July, the last day before the summer recess, battered but relieved ministers, their policy of retention rejected by the elected House but upheld by the hereditary peers, saw the Act finally onto the statute book in largely the same form as it had been introduced nine months earlier.

The predicament of the Attorney General during the protracted proceedings had been particularly awkward. Unlike Attlee or Morrison, Shawcross had been firmly opposed to the death penalty for many years as a result of his experience as counsel in a number of murder cases, usually acting for the prosecution.[59] Before the Cabinet reached its final decision, Shawcross asked for a private meeting with the Prime Minister and Morrison in which he strongly pressed his point of view:

Attlee, for his part, was equally strong in urging me to accept the majority opinion. In the end I agreed to do this but I remember leaving the meeting literally, I am afraid, in tears and saying that although I would obey the majority I would resign from the Government afterwards as quietly as I could because I should have failed to uphold an almost lifelong conviction ... As to the compromise clause, I think there is no doubt that Morrison was the initiator of this proposal. I myself thought that the matter was one on which no degrees of murder could be properly invented and was very loath to move the clause, but I was the Attorney-General at the time and it was my duty as Chief Law Officer to carry out the decision of the Cabinet. Churchill had a great time in leading for the Opposition and made what I thought was a splendid speech—but then he usually did.[60]

Once Shawcross had agreed to lead for the Government in the debate on the compromise clause, the possibility of a damaging resignation receded. Perhaps Morrison had foreseen this, yet in the event it was a considerate and generous letter, sent from 10 Downing Street in Attlee's own hand,[61] which helped to avert the potential

[58] *Parl. Debates*, HC, 454 (5th ser.), col. 752, 22 July 1948.
[59] He had also worked before the Second World War with Margery Fry in the Howard League for Penal Reform.
[60] Letter from Lord Shawcross, 19 Nov. 1991.
[61] Bodleian Library, Oxford: MS Eng. c. 2720, fol. 20; Private and Personal letter to the Attorney General from the Prime Minister, 26 July 1948. Quoted with the permission of the 3rd Earl Attlee.

embarrassment of losing from his Government not only the Attorney General, but also one of Labour's coming men. Noting that Shawcross had voted with the Government in not opposing the Lords amendments on 22 July, Attlee said that he was very grateful as he knew the strength of Shawcross's views. In fact he had sent a message via the Chief Whip telling him that if he felt he must abstain he was at liberty to do so. The letter continued:

You may, perhaps, have thought that I put my point of view too emphatically to you on a matter on which you hold strong views, whereas I am not a partisan on the question of the death penalty.

Long experience has, however, shown to me the danger of the good being lost through the devotion of some to what they think to be the best. I was, therefore, necessarily concerned to put the matter before you in what I considered to be its right perspective. This is the inevitable duty of a Prime Minister or Leader of a Party who wants to keep the team together, having regard to the major objectives of the Party.

We shall now have to consider what is the best approach to the subject in the light of existing circumstances.

With all good wishes,

Yours sincerely
C R Attlee

IV

In addition to ending corporal punishment as a penalty available to the courts, the Criminal Justice Act 1948 abolished penal servitude and hard labour; established new arrangements for the supervision of discharged prisoners; put preventive detention and borstal training on to a new footing; introduced corrective training, detention centres, and attendance centres; and revised the law on probation. Of direct interest only to the most rarified of all constituencies of criminal justice was the abolition of the privilege of peers to be tried before a special court composed of members of the House of Lords if charged with the commission of certain crimes. A new clause, proposed by Lord Simon, the former Lord Chancellor,[62] had been added at Committee Stage. The Home

[62] Viscount Simon was Lord Chancellor, 1940–5. He had been twice Home Secretary, 1915–16 and 1935–7; Foreign Secretary, 1931–5; and Chancellor of the Exchequer, 1937–40.

Secretary had previously informed the Cabinet that he would have included a provision to this effect in the Bill if he had not thought it preferable to leave it to the Lords to take the initiative.[63]

These measures had resulted from a long period of maturation and fitted into Morrison's 1944 vision of a 'legislative programme of social reconstruction' after the war had ended. Less certain was whether the measures themselves fitted the changed nature and mood of post-war British society. In the mid-1930s, when the policies were taking shape, the numbers sentenced to imprisonment had declined, the annual prison intake having fallen by more than two-thirds between 1910 and 1934.[64] Prisons and institutions for young offenders were closing down, probation was thriving, and more time was allowed to pay fines. As a later report on the prisons was to claim: 'In a variety of ways in the inter-war period, Britain became the centre of the prison reform movement'.[65] Constructive ideals of training and rehabilitation were translated into penal policies that appeared to be meeting their objectives. The reformist outlook on the aims of punishment was not seriously challenged by the slow, but continuously upward, movement of indictable crime throughout the 1920s and 1930s. In 1938, however, a higher proportion of prisoners (51.3%) was still serving sentences for non-indictable offences than for indictable offences (48.7%).[66]

By 1945 the picture was very different. Indictable offences known to the police had risen by 69% since 1938, reaching a total of 478,394 compared with 283,220 in 1938. In 1947, when the Cabinet was preoccupied with the death penalty, the trend was still rising, with an emphasis on crimes against property. For that year the comparable figure fell just short of half a million at 498,576.[67] 'The prevalence of crime', *The Times* reported, and particularly its

[63] CM (48) 30th Conclusions.

[64] Wiener, *Reconstructing the Criminal*, p. 380.

[65] Committee of Inquiry into the United Kingdom Prison Services, *Report* (Cmnd. 7673), HMSO, London, 1979, p. 15.

[66] Home Office, *Report of the Commissioners of Prisons and the Directors of Convict Prisons for the Year 1948* (Cmd. 7777), HMSO, London, 1949, p. 11.

[67] Home Office, *Criminal Statistics England and Wales 1947* (Cmd. 7528), HMSO, London, 1948, p. xvi. The causes of the increase in criminality are analysed by category of offence in Morris, *Crime and Criminal Justice since 1945*, pp. 34–7. There is a typographical error in the total of indictable offences known to the police in 1945 which should be 478,394 and not 478,349. (Table 3.1 on p. 35.)

increase since the end of the war, was 'causing grave concern over the whole of the country'.[68]

More frequent criminal offending led to more people being sentenced to imprisonment, although not pro rata because of the distinction between indictable and non-indictable offences. The higher proportion of the prison population which had been sentenced to imprisonment for offences triable on indictment[69] meant that the sentences served were longer than before, with a consequent increase in the size of the prison population overall. The daily average population surged from 12,915 in 1944 to over 17,000 in 1947, compared with pre-war prison population figures in the range between 10,000 and 11,000. By 1948 another sharp increase to 19,765 had occurred, with the average daily population exceeding 20,000 in July of that year. Nothing on a similar scale had been seen since 1911.[70] Whereas the increase up to and including 1946 was not attributed to more people being sent to prison each year, thereafter the pattern changed with a substantial rise in the number of convicted and sentenced offenders being received from the courts.[71] Prisons, such as Preston and Portsmouth, which had been closed as civil prisons since the 1930s, had to be reopened to contain the larger numbers.

While the grave concern about the prevalence of crime noted by *The Times* was often articulated, it was not yet politicized. Terence Morris has described how the problem of crime:

was not regarded as a political issue in the sense that it had an important place on the agenda of party politics. Rather, it was a kind of backdrop to everyday life. It did not touch as many people as it does today and it would have been difficult to see precisely what kind of partisan gloss could have been put on the matter. In the years immediately after the war there were other, infinitely more pressing, problems facing government ... The predominant atmosphere was that of social reconstruction.[72]

[68] *The Times*, 23 Jan. 1948.
[69] In 1947 the proportion of receptions on conviction for indictable offences carrying longer sentences was 76.6%, compared with 23.4% for non-indictable offences. *Report of the Commissioners of Prisons and Directors of Convict Prisons for the Year 1948* (Cmd. 7777), p. 11.
[70] Ibid.
[71] Ibid.
[72] *Crime and Criminal Justice since 1945*, p. 27. Dr Morris is Professor of Social Institutions at the London School of Economics and Political Science; previously Reader and Professor of Sociology with special reference to criminology. Vice-President of the Howard League for Penal Reform, 1986– .

Although subjected to heavy pressure from abolitionists, most of them on their own benches, the Labour Government had avoided giving any commitment on the future of the death penalty. At the start of the next session, mindful of the head of steam that had built up on the issue, Ede announced that the Government had decided to recommend the appointment of a Royal Commission to inquire into the possible limitation or modification of the death penalty.[73] A few weeks later when the Prime Minister informed the House of the name of the chairman and the terms of reference,[74] it became clear that the remit to consider ways of 'limiting' or 'modifying' capital punishment for murder excluded the outright abolition of the death penalty. That, Attlee insisted, was a matter for Parliament to decide and was not suitable for a Royal Commission.[75]

Overshadowed by the intensity of the debates on the death penalty, the ending of judicial corporal punishment was a notable step towards the debrutalizing, if not the humanizing, of criminal justice. Thenceforth, although punishment was still sometimes described by criminologists in terms of the 'pain' endured by a convicted offender as a consequence of the harm he had done, it was no longer true in the literal sense of the lawful infliction of physical injury by the punisher on the punished. The controversy smouldered on for several years fuelled by the entrenched views of some of the judges.[76] Speaking in the House of Lords, the most

[73] *Parl. Debates*, HC, 458 (5th ser.), col. 565, 18 Nov. 1948.

[74] Sir Ernest Gowers, one of the great public servants of the time, was named as chairman. The terms of reference were: 'To consider and report whether liability under the criminal law in Great Britain to suffer capital punishment for murder should be limited or modified, and if so, to what extent and by what means, for how long and under what conditions persons who would otherwise have been liable to suffer capital punishment should be detained, and what changes in the existing law and the prison system would be required; and to inquire into and take account of the position in those countries whose experience and practice may throw light on these questions.' *Parl. Debates*, HC, 460 (5th ser.), col. 329, 20 Jan. 1949. The Royal Commission sat for four years and reported in 1953 (Cmd. 8932).

[75] *Parl. Debates*, HC, 460, cols. 329–31. The composition of the Royal Commission caught the Prime Minister's eye and evoked a characteristically terse Minute to the Home Secretary on 23 January 1949: 'I have your Minute of 21 January in which you submit names of persons to be considered for memberships of the Royal Commission on Capital Punishment. I am not much impressed by this list, nor I think, will be public opinion. I would like to discuss names with you.' (Kenneth Harris, *Attlee*, Weidenfeld and Nicolson, London, 1982, Appendix IV, p. 601.)

[76] The Advisory Council on the Treatment of Offenders reported in 1960 that a majority of judges in the Queen's Bench Division agreed with the Lord Chief Justice

formidable of all criminal judges, the Lord Chief Justice, Lord Goddard,[77] had declared: 'Do away with the brutality of the "cat", but keep the birch, which may hurt, which will not injure and which will bring ridicule on the person who receives it.'[78]

V

With corporal punishment abolished as a judicially imposed sentence, and capital punishment diverted, at least for a time, to a committee room in Whitehall,[79] the decks were cleared for the first

that the reintroduction of judicial corporal punishment might be desirable in certain circumstances, although there was a minority who disagreed. Enquiries made by the Council's chairman, Mr Justice Barry, of judges of other divisions of the High Court and of the Court of Appeal, and of the judicial members of the House of Lords, revealed 'a great divergence of views'. *Corporal Punishment*, p. 7.

[77] Already a Lord of Appeal in Ordinary at the time he became Lord Chief Justice of England in 1946, Goddard's appointment marked a departure from the practice of promoting the holders of political office, usually the Law Officers. The exception was Mr Justice Lawrence, ennobled as Lord Trevethin at the age of seventy-seven, and Chief Justice for less than a year when standing in as caretaker for the Attorney General, Sir Gordon Hewart, in 1921–2. Before going to the House of Lords, Goddard had been a Lord Justice of Appeal 1938–44. He resigned as Lord Chief Justice in 1958 aged eighty-one. All of his successors have been drawn from the ranks of the higher judiciary.

[78] Goddard had taken part in the debates on the Criminal Justice Bill, carrying an amendment in the Lords, subsequently rejected by the Commons, which would have left with the courts the power to order birching for garrotting, living on immoral earnings, and robbery with violence. *Parl. Debates*, HL, 156 (5th ser.), cols. 191–215, 2 June 1948.

[79] The Royal Commission reported in 1953. Its main conclusion was that a workable procedure could be devised for giving the jury in a murder trial discretion to decide, after conviction, whether or not there were extenuating circumstances of a kind that would justify the substitution of a sentence of imprisonment for the death penalty. This was the only practicable way of enabling the courts, instead of the Executive, to take account of extenuating circumstances so as to correct the rigidity which was the outstanding defect of the existing law. Little more could be done to limit the liability to suffer the death penalty, the real question being whether capital punishment should be abolished or retained. The Report proposed ending the doctrine of constructive malice and, by a majority of one, the raising of the minimum age for execution to twenty-one. Although the Report was never implemented, the Royal Commission's work was not wasted. Hampered by its restrictive terms of reference, the existence of the Royal Commission kept capital punishment at the forefront of penal policy, but contained within a non-political framework in which neutral and thorough examination could take place. The doctrine of constructive malice was abolished by the Homicide Act 1957, the same statute importing the Scottish concept of diminished responsibility into English law.

real post-war scrutiny of penal policy and methods. The need for reappraisal in the 1950s was underlined by accumulating evidence that rising standards of material prosperity, education, and social welfare had not been matched by any corresponding decline in offending.[80] On the contrary, the high levels of crime recorded during the war years had been maintained, and in several categories increased. Two particularly disturbing trends had emerged. One was that the total of indictable offences against the person, that is crimes of violence and sexual offences, had continued to move upwards since the end of the war. The number was still small compared with offences of dishonesty, but it had increased persistently every year.[81]

Second was a startling growth in convictions of young men aged between sixteen and twenty-one. Offenders in this category had been responsible for more than their share of the increase in crimes of violence, but the enhanced rate of offending at these ages extended to crimes of all kinds.[82] Overcrowding, an ominous phenomenon, began to occur in some prisons. It was claimed that this was caused by the greater number of convictions, and the speed at which the increase took place, rather than from any perceptible changes in sentencing practice.[83] Overstrain in the resources of other criminal justice agencies, the courts, Borstals, approved schools, and the Probation Service, also became apparent. From now on, the twin claws of the pincer that was to hold the development of penal policy fast in its grip were the remorseless increase in the incidence of crime, and the overcrowding in the prisons. For the better part of the next forty years they were to be the decisive restraints.

The Home Office, in the skilful hands of R. A. Butler from 1957,[84] responded rationally and empirically. In the opinion of a senior civil servant of the day, Butler 'had a genuine desire for prison reform without any very clear concept himself of what he

[80] Home Office, *Penal Practice in a Changing Society: Aspects of Future Development (England and Wales)* (Cmnd. 645), HMSO, London, 1959, p. 1.

[81] Ibid.

[82] Ibid.

[83] Ibid., p. 2.

[84] R. A. Butler became Home Secretary in 1957, having failed to secure the premiership in that year when Harold Macmillan was preferred as Sir Anthony Eden's successor. He remained at the Home Office until 1962. After another unsuccessful leadership bid, he served as Foreign Secretary under Sir Alec Douglas-Home in 1963–4. Butler left politics with a life peerage to become Master of Trinity College, Cambridge in 1965.

wanted to achieve'.[85] Generally benevolent intentions, but imprecise objectives, were reflected in a White Paper published in February 1959 under the title *Penal Practice in a Changing Society*. The stated aim was to relate penal methods to the purposes which they were required to serve:

We need periodically to consider whether existing methods are the best that can be devised for dealing with crime in the context of society as it is at a given time. As crime is related to the pattern and outlook of the society in which it occurs, so penal methods may need to be adapted to the society in which they must operate.[86]

The White Paper called for a fundamental re-examination of penal methods 'based on studies of the causes of crime, or rather of the factors which foster or inhibit crime', supported by reliable assessments of the results achieved by existing methods. Such a re-examination could be 'a landmark in penal history and illumine the course ahead for a generation'.[87] More information was to be obtained on offenders, and their backgrounds, in order that the courts might select methods of disposal 'most likely to achieve the ends of justice in relation to the individual offender'.[88] Research into the causes and treatment of delinquency was to be encouraged. The Home Office had set up its own Research Unit in 1957,[89] in addition to supporting criminological research in the universities and elsewhere. Interest was aroused when the University of Cambridge declared that it was prepared, if the necessary funds could be made available, to consider the establishment of an Institute of Criminology. Soon after a gift was announced of £150,000 by the Wolfson Foundation for a chair, and in 1960 the Institute was

---

[85] Lord Allen of Abbeydale in Longford, *Punishment and the Punished*, p. 35.
[86] *Penal Practice in a Changing Society*, p. 6.
[87] Ibid., p. 7
[88] Ibid., p. 3
[89] See T. S. Lodge, 'The Founding of the Home Office Research Unit' in Roger Hood (ed.), *Crime, Criminology and Public Policy: Essays in Honour of Sir Leon Radzinowicz*, Heinemann, London, 1974, pp. 11–24. The decision to establish the unit had been foreshadowed by Butler when, in the course of a Supply Day debate on prisons in the House of Commons, he referred to the need to supplement knowledge of how to treat offenders: 'we must also make the best use of the tools which the sciences of statistics and sociology have put into our hands ...'. *Parl. Debates*, HC, 566 (5th ser.), col. 1143, 13 Mar. 1957.

established under the directorship of Professor Leon Radzinowicz.[90] Besides carrying out a programme of research, the Institute provided full-time courses of study for postgraduate degrees in criminology and part-time courses for criminal justice practitioners.

A sterner note prefaced another statement of intent, the setting up of a Standing Committee on Criminal Law Revision:[91] 'In order that those deserving punishment shall not escape owing to defects in the criminal law'.[92] Because of their higher rate of offending, the White Paper placed special emphasis on the treatment of young male offenders between the ages of sixteen and twenty-one. Perversely, as it must have seemed to penal reformers, the opportunities offered by borstal training, with its reformative aims, were all too often spurned by young offenders, many of whom preferred a prison sentence to borstal training on the grounds that it was usually shorter and for a more certain period.[93]

Detention centres, dating from 1952, provided a strict regime for selected young offenders, although better suited to those without previous experience of institutional custody. To avoid any but the worst young offenders being sent to prison, the Prison Commissioners proposed to accelerate the provision of detention centres, backed up by a new sentence of custodial training for a maximum of two years with the chance of being released on licence, subject to after-care, after six months. The implications of introducing a national scheme of criminal injuries compensation for the victims of violent crime, one of the last causes espoused by Margery Fry,[94]

[90] Previously Director of the Department of Criminal Science at Cambridge, Dr Radzinowicz was a member both of the Royal Commission on Capital Punishment and the Home Office Advisory Council on the Treatment of Offenders. He was knighted in 1970.
[91] The first chairman was Lord Justice Sellers. Initial subjects for review were the law of larceny and related forms of fraud, and defects in the law relating to indecent behaviour towards children, not amounting to indecent assault. [1959] Crim. L.R. 159.
[92] *Penal Practice in a Changing Society*, p. 4.
[93] Since the Criminal Justice Act 1948 there had been a restriction on the imposition of imprisonment upon a person under twenty-one years of age, unless the court was of the opinion that no other method of dealing with him was appropriate. Further prohibitions or restrictions on the imprisonment of offenders of certain ages were contained in the Magistrates' Courts Act 1952 and the Criminal Justice Act 1961.
[94] Margery Fry (1874–1958), penal reformer and educationalist, had died the previous year at the age of eighty-four. Always interested in new developments, she had also encouraged the study of criminology and penology in universities.

were to be investigated to see if a workable scheme could be devised.[95]

Penal Practice in a Changing Society stands as the high watermark of what later became known as the treatment model. Eschewing undue optimism, the constant pressure from the pincers precluding any such temptation, the White Paper irradiated a belief in the importance of scrutinizing the causes of crime, calmly and dispassionately, in order to ascertain more effectively methods of combating it. In doing so, it was a true reflection of the outlook and political style of the Home Secretary. Butler had shown a keen personal interest in the preparation of the White Paper which underwent at least four drafts before it reached the finished version. In his eyes it came to rank on a par with his Education White Paper of 1943.[96]

In the summer of 1958 the Home Secretary served notice to his ministerial colleagues that he would be making demands on the Government's expenditure programme to finance his plans for a wholesale prison-rebuilding scheme. He took the precautionary step of warning the Prime Minister in advance that he had 'no intention of embarrassing the Chancellor by making unreasonable demands on the Exchequer'.[97] Macmillan replied urbanely that he was all for the plan, adding:

No doubt it will cost money, but I do not suppose the money will be spent very quickly. I take it, it will mostly be building new prisons, but they will take some time, especially if the Ministry of Works have anything to do with the plans.[98]

The Prime Minister's reply was prescient. Two decades were to pass before the prison-building programme reached a scale that was to become significant in terms of public expenditure.[99]

[95] *Penal Practice in a Changing Society*, p. 7.
[96] 'Mr Butler saw this White Paper as comparable in importance with his 1943 White Paper on Education Policy': letter from Sir Charles Cunningham, 18 Aug. 1991. The same point is made by Butler's biographer, Anthony Howard, in *RAB: The Life of R. A. Butler*, Jonathan Cape, London, 1987, pp. 255–6.
[97] Ibid., p. 263.
[98] Prime Minister's Personal Minute dated 28 June 1958. Quoted in *RAB: The Life of R. A. Butler*, p. 264.
[99] When explaining the Criminal Justice Bill on Second Reading in November 1960, the Home Secretary told the House of Commons that in the seventeen months since the publication of *Penal Practice in a Changing Society* three new open prisons had been completed, and three detention centres for young offenders would be

VI

Butler postponed publication of the White Paper's proposals until after the Conservative Party Conference had met at Blackpool in the Autumn of 1958. He was not the first, or the last, Home Secretary to be apprehensive of the clamourous demands he was likely to face. In the event, he survived the Conference debate on crime and punishment without much difficulty, although in the following year back-benchers on his own side of the House of Commons forced open again the politically sensitive question of corporal punishment. The Home Secretary deftly referred their claims to the expert, and non-political, Advisory Council on the Treatment of Offenders. While recognizing that opinion was divided on the issue, the Council firmly came out against the reintroduction of any form of corporal punishment as a judicial penalty for any criminal offence.[100]

The report noted that advocates of reintroduction did not wish simply to limit the penalty to the same offences as those to which it had applied between 1861 and 1948. Rather they wanted to extend it, either to offences of all kinds, or at any rate to offences involving violence against the person, especially those committed by young hooligans.[101] If that were to be the outcome, it would mean putting the clock back not twelve years, but a hundred years.[102] Following in the footsteps of an earlier Departmental Committee,[103] the Advisory Council painstakingly analysed the subsequent criminal careers of men who had been flogged, comparing them with those who had been subjected to other forms of penalty. The conclusion was unchanged: namely, that the evidence did not point towards judicial corporal punishment as having any special or unique influence, and that it was unlikely to affect the incidence of crime.[104]

The Advisory Council's report was published in November 1960, the same month as a Criminal Justice Bill brought before Parliament

opened in the next three months. With work in progress at other prisons, the total amount of building construction had reached a figure more than four times that of two years before. *Parl. Debates*, HC, 630 (5th ser.), col. 568, 17 Nov. 1960.

[100] *Corporal Punishment*, p. 26.
[101] Ibid.
[102] Ibid.
[103] Departmental Committee on Corporal Punishment, *Report* (Cmd. 5684), 1938.
[104] *Corporal Punishment*, p. 16.

in legislative shape the main proposals contained in the White Paper. The timing made it inevitable that corporal punishment, nowhere mentioned in the Bill, should dominate the debates, and it did. The Annual Report of the Howard League for Penal Reform noted:

Despite the reasoned arguments... based on evidence from all who cared to submit it (including a high proportion of individuals and organizations with direct experience of offenders), demands for corporal punishment became even more vociferous and several amendments to the Criminal Justice Bill were introduced with this in view. The League supplied factual information on the subject to all Members of Parliament who wanted it and the amendments were soundly defeated in both Houses.[105]

In the face of some trenchantly expressed disapproval from the Conservative benches, the Government refused to yield. The main challenge came on the floor of the Commons at Report Stage when a new clause, giving the courts power to pass sentences of corporal punishment on young male offenders convicted of crimes of violence on second or subsequent conviction, was rejected by 259 votes to 67.[106] The hurdle of the Conservative Party Conference was still to come. In surmounting it, Butler established ascendancy over his critics. His recollection of the Conference debate that autumn, not untypically, combined boastfulness with political insight:

I spoke for forty minutes and carried the whole audience after a prolonged debate. Iain Macleod had tears in his eyes when he came up to congratulate Mollie. But, though they hesitated to return to the assault, many members of the party continued to hold this stand against me.[107]

What became the Criminal Justice Act of 1961 was a relatively short statute of forty-five sections sections and six schedules, with more of a coherent theme than is usually found in comparable legislation. It was a progressive measure, ministering to the conditions of Churchill's 'gentler age'. Its main thrust was directed towards revising the powers of the courts to deal with young offenders; their detention and treatment in a range of institutions

[105] Howard League for Penal Reform, *Annual Report*, 1960–1, p. 3.
[106] MPs voting for the new clause included one of the new intake at the 1959 General Election, Margaret Thatcher. *Parl. Debates*, HC, 638 (5th ser.), cols. 145–6, 11 Apr. 1961.
[107] *The Art of the Possible: The Memoirs of Lord Butler*, Hamish Hamilton, London, 1971, p. 201.

other than prisons, notably detention centres, Borstals or approved schools; and their supervision in the community by the Probation Service. All young offenders released from a detention centre were to get one year's compulsory after-care.

VII

Apart from the provisions on young offenders, the Act contained administrative changes, including one dear to the heart of the Home Office which had been tried before, but withdrawn by the Home Secretary in the face of strong criticism when the Criminal Justice Bill 1947 was considered at Committee Stage in the Commons. Despite some persistent opposition, inside and outside Parliament, the 1961 Act gave a power to make an Order in Council paving the way for the transfer to the Home Office of the functions of the Prison Commission.[108] Although they were public servants answerable to the Home Secretary, the Prison Commissioners had a separate existence going back to the reforms of the late nineteenth century. Under the Prison Act 1877, three Prison Commissioners had been appointed to reorganize and administer English county and borough prisons. The following year these prisons came under central government control, their number being reduced by half. Rules were made uniform, a standardized system of discipline adopted, and the staff co-ordinated into a single service with a regular system of promotion. For some years the convict prisons, already the responsibility of central government, remained technically distinct entities, but both were brought under the dominant authority of one man, Sir Edmund Du Cane.[109] From 1898 the Prison Commissioners became, as their chairman already was, Directors of Convict Prisons in addition to their responsibilities for the local prisons.[110]

Du Cane was the first in a line of redoubtable and prominent penal administrators of the stature of Sir Evelyn Ruggles-Brise,[111]

[108] The Commission was dissolved by the Prison Commissioners Dissolution Order 1963 (SI 1963 No. 597) which came into effect on 1 Apr. 1963.

[109] Inspector-General of Military Prisons and Chairman, Board of Directors of Convict Prisons, 1869; Chairman of the Prison Commissioners, 1877–95.

[110] Committee of Inquiry into the United Kingdom Prison Services, *Report* (Cmnd. 7673), HMSO, London, 1979, p. 9.

[111] Prison Commissioner, 1892; Chairman of the Prison Commission, 1895–1921.

Sir Alexander Paterson,[112] and Sir Lionel Fox.[113] Over the years the pattern of recruitment changed with rising Home Office officials being seconded as Commissioners for a spell on their way to the top in Whitehall. After 1948, the Chairman, with the rank of an Assistant Under-Secretary of State, reported to the Home Secretary through the Permanent Under-Secretary of State at the Home Office, instead of, as previously, through the Criminal Division at the Home Office.[114]

Centralizing tendencies were already evident in the late 1940s, but they were reinforced by the arrival at the Home Office of Sir Charles Cunningham as Permanent Under-Secretary in 1957.[115] Formerly Head of the Home Department at the Scottish Office, Cunningham was accustomed to a fully integrated system.[116] Although one consequence of their detached status was that the Commissioners tended to be remote from the day-to-day process of policy formulation in the higher echelons of the Home Office, they had the advantage of being perceived by the Prison Service as providing a collective leadership in which the professional element in the service could and did play a significant part. While the Commissioners were not drawn exclusively from within the Prison Service, by convention three key posts were reserved for people who had been promoted from prison governor grades. These were the Directors of Prison and Borstal Administration, and the Woman Director. In the words of Sir Frank Newsam,[117] Cunningham's predecessor as Permanent Secretary at the Home Office, the Directors stood 'under the Chairman, at the head of a hierarchical service through which the normal flow of promotion may carry a qualified officer from the lowest rank to be a Commissioner'.[118]

Few, if any, rose from the lowest rank, but none the less there

[112] Prison Commissioner, 1922–47. Many of the ideas and experiments leading to the main provisions of the Criminal Justice Act 1948 were attributed to Paterson.

[113] Secretary to the Prison Commission, 1925–34; Deputy Receiver to Metropolitan Police District, 1934–42 (Acting Receiver 1941–2), Chairman, the Prison Commission, 1942–60.

[114] Committee of Inquiry into the United Kingdom Prison Services, *Report*, p. 21.

[115] Permanent Under-Secretary of State, Home Office, 1957–66; Secretary, Scottish Home Department, 1948–57.

[116] The Scottish Prison Commission had been abolished in 1928, being replaced by a Prisons Division of the Scottish Home and Health Department under the Secretary of State's direct control.

[117] Permanent Under-Secretary of State, Home Office, 1948–57.

[118] Sir F. Newsam, *The Home Office*, Allen and Unwin, London, 1954, p. 160.

was a career path open to prison governors to progress through the intermediate rank of Assistant Commissioner to a full Commissionership. Promotion above the rank of governor did not take the successful aspirant out of his own service into a vaster bureaucracy. On the contrary, it was the administrators coming to the Commission from the Home Office who were seen (and saw themselves) as making a transition, even if a temporary one. Prison staff felt towards abolition much as the employees of an old established family firm would feel towards merger into an international conglomerate.

While tensions had existed between the Prison Service in the field, their headquarters, and the Home Office since the days of Du Cane and Ruggles-Brise, they were exacerbated by the centralization that took place in the 1960s and 1970s. Under the new system of administration resentment and lack of trust became commonplace, a situation which was not alleviated by the measures taken in the light of the May Committee's recommendations in 1979 to give the Prison Department greater autonomy. On the state of the relationship between the Prison Service and the Home Office, the May Committee commented:

We cannot escape the conclusion that many of those employed in the Service feel a deep sense of dissatisfaction with the organisation and management of it as a whole and that a gulf has grown up between the establishments in the field and the staff who work in them on the one hand and headquarters at the Home Office in London on the other.[119]

In quoting this extract twelve years later, the Report of the Inquiry into Prison Disturbances by Lord Justice Woolf found that the management changes which had taken place since 1979 had done nothing to reduce the deep-felt sense of dissatisfaction, and that in many establishments there was a strong feeling of distrust of headquarters.[120] Prison Department divisions were widely criticized by governors for appearing to operate in isolation, each pursuing their own areas of interest without regard to the priorities of other divisions and establishment needs. Animosity prevailed

[119] Committee of Inquiry into the United Kingdom Prison Services, *Report*, pp. 75–6.
[120] *Prison Disturbances April 1990*. Report of an Inquiry by Lord Justice Woolf (Parts I and II) and Judge Tumim (Part II) (Cm. 1456), HMSO, London, 1991, pp. 287–8. Lord Woolf became a Lord of Appeal in Ordinary in 1992.

between headquarters and the field, heightened by the different career backgrounds characterizing the two groups. Those whose careers were wholly tied to the Prison Service looked on the generalist civil servants at headquarters as lacking in commitment to the service. Because their tour of duty usually lasted no more than three or four years their primary loyalties were thought to be to their careers in the Home Office at large. Conversely, many headquarters staff saw those in the field as too narrowly concerned with the running of their own prison establishments, and resistant to any suggestion that they should be called to account for the extent to which they implemented nationally agreed policies.

The strained relationship between prison governors and the Home Office Prison Department was overshadowed by the even more turbulent staff relations between management and prison officers which came to a head in widespread industrial action in 1978. It would be a misleading over-simplification to attribute the continuing erosion of morale in the administration of the prisons to the abolition of the Commission in 1963. Many of the pressures were already latent and would have come to the surface irrespective of the organizational structure. Yet it is structure which gives to any undertaking its distinctive shape and identity. A visible structure influences style, facilitating the emergence of shared aims and values, and bearing strongly on the potential for leadership within the organization.

The issue must have seemed finely balanced at the time, but the troubled history of the prisons in the years that followed suggests that Butler was wrong to have accepted Cunningham's advice that the Commission was no longer an adequate body to handle the complexity of the tasks to be performed. The contention was that a co-ordinated approach was needed towards the treatment of offenders, and that it was not appropriate for the Home Secretary's responsibilities for prisoners to be on a different basis from his other responsibilities. Additional arguments deployed were that amalgamation with the Home Office would provide a larger pool of staff on which to draw; that it would be more efficient and economical for the establishment, finance, and other specialist services of the two bodies to be combined; and that the Scottish precedent had been 'fully successful'.[121]

---

[121] Committee of Inquiry into the United Kingdom Prison Services, *Report*, pp. 21–2.

The era of the Prison Commission was by no means the golden age that nostalgia sometimes portrayed it to have been, but the verdict must be that its abolition magnified rather than minimized the deepening crisis into which the Prison Service was falling. By 1991, prompted by ministerial exasperation with continuing industrial action and union-led recalcitrance to changed working patterns, the future of the Prison Service was again in the melting pot. Official policy was swinging back towards the model of a freer-standing organization, in the shape of an agency fashioned under the Government's 'Next Steps' initiative:

> The Government intends to develop the structure of the management of the Prison Service progressively in a manner that is consistent with the principles of 'Next Steps'. It will review the question of when agency status for the Prison Service might be appropriate as the changes set out in this White Paper are introduced.[122]

In an interview soon after his appointment as Director General, Joe Pilling, a senior civil servant, remarked that the conversion of the Prison Service into an executive agency would help to distance it from the Home Office and achieve greater operational freedom, adding: 'One of the problems with the prison service is that it is directly driven by civil servants and largely made up of civil servants. This can produce a certain ambiguity of role for us.'[123]

A 'hands off' approach was regarded as crucial by Sir Raymond Lygo who was appointed by the Home Secretary in August 1991 to undertake a review of the management of the Prison Service. A personal letter to Kenneth Baker forwarding his report and recommendations began unambiguously:

> When you asked me to undertake a review of the management of the Prison Service, I told you that I thought my recommendations would be easier for me to make than for you to implement, but you assured me you believed the climate was ready for some radical change.
> As we discussed at our first meeting and as I subsequently discussed with Angela Rumbold, it was very clear that unless there was a preparedness on the part of the Home Office to take its hands off the management of

---

[122] Home Office, *Custody, Care and Justice: The Way Ahead for the Prison Service in England and Wales* (Cm. 1647), HMSO, London, 1991, p. 31.
[123] *The Times*, 25 Oct. 1991. In January 1993 Pilling was replaced by a Director General (and Chief Executive designate) recruited from the private sector.

the Prison Service in its day to day business and allow itself to be constrained by matters of policy only, then it would not be possible to effect the changes which you deem desirable and which have become very clear to me as being necessary during the talks I have had and the visits I have made.[124]

Baker lost little time in accepting the majority of Lygo's recommendations, announcing in March 1992 that the Prison Service for England and Wales would become an agency from 1 April 1993. Consultations with the trade unions and other interested parties would begin shortly. In line with the recommended structure a Supervisory Board would be created, which would have responsibility for advising the Home Secretary on strategic and resource questions affecting the service. This Board would be chaired by the Home Office minister handling prison matters. A Chief Executive, appointed by open competition, and directly responsible to the Home Secretary, would chair a Management Board, rather than the part-time, non-executive chairman proposed in the report. Executive agency status, Baker declared, would constitute:

the right framework for placing the management of the service on a more professional footing, providing the most positive environment for staff to work in and, above all, ensuring the delivery of an improved service both to the public and those held in custody.[125]

Many unresolved problems lie ahead. What policy advice will the Home Secretary take on prison matters, for example the use of police cells and contracting with the private sector, which are distinct from the operations of the Prison Service, and by whom should it be given? What will be the relationship between the Supervisory Board, the Management Board, and the central Home Office? Will reserve powers be retained by the Secretary of State? What are the implications for the policy of contracting out and privatization?[126] Will the new agency be expected to make contracts with private sector companies for the management of what would in effect be rival penal establishments, or will this function continue to be performed by the Home Office? What, if any, legislation will be called for?

---

[124] Letter from Admiral Sir Raymond Lygo to Kenneth Baker, 12 Dec. 1991.
[125] *Parl. Debates*, HC, 205 (6th ser.), col. WA 567, 11 Mar. 1992.
[126] See Chapter 6.

Important as they are, such organizational questions are over-shadowed by what Lygo correctly identified as the main issue. Will ministers be prepared to surrender the close degree of control over the Prison Service to which they have grown accustomed, and to the extent necessary to allow a Chief Executive the freedom required for true agency status? Ministerial accountability to Parliament is often cited as a stumbling block, but it is not insurmountable. Chief Executives of a growing number of agencies are now politically accountable in a variety of ways.[127] Detailed scrutiny of large-scale and complex undertakings on a continuing basis is not a task for which most MPs have either the inclination or the time. What matters is that ministers should be ready and willing to come to the House of Commons when expected to do so in order to answer questions from elected representatives on matters of genuine public interest and importance.

In this sense the conferring of an enlarged degree of operational freedom on a professionally directed body need not mean any diminution of true public accountability. The police have far more operational independence from the Home Office than the Prison Service has ever enjoyed. No distinction is made for the Metro-politan Police, much the largest force in the country, where the Home Secretary has formal responsibility as the police authority.[128] The Commissioner is a recognizable national figure, in modern times invariably a career police officer of high ability. Nevertheless, it is the Home Secretary who has to face Parliament when things go wrong, whether incidents occur in the Metropolitan Police area or elsewhere. Accountability is not confined to policy matters, as

[127] Chief Executives of agencies are accounting officers and as such answerable to the Public Accounts Committee for the resources allocated to them by Government. They also appear before and give evidence to departmental Select Committees in the House of Commons, and reply in writing to Parliamentary Questions on operational matters which are referred to them by ministers. For an analysis of the issues of managerial freedom versus public accountability, see G. Jordan, *Next Steps Agencies: From Managing by Command to Managing by Contract?*, Aberdeen Papers in Accountancy, Finance and Management, University of Aberdeen, 1992. Grant Jordan is Professor of Politics at the University of Aberdeen.

[128] 'The Home Secretary... approves the broad policing policy of the force, which is published in the Commissioner's strategy statement. As the police authority, the Home Secretary is responsible for satisfying himself that the force is using resources to the best effect, and is answerable to Parliament for this and other aspects of his role.' Home Office, *Annual Report 1991*, The Government's Public Expenditure Plans 1991–2 to 1993–4 for the Home Office and the Charity Commission (Cm. 1509), HMSO, London, p. 13.

William Whitelaw found when he had to report to an astonished House of Commons that an intruder had got into the Queen's bedroom at Buckingham Palace.[129] Indeed, he took his responsibility so seriously that he had to be dissuaded from resignation.[130]

VIII

Alongside the milder reforms of the 1950s and early 1960s surged the powerful forces evoked by the death penalty. The lengthy period of Conservative government from 1951 to 1964 made it easier for Labour MPs, released from electoral inhibitions, to press for abolition. Speaking in a House of Commons debate on the Report of the Royal Commission on Capital Punishment in 1955,[131] Chuter Ede declared that his time as Home Secretary had not persuaded him either way of the arguments for or against deterrence. The case of Timothy Evans, however, who had been hanged in 1950 after conviction for murder partly on the evidence of John Christie, also convicted and executed for murder three years later, had convinced him that mistakes could occur. As Home Secretary, it was Ede who had written on Evans's papers when considering whether there were any circumstances to justify a reprieve: 'The Law must take its course'. In the light of the facts which emerged subsequently, he believed that Evans's execution was not justified and that a mistake had been made.[132] In the following year, Ede moved an amended Commons motion:

That this House believes that the death penalty for murder no longer

[129] *Parl. Debates*, HC, 27 (6th ser.), col. 645, 12 July 1982.

[130] The involvement of the Metropolitan Police was a factor that influenced Whitelaw in his initial reaction that he ought to resign at once as he had 'failed the Queen so dismally' (see *The Whitelaw Memoirs*, Aurum Press, London, 1989, p. 212). It was discounted by the Prime Minister and others, including Home Office officials, who dissuaded him, arguing that the Home Secretary could not be regarded as directly responsible for the operational actions of members of the many organizations for which he had overall responsibility. But there was no doubt that Whitelaw regarded himself as answerable to Parliament on a matter of unquestioned public interest and importance.

[131] *Parl. Debates*, HC, 536 (5th ser.), cols. 2076–84, 10 Feb. 1955.

[132] Following an inquiry by a High Court Judge, a posthumous free pardon was granted to Evans on the recommendation of the Home Secretary in 1966. See Home Office, *The Case of Timothy John Evans*, Report of an Inquiry by the Hon. Mr Justice Brabin (Cmnd. 3101), HMSO, London, 1966.

accords with the needs or the true interests of a civilised society, and calls upon Her Majesty's Government to introduce forthwith legislation for its abolition or for its suspension for an experimental period.[133]

On a free vote the amendment was carried by 292 votes to 246, a majority of 46. Ede was not the only former minister to change his mind. Each of the retentionist members of the Labour Cabinet in 1947–8 who still sat in the Commons voted for abolition. They were Herbert Morrison, George Isaacs, Tom Williams, and Arthur Woodburn. As a result of the expression of Parliamentary opinion, which the Prime Minister, Sir Anthony Eden, undertook to respect, the Government provided time for Sydney Silverman's Private Member's Bill for the abolition of the death penalty. The Second Reading was carried on 12 March 1956 by 286 votes to 262,[134] a majority of 24, and passed through all its remaining stages in the Commons, before being heavily defeated once more in the Lords.[135] Faced with the need to take some action, and willing to restrict the death penalty but not to abandon it completely, a classic step on the road to abolition,[136] the Government turned again to the idea of categorizing murders which the Labour Government had attempted, fruitlessly, as a way out of a previous Parliamentary impasse in 1948. Since then it had been closely examined, but once more rejected, by the Royal Commission on Capital Punishment.

The Government Bill which became the Homicide Act 1957 restricted the death penalty to five categories of capital murder. They were: (*a*) murders in the course or furtherance of theft, (*b*) murders by shooting or causing an explosion, (*c*) murders in the course or for the purpose of resisting lawful arrest or of escaping from legal custody, (*d*) murders of police officers in the execution

[133] *Parl. Debates*, HC, 548 (5th ser.), col. 2556, 16 Feb. 1956.
[134] *Parl. Debates*, HC, 550 (5th ser.), col. 146, 12 Mar. 1956.
[135] The Bill was rejected on Second Reading by 238 votes to 95, a majority of 143 against. *Parl. Debates*, HL, 198 (5th ser.), cols. 839–42, 10 July 1956.
[136] In a paper drawing on the findings of an international survey of the death penalty commissioned by the United Nations in 1987, Dr Roger Hood commented: 'It is well known that the process towards abolition in many states often begins with a restriction in the categories of crime subject to capital punishment and then proceeds to a further restriction to particular types of murder. This is frequently a path taken by governments where there appear to be strong sentiments expressed in favour of retaining the death penalty.' *The Death Penalty in International Perspective*, Amnesty International Seminar on the Death Penalty, CSCE Parallel Conference, Moscow, 16 Sept. 1991, p. 6.

of their duty and persons assisting them, and (*e*) murders by prisoners of prison officers in the execution of their duty and persons assisting them. The death penalty was retained for repeated murders, while a new defence of diminished responsibility, imported from Scotland, allowed a charge of manslaughter to be substituted for murder if a defendant 'was suffering from such abnormality of mind... as substantially impaired his mental responsibility for his acts...'.[137]

The measure was inherited by R. A. Butler who became Home Secretary while the Bill was going through Parliament.[138] Unlike other speakers in the debates, he made no attempt to justify the classification according to any degrees of heinousness or dreadfulness, claiming instead that the categories had been based upon 'the different principle of reducing the scope of capital punishment to the minimum necessary for that preservation of law and order, and confining it to those forms of murder for which it is not only a particularly necessary, but is also believed to be a particularly effective, deterrent'.[139]

In Parliament and outside, the distinction between capital and non-capital murders was subjected to much criticism. Despite its imperfections, which were soon to become well ventilated by the circumstances of individual cases coming before the courts, there were two outcomes which could not be ignored. The first was that the large majority of intentional killings within the family, or other existing personal relationships, were excluded from the death penalty, leading Professor Glanville Williams to remark: 'The Homicide Act has performed the service of removing capital punishment from the picture in nearly all killings of passion and depression'.[140] The second consequence was to limit the number of executions by the early 1960s to no more than three or four a year, so bringing nearer the prospect of total abolition by the familiar,

---

[137] Homicide Act 1957, Section 2. See also *Responses to Crime*, vol. 1, pp. 122–7.

[138] In his first speech as Home Secretary, Butler succeeded in uniting the disparate factions in a Committee of the Whole House to defeat by 346 votes to 2 an amendment to add death by poisoning to the categories of capital murder. *Parl. Debates*, HC, 563 (5th ser.), cols. 266–71, 23 Jan. 1957.

[139] *Parl. Debates*, HC, 563, col. 267.

[140] 'The Working of the Homicide Act', (1961) 10 *Howard Journal of Criminal Justice* 298. Glanville Williams QC was Rouse Ball Professor of English Law at Cambridge, 1968–78.

if inglorious, means of English penal reform: diminution, disuse, abandonment.[141]

It was the first two categories of capital murder in particular that discredited the Homicide Act.[142] The death penalty for murders committed in the course or furtherance of theft was intended as a deterrent against the use of physical violence in offences of burglary, housebreaking, and robbery. But away from the highly coloured examples used by both sides to illustrate their arguments in the debating chamber, experience showed that 'most of the theft-murders that have resulted in capital convictions since the Act have been committed by stupid persons, who had not the sense to see how easily they could be caught, and how much safer it would have been to do the job in a different way'.[143]

Murder can never be anything but a most serious crime, although committed in conditions of infinite variety, whereas thefts can be trivial in the extreme. In 1958, a year after the Homicide Act, for example, a man was hanged for capital murder having quarrelled with an elderly lady about the amount of wages he was to receive for working in her garden. As she was kneeling to get some tools out of a cupboard he struck her on the head with a hammer, apparently on the impulse of the moment, and then stole a wallet which he found in the house.[144] It was the last, far more trivial act, that led to his execution, rather than the brutal killing which would not otherwise have attracted the death penalty.

Clamorous criticism of this category of capital murder came simultaneously from an opposing tendency. Retentionists could not accept that a rapist who breaks into a house, violates his victim, and then kills in order to prevent her giving evidence against him,

[141] A survey for the United Nations covering the years up to 1960, carried out by the French jurist, Marc Ancel, listed twenty-four countries plus one state in Australia and six states in the United States of America as abolitionist *de jure*, with four more categorized as abolitionist *de facto*. (Department of Economic and Social Affairs, *Capital Punishment*, United Nations, New York, 1968, p. 10.) At the time of Dr Hood's report in 1988 the number of abolitionist countries had increased from twenty-four to fifty-three, plus fifteen states of the USA. Another eleven countries were listed as abolitionist *de facto*, at least since 1972. *The Death Penalty in International Perspective*, p. 3.

[142] Christopher Hollis, a former Member of Parliament who had taken a leading part in the earlier debates on capital punishment, published a critical account of the way the provisions of the Homicide Act 1957 had worked in practice. See *The Homicide Act*, Gollancz, London, 1964.

[143] (1961) 10 *Howard Journal of Criminal Justice*, 298 at 299.

[144] *R. v. Stokes* [1958] Crim. L.R. 688.

should be treated as having committed a lesser offence than a burglar who kills in the course of theft. Murder by shooting also led to indefensible anomalies. Its inclusion in the categories of capital murder had originally been defended by the Government on the grounds that the presence of a gun was an indication of a premeditated offence, but in practice it proved impossible to maintain the distinction between deliberate killings committed with a gun, or a knife or other weapon. Moreover, death caused by poisoning, the most premeditated of all murders, was exempted from liability to capital punishment.

IX

By the mid-1960s the long campaign for ending capital punishment was nearing a climax. Procrastination, compromise, and delay had been the response of successive governments of both political parties. But while a majority of informed public opinion, the target of persistent lobbying over so long a period,[145] moved decisively towards outright abolition, fortified by the anomalous penalties resulting from the 1957 Homicide Act, the views of the general public continued to be hostile and mostly out of sympathy with the prevailing climate at Westminster and Whitehall. A Gallup Poll in March 1960 showed that 78% of those questioned favoured the death penalty, with 73% believing that complete abolition would lead to a rise in the number of murders.[146]

There is always a risk that legislative reforms which outpace public opinion will be undermined by reaction. Timing and preparation of the ground is vital. Frustrating as the long-drawn-out debates since 1948 had been for the abolitionists, when the moment eventually came no one could claim that Parliament was acting precipitately or foisting a highly controversial measure onto a

---

[145] A National Council for the Abolition of the Death Penalty had been formed in 1925 to campaign against capital punishment. Following the Second World War it was succeeded by the National Campaign for Abolition of Capital Punishment. The publication of the Royal Commission's report in 1953 inspired a new attempt to change the law headed by Gerald Gardiner, QC (later Lord Gardiner) and (Sir) Victor Gollancz. See an article by F. Dawtry, who had been active in the campaign, in (1966) 6 *British Journal of Criminology* 183.

[146] J. E. Hall Williams, 'Developments Since the Homicide Act, 1957', included in Tuttle, *The Crusade against Capital Punishment in Great Britain*, p. 163.

nation that was unprepared. The history of large reforms has been
marked by resistance to novelty; people need time to get used to
ideas, even if they come to oppose them. The painstaking and
unbiased work of the Royal Commission, the failure of the 1957
alternative, the well-directed flow of abolitionist propaganda,
and the reliance on factual evidence as well as moral arguments, in particular the recognition that mistakes could occur,
and in all probability had occurred, led to the progressive
conversion of Parliamentary opinion. This was especially
noticeable amongst younger Conservatives in the Commons, and
amongst the life peers who had begun to join the Upper House
in increasing numbers since the Life Peerages Act in 1958. Co-
incident with the changing Parliamentary climate was a more
positive attitude towards abolition on the part of the Labour
Government.

Unlike the Homicide Act seven years earlier, the Murder
(Abolition of Death Penalty) Bill of 1964, introduced by the
indefatigable Sydney Silverman once again, was not a Government
Bill backed by the Government Whips. Although a Private Member's Bill, it had been included in the Government's programme set
out in the Queen's Speech. On a free vote, it received a second
reading in the Commons by 355 votes to 170.[147] Telling speeches in
support of abolition were made from the Conservative benches by
Sir Edward Boyle[148] and Henry Brooke,[149] another Home Secretary who had become persuaded by the arguments against
capital punishment once free of the cares of office. The
overwhelming support, however, came from Labour members,
with the Prime Minister and most of the Cabinet voting for
the Bill.

The Government's business managers had to come to the
rescue when it looked as though the Bill might be lost at
Committee Stage. The process of scrutiny and amendment which
had begun in the usual way in a Standing Committee upstairs,

[147] *Parl. Debates*, HC, 704 (5th ser.), cols. 1001–6, 21 Dec. 1964.
[148] *Parl. Debates*, HC, 704, cols. 983–92. Financial Secretary to the Treasury,
1959–62; Minister of Education, 1962–4. Life peerage as Lord Boyle of Handsworth
in 1970. Vice-Chancellor of Leeds University, 1970–81.
[149] *Parl. Debates*, HC, 704, cols. 905–15. Home Secretary, 1962–4; Financial
Secretary to the Treasury 1954–7; Minister of Housing and Local Government,
1957–61; Chief Secretary to the Treasury and Paymaster General, 1961–2. Life
peerage as Lord Brooke of Cumnor, 1966.

was interrupted when the Bill was returned unexpectedly to the floor of the House. With an overall majority of only three, the entire legislative programme of the session was jeopardized by the extra demands on the Parliamentary timetable. The day was saved by the Government's willingness for the House to meet, exceptionally, in the mornings until the Committee Stage of the Bill had been completed. In the event, no more than a single amendment was made in the Commons. It was a highly significant one. On 26 May 1965 a new clause proposed by Brooke, with support coming mainly from Conservative members, was carried by 176 votes to 128 which had the effect that the Act should expire on 31 July 1970, unless Parliament by affirmative resolution of both Houses otherwise determined.[150]

In the Lords the shift in opinion since the earlier attempts to abolish the death penalty had been rejected was even more striking. After a two-day debate, the Bill received a Second Reading, on a free vote, by a majority of exactly 100: 204 voting in favour and 104 against.[151] Symbolic, perhaps, of a 'gentler age' was the presence of the Archbishop of Canterbury and eleven bishops in the Division lobbies, all of them supporting the Bill, in contrast with the solitary bishop (Chichester) who had voted for abolition in 1948. In Committee, the Lord Chancellor, Gardiner, a prominent campaigner against capital punishment, tried unsuccessfully to lessen the impact of the Commons amendment by proposing that the five-year experimental period should expire on 31 July, only if Parliament so determined by affirmative resolution of both Houses.[152] At the initiative of the Lord Chief Justice, Lord Parker of Waddington, who, unlike his predecessor in 1948, had voted for abolition,[153] the Lords debated at Committee stage whether the penalty of life imprisonment for murder should be mandatory or discretionary. The implications of this question, transformed by the reprehensible way in which the administration of life imprisonment had developed over the intervening years, were to be

---

[150] *Parl. Debates*, HC, 713 (5th ser.), cols. 529–68, 26 May 1965.
[151] *Parl. Debates*, HL, 268 (5th ser.), cols. 711–14, 20 July 1965.
[152] *Parl. Debates*, HL, 268 (5th ser.), cols. 1251–70, 27 July 1965.
[153] In his speech on Second Reading, Lord Parker of Waddington explained that he was in favour of abolition not on moral grounds, but because of the 'complete absurdities' resulting from the working of the Homicide Act 1957. *Parl. Debates*, HL, 268 (5th ser.), cols. 480–1, 19 July 1965.

subjected to critical review by a Lords Select Committee in 1988/9.[154]

The Bill was given a Third Reading in the House of Lords on 26 October 1965 by 169 votes to 75.[155] Two days later, the Commons accepted the Lords amendments. On 9 November, the Murder (Abolition of Death Penalty) Act 1965 came into effect, suspending rather than abolishing the death penalty for those categories of murder that had been capital.[156] The decisive step had been taken, however, and the unworkability of the Homicide Act 1957 was still relatively fresh in legislative memory when the time came for Parliament to consider the continuation of abolition. In December 1969, after Conservative protests had been disposed of that Parliament was being asked to reach a decision at an unnecessarily early stage (a General Election was in the offing), both Houses agreed that the 1965 Act should not expire.[157]

By this route, indirect and long-drawn-out as it had been, the penalty of capital punishment for murder was ended. The decision was one of the most conspicuous, and courageous, ever taken by Members of Parliament, irrespective of party, in the knowledge of the widespread extent of disapproval for their actions. So firm,

---

[154] House of Lords, Session 1988–9, *Report of the Select Committee on Murder and Life Imprisonment* (HL Paper 78–I), HMSO, London, 1989. For the origins of the Committee and its recommendations, see Chapter 7.

[155] *Parl. Debates*, HL, 269 (5th ser.), cols. 553–8, 26 Oct. 1965.

[156] The death penalty remained unchanged for certain other criminal offences: treason: Treason Act 1814 (c. 146), Section 1; offences against the Treachery Act 1940 (c. 21), since repealed by the Statute Law (Repeals) Act 1973 (c. 39); piracy with violence: Piracy Act 1837 (c. 88), Section 2; setting fire to ships of war: Dockyards etc. Protection Act 1772 (c. 24), since repealed by the Criminal Damage Act 1971 (c. 48). No one has been executed in the twentieth century for any peacetime offence except murder. The number of persons executed for other offences committed in wartime is: in the First World War, one for treason; in the Second World War, two for treason and fifteen for offences against the Treachery Act: see Newsam, *The Home Office*, p. 117. These figures exclude persons on whom the death penalty was inflicted under naval, military, or air force law.

[157] After a Conservative motion deploring its early introduction had been defeated by 303 votes to 241, the Commons decided by 343 votes to 185 that the Murder (Abolition of Death Penalty) Act 1965 should not expire as otherwise provided by that Act. (*Parl. Debates*, HC, 793 (5th ser.), cols. 939–1062, 15 Dec. 1969, and cols. 1148–1298, 16 Dec. 1969.) In the Lords, an amendment by Viscount Dilhorne extending the experimental period by a further three years was defeated by 220 votes to 174. The Lord Chancellor's motion that the 1965 Act should not expire was then agreed without a division. *Parl. Debates*, HL, 306 (5th ser.), cols. 1107–322, 17 and 18 Dec. 1969.

however, was the hold of the death penalty on the imagination of the public, rivalling if not exceeding the appeal of corporal punishment, that abolition by Parliament did not end the controversy. On fourteen consecutive occasions since 1969 the House of Commons has rejected by substantial majorities the reintroduction of capital punishment,[158] yet the retentionist cause still flourishes. Although the substance was eliminated, the shadow remains.

[158] A table showing the result of votes in the House of Commons on capital punishment 1955–87 is contained in *Responses to Crime*, vol. 1, at pp. 158–9. Three more votes took place between 1987 and 1991: *Criminal Justice Bill 1987/8*. Report Stage, new clause allowing a jury to recommend the death sentence where a person has been found guilty of murder: *defeated* 218 : 341 (*Parl. Debates*, HC, 134 (6th ser.), cols. 814–18, 7 June 1988.) *Criminal Justice Bill 1990/1*. Committee Stage, new clauses moved seeking to reintroduce capital punishment: *defeated* 215 : 350 (murder of a police officer); 182 : 367 (death penalty for murder if upheld by Court of Appeal); 186 : 349 (murder caused by firearms, explosives, or an offensive weapon, or murder of a police or prison officer). New clause seeking to abolish capital punishment for treason or piracy *defeated* 257 : 289. (*Parl. Debates*, HC, 183 (6th ser.), cols. 112–28, 17 Dec. 1990.) *Armed Forces (Re-committed) Bill 1991*. Committee Stage, new clause to abolish capital punishment for certain military offences: *defeated* 124 : 228. (*Parl. Debates*, HC, 193 (6th ser.), cols. 83–6, 17 June 1991.) The offences are: serious misconduct in action; communicating with the enemy, or furnishing supplies, or aiding the enemy having been captured; obstructing operations or giving false air signals; mutiny or incitement to mutiny; and failure to suppress a mutiny. With the exception of mutiny and incitement to mutiny, the death sentence may be passed only when the offences are committed with intent to assist the enemy. The death penalty for these offences is discretionary and not mandatory. (*Parl. Debates*, HC, 193, col. 55.)

3

Changing within the Consensus, 1964–79

I

The abolition of the death penalty was a political, not an administrative, reform. Demand for the restoration of capital punishment is regarded to this day by many politicians as a powerful torrent capable of bursting its banks and flooding the adjoining landscape. For most of the time since 1965 it has been contained in a separate channel isolated from the rest of criminal justice policy-making. While the politicians were preoccupied with the death penalty and corporal punishment in the late 1950s and early 1960s, the civil servants were paddling in the mainstream, adjusting to the implications of the higher volume of crime[1] and trying to get a grip on what was to become a perennial problem for the next quarter century, the growth in the number of persons appearing before the courts charged with criminal offences.[2] To describe the process as reform would be to claim too much. Evolutionary modification, generally contained within a broad consensus, is nearer to the mark.

A short (eleven pages of text) and inexpensive (1s. 3d.), but resoundingly entitled, White Paper, *The War Against Crime in*

---

[1] The total number of indictable offences recorded by the police rose by 43% between 1958 and 1962. Convictions of indictable offences increased by 39% over the same period. One-third of all those found guilty of indictable offences each year were under the age of seventeen, and one-half under twenty-one. Two-thirds of those found guilty of breaking and entering were under twenty-one. Home Office, *The War Against Crime in England and Wales 1959–64* (Cmnd. 2296), HMSO, London, 1964, p. 3.

[2] Appendix 5 of the **Report** of the Royal Commission on Assizes and Quarter Sessions (Cmnd. 4153), HMSO, London, 1969, demonstrated the escalation that had taken place in the case load of the higher courts, comparing the statistics for 1938 with 1957–67. In addition to the sharp increase in the number of persons tried on criminal charges, more persons were sentenced in the higher courts after summary conviction, and there were also more appeals from summary conviction. Greatly extended legal aid meant that more criminal cases were fought resulting in heavier demands on court time (pp. 33, 161–2).

England and Wales 1959–64,[3] was published in April 1964 in the
dying days of the Conservative Administration which had taken
office in 1959. The Home Secretary was Henry Brooke, previously
Chief Secretary to the Treasury and Minister of Housing and Local
Government, who had replaced Butler in July 1962. A conscientious
but unimaginative minister, Brooke never found the touch needed
to be a successful Home Secretary.

Although not comparable with *Penal Practice in a Changing
Society* in breadth of vision nor in quality of argument, his White
Paper adopted a confident tone. In doing so it reflected Brooke's
belief that the nation was on course to solving the problems
of crime through a combination of diligent police methods and
technology, the observation and classification of offenders, better
informed sentencing decisions, improved treatment regimes in penal
institutions, and social work with young offenders and ex-offenders
in the community.[4] A study had been launched into the recording,
reporting, and presentation of criminal statistics,[5] and research 'into
the causes of crime and the effectiveness of the means of dealing
with the criminals' was going ahead.[6] As to the judiciary, the
prevailing Home Office view was that the need was simply to get
the judges to grasp the facts, revealed by criminological research
and the experience of the Prison and Probation Services, about the
suitability of various sorts of offenders for the different forms and
lengths of sentence which were at their disposal. The innovation of
pre-trial social inquiry reports, prepared by the Probation Service
to assist the sentencing decisions of judges in the higher criminal
courts, was a part of this approach.

Yet the presentational imperative to project the policies of
government in a positive light masked the existence of inner doubts.
Questioning of the effectiveness of the accepted methods, and the
justification for them, was not confined to penal reformers, being
shared by no less a figure than the all powerful Permanent Secretary

[3] Cmnd. 2296.
[4] In an uncharacteristic attempt to catch the mood of the times, Brooke had set
up an Advisory Committee on Juvenile Delinquency whose members included a
pop singer and a young man who had written a magazine article about his experience
of life in a detention centre. It was soon overtaken by the 1964 General Election,
and the new Home Secretary accepted advice from officials to terminate its existence.
[5] The report was published in 1967: Home Office, *Report of the Departmental
Committee on Criminal Statistics* (Cmnd. 3448), HMSO, London, 1967.
[6] *The War against Crime in England and Wales 1959–64*, p. 14.

at the Home Office, Sir Charles Cunningham. His recollection of what lay behind the next step, the establishment of an ill-fated Royal Commission, is illuminating:

By the early sixties ... it was clear that neither the efforts made in the first post-war decade nor the developments outlined in Mr Butler's White Paper were reducing—or were likely to reduce—the volume of crime or the numbers of persistent offenders. This led to increasing criticism of the ineffectiveness of crime prevention and of the accepted forms of penal treatment as well as of the philosophy underlying them. The results of research were not encouraging. The old belief that one major source of crime was to be found in poor social conditions, for example, was not supported ... The demands for something to be done were strong and understandable. But what? Could new approaches promising better results be found?

The Home Office had, of course, many existing sources of advice ... But there had been no overall review in recent times of the problem of crime and criminals by an independent and authoritative body. It was thought to be important that Parliamentary and public opinion—and concern—should be reassured by having a comprehensive review carried out by such a body. At best it might produce recommendations for new and hopeful initiatives. At worst it could conclude that the Home Office pianist was doing his best and need not be shot. It was therefore decided to set up a Royal Commission to review the whole problem of criminal behaviour and of the means of dealing with it.[7]

Translated into the sonorous language of the White Paper the stated reasons were:

The fundamental review of the whole penal system for which, in the Government's view, the time is now ripe is of such importance and magnitude that it needs to be carried out by a Royal Commission. There has been no comprehensive study of this kind since the Gladstone Committee of 1895. A purpose will be to reassess the value of our penal system as it has been built up until now—but much more than that. With that as the background, it is the time for a deep study of the philosophy underlying the system—to determine afresh what we ought to be seeking to achieve, to examine how far and in what manner the results of our present practice fall short, and to sift new ideas in order to judge which of them appear both constructive and practicable in operation.[8]

Far more limited in scope, but of immediate practical import,

[7] Letter from Sir Charles Cunningham, 18 Aug. 1991.
[8] *The War against Crime in England and Wales, 1959–64*, para. 54, p. 13.

was the question of the reorganization of the courts. The Whitehall demarcations described in Chapter 1 assigned responsibility for the criminal law and penal establishments to the Home Office, as well as the oversight of certain agencies of criminal justice: notably the police and the Probation Service. In the absence of any unified court service, responsibilities for different aspects of the courts of justice were distributed between various ministers and local authorities. Judges were appointed by the Crown on the advice of the Lord Chancellor, and magistrates by the Lord Chancellor on the recommendation of locally based advisory committees. The administration and financing of 842 Magistrates' courts, presided over by about 18,500 lay justices of the peace,[9] assisted by clerks who were mostly full-time and salaried, was in the hands of local Magistrates' courts committees, with the aid of a grant from the Home Office. The higher courts, Assizes and Quarter Sessions, and the High Court of Justice in London, were independent of central Government.

By the mid-1960s the need was becoming urgent for an overhaul of the traditional tribunals in which the more serious indictable crimes were tried before a High Court Judge, part-time Recorder or chairman of Quarter Sessions, and in 1966 the Government decided that there was substance for another Royal Commission. Only five years before, an interdepartmental committee set up jointly by the Home Office and the Lord Chancellor's Department, under the chairmanship of a High Court judge, had rejected the solution of permanent Crown Courts to handle the much increased workload of criminal cases and to reduce the time spent by defendants awaiting trial.[10] Legal opinion was generally opposed to exclusive concentration upon criminal work on the grounds that the monotony tended to cause staleness, in judges and in counsel, leading to decreased competence and possibly a tendency on the part of judges to become 'prosecution-minded'. Other factors were deployed, but the standpoint of the report was predominantly that

---

[9] Some Magistrates' courts were presided over by full-time stipendary magistrates recruited from practising barristers or solicitors. In 1969 there were forty-seven stipendaries, the majority being in London.

[10] Home Office and Lord Chancellor's Office, *Report of the Interdepartmental Committee on the Business of the Criminal Courts* (Cmnd. 1289), HMSO, London, 1961. The chairman was Mr Justice Streatfeild.

of the legal profession and local affinities,[11] rather than the interests of the accused or the more efficient dispatch of business.

For the chairman of the Royal Commission Labour ministers turned away from the legal profession, appointing instead an experienced businessman and ICI director, Dr Richard Beeching. As chairman of the British Railways Board (1963–5), Beeching had made his reputation in the public sector by the impressive way he had tackled the thankless job of modernizing the outdated rail network. Lord Gardiner regarded him as being well qualified by this experience to advise on the renewal of another, even more antique, part of the national heritage: the hallowed courts of justice. In courteously making a special journey to Beeching's home to induce him to accept the invitation, Gardiner incurred the Prime Minister's displeasure: Dr Beeching should have been invited to call on the Lord Chancellor.[12]

The Royal Commission on Assizes and Quarter Sessions was enjoined to inquire into the arrangements for the administration of justice at Assizes and Quarter Sessions, and 'to report what reforms should be made for the more convenient, economic and efficient disposal of the civil and criminal business at present dealt with by these courts'.[13] After bluntly pointing out the shortcomings of the existing system, the Royal Commission recommended a restructuring in which the criminal and civil work of the High Court would be separated. Ministerial responsibility for running the higher courts, both civil and criminal, should in future be placed in the

[11] In a review of the development of criminal justice policy 1945–70, Anthony Bottoms and Simon Stevenson cite the report of the Streatfeild Committee as an example of the strength of traditional values and local affinities which constituted one of the main factors in what went wrong. The authors identified four other central problems. They were: the political climate created by, and the practical results of, the continuing growth of recorded crime; problems of manpower for criminal justice agencies in a full employment economy; the beginnings of uncomfortable research results; and a series of individual incidents revealing underlying imperfections in the system. 'What Went Wrong? Criminal Justice Policy in England and Wales 1945–70', in D. Downes (ed.), *Unravelling Criminal Justice*, Macmillan, London, 1992, p. 10. Professor Bottoms is Director of the Institute of Criminology at the University of Cambridge. Simon Stevenson was formerly a Research Associate at the Institute.
[12] R. F. V. Heuston, *Lives of the Lord Chancellors 1940–1970*, Clarendon Press, Oxford, 1987, p. 227.
[13] Royal Commission on Assizes and Quarter Sessions, 1966–69, *Report* (Cmnd. 4153), HMSO, London, 1969, p. 4.

hands of the Lord Chancellor.[14] These recommendations were accepted[15] and incorporated into the Courts Act 1971 which merged Assizes, Quarter Sessions, and the Central Criminal Court[16] into one Crown Court with two tiers of full-time judges, together with part-time recorders and assistant recorders. While permanent courts were established in the main centres of population, High Court judges continued to be itinerant, backed up by circuit judges sitting continuously in the main centres.[17] As recommended by Beeching, the Lord Chancellor assumed overall responsibility for the construction and administration of all courts above the level of the Magistrates' courts.

The reorganization of the courts of justice, long recognized as necessary but not previously attempted, owed much for its implementation to the perseverance of Gardiner. One of the few lawyers in modern times to have reached the Woolsack other than via membership of the House of Commons and ministerial office,[18] Gardiner was a visionary who came to government late in his career, with the result that his idealism had not been exhausted by previous struggles to get things done. Joining the House of Lords as a life peer only in 1963, he became Lord Chancellor in the following year when the Labour Administration was formed, remaining in office until 1970. His abiding concern for law reform

[14] Ibid. The report contains a summary of main conclusions and recommendations at pp. 139–47.

[15] Broad all-party support was indicated in a report by a committee of the Society of Conservative Lawyers chaired by (Sir) Geoffrey Howe, QC. It concluded that the Beeching proposals were in their essentials not only necessary, but overdue.

[16] The Central Criminal Court at the Old Bailey is staffed by its own permanent judges, headed by the Recorder of London and the Common Serjeant, supplemented by judges of the Queen's Bench Division of the High Court who preside over trials on the most serious charges. The accommodation is provided by the City of London.

[17] In 1991 there was a total of ninety Crown Court centres in England and Wales. Eight were in London and eighty-two outside. Some Crown Court centres, in addition to their own courtrooms, used courtrooms at other locations. *Parl. Debates*, HL, 533 (5th ser.), col. WA 23, 9 Dec. 1991.

[18] Lords Maugham and Simonds, both of whom had been judges, were the only previous exceptions in the twentieth century. Simonds, who had been a Lord of Appeal in Ordinary since 1944, was an unexpected appointment as Lord Chancellor when Churchill returned to office as Prime Minister in October 1951. He remained on the Woolsack until replaced by the Home Secretary, Sir David Maxwell Fyfe (Lord Kilmuir) in 1954, being reappointed as a Lord of Appeal in Ordinary and continuing in that capacity until 1962. In 1987 Lord Mackay of Clashfern, Lord Advocate of Scotland 1979–84 and a Lord of Appeal in Ordinary 1985–7, became Lord Chancellor.

led to the creation of permanent institutional machinery in the form of separate Law Commissions, one for England and Wales and another for Scotland, with full-time Commissioners and supporting staffs.[19] Resolutely opposed by two of Gardiner's less enlightened predecessors as Lord Chancellor, Simonds and Dilhorne, the Law Commission under its first chairman, Sir Leslie Scarman,[20] soon earned acceptance as a valuable strengthening of the hitherto piecemeal procedures for revising laws which had become outdated or unsatisfactory in practice.

Ignoring the traditional possessiveness of the Home Office towards the content of the criminal law as well as its administration,[21] the Law Commission declined to confine itself to civil law matters. As if to make the point, the first published report put forward proposals to abolish certain obsolete criminal offences; the Commission's recommendations being implemented in the Criminal Law Act 1967. Further reports followed on imputed criminal intent (1966), damage to property (1970), forgery (1973), conspiracy and public order offences (1976), defences of general application (1977), the mental element in crime (1978), the territorial extent of the criminal law (1978), and interference with the course of justice (1979).

The Criminal Law Revision Committee, a by-product of *Penal Practice in a Changing Society* in 1959, continued its work in parallel with the Law Commission, but under the aegis of the Home Office. Unlike the Law Commission, the Criminal Law Revision Committee was a standing committee that was only activated as a result of specific references by the Home Secretary. In a review of

[19] Section 1 of the Law Commissions Act 1965 provided for the Lord Chancellor to appoint for England and Wales a Law Commission consisting of a Chairman and four other Commissioners, the qualification for appointment being that the candidate holds judicial office or is a barrister or solicitor or a university teacher of law. The Act also provided for a separate Law Commission for Scotland, where the minister responsible is the Lord Advocate. The function of each Commission is to keep under review the whole of the law with which it is concerned 'with a view to its systematic development and reform', including codification and generally the simplification and modernization of the law.

[20] Later Lord Scarman. A Judge of the Probate, Divorce, and Admiralty Division from 1961, he was seconded as full-time chairman of the Law Commission, 1965–73. Scarman became a Lord Justice of Appeal in 1973, and was a Lord of Appeal in Ordinary, 1977–86.

[21] Gardiner was open in his references to departmental rivalries: 'Metaphorically at least, outside the Home Office there are large notices saying "Lord Chancellors keep out".' Quoted in *Lives of the Lord Chancellors 1940–1970*, p. 234.

its work over the first ten years, its chairman, Lord Justice Sellers, claimed that the two institutions 'worked side by side in complete harmony and with some mutual assistance'.[22] Improbably cosy though the claimed relationship sounds, there is no evidence of rivalry or bad feeling. Eventually the Committee was to wither on the vine; the last reference resulting in its Eighteenth Report on *Conspiracy to Defraud*[23] in 1986.

Gardiner's zeal was matched by the transition to the Home Office of one of the most promising of the new generation of Labour Ministers, Roy Jenkins. Succeeding the ailing Sir Frank Soskice[24] as a young Home Secretary in December 1965, at the age of forty-five Jenkins was on the threshold of a dazzling career.[25] Always more interested in obtaining results than in political theorizing, the new Home Secretary, in his first Cabinet post (one that he coveted) lost no time in setting his stamp on a Department that had become accident prone. His arrival precipitated an immediate clash with Cunningham who, in Jenkins's eyes, represented

the guardian, not so much of particular Home Office policies, as of a certain Home Office approach to life which I was convinced had to be broken if future Home Secretaries were to avoid the St. Sebastian-like fate of Brooke and Soskice. An air of dutiful defeat had become the most appropriate demeanour for a Home Secretary. 'Poor old Home Office', Soskice had minuted on one file: 'We are not always wrong, but we always get the blame'.[26]

The battlefield between the incoming Home Secretary and the veteran civil servant is vividly depicted in Jenkins's memoirs.[27] His requirements were crystallized into a list of specific organizational demands, twenty-two in all, each one of them hard fought. Behind his insistence that the intensely hierarchical system of submissions be changed, lay Jenkins's determination that the Home Secretary

[22] 'The First Ten Years of the Criminal Law Revision Committee', [1969] Crim. L.R. 302 at 311.
[23] Cmnd. 9873, HMSO, London, 1986.
[24] Home Secretary from Oct. 1964 to Dec. 1965. Solicitor General, 1945–51, Attorney General, 1951. Life peer as Baron Stow Hill, 1966.
[25] Minister of Aviation, 1964–5; Home Secretary, 1965–7, and again in 1974–6; Chancellor of the Exchequer, 1967–70. President of the Commission of the European Communities, 1977–81. Chancellor of the University of Oxford since 1987. Life peer as Lord Jenkins of Hillhead, 1987.
[26] Roy Jenkins, *A Life at the Centre*, Macmillan, London, 1991, p. 181.
[27] Ibid., pp. 179–84.

had to be allowed sufficient scope to use his political judgment in weighing up alternative courses of action. Cunningham's centralized system did not permit this since all submissions to the Home Secretary were channelled through him, with only one course of action being recommended. The submissions were brief and lucid, economical of ministerial time, but unaccompanied by any files or background papers from which alternatives could be devised or warning signals detected.[28]

Sir Charles, a man of mettle, did not surrender his system without a struggle:

Cunningham defended it with every weapon he could muster. He threw his whole authority and experience behind it. I remember that at one stage ... his eyes filled with tears. I almost wavered. Was it right at the end of a distinguished public servant's long career to reduce him to such misery? It was only later that I realized that the tears were caused by rage and not by sadness.[29]

Jenkins was fortunate that he brought with him to the Home Office an intuitive understanding that it is how issues and incidents are handled, more than the policies which are decided upon, that can make or break a Home Secretary's reputation. It is a lesson which has been painfully learned, or sometimes never learned, by several of those who went before and came after.

Following a General Election in March 1966, which confirmed Labour in power for another Parliament, three main policy objectives engaged the Home Secretary. The first was a resolute attempt to accelerate the pace of police reorganization, reducing the number of separate police forces from 117 to 49. The second was to make greater headway in the field of community relations, enhancing the pioneering role of the Race Relations Board, and preparing for fresh legislation. The third was the prospect of a new Criminal Justice Bill. Work on several aspects of policy for the Bill had already been put in hand in Soskice's time. In 1965, two White Papers were published: *The Child, The Family and The Young Offender*[30] in August, followed by *The Adult Offender*[31] in December. The appearance of the two documents, and the Government's

---

[28] Cunningham took offence at Jenkins's version of his methods and sent his own account of these events to be lodged in the Home Office records.
[29] *A Life at the Centre*, p. 183.
[30] Cmnd. 2742, HMSO, London, 1965.
[31] Cmnd. 2852, HMSO, London, 1965.

intention to legislate upon the proposals they contained, dealt a
sideways, but none the less mortal, blow to Brooke's Royal Commission which was simultaneously subjecting the entire penal system
to critical review.

II

Even without the change of Government which brought Labour to
power in October 1964 after thirteen years in Opposition, the Royal
Commission on the Penal System would have been grievously
hampered by its over-ambitious terms of reference and a divided
membership. The terms of reference were:

In the light of modern knowledge of crime and its causes and of modern
penal practice here and abroad, to re-examine the concepts and purposes
which should underlie the punishment and treatment of offenders in
England and Wales; to report how far they are realised by the penalties
and methods of treatment available to the courts, and whether any changes
in these, or in the arrangements and responsibility for selecting the sentences
to be imposed on particular offenders, are desirable: to review the work of
the services and institutions dealing with offenders, and the responsibility
for their administration: and to make recommendations.[32]

It was a vast task. The Commission was being asked to frame a
philosophy for criminal justice and to measure the performance of
penal proceedings against it. The remit extended to offenders of all
ages. It called not only for an investigation of the sentencing powers
and practice of the criminal courts, but of the sentencing process
itself. The injunction to review the work of the services and
institutions dealing with offenders included the prisons, young
offender institutions, approved schools, and the Probation Service.
The endeavour was set in an international context, the Commission
being charged with acquainting itself with modern penal practice
abroad.

The sixteen strong membership,[33] headed by a former minister,

---

[32] *Parl. Debates*, HC, 693 (5th ser.), cols. 601–2, 16 Apr. 1964.
[33] The full membership was: Viscount Amory (chairman), Lady Adrian, David
Basnett, Mr Justice Edmund Davies, Hon. Sylvia Fletcher Moulton, Dr T. C. N.
Gibbens, T. L. Iremonger MP, R. E. Millard, Professor J. N. Morris, Rt. Rev. R.
C. Mortimer, Professor Leon Radzinowicz, Mrs B. Serota, Sam Silkin MP, Mrs E.
Warburton, Lord Wheatley, Baroness Wootton of Abinger.

Viscount Amory,[34] contained two judges, a bishop, two Members of Parliament, a trade union leader, several magistrates, and two of the foremost criminologists of the day, Sir Leon Radzinowicz and Baroness Wootton of Abinger.[35] From the start there were differences in approach and attitude. To Professor Radzinowicz and Barbara Wootton, both strong characters unaccustomed to taking no for an answer, any thorough re-examination of the concepts and purposes underlying the punishment and treatment of offenders in the light of modern knowledge of crime and its causes was worthless without systematic research, including field-work by qualified staff, taking anything up to four years to complete. Other members were conscious of the need to make progress more urgently if the whole enterprise was not to be overtaken by events. Amory, a likeable and popular man, had been one of the few Conservative MPs to be active in the campaign to end capital punishment in the late 1940s. For all his experience, he was ill at ease in the chair, and unsuccessful in holding a fissiparous membership together.

At the time of its establishment the Commission had been asked to give first priority to a study of young offenders under twenty-one and their treatment. Little had been accomplished before the emergence of the new Government's proposals for the treatment of young offenders, spelling the end of approved schools. A few months later, in the White Paper on adult offenders, the Home Office brought out proposals for the abolition of the special sentences of corrective training and preventive detention, and for the release of prisoners on parole, without making any mention of the Commission. Assured by the Home Secretary that a report would still be of value, the Royal Commission pressed on with its work, abandoning the young offender study and turning its attention to other things. Disillusion set in as awareness spread that the Government had its own agenda, much of the groundwork having been prepared in opposition by a Labour Party study group which shortly before the election had published a report titled *Crime: A*

[34] Derick Heathcoat-Amory: Minister of Pensions, 1951–3; Minister of State, Board of Trade, 1953–4; Minister of Agriculture, 1954–8; Chancellor of the Exchequer, 1958–60. Created a peer as Viscount Amory, 1960.
[35] Barbara Wootton was Professor of Social Studies, 1948–52, and Nuffield Research Fellow, 1952–7, at London University. Created a life peer in 1958, she sat as a magistrate in the Metropolitan Courts from 1926–70, and was a member of four Royal Commissions.

Challenge to Us All.[36] Several members of the Government, notably Gardiner and Sir Elwyn Jones, the Attorney General, had served on the study group. The Minister of State at the Home Office, Alice Bacon, who sat on the Labour Party's National Executive,[37] had been a member, while two others, Mrs Serota[38] and Dr T. C. N. Gibbens,[39] were included amongst the membership of the Royal Commission.

In the Spring of 1966, six of the Commissioners, led by Radzinowicz and Wootton resigned, having become persuaded that, with substantial legislation pending, and in the absence of conclusive research to support recommendations likely to last for a lengthy period, the opportunity no longer existed for the Commission to make a comprehensive report capable of setting the direction for a generation. According to Cunningham, 'The Home Secretary—and the Home Office—were greatly concerned about the Commission's almost unprecedented decision; but it had to be accepted.'[40]

On 27 April the Prime Minister, Harold Wilson, informed the House of Commons that on his advice the Queen had approved the dissolution of the Royal Commission. In its place, the Home Secretary would appoint a standing Advisory Council to report and make recommendations from time to time on such aspects of penal treatment as he might refer to it or as the Council itself, having consulted the Home Secretary, felt that it ought to consider.[41]

Wilson disclosed the split into equally balanced factions when he said that two further members had also resigned on the grounds that a weakened Commission could no longer usefully continue.

[36] It was the report of this study group, under the chairmanship of Lord Longford, which had first recommended parole (pp. 43–4). It also advocated the establishment of a body of whole-time Law Commissioners to carry out a review of the criminal law (p. 39). Neither proposal featured in the Labour Party Manifesto for the 1964 General Election.

[37] Chairman of the Labour Party, 1950, and of the Labour Party Conference, 1951; Minister of State: Home Office, 1964–7, Department of Education and Science, 1967–70. Created a life peer as Baroness Bacon, 1970.

[38] Chairman, Children's Committee, London County Council, 1958–65; Chief Whip, Greater London Council, 1964–7. Life peerage for services to children, 1967. Minister of State (Health), Department of Health and Social Security, 1969–70. Founder Chairman, Commission for Local Administration, 1974–82.

[39] Professor of Forensic Psychiatry, Institute of Psychiatry, University of London, 1967–78; Hon. Consultant, Bethlem Royal and Maudsley Hospitals. Member of the Parole Board, 1972–5.

[40] Letter to the author, 18 Aug. 1991.

[41] *Parl. Debates*, HC, 727 (5th ser.), cols. 703–4, 27 Apr. 1966.

The remaining eight, including the hapless chairman, disagreed. They believed that a fundamental and searching reappraisal of the purposes of a modern penal system, and the methods by which those purposes should be translated into practice, was still entirely feasible. In their view the Commission should be allowed to complete its task, and new appointments should be made to replace the members who had resigned.[42]

The same course was endorsed by the Leader of the Opposition, Edward Heath. Expressing disappointment at the decision to dissolve the Royal Commission, for which the new Advisory Council would be no substitute, Heath contended that such a serious outcome could have been avoided if, after the resignation of the initial six members, the Prime Minister or the Home Secretary had said firmly that they would appoint others to take their place. Wilson rejected the argument, replying that the Commission had broken down because it was no longer practical to contemplate a once for all look at something that was changing so rapidly.[43]

Given the rambling terms of reference, and the clash of opinion between its members as to how they should be interpreted, the Commission would have faced a bumpy ride at the best of times. Yet the immediate cause of its demise was the change in Government. Labour ministers, newly in office, were raring to go with their own legislative programme. They were disinclined to be held back by the deliberations of a slow-moving and ponderous Commission. This conclusion is devoid of party political implication; the situation might easily have been the same if the parties in opposition and government had been transposed. In such circumstances it is natural that ministers should want to implement without undue delay policies for changes in the legal framework of the criminal law and for dealing with offenders which they may have espoused before coming to power.

The sole memorial left behind by the stricken Royal Commission was the Advisory Council on the Penal System (ACPS). The presence of an independent standing group to advise the Home Secretary was no novelty since an Advisory Council on the Treatment of Offenders had been set up by Herbert Morrison as early

---

[42] Ibid., col. 704.
[43] Ibid., cols. 704–5.

as 1944 as part of the plans for post-war reconstruction.[44] By 1966 the earlier body was dormant, its last flicker of life being a report on after-care in 1963.[45] The report was not without influence, as it contributed to the transition of the probation service from a group of self-employed social case workers into a nationally organized and publicly funded service.

Three members of the dissolved Royal Commission transferred their loyalties to the ACPS with good grace. Radzinowicz and Wootton were joined by Mrs Serota, who was to succeed to the chairmanship after the death of the first chairman, a former Labour minister with a keen interest in penal policy, Kenneth Younger.[46] Avoiding the perils of the grand design, and eschewing broader questions of penal philosophy, the ACPS concentrated its attention on specific references. For the next twelve years, its reports were to form an important strand in the formulation of policy.

The first remits to the ACPS were reparation by the offender to the victim for the harm he had done, and non-custodial penalties.[47] There was no evidence at the time, and very little since, that victims actually wanted reparation, although it was a theme with some appeal to Conservatives in Parliament. Indeed when in Opposition amendments had been moved unsuccessfully to give greater effect to reparation during the passage of the Criminal Justice Bill in 1966/7. The advantages of non-custodial penalties had long been propagated by penal reformers of a progressive liberal disposition, and had been the subject of two previous reviews by the Advisory Council on the Treatment of Offenders.[48] Now, once again, the topic was timely as a substantial area of policy that had been within the ambit of the Royal Commission, but one which had not been

[44] The first chairman was Mr Justice Birkett who, in 1945, was alternate British member (to Lord Justice Lawrence) of the International Tribunal for the trial of war criminals at Nuremberg. Celebrated as an advocate, Birkett became a Judge of the King's Bench Division of the High Court of Justice, 1941–50, and a Lord Justice of Appeal, 1950–7. He was created a Baron in 1958.

[45] Home Office, *The Organization of After-Care*, Report of the Advisory Council on the Treatment of Offenders, HMSO, London, 1963.

[46] Under-Secretary of State, Home Office, 1947–50, Minister of State, Foreign Office, 1950–1. Director, Royal Institute of International Affairs, 1959–71. Chairman of the Howard League for Penal Reform, 1960–73, and Chairman of Advisory Council on the Penal System, 1966–76. Knighted in 1972.

[47] *Parl. Debates*, HC, 736 (5th ser.), col. WA 377, 25 Nov. 1966.

[48] Home Office, *Alternatives to Short Terms of Imprisonment*, Advisory Council on the Treatment of Offenders, HMSO, London, 1957; and *Non-residential Treatment of Offenders under 21*, HMSO, London, 1962.

pre-empted by Government intentions for legislation.[49] Pragmatists too were attracted by the potential they saw in non-custodial penalties as a method of easing the ominous pressures being caused by the rising prison population.

III

Although political ideology can play a significant part in reshaping the penal system, as it did in 1964 through the influence of *Crime: A Challenge to Us All*, and to a lesser extent as it would have done had the Conservatives regained office in 1966, incoming governments customarily do not pack in their baggage detailed blueprints on criminal policy. Unlike the economic and social controversies which dominated the election campaigns of the period, and the policy-making preliminaries which preceded them, in penal matters the underlying objectives were accepted by each of the two main parties. The paramountcy of the rule of law, the maintenance of public order, and the goal of an efficient and humane penal system, were not in question. Differences occurred as to means, but examination of the electoral manifestos throughout the 1960s and 1970s shows a reluctance to politicize issues which, given the intractable nature of crime and the limited efficacy of measures to counter it, would only have had the effect of exciting popular expectations beyond the capacity of any government to fulfil.

Considerations of this sort dictate that the political impetus accompanying ministers on arrival at their departments after an election is usually a good deal less noticeable at the Home Office than elsewhere in Whitehall. Roy Jenkins in 1965 was an exception, having gone on record in a book written for the 1959 General Election with his personal, and unauthorized, programme for 'the wholesale reform of which the Home Office is still in urgent need'.[50] The accent was on lifting restrictions on individual liberty. Apart from capital punishment, the laws on homosexuality and abortion, and the decriminalization of suicide, there was no mention of

[49] See M. J. Moriarty, 'The Policy-Making Process: How it is seen from the Home Office', in N. Walker (ed.), *Penal Policy-Making in England*, University of Cambridge Institute of Criminology, Cambridge, 1977, p. 136.
[50] *The Labour Case*, Penguin Books, Harmondsworth, 1959, p. 136. See also, *A Life at the Centre*, pp. 180–1.

reform of the penal system, or of the prisons. In implementing such a programme, Jenkins predicted:

A great deal would depend on the reforming zeal and liberal spirit of the man who became Home Secretary. And however well endowed he was with these qualities, he might still have difficulty on some points.[51]

More typically, as a senior official writing from first-hand knowledge observed:

time and again the Ministerial contribution to penal policy-making ... lies not in the Minister's bringing in his own fresh policy ideas, but in his operating creatively and with political drive upon ideas, proposals, reports, etc., that are, so to speak, already to hand, often within the department but sometimes in the surrounding world of penal thought.[52]

Until the watershed of 1979, few restraints on a Home Secretary's freedom of action in the mainstream stemmed from the political ideology of his party or ministerial colleagues. For Conservative governments as much as for Labour, it was far more common that the inadequacy of resources for allocation to programmes with limited political appeal, in competition with spending programmes by other departments holding out more evident social or financial benefits, set the limits on what could be done. One constant factor, unaffected by change of government, but never far below the surface, was an extreme sensitivity about the degree of public support for policies which tended to be perceived (however misguidedly) as 'soft' on crime.[53]

The period saw few radical departures in penal policy. When this happened, as it did with parole and financial compensation for criminal injuries, the seed-bed was usually found in 'the surrounding world of penal thought', rather than in any party political objectives. Whilst it is true that parole was advocated in *Crime: A Challenge to Us All*, it is true also that in the consensual politics of the day party study groups drew freely upon the available sources of expertise and received wisdom: the penal services themselves, the legal and academic communities, penal reform and other related

[51] *The Labour Case.* p. 140.
[52] *Penal Policy-Making in England*, p. 133. M. J. Moriarty was Head of the Home Office Crime Policy Unit in 1974–5, and Assistant Under-Secretary of State in charge of criminal policy, 1975–9. UK representative on the Council of Europe Committee on Crime Problems, 1976–9; Chairman, 1978–9.
[53] Ibid., p. 132.

interest groups, and published material from official or academic sources.[54] Parole was not a new idea,[55] having existed in parts of the United States since early in the twentieth century, and had been canvassed down the years. But support had been no more than patchy until it was taken up by such a strong party group on the eve of electoral victory. Then, at last, its hour had come.

In the 1965 White Paper on *The Adult Offender* the Government had declared:

> prisoners whose character and record render them suitable ... should be released from prison earlier than they are at present. Prisoners who do not of necessity have to be detained for the protection of the public are in some cases more likely to be made into decent citizens if, before completing the whole of their sentence, they are released under supervision with a liability to recall if they do not behave. Other countries have used systems of this kind with success and the Government have concluded that the time has come to ask for powers to adopt a system of early release on licence in this country.[56]

Criminal injuries compensation, the precursor of policies which two decades later were to be matched more closely to the actual situation of victims of crime, their needs and desires, had a mixed provenance towards which penal reform groups, official thinking, and party political interests each contributed.[57] After a long and uphill struggle, lasting for most of the 1950s, Margery Fry had persuaded the Howard League and the newly formed JUSTICE[58] to take up the cause of monetary restitution to be paid out of public funds to those who had suffered personal injury from acts of criminal violence. Parliamentary support began to coalesce, deriving mainly from the analogy which was seen between compensation for criminal injuries and the existing welfare provision for people who had sustained injuries in the course of their work. MPs familiar with claims for workmen's compensation, or the

[54] Ibid.

[55] See *Responses to Crime*, vol. 1, pp. 252–3.

[56] Cmnd. 2852, p. 3.

[57] For an informative account of criminal injuries compensation as the first major piece of policy-making for victims, see Paul Rock, *Helping Victims of Crime: The Home Office and the Rise of Victim Support in England and Wales*, Clarendon Press, Oxford, 1990, pp. 46–90.

[58] JUSTICE was founded in June 1957 as an alliance of lawyers from the three main political parties, becoming the British Section of the International Commission of Jurists.

operation of the Industrial Injuries Compensation Scheme, took a leading part.

Gradually the Home Office reacted; first with a tentative mention in *Penal Practice in a Changing Society*; then with a lukewarm report from a working party in 1961; and finally, when all-party pressure was at its height, with a White Paper on *Compensation for Victims of Crimes of Violence*,[59] published shortly before the 1964 General Election. In between, both JUSTICE and the Conservative Political Centre brought out reports urging that the state should compensate financially the victims of certain violent offences. Once the principle had been accepted, the main practical difficulty was seen as how to distinguish between innocent victims of assault and 'fraudulent and guilty' victims, such as criminals fighting over their spoils or men beating each other up in gang warfare.[60]

The solution adopted by Brooke was oblique. Instead of conferring entitlement by way of primary legislation, compensation would be paid *ex gratia* without the presumption of state liability. An experimental and non-statutory scheme would be set up, administered by a board composed of lawyers who would make discretionary awards based on common law damages. The offences causing the injury were not specified, although offences committed against a member of the offender's own family would not be compensated.[61] After a debate in the House of Commons on the White Paper's proposals, which were accepted without dissent, an amended scheme was announced in June[62] which came into effect on 1 August 1964. Administrative delays and mounting cost were the principal features which marred the subsequent development of what was to become one of the most extensive, and expensive, of all instruments of criminal justice.[63]

[59] Cmnd. 2323, HMSO, London, 1964.
[60] Rock, *Helping Victims of Crime*, pp. 78–81.
[61] Ibid., p. 82.
[62] *Parl. Debates*, HC, 697 (5th ser.), cols. WA 89–94, 24 June 1964.
[63] Financial compensation for criminal injuries was placed on a statutory basis by Sections 108–17 of the Criminal Justice Act 1988, although four years later this part of the Act had still not been brought into effect. See Chapter 4.

IV

The legislation which was to become the Criminal Justice Act 1967, a long statute of 106 sections and seven schedules, was the most comprehensive since the 1948 Act. Earlier the same year it had been preceded by a Criminal Law Act which brought to an end the time-honoured division of crimes into felonies and misdemeanours, as well as abolishing certain obsolete crimes and the torts of maintenance and champerty on the recommendation of the Law Commission. The Criminal Justice Act was more wide ranging, making changes in criminal procedure and the powers of the courts to deal with offenders.

A new power to suspend sentences of imprisonment was added by Jenkins, at the instigation of the judiciary. Once again, the proposal was not original, having twice been considered by the Advisory Council on the Treatment of Offenders in the 1950s, but rejected on both occasions.[64] Nevertheless, the Home Secretary was persuaded that anything which might help towards countering the rising prison population by keeping out of prison those who need not be there was worth trying:

By this means [the suspended sentence] we shall substantially avoid sending people to prison for the first time unnecessarily. Whichever way the outcome goes in an individual case, I do not believe that society can lose. If no further offence is committed, the deterrent has worked, prison space has been saved, and the offender has not been made used to prison conditions. If a further offence is committed, the offender will be punished, certainly and surely, both for the earlier and the subsequent offence. This is a sensible but by no means necessarily a lenient proposition.[65]

On passing a sentence of imprisonment of two years or less the Act empowered a court to suspend the sentence by ordering that it should not take effect unless during a specified period the offender committed another offence punishable by imprisonment. In the case of a sentence of six months or less, with certain exceptions such as where the offence involved violence, the possession of firearms, explosives, or offensive weapons, or indecent conduct with a person aged under sixteen, the court was obliged to suspend the sentence.[66]

[64] Home Office, *Alternatives to Short Terms of Imprisonment*, Advisory Council on the Treatment of Offenders, HMSO, London, 1957.
[65] Parl. Debates, HC, 738 (5th ser.), col. 66, 12 Dec. 1966.
[66] Criminal Justice Act 1967, Section 39.

Since the maximum term of imprisonment which might be imposed in the Magistrates' court for a single offence is six months, the Act effectively took out of the hands of the magistrates the power to impose sentences of immediate imprisonment on the majority of offenders who had not previously been sentenced to imprisonment or Borstal training.[67] The change was much resented, and the Magistrates' Association, 'by now a powerful body, and far removed from the fledgling organization founded by Margery Fry almost half a century before, campaigned ceaselessly until the law was subsequently amended ... '.[68]

Before long malfunctions began to appear as it became evident that suspended sentences of imprisonment were being used in place of non-custodial penalties, especially probation orders and fines.[69] Probation Officers were overworked, and a suspended sentence was a way of avoiding adding to their case loads. Fines often went unpaid. The suspended sentence had the disadvantage of seeming to be not quite one thing or the other, with some sentencers succumbing to the temptation of adding to the length of the term of imprisonment which would have been imposed immediately, so balancing the act of suspension with greater severity in the event of a breach. Because those who re-offended went to prison automatically, without the possibility of a non-custodial sentence the next time they were convicted of an imprisonable offence, they might remain in custody for a longer time than would otherwise have been the case. Some might not have found their way to prison at all. All in all, it was a classic example of what criminologists define as net-widening, leading to consequences quite different from those envisaged.

Other factors beside the suspended sentence bore on the size of the prison population in the early 1970s, and the trends were not

[67] Mandatory suspension did not apply if an offender had at any time before the commission of the offence been sentenced to, or served any part of, a sentence of corrective training, imprisonment, or borstal training previously passed for another offence or been subject to a suspended sentence (Criminal Justice Act 1967, Section 39(3)(*e*)).

[68] T. Morris, *Crime and Criminal Justice since 1945*, Basil Blackwell, Oxford, 1989, p. 115. The mandatory suspension of shorter sentences was abolished by the Criminal Justice Act 1972, Section 11(1).

[69] R. F. Sparks, 'The Use of Suspended Sentences', [1971] Crim. L.R. 384. See also A. E. Bottoms, 'The Suspended Sentence After Ten Years: A Review and Reassessment', *Occasional Paper No. 2*, Centre for Social Work and Applied Social Studies, University of Leeds, 1980.

encouraging. After reaching a peak of 40,000 in 1970 and 1971, the numbers in prison fell in 1972 and 1973, but the 40,000 threshold was exceeded again in 1975. July of that year saw a post-war peak of 40,808.[70] The 1967 Act (in Section 65) also brought to finality one of the most contentious chapters in English penal history. The last vestige of corporal punishment was eradicated by repealing Section 18 of the Prison Act 1952, which had allowed the infliction of corporal punishment in Prison Service establishments. No such punishment had been confirmed by any Home Secretary since June 1962,[71] and it had been used only sparingly before that.

Whilst the provisions authorizing the early release on parole of prisoners under supervision and subject to recall had been generally welcomed in Parliament, as was the power to suspend sentences, two items provoked controversy. These were the introduction of majority verdicts to avoid the necessity for new trials when juries could not reach unanimous verdicts, and the extension of firearms certificates to shotguns. The latter was unpopular with farming and sporting interests and was strongly opposed by Conservative members.

Majority verdicts, a mechanical adjustment to the process of criminal trials rather than a genuinely new policy, touched a nerve in the body politic as matters concerning juries often do. Unlike other more intricate proposals in the Bill, altering the rule that jury verdicts in England and Wales must be unanimous could be, and was, presented by its critics in populist terms as removing a brick from the bastion of liberty. Press reaction and the Criminal Bar were generally hostile, fed by heightened fears of jury nobbling emanating largely from police circles. In Parliament Jenkins, whose personal initiative it was,[72] had taken the precaution of conferring in advance with the Conservative front-bench spokesman on Home Affairs. In Quintin Hogg[73] he found a trustworthy ally. The future Lord Chancellor promised

---

[70] *Report on the Work of the Prison Department 1974* (Cmnd. 6148), HMSO, London, 1975, p. 3.

[71] The dying embers of the argument flared up in 1966 when Jenkins set aside a magistrates' decision to order the birching of a young prisoner at Maidstone Prison.

[72] Home Office opinion was mostly against, although Jenkins had been influenced by (Sir) Robert Mark, later to become Commissioner of the Metropolitan Police (1972–7). Mark was Assistant Commissioner 1967–8 and Deputy Commissioner 1968–72, having been brought in to the higher reaches of New Scotland Yard at the insistence of Jenkins.

[73] Viscount Hailsham had disclaimed his hereditary peerage and returned to the

to back him through thick and thin, but not before I had consulted the
eight or nine senior legal Members (some of them more distinguished at
the Bar than myself) and got their promises of support. In the end,
overcome by the superstitious public outcry, all these ratted and voted the
other way. I kept my word to Jenkins and backed his proposals for all I
was worth as a welcome, if minor, rationalization of the creaking old eighteenth-century ox-wagon of our criminal law. Ten to two seemed to be a
perfectly adequate majority with the proper safeguards Jenkins offered ... [74]

Deserted by Hogg's senior legal colleagues on the Conservative
benches, and with a strong challenge mounted by the libertarian
left on the Government side, the clause looked in danger. But at
the end of the day, due to skilful management by Jenkins combined
with the staunchness of the shadow Home Secretary, the clause
survived at Report Stage by 180 votes to 102.[75] Supporters of the
change were fortified by the knowledge, revealed by the Home
Secretary in his speech, that of the thirty-five judges in the Queen's
Bench Division (including the Lord Chief Justice who conducted
the poll), twenty-five were in favour of majority verdicts, provided
that the majority did not fall below ten to two. Eight were against,
with two undecided and prepared to follow the majority.[76] It is an
error to assume that the higher judiciary is always against reform.
On several occasions when their views have been canvassed, the
judges of the High Court and the Court of Appeal have shown
themselves capable of accepting changes that do not necessarily
coincide with popular or professional opinion. A later example can
be found in the proposal to substitute discretionary sentences
(including life imprisonment) for the mandatory life sentence in
cases of murder.[77]

It was the concept of parole, originally at the discretion of the
Home Secretary, but amended in the course of the passage of the
legislation through Parliament so that he could grant early release
on licence to a prisoner only if advised to do so by a statutory Parole
Board, that commanded the keenest interest of penal reformers and

---

House of Commons as Quintin Hogg in 1963. He was created a life peer in 1970 as
Lord Hailsham of St. Marylebone and appointed Lord Chancellor. In 1967 he was
Shadow Home Secretary in the House of Commons.

[74] *A Sparrow's Flight: The Memoirs of Lord Hailsham of St. Marylebone*, Collins,
London, 1990, p. 364.

[75] *Parl. Debates*, HC, 745 (5th ser.), cols. 1899–902, 27 Apr. 1967.

[76] *Parl. Debates*, HC, 745, (5th ser.), col. 1779, 26 Apr. 1967.

[77] See Chapter 9.

had the most widespread effect.[78] Although presented mainly as a measure of penal reform that was desirable for its own sake, officials were more sanguine that parole might lead to the hoped for reduction in the prison population than the dubious promise of the suspended sentence.

The advice of senior civil servants was especially influential at this period. In preparing the Bill and seeing it through Parliament, Jenkins had at his right hand Cunningham's successor as Permanent Under-Secretary of State, Sir Philip Allen. A former deputy chairman of the Prison Commission, Allen was a sophisticated Whitehall practitioner, knowledgeable about and deeply interested in the reshaping of penal policy. In their efforts to weld together into a coherent master plan proposals deriving from several different sources: party politics, expert advisers, and Home Office know-how, Jenkins and his first civil service adviser constituted an unusually perceptive and skilful partnership. Yet in the outcome the Criminal Justice Act 1967, with over 300 amendments to the original Bill having been debated for more than sixty hours in the Commons Standing Committee, suffered the fate of those that went before and came after. In Allen's own words, 'however worthy the original intention it is almost inevitable that one ends up with a pretty fair rag-bag and that a carefully drawn long title offers no real defence'.[79]

V

Out of office for the first time since 1951, the Conservatives threw themselves into policy-making after the 1964 election defeat. The new chairman of the Party's Advisory Committee on Policy, an appointment long held by R. A. Butler, was Edward Heath.[80]

---

[78] See *Responses to Crime*, vol. 1, pp. 251–85, for an account of the growth of the parole system from its inception in 1967 until 1986. By 1987, 24,432 prisoners were eligible for early release of whom 13,994 (58.9%) were granted parole, *The Parole System in England and Wales: Report of the Review Committee* (Cm. 532), HMSO, London, p. 145, Table 2. The Criminal Justice Act 1991 implemented changes in the operation of the parole system which are described in Chapter 9.

[79] Letter from Lord Allen of Abbeydale, 12 Mar. 1990.

[80] At the time of the 1964 General Election, Edward Heath was Secretary of State for Industry, Trade, and Regional Development, and President of the Board of Trade. He had served previously as Lord Privy Seal, with Foreign Office responsibilities, 1960–3; Minister of Labour, 1959–60; Government Chief Whip, 1955–9; Prime Minister, 1970–4.

During the short period of nine months which elapsed before he succeeded Sir Alec Douglas-Home as Leader of the Opposition on 2 August 1965, Heath set up policy groups oriented towards issues with strong electoral appeal. In a letter to a member of the group on crime who had expressed an interest in foreign affairs, Heath replied:

the difficulty quite frankly is that everybody wants to join the Study Groups on foreign affairs or economic policy and I am not at all sure that electorally these are the two most important. Indeed I am rather coming round to the view that the trouble last year was not that we failed to produce as good policies as our opponents but that we failed to produce policies for the issues the electorate was most interested in.[81]

The terms of reference of the policy group on crime were 'to assess post-war trends in crime and their probable cause, to evaluate current and proposed new methods for the prevention of crime and the treatment of offenders and to make recommendations.'

Initially the chairman was Sir Edward Boyle, followed by the shadow Home Secretary, Peter Thorneycroft,[82] when Boyle moved on to become deputy chairman of the Advisory Committee on Policy. Heath took a keen interest in the group's composition, sending out personal letters of invitation. Because of the necessity to keep in step with the Parliamentary Party, the membership contained four MPs (William Deedes, Edward Gardner QC, William Rees-Davies, and Mark Carlisle), as well as the chairman. There was a former junior Home Office Minister, Earl Jellicoe, from the Lords; with the voluntary side of the Party being represented by Mrs Adelaide Doughty, chairman of the National Women's Advisory Committee, and Mrs Lucille Iremonger, a journalist and wife of a Conservative MP. Heath was determined to broaden the range of experience and attitudes represented on the group and added Ian Trethowan,[83] then a political commentator for the BBC; Beryl

[81] Conservative Party Archive, Bodleian Library, Oxford. Conservative Research Department papers, file CRD 3/19/6, letter dated 9 Feb. 1965 from Heath to Earl Jellicoe.

[82] President of the Board of Trade, 1951–7; Chancellor of the Exchequer, 1957–8 (resigned); Minister of Aviation, 1960–2; Minister of Defence, 1962–4. After losing his seat in 1966, Thorneycroft became a life peer in 1967, returning to national politics as Chairman of the Conservative Party, 1975–81.

[83] Managing Director, BBC Radio, 1969–75; Managing Director, BBC Television, 1976–7; Director General of the BBC, 1977–82. Chairman: Horserace Betting Levy Board, 1982–90; and Thames Television, 1987–90. Knighted 1980.

Cooper, a barrister; Timothy Raison,[84] Editor of *New Society*; Dr Bryan Wilson, an Oxford sociologist and Fellow of All Souls College; and Dr William Belson from the London School of Economics.

Responding to Heath's invitation, Wilson wrote that he was not a member of the Conservative Party, or of any political party, and while he was willing to assist the Advisory Committee by participating in the work of its study group on post-war crime, he would not wish to do so if the implication of his participation was to become politically committed. Heath replied promptly and reassuringly:

I have always felt that on these policy study groups we must avoid restricting ourselves to those who are already fully committed politically to the Conservative Party. Certainly so far as we are concerned we would completely recognise your position and we are in fact, since your position is shared by several other experts in their respective fields who have been good enough to assist us in this venture, doing our very best to see that the names of those who are taking part in the policy study groups do not become public property.[85]

In the event, Wilson not only joined the policy group, preparing two closely reasoned papers on which the analysis of the social causes of the rising crime rate in the group's report was based, but agreed that his name should be included amongst the authors of the published version.[86] Only Trethowan's name was omitted, presumably more for reasons of his public reputation as an interviewer and commentator than for any lack of enthusiasm for the Conservative cause. Indeed, he had urged Heath to set up a policy group on crime, writing:

What, I suggest, is really disturbing people is the problem of law enforcement, something which the Conservatives are traditionally concerned about and the Labour Party is traditionally rather wet about.[87]

The group's secretary was Carol Mather, a retired Guards' officer

[84] Later MP for Aylesbury, 1970–91; Minister of State: Home Office, 1979–83; Foreign and Commonwealth Office and Minister for Overseas Development, 1983–6. Knighted 1991.
[85] CRD 3/19/6; Wilson to Heath 3 Feb. 1965; Heath to Wilson 8 Feb. 1965.
[86] *Crime Knows No Boundaries*, Conservative Political Centre, London, CPC No. 334, 1966.
[87] CRD 3/19/6; Trethowan to Heath 4 Jan. 1965.

employed by the Conservative Research Department and a future MP for Esher. The working methods were described by the politically uncommitted Wilson: 'My impression was of a group of people who were seriously interested in the subject and deeply concerned about it. Our discussions were serious and, I thought, well informed.'[88]

Heath's most ambitious fly was cast over a serving senior police officer, Colonel Eric St. Johnston,[89] then Chief Constable of Lancashire. In his reply St. Johnston said that the Chief Inspector of Constabulary at the Home Office, whom he had consulted, did not think he should accept the invitation to join the working party, but that there would be no objection to his attending any meeting to which he might be invited. He added that he would be speaking only as an individual and not as a representative of the Chief Police Officers' Association. His letter is minuted tersely in Heath's hand: 'They could invite him to every meeting as consultant. He is a Tory. E.H.'.[90]

Tory or not, there is no evidence that St. Johnston, who himself became HM Chief Inspector of Constabulary in 1967, overstepped the boundaries of propriety. The minutes of the crime policy group record that, in common with various other expert witnesses, he attended one meeting of a sub-committee which was considering crime prevention. Accompanied by the Deputy Chief Constable of Lancashire, he opened challengingly, saying that he understood the Committee had already heard the views of the Metropolitan Police Commissioner and the Chief Inspector of Constabulary. These represented the establishment; whereas the views of his deputy and himself represented those of the rebels.[91] Members of the policy group later visited the Lancashire Constabulary Headquarters on 18–19 July 1965 for a briefing by the Chief Constable and his senior officers and saw a demonstration of the work of the force.

The first meeting, under Boyle's chairmanship, took place at the Conservative Research Department on 16 February. On 1 June, Thorneycroft warned that because of the possibility of an autumn

[88] Letter to the author, 2 June, 1990.
[89] Chief Constable: Oxfordshire, 1940–4; Durham County, 1944–50; Lancashire, 1950–67. HM Chief Inspector of Constabulary, 1967–70. Knighted 1967.
[90] CRD 3/19/6; St. Johnston to Heath 8 Feb. 1965, and manuscript minute 10 Feb. 1965.
[91] CRD 3/19/4; Minutes of Prevention Sub-Committee, 11 May 1965.

election, Heath had asked for interim reports by the end of the month. In Heath's personal and confidential letters to chairmen of policy groups he said that interim reports should concentrate on points that might be considered for inclusion in a manifesto for an autumn election. His letter went on to outline the procedure, a model of its kind, for presenting the fruits of policy research to the Conservative Party in Opposition:

The reports should be sent in the first instance to me for submission to the Advisory Committee on Policy. The ACP will then consider the report at its next meeting, and it may be that you would like to be present at that meeting. After the reports have been discussed by the ACP I pass the report, together with the views of the ACP to the Leader of the Party who no doubt will then wish to discuss it with his Consultative Committee.[92] The ACP does, I realise, add to the length of the procedure but it is important. It is the only method we have of associating with our policy the Party as a whole through a body that is representative of the front and back benches and the Party in the country as well as the Party in the House.[93]

A preliminary draft of the Crime Policy Group's interim report was ready by 23 June, with a second draft following on 29 June. By 6 July the final version was circulated by the Conservative Research Department, and on 13 July Thorneycroft sent the interim report to Heath, with copies to Sir Alec Douglas-Home and the Advisory Committee on Policy. In a covering letter he said that some further amendments would be needed, 'including particularly, in the light of recent events, a paragraph on prison security on the general lines that prisons should be better to live in and harder to get out of'.[94]

The possibility of publication was raised by Thorneycroft who suggested not only that it would demonstrate the thinking that had been done, but tactically that it would 'in some degree pre-empt any White Paper which the Socialists may be thinking of producing

[92] The Leader's Consultative Committee acts as the Shadow Cabinet when the Conservative Party is in Opposition.
[93] CRD 3/19/6; Heath to Thorneycroft 3 June 1965.
[94] CRD 3/19/6; Thorneycroft to Heath 13 July 1965. Five days earlier, on 8 July 1965, Ronald Biggs, serving a thirty-year sentence for his part in the great train robbery, escaped from Wandsworth prison with three other prisoners. Eleven months before, another of the convicted train robbers, Charles Wilson, also serving thirty years, had escaped from Winson Green prison at Birmingham.

based on Longford'.[95] If the report were to be published, he forecast that most members would be willing to let their names go on it. In reply, Heath expressed his 'really very warm thanks' to the members of the policy group. It was, he said, 'no inconsiderable sacrifice to put in the time and effort that this sort of work requires, particularly when, as I fear has been the case so far, it has to be pursued at rather a breakneck speed'.[96]

Heath's initial reaction was favourable to the idea of publication, subject to the report's reception by the Advisory Committee on Policy and the advice of 'our publicity pundits'.[97] As Leader of the Opposition, in November 1965 he decided against signing personally a foreword to the report which it had been agreed should be published as a pamphlet by the Conservative Political Centre. He did, however, ask to see and approve the proposed wording,[98] and on 30 December sent some comments on the proofs accompanied by a brisk command to 'get this sorted out and cleared as soon as possible'.[99]

Under the title *Crime Knows No Boundaries* the report was published on 19 January 1966, less than a year after the inception of the policy group. It contained a comprehensive study of the causes, prevention, and treatment of crime. The implications of some of the social causes were frankly stated as being 'not particularly comforting, since many of the goals which we as a nation set ourselves, the policies which we pursue and the material objectives to which we attach importance tend to increase rather than to diminish the incidence of crime.'[100]

Specific recommendations were aimed at strengthening the police, in manpower, efficiency, and pay, and speeding up the process of amalgamating local forces. The case for a separate traffic corps, strongly resisted by the police, was not worth pursuing. Arrange-

[95] The reference is to *Crime: A Challenge to Us All*, the report of the Labour Party study group under the chairmanship of Lord Longford.
[96] CRD 3/19/6; Heath to Thorneycroft 19 July 1965.
[97] Ibid.
[98] Ibid.; John MacGregor, Political Secretary to Edward Heath (later Secretary of State for Agriculture, 1987–9, for Education and Science, 1989–90, and Transport, 1992– ; Lord President of the Council and Leader of the House of Commons, 1990–2), to Conservative Research Department 30 Nov. 1965.
[99] Ibid.; Anne Tillard, Private Secretary to Edward Heath, to the Directors of the Conservative Research Department and the Conservative Political Centre, 30 Dec. 1965.
[100] *Crime Knows No Boundaries*, p. 11.

ments for committal proceedings should be reviewed, and short-
term imprisonment discouraged as being expensive and of little
reformative value. Powers should be given to the courts to sentence
adult offenders to attendance centres. More probation hostels were
urgently needed for young persons, and hostels should be provided
for adult offenders who required strict supervision. The report
concluded that substantial financial support should be given to
research promoted and co-ordinated by the Home Office and carried
out in the universities and by other agencies. The early release
of prisoners serving long sentences of determinate duration was
supported, although in the same way as the Longford report to the
Labour Party eighteen months before, the policy group added a
proviso that the Home Secretary should in all cases consult an
advisory body before doing so.

A leading article in *The Times* found the general approach
tentative, but did not offer any criticism on those grounds. On the
contrary, it commended the authors for resisting the temptation to
turn the increases in offences against property and the person into
highly inflammable political material with corresponding demands
for 'hard' as opposed to 'soft' dealings with offenders.[101] The tone
of the publication was firm but moderate and thoughtful; a true
reflection of the Heathite aspiration towards social policies that
aimed to be humane, practical, and vigorous. The forces of counter
revolution had not yet gathered strength.

VI

The Government formed by Edward Heath in June 1970 enacted
the main criminal justice legislation of the decade in 1972. A
stronger law and order ticket, although a feature of the Conservative
appeal to the electorate, was given no great prominence. Before the
General Election there had been some talk of revising *Crime Has
No Boundaries*, after Quintin Hogg had written to Heath calling
for a 'refurbishment' of policies towards crime.[102] Patrick Cosgrave,
then at the Conservative Research Department, listed the changes
he thought necessary in the text,[103] but the Director of the Research

[101] *The Times*, 20 Jan, 1966.
[102] CRD 3/19/7; Hogg to Heath 25 Nov. 1969.
[103] Ibid.; Cosgrave to Heath 9 Dec. 1969.

Department, Brendon Sewill, was not happy about the suggestion. What would be the status of a new document? Who would sign it? Was it to be an official Party document or a pamphlet in the name of Quintin Hogg? If the latter, Mr Hogg would be likely to want to write it himself and not be content simply to sign it. While the Party wished to give the minimum of specific policy commitments, yet conveying the impression that a Conservative Government would be full of ideas, such a stance would be insufficient to satisfy the press.[104]

The Party officials had their way and with the imminence of the Election the debate became subsumed in the drafting of the manifesto. No mention of crime occurred until page 26 of the thirty-page manifesto, where police recruitment, public order offences, prison-building, and secure detention for the most dangerous criminals were itemized. Even the reference to an 'age of demonstration and disruption' was balanced by an addendum representative of the Leader's outlook: 'A tolerant and civilized society must continue to permit its citizens to assemble, march and demonstrate in support of the ideals and principles they believe in.'[105]

The change in the political complexion of the Government after the Election did not lead to any sharp change of direction in the thrust of criminal policy. Although it is arguable that the seeds of dissensus had already taken root in the surrounding world of penal thought, dividing those who advocated a welfare philosophy from those who inclined to place confidence in penalties and the traditional legal apparatus, in the Home Office at least the consensus still held. The wise hand of Philip Allen was still evident; Reginald Maudling, the new Home Secretary, was an experienced and tolerant man, if no longer the force he had once been.[106] So it was that the most innovative proposal in the Criminal Justice Bill presented to Parliament on 10 November 1971 stemmed not from the Tory manifesto, nor from *Crime Has No Boundaries*, but from an official committee chaired by a Labour life peer.

As long before as November 1966, Jenkins had asked the Advis-

[104] Ibid.; Sewill to Douglas (Deputy Director), copied to Cosgrave 15 Apr. 1970.
[105] *A Better Tomorrow*, Conservative and Unionist Central Office, London, 1970, p. 26.
[106] President of the Board of Trade, 1959–61; Secretary of State for the Colonies, 1961–2; Chancellor of the Exchequer, 1962–4; Home Secretary, June 1970–July 1972 (resigned). Maudling's ministerial career ended over an imprudent business relationship with John Poulson whilst he was out of office between 1964 and 1970.

ory Council on the Penal System to consider what changes and additions might be made in the range of non-custodial penalties that were available to the courts. For adult offenders these had for many years been confined to absolute or conditional discharges, fines, and probation orders. There was a widely held view amongst sentencers at the time that these powers were too limited;[107] while the furtherance of types of punishment not necessitating the deprival of liberty had been a perennial cause of penal reformers. The 1967 Criminal Justice Act had added the suspended sentence which had been pressed on the Home Secretary by an enthusiastic judiciary. Unlike a probation order, which was not regarded as a sentence of the Court, a suspended sentence ranked not merely as a sentence, but as a sentence of imprisonment, with a condition attached which activated the element of custodial confinement only if another offence was committed within a stated period of not less than one year nor more than two (originally three) years.

The ACPS had set up a sub-committee, under the chairmanship of Baroness Wootton of Abinger, to carry out the review. A weighty report was completed by May 1970 covering fines, service to the community, deferment of sentence, attendance centres, disqualification from driving or certain occupations, forfeiture of property, intermittent custody, and the combination of probation with other orders. One of the earliest communications on penal matters received by Maudling, after taking office as Home Secretary on 20 June 1970, was a letter signed by the Chairman of the Advisory Council on the Penal System dated 30 June. In it, Younger stressed the need for additional alternatives to custodial sentences, which had been implicit in the decision to ask the Council to undertake the inquiry. Efforts should be directed not merely towards keeping offenders out of prison, but towards changing their attitudes to society. The most 'imaginative and hopeful' of the sub-committee's proposals were that:

the criminal courts should be empowered to require offenders to carry out service to the community. The Council feel that this scheme, with its emphasis on the reformative value of service in association with volunteers, is likely to be a promising form of new non-custodial penalty and that its

---

[107] Home Office, *Non-Custodial and Semi-Custodial Penalties*, Report of the Advisory Council on the Penal System, HMSO, London, 1970, p. 3.

effectiveness is likely to be all the greater because it involves the positive co-operation of the offender.[108]

'Operating creatively' on a proposal which intrinsically was another version of reparation, although this time to the community as a whole, Maudling echoed the sentiments of the ACPS in his speech commending the Criminal Justice Bill to the House of Commons on Second Reading. There was nothing in the Bill which was in any way dramatic or spectacular, he said, rather it was the culmination of much work and thought over many years by people inside and outside the House who were concerned with the problems of crime and punishment and penal treatment generally.[109]

The Bill also incorporated recommendations made by another sub-committee of the ACPS, chaired by Lord Justice Widgery,[110] extending and rationalizing the powers of the courts to require a convicted offender to make financial reparation to his victim. Criminal bankruptcy orders, designed to ensure that those who committed large-scale crimes, especially fraud, should not be able to benefit from the fruits of their criminal activities, were also included. Maximum penalties for firearms offences were to be increased. As an alternative to imprisonment, the courts would have discretion to sentence offenders, with their consent, to between 40 and 240 hours of community service work. To the Home Secretary the idea was

a wholly novel concept in this country. It has been tried experimentally in other countries, but it is new to us. I have high hopes for it ... I like the idea of sentenced persons doing something useful for their fellow citizens rather than mouldering inside a prison. In fact, such voluntary activity might well lead to their continuing to do it in the future of their own free will.[111]

To the politicians of the early 1970s, the notion of community service by offenders was an attractive one. Combining relative novelty with practicality, it seemed evidently constructive as a way of repaying society for a wrong done, while at the same time

---

[108] Ibid., p. v.
[109] *Parl. Debates*, HC, 826 (5th ser.), col. 965, 22 Nov. 1971.
[110] Home Office, *Reparation by the Offender*, Report of the Advisory Council on the Penal System, HMSO, London, 1970. Lord Widgery succeeded Lord Parker of Waddington as Lord Chief Justice in 1971, retiring due to ill-health in 1980.
[111] *Parl. Debates*, HC, 826, col. 973.

bringing the offender within reach of the voluntary organizations which are a peculiarly English way of providing services of value to a wider community. Perhaps the difficulties of finding suitable work for offenders, and ensuring that tasks were properly performed, were underestimated in the enthusiasm of the initial response. Nevertheless a new, and in the event permanent, penal instrument had been forged. As we shall see in a later chapter, much of the same reasoning was to recur towards the end of the 1980s in the search for ways of implementing punishment in the community.

The motivation behind the Criminal Justice Act 1972 lay in the desire of ministers to be seen to be taking action in the field of criminal justice without any ideologically dominant objectives to fuel the legislation. While there were some deeply held opinions, as shown in the controversy over the provisions in the 1967 Act which had made the suspension of certain short sentences mandatory,[112] they provided insufficient grist for the legislative mill. The raw material was stored within the department. Some of it, notably parts of the two reports from the ACPS, chimed with, although were not attributable to, the political beliefs of a number of Conservatives on the back benches in the House of Commons. The moderate Home Secretary was not alone in contending that offenders should recompense their victims, and through the performance of tasks of value to the community make reparation for the harm they had done. In the form in which the proposals on community service appeared in the Bill they owed something also to the Government's hope that the new measure would be seen as a credible alternative to custodial sentences, thus contributing towards the aim of bringing down the prison population.

It would be an overstatement to interpret the 1972 Act as a planned and conscious attack on the size of the prison population.[113] The gravitational field generated in its productive phase by the legislative cycle attracted items from several diverse sources. The Wootton and Widgery proposals came to hand at the right time;

[112] Lord Gardiner, who at the time of the Criminal Justice Act 1967 had been doubtful whether it was right to make it mandatory for a court to suspend sentences of imprisonment of not more than six months, later changed his mind and moved an amendment to the Criminal Justice Bill in the House of Lords to retain the mandatory requirement, subject to some exceptions. His amendment was defeated by 77 votes to 50. *Parl. Debates*, HL, 333 (5th ser.), cols. 531–58, 17 July 1972.
[113] 'The Policy-Making Process: How it is seen from the Home Office', p. 137.

there were pressures from bodies such as the Magistrates' Association and the Justices' Clerks; while the prospect of legislation prompted a clearing out of the pigeon holes of Whitehall. Parliamentary proceedings, second thoughts about the drafting, and the addition of makeweight provisions, added to and varied the original core as the Bill progressed. As enacted, a Home Office official[114] traced the origins of the twenty-four Sections comprising Part I of the Act, entitled 'Powers for Dealing with Offenders', in the analysis reproduced in Table 3.

TABLE 3. *Criminal Justice Act 1972: origins*

Section	Subject	Origin
1–6	Compensation	Widgery Report
7–10	Criminal bankruptcy	Widgery Report
11–14	Suspended prison sentences, etc.	Ministerial/ Departmental
15–19	Community service	Wootton Report
20	Day training centres	Departmental
21	Breach of probation	Departmental
22	Deferment of sentence	Wootton Report
23	Forfeiture of property	Wootton Report
24	'Criminal' driving disqualification	Wootton Report

VII

After the passage of the 1972 Act there was no further criminal justice legislation for five years. In the interval, problems multiplied more rapidly than the policies to counter them. Delegated legislation, decisions of the courts, and changing administrative practice, amounted to a sluggish dynamic for speeding up the ability of the criminal justice system to respond. The design and building of a series of new prisons and detention centres, the first comprehensive programme since Victorian times, was embarked upon following Butler's initiative, but after the early stages fell prey to cutbacks

[114] M. J. Moriarty. Ibid., pp. 137–8.

for economic reasons. The most keenly felt was a condition attached to a large scale loan from the International Monetary Fund in 1976 requiring a reduction of £1 billion in public expenditure to support the external value of sterling. The prison-building programme was among the casualties. Even the contorted prose of the Prison Department's report for that year could not disguise the import:

the on-going place producing programme begun in 1970 was suspended indefinitely and expenditure is now limited to completing major place producing and redevelopment projects already under way. Improvements at existing establishments have also been curtailed and will be necessarily confined in the years ahead to the renewal of essential services and repairs to enable establishments to continue in full operation.[115]

Other developments, to become increasingly portentous as time went on, primarily the moves towards stricter control over police powers of arrest and questioning of suspects, and the inauguration of an independent prosecution service, were in their embryonic stages. A review of the constitutional position of the police and the 'arrangements for their control and administration', had been carried out by a Royal Commission under the chairmanship of Sir Henry Willink whose final report had been published as early as May 1962.[116] Although some well-publicized scandals had begun to undermine the respect which the police still generally enjoyed, the majority recommended no fundamental change,[117] contenting themselves with drawing attention to 'a body of evidence, too substantial to disregard, which in effect accused the police of stooping to the use of undesirable means of obtaining statements and of occasionally giving perjured evidence in a court of law'.[118] Against these criticisms, the Royal Commission noted that it had heard from 'witnesses representing a wide range of interests a great many tributes to the integrity of the police'.[119] Conventional and gradualist as its recommendations tended to be, the Royal Commission can take credit for laying the foundations of the practice

[115] *Report of the Work of the Prison Department 1976* (Cmnd. 6877), HMSO, London, 1977, p. 1.
[116] Royal Commission on the Police 1962, *Final Report* (Cmnd. 1728), HMSO, London, 1962.
[117] In a powerfully argued memorandum of dissent, Dr A. L. Goodhart proposed a centrally controlled police force on a regional basis. Ibid., pp. 157–79.
[118] Ibid., p. 110.
[119] Ibid., p. 112.

of bringing in a senior officer from another force to investigate complaints against the police. It also recommended the appointment of a Chief Inspector of Constabulary answerable to the Home Secretary, and that the post be filled without delay.

By the later 1960s and throughout the 1970s uneasiness over police impropriety in investigating crime grew rather than diminished. Disquiet arose from a number of notorious incidents, in particular the Maxwell Confait murder case. In that case the conviction of three youths in 1972 was later overturned by the Court of Appeal in a judgment which by implication raised disturbing questions about police interrogations, especially of juveniles and the mentally handicapped. The case was the subject of an inquiry by a former High Court judge, Sir Henry Fisher, whose report included forceful criticisms of police officers and of a lawyer in the DPP's Department. In making specific recommendations on the wording and application of the Judges' Rules and other matters, Fisher observed cautiously, but correctly:

An inquiry such as mine into a particular case is not a sufficient foundation for fundamental changes in the law relating to police investigation and prosecution (such, for instance, as the introduction of a system like that prevailing in Scotland). If such changes are to be contemplated, then something like a Royal Commission, which could go into all aspects of any proposed changes (including the cost) would be required.[120]

In June 1977, six months before Fisher's report was published, the tide of opinion was running so strongly that the Prime Minister announced the appointment of a Royal Commission on Criminal Procedure. The time had come, James Callaghan said, for the whole criminal process, from the start of investigation to the point of trial, to be reviewed.[121] The remit extended to the prosecution as well as the investigation of crime. The inclusion of the former originated less from public concern over any alleged malpractice than from lack of confidence, felt mainly but not wholly within the legal profession, in procedures whereby ultimate responsibility for prosecuting as well as investigating in the vast majority of cases rested with the police. Objections were both of principle and of a practical nature. More than a century earlier, in 1856, a Select Committee of the House of Commons had heard arguments remark-

---

[120] HC 90, Session 1977–8, pp. 6–7.
[121] *Parl. Debates*, HC, 933 (5th ser.), cols. WA 603–5, 24 June 1977.

ably similar to those which were to convince the Royal Commission:

The Attorney General for England states that cases are often brought to trial which, from being imperfectly got up, break down, and thus cause the acquittal of guilty parties. Many cases are likewise brought into court, where, on account of the trivial nature of the offence imputed, or the deficiency of proof adduced, prosecutions are undesirable ... Policemen assume the functions of public prosecutors; a practice liable to abuse. There may often be a good case for conviction, and no deficiency of evidence, yet acquittal ensues because the prosecutor, acting without advice, is not sufficiently informed as to the precise nature of the proof required by law.[122]

In 1970 JUSTICE had published a report of a working party, chaired by Lewis Hawser QC and Basil Wigoder QC,[123] recommending an equivalent of the Scottish prosecution system. When the idea of a Royal Commission was in circulation, lawyers within the ranks of the Government, notably Sam Silkin, the Attorney General and one of the few front-benchers on either side to have taken a close interest in penal reform,[124] and Alex Lyon, a Minister of State at the Home Office, pressed for the opportunity to be grasped to make an authoritative assessment of the arguments for a public prosecution service independent of the police. The chance to convert a proposal long mooted into reality was too precious to let slip.

The selection of members[125] was a slow business and the Commission did not begin work until February 1978. By then it was inevitable, given such wide terms of reference and the thoroughness expected of an inquiry by a Royal Commission, that its report

[122] HC, 206, Session 1856, p. iv.

[123] QC, 1966; life peer 1974. Liberal Chief Whip, House of Lords, 1977–84.

[124] QC, 1963; Attorney General, 1974–9. Created a life peer as Lord Silkin of Dulwich in 1985.

[125] The appointment as chairman of Sir Cyril Philips, Professor of Oriental History in the University of London (1946–80), was imaginative and successful. Between them the other members covered a diverse range of experience and opinion: a Lord Justice of Appeal; four magistrates, one being General Secretary of the Fabian Society and another a black Canon of the Anglican diocese of Southwark; a former Chief Constable and a former Secretary of the Police Federation; a retired Permanent Under-Secretary of State at the Home Office; three lawyers—one a barrister, one a solicitor, and one an academic; a Professor of Sociology; the General Secretary of the Transport and General Workers' Union; the Managing Director of Yorkshire Television; and a senior executive of the North Eastern Co-operative Society.

TABLE 4. *Royal Commissions, 1960–81*

Subject	Date established	Chairman	Terms of reference	Date of report
Police	1960	Sir Henry Willink	To review the constitutional position of the police throughout Great Britain, the arrangements for their control and administration and, in particular, to consider: (1) the constitution and functions of local police authorities; (2) the status and accountability of members of police forces including chief officers of police; (3) the relationship of the police with the public and the means of ensuring that complaints by the public against the police are effectively dealt with; and (4) the broad principles which should govern the remuneration of the constable, having regard to the nature and extent of police duties and responsibilities and the need to attract and retain an adequate number of recruits with the proper qualifications.	1962
Penal system	1964	Viscount Amory	In the light of modern knowledge of crime and its causes and of modern penal practice here and abroad, to re-examine the concepts and purposes which should underlie the punishment and treatment of offenders in England and Wales; to report how far they are realized by the penalties and methods of treatment available to the courts, and whether any changes in these, or in the arrangements and responsibility for selecting the sentences to be imposed on particular offenders, are desirable; to review the work of the services and institutions dealing with offenders, and the responsibility for their administration: and to make recommendations.	dissolved without reporting 1966

Table 4. *Royal Commissions, 1960–81—continued*

Subject	Date established	Chairman	Terms of reference	Date of report
Assizes and Quarter Sessions	1966	Lord Beeching	To inquire into the present arrangements for the administration of justice at Assizes and at Quarter Sessions outside Greater London; to report what reforms should be made for the more convenient, economic and efficient disposal of the civil and criminal business at present dealt with by those courts and to consider and report on the effect these will have on the High Court, the Central Criminal Court, the Courts of Quarter Sessions in Greater London, and the County Courts throughout England and Wales.	1969
Criminal procedure	1978	Professor Sir Cyril Philips	To examine, having regard both to the interests of the community in bringing offenders to justice and to the rights and liberties of persons suspected or accused of crime, and taking into account also the need for the efficient and economical use of resources, whether changes are needed in England and Wales in (1) the powers and duties of the police in respect of the investigation of criminal offences and the rights and duties of suspects and accused persons, including the means by which these are secured; (2) the process of and responsibility for the prosecution of criminal offences; and (3) such other features of criminal procedure and evidence as relate to the above; and to make recommendations.	1981

could not be completed and delivered until after a General Election
had taken place and, as it turned out, a new Government had come
into power. The Commission was the fourth to be established since
1960. Details of each are given in Table 4. Mrs Thatcher did not
look with favour on Royal Commissions as a method of resolving
difficult issues, and none was set up during her premiership between
1979 and 1990.

VIII

Over the five years since the 1972 Act, the list of items calling for
legislation was lengthening. In the Criminal Law Bill planned for
the session 1976/7 Home Office officials saw a vehicle capable of
travelling beyond its original destination, the modernization of the
outdated state of the law on conspiracy and trespass, by hitching
on proposals dealing with the powers of the courts, the distribution
of business between the Crown Court and the Magistrates' courts,
penalties, and a number of procedural changes. Ministers agreed,
and a Bill was duly introduced in the House of Lords. With the
unforeseen addition of partly suspended sentences when the Bill
reached the Commons, the resulting measure became the Criminal
Law Act 1977, finally amounting to sixty-five sections and fourteen
schedules. Even the Home Secretary, Merlyn Rees, in his Second
Reading speech commending the measure to the House, volunteered
that it had no theme.[126] Other commentators depicted the Act less
flatteringly as yet another example of 'dustbin legislation'.[127]

The law reform parts of the Act were opportune and important.
Conspiracy was an old common law offence, frequently charged
and much in need of bringing up to date. Trespass was, and
generally so remains, a civil wrong. The Act buttressed the law on
trespass with two new criminal offences: using or threatening
violence in order to obtain entry to any premises, and occupying a
house or flat and refusing to leave at the request of the rightful
occupier. Films, whether shown in public cinemas or cinema clubs,
were brought within the scope of the Obscene Publications Act

---

[126] *Parl. Debates*, HC, 931 (5th ser.), col. 237, 3 May 1977.
[127] T. M. Aldridge, *Criminal Law Act 1977*, Annotated Legislation Service Vol.
249, Butterworths, London, 1978 p. 1.

1959. New offences were created to counter the menace of bomb hoaxes and the reality of threats to kill, whether by the planting of bombs or other means. The offences of dangerous driving and causing death by dangerous driving, those convicted of the latter regularly killing more people on the roads each year than those convicted of murder, were abolished, being replaced by reckless driving and causing death by reckless driving.[128]

The procedural and administrative changes affected remands, young offenders, the disclosure of prosecution evidence to accused persons or those representing them, and coroners' courts. Inflation called for an uplift in many maximum fines, with a power being conferred upon the Home Secretary to adjust financial limits in the future by order, having first obtained the approval of both Houses of Parliament, so as to keep them in step with subsequent changes in the value of money. The power was brought into force on 17 July 1978.

By the mid-1970s the purity of Gardiner's reorganization of the criminal courts was jeopardized by the Crown Court becoming overburdened with trials for large numbers of relatively trivial offences. Lengthy delays occurred; there were about 8,000 cases awaiting trial in the Crown Court in 1974, growing to 12,000 by September 1976. The Government had responded by setting up an interdepartmental committee under the chairmanship of Lord Justice James to review the distribution of criminal business between the Crown Court and the Magistrates' courts. The Committee reported in 1975, and its recommendations formed the basis of the reorganization effected by the Criminal Law Act 1977.[129] All of the existing types of offence were reduced to three categories, classified by the method of trial. They were: offences triable only on indict-

[128] The provision in the Criminal Law Act 1977 was replaced by the Road Traffic Act 1988, which in its turn was repealed by the Road Traffic Act 1991. The current offences are now once again described as dangerous driving and causing death by dangerous driving. The definition in Section 1 of the Road Traffic Act 1991 is causing the death of another person by driving a mechanically propelled vehicle dangerously on a road or other public place in a way that falls so far below what would be expected of a competent and careful driver that it would be obvious to such a driver that driving in that way would be dangerous. The 1991 Act also created a new offence of causing death by careless driving when under the influence of drink or drugs. These provisions came into force on 1 July 1992.

[129] Home Office and Lord Chancellor's Office, *The Distribution of Criminal Business between the Crown Court and the Magistrates' Courts* (Cmnd. 6323), HMSO, London, 1975.

ment; offences triable only summarily; and offences triable either
way.

A procedure was laid down to determine whether an 'either
way' offence was to be tried summarily or on indictment. The
Magistrates' court must first form a view on which mode of trial
appears more suitable, having regard to the nature of the case;
whether the circumstances make the offence one of a serious
character; and whether Magistrates' powers of sentencing would
be adequate. The case can be tried summarily only if the accused
consents. This proviso allows a measure of latitude to opt for jury
trial on indictment to a person accused of a more serious offence,
or one which could have profound effects on him if found guilty.[130]

The decks had not been cleared, however, for a further innovation. The partly suspended sentence of imprisonment had been
omitted from the Bill which had passed through all its stages in the
Lords, although it had been under consideration by the ACPS.[131]
Its addition was due to a debating coup by a junior Opposition
spokesman, Patrick Mayhew,[132] during Standing Committee in the
Commons. The Minister of State, Brynmor John, who was taking
the Bill through the Committee on behalf of the Home Secretary,
unexpectedly accepted the amendment to the surprise of his officials.
On the floor of the House at Report stage, the Government tabled
a redrafted new clause which received all-Party support and was
agreed without a division.[133] Only two MPs, Emlyn Hooson, a

[130] Offences triable either way included bigamy, some forms of perjury (but not
in respect of evidence given in court), forgery, burglary (except where violence was
used or threatened towards the occupants of a dwelling), unlawful sexual intercourse
with a girl aged under sixteen, and indecency between men.

[131] Home Office, *Sentences of Imprisonment: A Review of Maximum Penalties*,
HMSO, London, 1978, pp. 118–23. The Council had been attracted by what it
regarded as 'the penological arguments' in favour of partial suspension, and had
intended to recommend a new power to suspend part of a prison sentence in its
final report. The intention was overtaken by events at the Committee stage of the
Criminal Law Bill in the House of Commons.

[132] QC, 1972. Minister of State at the Home Office, 1981–3; Solicitor General,
1983–7; Attorney General, 1987–92; Secretary of State for Northern Ireland, 1992– .
Knighted 1983.

[133] The clause which became Section 47 of the Criminal Law Act 1977 provided
that where a court passes on an adult a sentence of imprisonment for a term of not
less than six months and not more than two years, it may order that, after he has
served part of the sentence in prison, the remainder of it shall be held in suspense.
The part held in suspense shall be not more than three-quarters, and not less than
one-quarter of the whole term. If he is convicted of an offence punishable with
imprisonment and committed during the whole period of the original sentence, the

Liberal QC,[134] and Leo Abse, a Labour back-bencher, sounded a warning.

Since the Criminal Justice Act 1967, the Courts had been able to suspend a sentence of imprisonment, but not to require part of it to be served in custody with part suspended. Conceptually it was tempting to argue that greater flexibility would allow the sentencing court more discretion if it concluded that full suspension could not be justified, but that a brief experience of imprisonment might have some deterrent effect without first offenders remaining long enough in prison to become acclimatized. The ACPS saw in this a double deterrent: the deterrent element of actual custody, and a postponed deterrence during the suspension period.[135] In the Commons debate a sponsor of Radical Alternatives to Prison, Robert Kilroy-Silk, said that penal reformers (he mentioned the Howard League, NACRO, and the ACPS) were in favour of partly suspended sentences, as he was himself, on the grounds that the length of the sentence had little deterrent effect.[136]

The Minister of State spoke about overcrowding and the cost of adding a supervision requirement to the new sentence;[137] with Mayhew, in a phrase that was to gain increasing currency on the Conservative benches, pronouncing that whereas a great many people who get a suspended sentence, and their friends, think that they have got away with their crime, the effect of 'a short, sharp and I hope, nasty taste of prison'[138] would linger on. Far from being a soft option, he contended, the partly suspended sentence would enable the courts to deal more severely with 'people who need to have the deterrence of a taste of prison at what is relatively the outset of their criminal experience'.[139]

The possibilities of a more stringent regime during their stay in prison, Mayhew added, should also be considered. This was the language of the Conservative Right, and it is seldom that it sychronizes with the tenets of the reformist Left. The irony was

court may restore the part of the sentence held in suspense and order him to serve it in prison.

[134] Emlyn Hooson was created a life peer in 1979, and became an authoritative participant in House of Lords debates on criminal justice.

[135] *Sentences of Imprisonment*, p. 118.

[136] *Parl. Debates*, HC, 935–1, (5th ser.), cols. 475–6, 13 July 1977.

[137] Ibid., cols. 462–3.

[138] Ibid., cols. 464–5.

[139] Ibid., col. 465.

that the two conflicting strands should converge on a proposal that was so unlikely to achieve its ill-defined and contradictory aims.

In the event, the life of the partly suspended sentence was short and inglorious. Section 47 of the Criminal Law Act 1977, was not brought into force for another five years until 1982, ministers of both parties having accepted the advice of Home Office officials that the provision was too risky to implement at a time of acute overcrowding in the prisons. Their doubts arose from the inability to predict or control how the courts would use the power. A term of x years' imprisonment to be served and y years' suspended might be imposed, when previously x would have been thought sufficient. If this were to happen, the activation of only a proportion of suspended terms would amount to a heavy extra burden on the prisons. Moreover, the workings of the partly suspended sentence were complex and difficult to explain to those who had been convicted; the sentence was not available for young offenders under the age of twenty-one; and there were confusing anomalies with parole entitlement.[140]

Unlike the fully suspended sentence which had become popular, in some ways too popular with the initial enthusiasm of the courts having to be reined in by the Court of Appeal,[141] the partly suspended sentence never caught on. In 1987 and 1988 only some 2,700 partly suspended sentences were imposed in the whole of England and Wales. In 1988 magistrates gave 15,900 fully suspended sentences and the Crown Court another 15,000. Two-thirds of the suspended sentences imposed by the Magistrates' courts were for

---

[140] The custodial portion of a partly suspended sentence attracted remission and parole entitlement, which became relevant after the reduction in 1983 of the minimum qualifying period for parole from twelve months to six months. For an exposition of the anomalies that arose, see *The Parole System in England and Wales: Report of the Review Committee* (Cm. 532), HMSO, London, 1988, pp. 117–18.

[141] In *R. v. O'Keefe* [1969] 1 All ER 426, Lord Parker CJ held that before passing a suspended sentence the court must go through the process of eliminating other possible courses, and only when, having considered the alternatives, it decides that the case in question is one of imprisonment should the option of the suspended sentence be considered. In particular a suspended sentence should not be given when a probation order was the proper order to make. His judgment was the genesis of the restriction enacted in Section 11(3) of the Criminal Justice Act 1972: 'An offender shall not be dealt with by means of a sentence of imprisonment suspended under Section 39 of the said Act of 1967 unless the case appears to the court to be one in which a sentence of imprisonment would have been appropriate in the absence of any power to suspend such a sentence.'

up to three months. In the Crown Court over 90% were for up to a year, and 50% under six months.[142]

In November 1988 the Carlisle Committee's review of the parole system found the partly suspended sentence to be 'wholly incompatible' with the scheme proposed for conditional release in the future, and recommended its abolition.[143] In the White Paper on *Crime, Justice and Protecting the Public*, which outlined the Government's plans for legislation in 1990/1, the recommendation was accepted.[144] Section 47 of the Criminal Law Act 1977 was duly repealed by the Criminal Justice Act 1991.

IX

An insight into the relevance of presentation to parties in Opposition can be found in Conservative policies towards law and order in 1978. Since May 1977 Labour no longer had an overall majority in the House of Commons, depending on Liberal or Nationalist support to remain in office. An election could come at any time, and policies across the board were being honed in readiness. At a Shadow Cabinet meeting held in the Leader's Room at the Commons on 1 March 1978 a policy paper titled *Law and Order: A New Resolve* was submitted for approval.[145] Drafted by the Conservative Research Department, it was presented by William Whitelaw, the Shadow Home Secretary, and David Howell, formerly a junior minister who had worked under Whitelaw at the Northern Ireland Office and was at the time a front-bench spokesman on Home Affairs.[146] Mrs Thatcher was in the chair, with fourteen other members of the Leader's Consultative Committee present. None had previously served as Home Office ministers,

[142] *Crime, Justice and Protecting the Public: The Government's Proposals for Legislation* (Cm. 965), HMSO, London, 1990, p. 16.
[143] *The Parole System in England and Wales*, p. 118.
[144] Cm. 965, p. 16.
[145] A copy of the minutes of the 194th Meeting of the Leader's Consultative Committee is held in the Conservative Party Archive at the Bodleian Library (LC 78/194).
[146] Parliamentary Secretary, Northern Ireland Office, 1972; Minister of State, 1972–4; Minister of State, Department of Energy, 1974. Secretary of State for Energy, 1979–81; for Transport, 1981–3. Chairman, House of Commons Select Committee on Foreign Affairs, 1987– .

although Lord Thorneycroft had chaired the policy group which had produced *Crime Knows No Boundaries* in 1966. Opposition Whips, Party officials, and the Head of the Home Affairs Section of the Conservative Research Department were in attendance.

Introducing the paper, Whitelaw suggested that in place of 'Law and Order' it should be retitled 'The Protection of the Citizen'. There is no record of the reaction to this suggestion, but the phrase 'law and order' was too deeply engrained to be displaced from general currency. The discussion covered police pay, seen as an important but potentially costly commitment, and the undesirability of a referendum on capital punishment 'because of its implications for other policy areas and the danger of undermining Parliamentary government'.[147] Suggestions were put forward on corporal punishment, a crime of vandalism, special constables, violence on television, community homes, school activities, controlling obscene displays, and parental responsibility. It was agreed that the paper should be redrafted and circulated, and that any published statements of policy should make it clear Conservatives 'did not believe additional resources alone to be the answer to law and order problems, but that the humanizing of our society had an important contribution to make'.[148] The claim that 'the shorter the sentence is, the better', was regarded as being open to misinterpretation, and should be rephrased.

Although the 1978 policy paper was never published, its main features were incorporated in the manifesto, and the supplementary briefing that accompanied it, for the General Election which came in May of the following year. The commitments are listed in the next chapter, but they need to be put in the context of their presentation and the way the law and order issue was handled during the election campaign. A meeting to draw up plans took place in the Chairman's room at the Conservative Central Office on 7 July 1978.[149]

Thorneycroft (the Party Chairman), Whitelaw, and Howell were joined by a group of mostly younger professional advisers and party officials. Gordon Reece, a public relations consultant and personal adviser to Margaret Thatcher, was at the time Director of Publicity at the Central Office. Tim Bell was Chairman and

[147] LC 78/194.
[148] Ibid.
[149] CRD 4/10/24 contains a copy of the minutes of the meeting.

Managing Director of the Party's advertising agency, Saatchi and Saatchi Garland-Compton. Christopher Patten was Director of the Conservative Research Department, accompanied by Nicholas True from the Home Affairs Section. Tristan Garel-Jones and Alan Howarth were on the Chairman's staff at Central Office. Patten, Garel-Jones, and Howarth were later to become MPs and hold office as ministers under Mrs Thatcher; all were aged in their mid-thirties. Bell and Reece continued as key advisers to the Prime Minister, on the communication of policy as well as on her personal projection, throughout the election campaigns of the 1980s. Both were knighted, becoming famous names in the world of public relations.

The discussion concentrated upon the imperatives of effective political communication: the need to prepare a 'distillation' of policy in a form that could be used as background for press conferences, speeches, and broadcasts, and the language and basic terms that should be employed. The phrase 'law and order' continued to provoke differing opinions.[150] The Party might talk of 'safety in the streets', or 'violence in the streets', or 'protecting the citizen', or 'safety in the home'. Notwithstanding the reservations expressed by Whitelaw amongst others, especially about the impact on younger people, it was hard to find a better comprehensive phrase than 'law and order'. What was it that people responded to? Presumably it depended on who they were. A pensioner might be particularly concerned about safety in the streets. A resident in a tower block might be concerned about vandalism. A parent might be concerned about discipline in the schools. It was agreed that systematic use should be made of the words 'safety', 'security' (a word Labour was believed to be fond of and which might therefore be turned to advantage), and 'support'. Society might be described as 'overregulated and underprotected'.

Five items identified for use at a press conference and for speeches and broadcasts were:[151]

1. The Government must support the police. The police had not

---

[150] Poll data from a 1978 survey conducted for the Conservative Party by ORC indicated that 'law and order' was 'very variously interpreted'. It also suggested that a substantial majority of the electorate did not believe that the Labour Government were giving the police adequate support. Ibid.

[151] CRD 4/10/24.

received proper support from Labour ministers, leading to poor pay and loss of experienced manpower.

2. People guilty of crimes must be convicted. The period between arrest and trial for serious offences must be shortened and the question of bail should be looked at.

3. Punishments must make sense. The political background was likely to be a country clamouring for tougher punishments and wanting to be convinced that crime will be dealt with, while expert reports called for less resort to prison sentencing. Against this background, Conservatives should say: too many prison sentences are given to the wrong people (e.g. alcoholics); prison regimes are too often wrong, with prisoners staying inside in relatively soft conditions for relatively long sentences; too often violent criminals do not get sent to prison as they should; for young thugs short spells are advocated in glasshouse-type detention centres with a very tough physical regime (but good food); otherwise there should be a greater emphasis on fines, representing a more humane and economical approach.

4. The treatment of offenders is important as well as punishment. The Conservative leadership should show itself as compassionate and imaginative as well as tough where necessary. The public will not be reconciled to compassion and rehabilitation until they are confident that criminals are in fact being caught and punished. Firm action is necessary on law and order. Deprivation must not be an excuse for everything. Compassion for the victim should come before compassion for the criminal.

5. As an addendum, it might be worth saying something positive, following public statements by the Metropolitan Police Commissioner, Sir David McNee, about the need for improved discipline in schools and the high proportion of offences committed by 10–16-year-old children. This should be discussed with the Shadow Cabinet spokesman on Education.

It was decided that capital and corporal punishment should not be volunteered for the list of topics to be projected. The line to take on capital punishment was that what urgently mattered was not the form of punishment, but making sure that people can live in safety and without fear. Conservatives were concerned that an old lady can go and collect her pension without coming back to find her gas meter has been robbed, and that a mother can send her child round to a local shop without fear that the child will be molested. It was important that members of the Party should not come out with calls for a referendum on capital punishment, as some candidates were reported to have done. Mr Whitelaw would personally repudiate such demands if they were made again. The question of capital punishment had always been a matter for individual conscience on a free vote in the House of Commons. It was not thought that there was much demand for corporal punishment. Mr Whitelaw dealt with the question normally by saying that it was no doubt a suitable kind of punishment for schoolboys, but it did not make sense for judicial use, especially because of the delay between offence and punishment.

A press advertisement prepared by Saatchi's on the theme: 'Is it safe to vote for another Labour Government?' was approved. The copy featured the rise in crime that had taken place under Labour, stressing the need to support the police and the protection of people and property. As regards television, it was noted that the broadcasting authorities were not willing to make newsfilm of the incidents outside the Grunwick factory available for party use. Mr Whitelaw would pass on to Mrs Thatcher the proposals for phrases and the presentational priorities, suggesting to her that she might wish to hold a meeting on the subject. Although there were some variations as the election campaign unfolded, the thrust of the Tory message on law and order did not deviate from the plan drawn up at the meeting on 7 July 1978.

X

Public policy over the three decades separating 1947 and 1979, represented, on the whole, the upholding of a consensual approach towards criminal justice. The great issues, the ending of capital and corporal punishment as judicial penalties, cut across the parties and were treated as matters of individual conscience distinct from party politics. At general elections the differences between the parties were magnified, but even in 1979, when the degree of politicization was greater than previously, the divide was more one of presentation and emphasis than substance. With few exceptions, not all of which were as abortive as the partly suspended sentence, the ground for legislative change was usually prepared by Royal

Commissions, Committees of Inquiry, or reports from the ACPS
or other advisory bodies. The special interest groups were influential
and research was encouraged into the causes of crime and the
treatment of those who had offended. The courts were reorganized
and criminal offences reclassified, reforms which affected large
numbers of people, but which had been achieved with a minimum
of political controversy.

Punitive trends could be identified in the increase of maximum
sentences of imprisonment for offences of violence against the
person. Firearms controls were tightened. In sentencing, indeterminacy fell out of fashion sweeping away borstal training in its
tide. Detention centres survived, despite the erosion of evidence to
support the ideals of retribution and deterrence which they epitomized. The more liberal values of the 1960s were sustained in an
unobtrusive, yet pervasive, climate of common attitudes shared by
Home Office officials, special interest groups, and a respectable
body of informed opinion. In this environment, the Probation
Service was shaped into a discernible national system. Financial
compensation became available for the first time for criminal
injuries; the community service order raised hopes as an alternative
to custody; and an elaborate system of parole, later greatly
expanded, was instituted.

These progressive changes in penal policy were not matched by
changes for the better within the prison system. The building of
new prisons and the improvement of old ones were low priorities
in the aftermath of the world war when scarce resources were
concentrated upon houses, schools, hospitals, and roads. Ministers
were touchy on accusations of spending public money on making
the prisons more comfortable for criminals while so many deserving
people were suffering hardship or deprivation. Home Office officials
knew what needed to be done, but were inhibited by the political
weather from doing it.[152] As a result, their efforts were diverted
more towards devising non-custodial alternatives than facing up
to the intractable problems of institutional confinement. Some
sensational prison escapes in the mid-1960s (including four of the

---

[152] Letter from Lord Allen of Abbeydale, 30 Apr. 1990: 'the Home Office was
perfectly well aware of what was wrong, but what hope was there in the post-
war years of persuading Ministers (and the public) that scarce resources should be
given to the prisons when the country was crying out for more houses, schools,
roads ...'

great train robbers and the spy George Blake),[153] led to heightened security and control at the cost of treatment, training, and education. The Report of the Prison Department for 1967 commented:

Staff who had long been encouraged to develop treatment relationships towards prisoners had little time left for this important work after discharging tasks arising from the need to concentrate on security. There was some curtailment of prisoners' activities, a reduction in the number of outside working parties and of educational classes.[154]

New closed prisons were built for convicted offenders serving long fixed sentences or life imprisonment for the most serious crimes. In the five years from 1966 to 1971 maximum security prisons at Gartree (opened 1966), Albany (1967),[155] and Long Lartin (1971) took their places alongside such grim old gaols as Parkhurst, Wakefield, and Wormwood Scrubs. Their regimes may have been impoverished by the emphasis on security and restrictions on movement within the prison, but at least the physical settings avoided the squalor and overcrowding which worsened in the local prisons. There the higher number of offenders sentenced to imprisonment, augmented by a burgeoning population of unconvicted persons remanded in custody awaiting trial, regularly exceeded the capacity of the prison system to contain them in acceptable conditions. Before the financial axe fell in 1976, occasional shafts of light shone through the darkening sky: the old women's prison at Holloway was demolished and replaced on the same site by a completely new prison stressing medical supervision; whilst at Grendon Underwood the Prison Service pioneered a special establishment for the treatment and management of mentally abnormal offenders who had been sentenced to imprisonment.

The looming prison crisis dominated penal thinking in the latter part of the period. The nightmare of a breakdown in the prisons, leading to riots and disorder as the pressure of numbers mounted,

[153] These incidents led to an inquiry and report by Lord Mountbatten on escapes and security which had far-reaching repercussions on the prison system. See Morris, *Crime and Criminal Justice since 1945*, pp. 129–35. Also *Responses to Crime*, vol. 1, pp. 236–8.

[154] Report on the Work of the Prison Department 1967 (Cmnd. 3774), HMSO, London, 1968, p. 5.

[155] In 1992 the Home Office announced that Gartree and Albany were due to be phased out of the dispersal system over the next twelve months. A new top-security prison, with 534 places, was opened at Whitemoor in Cambridgeshire in January 1992.

haunted thoughtful Home Office officials from the most senior to the most junior. Few had any great faith in prisons as institutions for the reform of the inmates they contained, nor of imprisonment as a means of controlling crime. Yet the Home Office was powerless to affect the sentencing decisions of the courts. In reaction it turned to a whole gamut of strategies advocated by advisory committees and penal reform groups in an attempt to counter and check the rising tide of custodial sentences. The roll call was a lengthy one: fines, probation, parole, community service, compensation, reparation, suspended sentences. Such unity as they had, however, arose more from the situation in the prisons than from any co-ordinated plan to alter the course of a penal policy that was increasingly being called into question.

Despite the high hopes of *Penal Practice in a Changing Society*, recognizable authority in the shape of detection, arrest, and prosecution still counted for more than prevention. Warning signs began to flash that abuses could occur in the police investigation of serious crime. The stimulant of efficiency led to local police forces being reorganized and amalgamated.[156] Police pay and conditions were improved, although not to levels that satisfied the Police Federation and its members. As part of the drive for greater effectiveness the police embraced technology as a means of countering the expanding sophistication of crime.

Officers were switched to specialist tasks leading to a reduction in police presence and visibility on the streets. Whether or not routine patrolling of neighbourhoods was an economical use of manpower, there was no doubt that it reflected a heartfelt public desire to see more policemen on the beat.[157] Roy Jenkins, usually so percipient an interpreter of the public mood, became caricatured in popular legend as the libertarian Home Secretary who wanted

---

[156] The number of separate forces in England and Wales was reduced from 159 in 1945 to forty-nine in 1970, and later to forty-three (the present total). After 1964 the stimulant of efficiency was reinforced by powers granted to the Home Secretary in the Police Act of that year to promote compulsory amalgamations. A spurt came when Jenkins set a timetable in May 1966: 'I hope that we can proceed, not in a rush, but, none the less, pretty fast. I hope that many of these amalgamations will be ready to come into operation by 1st April next year, and that they will be pretty well all through by a year further on from then.' *Parl. Debates*, HC, 728 (5th ser.), col. 1345–6, 18 May 1966.

[157] For the public reluctance to accept moves away from the traditional foot beat system as the main method of operational policing, see Bottoms and Stevenson in Downes (ed.), *Unravelling Criminal Justice*, pp. 28–32.

to insulate policemen in Panda cars. Whatever generalizations might have been true at the level of national policy, it was becoming evident towards the end of an era that had been marked by political consensus that in Greater London and some of the other metropolitan areas the public accountability and operational methods of the police were no longer consensual.[158]

---

[158] The politicization of the police during the 1970s is well described by R. Reiner in *The Politics of the Police*, Wheatsheaf Books, Sussex and St Martin's Press, New York, 1985. Robert Reiner is Professor of Criminology at the London School of Economics.

4

Conservatives Ascendant, 1979–88

I

By the time of the General Election in May 1979, which brought the Conservatives to power for a period lasting into the 1990s, the legislative cycle described in the opening chapter had settled into a regular rhythm. The continuing momentum of the drive towards the creation of fresh criminal justice legislation at regular intervals should not be underestimated. General elections provide milestones and signposts pointing to changes in direction and priority, but they rarely presage the most significant developments in policy. More often these result from longer-term forces activated by factors that may not be apparent in the feverish atmosphere engendered by elections, or from shorter-term and more acute forces released by untoward incidents attracting adverse publicity in Parliament and the press, such as prison riots or escapes, miscarriages of justice, public disturbances or disasters, sometimes leading to an inquiry. The report of the inquiry then sets an agenda for future political action.[1] For all these reasons, as well as the risks of giving hostages to fortune, the statements on criminal policy made by the main parties at election time tend to rely more on generalities than on specific proposals.

The Conservative campaign of 1979, the first of three under Mrs Thatcher's leadership, made more of law and order, and in a more strident and populist way, than hitherto. It exploited what it described as Labour's record of failing to counter the growing disrespect for the rule of law which amounted to 'The most disturbing threat to our freedom and security', declaring roundly that: 'In government, as in opposition, Labour have undermined

---

[1] Some examples are cited by Anthony Bottoms and Simon Stevenson in D. Downes (ed.), *Unravelling Criminal Justice*, Macmillan, London, 1992, pp. 23–7.

it.'[2] Conservatives intended to restore respect for the rule of law, reestablishing the supremacy of Parliament and giving the right priority to the fight against crime. In their constituency election addresses 87% of Conservative candidates committed themselves to strong action on law and order, this being the second most important topic after tax cuts. Opinion polls indicated that it was the major policy issue on which the Conservatives had the most decisive lead over Labour.[3]

Away from the hubbub of the General Election, the deeper currents of opinion were shifting perceptibly. Progressive liberal beliefs, so long dominant in penal ideology, were faltering. The ability of the state to order its affairs in such a way as to diminish the incidence of crime, striving whenever possible to rehabilitate those who had offended against its laws, was no longer taken for granted. Ironically it was the unexpected findings of the empirical research favoured in the days of Butler and Brooke that served to undermine some of the most cherished assumptions.[4] Quieter and more reflective voices began to move in the same direction as the 'loud angry crowd. Very angry and very loud',[5] whose constant chant was that the only way to control crime was by strengthening the police, improving the rates of detection, and punishing criminals more severely.

The fissure in popular opinion was mirrored in the decline of consensus among the informed. Professional practitioners engaged in criminal justice, academic writers and commentators, and penal reform groups were still consulted by civil servants, and their advice was still listened to, but the cumulative impact was greatly reduced after 1979. Although occasional committees were set up with independent members, the habit of seeking disinterested expert advice fell out of favour with the party in power, although not

[2] *The Conservative Manifesto, 1979*, Conservative Central Office, London, 1979, p. 19.
[3] P. Riddell, *The Thatcher Government*, Martin Robertson, Oxford, 1983, pp. 193–4.
[4] See *Unravelling Criminal Justice*, p. 22: 'Two of the cornerstones of early post-war thought in English criminal justice were, first, belief in the crime-preventive effectiveness of traditional police beat work, and secondly, belief in the considerable reformative possibilities of various kinds of penal treatment (either in custodial or in non-custodial settings). Both these cornerstone beliefs were to come under very serious fire as a direct result of empirical research results.'
[5] See the quotation from W. H. Auden which forms the epigraph to *Responses to Crime*, (vol. 1).

with the Labour Opposition which continued to look to the penal reform groups such as NACRO and the Howard League for guidance and briefing.

The fate of the Advisory Council on the Penal System (ACPS) epitomized the new spirit permeating Whitehall. Set up after the collapse of the Royal Commission on the Penal System in 1966, it soon became a significant contributor to the formulation of policy. The distinction of its expert, and non-party political, composition coincided with a period when party ideology was relatively weak as a source of innovation. From its early days the ACPS was more than an independent group playing with new ideas. It became a clearing house in which proposals could be assessed and tested against a formidable corpus of knowledge and experience before being recommended for legislation or implementation in administrative practice. For a decade, under both Labour and Conservative administrations, the ACPS enjoyed unusual authority. Summarized below is the outcome of the Council's reports published between 1968 and 1978.

REPORTS OF THE ADVISORY COUNCIL ON THE PENAL SYSTEM, 1968–78

Detention of Girls in a Detention Centre (1968)

Recommendation that the one detention centre then available for girls should be closed was accepted.

Regime for Long-Term Prisoners in Conditions of Maximum Security (1968)

Recommendations for dispersal (not concentration as proposed by Lord Mountbatten) accepted. Legislation not required.

Detention Centres (1970)

The main recommendations were that there should be a general review of methods of treatment for young offenders and that, pending such a review, existing powers to sentence young offenders to detention in a detention centre or short-term imprisonment should be retained. Various minor recommendations, not requiring legislation, were mostly accepted.

Non-Custodial and Semi-Custodial Penalties (1970)

Recommendations implemented in the Criminal Justice Act 1972 were for the courts to have power to make community service orders (Sections 15–19); defer sentence (S. 22); deprive an offender of property used to commit an offence (S. 23); and disqualification from driving where vehicle used to commit an offence (S. 24). Other recommendations not accepted were for the setting up of an Enforcement Office to enforce the collection of overdue fines and of civil debts; an experimental attendance centre for adult traffic offenders; and the introduction of weekend imprisonment 'as soon as circumstances permit'.

Reparation by the Offender (1970)

The recommendations, implemented in the Criminal Justice Act 1972, were for the courts to have a single comprehensive power to make compensation orders (Sections 1–5) and for a criminal bankruptcy scheme (Sections 7–10).

Young Adult Offenders (1974)

A single custodial sentence ('the custody and control order') was recommended for offenders under the age of twenty-one. The Council's recommendations provided the basis for a Green Paper published in 1978 by the Labour Government, although the subsequent Conservative Government legislated on different lines in the Criminal Justice Act 1982, retaining the detention centre order as a separate sentence. A unified custodial sentence for young offenders was later introduced by the Criminal Justice Act 1988.

Powers of the Courts Dependent on Imprisonment (1977)

The report examined various powers of the police and the courts exercisable only in relation to offences punishable with imprisonment. It recommended that most of them should remain subject to this restriction, but that some should be freed from it. No legislation resulted from this report.

The Length of Prison Sentences: Interim Report (1977)

Recommendations to reduce the length of prison sentences for average offenders were addressed to the judiciary, with Government support. No legislative changes were proposed. The report did not deal with lengthy sentences passed by the courts in cases such as armed robbery or serious crimes of violence.

Sentences of Imprisonment: A Review of Maximum Penalties (1978) Recommendations not accepted.

What turned out to be the Council's last report, a review of maximum penalties, was its least successful. The new maxima recommended by the ACPS were judged by the Home Office to be unacceptable to the preponderance of Parliamentary, judicial, and public opinion. The report was left unimplemented, and was followed by a lull in which no further reference was made before the 1979 General Election. In consequence, the Council was not active at the time the Conservatives returned to office.

In the ordinary way, no incoming Home Office minister, least of all one with the qualities and style of William Whitelaw, nor the officials advising him, would have contemplated abolishing the ACPS. Despite a recent hiccup, it was patently a body of good standing that had done valuable work. But the times were not ordinary. One of the earliest targets in the new Prime Minister's sights was the large cluster of non-departmental bodies which had proliferated during the years of consensus. In her scornful view many such bodies, known as quangos,[6] were not simply unnecessary but represented an insidious spread of patronage, concealing at the same time the growth that had taken place in the apparatus of central government. The growth, moreover, was one that was not disclosed in the statistics on the size of the Civil Service.[7] No time was lost in recruiting a recently retired Permanent Secretary[8] to carry out a critical review of the whole range of non-departmental bodies with the aim of 'eliminating any which had outlived their usefulness or which could not be justified in the context of the

[6] The acronym 'quango', was generally understood to stand for quasi non-governmental organization. For a survey of the ways in which these and other types of organization can influence public policy-making, see Anthony Barker (ed.), *Quangos in Britain*, Macmillan Press, London and Basingstoke, 1982.

[7] *Report on Non-Departmental Public Bodies* (Cmnd. 7797), presented to Parliament by the Prime Minister, HMSO, London, 1980, p. 4.

[8] Sir Leo Pliatzky, Deputy Secretary, 1971–6, Second Permanent Secretary, HM Treasury, 1976; Permanent Secretary, Department of Trade, 1977–9.

Government's objectives of reducing public expenditure and the size of the public sector'.[9]

Each minister in charge of a Department was instructed to consider the full list of public bodies in the field for which he was responsible in the light of four questions:

(i) Is the function which is being carried out essential? Or, if not, is it valuable enough to justify the time and money spent on it?
(ii) If the answer is that the function is either essential or sufficiently valuable, is it best carried out by the non-Departmental body in question rather than by another means?
(iii) Is it being carried out well and economically?
(iv) Conversely, would there be any substantial loss or disadvantage if the body were wound up?[10]

Direct answers to the questionnaire turned on the interpretation of value. Even when in full flood the cost of the ACPS was modest. Neither the chairman nor members were paid any fees,[11] the main expenditure being incurred in the preparation and publication of their reports. But what was the non-financial worth of its work? How did it measure up to the tests of being 'essential' or 'sufficiently valuable'? Most important of all in the minds of ministers and senior civil servants was the answer to the unspoken question: how should Whitehall react to the new broom at Number 10?

It was the chance that the ACPS was temporarily inactive which made it vulnerable. Could the Home Office justify reactivating it once the review was underway and, if so, for what purpose? If not, was it realistic to hope to get away with leaving it inactive? From the standpoint of the Home Secretary, and the Department as a whole, the priority was to preserve those bodies which were likely to be of the greatest utility. To claim that all Home Office quangos should be spared would leave the Home Secretary in an uncomfortably exposed, and probably untenable, position.

This was the background against which officials had to consider parting with an old friend, if one less frequently seen lately. Their reasoning was that the benefit obtained from the Advisory Council's previous work was relevant to the review only in so far as it

[9] *Report on Non-Departmental Public Bodies*, p. 4.
[10] Ibid., p. 5.
[11] Travelling and subsistence expenses of members were refunded in accordance with standard civil service procedure.

suggested what further advantages would be gained if the Council survived. The dominant issue of penal policy at the time was whether and how the courts could be induced to curtail the use of imprisonment, both by reducing sentence lengths and by making even more use of alternatives to custody. Thanks in part to the Council itself, a wider range of non-custodial measures was available, and it was difficult to identify any possible extensions of the range that might be worth exploring. In its interim report on sentence lengths, the Council had done as much as reasonably could be expected of such a body to make a case for reduction. In 1979 (as later) the need was seen as being to communicate the case persuasively to the judiciary and to the Government's own supporters. The Home Office was not convinced that any further references to the Council would assist in making progress towards that goal, or that there were other subjects which could profitably be referred at the time, or which could then be foreseen as needing to be referred in the future.

Still less did officials see how the Home Secretary could make a convincing case for keeping the Council in being with no early prospect of a further remit. Some put more weight than others on the prestige and public reputation of the ACPS, but none argued strongly for it to be retained if the Home Secretary felt that sacrifices had to be made. He did.

The final cull of advisory bodies amounted to 211. Of these five Home Office bodies were earmarked for immediate abolition, with another eight following in due course. The Advisory Council on the Penal System headed the list, the saving being described as negligible since the Council was 'in abeyance'.[12]

A more polemic explanation is provided by the noted penal reformer, Louis Blom-Cooper, who served as a member of the Advisory Council throughout its life:

ACPS was dissolved because of the Conservative Government's distaste for independent advice. It was not axed because it was ineffective. Apart from its last report, every other report ultimately found its way either on to the statute book or to a change in penal practice. Even the recommendations of the Young Adult Offender report of 1974 was in effect enacted in the Criminal Justice Act 1988. Looking back on the work of the Council, I have no hesitation in saying that it was a valuable instrument

---

[12] *Report on Non-Departmental Public Bodies*, p. 87.

for identifying and suggesting changes in penal policy and practice. I am convinced that Ministers of both parties (up until 1979) and Home Office officials all valued the Council and would have argued for its retention. Had the Council continued after 1979 issues such as Boards of Visitors and Parole could have been reported on without having to set up separate departmental Committees. Other penal issues that aroused controversy— such as censorship of prisoners' mail, the categorisation of prisoners, the privatisation of the remand system—could usefully have been referred to the ACPS.[13]

II

Penal policy featured less prominently in the Conservative manifesto than it did in the election campaign. The difference was due more to tone of voice than to substance. In presenting the Conservative case to the electorate the manifesto draftsmen did not stray far from the familiar paths of party politics. While disparaging the policies, record, and attitudes of their Labour opponents in the manner customary to election campaigns, they were aware of the dangers of being too specific. Commitments were few in number and kept in a low key: 'Britain needs strong, efficient police forces with high morale ... Surer detection means surer deterrence. We also need better crime prevention measures and more flexible, more effective sentencing.'[14] The potentially divisive subject of capital punishment for murder was mentioned, but only tentatively. The issue must remain a matter of conscience for Members of Parliament, the manifesto stated, and the new House of Commons would be given an early opportunity for a free vote. While the emphasis on enforcement and penalties was quintessentially Tory, there was limited opportunity for political challenge to the policies themselves. Indeed, the most fertile ground for controversy was to be found within the Conservative Party itself. In many constituencies attitudes towards the death penalty were a factor when local Associations selected their Parliamentary candidates. Despite forebodings to the contrary, the post-election vote in the House of Commons

[13] Letter dated 29 Aug. 1991.
[14] *The Conservative Manifesto, 1979*, p. 19.

on a motion to reintroduce capital punishment was defeated decisively by 362 votes to 243.[15]

During the election campaign six commitments were given or repeated, some already having been announced. The full list, as circulated by the Conservative Research Department for guidance to candidates in the week before polling, was as follows:

1. We shall amend the Children and Young Persons Act 1969 to provide magistrates with the power to make residential and secure care orders on young offenders.

2. We shall toughen the regime in some detention centres on an experimental basis as a short, sharp shock to violent young thugs.

3. We shall expand the use of attendance centres—particularly for the 18–21 year olds—as a cheap method of invading the leisure time of hooligans and vandals.

4. We shall amend the Criminal Justice Act 1961 to allow courts to impose six month to three year prison terms on 17–21 year old offenders.

5. We shall encourage more frequent use of shorter prison sentences for the less serious crimes, while insisting that violent offenders face a long spell inside.

6. We shall in the light of the May Committee Report take firm action to deal with the serious problems of our prisons—in relieving over-crowding and supporting prison officers, and in improving facilities as resources allow.[16]

An additional manifesto commitment endorsed the undertaking given in 1978 to implement in full the award on police pay which had been recommended by an independent inquiry under the chairmanship of Lord Edmund-Davies.[17] The Labour Government had set up the committee because of escalating discontent and belligerence on the part of the police, culminating in a resolution

[15] *Parl. Debates*, HC, 970 (5th ser.), col. 2122, 19 July 1979. For an analysis of votes in the House of Commons on capital punishment 1955–87, see *Responses to Crime*, vol. 1, Table 8, pp. 158–9.

[16] *Daily Notes*, No. 10, 26 Apr. 1979, p. 149.

[17] Lord Edmund-Davies was a Lord of Appeal in Ordinary, 1974–81. Previously he had been a Judge in the Queen's Bench Division of the High Court, 1958–66, in which year he conducted the Tribunal of Inquiry into the Aberfan Disaster. He was a Lord Justice of Appeal, 1966–74. The commitment on behalf of the next Conservative Government to implement in full the pay increases was given by William Whitelaw, then Opposition spokesman on Home Affairs, in the House of Commons on 17 July 1978. *Parl. Debates*, HC, 954 (5th ser.), col. 33.

by the Police Federation demanding the right of the police to strike.[18] Although the spark which ignited the crisis was a single, and arguably miscalculated, decision on the application of the Government's pay policy, police morale and manpower was already combustible material. Caught between the committee's recommendation of substantial pay increases for the police, and the wider implications for their policy of pay restraint, Labour ministers had compromised, accepting the recommendations but phasing them over two years.

The election won and Whitehall reoccupied, the party in power had to reconcile itself with the constraints described in Chapter 1: the pressure on Parliamentary time, practical experience and priorities within Departments, and the need for consultation with affected interests. The demands made by other ministers on the timetable, and the fact that the cycle was not yet complete, meant that there was no legislation on criminal justice included in the programme for the first two Parliamentary sessions. For the Home Office, 'still a legislatively dominated administration' as the Permanent Secretary in the early 1980s assured Paul Rock,[19] a passive phase provides a breathing space, although one in which *ad hoc* decisions on specific issues tend to take precedence over systematic work on more far-reaching policies covering interrelated matters.

The new Home Secretary, William Whitelaw, was quickly off the mark in implementing the pledge on police pay. On 9 May, five days after the election, he announced that the Government had accepted the Edmund-Davies proposal in full, and thereafter police pay would be based on a formula linking increases to movements in the index of average earnings during the previous twelve months. The decision had been taken at the first Cabinet Meeting of the session held the previous day. Whitelaw later admitted: 'I knew that the Treasury would not like it, and so I obtained my colleagues' agreement at the earliest possible moment.' He added candidly: 'I have never regretted that decision, because at that time police recruiting was poor and standards of policing were suffering. But

---

[18] Since the Police Act 1919 police officers had been prohibited by Section 2 from being members of trade unions or withholding their services. The same Act in Section 1 had established the Police Federation, to which, coincidentally, the Prime Minister, James Callaghan, had been Parliamentary Consultant between 1955 and 1964.

[19] *Helping Victims of Crime*, Clarendon Press, Oxford, 1990, p. 7.

I confess to some disappointment when a great improvement in police conditions of service was not followed by a corresponding improvement in police efficiency.'[20]

For a party embarking on an extended spell in government that was to carry it throughout the 1980s and beyond, although there was no knowing it at the time, the electoral commitments were limited in scope and, with the exception of the regime in detention centres, of no great political import. Discordance existed, however, between the emphasis on custodial penalties which was evident in the Conservative guidance to candidates and the Home Office objective of persuading the courts to curtail sentence lengths and make more use of alternatives to custody. Therein lay one of the underlying causes of the resistance Whitelaw encountered within his own party, inside and outside Parliament, throughout his time as Home Secretary.

On taking office, Whitelaw knew that he had to tread carefully. In the same way as most, if not all, of the Home Secretaries who preceded him throughout the 1970s: Maudling, Carr, Jenkins (for the second time), and Rees, he saw his role, in the manner familiar from the last chapter, as working creatively on the material already to hand, particularly the measures to reduce the size of the prison population. At the same time he was well aware of the importance of keeping a weather eye open for unpredictable events and crises, and the necessity to handle them in such a way as to command the confidence of the general public and his own party. It may not sound much of an aspiration compared with the higher ground occupied by Butler and Jenkins, but in retrospect it stands out as a courageous attempt to maintain the policy of trying to proceed whenever possible within a framework of conciliation and consensus at a time when many of his colleagues in the Government, led by the Prime Minister, were moving in the opposite direction.

Once police pay was off the agenda the largest and most immediate topic calling for a positive response was the pending report of a committee under the chairmanship of a High Court judge which had been deliberating in the same part of London at the same time as the Conservative manifesto was being given the finishing touches.

---

[20] *'Some of the Lessons I Learnt in 4 Years as Home Secretary'*, unpublished manuscript supplied to the author by Viscount Whitelaw, based on a speech to the Howard League for Penal Reform in 1990, p. 2.

On 17 November 1978 the Labour Home Secretary, Merlyn Rees,[21] on behalf of the Secretaries of State for Scotland and Northern Ireland as well as himself, had set up a departmental committee of inquiry into the United Kingdom prison services under the chairmanship of Sir John May.[22]

The deteriorating state of industrial relations in the prisons, verging on open hostilities or even anarchy in the words of one experienced commentator,[23] had given the inquiry its original impetus. The Home Secretary stressed the urgency of the review, initially asking the committee to report in the unrealistically short time of six months. Due to the number and complexity of the problems facing the Prison Service, and the desire of the committee to explore the underlying causes including the way the prisons were organized and managed, the state of the buildings, and the conditions in which staff and inmates were required to live and work, the report took twelve months to prepare rather than six. It was still a remarkable achievement for a committee which had met on fifty-three days, visited a large number of establishments throughout the United Kingdom, as well as in France and Scandinavia, and received voluminous evidence.

The May report presented to Whitelaw in October 1979[24] furnished him with a detailed plan for action on one of the most troubled of all his new responsibilities. The inquiry reached many conclusions which he shared: in its arguments for more imaginative alternatives to custody and shorter sentences for non-violent offenders; in its call for a substantial programme of prison-building; and in the proposals for reorganizing the Prison Department and conferring a greater degree of independence upon the Inspectorate of Prisons.[25]. All of the major recommendations were accepted, and the report strengthened the Home Secretary's hand, adding weight to

[21] Parliamentary Under-Secretary of State at the Home Office, 1968–70; Secretary of State for Northern Ireland, 1974–6; Home Secretary, 1976–9. Life peer, 1992.
[22] Judge of the Queen's Bench Division of the High Court, 1972–82; Member of the Parole Board, 1977–80 (Vice-Chairman 1980); Lord Justice of Appeal, 1982–9. In 1989 Sir John May was appointed to inquire into the circumstances surrounding the convictions arising out of the bomb attacks in Guildford and Woolwich in 1974.
[23] Professor Michael Zander. For a fuller account of the May Report and the conflict between staff and management in the Prison Service, see *Responses to Crime*, vol. 1, pp. 239–43.
[24] Committee of Inquiry into the United Kingdom Prison Services, *Report* (Cmnd. 7673), HMSO, London, 1979.
[25] *The Whitelaw Memoirs*, Aurum Press, London, 1989, p. 170.

his arguments for the resources needed to embark on a large-scale programme of building new prisons and refurbishing old ones.[26]

By April 1980 a reorganization of the Prison Department of the Home Office had been announced, and in the Criminal Justice Act 1982 the office of Chief Inspector of Prisons, and his duty to inspect and report upon prisons, was given statutory backing and greater independence.[27] In the 1980s, largely as a result of the tenacity and plain speaking of the two successive Chief Inspectors, Sir James Hennessy[28] and Judge Tumim,[29] the inspectorate became increasingly relevant as an instrument of penal reform. A continuous stream of trenchant reports, all of which were published causing periodic embarrassment to the Prison Department, constituted a significant strand in the changing climate of public opinion. Personalities count, and Tumim in particular brought to a hitherto lacklustre public office a colourful personality and arresting turn of phrase which served him well in attracting attention to numerous defects in need of remedy.

III

The commitment to amend the Criminal Justice Act 1961 in order to allow the courts to impose fixed sentences of up to three years' imprisonment on young offenders had a chequered history. The restrictions contained in the 1961 Act on the power of the courts

---

[26] For details of the building programme, and arguments against the reductionist case, see *Responses to Crime*, vol. 1, pp. 226–32.

[27] As strongly urged by the Mountbatten report in the aftermath of the prison escapes in the mid-1960s. See *Report of the Inquiry into Prison Escapes and Security by Admiral of the Fleet Earl Mountbatten of Burma* (Cmnd. 3175), HMSO, London, 1966.

[28] British High Commissioner to Uganda, 1973–6; Governor and Commander in Chief, Belize, 1980–1; HM Chief Inspector of Prisons for England and Wales, 1982–7.

[29] Stephen Tumim, a Circuit Judge since 1978 and author of *Great Legal Disasters* (1983) and *Great Legal Fiascos* (1985), was appointed as HM Chief Inspector by Douglas Hurd in 1987, the first judge to be chosen. In July 1990 Judge Tumim joined the inquiry under the chairmanship of Lord Justice Woolf to investigate the disturbances at Strangeways and other prisons which had occurred in April. With Lord Justice Woolf he was joint author of Part II of the Report, *Prison Disturbances April 1990* (Cm. 1456), HMSO, London, 1991. This part examined the role of the prison service and the way prisons were run, reviewing what action should be taken to divert from prison those persons who do not need to be there.

to pass medium-term prison sentences on young adults had originated from proposals made by the Prison Commissioners with the support of the then Advisory Council. The reasoning was that short or medium-length sentences of imprisonment were of doubtful deterrent effect compared with the indeterminate sentence of borstal training. The judiciary had resented these restrictions, which over a wide range of cases deprived them of the power to pass a determinate sentence, while borstal training proved incapable in practice of adapting its theoretical indeterminacy to the variety of individual offenders. Consequently, the 1961 Act enacted by a Conservative Government had the unusual distinction of having one of its principal provisions singled out for repeal in a subsequent Conservative manifesto; the about-turn being accomplished in the Criminal Justice Act 1982.

From the relatively short list of items appearing under the manifesto rubric *Deterring the Criminal*, the one regarded with the greatest scepticism by Home Office officials was the commitment to experiment with tougher regimes in certain detention centres as 'a short, sharp shock for young criminals'. The phrase was far from new,[30] but it had become part of the rhetoric of the election campaign, evoking a warm response in many a Conservative breast. The new Home Secretary had no alternative but to insist on its implementation. Since it was never questioned that an experimental scheme could be established under existing legislation (although it precluded experiments of less than three months' duration), the initial hurdles to be surmounted by Whitelaw were departmental rather than Parliamentary. Here he had a piece of good fortune in inheriting as Director General of the Prison Service, Dennis Trevelyan,[31] a senior civil servant with whom he had previously

[30] The notion of a brief period of confinement as a short, sharp shock for young offenders sent to a strictly disciplined regime lay behind the establishment of the original detention centres sanctioned by Parliament in the Criminal Justice Act 1948. Some MPs then and later looked towards detention centres as a substitute for corporal punishment, seeing in them a lawful way of inflicting a degree of physical pain and suffering on young men in the hope that the experience would 'bring them to their senses', thus acting as a deterrent from further offending. See J. E. Hall Williams, *The English Penal System in Transition*, Butterworths, London, 1970, pp. 330–7.

[31] D. J. Trevelyan was Assistant Under-Secretary of State, Northern Ireland Office, 1972–6; Deputy Under-Secretary of State and Director General of the Prison Service, 1978–83; First Civil Service Commissioner, 1983–9. Principal of Mansfield College, Oxford, since 1989.

worked harmoniously at Stormont Castle when he had been Secretary of State for Northern Ireland.

The Director General was as antipathetic towards the idea as the
other officials with experience of dealing with young offenders, but
the close relationship between Whitelaw and himself permitted a
bargain to be struck. Trevelyan would apply to the task his
considerable ingenuity in translating the wishes of politicians into
practical administration (he had been one of the authors of the
power-sharing agreement in Northern Ireland in 1973/4). In return,
the Home Secretary would support his aim to achieve positive
policies towards more humane standards in establishments which
were threatened by a rapidly rising population, a worn-out and
inadequate prison estate, and a collapse of belief in the capacity of
the penal system to rehabilitate. The resumption of prison-building,
suspended because of economic adversity in 1976, was initially at
the rate of two major project starts a year, beginning in 1981/2.[32]
Looking back Whitelaw recalled:

I was determined to increase the amount of money spent on new prison
building and on the modernization of existing prisons. This has never been
a popular course and yet I was convinced that many years of neglect made
such action essential. The conditions in some of our older prisons were
deplorable and despite considerable expenditure since, remain so today.[33]

Common attitudes towards the sparing use and limited potential
of imprisonment brought the minister and his chief prison admin-
istrator together into an unusually intimate partnership. As a result
of the pact, a greater degree of outspokenness was afforded to
Trevelyan than any of his predecessors since the abolition of the
Prison Commission. It was a licence he used boldly, condemning
the conditions in the decaying prisons for which he was responsible
as 'an affront to a civilised society'.[34] The contrast with the normally
anodyne phraseology of the annual report on the work of the
Prison Department bore out the confidence placed in the Director
General by the Home Secretary.

By 15 November 1979 Whitelaw was able to tell the House of
Commons that he was ready to set up a pilot project for persistent

[32] *Report on the Work of the Prison Department, 1980* (Cmnd. 8228), HMSO,
London, 1980, p. 3.
[33] 'Some of the Lessons I Learnt in 4 years as Home Secretary', p. 4.
[34] *Report on the Work of the Prison Department, 1980*, p. 4.

young offenders in two detention centres. A senior detention centre in West Yorkshire (New Hall) for offenders aged between seventeen and under twenty-one and a junior detention centre in Surrey (Send) for offenders aged fourteen and under seventeen had been selected, although not without difficulty because of staff opposition. In them young offenders would undergo a rigorous regime unless they were physically or mentally unfit, or had received more than a three-month minimum sentence. Those sentenced to between three months and six months were sent to other detention centres. The regime would place emphasis on briskness, discipline, and respect for those in authority; there would be drill, parades, and inspections. The project would be carefully evaluated, and would start in the spring of 1980.[35] Then and later the Home Secretary had to withstand strong criticism in Parliament that he was pandering to a vociferous law and order lobby and engaging in 'unnecessary barbarity'.[36]

One of Whitelaw's endearing handicaps was that when his heart was not in something, it showed. Behind the bark of a sergeant major and the Parliamentary guile of a former Chief Whip was a kindly and tolerant man, ready to listen to the advice of those whom he trusted, and suspicious of extremism in most of its forms. The idea had not been his own, but had originated from the Conservative Research Department during the years in Opposition. Whitelaw had acquiesced in the proposal as an experiment worth trying on the pragmatic grounds that since the existing methods of dealing with young offenders had been ineffective, an open mind should be maintained towards other approaches.[37] Faced with the outright hostility of the Opposition parties in Parliament, shared by most of the penal reform groups, and the reluctance of the civil servants in the Home Office and Prison Service, he knew that he could not afford to renege on a clear electoral commitment. Whitelaw's tactic was to move slowly and cautiously, taking no further than he judged was strictly necessary a policy about which he had increasingly come to harbour misgivings.

[35] *Parl. Debates*, HC, 973 (5th ser.), cols. 1493–5, 15 Nov. 1979.

[36] Ibid., col. 1494.

[37] Manifesto briefing material prepared by the Conservative Research Department for the 1979 General Election contained a hint of reservation under the heading 'Detention Centres': 'Mr Whitelaw no longer wishes the term "glasshouses" to be used'. CRD 4/10/27.

Two more detention centres were added to the experiment in September 1981, but it was not until after the 1983 Election was safely out of the way that any evaluation was published. By then Whitelaw had left the Home Office, being succeeded as Home Secretary by Leon Brittan.[38] Unlike his predecessor, Brittan was personally committed to the idea of tougher regimes in detention centres. However, the report of the Young Offender Psychology Unit of the Prison Department,[39] overseen by a committee with two outside academic members,[40] provided him with no encouragement, finding that 'the introduction of the pilot project regimes had no discernible effect on the rate at which trainees were re-convicted'.[41] In the least conspicuous form of statement to the House of Commons, a reply to a prearranged Question for Written Answer, Brittan said that the conclusion was not surprising seen against the general background of research findings on the identifiable deterrent effect of particular sentences.[42] More than half of those sent to detention centres had been reconvicted within a year, irrespective of whether their sentence had been served at one of the experimental centres or not. It appeared that for most of the trainees drilling had been an enjoyable, if at first unfamiliar, experience. It was the mundane work tasks with an element of dirt or drudgery about them that were least liked: 'The drill was by comparison popular and aspects of physical education positively attractive.'[43]

Since the findings produced nothing to support the Tory credo underlying the short, sharp shock, the Home Secretary was left holding a distinctly warm potato. Brittan responded by abandoning the drill and physical education, but extending to the remaining detention centres some other elements of the regime, such as the parades and inspections, the 'brisker tempo', and initial restrictions on association and outside activities. In future there would be a consistent regime for the whole detention centre system, and the

[38] (Sir) Leon Brittan was Minister of State, Home Office, 1979–81; Chief Secretary to the Treasury, 1981–3; Home Secretary, 1983–5; Secretary of State for Trade and Industry, 1985–6 when he resigned. Vice-President of the Commission of the European Communities since 1989. Knighted in 1989.

[39] Home Office, *Tougher Regimes in Detention Centres*, HMSO, London, 1984.

[40] (Sir) David Cox, Professor of Statistics at Imperial College of Science and Technology, and later Warden of Nuffield College, Oxford, and Gordon Trasler, Professor of Psychology at the University of Southampton.

[41] *Tougher Regimes in Detention Centres*, p. 243.

[42] *Parl. Debates*, HC, 64 (6th ser.), cols. WA 575–7, 24 July 1984.

[43] *Tougher Regimes in Detention Centres*, p. 242.

experiment was concluded.[44] The political damage was limited, but it is hard to avoid the verdict that sound penal administration had been made to serve the needs of a defective icon of political ideology.

IV

Any understanding of criminal behaviour acknowledges the importance of age as a characteristic of offending. The early years of childhood and schooling are usually influenced by parents, adult relatives, and teachers exercising powerful controls on behaviour.[45] As James Q. Wilson and R. J. Herrnstein demonstrate, it is only later, in adolescence and beyond, that

most people run into 'bad influences' able and willing to reinforce antisocial activities. The major sources of reinforcement for criminal behaviour— money, sex, intense and lasting hostility toward others, antisocial peer pressure, and various forms of substance abuse—are absent or relatively weak in childhood. The appetite for sex or money takes time to reach full power, as do the cravings of various addictions.[46]

In Britain, as in the United States and other societies, particularly although not exclusively those with large concentrations of population in urban areas, the peak of offending by males occurs between the ages of fourteen and twenty-one. Throughout the period 1978– 87 the highest rate of known offending per 100,000 population in England and Wales was amongst males aged fourteen and under seventeen, amounting to about six times as high as the overall rate of male offending irrespective of age.[47] Existing research, periodically updated, indicated that nearly one-third of the entire male population born between 1953 and 1963 had been convicted

---

[44] *Parl. Debates*, HC, 64 col. WA 576.

[45] For a survey of research findings and an interpretation of the age effect, see ch. 5 in J. Q. Wilson and R. J. Herrnstein, *Crime and Human Nature*, Simon and Schuster, New York (Touchstone edn.), 1985, pp. 126–47; also ch. 6 on 'Youth, Delinquency and Drugs' in *Responses to Crime*, vol. 1, pp. 174–210.

[46] *Crime and Human Nature*, p. 144.

[47] Home Office, *Criminal Statistics England and Wales, 1988* (Cm. 847), HMSO, London, 1989, p. 88.

of a standard list offence (broadly equivalent to an indictable offence) before reaching the age of thirty-one.[48]

Well known as they were to officials in the Home Office and those taking an informed interest in penal matters, these characteristics attracted no more than intermittent attention from politicians. The first detention centre for offenders aged below seventeen opened in 1952, under the management of the Prison Commissioners, who wished to keep the centres separate from the ambience of prison. By 1958 the punitive currents that had been not far beneath the surface in the Parliament which passed the Criminal Justice Act in 1948, from which detention centres originated, had moderated to the extent that a First Offenders Act reached the Statute Book, having been promoted by the Howard League for Penal Reform to discourage courts from sending an offender to prison for the first time.[49] The judicially unpopular restrictions on the power of the courts to pass medium-term prison sentences on young adults, as already noted, followed in 1961, and each Criminal Justice Act thereafter (with exception of the truncated 1987 Act) contained some provisions relating to young offenders.

The report in 1974 from the Advisory Council on the Penal System on young adult offenders, referred to earlier in this chapter, had recommended the replacement of sentences of borstal training, detention centre, and imprisonment by a single generic sentence of a custody and control order, with a short period (not exceeding six months) of compulsory supervision by the Probation Service following release. The separate establishments catering for the three sentences should be merged into a single system.[50] The report also proposed a local or neighbourhood pattern of young adult offender establishments similar to what was advocated by Lord Woolf for the Prison Service after his inquiry into the causes of the serious disturbances in 1990. The ACPS report was far-sighted, but ahead

[48] Home Office, *Statistical Bulletins* 7/85 and 32/89 summarize the results of detailed studies into the criminal and custodial careers of those born in 1953, 1958, and 1963.

[49] See L. Blom-Cooper, *The Penalty of Imprisonment*, Tanner Lectures on Human Values, IX, University of Utah Press/Cambridge University Press, 1988, p. 302. Louis Blom-Cooper was chairman of the Howard League, 1973–84, and was knighted in 1992.

[50] Home Office, *Young Adult Offenders*, Report of the Advisory Council on the Penal System, HMSO, London, 1974, pp. 21–3.

of its time. It is interesting to see how much of it has since been implemented or revived.

Lengthy deliberations followed its publication in 1974, the chief delaying factors being reservations on the part of the judiciary over the degree of executive discretion inherent in the transfer from custody to supervision, and reservations on the part of the Probation Service over the manpower implications of supervision of a more intensive nature. Eventually enough progress was made to enable the Labour Government to accept in principle the recommendation for a new custodial sentence in a Green Paper in 1978, with the proviso that full implementation would not be possible without additional resources which were not currently available.[51] One of the immediate responses was the contention that government, especially a Labour government, should be more concerned with developing alternatives to custody than in occupying itself with changing the pattern of custodial sentencing.

While there was some force in this criticism in terms of expressed values, the fact was that there existed already a wide, arguably too wide, range of non-custodial sanctions available to the courts. They included conditional discharge, fines, probation orders, and powers to require attendance at a day centre, to make community service orders, and to suspend sentences. The real issue was not the availability of alternatives to custody, but the wider use of those that were currently at the disposal of the courts. This was a situation calling for persuasion and exhortation rather than legislation.

In the year after the General Election of 1979 a White Paper[52] honoured an undertaking in the Queen's Speech to bring forward before the end of the session proposals for strengthening the law relating to juvenile and young offenders in England and Wales.[53] The note of urgency reflected the intention of the new Government to implement its manifesto and electoral commitments, and to respond to the re-emergent punitive sentiments it perceived amongst its supporters, inside and outside Parliament. Within the Parliamentary party critical opinion hardened in March 1982 in an

[51] Home Office, *Youth Custody and Supervision: A New Sentence* (Cmnd. 7406), HMSO, London, 1978, p. 1.
[52] Home Office (and others), *Young Offenders* (Cmnd. 8045), HMSO, London, 1980.
[53] Ibid., p. 1.

unsuccessful attempt by Whitelaw's detractors to get rid of him as Home Secretary.[54]

The White Paper, and the legislation which followed in the next session, confirmed the decision of the Labour government to introduce a new sentence of youth custody. But, contrary to the ACPS recommendation, it retained a symbolic attachment to the detention centres which were greatly disliked by penal reformers and would have been subsumed into the generic sentence under the previous proposals. The duration of an order for detention at a detention centre was altered from a maximum period of six months and a minimum of three months, to a maximum of four months and a minimum of three weeks. The explanation given for the reduction in the maximum period was that offenders sentenced to more than four months in custody might reasonably be expected to benefit from some kind of training, whereas the disciplined but limited regime in a detention centre was not appropriate for more than a few weeks.[55]

All young male offenders aged between fourteen and twenty one, who had been convicted of an offence punishable with imprisonment in the case of a person aged twenty one or over, and received a sentence of more than four months in duration, would in future be sentenced to youth custody. Such sentences were to be served in the existing accommodation available to the Prison Department varying from former Borstal institutions and young prisoner centres, to young prisoner wings, or when unavoidable, to other accommodation in adult prisons.

The rationalization concealed a rift that had opened between the then Minister of State, Brittan, and the officials responsible for the preparation of the legislation. Since the courts would have restored to them the power to pass custodial sentences for fixed terms, Brittan argued strongly that, in relation to shorter terms, they should have the freedom to choose between detention centres and youth custody. This greatly worried the Prison Department because it would require the duplication of provision made for offenders among whom no distinction could be made on any objective basis. It also seemed likely that Magistrates' courts might be unduly attracted by the punitive appearance of the detention centre regime,

[54] *The Whitelaw Memoirs*, pp. 199–200.
[55] *Young Offenders*, p. 6.

consigning to it offenders more suitable for regimes with a larger component of education and training. Ministers were not prepared to countenance any arrangement under which offenders were allocated to detention centres or youth custody by administrative action after sentence, rather than by order of the courts. Eventually a compromise was worked out whereby allocation depended simply on the length of the sentence: four months or less meant going to a detention centre, longer than four months meant youth custody.

V

Moving the Second Reading of the Criminal Justice Bill in January 1982, Whitelaw echoed the words of the election manifesto saying that the primary purpose of the Bill was to provide the courts with more flexible and effective powers for dealing with the diversity of offenders. His overriding concern was that punishment should not only fit the crime, but that it should also be effective in dealing with the individual criminal. It was a well-intentioned formula which nevertheless encapsulated two different concepts. On the one hand was what became known as the justice model, i.e. retribution in proportion to the harm done;[56] on the other, a treatment model aimed at future prevention. Whether the two objectives were capable of being pursued simultaneously, or whether internal contradictions made them exclusive alternatives, was a question that was to dominate penal thinking throughout the 1980s.

The treatment model was embodied in clauses relating to probation, the suffix 'after care' being deleted from the designation of the Probation Service, Probation Committees, and Probation Areas. Social inquiry reports would in future have to be prepared by a probation officer on any offender who had not previously served a prison sentence in order that the court might decide whether there was any appropriate way of dealing with him other than by means

---

[56] Proportionalist sentencing theory, symbolized by the phrase 'just deserts', became penologically fashionable in the United States after the publication of Andrew von Hirsch's work, *Doing Justice: The Choice of Punishments*, Hill and Wang, New York, 1976. Professor von Hirsch, from the School of Criminal Justice at Rutgers University, has been a tireless advocate for policies based upon just deserts. See also his book, *Past or Future Crimes: Deservedness and Dangerousness in the Sentencing of Criminals*, Manchester University Press, 1986.

of a custodial sentence. A leaning towards the justice model,
however, could be detected in a concession made to the opinion of
judges and magistrates that in certain cases a social inquiry report
would serve no useful purpose because the offence was such that a
non-custodial sentence could not be justified.[57]

Changes in the legislation on probation would be introduced to
require selected offenders, as a condition of a probation order, to
participate in specified activities for a limited period not exceeding
sixty days. The provision arose from an intervention by the courts
in the way that non-custodial penalties were administered, the
House of Lords having upheld a majority judgment in the Divisional
Court that there was no power to require attendance at a day
centre, distinct from a statutory day *training* centre, as a condition
of a probation order.[58] Day centres, about seventy in number,
differed from the day training centres which had been authorized
by the Criminal Justice Act 1972 in providing less intensive forms
of supervision and training. Originally designed to meet the needs
of inadequate recidivists, four day training centres had been set up
in Liverpool, London, Sheffield, and Pontypridd, initially as a
two-year experiment, although they remained open (still on an
experimental basis) for nearly nine years. The research results were
not encouraging. Costs were high; sixty days' attendance costing
from four to ten times more than a community service order
running for a year. The drop-out rate was between 10% and 26%,
and the reconviction rate between 40% and 65%.[59] Eventually the
experiment was terminated, the Probation Service having developed
instead a larger number of additional day centres with the more
modest objective of keeping less serious offenders off the streets
and out of trouble.

The power to require selected offenders to participate in specified
activities for a limited period as a condition of a probation order

[57] Under Section 62 of the Criminal Justice Act 1982 the requirement to obtain
a social inquiry report did not apply if, in the circumstances of the case, the court
was of the opinion that it was unnecessary.

[58] *Cullen* v. *Rogers* [1982] 2 All ER 570. The dissenting judgment in the Divisional
Court of the Queen's Bench Division was delivered by Lord Justice Waller, at the
time one of the few judges sympathetic to penal reform amongst the higher judiciary.
He was a member of the Parole Board 1969–72, serving as Vice-Chairman 1971–2,
and of the Advisory Council on the Penal System, 1970–3 and 1974–8.

[59] L. J. F. Smith, 'Day Training Centres', (1982) 14 *Home Office Research Bulletin*,
34–7.

opened the way for non-custodial supervision of a more demanding kind. This was to adapt for young adults the idea of intermediate treatment, hitherto confined to juvenile offenders under the age of seventeen. Since the Children and Young Persons Act 1969[60] juvenile courts, when making a supervision order, had been enabled to authorize the supervising officer to require the child or young person to attend specific places and be involved in organized activities for a period not exceeding ninety days. The nature of these activities varied widely from area to area, but the emphasis typically was on group work. Methods were evolved to confront young people with the consequences of their behaviour, bringing home to them the damage caused to victims, families, and friends. Intensive, and sometimes painful, discussions probed the causes of offending by each individual member of the group, demonstrating how criminal anti-social conduct could be avoided in the future.

The term 'intermediate treatment' had its origins in a White Paper of 1968:

Existing forms of treatment available to the juvenile courts distinguish sharply between those which involve complete removal from home and those which do not. The juvenile courts have very difficult decisions to make in judging whether circumstances require the drastic step of taking a child away from his parents and his home. The view has often been expressed that some form or forms of intermediate treatment should be available to the courts, allowing the child to remain in his own home but bringing him also into contact with a different environment.[61]

Over the years, intermediate treatment, nourished in particular by the interest and funding of the Department of Health and Social Security, was a success story. By 1988 in excess of £15 million had been made available in grants for the development of intensive intermediate treatment projects aimed at the more serious juvenile offenders. Between 1983 and 1987 3,389 places were provided by voluntary bodies in sixty-two local authority areas aided by the DHSS initiative. Funds were also made available to NACRO to monitor the initiative and make sure that the projects achieved effective diversion from care and custody.[62] Partly as a consequence

---

[60] Later amended by the Criminal Law Act 1977 and the Criminal Justice Act 1982.

[61] Home Office, *Children in Trouble* (Cmnd. 3601), HMSO, London, 1968, p. 9.

[62] R. Allen, 'Out of Jail: The Reduction in the Use of Penal Custody for Male Juveniles 1981–8', (1991) 30 *Howard Journal of Criminal Justice* 30 at 48.

of intermediate treatment, day centres and other elements forming part of the treatment model working together rather than against one another, the Home Office was justified in pointing out in a Green Paper published in 1988 that proportionately fewer juveniles had been brought before the courts and that the use of custody was declining.[63] Germane as intermediate and other forms of treatment had been in contributing towards the proportionate decline in the use of custody for younger people, other and more powerful forces had also been at work.

In his speech on Second Reading of the 1982 Bill, Whitelaw had stressed the need for a sentencing structure which, while recognizing that custody may be essential, secured that it be used only where necessary.[64] The general intention was reflected in clause 1 which stated that no court may impose any custodial sentence on a person under twenty-one years of age unless it was satisfied that 'no other method of dealing with him is appropriate'.[65] As originally drafted, the Bill stopped short of including any criteria to guide the court on the interpretation of the restriction. The wording lacked the degree of precision sought by some penologically interested members of both Houses of Parliament. In a published report the previous year the Parliamentary All-Party Penal Affairs Group (PAPPAG) had urged that:

legislation should provide that a youth custody sentence should be imposed only when the offender is a real danger to society or has shown himself

[63] *Punishment, Custody and The Community* (Cm. 424), HMSO, London, 1988, p. 6.

[64] *Parl. Debates*, HC, 16 (6th ser.), col. 294, 20 Jan. 1982.

[65] The restriction on custodial sentences for young offenders was not new as the Powers of Criminal Courts Act 1973, consolidating provisions formerly in the Criminal Justice Act 1948 as amended by the Criminal Justice Act 1961, prohibited a court from sentencing a person aged seventeen but under twenty-one to imprisonment unless it was of the opinion that no other method of dealing with him was appropriate. Debating the Criminal Justice Bill 1982 in the House of Lords a leading member of the Criminal Bar, Lord Hutchinson of Lullington QC, gave a telling account of his experience of this provision in the Magistrates' courts: 'What happens in magistrates' courts very often is that the clerk, after the magistrate has sentenced the person to imprisonment of some kind, looks up and simply says: "No other method appropriate?" The magistrate nods and then that is entered on the record. It becomes a pure formality. Exactly the same thing has happened with not sentencing first offenders to prison. Again you have to state your reasons and once again off goes the person to prison and the clerk says: "Seriousness of offence?", and the magistrate nods, and down goes "seriousness of offence".' *Parl. Debates*, HL, 431 (5th ser.), col. 948, 22 June 1982.

unwilling or unable to respond to non-custodial penalties. A court on passing a youth custody sentence should give its reasons for this conclusion, and this part of the process should form grounds for appeal.[66]

During the Committee stage of the Bill in the House of Commons, Robert Kilroy-Silk, a Labour MP and chairman of PAPPAG, cobbled together an amendment out of the wording of the Bill and the PAPPAG report. It stipulated that custodial sentences could be passed on an offender under twenty-one only if the court considered that no other sentence was appropriate because he had shown himself to be unable or unwilling to respond to non-custodial methods of treatment, or because a custodial sentence was necessary for the protection of the public. After being debated at length, but opposed by the Government, the amendment was withdrawn. One of the criticisms in the Standing Committee debate was that the amendment would make it impossible to imprison a first offender who had committed a very serious offence in circumstances where there was little likelihood of repetition.

PAPPAG then discussed the matter again before the Bill reached the House of Lords and, at the suggestion of the former Attorney General, Sam Silkin, who had been a member of the working party which had drafted the report, the amendment was expanded to include a third criterion: that the offence was 'so serious that a non-custodial sentence cannot be justified'. In its revised form the amendment was tabled in the Lords by Baroness Faithfull, another member of the working party, and debated during the Committee stage. Unlike Kilroy-Silk in the Commons, Baroness Faithfull spoke from the Conservative benches. She obtained strong support from Opposition speakers, as well as from some peers on her own side of the House. The amendment was opposed by a Home Office minister, Lord Elton,[67] but carried on a division by 102 votes to 81.[68] The Government did not seek to overturn the set-back when Lords amendments were considered in the Commons, with the result that the guide-lines were incorporated in what became Section 1(4) of the Criminal Justice Act 1982.

As amended, the final wording of the Act elaborated the original

[66] *Young Offenders: A Strategy for the Future*, Barry Rose, Chichester and London, 1981, p. 64.
[67] Parliamentary Under-Secretary of State, 1982–4; Minister of State, Home Office, 1984–5.
[68] *Parl. Debates*, HL, 431 (5th ser.), cols. 955–6, 22 June 1982.

provision in the Bill by requiring the court to base its opinion on one of three possible grounds: the failure of non-custodial penalties, the need to protect the public, and the seriousness of the offence. In supporting the amendment in the House of Lords the former Lord Chancellor, Lord Elwyn-Jones, said that the issue was a proper one on which Parliament should give guidance to the courts. He did not believe that the judiciary would object to being given such guide-lines.[69] A succession of judgments enforcing the statutory criteria by the Court of Appeal from 1983 onwards bore out the accuracy of his prediction.[70]

Although the courts initially were slow to digest the import of the new legislation, the statutory restrictions on custodial sentences for young offenders gradually began to bite.[71] In the first full twelve-month period of the operation of the Act, 1984, compared with the base year of 1982, the number of custodial sentences imposed on juveniles aged fourteen and under seventeen fell by 6.85%. It took longer to check, and then reverse, the previously rising trend of custodial sentences passed on young adults aged seventeen and under twenty-one, but enough of a pattern had emerged for there to be mounting pressure to sharpen the guide-lines in the next legislation. By 1988, when the next criminal justice legislation was completing its long-drawn-out progress through Parliament, the reduction in the number of young male offenders receiving custodial sentences had reached 13.36% between the ages of seventeen and under twenty-one, and no less than 54.79% between fourteen and under seventeen. A statistical profile over the years 1982–90 is given in Table 5.

The steady decline in the number of young male offenders sentenced to custody which occurred throughout the 1980s is one of the most remarkable post-war achievements of deliberate legislative enactment. That it owed so little to the Government, and so much to independent-minded members of both Houses of Parliament, was later acknowledged in a generous tribute to Baroness Faithfull by Elton: 'I look at my Noble Friend Lady Faithfull

[69] Ibid., col. 954.
[70] In briefing paper 69, titled *Criteria for Custody*, NACRO summarized selected Court of Appeal judgments from 1983 to 1988 in which appeals against sentence were allowed on the grounds that the lower court had not correctly applied the requirements of Section 1(4) of the Criminal Justice Act 1982.
[71] See Elizabeth Burney's study in twelve petty sessional divisions, 'All Things to All Men: Justifying Custody under the 1982 Act', [1985] Crim. L.R. 284.

TABLE 5. *Young male offenders sentenced to immediate custody, 1982–1990*

	Number	Difference from 1982 figure expressed as % of that figure
Aged 14 and under 17		
1982	7,300	—
1983[a]	6,900	−5.48
1984	6,800	−6.85
1985	6,100	−16.44
1986	4,400	−39.73
1987	4,000	−45.21
1988	3,300	−54.79
1989	2,300	−68.49
1990	1,700	−76.71
Aged 17 and under 21		
1982	23,200	—
1983[a]	23,500	+1.29
1984	24,200	+4.31
1985	25,700	+10.78
1986	21,700	−6.47
1987	21,600	−6.90
1988	20,100	−13.36
1989	16,300	−29.74
1990	14,100	−39.22

[a] Part 1 of the Criminal Justice Act 1982 came into operation on 24 May 1983.
Source: Home Office, *Criminal Statistics England and Wales.*

because that touches the part of the 1982 Act which she carried into Section 1 against my advice. I concede now that she was right.'[72]

Official endorsement that the public safety was not endangered by the presence in the community of so many youths who previously might have expected to be in custody could be found in the deployment of the statistics indicating that overall offending by known juveniles had fallen significantly over the same period. Thus by the time the Government was ready to bring forward its plans

[72] *Parl. Debates*, HL, 524 (5th ser.), col. 507, 12 Dec. 1990.

for the 1990/1 legislation it was able to claim: 'The number of known juvenile offenders has dropped from about 174,000 in 1981 to about 119,000 in 1988. This is a greater reduction than would be expected from the reduction in the number of those in this age group.'[73]

The story of how the tide was turned gave heart to penal reformers, as well as having a marked influence on the contents of the Criminal Justice Acts of 1988 and 1991. Twice more ministerial backbones needed to be stiffened and judicial doubts overcome. But the evidence was there, in the Home Office's own statistics, and before long in the public domain. It is true that other factors besides the statutory restrictions on the sentencing of young offenders contributed to the decline. The increased use of cautions by the police was significant, as was the greater disposition of magistrates to consider intermediate treatment as they, and equally important their clerks, became more closely involved in its planning with the Probation Service and voluntary organizations. Other relevant changes during the period were the extension of community service orders to sixteen year-olds and the provision of probation day centres for offenders aged seventeen and over.

A reminder of a less happy Parliamentary initiative recurred when the 1982 Act was in preparation. The partly suspended sentence, discussed in the previous chapter, had still not been brought into effect. The Home Office had hesitated

because of fears that the new sentence would be used to give a 'taste of imprisonment' in cases where at present the courts would impose a fully suspended sentence or a non-custodial sentence. Inevitably, too, in a proportion of cases the suspended part of the sentence would be sub-sequently activated. Thus there can be no certainty that implementing section 47 would achieve any reduction in numbers in custody and would not confer any advantage in the treatment of individual offenders.[74]

Home Office officials had tried to persuade ministers, in vain, that the provision should be repealed. The presence of Patrick Mayhew, now Minister of State, meant that his hobby-horse was preserved when the Bill was in draft. The 1982 Act made certain

---

[73] Home Office, *Crime, Justice and Protecting the Public* (Cm. 965), HMSO, London, 1990, p. 45.

[74] Home Office, *Review of Parole in England and Wales*, May 1981, p. 14.

relatively minor changes to the 1977 legislation,[75] but the die was cast and the new sentence was brought into effect by the Criminal Law Act 1977 (Commencement No. 11) Order 1982. By then, the political weather had changed again since Whitelaw had run into difficulties over his plan to reduce the prison population by way of supervised release. At the eleventh hour he had to find a face-saving substitute. The partly suspended sentence was ready to hand.

VI

When preparing the legislation, and in his consideration of sentencing practice, Whitelaw had been anxious to consult, and if possible carry with him, the higher judiciary. As his office befitted, Lord Lane, appointed Lord Chief Justice of England in 1980,[76] was a robust upholder of judicial independence and wary of politicians whose priorities and objectives not infrequently diverged from those of the judiciary.

The traditional view, widely accepted in Whitehall and Westminster as well as at the Temple, was that sentencing in the Crown Court was entirely a matter for the judiciary and no one else. Parliament set maximum penalties for each offence, and if the trial judge strayed too far out of line with the prevailing practice, the Court of Appeal had the power to reduce and, after 1988, to increase the sentence in the interest of consistency. Of the few exceptions to sentencing discretion, murder was far and away the most important. Where the jury returned a verdict of guilty to a charge of murder, or a defendant pleaded guilty, the penalty of life imprisonment was prescribed by statute. The trial judge's function was to pronounce the sentence required by law, recommending to

[75] Section 30 of the Criminal Justice Act 1982 differed from Section 47 of the Criminal Law Act 1977 in that it reduced the minimum sentence which could be partly suspended from six months to three months. It also provided (1) that the Court should not make an order of partial suspension unless it was satisfied that a wholly suspended sentence would be inappropriate, and (2) that it was subject to the restrictions on sentences of imprisonment upon persons who had not previously served custodial sentences which were contained in the Powers of Criminal Courts Act 1973.

[76] Judge of the High Court of Justice, Queen's Bench Division, 1966–74; Lord Justice of Appeal, 1974–9; Lord of Appeal in Ordinary, 1979–80. Lord Chief Justice of England, 1980–92. Member of the Parole Board, 1970–2 (Vice-Chairman, 1972).

the Secretary of State in open court if he thought the circumstances of the case warranted it a minimum period of time which should elapse before release on licence.[77] The power to make a minimum recommendation when pronouncing sentence was seldom used. As time went on, the real significance of the judicial contribution to sentencing for murder became diverted into the private process of setting a tariff, that is the term of imprisonment which must be served to satisfy the requirements of retribution and general deterrence before questions of risk and public safety were considered. The way this procedure evolved, and the strong objections to it, are set out in Chapter 7.

In the 1980s two external forces were converging to define more rigorously the sentencing discretion of the individual judge in criminal trials. The first was appellate review by the Court of Appeal; the second the concentration on sentencing in the training provided for Crown Court judges by the Judicial Studies Board.[78] Induction seminars were compulsory for newly appointed Assistant Recorders, supplemented by quinquennial refresher seminars for Recorders and Circuit judges, and by circuit sentencing conferences. There is no compulsory training for newly appointed High Court judges, although previously many of them will have sat as Recorders or Assistant Recorders.

The scope of appellate review was deliberately extended by the Criminal Division of the Court of Appeal by means of guide-line judgments in which the court laid down a scale of penalties related to the gravity of a particular type of crime. These judgments went beyond the facts of the actual case before the court, exploiting the opportunity to enunciate general sentencing principles, sometimes accompanied by a scale of penalties which the judges in the Crown Court were expected to follow. Since 1980 guide-line judgments, normally by the Lord Chief Justice, indicated graduated levels of penalty, *inter alia*, for the illegal import and supply of controlled drugs, causing death by reckless driving, rape, incest, riot, social security frauds, theft in breach of trust, and involuntary man-

[77] Murder (Abolition of Death Penalty) Act 1965, Section 1(2).
[78] The Judicial Studies Board was set up in 1979. For a note on its terms of reference and origin, see *Responses to Crime*, vol. 1, p. 15. Three increasingly informative reports on the Board's work have been published: *Judicial Studies Board Report for 1979–1982*, HMSO, London, 1983; *Judicial Studies Board Report for 1983–1987*, HMSO, London, 1988; and *Judicial Studies Board Report for 1987–91*, HMSO, London, 1992.

slaughter.[79] The Court of Appeal's guide-line judgments are compiled and circulated to every judge sitting in the Crown Court
throughout England and Wales. The Magistrates' Association also
promulgates sentencing guide-lines for use in the courts of summary
jurisdiction.

The Court of Appeal did not confine itself to fabricating relative
scales of punishment, Lord Lane showing himself at the start ready
to give forthright guidance on the use of imprisonment. In *Upton*,
one of the earliest cases that came before him as Lord Chief Justice
in March 1980, he referred to the undesirability of certain types of
petty offender taking up the limited amount of prison accommodation:

the time has come to appreciate that non-violent petty offenders should
not be allowed to take up what has become valuable space in prison. If
there really is no alternative ... to an immediate prison sentence, then it
should be as short as possible. Sentencing judges should appreciate that
overcrowding in many of the penal establishments in this country is such
that a prison sentence, however short, is a very unpleasant experience
indeed for the inmates.[80]

Later in the year, in the case of *Bashir Begum Bibi*, Lane CJ
returned to the same theme:

it is no secret that our prisons at the moment are dangerously overcrowded.
So much so that sentencing courts must be particularly careful to examine
each case to ensure, if an immediate custodial sentence is necessary, that
the sentence is as short as possible, consistent only with the duty to protect
the interests of the public and to punish and deter the criminal.[81]

The judgment gave examples of the sort of case where shorter
sentences would be appropriate, and those which called for a
medium or longer sentence. Emphasizing that much will depend on

---

[79] Illegal import and supply of controlled drugs: *Aramah* (1983) 4 Cr. App. R.
(S) 407; [1983] Crim. L.R. 271; *Bilinski* (1987) 9 Cr. App. R. (S) 360; *Satvir Singh*
(1988) 10 Cr. App. R. (S) 402. Causing death by reckless driving: *Boswell* (1984) 6
Cr. App. R. (S) 257. Rape: *Billam* (1986) 8 Cr. App. R. (S) 48. Incest: *Attorney
General's Reference (No.1 of 1989) under Criminal Justice Act 1988 section 36*
(1989) 11 Cr. App. R. (S) 409. Riot: *Keys* (1986) 8 Cr. App. R. (S) 444. Social
security frauds: *Livingstone Stewart* (1987) 9 Cr. App. R. (S) 135. Theft in breach
of trust: *Barrick* (1985) 7 Cr. App. R. (S) 142. Involuntary manslaughter: *Coleman*
(1992) 13 Cr. App. R. (S) 508; [1992] Crim. L.R. 315.

[80] *Upton* (1980) 71 Cr. App. R. 102 at 104.

[81] *Bibi* (1980) 71 Cr. App. R. 360 at 361.

the circumstances of each individual offender and each individual offence, Lane CJ continued:

What the Court can and should do is to ask itself whether there is any compelling reason why a short sentence should not be passed. We are not aiming at uniformity of sentence; that would be impossible. We are aiming at uniformity of approach.[82]

Judicial training, already well established for magistrates,[83] was gingerly handled when it was extended to the professional judiciary in 1979, following the report of a working party chaired by Lord Bridge, then an Appeal Court judge.[84] The term judicial studies was preferred to judicial training, the report taking pains to explain that no 'indoctrination' or 'conditioning' of newly appointed judges towards any prescribed line was intended.[85] Although there was apprehension that the Judicial Studies Board might inhibit the freedom of an individual judge to pass whatever sentence he thought right having heard the evidence and seen the defendant in court, it gradually abated as an awareness spread that the Board's aims were to enhance judicial performance and encourage consistency in sentencing, so that the penalties imposed for similar offences did not vary markedly from one court to another.

The Board was reconstituted in 1985, its functions being expanded to cover the civil and family jurisdictions, in addition to taking on

[82] *Bibi* at 361–2. Following the *Upton* and *Bibi* judgments, the Home Office estimated that reduced sentence lengths led to a short-term reduction of 2,000–3,000 in the prison population. Home Office, *Statistical Bulletin* 33/90, p. 6.

[83] The Justices of the Peace Act 1949 set up Magistrates' Courts Committees with responsibility for the administration of Magistrates' courts in their areas. Section 17 of the Act required each of these committees to make and administer schemes of instruction in accordance with arrangements approved by the Lord Chancellor. The Section was not brought into operation until April 1953, and the response both from the committees and from individual magistrates, although mainly acceptable, was not regarded by the Home Office as wholly satisfactory. In 1962 the Magistrates' Association's annual general meeting passed a resolution in favour of 'a basic form of obligatory training'. The Government eventually took up the idea, and obligatory basic and juvenile court training was introduced for all magistrates appointed from 1 January 1966. Periodical refresher training was later added, and is obligatory for all those appointed from 1 January 1980. For a more detailed account, see Sir Thomas Skyrme, *The Changing Image of the Magistracy*, Macmillan, London, 2nd edn., 1983, pp. 68–83.

[84] Working Party on Judicial Training and Information, Consultative Working Paper, HMSO, London, 1979.

[85] A. Ashworth, 'Judicial Independence and Sentencing Reform' in D. A. Thomas (ed.), *The Future of Sentencing*, University of Cambridge Institute of Criminology, Occasional Papers No. 8, 1982, pp. 52–3.

the supervision of training for magistrates and judicial chairmen and members of tribunals. By then the lingering resistance of a few stubborn judges had virtually disappeared, opening the way for induction and refresher courses that amounted to vocational training. The report on the Board's work between 1983 and 1987 was sufficiently confident to predict: 'We doubt whether a change of name to the Judicial "Training" Board would nowadays raise many eyebrows.'[86]

The report went on to maintain that the word 'studies' in its title was not simply a euphemism. Apart from instruction via the imparting of information, the aim was to provide opportunities for its clientele to exchange views and impressions with their colleagues, many of whom worked in relative isolation. The emphasis was placed squarely upon enabling individual judges, both lay and professional, to perform their duties more effectively.[87] The commissioning of studies into the substance of the law or the administration of justice was apparently ruled out: 'the purpose of the Board is to further studies of others, not itself to engage in them.'[88] Any hint of policy-making, for example in suggesting topics on which guide-line judgments should be given, was eschewed. Similar sentiments were expressed in the report for the years 1987–91, in which the Board tentatively put forward the possible establishment of a Judicial College in the longer term.[89]

Did such a cautious approach mean that the chance was missed to establish a connecting link between the Home Office with its responsibility for the content of the criminal law and the judges who were responsible for administering it? Although the Judicial Studies Board had been constituted under the wing of the Lord Chancellor's Department, the Home Office had established a bridgehead in the shape of a senior official on the main Board since its inception. As specialist committees followed, representation was also secured on the Criminal and Magisterial Committees, and in due course an Advisory Committee on Ethnic Minorities which was added in 1991. Throughout its existence, however, the Board confined itself to organizing the training, in the broader sense of the term, of the judiciary and others exercising judicial functions,

---

[86] *Judicial Studies Board Report for 1983–1987*, p. 13.
[87] Ibid., pp. 12–13.
[88] Ibid., p. 14.
[89] *Judicial Studies Board Report 1987–91*, p. 53.

largely conducted by the judiciary, with a view to improving their performance. A feature was the care that was invariably taken to act on lines believed to be acceptable to the Lord Chief Justice and his senior brethren.

A curious episode in the mid-1980s brought the Judicial Studies Board fleetingly within the ambit of legislative design. Although there was no need for a body set up to promote judicial studies and training to have the imprimatur of Parliament, it was proposed that the Board should have conferred upon it a statutory responsibility to promulgate guide-line judgments. Since this was happening entirely satisfactorily already, there had to be a special reason why it was thought necessary to seek Parliamentary endorsement.

The explanation lay in the controversy over lenient sentences which began during the debates on the setting up of the Crown Prosecution Service in 1985, and continued over the next two or three years. As published, the Prosecution of Offences Bill contained a clause enabling the Attorney General to refer to the Court of Appeal for its opinion any sentence passed by the Crown Court for an indictable offence which was considered to be too lenient. Although the defendant could not have his sentence increased, the Court of Appeal would be given an early opportunity to review and pronounce upon what the proper penalty should have been. The clause was strongly criticized in the House of Lords and, despite an eloquent defence by the Lord Chancellor, Lord Hailsham, it was rejected by 140 votes to 98.[90] The Government did not try to reinstate it in the Commons.

In the Criminal Justice Bill of 1986/7 another attempt was made to confer on the prosecution the right to ask for a review by the Court of Appeal of any sentence passed by the Crown Court on a trial on indictment which the Attorney General considered raised a question of public importance. As before, the sentence passed on the defendant in the Crown Court would be left undisturbed. The Court of Appeal was to be charged instead with laying down the principles to be observed in sentencing in similar cases in the future. Such rulings would be promulgated by the Judicial Studies Board which was given 'a statutory duty to assemble and publish, for the benefit of the judges and for the information of the wider public,

---

[90] *Parl. Debates*, HL, 459 (5th ser.), col. 404, 24 Jan. 1985.

the Court of Appeal's guidelines as they apply to particular classes of offence or particular classes of offender'.[91]

This time the proposal was subjected to forthright condemnation by Lane, who had been the prime source of the demand for the Court of Appeal to be given a power to increase sentences that were 'manifestly too light':[92]

The suggestion that the Judicial Studies Board should have some statutory authority fills me with horror. It already collates and publishes the necessary decisions and there is no need to give it any statutory power to do that. Clause 29 will do nothing to show the public that a miscarriage of justice has been put right for the simple reason that it has not been put right.[93]

The Board itself had no objection to being put on a statutory basis, but would have preferred to see any such recognition cover the whole range of its activities, and to be enacted on its own merits, rather than from what might well be regarded as an ulterior motive. In the outcome, the second proposal fared no better than its predecessor. Before the matter reached a decision in the Lords, a General Election was called and only the first part of the Bill, dealing with offences of serious fraud, was enacted as the Criminal Justice Act 1987.

After the Conservative victory the remaining parts were reintroduced into the House of Lords. Douglas Hurd, reappointed as Home Secretary, decided that the time had come to escape from the cross-fire to which he and his ministers had been exposed and that the complicity of the Judicial Studies Board was no longer required. He remained convinced, however, that the harm to public confidence which the occasional over-lenient sentence could cause was too corrosive to be ignored. The prolonged debate had not been in vain, for it had established, contrary to the initial Whitehall assumption, that there was a majority in Parliament for the sentence passed on the actual offender to be increased by the Court of Appeal in appropriate cases, rather than the Court merely proclaiming the principles it raised.

[91] Home Office, *Criminal Justice: Plans for Legislation* (Cmnd. 9658), HMSO, London, p. 7.

[92] In the House of Lords debate Hailsham declared: 'This [clause] does not have its origin in press criticism. It does not have its origin in party conferences. It does not have its origin even in women's organizations ... It has its origin in the Lord Chief Justice. No less; no more.' *Parl. Debates*, HL, 459, cols. 398–9.

[93] *Parl. Debates*, HL, 486 (5th ser.), cols. 1295–6, 27 Apr. 1987.

As enacted, the legislation conferred on the Attorney General a power to refer to the Court of Appeal any sentence passed by the Crown Court where it appeared to him to be unduly lenient. The leave of the Court of Appeal would be required. On considering a reference under the new procedure the Court would be able to quash the sentence and substitute for it whatever sentence it thought appropriate which the court below had the power to pass. The Minister of State assured the House of Lords that the power to refer sentences to the Court of Appeal for review would be used only 'sparingly' by the Attorney General.[94] On Report, the Government accepted an amendment to the wording of what became Section 36 of the Criminal Justice Act 1988, following criticisms made in Committee by Lane and myself. The amendment had been drafted by Parliamentary Counsel to meet the point and was offered to me to put down. It was accepted without dissent.[95]

Once the idea of linking the Judicial Studies Board to the prosecution right to appeal had been abandoned, the Board reverted to its settled role. In essence, despite the presence of some non-judicial members, it preserved the character of a judicial enclave in the wider world of criminal policy. Institutional antagonism towards the executive branch of government, veiled by courteous personal relationships, was sufficient to keep the civil servants in check. The access that their membership brought was useful enough as a sounding board to test the temperature of judicial opinion, and a Home Office minister or senior official was regularly invited to speak about current legislation or policy developments at the refresher seminars held three times a year for Crown Court judges. Throughout these exchanges a wary eye was kept on any policies, overt or covert, which might have the effect of limiting the sentencing discretion of the courts. In particular, the idea of a sentenc-

[94] *Parl. Debates*, HL, 489 (5th ser.), col. 316, 26 Oct. 1987. Between 1 Feb. 1989, when this part of the Act came into force, and 19 Dec. 1991, fifty-nine applications were made by the Attorney General for leave to refer Crown Court sentences to the Court of Appeal under the provisions of Sections 35 and 36 of the Criminal Justice Act 1988. Out of this total, six applications were withdrawn by the Attorney General before consideration by the Court of Appeal; one was refused; one was not considered as a retrial was ordered; and fifteen were pending. Of the remainder, thirty-one resulted in an increase in sentence; four in the sentence passed in the Crown Court being confirmed; and one varied from a suspended sentence to a probation order. *Parl. Debates*, HL, 533 (5th ser.), col. WA 85, 19 Dec. 1991. See also [1992] Crim. L.R. 142.

[95] *Parl. Debates*, HL, 490 (5th ser.), cols. 179–81, 17 Nov. 1987.

ing council, never adopted by the Government but pressed by the
Opposition during the passage of the Criminal Justice Act 1991,
was so disliked by the higher judiciary that there was a tendency
to see in almost any proposal put forward by the Home Office a
disguised attempt to create one.

The reality was that the Board had not been designed as an
instrument for refining one of the most crucial of all relationships
in the process of criminal justice, and it was unwilling to adapt
itself to that end. The ideal of judicial independence continued to
be interpreted in such a way that no common ground could be
marked out where judges and government could come together in
joint endeavour, above all to relate the penalty imposed by the
court to the availability of resources required to make it achieve
its intended ends. Could ministers do better?

VII

The *Upton* and *Bibi* judgments corresponded so closely with the
Home Secretary's outlook that an opportunity beckoned to open
an informal channel for the exchange of ideas in private, and at
the highest level, between the executive and the judiciary. A Deputy
Under-Secretary of State, Anthony Brennan, at the time in charge
of the Criminal Department at the Home Office, who had got to
know Lane when both were promoting the newly established Parole
Board in the 1960s, was entrusted with the diplomatic task of
making the first approach to the Lord Chief Justice to ascertain if
he would be willing to meet the Home Secretary. The answer was
favourable and in the Autumn of 1980, in conditions of great
secrecy, a dinner party was held on neutral ground in a private
room at a West End Club. The Lord Chief Justice was accompanied
by his deputy, Lord Justice Watkins, with the Home Office team
consisting of Whitelaw, Brittan, then Minister of State, Sir Brian
Cubbon, the Permanent Secretary, and some other senior officials.

The meeting was sufficiently successful for it to be agreed that it
should be followed up by a series of buffet suppers at which Brittan,
accompanied by some of the Home Office officials, would meet a
number of judges for off-the-record discussion. Only one of the
projected series of four had taken place when the fragile concord
was shattered by a disagreement arising out of media coverage of

a change in policy. A second working supper, which had been arranged previously, took place at York shortly after the publication in the *Sunday Times* and elsewhere of reports which were much resented by Lane. No more was heard about plans for any further meetings.

The antecedents of the breach were to be found in an internal *Review of Parole in England and Wales* prepared by Home Office officials and circulated to interested parties in May 1981. As something of an afterthought, the review had canvassed the possibility that all offenders sentenced to less than three years, but more than six months' imprisonment, should be released automatically after serving one-third of their sentence. A period of compulsory supervision by the Probation Service would follow in the second portion of the sentence, with the final third being remitted.[96] The proposal for automatic release, although after one-half of the sentence had been served, was to re-emerge in a somewhat different form in a recommendation of the far more exhaustive Review Committee chaired by Lord Carlisle of Bucklow in 1987/8,[97] and was incorporated in the Criminal Justice Act 1991. Ten years earlier it was in advance of its time and was regarded as an unacceptable erosion of the duration of the sentence passed by the court. Brennan raised the idea tentatively as a possible change under consideration within the Home Office at a seminar of the Judicial Studies Board, where it was poorly received.

Wind of the tentative proposal reached the press and broadcast media. The idea, never formally taken up by the Government, was greeted with enthusiasm as a promising new initiative which could amount to a revolution in the prison system, cutting at a stroke as many as 7,000 people from a prison population standing at near to 44,000.[98] On 11 November 1981 *The Times* reported that Whitelaw was 'on the point of dumping a proposal by which he and his colleagues have previously set great store; the idea of automatic supervised release for shorter sentence prisoners'. At the Annual Meeting of the National Association for the Care and Resettlement of Offenders (NACRO), the Home Secretary disclosed that he was considering instead bringing back to life the dormant Section 47 of

[96] Home Office, *Review of Parole in England and Wales*, pp. 14–15.
[97] *The Parole System in England and Wales*, Report of the Review Committee (Cm. 532), HMSO, London, 1988.
[98] Hugo Young, *Sunday Times*, 17 May, 1981.

the Criminal Law Act 1977 enabling the courts to suspend part of a prison sentence. On 22 November the *Sunday Times* carried the report which led to the breakdown in relations with the judiciary:

Britain's judges and magistrates have thwarted a penal reform proposed by the Home Secretary which would have dramatically reduced the number of prisoners in the country's overcrowded jails. William Whitelaw had hoped to introduce automatic release for prisoners who had served one-third of their sentences. But judges and magistrates, he told the *Sunday Times*, 'were unanimously against it'. They warned him that if he pushed his proposal through they would increase sentences to compensate.

The claim that Whitelaw had been thwarted in a brave new initiative towards reducing prison overcrowding because of the diehard opposition of the judiciary was not the whole truth. Although what had been perceived as judicial resistance to constraints on their ability to determine the amount of time actually to be spent in prison by an offender had undoubtedly influenced the Home Secretary's change of heart, there were other compelling factors. An intransigent current of Tory opinion simultaneously was hardening against Whitelaw, culminating in a very public reverse at the Party Conference in October.[99] Thus it was not correct to infer it was the opposition of the judges alone, relayed by Lane with an implied threat of retaliation, that had forced his hand.

Lane particularly deprecated that the *Sunday Times* story was directly attributed to Whitelaw himself, and was furious. Although the two men had got on well when they had met, their relationship was still guarded and not firmly rooted enough to withstand an early squall. To Lane, the episode bore out what he had always suspected; that no politician could be trusted, that political expediency would always come first, and that all were the same under the skin. His anger became known quite widely in the Inns of Court, and was relayed to Whitelaw. The Home Secretary, taken aback by what he regarded as no more than a misunderstanding, was hurt by the accusation of duplicity. Intermediaries in the shape of the Attorney General, Sir Michael Havers,[100] and Patrick Mayhew, did what they could to restore harmony, but in the end it was the magnanimity of Lane which achieved a rapprochement. On 25

[99] *The Whitelaw Memoirs*, pp. 195–8.
[100] Solicitor General, 1972–4; Attorney General, 1979–87; Lord Chancellor, 1987.

January 1983 the Chairman of the BBC Board of Governors, George Howard, a close personal friend of Whitelaw, gave a dinner party in honour of the Home Secretary and his wife at the BBC Television Centre. Lane, whose very heavy duties in court meant that he seldom dined out, was among the guests. His mode of speech, as well as his presence, made it clear that the incident was over.

Formal relations between the Home Secretary and the Lord Chief Justice were not resumed until 1986. By then Douglas Hurd, who had succeeded Brittan as Home Secretary the previous year, was embarking upon the early stages of his grand design which was subsequently outlined in the Green Paper on *Punishment, Custody and the Community*.[101] Regular meetings, less clandestine than that of 1980, were held with Lane and his deputy in the Home Secretary's room at Queen Anne's Gate. As before, there were matters of substance to discuss on which it was desirable to hear from the Lord Chief Justice while the Government's plans for legislation were still at the formative stage. The value of a functional relationship between the executive and the judiciary was openly recognized when the Lord Chief Justice, together with the Lord Chancellor and Attorney General, attended the first of a series of national conferences on criminal justice launched by the Home Secretary at Ditchley Park in September 1989. After this meeting the tenuous relationship that had been developed was subsumed into a setting of enhanced co-operation between the main services which make up the system of criminal justice. Sentencing reforms were no longer the chimera they had been for so long, and walking the tightrope of bilateral relations was made less perilous for both parties by the construction of a broader platform.[102]

[101] Cm. 424, HMSO, London, 1988.
[102] The Ditchley meeting was followed by a series of national and regional conferences organized by the Home Office which were designed to bring together experience and expertise from all parts of the criminal justice system and other relevant disciplines. Participants regularly included Home Office ministers and officials; judges; members of the Crown Prosecution Service, the police, and the Prison Service; court administrators; magistrates; and probation officers.

VIII

Looking back, the 1982 Act with its rationalization of custodial sentences for young offenders and the adoption of criteria restricting their imprisonment, stands out as a momentous step in the evolution of criminal policy. The legislation also contained the seeds of more far-reaching policies towards the sentencing of adults that were to come to fruition at the end of the decade. Before then, in the mid-1980s, Parliament enacted three other important statutes. Chronologically the Police and Criminal Evidence Act came first in 1984, followed by the Prosecution of Offences Act in 1985 which led to the setting up of a Crown Prosecution Service independent of the police with the aim of securing greater consistency in prosecution decisions. The pressure for an independent prosecution service was noted in Chapter 3. The third statute was the Public Order Act 1986.

The Police and Criminal Evidence Act had a protracted and difficult birth, attended by controversy over the legitimacy and effectiveness of the police that was such a pronounced feature of the period. Conceived by a Royal Commission established by the Labour Government in February 1978, and delivered by a Conservative Government six years later, having suffered a miscarriage in the Parliamentary session 1982/3 when the Bill had not completed its passage through the Commons by the time a General Election intervened, the Bill generated fierce criticism inside and outside Parliament. To the Government it represented 'a long overdue reform and modernisation of the law governing the investigation of crime'.[103] Libertarians saw it in a different light, being alert to the challenge it posed to the rights and liberties of individuals suspected of having committed a criminal offence. Intercalated between the two were the powers and obligations of that most formidable of vested interests, the police, when investigating crimes and bringing offenders to justice.[104]

Steering its way through the minefield, the Royal Commission

[103] See Sir Leon Brittan's foreword to the 1st edn. of Professor Michael Zander's commentary on *The Police and Criminal Evidence Act*, London, Sweet and Maxwell, 1985, reprinted in the rev. 2nd edn., 1990, p. vii.
[104] For an account of the sequence of events between the publication of the Royal Commission's report and the passing of the Act, and more generally on police powers and accountability, see R. Reiner, *The Politics of the Police*, Wheatsheaf Books, Sussex, and St Martin's Press, New York, 1985, pp. 167–96.

on Criminal Procedure succeeded in producing a near unanimous set of recommendations covering the criminal process from the start of the investigation to the point of trial. In pursuing a balance between suspects' rights and the powers of the police, the price was vagueness on certain issues, with two of the members, Jack Jones, a leading trade unionist[105] and the Revd Canon Wilfred Wood, dissenting on some proposals which they considered to be too favourable to the police. When the Commission's report was published in January 1981[106] it met with a mixed reception. Civil liberties groups and most of the political Left condemned it as a triumph for the law and order lobby.[107] The police, on the other hand, having awaited the report with pessimism and trepidation, were pleasantly surprised, and gave the recommendations a guarded welcome. The Bar and Law Society responded favourably to the report as a whole, although with reservations as to its detail. To the Conservative Government which had inherited the Royal Commission, the polarization of the reactions made the report in some ways the more attractive a topic for legislation; a reforming measure which, in so far as it proved contentious, would reflect a distinctive policy of support for the forces of law and order. The initial steps, nevertheless, were cautious: a non-committal consultative memorandum being issued in August 1981, followed by a Commons debate in November.[108]

The drafting of the legislation occupied the early months of 1982. With some modifications, the resultant Bill accepted the Royal Commission's proposals for rationalizing and modernizing police powers for the investigation of crime. The principal coercive powers were to stop and search persons, to arrest them, to enter and search premises and seize material as evidence, and to take fingerprints or body samples without consent. For the first time, specific provision was made for the detention of suspects for questioning without their being charged for a period extendable up to a maximum of ninety-six hours.

The powers were not in themselves novel. Most existed in some

---

[105] General Secretary, Transport and General Workers' Union, 1969–78; Member, TUC General Council, 1968–78. Deputy Chairman, National Ports Council, 1967–79.
[106] Royal Commission on Criminal Procedure, *Report* (Cmnd. 8092), HMSO, London, 1981.
[107] *The Politics of the Police*, p. 167.
[108] *Parl. Debates*, HC, 13 (6th ser.), cols. 527–90, 20 Nov. 1981.

form already, but as they were limited to particular offences, circumstances or places, they were haphazard in application. For example, although there was power to search for a variety of items including dangerous drugs, firearms, or the eggs of protected birds, it did not extend to offensive weapons or articles which it was an offence to carry. Powers were available in the Metropolitan Police district and certain urban areas to search persons and vehicles for stolen goods, but not elsewhere. The most commonly used power of arrest applied only to offences carrying a maximum penalty of at least five years' imprisonment. There were powers relating to other offences of differing degrees of gravity, but not for instance indecent assault, then carrying a maximum penalty of two years' imprisonment, since increased to ten. Powers of entry to premises for the purposes of search applied more to the proceeds of crime than to obtaining evidence of offences, up to the most serious. Thus there was no power, even under warrant, to enter and search the scene of a murder or kidnap. Law and practice on the period of time during which a suspect could be kept in custody without being charged was uncertain.

Greater novelty was attached to the statutory safeguards contained in the Bill since nothing comparable had existed previously. In future an elaborate system of record-keeping would be required, recording the reasons for the exercise of each coercive power and of every stage in the handling of a suspect in detention. In addition, the Bill took over some relatively uncontroversial proposals from an earlier report on evidence by the Criminal Law Revision Committee.[109] It also embodied changes in police complaints and disciplinary procedures, and provided for that consultation between the police and local communities which Lord Scarman had recommended in his report on the Brixton riots[110] with the aim of securing better co-operation with the police in preventing crime. The

[109] Criminal Law Revision Committee, *Eleventh Report* (Cmnd. 4991), HMSO, London, 1972.
[110] *Report on the Brixton Disorders 10–12 April 1981* (Cmnd. 8427), HMSO, London, 1981. Section 106 of the Police and Criminal Evidence Act 1984 requires arrangements to be made in each police area for obtaining the views of the local population on its policing. Research findings on the setting up and operation of police consultative committees are summarized by R. Morgan, 'Talking about Policing', in Downes (ed.), *Unravelling Criminal Justice*, pp. 165–83. Rod Morgan is Professor of Criminal Justice at Bristol University and acted as an assessor to Lord Justice Woolf's inquiry following the disturbances at Strangeways and other prisons in 1990.

Royal Commission's recommendations for a prosecution service independent of the police were left aside as requiring further thought, and as substantial enough to justify separate legislation.

Publication of the Bill drew fresh criticism from civil liberties groups, now reinforced by a wider range of academic and legal opinion, complaining that the Bill upset and distorted the balance between police powers and suspects' rights which the Royal Commission had striven to achieve. From the Government front bench, Whitelaw opened the debate on Second Reading:

This is a long Bill and is directed largely to the police service. At the end of the day, however, the Government are anxious that no one should lose sight of the vital part that the community at large plays in the prevention and detection of crime. That has two consequences. First, it has influenced how we have sought to construct the main proposals and support them with provisions relating to community consultation and police complaints procedures. Secondly, it means that Parliament, which represents the community at large, bears a heavy responsibility. That is because not only must it see that the long-outstanding overhaul of the law relating to the investigation of crime and the treatment of suspects is conducted with success, but it must ensure that that technical success is matched by a regard for the need in a free society to win the support of the population at large. That support alone can guarantee a workable and lasting resolution of all the important issues in the Bill that go so close to the heart of maintaining the civil peace in our society.[111]

For the Opposition Roy Hattersley[112] was unimpressed and retorted succinctly:

The Opposition will divide the House against the Bill for three distinct, but directly related, reasons. First, we believe that the Bill contains proposals concerning arrest, detention and interrogation that are, or ought to be, unacceptable in a free society. Second, the Bill proposes extensions of police powers that will alienate the police from the public whom they serve, thus making the prevention of crime and the apprehension of criminals more rather than less difficult. Therefore the Bill seems to us to be wrong both in practice and in principle. Third, we believe that it is an opportunity lost.[113]

[111] *Parl. Debates*, HC, 33 (6th ser.), col. 157, 30 Nov. 1982.
[112] Minister of Defence for Administration, 1969–70; Minister of State, Foreign and Commonwealth Office, 1974–6; Secretary of State for Prices and Consumer Protection, 1976–9. Principal Opposition spokesman on Treasury and economic affairs, 1983–7; on home affairs, 1980–3 and 1987–92. Deputy Leader of the Labour Party, 1983–92.
[113] *Parl. Debates*, HC, 33, col. 157.

On a Division the Bill was given a Second Reading by 273 votes to 187. It then went to a Standing Committee off the floor of the House where some 300 amendments were either made or promised by the Government for later stages. On Report only forty amendments had been considered when a General Election was called in May 1983, and the Bill had to be abandoned.

After the Conservatives returned to office, the new, comparatively young, Home Secretary, Leon Brittan,[114] made the Bill his first priority. He set in train a root-and-branch review of its contents, taking the chair at a series of meetings with junior ministers and officials at which the text was examined clause by clause, with particular attention paid to the points that had been causing the most difficulty at the end of the previous Parliament. The revised Bill presented to the Commons in October 1983 was still obnoxious to civil liberties groups, but the changes that had been made ensured it a better reception from the Bar and the Law Society, although as an inevitable consequence, a much less enthusiastic one from the police.

Among the principal concessions was the definition of a 'serious arrestable offence'. This was a matter of some significance because certain police powers (road checks, detention beyond twenty-four hours, delaying access to a solicitor, and taking intimate samples) were to become as they now are, exercisable only in the investigation of such an offence. The Royal Commission had put forward a similar concept of a 'grave offence', but had been unable to offer a satisfactory definition.[115] In the first Bill, such an offence was defined in subjective terms as 'an arrestable offence which the person contemplating the exercise of the power considers to be sufficiently serious to justify his exercising it'. In the revised Bill, this was replaced with a definition on lines which the Law Society had suggested, taking account of the consequences of the offence (e.g. death or serious injury, substantial financial gain, or serious financial loss). The later version also converted what had previously been powers for the Home Secretary into duties: in particular the issue of codes of practice for the exercise of police powers, and

---

[114] Brittan was aged forty-three when he became Home Secretary. He had been in practice at the Bar before joining the Government as Minister of State at the Home Office after the 1979 General Election.

[115] Royal Commission on Criminal Procedure, *Report*, p. 24. The report categorized those offences which it regarded as covered by the term 'grave offences'.

making the tape-recording of police interrogations compulsory.

It is interesting to compare Brittan's sharper presentation of the revised Bill on Second Reading with Whitelaw's on the original. What both sought to convey, however, was a clear implication that it was Conservative ministers, and those behind them, who stood for law and order:

This is, then, a wide-ranging measure, raising issues of vital concern in a free society. It is needed for three very simple reasons. Each provides a strong case in itself, but taken together I believe that the case is compelling. First, the present state of the law is unclear and contains many indefensible anomalies. Secondly, the police need to have adequate and clear powers to conduct the fight against crime on our behalf and the public need to have proper safeguards against any abuse of such powers if they are to have confidence in the police. Thirdly, these measures play an essential part in an overall strategy designed to create more effective policing. They do not solve, or pretend to solve, all the problems of policing in Britain today, but they have an important part to play alongside administrative and other measures needed or being dealt with already to ensure that the police can operate efficiently, fairly and with the active support of the public.[116]

As it was bound to do, Labour opposed the revised Bill on Second Reading in the Commons, claiming that it would do little if anything to give the nation the protection from crime which the Government promised but had failed to provide. From the front bench, Gerald Kaufman, who had replaced Hattersley as Home Affairs spokesman, added the comment that the Bill would 'seriously undermine civil liberties in ways which again are unprecedented in modern history'.[117]

When it reached the Lords there was renewed controversy, but with the focus shifting from the police to court procedure. One of the principal topics was to have much relevance in the light of the grave miscarriages of justice which only later emerged. Confessions by accused persons, and the extent to which they are admissible as

[116] *Parl. Debates*, HC, 48 (6th ser.), cols. 25–6, 7 Nov. 1983.
[117] Ibid., cols. 42–3.

evidence in court, have always raised difficult issues.[118] The question exercising the House in the early 1980s was whether the courts should have a general discretion to exclude evidence on the ground that it had been obtained unfairly. The Royal Commission had come down firmly against the exclusion of material obtained illegally or unfairly, save for confessions procured by the use or threat of violence. The Government accepted that there needed to be stricter control over the admission of confessions, and decided to adopt the dual test recommended by the Criminal Law Revision Committee. As enacted in Section 76 of the 1984 Act, this required a confession to be excluded if it was obtained either by oppression (defined as torture, inhuman or degrading treatment, or the use or threat of violence), or in consequence of anything said or done which was likely in the circumstances to render a confession unreliable.

The dispute in the Lords went wider than confessions, raising the possibility that the courts might be given an exclusionary discretion extending to evidence obtained by other means. The proposal did not command universal support, Lord Denning roundly declaring 'let us leave our common law as it is and let us leave our judges to develop it'.[119] Undeterred, Lord Scarman moved an amendment on Report, and carried it against the Government.[120] The effect was to make any evidence, other than a confession, inadmissible if it had been obtained improperly or in breach of the codes of practice, unless the breach was trivial, or unless the charge was serious and the evidence was of high probative value. Despite the eminence of its provenance, the wording did not survive into the Act, being displaced by a provision drafted by the Lord Chancellor personally which became Section 78(1):

In any proceedings the court may refuse to allow evidence on which the prosecution proposes to rely to be given if it appears to the court that, having regard to all the circumstances, including the circumstances in which the evidence was obtained, the admission of the evidence would

---

[118] Under common law a confession was only admissible if the prosecution could show that it was voluntary in the sense that it had not been induced by fear of prejudice or hope of advantage exercised or held out by a person in authority. Nor must confessions have been obtained by oppression. See M. Zander, *The Police and Criminal Evidence Act 1984*, rev. 2nd edn., 1990, p. 187.

[119] *Parl. Debates*, HL, 455 (5th ser.), col. 660, 31 July 1984.

[120] Ibid., cols. 653–74. 125 peers voted Content and 118 Not Content.

have such an adverse effect on the fairness of the proceedings that the court ought not to admit it.

Looking back in his memoirs at the passage of the Police and Criminal Evidence Act, Whitelaw wrote:

> I personally am particularly disappointed with the effects of the Police and Criminal Evidence Act. Perhaps it is much too early to form a judgment on the achievements of such a recent Act. My doubts probably arise because I was so sure that it was right at the time of its introduction.... Many of its provisions were widely accepted and in theory they should have contributed to better relations between police and public. So far this does not seem to have happened. Indeed, the Act tends to be blamed in police circles for increased bureaucracy, wasting valuable police time on the streets in pursuit of criminals.[121]

It is a paradox that the deeply disturbing cases of the Guildford Four and the Birmingham Six, both stemming from convictions before the provisions of the Act were in force, should have caused the police to revise their opinion. While no framework of regulation can eradicate all unacceptable practices or abuse, at least it reduces the scope for them, and hence the harm done to the reputation of the police. Like many statutes the Act has had unexpected results. The police sub-culture, with behaviour strongly conditioned by traditional methods of investigating crime,[122] has been slow to change. But one change there has been. Today the tape recording of interrogations of suspects is looked on by the police as being as much of a protection for them as it is for the suspect.

The third Act of the mid-1980s reached out to a wider public than either the Police and Criminal Evidence Act 1984 or the Prosecution of Offences Act the following year. Violent public disorders, often graphically seen on the nation's television sets, had begun with the disturbances at the Grunwick plant and at Lewisham in 1976/7, continued at Leicester and Southall in 1979, escalated with the street riots of 1981 at Brixton and Toxteth, and came to a head in the bitter and sometimes violent clashes which occurred (including the death of a miner going to work under police escort in

---

[121] *The Whitelaw Memoirs*, pp. 230–1.

[122] 'It is the police sub-culture which is the key to understanding police actions. This sometimes amounts to an extreme rule scepticism.' Reiner, *The Politics of the Police*, p. 175. See also M. McConville, A. Sanders, and R. Leng, *The Case for the Prosecution*, Routledge, London and New York, 1991, pp. 36–55.

South Wales) during the long-drawn-out miners' strike in 1984/5.[123] Football hooliganism also became endemic in the 1980s, leading to inquiries, reports, and separate legislation.

The Public Order Act 1986 was unusual in that it was both an expeditious response to public demand and a law reform measure which had been long in the making. In 1980 the Home Office and Scottish Office had published a Green Paper on their review of statutory public law offences,[124] followed by a White Paper in 1985.[125] In between came a report by the House of Commons Select Committee on Home Affairs[126] and Lord Scarman's seminal report on the Brixton disorders.[127] The Law Commission too had been diligent, in 1983 bringing out a report on common law offences relating to public order which had been preceded by a working paper the previous year.[128] All of these reports were unanimous in concluding that the common law misdemeanours of riot, rout, affray, and unlawful assembly, supplemented by powers of regulating public processions in the Public Order Act of 1936, were no longer adequate to meet changed conditions. The majority of their recommendations were accepted in the 1985 White Paper, and incorporated in a new Act the following year. Three new statutory offences—riot, violent disorder, and affray—were substituted for the old common law offences. The Public Order Act 1986 also reformed the law on processions, assemblies, and incitement to racial hatred, and gave courts in England and Wales power to make orders excluding offenders from football grounds.

Closest to the hearts of some MPs representing constituencies afflicted by the problems of decaying inner cities and urban violence was a new offence of using threatening, abusive, or insulting words or behaviour, or disorderly behaviour, or displaying any writing, sign, or other visible representations which are threatening, abusive,

---

[123] This sequence of events is cited by Professor R. Card in his review of the antecedents of the Public Order Act 1986. See *Public Order: The New Law* (Annotated Legislation Service vol. 314), Butterworths, London, 1987, p. 3.

[124] *Review of the Public Order Act 1936 and Related Legislation* (Cmnd. 7891), HMSO, London, 1980.

[125] *Review of Public Order Law* (Cmnd. 9510), HMSO, London, 1985.

[126] *Report on the Law Relating to Public Order*, Fifth Report, HC 756—I and II, 1980.

[127] *Report on the Brixton Disorders 10–12 April 1981* (Cmnd. 8427).

[128] *Report on Criminal Law: Offences Relating to Public Order*, Law. Com., No. 123, 1983, and *Working Paper on Offences against Public Order*, Working Paper No. 82, 1982.

or insulting to a person likely to be caused harassment, alarm, or distress. The provision, which attracted lively cross-party interest, was aimed at curbing rowdy and intimidating behaviour by youths on problem housing estates and in public places.

Section 5 of the Public Order Act 1986 had originated from the police, whose chief officers had argued the need for an offence covering minor acts of incivility or disorderly conduct, falling short of actual violence, but which nevertheless caused intimidation or distress. The Act came into force on 1 April 1987 and Section 5 has been well used since. The total number of prosecutions and convictions is shown in Table 6.

TABLE 6. *Prosecutions and convictions, 1987–90, under Section 5 of the Public Order Act 1986*

Year	Prosecutions	Convictions
1987[a]	12,660	9,490
1988	32,493	24,079
1989	37,384	26,802
1990	36,632	25,193

[a] Part year only.

Source: Home Office, *Criminal Statistics England and Wales.*

Despite the upward statistical trend, police officers interviewed for a Home Office survey did not feel that there had been an increase in public disorder since the passing of the Public Order Act:

If anything, some felt that the opposite was the case. When asked to explain what might lie behind a possible rise in the number of recorded public order offences they tended to suggest that this was due more to the nature of the legislation. To a great extent this came down to the incorporation of certain forms of minor misbehaviour, which the police might not previously have had powers to deal with formally, within the ambit of S.5 of the Act. Included among such misbehaviour was 'rowdiness' and 'failure to heed warnings to move on'.[129]

[129] T. Newburn, D. Brown, D. Crisp, and P. Dewhurst, 'Policing the Streets', (1990) 29 *Home Office Research Bulletin* 10. The study was based on a sample of 470 public order cases drawn from 1988 records at five stations in two police areas.

IX

Hard on the heels of these three statutes in the latter part of the 1980s came a second, and in the event third, Criminal Justice Act since the legislation introduced early in the 1986/7 session had not completed its passage through Parliament when the General Election was called in May 1987. The Criminal Justice Acts of 1987 and 1988 were workmanlike responses to an unusually large and diverse number of proposals already accepted in principle by the Government which were awaiting legislation. The original provenance of the legislation was the necessity to implement a detailed report by the Fraud Trials Committee set up under Lord Roskill's chairmanship in 1983;[130] to reform the law on extradition as forecast in a Green Paper in 1985;[131] to empower the courts to freeze and confiscate the proceeds of all forms of profitable crime; to remedy the chronic overloading of the Crown Court; and to place the criminal injuries compensation scheme on a statutory basis.[132]

The desirability of giving effect to these well-thrashed-out policies (most of which he had inherited) coalesced in Hurd's mind with what he saw as the key political themes of the day. These were: fraud, victims, juries (challenges and increasing the age limit for jurors), lenient sentences, increased severity in sentencing for crimes of violence, and confiscation of the profits of crime.

The report on fraud trials had made over one hundred recommendations, many of them requiring legislation, aimed at tackling the growing menace of large-scale fraud. The most contentious proposal, supported by a majority of the Roskill committee, was to replace jury trial in lengthy and complex fraud cases with trial by a judge and two assessors possessing business expertise. In the first volume of *Responses to Crime* the arguments for and against the right to jury trial in cases of complex fraud were rehearsed.[133] In the outcome, the proposal to abolish it was omitted from the Bill, although supported by several ministers including

---

[130] *Fraud Trials Committee Report*, HMSO, London, 1986.

[131] *Extradition* (Cmnd. 9421), HMSO, London, 1985.

[132] The Government's plans for legislation were set out in a White Paper published in Mar. 1986, *Criminal Justice: Plans for Legislation* (Cmnd. 9658), HMSO, London, 1986.

[133] pp. 90–4.

the Prime Minister and the Chancellor of the Exchequer,[134] as well
as their political advisers. It proved incapable of gaining sufficient
Parliamentary support, however, being opposed in particular by
lawyers on the Conservative back benches.

Extradition is the procedure which enables the authorities of one
state to return to the authorities of another state a person accused
or convicted of committing an offence within the jurisdiction
of that other state. The principal domestic legislation governing
extradition between the United Kingdom and foreign states was
over a century old,[135] and in two major respects was out of line
with the law of member states of the Council of Europe. First, a
request for the surrender of an alleged fugitive from justice was
admissible only if he was accused or had been convicted of one of
the 'extradition crimes' listed in the statute. This contrasted with
the more flexible approach of the European Convention on Extradition,[136] governing co-operation between most continental
members of the Council of Europe, which allows extradition for
any offence punishable under the law of both states with at
least twelve months' imprisonment. Secondly, the state seeking
extradition from the United Kingdom had to meet the same
requirement to establish a prima-facie case as the prosecution can
be required to meet in England and Wales when seeking to have a
defendant tried in the Crown Court.

For European states with fundamentally different systems of
criminal procedure and rules of evidence this requirement caused
great difficulty, resulting in some ill feeling. Between Spain and the
United Kingdom in particular, it led to a complete breakdown in
extradition arrangements for several years. In defining 'extradition
crime', the Bill adopted the same criterion as the European Convention. It also permitted the Government to dispense with the
prima-facie requirement in relation to any particular foreign state
or group of states, a proposal which was to encounter opposition
in Parliament as a diminution of the rights of fugitives at risk of
return for trial in another state. Such a dispensation was only
granted initially to states which were parties to the European
Convention.

The changes in the law on extradition made in the Criminal

---

[134] See Chapter 1.
[135] Extradition Act 1870 (c. 52).
[136] Concluded at Paris on 13 Dec. 1957.

Justice Act 1988[137] enabled the United Kingdom to ratify the Convention,[138] so promoting closer and more effective co-operation with Europe in face of the vast expansion in international crime, particularly terrorism, drug trafficking, and international fraud. Such concerns were increasingly to dominate ministerial attitudes in the future.

The legislation introduced in 1986 reflected a growing public interest in another contemporary figure on the stage of criminal justice: the victim who had suffered injury, loss, or damage as a consequence of the criminal act of another. By the late 1980s the rapid voluntary growth of victim support schemes was beginning to receive some assistance from the Home Office, supplemented by a variety of central government programmes.[139] The main source of financial recompense, however, continued to come from court orders requiring offenders to pay compensation to their victims. Under the Bill these were to be extended to include the proceeds of the sale of forfeited property which could be used to compensate victims in appropriate cases. In addition, the court would be required to give reasons for not awarding compensation, most commonly because of the offender's lack of financial resources. Irrespective of the means of the offender, the new provision was intended to ensure that the possibility of compensation was not overlooked.

Apart from the proceedings in court, victims were applying in increasing numbers for compensation from public funds under the Criminal Injuries Compensation Scheme. In 1984/5 the scheme paid

---

[137] Besides introducing a new system of extradition to foreign states, designed to replace that established in 1870, the Act amended the system of extradition to dependent territories and independent Commonwealth countries provided for in the Fugitive Offenders Act 1967 (c. 68). The first change, concerning the range of offences for which extradition could be granted, was extended to the 1967 Act, thus giving effect in United Kingdom law to a decision agreed upon in 1986 by Commonwealth Law Ministers meeting in Harare. The other change, conferring power to dispense with the prima-facie requirement, was not carried over to the Commonwealth scheme. The argument was that the concept of a prima-facie case was well understood in other Commonwealth jurisdictions, whose legal systems were mostly derived from English law, and that no general difficulties had arisen from its application to extradition within the Commonwealth.

[138] The instrument of ratification was deposited in February 1991 and took effect on 14 May 1991.

[139] The growth of victim support, and the development of public policy towards the victims of crime in England and Wales, has been charted with a wealth of detail by Paul Rock in *Helping Victims of Crime.*

over £35 million in compensation to 19,771 victims and their dependants.[140] In the next financial year the amount paid in compensation had reached £41.5 million, with the total number of applicants rising from 34,890 to 39,697, an increase of 13.8%.[141] After long arguments, the complement of staff authorized by the Home Office was increased to 218 by September 1986[142] in order to service the upsurge in new applications. The 'experimental' scheme, set up in 1964 with the consent of Parliament, but with little thought of its potential costs, had grown into an enormous undertaking. Large total amounts were being expended each year by the Criminal Injuries Compensation Board without any statutory authority.

The Home Office was uncomfortable about the propriety of this arrangement, and as early as 1983 the Government had announced its intention to place the scheme on a statutory basis as soon as a suitable opportunity occurred.[143] Legislation would bestow upon eligible applicants a right to receive compensation and confer Parliamentary authority for the expenditure incurred. The fact that Parliamentary legitimacy came at a time when a backlog had built up amounting to some 51,000 cases outstanding on 31 March 1986,[144] with costs rising seemingly irreversibly, meant that a gulf opened between the intentions of Parliament and the degree of practicability required for their bringing into force. In 1992, four years after the passing of the Criminal Justice Act 1988, and twenty-eight years after the original non-statutory scheme was introduced in 1964, the legislation putting the Criminal Injuries Compensation Scheme onto a statutory basis had still not been brought into effect.

In December 1989 the Home Secretary informed the House of Commons that to make the scheme statutory at that time would, in the opinion of the Criminal Injuries Compensation Board, 'disrupt work and add to arrears'.[145] The Government accepted that judgment. In view of the urgent need to tackle the backlog[146]

---

[140] Criminal Injuries Compensation Board, *Twenty-First Report* (Cmnd. 9684), HMSO, London, 1985, pp. 8–10.

[141] Criminal Injuries Compensation Board, *Twenty-Second Report* (Cm. 42), HMSO, London, 1986, pp. 2–7.

[142] *Parl. Debates*, HC, 106 (6th ser.), col. WA 714, 4 Dec. 1986.

[143] *Parl. Debates*, HL, 446 (5th ser.), col. 308, 14 Dec. 1983.

[144] *Twenty-Second Report*, p. 2.

[145] *Parl. Debates*, HC, 163 (6th ser.), col. WA 411, 8 Dec. 1989.

[146] During the year ended 31 Mar. 1991 the Criminal Injuries Compensation

and improve the Board's service to present and future claimants, the scheme would not yet be made statutory. Instead, changes would be introduced into the non-statutory scheme so as to 'streamline' it. A revised scheme came into effect on 1 February 1990.

Since then, criminal injuries compensation has been investigated by the House of Commons Select Committee on Home Affairs and by a review team drawn from the Home Office, the Treasury, and a private firm of management consultants. The Commons Select Committee reported that 'a dismal picture of under-resourcing' emerged from the evidence. It was particularly critical of the delays, commenting that the 'scandalous backlog' which had built up meant that a system designed to help victims was instead frustrating them.[147] The review team raised some fundamental questions about the scheme, both as it is and as it would be if made statutory as Parliament intended. These included whether the provision for rights of appeal is over-elaborate; whether lower-level awards might be banded in order to simplify and speed up the process of dealing with claims; and whether the whole scheme might be contracted out to the insurance industry, or combined in a public/private sector partnership, for example with the Motor Insurers' Bureau or the industrial injuries system.[148]

By mid-1992 the prospect of bringing into force the statutory authority for payments made by the Criminal Injuries Compensation Board which had been conferred by the Criminal Justice Act 1988 was as remote as ever. The size of the backlog and the

Board increased its productivity, resolving 53,384 cases, 38% more than in the previous year. For the first time in ten years the number of cases resolved exceeded the number of new applications, so reducing the backlog of applications awaiting action which had reached a high point of 87,000 by the end of 1989/90. The total amount paid in compensation from the introduction of the scheme on 1 Aug. 1964 until 31 Mar. 1991 was £613,584,928. Over the same period the total number of applications was 603,043, of which 507,390 had been resolved. Criminal Injuries Compensation Board, *Twenty-Seventh Report* (Cm. 1782), HMSO, London, 1991, pp. 1–4. In 1991/2, the Board resolved 60,113 cases, 12.6% more than in 1990/1. But the number of applications received went up to 61,400, an increase of 22% over the previous year. (Letter from the Director, Criminal Injuries Compensation Board, 8 June 1992).

[147] House of Commons, Session 1989/90, Home Affairs Committee, Second Report, *Compensating Victims Quickly: The Administration of the Criminal Injuries Compensation Board* (HC 92), HMSO, London, 1990, pp. vii and xvi.

[148] Home Office Management Advisory Services with Capita Management Consultancy, *Management Review of the Criminal Injuries Compensation Board*, June 1991.

high overall cost of compensating victims of crime continued to dominate the minds of ministers and civil servants, not least in the Treasury. A move away from the link with common law damages towards a fixed tariff structure of payments was forecast, but it was not anticipated that this or any other new arrangements would begin to operate before 1994.

As with earlier criminal justice legislation, the 1987 Bill contained further provisions for the treatment of young offenders. At long last detention centre orders and sentences of youth custody were to be amalgamated into a single custodial sentence of detention in a young offender institution for males aged fourteen to twenty and females aged fifteen to twenty. Once the Act came into force, separate detention centres ceased to exist. Few mourned their passing.

With the exception of children and young persons sentenced to detention under Section 53 of the Children and Young Persons Act 1933 for murder or manslaughter or certain other grave crimes, the only custodial sentence which a court would be able to pass on convicted persons under the age of twenty-one was the new sentence of detention in a young offender institution or, if the offence was one for which an adult would be liable to a maximum or mandatory penalty of life imprisonment, custody for life. The length of the sentence of detention was to be limited in the case of offenders under the age of seventeen, and revised criteria were set out which had to be satisfied before a sentence of detention was imposed on a young offender. The criteria clarified and strengthened the restrictions on the use of custody contained in the 1982 Act, adding a duty for the Crown Court or Magistrates' court when passing a sentence of detention to state in open court that it is satisfied a young offender qualified for a custodial sentence, and to explain in ordinary language why it is passing a custodial sentence on him.

The Parliamentary pressure group which had been instrumental in accomplishing the adoption of statutory criteria in 1982 had remained active. In 1985 PAPPAG brought out a consultative paper outlining some possible ways of strengthening the criteria[149] and sent it to organizations in the criminal justice arena for comment. As a result of this exercise the Group drafted a Criminal

[149] Parliamentary All-Party Penal Affairs Group, *Statutory Restrictions on the Use of Custody for Young Offenders: A Consultative Paper*, Dec. 1985.

Justice (Amendment) Bill which was introduced in the Lords in 1986 as a Private Member's Bill by Lord Silkin of Dulwich. It received a formal First Reading, but proceeded no further.[150] When the 1987 Criminal Justice Bill was introduced into Parliament, the Group discussed its proposals for tighter criteria with David Mellor, then a Home Office minister,[151] and officials. The minister said the Government would be willing to consider an amendment to this end. No member of PAPPAG's Executive Committee was on the House of Commons Standing Committee on the Bill, but Home Office officials informally indicated that ministers would be likely to accept the All-Party Group's amendment if the Opposition tabled it. This was duly arranged.

Clive Soley, a Labour MP and ex-senior probation officer, who had been a member of PAPPAG before he took on front-bench responsibilities, agreed to put down the amendment. On 10 March 1987 he moved a comprehensive new clause setting out the restrictions on the custody and detention of persons under twenty-one, including the giving of reasons when a court sentenced a young person to custody. Replying for the Government, the Parliamentary Under-Secretary, Douglas Hogg,[152] accepted the desirability of tightening the criteria that should apply when making custody orders for young people. He was uneasy about the wording of the proposed new clause, and undertook to revise the drafting and come back on Report with an amendment satisfactory both to the Opposition and the Government.[153]

In its original form the 1986/7 Bill ran to 128 clauses and 10 schedules, being the first in the post-1945 series of Criminal Justice Bills to start its passage through Parliament with more than one hundred clauses. In the early summer of 1987, having completed its passage through the Commons, the Bill was still undergoing scrutiny in the Lords when the calling of a General Election

---

[150] Parliamentary All-Party Penal Affairs Group, *The Case for the Criminal Justice (Amendment) Bill*, Oct. 1986.

[151] Parliamentary Under-Secretary of State, Home Office, 1983–6. Minister of State: Home Office, 1986–7; Foreign and Commonwealth Office, 1987–8; Department of Health, 1988–9; Home Office, 1989–90. Minister for the Arts, 1990; Chief Secretary to the Treasury, 1990–2. Secretary of State for National Heritage, 1992.

[152] Parliamentary Under-Secretary of State, Home Office, 1986–9. Minister of State: Department of Trade and Industry, 1989–90; Foreign and Commonwealth Office, 1990– .

[153] *Parl. Debates* (HC), SC (1986–7), III, col. 1000, 10 Mar. 1987.

terminated the life of the Parliament. By agreement between the parties, the early clauses covering the setting up of a Serious Fraud Office, the transfer of complex cases of fraud direct to the jurisdiction of the Crown Court without the need for committal proceedings, and a system of formal preparatory hearings which were to be part of the trial before the jury was sworn, were completed before the dissolution of Parliament on 18 May 1987. All the other clauses were negatived on Government amendments, leaving Part I of the Bill to be enacted as the Criminal Justice Act 1987.

The remaining parts were reintroduced in the Lords shortly after the Election. In the interim, the revised restrictions on the custody and detention of young offenders were reworded by Government draftsmen. Home Office officials had consulted the Clerk to PAPPAG, Paul Cavadino, over this further version and the criteria as redrafted were included in the Bill when it came back to Parliament. An editorial in the journal *Justice of the Peace* welcomed the clause as 'a much clearer, emphatic and structured approach to the task in hand—and one which we would guess courts would find easier to operate'.[154] The Committee and Report stages followed in November, and early in 1988 the Bill returned to the Commons for the second time. After some further consideration, the Criminal Justice Act eventually reached the statute book in July. Thus for twenty months, a much longer span than usual, Parliamentary opportunities existed to legislate on criminal justice issues. Full advantage was taken of the protracted timetable to amend or add to the Bill's original contents. While the endorsement and extension of the principle of restricting custody for young offenders was the most important of the Act's sentencing provisions, it was not widely publicized. Controversy centred around jury challenges,[155] lenient sentences, and, as a foretaste of events that were to surface so dramatically before the Parliament was out, compensation for miscarriages of justice.

[154] 3 Oct. 1987.
[155] Section 118 of the Criminal Justice Act 1988 abolished the right to challenge jurors without cause in proceedings for the trial of a person on indictment. Section 119 extended the qualification for jury service from the age of sixty-five to seventy.

X

Apart from the accretions which were added as the legislation wound its way through two successive sessions of Parliament,[156] several large and important issues raised in the debates were left to one side. The main reason for their omission was the very bulk of the Bill. Unlike the previous Criminal Justice Bills since the Second World War, the 1986–8 legislation was not concerned primarily with sentencing policy and the treatment of offenders. It would have been difficult, indeed probably not possible, for the Government to have embodied its still inchoate policies towards the sentencing of adult offenders in the original Bill, even if ministers' thoughts had taken sufficient shape to enable them to be translated into instructions to draftsmen. An additional reason, in the opinion of the Home Secretary, Douglas Hurd, and his official advisers, was that several of the most awkward issues called for further study.

This was no temporizing tactic to catch a more favourable political wind, but a recognition of the depth of some of the subjects and their practical significance to the operation of criminal justice. The parole system, under review by Lord Carlisle's committee since 1987, handled 23,778 cases in that year.[157] The uncertain state of the law on murder, which had been reviewed by the Criminal Law Revision Committee[158] and the Law Commission,[159] was included in the remit of a House of Lords Select Committee appointed after debates on the penalty for murder and life sentences during the passage of the 1987 Bill. The Select Committee on Murder and

---

[156] Obligations incurred under international treaties were honoured in Section 134 of the Criminal Justice Act 1988 which created a new criminal offence of torture. New clauses were introduced at Report Stage in the House of Commons after the Government had agreed to consider amendments proposed by an Opposition spokesman, Peter Archer, a former Solicitor General, to enable ratification of the United Nations Convention against Torture and other Cruel, Inhuman, or Degrading Treatment or Punishment to which the UK was a signatory. Although the UK was already a party to the European Convention on Human Rights, Article 3 of which prohibited torture, the UN Convention required every signatory to ensure that all acts falling within the wide definition of torture contained in the Convention, committed anywhere in the world, were punishable as criminal offences under its law.

[157] *The Parole System in England and Wales*, p. 40.

[158] *Offences against the Person*, Fourteenth Report of the Criminal Law Revision Committee (Cmnd. 7844), HMSO, London, 1980.

[159] *A Criminal Code for England and Wales*: Draft Criminal Code Bill and Commentary, Law Com., No. 177, 1989.

Life Imprisonment reported after a very full Parliamentary inquiry, extending to Scotland as well as England and Wales, in the session 1988/9.[160] Its impact on the 1990/1 legislation is discussed in Chapter 9.

Hurd himself took the initiative in raising the issue of the right of silence in a lecture to the Police Foundation in July 1987. The reaction from the police organizations was favourable, as he had anticipated it would be, but the legal profession was generally cool. In deciding to revive the debate on what he knew was a sensitive subject Hurd had been influenced by the view of the Association of Chief Police Officers that the implementation of the recommendations of the Royal Commission on Criminal Procedure in the Police and Criminal Evidence Act 1984 had tilted the balance too far in favour of the suspect and against the police. Accordingly in May 1988 he set up a working group under the chairmanship of Bill Bohan:

There has been a lively debate, and I have listened carefully to the arguments for and against change. I am not convinced that the protection which the law now gives to the accused person who ambushes the prosecution can be justified. The case for change is strong. But I am persuaded by some of the comments which have been made that more careful work needs to be done before we can bring forward with confidence a specific proposal for legislation. I do not see the Criminal Justice Bill, which is already long and detailed, as the right vehicle for such a proposal.[161]

The terrain was not unfamiliar having already been traversed by the Criminal Law Revision Committee in 1972,[162] as well as by the Royal Commission on Criminal Procedure later in the decade. The working group, which included representatives of the legal profession, the Crown Prosecution Service, and the police, was conscious of the lack of authoritative research data, an essential preliminary to an inquiry where each of the directly involved parties, the police and the suspects, had a strong vested interest. Although the deadline for reporting precluded the working group from commissioning any research itself, the Home Office Research Department sponsored some research at the University of Kent

[160] HL Paper 78-I, Session 1988–9, HMSO, London, 1989.
[161] *Parl. Debates*, HC, 133 (6th ser.), col. WA 466, 18 May 1988.
[162] *Eleventh Report: Evidence (General)* (Cmnd. 4991), HMSO, London, 1972.

into police interviewing techniques in cases where suspects exercised their right of silence, and the outcome in court.[163]

Well before the results became known the political mood was changing. Hurd was soon to move on to the Foreign Office, but his initiative already had been overtaken by events: the unexpected incidents which make a Home Secretary's ministerial life so unpredictable. By the time the working group reported in July 1989,[164] mounting public agitation was matched by private unease about the lawfulness of the convictions of the Guildford Four.[165] No Home Secretary would have felt confident about going ahead with measures to strengthen the hands of the police and prosecution in questioning suspects at such a time.

The right of silence thus merged with the wider, and acutely disturbing, topic of miscarriages of justice. Eighteen months later, in a statement on the setting up of a Royal Commission to review all stages in the criminal process, made in the House of Commons on the same day as the Court of Appeal's decision to quash the convictions of six men for murder following bomb explosions at a Birmingham public house in November 1974, Kenneth Baker confirmed that the review would include 'the place of the right to silence in criminal proceedings'.[166]

Another issue that had been held over was the giving of evidence by children in criminal proceedings. The 1988 Act had contained a provision enabling the evidence of child witnesses in cases of violent or sexual offences to be given via a live video link.[167] Within the Home Office the first move had come from Hurd's political adviser, Edward Bickham, who had seen in the Roskill Committee's recommendation for overseas evidence in fraud trials to be given through live television links a precedent to extend a similar facility

---

[163] The findings were due to be published in 1992 under the title 'The Incidence, Antecedents and Consequences of Suspects' Use of the Right to Silence' in the journal *Criminal Behaviour and Mental Health*.

[164] Home Office, *Report of the Working Group on the Right of Silence*, 13 July 1989.

[165] Their convictions were quashed three months later by the Court of Appeal in October 1989.

[166] *Parl. Debates*, HC, 187 (6th ser.), col. 1110, 14 Mar. 1991.

[167] Section 32 of the Criminal Justice Act 1988 enabled a witness under the age of fourteen, with the leave of the court, to give evidence through a live television link on a trial on indictment or an appeal to the Criminal Division of the Court of Appeal where the offence charged is one of a number of specified assaults or cruelty or sexual offences.

to relieve child victims from the harrowing experience of giving evidence in the courtroom. Reconciling the interests of child victims or witnesses with the legitimate rights of an accused person to question evidence brought against him was appallingly difficult, and the Government had resisted pressure to go further and allow video recordings of pre-trial interviews with children to be made admissible in evidence.

This vexed question was passed to an advisory group including representatives of the police, social services, and the Bar under the chairmanship of the Common Serjeant of London, Judge Pigot. In December 1989 the group recommended that video-recorded interviews with children under the age of fourteen should be admissible as evidence in Crown Court trials for violent and sexual offences and offences of cruelty and neglect, and at comparable trials in the juvenile courts. Where the offence charged was of a sexual nature the provision should extend to child witnesses under the age of seventeen. Interviews should be conducted in accordance with a statutory code of practice, and the judge should be required to take account of the code of practice when deciding whether to admit a video recording in evidence.[168]

Still in the distance, storm clouds were gathering over the most divisive of all non-party political issues: whether or not it was right to pursue the prosecution of war crimes alleged to have been committed by men who had since become British citizens or who had taken up residence in the United Kingdom. In such cases, prosecution would not be possible without fresh legislation. The Government decided that there ought first to be an inquiry to ascertain the number of cases likely to arise, and to find out whether there would be sufficient evidence to support prosecutions if the law were changed. This delicate task was undertaken with impartiality and thoroughness by Sir Thomas Hetherington (a former Director of Public Prosecutions) and William Chalmers (formerly Crown Agent for Scotland). Their report was published in July 1989,[169] and led to a breach between the two Houses of Parliament when the resulting Bill was twice rejected by the Lords having been twice passed by the Commons. For the first time since 1949 the

---

[168] Home Office, *Report of the Advisory Group on Video Evidence*, Dec. 1989, p. 69.

[169] *War Crimes*, Report of the War Crimes Inquiry (Cm. 744), HMSO, London, 1989.

procedure contained in the Parliament Acts of 1911 and 1949 was invoked, and the measure submitted for the Royal Assent without the consent of one of the Houses of Parliament.

XI

By the late 1980s numerous criminal justice issues, some of them pregnant with controversy, were crowding around the Home Secretary. Even before the extended legislation of 1986–8 had been completed, the cycle was moving forward again, gathering momentum in the accumulation of fresh topics. The years of Conservative ascendancy from 1979 to 1988 had been marked by a formidable programme of law-making. Three Criminal Justice Acts, as well as the Police and Criminal Evidence Act 1984, the Prosecution of Offences Act 1985, and the Public Order Act 1986, had been supplemented by laws on drug trafficking and firearms. The Repatriation of Prisoners Act 1984 had enabled prisoners from the United Kingdom who were convicted abroad to be returned voluntarily to serve their sentences in this country. The Advisory Council on the Penal System had been wound up, while the Judicial Studies Board developed into a new, if narrowly channelled, fount of influence.

Ceaseless activity, however, does not result in a broadening of vision; indeed the opposite is more likely to occur. The pace had to slow down. A pause was needed for reflection and digestion. Above all, an opportunity had to be found to make a penetrating, unprejudiced, and sustained effort to get to grips with the thirty-year rise in crime which, in common with most other countries in Western Europe, continued to disfigure British society and diminish the way of life of so many of its citizens.

In the making of policy it is always as well to recognize the truism that institutions come to have lives of their own and nowhere is this more evident than in criminal justice. The criminal law and its machinery for enforcement: the judicature, the courts, the police, the prisons, and the Probation Service, all stand as monuments to successive attempts to counter offending. Without them, we have come to believe, no orderly and civilized society would be sustainable. Nevertheless their presence does not imply solutions; indeed too great an emphasis on legislation, and the functions and procedures of institutions, can divert concentration from objectives and the results of the policies that have been pursued. Some of the institutions had been subjected to critical scrutiny and change in the 1980s. A new Crown Prosecution Service had come into being, and fetters, as they were seen by many policemen, had been placed on the police in the gathering of evidence and the questioning of suspects as a result of the Police and Criminal Evidence Act 1984. The Public Order Act 1986 may have coincided with deeper forces already present in society, but by the end of the decade the tumultuous riots and street disturbances which had reached their zenith at Brixton and Toxteth had not been replicated. Yet the most intractable inheritance from the past remained virtually untouched.

The habitual focus on the prisons, and the urgent necessity to improve the disgraceful conditions which persisted in them, had distracted attention away from imprisonment. The belief that imprisonment was the proper penalty for all save the most minor or out-of-character criminal offences remained deeply embedded in the penal culture. The burden of Lane's judgments in *Upton* and *Bibi* was not repeated in subsequent cases coming before the Court of Appeal, and had no lasting effect on sentencing practice. As the 1980s progressed, so did the average length of sentence passed on adult males by the Crown Court increase.[170]

In 1982 a small, and at the time almost unnoticed by the general public, adjustment had been made in the relationship between young offenders, statute law, and the sentencing courts. The change had been perpetuated, accepted and refined by the judiciary, consolidated and extended by Parliament in 1988, again with a minimum of public attention. Was this the way forward? Could a similar policy, handled with care, reach out to embrace the generality of adult offenders?

---

[170] The average length of sentence imposed on adult males by the Crown Court, which had risen from 16.6 months in 1984 to 18.8 months in 1988, rose to 19.7 months in 1989. Also significant was the increase in the proportion of offenders sentenced for indictable crimes in the Crown Court instead of the Magistrates' courts from 20% in 1985 to 25% in 1988 and 1989. Home Office, *Statistical Bulletin*, 20/90.

5

The Quest: Punishment in the Community, 1987–90

The man and the moment came together in the aftermath of the General Election in June 1987. While the interrupted Criminal Justice Bill resumed its progress towards the statute book; while the committees and inquiries listed in the last chapter were busy garnering evidence; the Home Secretary stood back and took stock.

Douglas Hurd had already been Home Secretary for nearly two years. Coming to the Home Office from the thankless assignment of Northern Ireland Secretary, his first Cabinet post, he had spent fifteen months' apprenticeship as a Minister of State at the Home Office between 1983 and 1984. With the uncertainties of the General Election and the formation of the new Government behind him, it was a pensive man who returned to his room in Queen Anne's Gate on 11 June to study the comprehensive brief drawn up by the Permanent Under-Secretary for incoming ministers after each Election.

By now Hurd had got a feel for the ways of the great department of state which he headed. He knew that a Home Secretary who displayed a sure touch, with the capacity to make decisions that were well thought-out, fair, and defensible, could earn a reputation with his officials inside the department, and his ministerial colleagues outside it, that would enable him to use his political skill to achieve something of enduring worth. The confidence of colleagues elsewhere in the Government is especially important for a Home Secretary, as most of the policies he promotes in their name owe more to his judgment or departmental advice than to collective decisions of the Cabinet or its Committees. Amongst the Conservative MPs in the House of Commons too, who had imposed such limitations on Whitelaw's scope for action, Hurd had built up a reputation as a safe pair of hands.

Cautious and pragmatic rather than visionary in outlook, but aware of the dangers of floating on the tide, Hurd, like Butler and Jenkins before him, had a gift for spotting openings. He perceived that moments came and went when, with skill and determination, the bounds of what was possible politically could be expanded to the public benefit and the advantage of the Government. There is an adage in the Home Office that after a General Election changes in ministerial personalities can be just as significant as changes between the parties in power. A minister who is re-appointed, returning with enhanced reputation and authority, is in the optimum situation to get things done if he knows what he wants to do.

In 1987 Hurd sensed that the time was ripe to draw together several strands of policy, weaving them into a coherent pattern and projecting them as a whole. Twenty years before Jenkins had approached the 1967 Criminal Justice Act in the same spirit. Although lip service was paid to the interdependence of the four cornerstones of criminal justice—the courts, the prisons, the police, and the Probation Service, there was still a long way to go towards the development of co-ordinated action in the pursuit of common objectives and monitoring how far the objectives were being achieved in practice. Leon Brittan had fostered the idea of a more systematic and better managed structure for criminal justice, capable of responding to strategic planning, and it was one which appealed to the orderly and rational side of Hurd's nature. Moreover it was consistent with Government policies elsewhere in Whitehall and accorded with the ethos of the Financial Management Initiative.[1]

Yet the Home Secretary's insight extended beyond the organizational import. Hurd saw in the creation of a system of criminal justice, however loosely structured, an opportunity to move away from the single issue narrowness embedded at the heart of the penal

[1] The Financial Management Initiative was launched in May 1982 and announced in Cmnd. 8616 (*Government Observations on the Third Report from the Treasury and Civil Service Select Committee*, Session 1981–2, HC 236). Its purpose was 'to improve the allocation, management and control of resources throughout central government', see *Financial Management in Government Departments* (Cmnd. 9058), para. 2. Each Department was required to draw up, implement, and keep under review a plan for making managers at all levels responsible for control of the resources they consumed and for the results they achieved. Important elements in such a plan were a detailed financial information system and, where practicable, the development of performance indicators and output measures.

system and implicit in its description. While recognizing the power and responsibility of the state to discipline and punish those who had committed criminal offences, to the current occupant of the Home Secretary's room it was as important to reduce crime as it was to punish the offenders. In the Election campaign, for instance, Hurd personally had insisted that crime prevention and better provision for victims had a place in the Conservative manifesto.[2]

After the Election the Home Office ministerial team was strengthened by a new, and at first reluctant, recruit. John Patten, aged forty-one, was previously Minister of State for Housing, Urban Affairs, and Construction. In that office he had been marked as a rising star with ample Parliamentary and public exposure. A sideways move to the Home Office as Minister of State was not the promotion he had hoped for. It came about as a consequence of a proposal, formulated before the outcome of the Election was known, as part of the departmental submission for the next administration making the case for a new portfolio at Minister of State level, answerable to the Home Secretary for crime prevention, victims of crime, criminal justice policy, and race relations. A minister with imagination and presentational skills was called for who, without the burden of detailed responsibility for prisons, the police or immigration, the three most time-consuming and arduous of Home Office departments, would be able to concentrate single-mindedly on the development and promotion of policies designed to make a dent in the seemingly intractable problems of ever-rising crime rates and how best to counter them. Energetic and persuasive, it was a commission for which Patten was ideally equipped. Little time elapsed before he was firmly established as the Home Secretary's lieutenant on all matters concerning criminal policy.

Patten's tenure was prolonged beyond that of many Ministers of State, remaining as he did at his post after Hurd moved to the Foreign Office in October 1989. Ultimately he was the only one of the original group of ministers and senior officials to survive from the pre-legislative stages in 1987 until the Bill introduced in November 1990 reached the statute book in July of the following year as the Criminal Justice Act 1991. So engrossed had he become

[2] Douglas Hurd had chaired a study group from which the manifesto commitments on freedom, law, and responsibility had emanated.

with the task, that the quondam reluctant minister was believed to have resisted more than one opportunity for a change of scene, until finally obtaining Cabinet Office as Secretary of State for Education after the General Election in April 1992.

The Permanent Under-Secretary of State, Sir Brian Cubbon, having seen many earlier policies blighted in the course of a lengthy career at the Home Office and Northern Ireland Office, was nearing retirement.[3] Although his immediate subordinates did not find him an easy man to work with, there was no slackening with Cubbon keeping a particularly watchful eye on any matter affecting the prisons. His main interest in this period was inculcating an integrated view of the criminal justice system, extending beyond the Home Office and trying to raise its sights above the level of crisis management. Trevelyan's successor as Director General of the Prison Service, Christopher Train,[4] had his hands full coping with recurrent and often acute crises in the prisons, at the same time as implementing the May reforms and pushing forward the slow-moving building programme.

The senior official working directly with Hurd and Patten on the construction of new policies for criminal justice was David Faulkner, the Deputy Under-Secretary of State in charge of the Criminal and Statistical Departments, and the Research and Planning Unit. He too was the right man in the right place at the right time. Well experienced in penal matters and with a subtle intelligence, Faulkner was exceptional in his clarity of vision and openness to outside opinion. Three Assistant Under-Secretaries answered to him. Michael Head was in charge of the Criminal Justice and Constitutional Department, on the criminal justice side dealing with Magistrates' courts, bail, and probation; Bill Bohan headed the Criminal Policy Department overseeing the sentencing powers of the courts, penalties, criminal law and procedure, and Prerogative of Mercy, the treatment and release of mentally disordered offenders, the control of drug misuse, and the preparation of legislation; and Dr Rita Maurice, a professional statistician, was in

[3] Cubbon was Permanent Under-Secretary of State at the Home Office, 1979–88, holding the same appointment at the Northern Ireland Office, 1976–9. He was injured in the same bomb blast which killed the British Ambassador to the Republic of Ireland, Christopher Ewart-Biggs, in 1976.

[4] Deputy Under-Secretary of State, Home Office, and Director General of the Prison Service, 1983–91. Secretary, Royal Commission on Criminal Procedure, 1978–80; Assistant Under-Secretary of State, Home Office, 1980–3.

charge of the Statistical Department. The Head of the Research and Planning Unit, Mary Tuck, was also influential, externally as well as inside the Home Office, being particularly effective with the Right-wing think-tanks. Within the public service, Faulkner was the main point of contact with the higher judiciary, the Lord Chancellor's Department, the Law Officers' Department and the Crown Prosecution Service.

In the week after the General Election (but arranged before it) a dozen or so Home Office staff assembled on a cold midsummer day for a two-day seminar at the Ship Hotel, Brighton, under Faulkner's chairmanship. Unusually, the Home Secretary's Special Adviser, Edward Bickham, had been invited to attend for part of the meeting. Following a review of progress in the main areas of policy, two projects were selected for further work and submission to ministers. The titles chosen were Safer Cities and Action for Youth. The Safer Cities programme, although devised before it, was held back for some weeks in order to be absorbed into a wider governmental initiative, known as Action for Cities, in which the activities of various ministries were brought together with the aim of reversing social and economic decline and strengthening regeneration in some of the most hard-pressed urban areas.

While maintaining a place on the Home Office agenda of steps to reduce crime, overall responsibility for community development was keenly contested by the two lead departments: the Department of the Environment and the Department of Trade and Industry. The more nebulous Action for Youth never came to anything, partly due to a lack of interdepartmental commitment. It had two main aspects: encouragement and opportunities for young people generally (education, training, employment, the Youth Service); and community-based measures, related to those opportunities, specifically aimed at young people in trouble. The second aspect was diverted into the development of the White Paper which preceded the 1990/1 legislation, and the changes in the Probation Service. The first, so far as it bore on Home Office interests, was left on the shelf for some time to come.

A parallel development, with party political implications, was crime prevention, particularly precautions against domestic theft or break in. Whereas most forms of police activity contribute to crime prevention in its broadest sense, policing had been augmented by a spontaneous expansion in the number of locally based neighbourhood watch schemes.[5] Despite some reservations on the part of the police, and a lack of conclusive research findings on its effectiveness, neighbourhood watch touched a responsive nerve in many localities. Over the five years between 1982 and 1987 the total number of schemes multiplied rapidly, with little official encouragement, to reach an estimated 43,000 schemes covering some two million households by the end of October 1987.[6] The Conservative election manifesto had fastened on to this striking manifestation of self-help stating: 'We are committed to the success of this popular anti-crime movement. We will build on the support of the public by establishing a national organization to promote the best practices in local crime prevention initiatives.'[7]

One of the few Conservative Members of Parliament to lose his seat at the General Election in 1987 was Steven Norris, defeated at Oxford East but soon to be returned at a by-election at Epping Forest. He was brought into the Home Office as an adviser by Hurd, at the suggestion of Patten, shortly after his electoral setback to design a new organization and consider how best it might be fitted into the bureaucracy. Norris was joined by David Birley, seconded to the Home Office from the NACRO Crime Prevention Unit, and together they worked on a report to implement the manifesto commitment. Although the Home Secretary at first inclined towards a loose federation of voluntary organizations aided by central government funding on the model of the National Association of Victim Support Schemes, other ideas under consideration included a national agency or some form of charitable organization.

[5] For an account of the origins of neighbourhood watch, and a review of situational crime prevention and other strategies to reduce crime, see Chapter 9 on 'Prevention and Crime Reduction' in *Responses to Crime*, vol. 1, pp. 286–313.

[6] Three years later, the total number of neighbourhood watch schemes had almost doubled to an estimated 85,000 schemes, covering approximately one household in every six (David Waddington speaking at a Crime Concern Conference in London on 18 Oct. 1990). Estimates of the number of schemes in England and Wales are compiled by the Home Office from data provided by the police. Although some may be defunct and others existed only on paper, the validity of the estimates has been broadly corroborated by research. The third British Crime Survey in 1988 found that only 4% of schemes could be classified as inactive, while the findings of another survey published in the same year identified very few schemes that had been discontinued. See P. Mayhew, D. Elliott, and L. Dowds, *The 1988 British Crime Survey*, Home Office Research Study No. 111, HMSO, London, 1989, p. 55; and M. S. Husain, *Neighbourhood Watch in England and Wales: A Locational Analysis*, Crime Prevention Unit Paper No. 12, Home Office, London, 1988.

[7] *The Next Moves Forward*, The Conservative Manifesto, 1987, p. 58.

Ministerial solicitude towards crime prevention, initially inspired by the phenomenal popular appeal of neighbourhood watch, led them to take a more analytical interest in the roots of crime: the physical conditions and management of problem housing estates; the criminality fostered by youth delinquency, drugs, and alcohol abuse;[8] and relationships within the family or other social groups. Such approaches were more questioning and less assertive than other politically inspired policies had been in the past,[9] and were underpinned by the empirical research on situational crime prevention which had been pioneered within the Home Office Research and Planning Unit. So by the time the Home Secretary decided to convene a strategy seminar of ministers and officials in the autumn of 1987 most of the spadework had been done. The political soil was ready for sowing.

II

The one-day seminar which took place on 28 September at Leeds Castle in Kent was not a starting-point. Rather it confirmed and strengthened a number of existing policies and trends, crystallizing others that were still in the pre-formative stages. None the less, the meeting soon came to be recognized as a milestone in the development of policies that had been consciously designed as part of a system of criminal justice, rather than a random collection of timely proposals for change.

Those attending were entirely from the Home Office. Hurd was in the chair throughout, accompanied by his four junior ministers: John Patten, the Earl of Caithness (responsible for the Prison Department), Timothy Renton (responsible for broadcasting policy and immigration), and Douglas Hogg (responsible for the police and for measures against drug misuse). Cubbon was supported by all six Deputy Secretaries, including Faulkner (Criminal Departments), Train (Prison Service), John Chilcot (Police), and the Legal Adviser, James Nursaw. Another Deputy Secretary, Michael Moriarty, Prin-

[8] See *Responses to Crime*, vol. 1, Chapter 6 on 'Youth, Delinquency, and Drugs', pp. 176–210.

[9] For example, the unsuccessful experiment with tougher regimes in detention centres as a result of the Conservative manifesto commitment in the 1979 General Election which is described in Chapter 4.

Punishment in the Community

cipal Establishment Officer since 1984, had much experience of the
subjects under review having previously been Head of the Home
Office Crime Planning Unit and in charge of the Criminal Policy
Department.[10] The Principal Finance Officer attended, so did
Bickham, with Norris taking part in the discussion on crime
prevention. The Principal Private Secretary and the Private Secretaries to the other ministers were present, as was Mary Tuck
from the Research and Planning Unit.

Crime prevention was the first of three main themes discussed.
The priority was seen as motivating a greater public involvement
by means of enhanced publicity to reinforce the work of the
Standing Conference on Crime Prevention[11] and of the Ministerial
Group.[12] Besides highlighting good practice and disseminating information on the diversity of preventive measures, publicity, it was
claimed, served to build confidence and generate a more receptive

[10] M. J. Moriarty had represented the UK Government on the Council of Europe
Committee on Crime Problems 1976–9, acting as chairman of the Committee in
1978/9. His valuable analysis of how the policy-making process was seen from the
Home Office, published by the Cambridge Institute of Criminology in 1977, is
referred to in Chapter 3.
[11] The Home Office Standing Conference on Crime Prevention is a national forum
which since 1985 has been chaired by a Home Office minister. It comprised
some forty numbers drawn from Government Departments, the local authority
associations, the insurance industry, the private security industry, the voluntary
sector, commerce, and the police. Through its working groups the Standing Conference makes recommendations to government, police, trade and industry, or other
interested groups.
[12] The Ministerial Group on Crime Prevention was established in March 1986
when the Prime Minister and the Home Secretary chaired two seminars on crime
prevention at 10 Downing Street. Its terms of reference were:

> to carry forward the Government's strategy for preventing crime and the fear of
> crime by reducing opportunities that exist for crime to occur, and to create
> confidence within the community that crime can be reduced, having particular
> regard to:
> (i) developing proposals for the more effective implementation of that strategy;
>   and
> (ii) the arrangements within and outside of government for the co-ordination,
>   development, and implementation of initiatives.

Twelve Government Departments were represented on the Group at ministerial and
official level. Before the 1987 General Election they were: Home Office, Scottish
Office, Northern Ireland Office, Welsh Office, Department of the Environment,
Department of Employment, Department of Health and Social Security, Department
of Education and Science, Department of Trade and Industry, Department of
Transport, Department of Energy, and the Treasury. The Group keeps in close
touch with the Association of Chief Police Officers. In June 1987, Patten took over
the chairmanship.

climate for all those (including the police) who were working to develop crime prevention at local level. A national publicity campaign, costing approximately £10 million over three years, with complementary handbook and circular, would concentrate upon successes and opportunities.

Important as publicity was, it had to be supported by action at the grass roots if the incidence of crime was actually to be reduced. The rationale of the Safer Cities programme depended upon local initiatives, and the implementation of local initiatives necessitated devising new administrative procedures. The shape these took was determined largely by the deterioration which had occurred in the relations between central and local government throughout the 1980s. In earlier, less confrontational, times the natural course would have been to confer powers, or even impose duties, on local authorities by statutory provision. No doubt such provisions would have been carefully framed so as not to encroach on the functions of Chief Constables who, like the local authorities, would have been consulted in advance.

The thrust of the Action for Cities initiative, which was announced by the Prime Minister personally in March 1988, was to establish a climate of enterprise in the inner cities, encouraging new businesses, and improving people's job prospects, motivation, and skills. Inner cities would be made more attractive to residents through a number of measures, including crime reduction, which aimed to render them safer and more pleasant places in which to live and work.[13] Like Action for Cities, whose enterprise orientated policies were anathema to many Labour-controlled local authorities, the less controversial Safer Cities programme followed a pattern of intervention by central government in the setting up, funding, and direct management of locally based activities. Local government in each area was subsequently involved in the crime prevention projects, but not as the primary agent.

Although the projected total of twenty urban areas, selected both because of their high crime rates and readiness to participate, was not reached until January 1991, Safer Cities extended further the action/research approach of an earlier experiment. Over an eighteen-month period demonstration projects in five towns (Bolton, Croydon, North Tyneside, Swansea, and Wellingborough) had

[13] *People in Cities*, Department of Environment, HMSO, 1990, p. 2.

tested the potential for concentrated inter-agency work in a chosen locality. Treasury expenditure was then authorized to fund sixteen Safer Cities projects for an initial period of up to three years.[14] As with the Five Towns experiment, the objective was to stimulate greater public awareness that crime, and the debilitating fear of crime, could be reduced through co-ordinated policies agreed and driven forward by local people.

In each project area locally recruited staff, led by a co-ordinator appointed by the Home Office,[15] was backed up by a steering committee representing the police, the Probation Service, and the local authority, as well as local businesses and voluntary groups. Detailed objectives were agreed and incorporated into an action plan on the basis of a localized crime profile and other surveys. Budgets were typically in the range of £250,000 p.a. In this way it was hoped to mobilize effective local action within a framework of national objectives prescribed by the Home Office. These were stated as: to reduce crime; to lessen the fear of crime; and to create safer cities within which economic enterprise and community life could flourish.[16]

The political commitment to set up some kind of national crime prevention organization was also discussed at the seminar. Norris and Birley's report was not yet complete, being received by the Home Office in November and reaching the Home Secretary, with departmental comments appended, on the 27th of the month. After Leeds Castle, Hurd kept a close eye on the work in progress, holding meetings in his room, and had no hesitation in approving

[14] Four additional areas (Derby, the London Borough of Hammersmith and Fulham, Leicester, and Middlesborough) were invited to join the Safer Cities programme in January 1991. Early in 1992, Patten announced that the sixteen original community based projects would be extended at least to March 1994, and that funding for the four more recently established projects would continue until 1995. Since the programme began more than 2,200 local crime prevention schemes had been supported financially, representing an investment of some £13.8 million. Home Office, *News Release*, 26 Feb. 1992.

[15] Co-ordinators were recruited locally from varying backgrounds including NACRO, the Probation Service, local authorities, or the police. An unforeseen difficulty in recruiting suitable staff was the main reason why most of the original projects did not get going until the late summer or autumn of 1989.

[16] For an analytical narrative on the origins, administration, and evaluation of the Safer Cities programme, see an unpublished paper by Nicholas Tilley, 'Opportunity Knocks! Crime Prevention and the Safer Cities Story', presented at the Social Policy Association Annual Conference at Nottingham University, July 1991. The Home Office published annual progress reports in 1989, 1990, and 1991.

the recommended solution. This was the most original and least interventionist of the options: the idea of setting up a charitable organization which would look to non-governmental sources for its support and, it was hoped, for the larger part of its funding. The attraction of a limited call on public expenditure and a harnessing of the private sector in the cause of crime prevention was irresistible. The title, Crime Concern was recommended in the report:

Although we use the term NCPO [National Crime Prevention Organisation] throughout this report for ease of identification, we strongly recommend that the organisation be titled

CRIME CONCERN TRUST LTD

to be promoted as

CRIME CONCERN

Response to this title has so far been excellent. It combines the central importance of tackling crime with the concept of concern by the community, professionals, officials, etc. In addition, the title fits ideally with the themes currently proposed for the National Crime Prevention Advertising Campaign.

On the financing of crime prevention, the report proposed that the new organization should:

- help match new schemes to existing statutory or voluntary sources of funding;
- stimulate the introduction of private sector sponsorship for local crime prevention initiatives;
- itself dispense 'a relatively small amount (£200,000) of pump-priming finance'.

An outline budget envisaged administration costs running at £600,000 a year. The report made no recommendation on how these costs should be met in the long term, although stating: 'It will be necessary for the Home Secretary as sponsoring Department to provide pump-priming finance for NCPO.'

Crime Concern was registered as a charity, in the form of a company limited by guarantee, with Norris as Chairman and launched in May 1988. A full-time chief executive, Nigel Whiskin, was appointed in September. The police, Probation Service, and local authorities were represented on an advisory board, together with some prominent businessmen. In discussion with the Home

Office a target was set of becoming self-financing within three years. Although the budget for raising funds for the sponsorship of specific crime prevention projects exceeded expectations, reaching £1.5 million by 1991, Crime Concern found it 'very difficult indeed to raise the core funding for its administration'.[17] Nevertheless, the fact that the Home Office continued to subsidize the costs of central administration was a tribute to what had been achieved in the formative years.

As the novelty wore off crime prevention began to change in character. Essentially defensive schemes like neighbourhood watch, often criticized for being a middle class preserve, particularly strong in the more prosperous suburban parts of the country, and making a heavy demand on police resources, were supplemented by numerous local initiatives in high-crime urban areas.[18] The stimulation of crime prevention initiatives in localities where community structures are poorly developed or have broken down has been a priority for Crime Concern. In its constant efforts to maintain the willing participation of the police, in its success in securing the active involvement of many national chains of retailers and service providers, and perhaps above all in its work with children and young people, Crime Concern has proved its worth. Although not attaining the status of an acknowledged national movement it has served a constructive purpose as a channel for the propagation of a simple message, namely that a high proportion of property crimes, especially household burglary and auto crime, can be prevented if more care is taken.

Returning to Leeds Castle, two other ideas which had been canvassed by the manifesto drafting group, the wider use of special constables and the provision of public funds for the purchase of domestic security equipment, were not pursued. The Police Federation was resolutely opposed to the expansion of special constables, and attempts to convince them of the utility of these part-time policemen to co-ordinate crime prevention (as had been done successfully in Bradford) were ineffectual. In spite of their opposition, interest was kept alive through the persistence of Douglas Hogg, the Parliamentary Under-Secretary and himself a

---

[17] Letter from Steven Norris, MP, 10 June 1991.
[18] See the Wythenshawe Crime Prevention Campaign in Manchester and other examples in S. Husain and J. Bright (eds.), *Neighbourhood Watch and the Police*, Crime Concern, Swindon, 1990.

former special constable, and revived later.[19] The proposal to make available public funds for domestic security equipment, although discussed by the Ministerial Group on Crime Prevention at various meetings between October 1986 and February 1988, foundered on the familiar rock that no Whitehall Department was ready to take the lead in funding such a scheme.

III

The severity of punishment and the reliance on imprisonment led the seminar into a consideration of sentencing policy as its second theme. Under the heading 'The Fight against Crime' the Conservative manifesto had declared:

The origins of crime lie deep in society: in families where parents do not support or control their children; in schools where discipline is poor; and in the wider world where violence is glamourised and traditional values are under attack.

Government *alone* cannot tackle such deep-rooted problems easily or quickly. But Government must give a lead: by backing, not attacking the police; by providing a tough legal framework for sentencing; by building the prisons in which to take those who pose a threat to society—and by keeping out of prison those who do not; and by encouraging local communities to prevent crime and to help the police detect it.[20]

This statement contained the kernel of the policy which was to reach its culmination in the Criminal Justice Act 1991. For years Conservative Home Secretaries from Butler onwards had advocated a dual or twin track approach to sentencing. Violent and serious crimes should be punished by the courts with appropriate severity, and Parliament invited to increase maximum penalties wherever it was necessary to demonstrate public disapprobation. Ministers pointed to the Criminal Justice Act 1988, in which maximum penalties had been increased for certain firearms offences, cruelty to children, bribery, and insider dealing. Another change categorized under the heading of severity was the procedure by which,

[19] On 2 Jan. 1991 *The Times* reported on a £1.5 million promotional campaign to increase the special constables' strength in England and Wales from 15,000 to 25,000 by 1994, coupled with a trial under which some specials would be paid between £400 and £900 a year 'as recompense for their dedication'.
[20] *The Next Moves Forward*, p. 55.

on a reference from the Attorney General, the Court of Appeal had been given power to increase the sentence passed in the Crown Court for offences triable on indictment if it was considered to have been unduly lenient. At the same time, the twin-track approach acknowledged that when dealing with less serious offences, a prison sentence could do more harm than good, particularly to first offenders or young people.

An eloquent opening paragraph of the Green Paper on *Punishment, Custody and the Community* published in the following year described the negative side of imprisonment in these terms:

for ... less serious ... offenders, a spell in custody is not the most effective punishment. Imprisonment restricts offenders' liberty, but it also reduces their responsibility; they are not required to face up to what they have done and to the effect on their victim or to make any recompense to the victim or the public. If offenders are not imprisoned, they are more likely to be able to pay compensation to their victims and to make some reparation to the community through useful unpaid work. Their liberty can be restricted without putting them behind prison walls. Moreover, if they are removed in prison from the responsibilities, problems and temptations of everyday life, they are less likely to acquire the self-discipline and self-reliance which will prevent reoffending in future. Punishment in the community would encourage offenders to grow out of crime and to develop into responsible and law abiding citizens.[21]

The problem faced by ministers in their public pronouncements throughout the 1980s had been that the tough denunciation of violent crime, and the condemnation of criminals, had overshadowed the commendation of non-custodial disposals for non-violent offenders. It was the shriller statements that had gained wider attention being seen, and sometimes intended to be seen, as the true embodiment of Tory resolve. To find ways of giving greater substance to the non-custodial track, without losing credibility with those of their supporters whose belief in punishment was unshakeable, was a quest calling for all the political dexterity of Hurd, Patten, and their advisers.

Leeds Castle provided a timely platform for a reappraisal of non-custodial penalties, attempting to relate them more closely to the ideal of punishment. Given the popular identification of punishment with imprisonment, was it possible to stiffen non-custodial options

[21] Cm. 424, HMSO, London, 1988, p. 1.

so that the aims of punishment, deterrence, and rehabilitation (to the extent that they were more than catch-phrases) were pursued not in prison but in the environment in which the offender would normally have to come to terms with every day life? The issue was more than one of political presentation, important as that was, since unless community penalties for less serious offences could be shaped in such a way as to command the confidence of the courts they would not gain wider currency.

As with many attempted reforms there was no single target-group to be persuaded, but three markedly different ones. The first was the Conservative Parliamentary Party, whose support would be needed to carry the legislation. Then came the judiciary, who would determine the use made of any additional sentencing powers conferred upon them by Parliament; and finally the Probation Service, or any substitute for it, which would be needed to supervise offenders in the community.

Bickham, who had worked with Hurd on the Home Affairs drafting group for the manifesto before the General Election, had absorbed some salutary lessons on the ineffectiveness of imprisonment to reduce the level of crime during a four-week study tour of the United States in the spring of 1987. As a result of his political contacts he believed that a majority of Conservatives were willing to accept the twin track policy, but only if they could be assured that the second track would be 'beefed up'. Crime prevention too was coming to be thought of as a dimension of criminal justice policy.[22] The Home Secretary and Patten agreed with this assessment. To follow through the decisions reached at Leeds Castle, Patten embarked on a prolonged programme of inviting back-bench Conservative MPs to working lunches at his room in the Home Office. These were intended to enable him to expound the twin-track policy and listen to reactions. For a period of just over a year, his Parliamentary Private Secretary invited groups of six to ten MPs at a time to visit the Home Office, until a total of some 150 of their party colleagues had contributed to the policy-making process.

At these meetings the Minister of State's stance was tentative and open-minded, indicating that he was trying out ideas while they were still in the formative stages. When the proposals were

[22] Letter from Edward Bickham, 9 Jan. 1990.

made public, there was widespread support on the Conservative benches, primarily because so many people felt that they had been part of the sequence which had led to their formulation.[23] In contrast to Whitelaw's experience at the beginning of the decade, the Home Office ministers had 'virtually a clean slate' with their Parliamentary colleagues for more than two and a half years from the 1987 Election until the disturbances that erupted at Strangeways and other prisons in April 1990.[24]

In the process of building support for their policies in the Commons, ministers were sustained by an unusually influential back-bencher, John Wheeler. As a former Assistant Governor in the Prison Service, Wheeler was well informed, moderate in outlook, and generally sympathetic to the Home Secretary's policies. His role was pivotal, since he occupied concurrently the chair of the House of Commons Select Committee on Home Affairs and the reformist Parliamentary All-Party Penal Affairs Group.[25] From 1987 onwards, Wheeler was also Vice-Chairman of the Conservative Parliamentary Home Affairs Committee. He was to prove the Home Secretary's staunchest ally. Hurd consulted him regularly, listened to what he had to say, and respected his judgment on the state of Parliamentary opinion, in the House as a whole as well as on the Tory benches.

Relations with the higher judiciary, and Hurd's tactful handling of discussions with the Lord Chief Justice, were recounted in the last chapter. Together with the input of officials to the sentencing seminars and committees of the Judicial Studies Board,[26] and a certain amount of 'shuttle diplomacy' by Faulkner acting as envoy on behalf of the Home Secretary, there were sufficient channels for the outlines of the evolving policies to be communicated to the judiciary in the course of the extended process of public consultation that preceded the drafting of a bill.

---

[23] Letter from Martin Brandon Bravo MP, Parliamentary Private Secretary to John Patten, 22 May 1990.

[24] Ibid.

[25] Wheeler was knighted in 1990 and relinquished the chair of the Home Affairs Select Committee in 1992.

[26] Faulkner was a member of the main Board, with the Head of the Criminal Policy Department (Bohan) sitting on the Board's Criminal Committee, and the Head of Home Office Division C2 (responsible for Magistrates' courts) on the Magisterial Committee.

IV

The most prickly, if not the largest, issue to which the Leeds Castle seminar bent its mind was the anticipated hostility of the Probation Service towards the 'beefing up' of community penalties. By training,[27] as well as what had become the customary way of looking upon their duties, probation officers regarded themselves as engaged in social work with and on behalf of a specialized group of clients, namely those who had been convicted of a criminal offence and sentenced in a court of law. Although answerable for the supervision of offenders subject to probation or community service orders, and responsible for bringing back before the court any offender who breached the conditions, probation officers typically saw their functions as being 'constructive' rather than 'punitive'.[28] Any proposals to convert supervision from a conscientious 'attempt to influence constructively the offender's future behaviour into a measure deliberately designed to impose irksome restrictions as a form of punishment'[29] would be repugnant.

However discordant with the culture of the Probation Service, it was precisely the importation of 'irksome restrictions' that was crucial to the chances of convincing the first two target groups of the Home Secretary's proposition that not all those sentenced to imprisonment for less serious offences needed to go to gaol. The conundrum was baldly stated in a paper prepared by the senior civil servant handling probation for the Leeds Castle seminar:

The extent to which the probation service can be used to divert more serious offenders from custody, is dependent on persuading the courts of the service's ability to hold and control serious offenders. An important issue for future consideration is whether more could and should be done to encourage the courts to have greater confidence in the service and the extent to which this might require a change in the probation service's

[27] On 19 Sept. 1990 John Patten announced the setting up of an efficiency scrutiny of in-service training for the Probation Service.

[28] See D. Garland in H. Rees and E. Hall Williams (eds.), *Punishment, Custody and the Community: Reflections and Comments on the Green Paper*, Suntory Toyota International Centre for Economics and Related Disciplines/London School of Economics, 1989, pp. 8–14.

[29] The General Secretary of the National Association of Probation Officers in *Punishment, Custody and the Community: Reflections and Comments on the Green Paper*, p. 88.

attitude to offenders away from 'advising, assisting and befriending' towards controlling.

The implication that probation officers no longer enjoyed the confidence of sentencers was one that was bound to cause despondency and resentment in the service, and it did. Much time and effort was to be given by ministers and officials in the pre-legislative stages to assuring the service that the plans for punishment in the community offered great opportunities for the future. In this endeavour, neither the carrot nor the stick were spared. In a keynote speech to the Annual Conference of the Association of Chief Officers of Probation in Leeds, Patten spoke of the importance of phraseology in communicating the message to the public:

Most people in the world outside probation quite naturally use words like 'punishment', 'control', 'tough and demanding'. They prefer 'offender' to 'client'. They are surprised when probation officers do not, and the seeds of unease and confusion are sown. In order to market your work to the courts and to the public, whose attitudes the courts must take into account, you have to use the clearest language you can. That means avoiding jargon and using words that ordinary people use.

In what has become a *locus classicus*, Patten went on to acknowledge:

there is an inherent tension between the concept of control—let alone punishment—and the roles of the probation service which are variously described as 'welfare', 'caring' or 'helping'—however these are defined. Of course this tension will be so great that it may rule out a non-custodial disposal completely. What I would want to argue very strongly is that there is no *necessary* reason why this tension should be destructive in the majority of cases that *are* likely to come under the probation services umbrella.

But I still use the word 'punishment'. My reason for this lies in some basic truths about the way the criminal justice system operates and how the public perceive it. Taking the public first, their concept of punishment, I suggest, is that of an offender being subject to restrictions on liberty, inconvenience and even to financial penalties; these restrictions to be proportionate to the degree of inconvenience the offender has caused for society or for his victims. They will be reflected in restrictions on his ability to do what he wants and when, and in the obligations which are put on him to face the reasons for his offending, the consequences for his victim and the need for reparation to society. The Green Paper recognises that in some cases the perception of punishment can be met only by a custodial sentence. It argues, however, that it would be adequately met in cases of significant other categories of offenders, by—and again I use the word without any sense of it being inappropriate—punishment in the community. *The fact is that all probation based disposals are already in varying degrees forms of punishment. For example, the offender who has to report to a probation officer, or work specified hours on community service, or spend 60 days at a day centre is clearly being punished. It is bizarre to scratch around to find polite euphemisms for what is going on.*

There is no reason for thinking that what you do at present—and what you would do under Part II of the Green Paper—could be regarded as anything less than presenting an offender with a set of demands and requirements which reflect society's disapproval of what he did, at the same time as enabling the probation service to carry out its traditional role of helping offenders to develop and surmount their individual problems.

I take very much the same approach on the question of *control*. This means exercising enough authority and supervision to ensure that the wishes of the court are carried out and that the public are protected. Here again, the probation service is already firmly in this kind of business. There are various ways in which the probation service is involved in control to one degree or another. Let me give some examples: probation officers exercise control through the authority derived from the court or various orders and licences; by setting tasks for offenders; by the use of formal warnings or breach proceedings; through counselling which attempts to set limits to particular forms of conduct, and, most importantly by ensuring that the offender observes the conditions or requirements imposed by the court.

Here again, I reject the view that this concept of control is incompatible with the traditional view of the probation process. Nor do I regard it as incompatible with that process to ask the probation service to exercise a degree of supervision and enforcement which matches the background of any offender who might be entrusted to them by the courts. We are after all asking the courts to undertake a significant act of faith. You are officers of the court. This does not require the probation service to exercise at all times a heavy-handed authoritarian approach which gets in the way of their traditional role. It does call for a flexible approach geared to the needs and circumstances of the individual offender which takes into account also the wishes of the court and needs of society.[30]

The post-Leeds Castle Green Paper[31] took an even less forthcoming line. In a passage to which Hurd personally had given much

---

[30] Home Office, *News Release* dated 15 Sept. 1988. Emphasis as in the original.

[31] *Punishment, Custody and the Community.*

thought, it raised the spectre that a new organization might be set up to manage punishment in the community. This possibility was preceded by an affirmation that in the short term there was no other existing service or organization better placed than the Probation Service to take on the task. The Government recognized that the proposed supervision and restriction order[32] would 'contain additional elements of control which some members of the probation service might perceive as inimical to their approach to working with offenders'.[33]

Eschewing threatening language, the Green Paper said that the Government did not envisage a new organization being set up to supervise offenders directly, preferring one that would contract with other services or organizations to do so:

The organisation could be part of the Home Office. Alternatively, it might be a separate non-departmental public body with a Director, a small permanent staff and possibly a governing Board drawn from those with relevant experience. The new organisation could contract for services from the probation service, the private or voluntary sector and perhaps for some purposes from the police or the prison service. The Prison Department already contracts in this way for services of probation officers in prisons, and the Central After-Care Association operated similarly until the probation service assumed direct responsibility for prison after-care in the 1960s. A new organisation would be able to set national standards and to enforce them, because they would be written into contracts.

The Government would welcome views on the possibility of setting up a new organisation to take responsibility for the arrangements for punishment in the community, and providing services through contracts with other organisations.[34]

A greater emphasis on control and the power to regulate was less objectionable, to Chief Officers of Probation at least, than the rhetoric of punishment. As Patten had argued, the word 'control' did no more than describe in plain language the existing relationship between probation officers and those whom they were supervising: 'If we have a special expertise', said the Chairman of the Association

[32] An order combining compensation, community service, residence (e.g. at a hostel), prescribed activities (e.g. at a day centre) and tracking or a curfew, possibly enforced by electronic monitoring, was outlined in the Green Paper but not pursued in the White Paper, *Crime, Justice and Protecting the Public*, which followed in Feb. 1990.

[33] *Punishment, Custody and the Community*, p. 17.

[34] Ibid., pp. 17–18.

of Chief Officers of Probation, 'it is in making sense to offender and community alike that the issue of control can sit alongside care and concern without either concept being damaged.'[35] Rather than risk the eclipse of their service, a majority of probation officers settled for unenthusiastic acquiescence. In the case of community service orders particularly, many in the Probation Service accepted the need to tighten up standards of supervision if the orders which had offered such promise when first introduced in 1973[36] were to continue to be used extensively by the courts.

V

It was the reparative notion of an offender giving something back to the community he had harmed, rather than the restrictions on personal freedom which were equally part of community service orders, that had caught the imagination of sentencers. Aimed at offenders who would otherwise be at risk of custody,[37] the orders had been widely used, especially by Magistrates' courts, with the result that in 1988 about 31,000 offenders were sentenced to community service, compared with 69,000 sentenced to immediate custody.[38] Close examination of sentencing patterns over the decade 1977–87 revealed that the proportion of offenders sentenced to immediate custody had continued to rise. The unavoidable inference was that community-based disposals had been used by some courts as alternatives to fines, rather than to deflect offenders from custody. In terms of cost-effectiveness, the more expensive options, probation and community service, had tended to be preferred to the less expensive option of a fine.[39] Nevertheless, any undermining of such a significant element of the penal system could have far-reaching results.

Once a survey by Her Majesty's Inspectorate of Probation had

[35] Graham Smith, Chief Probation Officer, Inner London Probation Service, *Punishment, Custody and the Community: Reflections and Comments on the Green Paper*, p. 115.
[36] See Chapter 3.
[37] A community service order could only be imposed for imprisonable offences.
[38] *Punishment, Custody and the Community*, p. 3.
[39] Committee of Public Accounts, Seventh Report, *Home Office: Control and Management of Probation Services in England and Wales*, HC 259, Session 1989/90, HMSO, London, p. xi.

confirmed impressions that the supervision of community service orders was inconsistent and patchy, with failures to carry out the work ordered by the court not always being reported, a further candidate for 'beefing up' appeared on the ministerial agenda. Complaints of unevenness of standards from some judges and magistrates had also been noted by the Home Office.

Community service, according to the Green Paper, should be rigorous and demanding, otherwise sentencers and the general public would not accept it was a punishment. The chosen method to achieve this objective was by setting national standards, and providing for monitoring and inspection to see that they were observed. Standards would prescribe the type of work to be done by offenders and the way the hours worked should be reckoned. Standards both of performance and behaviour were required, including a clear and consistent procedure to be followed if an offender failed to comply with the requirements of the order. Offenders would be expected to begin work promptly after the order was made, and attend for work regularly and punctually.[40] Although the Home Office claimed that national standards would extend the best existing practice to all schemes, they were denounced by the National Association of Probation Officers as having been drafted without consultation with those responsible for managing well-run and effective schemes, relying on an approach that was 'rigid and punitive' in order to bring community service into line with the Government's policy of punishment in the community.[41]

The existing legislation gave the Home Office sufficient latitude to overhaul the standards of supervision of offenders on probation as well as those receiving community service orders. To this end, a policy statement titled *Tackling Offending: An Action Plan* was circulated in August 1988 to Probation Services, police forces, the judiciary, justices' clerks, chairmen of Magistrates' benches, the Crown Prosecution Service, as well as some voluntary organizations and the representative organizations of the various professions.

By 1989 it was time to start mending the fences with the Probation Service. Although some sticking points remained where the opposition was total, electronic monitoring and curfews above all else, the arguments on both sides were more symbolic than central

[40] *Punishment, Custody and the Community*, p. 4.
[41] *Punishment, Custody and the Community: Reflections and Comments on the Green Paper*, p. 104.

to the achievement of the Government's aims. In his advocacy of punishment in the community, Faulkner was thoughtful and conciliatory:

Punishment must not mean rejection. When it takes the form of imprisonment it may mean temporary or sometimes prolonged removal, but even with imprisonment the offender should again become a full member of the community with all its resources and opportunities available to him on release—although we know only too well how difficult that can be. When it takes place in the community the links if they exist need not be broken, and if they do not, or if they are faulty—as too often happens—the task of constructing them can begin at once. Punishment in the community has been criticised as likely to reinforce society's instincts for repression and rejection, and I share the implied concern that we must not create an isolated, criminalised and potentially hostile underclass: but I would hope that these instincts are driven more by crime and fear of crime ... than they are by hatred for individual offenders. There is research evidence on this point. If properly applied, the notion of punishment in the community should help to reinforce the community's sense of responsibility for its misfits and failures.[42]

Although not marked by any clear break in the discussion, the third theme of the Leeds Castle meeting was the perennial one of how to prevent young people from becoming enmeshed in the criminal justice system. Under this heading the discussion covered the causes of criminality, the role of parents, and the use of custodial sentences. One of the most pregnant statistics deployed was that the proportion of the prison population aged between seventeen and twenty was currently 27% of the total for England and Wales, as against 13% in Germany.

Agonizing about young people and crime, at Leeds Castle and after, prompted renewed deliberation on the responsibilities of parents for the delinquent or criminal behaviour of their children. In 1987 it was estimated that about 6,000 recorded crimes were committed by children under ten, and consequently below the age of criminal responsibility. Patten took an especial interest in this subject and was attracted by the possibility of creating a new offence to signify the responsibility of parents for the misconduct of their children who, because of their age, were beyond the reach of the criminal law. There were, he believed, many reasons why a

[42] 'The Future of the Probation Service: A View from Government', Clarke Hall Conference, Cambridge, 3–5 July 1989.

child drifts into crime. They may be egged on by friends, immaturity may be a factor, as may be drink, drugs, or boredom. But to the minister the single most important factor was home life:

Parents, the first educators of their children, have a duty to teach their children the difference between right and wrong. Right to tell the truth, to respect other people's property and to look after those less fortunate than yourself. Wrong to lie, steal, to cheat or to bully.

These fundamental truths, properly instilled into children at an early age, not only help a child keep out of trouble as he or she grows up. They also help to bind the family itself together, creating a close-knit home in which people can trust and rely on one another, and therefore be trusted by others.

Parental responsibility must go further than that. It includes an obligation to prevent children from getting involved in hooliganism or criminal activity. No doubt in many cases, parents are blissfully unaware that their child has taken to shoplifting or is running with a gang of vandals. Often the parent may suspect or know, but is not in a position to take any preventive action, perhaps because the family structure has broken down, or because the child is simply beyond control.

However, there are some parents, who *could* cope, but simply choose not to: households where seemingly children are deliberately not taught the difference between right and wrong, where the parents are quite well aware of the child's criminal activity but make no attempt to stop it. There are even cases where the parent, actively or silently, condones or connives at crime. These are families which have failed not through misfortune or misjudgement, but through wilful neglect by parents of their responsibilities.

In such cases, the means should be available to make parents take those responsibilities seriously, both where the child is under 10 and hence completely outside the criminal justice system, and where the child is a juvenile, that is to say under 17.[43]

Such authentic Tory sentiments were an overtly political input to the formulation of policy. Officials counselled caution, pointing out that in protecting a child under ten from prosecution, and allowing one between ten and thirteen to be convicted only if proved to have known that what he did was seriously wrong, the law takes account of a child's limited understanding and moral and social immaturity. Such factors are intrinsic to the child, and are not good reasons for transferring criminal responsibility to its parents.

[43] Patten to Mrs P. Newbon, Parliamentary Liaison Officer of the UK Federation of Business and Professional Women, 30 Mar. 1989. Emphasis as in the original letter.

Other objections arose out of the concept of criminal responsibility. At common law, the *mens rea* that the prosecution must prove a defendant to have had at the time of committing a crime in order to secure a conviction requires either an intention to bring about a particular consequence, or recklessness as to whether such a consequence may come about. It is not unknown for the criminal law to make one person punishable for the act of another, for example the landlord of a public house can be prosecuted if his barman sells alcoholic drinks to persons under a minimum age. That relationship, however, is an adult one of employer and employee, and the landlord can reasonably be expected to keep a close watch on what is done in the course of business on premises licensed to him. He will not be held responsible if the barman damages or steals the cars of the customers on leaving the public house at the end of his shift.

After prolonged debate, in which the difficulties and options were argued out between special advisers and officials, as well as with Patten himself, the conclusion was reached that failure by parents to take due care to prevent a crime by their child was the least hazardous route to the ministerial destination. But even then obstacles stood in the way. If a parent were to be liable to penalty for failing to take due care to prevent offending by mini-criminals, in Patten's unfortunate phrase,[44] the parent's liability could be said to depend on some element of fault or oversight in his or her own conduct. But what standards of care would be implied? Probably most anti-social acts by children under ten could in theory be preventable by some restriction which might be imposed by their parents. Was a boy of nine to be confined to a flat in a tower block on a housing estate throughout the evening because other boys of that age had previously got into trouble in the locality after dark?

The idea behind the creation of a new offence of failure to prevent child crime, was flawed by an abstract and unrealistic view of family life and parental influence in the homes of many of the children who appeared before the courts. The frequent references to parents in the plural did not accord with the prevalence of breakdown in marriage as a precursor of delinquency in dysfunctional families.[45] Poor standards of housing, economic depriva-

[44] Ibid.
[45] See *Responses to Crime*, vol. 1, pp. 184–8 and *Cambridge Studies in Criminology*, vols. XXV, XXXIV, XXXV, L, Heinemann Educational Books, London, 1969–82.

tion, domestic violence, chronically disorganized households, and abandoned mothers, all contributed to settings in which punishing an often inadequate parent or parents was more likely to exacerbate than to improve relationships within the family. The chances were that children and young people from unhappy and disturbed backgrounds, whose parent or parents had been penalized because of their offending, would experience still greater feelings of rejection and lack of love, thereby increasing the possibility of leaving home and getting into even deeper trouble.

As the internal debate rumbled on, the Green Paper remained silent on offending by children. By the time the Government announced its plans for legislation in a White Paper early in 1990[46] the outright opposition of the magistracy, before whom most juveniles charged with criminal offences appeared, and the main children's and penal reform groups had merged with the legal and administrative difficulties to confine the proposals to strengthening the existing powers relating to parents when children over ten are brought before the criminal courts in their own right. The Government fell back on an intention to amend the law so as to ensure that at least one parent accompanied their child to court in a wider range of cases than previously. Under Section 34(1) of the Children and Young Persons Act 1933 parents already could be required to attend when their children appeared in court charged with a criminal offence, if the court regarded it as desirable that they should do so and unless it would be unreasonable to require their attendance. Experience in the courts showed that whereas some parents attended, others did not. In the previous year Patten had argued: 'I think we should seriously consider an extension of the law to make parental attendance compulsory in the absence of very good reasons for staying away.'[47]

When the Criminal Justice Bill was published in November 1990 it envisaged replacing the discretionary power of the court to require the attendance of parents with a statutory duty to require a parent or guardian to attend during all the stages in the proceedings against a child or a young person under the age of sixteen. The only exception was where the court was satisfied that it would be

---

[46] Home Office, *Crime, Justice and Protecting the Public* (Cm. 965), HMSO, London, 1990, p. 41.
[47] Patten to Mrs Newbon, 30 Mar. 1989.

unreasonable to require such attendance, having regard to the circumstances of the case.

On fines and other financial penalties (such as an order for compensation) the White Paper said that the current arrangements would be revised so that parents would have a formal obligation to pay in cases where juveniles were fined. In deciding the level of payment to be made, the courts would take account of the parents' means, and not just the means of their children. Legislation would be introduced requiring local authorities to pay compensation and fines when a juvenile in their care was convicted, and the court was satisfied that the offence followed a failure by a local authority to carry out its duties.[48] Restrictions would be removed which limited the use of the power to order the parents of juveniles convicted of criminal offences to enter into a recognizance of up to £1,000 to take proper care and exercise proper control over them. In future, courts would be required to consider binding over parents of juveniles convicted of criminal offences in every case, unless it would be unreasonable in the circumstances to expect them to be able to exercise the required degree of supervision and control.[49] These proposals were to be subjected to sustained challenge, in the House of Lords especially, when the Bill was going through Parliament.

Attempts to make parents share responsibility for wrongdoing by their children had a long history. Radzinowicz and Hood note that the idea was current in the 1880s in a variety of forms, finally reaching the statute book in the Youthful Offenders Act 1901 and the Children Act 1908.[50] Before then several proposals were canvassed, one being remarkably similar to Patten's version a century later. An unsuccessful Bill introduced in the House of Lords in 1890 sought to make general negligence in the care and control of a child a statutory offence, for which parents would be punished by a small fine, ordered to pay compensation, and be subject to imprisonment in default.[51] The legislation in 1901 was

---

[48] *Crime, Justice and Protecting the Public*, p. 42. In the Bill this intention was achieved by construing references to the responsibilities of parents and guardians for financial penalties as referring to local authorities when exercising parental responsibility for a child or young person.

[49] Ibid., p. 42.

[50] *A History of English Criminal Law and its Administration from 1750*, vol. 5: *The Emergence of Penal Policy*, Stevens, London, 1986, pp. 656–7.

[51] Ibid., p. 656.

more circumspect, going no further than empowering courts to summon parents to attend where there was reason to believe that they had 'conduced' to the commission of an alleged offence by failing to exercise due care and control over children in their care. If such failure was proved, the parents could be ordered to pay any fines, costs, or damages imposed on the child or young person.[52]

Radzinowicz and Hood's conclusion was that although in practice these provisions did not have a great deal of impact, they had social and political significance as a sign of 'the new perception of the responsibilities of the State, extending gradually but substantially its frontiers of intervention and control'.[53] In the closing years of the twentieth century the frontiers remained in much the same place, the episode illuminating the lasting nature of the quest for fresh solutions, and the ingenuity of officials threading a way through the administrative and legal thickets to enable the political intentions of ministers to be met, albeit not always in the manner originally intended.

VI

More than at any other time in the life of a Government a spirit of buoyancy and optimism prevails for a few weeks immediately after a decisive win at a General Election. For a brief moment of rapture, everything seems possible. The confident outlook of the ministers as they arrived at the handsome setting of Leeds Castle on a glorious autumn day after the summer holidays was soon dissipated.

On 30 September 1987 the prison population, including those in police cells, stood at 48,216 having broken through the psychological threshold of 50,000 three months earlier. At the end of July the numbers in prison and police cells reached a record of 50,979. Temporary measures were taken to stretch the available accommodation to its utmost limits, and in August 50% remission in place of the standard one-third had been introduced for all prisoners serving sentences of twelve months or less. Breathing space was provided by an almost immediate reduction of more than 3,000

[52] Ibid., p. 657.
[53] Ibid.

in the prison population. The building programme launched by Whitelaw in 1980, and maintained by Brittan, was progressing slowly, but the need to move prisoners out of existing accommodation so as to refurbish older prison blocks meant there had been little easing of the intolerable conditions of overcrowding which had led to Trevelyan's denunciation and to a well-publicized outburst by the Governor of Wormwood Scrubs prison, referring to himself as 'the manager of a large penal dustbin'.[54]

Before the Leeds Castle meeting turned its collective mind to the topic of prison overcrowding there had been a perceptible undertow in the current of the discussion that really what was called for was more toughness; that people should be sent to prison for longer, and that more offenders deserved to be sent to prison. Echoes of the hustings, although muted, could still be heard. The mood did not survive in the face of some devastating calculations on the size of the prison population by the Statistical Department of the Home Office. Their impact was the greater since the six-monthly forecasts had proved to be persistently too low for some time past.

The statistics showed that the average number of persons in 1985 held at Prison Service establishments and police cells in excess of the certified normal accommodation of the prisons (CNA) was 6,474. In 1986 it dropped to 6,078, but in 1987 the excess above CNA rose to close on 7,000 (6,969), despite the provision of more than 2,000 additional places in 1985–7. The forward projections indicated an increase to a peak of about 9,000 above CNA. It was that figure that had convinced the Home Secretary of the need to introduce half remission for shorter-sentenced prisoners. On the basis of the historical trend of $2\frac{1}{2}\%$ annual increase since 1946, and assuming no faster rate of growth, the forecast showed that the difference between the certified normal accommodation and the average number of persons held in custody could be expected to reach the same level as 1987 again in 1989, after allowing for the effects of half remission and the provision of further capacity.

The implications were chilling even before the impact of possible

---

[54] In a letter to *The Times* published on 19 Nov. 1982 the Governor, John McCarthy, wrote that he had not joined the Prison Service to manage 'overcrowded cattle pens', where the interests of the individuals had to be sacrificed continually to those of the institution, and where the staff were 'forced to run a society that debases'. Bearing in mind the substance of the criticisms, which were made public in breach of Civil Service regulations, Whitelaw wisely refrained from disciplinary action.

longer sentences was considered. Here the peak rose as high as 12,000 above CNA. That was seen as doomsday, a situation that prison administrators would find impossible to handle. Nor did the political risks need to be spelled out of having to set prisoners free by executive release[55] because the prisons could not cope. The method of calculation was important since CNA was not a static threshold, but one that took account of new prison places coming on stream as a result of the prison-building programme. When presented in round figures the picture was equally unacceptable: a prison population soaring from the 1987 average of 48,963 to well over 60,000 in the foreseeable future, possibly reaching 70,000 by the year 2000.

If there was any single moment at Leeds Castle when opinions

TABLE 7. *Population in custody*[a]*: annual averages and certified normal accommodation (CNA), 1984–90*

Year	Average number of persons in custody[b]	Certified normal accommodation on 30 June	Excess of col. 1 over col. 2[c]
1984	43,349	39,033	4,316
1985	46,278	39,804	6,474
1986	46,889	40,811	6,078
1987	48,963	41,994	6,969
1988	49,949	44,179	5,770
1989	48,610	45,427	3,183
1990	45,636	42,804	2,832

[a] Population in custody includes untried persons held on remand in Prison Service establishments and police cells, convicted but unsentenced offenders, sentenced prisoners (adults and young offenders), and non-criminal prisoners.
[b] Annual averages are calculated on the total population at month end.
[c] A large proportion of the excess of average population over CNA was concentrated in the local prisons.
Source: Home Office, *Prison Statistics England and Wales.*

[55] In the Criminal Justice Act 1982, Section 32, Whitelaw had obtained from Parliament a power to release by order up to six months earlier than they would otherwise be released prisoners in certain categories, provided the Secretary of State was satisfied that it was necessary to do so 'in order to make the best use of the places available for detention'. The power had first been taken, on a temporary footing, in the Imprisonment (Temporary Provisions) Act 1980. Up to the time of writing, it has never been used.

changed, it was at this point. Ministers and officials were united in their reaction that such a situation would be intolerable and must not be allowed to happen. The aim should be to find ways of reducing numbers in custody, not of increasing them. Sentence lengths should be reduced for property offenders wherever possible, and prison reserved for the most serious offences, especially those involving violence or sexual offences, where the crime was so outrageous that a non-custodial sentence would bring the process of justice into disrepute.

Public expenditure considerations also came into play. The costs were already vast. The expenditure on the building of new prisons and the improvement and expansion of old ones was nearing £1 billion, to which had to be added the recruitment of more prison officers. The annual Public Expenditure Survey, the method used by the Treasury to fix the amount of money made available to Departments for each programme and sub-programme for the coming year (the 'focus year'), and provisionally for each of the two following years, came immediately after the Leeds Castle meeting. The Home Office is accustomed to making statistical projections to support bids for additional expenditure to control crime or compensate the victims. For example, projected increases in the volume of reported crime, especially violent crime, have an effect both on police manpower and the number of applicants under the criminal injuries compensation scheme. Political judgments about the consequences of not increasing expenditure clash with the availability of public funds which are under pressure from many other quarters. But for prisons above all, because of the necessity of providing physical plant, expenditure is directly related to the numbers expected to be in custody. A set of projections was prepared on the size of the prison population reflecting statistical trends over a ten-year period, backed by assumptions about the incidence of crime and the responses of the police, the Crown Prosecution Service and the courts. In view of the stark implications of the projections presented at Leeds Castle, there was an urgent practical necessity for the Home Office to convince the Treasury that there were positive and realistic plans to take action to reduce the predicted scale of demand.

Two forces, therefore, converged. The penological arguments for sending fewer offenders to prison were joined by the increasingly unacceptable levels of cost and manpower that would be unavoidable if the existing patterns of offending and detection continued, and no changes were made in the sentencing of offenders by the courts. Not only was there an opportunity, but an imperative need, for a radical shift in policy. The status quo was no longer tenable. This was the context that made possible the adoption of the most adventurous of the specific solutions put forward by officials.

The general restrictions on the imprisonment of offenders aged under twenty-one, which had been incorporated in Section 1(4) of the Criminal Justice Act 1982, and re-enacted and strengthened in the 1988 Act, have already been described. Although the initial response of the courts had been slow, the White Paper laid emphasis on the fact that since 1983 the number of offenders under seventeen who had been sentenced to custody had halved, without any discernible increase in the number of offences committed by juveniles.[56] While it was true that other factors besides the statutory restrictions on the use of custody for young offenders contributed to the decline, judicial interpretation and practitioners' usage was crucial.

The developing body of case law was well exemplified by an appeal against sentence which came before the Criminal Division of the Court of Appeal in 1989.[57] The appellants were two seventeen-year-old youths, neither with previous convictions, who had pleaded guilty to charges of burglary from unoccupied dwellings during the day while the occupiers were away. Both received sentences of youth custody. In reducing their sentences, the Court of Appeal held that in cases of burglary it was not enough for the court to say that all domestic burglaries were serious, because of the effect on the occupants as well as the loss of property, and that therefore a non-custodial penalty could not be justified. The court had to have regard to the statutory framework dating from the Powers of Criminal Courts Act 1973, relating to first sentences of imprisonment and the use of community service orders, as well as satisfying itself that the facts of each case fulfilled the conditions set out in Section 1 of the Criminal Justice Act 1982.[58]

The White Paper also contained an unqualified statement, unthinkable in the climate of the early 1980s, asserting the ascend-

---

[56] *Crime, Justice and Protecting the Public*, p. 12.

[57] *Hearne and Petty* (1989) 11 Cr. App. R. (S.) 316.

[58] Another case in which the Court of Appeal held that the statutory criteria had to be applied to the circumstances of the actual offence, rather than a general category within which it fell, was *Poyner* (1989) 11 Cr. App. R. (S.) 173.

ancy of Government and Parliament, and rejecting the 'hands off' attitude towards any aspect of sentencing on grounds of judicial independence: 'sentencing principles and sentencing practice are matters of legitimate concern to Government, and Parliament provides the funds necessary to give effect to the courts' decisions'.[59]

By this time, a wholly unexpected turn of events had occurred. The prison population, instead of proceeding steadily upwards, had begun to go down. In the search for explanations, researchers were inclined to attribute part of the reason for the fall in the prison population since 1988 to the fact that fewer young people were being sentenced to imprisonment. The picture was obscured by the decline which had occurred simultaneously in the number of young offenders found guilty of, or cautioned for, indictable offences. The figures were not easy to interpret as fewer convictions and cautions could have resulted from the use of less formal means of dealing with offenders, rather than less involvement in crime.[60] Nevertheless, the proposition that the restrictions on the imprisonment of offenders under the age of twenty-one had worked to reduce the size of the prison population was one which became generally accepted.

VII

Could a great leap forward be made to extend the restrictions to all offenders, irrespective of age? Cautiously, the policy-makers in the Home Office moved towards an affirmative answer to this question. At a series of discursive meetings in Hurd's room, officials devised a scheme whereby restricting the use of custodial sentences for adult offenders would be confined to those convicted of less serious offences. This could, it was suggested, be achieved by excluding offences where the penalty was fixed by law, and the most serious offences triable only on indictment, possibly limiting the latter category to those who had already received a prison sentence. Restrictions on imprisonment would be partial and not total, and kept in line with the principle of just deserts, if (*a*) the

---

[59] *Crime, Justice and Protecting the Public*, p. 5.
[60] *Home Office, Criminal Statistics England and Wales 1989* (Cm. 1322), HMSO, London, 1990, pp. 93–4.

offence for which the offender had been convicted was so serious that only a custodial sentence could be justified, and (*b*) that only a custodial sentence would be adequate to protect the public from serious harm. To reach an informed decision on these considerations, courts would need social inquiry reports on a far larger group of defendants, thus bringing back into a central role the Probation Service whose duty it was to prepare them. In the same way as with young offenders, reasons should be given in open court whenever it was considered that a custodial sentence was justified.

The three years which followed the meeting at Leeds Castle saw many twists and turns as policies began to take legislative shape. Additional tributaries, such as the parole reforms resulting from the recommendations of the report of the review body under the chairmanship of Lord Carlisle, and the first trickle from the spring of privatization rising in the remote uplands of contracting out of court custody and escort services, fed into the main stream. Meanwhile, the prison population, defying all expectations, continued to fall, the forecasts failing to predict the lows, just as they had failed to predict the highs of earlier years. There were changes of people and emphasis, most significantly when David Waddington[61] succeeded Douglas Hurd as Home Secretary on 26 October 1989. The new Home Secretary, a barrister and one of the few supporters of capital punishment amongst the ranks of senior ministers, was not cast in the mould of a penal reformer. He stood for a different type of Toryism to Hurd,[62] but the impetus by then was irreversible.

While Hurd was still Home Secretary, the Government had begun to draw together its conclusions in the Summer of 1989. The next milestone was an important and unprecedented conference that took place in September 1989, again at a great country house. This time it was the Home Secretary, the Lord Chancellor, and the Attorney General who invited the Lord Chief Justice and his deputy, together with leading members of the magistracy and the

[61] Previously Government Chief Whip, 1987–9, Waddington had served as a Minister of State at the Home Office under Brittan and Hurd, 1983–7. He was Home Secretary for little over a year, before being created a life peer and Leader of the House of Lords in November 1990. He left the Government after the General Election in Apr. 1992, becoming Governor of Bermuda later in the year.

[62] Unlike John Patten, Sir John Wheeler, and Steven Norris, all of whom supported Douglas Hurd in the election for the leadership of the Conservative Party in Nov. 1990, David Waddington preferred John Major.

operational services to attend a two-day conference at Ditchley Park in Oxfordshire. As before, the ministers were accompanied by their senior officials. Patten too was present, although on this occasion, in deference to the judiciary, there were no political advisers. The purpose of the gathering was to review with those taking part the stage which the Government's programme had reached and to indicate the direction in which it was going.

After the Ditchley Conference, the Home Office got to work on drafting a White Paper for publication early the following year delineating the shape and content of the legislation to be introduced in the Parliamentary session 1990/1. In the forefront was the concept of a statutory framework of sentencing principles, with restrictions on the imposition of custodial sentences. Other central proposals included a redefinition and reconstruction of community sentences; reduced maximum penalties for certain offences, but increased sentencing powers for serious violent or sexual crimes; a wider jurisdiction for the Juvenile Court, to be renamed the Youth Court; the introduction of unit fines related to the means of the offender; and a restructuring of parole. One casualty was a plan close to Faulkner's heart for a National Institute of Justice. This was intended to serve two purposes: to improve the quality of leadership and management in the criminal justice system; and to generate and develop ideas for improving its operation. It would be partly a teaching institution, and partly a centre for discussion and deliberation from which it might develop an advisory function. The institute could, but need not in the first phase, have its own research capacity. In any event, it would keep abreast of current research and maintain contact with research institutions, abroad as well as in the United Kingdom.

The attractiveness of the proposal to ministers was their concern about the relative isolation of the operational services and professions which together made up the criminal justice system. Few of those on joining the services would have friends or acquaintances in other services who they knew from school or university. In their subsequent careers such training as they received would be given on a single service basis, with opportunities for wider social and professional contacts restricted by the circumstances of their jobs, and sometimes (particularly in the Prison Service) by individual inclination. As a result, it was not only possible but commonplace to rise to the top of a service with no more than a limited perspective of the wider system of which their service formed part. The reasoning went beyond the operational services—the police, prisons, probation, and the Magistrates' courts—applying equally to the legal profession, the judiciary, and the staff of Government Departments, including the Crown Prosecution Service and the Crown Court Service.

The proposal for a National Institute of Justice had been accepted in principle at Leeds Castle and Faulkner followed up with a more detailed outline in December. Hurd's reaction was that the idea was well worth pursuing, since the different components still jostled together without really understanding each other because each had a different intellectual formation. Some of the objectives coincided with the less ambitious plans for a series of week-long criminal justice conferences which were designed to complement the ministerial level Ditchley meeting. The special conference programme, organized by a unit within the Home Office, went ahead under Faulkner's direction, and it was decided to launch the institute from that programme if it was successful. Work was done on a possible structure as a 'Next Steps' agency, but enthusiasm was waning and eventually Hurd's ministerial successors decided that even as an agency an institute would have too much independence to be acceptable.

One of the speakers at the Ditchley conference was Sir Clive Whitmore, who had succeeded Cubbon as the Permanent Secretary the previous year. In a paper titled *Managing the Criminal Justice System* Whitmore argued that the key decision points which occurred throughout the criminal justice system represented step changes in the demand made on resources. He cited three examples: (1) in 1987/8 the average cost of a summary trial of an either-way offence for a guilty plea was £122, while the Crown Court costs for a guilty plea were £300. For a not guilty plea the costs in the Magistrates' court were £295; in the Crown Court they were £3,100. (2) The average cost per defendant to the Crown Prosecution Service in the Magistrates' court in 1987/8 was £45; in the Crown Court it was £390. (3) In 1987/8 the average cost of a probation order was about £1,300 and of a Community Service Order was about £570. The average cost of one week in custody was about £275.

Whitmore went on to disclose that the ministers present were currently in the middle of their annual bilateral negotiations with the Chief Secretary to the Treasury[63] on the cash to be made available for their programmes for the next three years. It was standard practice, he said, for the Chief Secretary to declare in his opening remarks at the first meeting each year, that the overall public expenditure position was very difficult, that the aspirations of individual spending ministers wildly exceeded the totals which could be tolerated within the Government's collective economic policy, and that departmental plans would have to be radically truncated. In the 1989 round, the Chief Secretary had told the Home Secretary that the position was probably more difficult than it had been in any year since 1980, and officials were not inclined to dismiss the remark as part of the opening negotiating tactics.

In Home Office terms, Whitmore said, there was a direct link between the strength of the Deutschmark and the number of prison places that could be provided. At the centre of Government, ministers collectively had to weigh how much could be spent on criminal justice in relation to the demands of other programmes such as education and health in making an essential contribution to the framework of society. Expenditure on the criminal justice system had risen by 72% in real terms over the eleven years since 1978/9. The increase resulted from the growing demands placed on the various services, particularly prisons and the police, as well as their intrinsic importance.

VIII

In a way that had not been seen since *Penal Practice in a Changing Society* thirty years before, the White Paper on *Crime, Justice and Protecting the Public*[64] was a classic statement of public policy. Well written, well argued, and politically courageous in places, it demonstrated a breadth of outlook not often found in official documents. Above all, the White Paper caught the spirit of the times. Each of its central tenets had a resonance in public opinion:

[63] Norman Lamont, Chief Secretary to HM Treasury, 1989–90, had previously been Minister of State, Department of Trade and Industry, 1981–5, for Defence Procurement, 1985–6, and Financial Secretary to HM Treasury, 1986–9. He became Chancellor of the Exchequer in Nov. 1990 and continued in that office after the 1992 General Election.

[64] Cm. 965.

that imprisonment should be reserved for the most serious crimes; that punishment should be in proportion to the seriousness of the offence;[65] that there should be a sharper distinction in the way the courts deal with violent and non-violent crimes; that community penalties should be strengthened to provide the courts with a realistic form of alternative punishment for the less serious offences; and that fines should be related to the means of the offender.

Taken as a whole *Crime, Justice and Protecting the Public* was generally well received by penal reformers and the quality press. 'The Government's proposals provide a new sense of purpose to the penal system', said *The Times*.[66] In the view of the Prison Reform Trust, the White Paper was 'an important step towards a more rational penal system, and one that is less reliant upon custody. Although many major issues are not addressed, both in its overall strategy and in many of its specific proposals the White Paper is consistent with much that we and the prison reform lobby in general have been saying for many years'.[67] Some of the vested interests, a majority of probation officers and the organizations representing members of the Prison Service being conspicuous amongst them, objected vociferously to parts of the White Paper and the underlying policies on which the proposals for legislation had been based. Any latent resistance from the most powerful vested interest of all, the judiciary, had been forestalled by the early

---

[65] Although 'the seriousness of the offence' slipped into the currency of sentencing jargon without dissent, few attempts have been made to define more closely the meaning of the phrase or how to measure relative harm. In the spring of 1991 Andrew von Hirsch and Nils Jareborg published a theory for assessing the degree of harm suffered by the victim as a consequence of a criminal act. It revolved around the standard or quality of a person's life, the most grievous harms being those which reduced the victim's sense of well-being most drastically. If certain conditions were met, the authors believed that their theory could be applied to sentencing law and practice in a systematic way. Although the strong tradition of judicial discretion to determine the sentence within the maximum permitted by Parliament makes improbable the adoption in England and Wales of fixed sentencing grids based upon harm scales, nevertheless this approach is a stimulus to think more deeply about the gravity of criminal offences from the standpoint of the harm suffered by the victim, and not simply the culpability of the offender. See 'Gauging Criminal Harm: A Living-Standard Analysis', (1991) 11 *Oxford Journal of Legal Studies*, 1–38.

[66] 7 Feb. 1990. The same edition of *The Times* published a feature article by the author headed 'More than just deserts'.

[67] Prison Reform Trust, *Comments on the White Paper 'Crime, Justice and Protecting the Public' (Cm. 965)*, Apr. 1990, p. 1.

endorsement of the sentencing proposals by the Lord Chief Justice, Lord Lane.

The process of consultation was not yet at an end. Another discussion paper, *Supervision and Punishment in the Community*,[68] followed shortly after the White Paper. This was aimed directly at the Probation Service, setting out proposals for structural reorganization and changes in working practices. The Home Office had been grappling with these outstanding issues for some time, but it was natural enough that the new Home Secretary should also wish to break some fresh ground in placing his imprint on the inheritance bequeathed to him by Hurd. Waddington's choice fell on the victims of crime, a subject on which much work had been done,[69] but relatively little said in the various official publications since legislation was not normally required.[70] The Home Office rallied swiftly, drafting a twenty-seven-page booklet as the third part of an 'integrated approach', the other two being the proposed improvements in the powers of the courts to deal with offenders, and how community penalties should be put into effect. The Victim's Charter,[71] published to coincide with European Victims' Day on 22 February 1990, set out in plain language the rights and entitlements of the victims of crime and provided a timely outline of the processes in which the victim was likely to find himself involved.

Less obviously, the message of the charter was also directed at the agencies with which victims would come into contact: the police, the Crown Prosecution Service, the courts, and Victim Support[72]

[68] Home Office, *Supervision and Punishment in the Community: A Framework for Action* (Cm. 966), HMSO, London, 1990.

[69] Summarized in Paul Rock, *Helping Victims of Crime: The Home Office and the Rise of Victim Support in England and Wales*, Clarendon Press, Oxford, 1990.

[70] Criminal justice legislation could, however, be of direct benefit to victims. Apart from the provisions relating to the payment of financial compensation for certain criminal injuries, the Criminal Justice Act 1988 permitted evidence from children under fourteen in cases of alleged violence or sexual abuse to be given over a live television link (Section 32) and extended anonymity for alleged victims of rape (Section 158).

[71] Home Office, *Victim's Charter*, A Statement of the Rights of Victims of Crime, Central Office of Information/Home Office, 1990.

[72] For the origins of the National Association of Victims Support Schemes in the 1970s and its formative development since, see Rock, *Helping Victims of Crime*; also *Responses to Crime*, vol. 1, on the role of victims in the criminal justice process and the argument for practical measures to ease their plight when attending court, pp. 27–61.

volunteers. A checklist of questions was given to test how well, or indifferently, victims of crime were treated at their moment of need. Court staffs were encouraged to consider the layout of the court, the waiting time, and the facilities available to victims, so as to reduce as far as possible the alienation so often experienced when victims attend court, either as witnesses in a criminal trial, or as observers. New buildings offered greater potential than old ones, and the Home Office was revising the Design Guide issued to Magistrates' Courts Committees to draw attention to witnesses' special needs in order that they might be considered when new buildings were being planned. In the Crown Court the latest design standards for new buildings provided for an ample number of witness waiting rooms per courtroom, and for separate entrances to courtrooms so that victims and other witnesses could avoid contact with the public when going to the witness box.

The charter contained a specific mention of the Victim in Court project which derived from the recommendations of a working party chaired by a former chairman of the Magistrates' Association, Lady Ralphs:

Victim Support has set up special projects in seven Crown Court centres. These projects are funded by the Home Office and are supported by the Lord Chancellor's Department. In each court centre there is a court based co-ordinator, employed by the local victim support scheme with a team of specially selected volunteers, trained to give practical and emotional support to victims of crime and other vulnerable witnesses attending court. This includes making contact with victims as soon as possible so that help can be given where necessary with such matters as childminding, liaison with employers or transport to court.[73]

On the day of publication, the Home Secretary announced his agreement to providing sixty additional staff for the Criminal Injuries Compensation Board, urgently requested by its new chairman, Lord Carlisle of Bucklow, to help deal with the backlog of claims that still persisted, together with an extra £17 million available for payment of compensation in the coming year.[74]

Further discussion papers followed, on the role of voluntary organizations in dealing with offenders in the community and their

[73] *Victim's Charter*, p. 10.
[74] For an account of the operation of the Criminal Injuries Compensation Scheme, see Chapter 4.

relationship with central Government and the statutory services,[75] and on court escorts, custody and security, published in April and July 1990. Including an earlier Green Paper on *Private Sector Involvement in the Remand System*[76] in July 1988, an important and politically contentious topic which is the subject of Chapter 6, the number of publications issued by the Home Office to prepare the way for the 1990/1 legislation amounted to six. The *Victim's Charter* and two further publications, on the remand of alleged juvenile offenders and the organization of the Probation Service in supervising community penalties, which were published while the legislation was before Parliament, brought the grand total to nine. The titles and dates of publication are shown in Table 8. It was permissible hyperbole for Patten to claim, as he did when the Bill finally reached a Standing Committee in the House of Commons, that it was 'the most carefully prepared and openly aired Criminal Justice Bill this century'.[77]

TABLE 8. *Home Office publications linked to the Criminal Justice Act 1991*

Title	Date
Punishment, Custody and the Community (Cm. 424)	July 1988
Private Sector Involvement in the Remand System (Cm. 434)	July 1988
Crime, Justice and Protecting the Public (Cm. 965)	Feb. 1990
Supervision and Punishment in the Community: A Framework for Action (Cm. 966)	Feb. 1990
Victim's Charter	Feb. 1990
Partnership in Dealing with Offenders in the Community: A Discussion Paper	Apr. 1990
Court Escorts, Custody and Security: A Discussion Paper	July 1990
The Remand of Alleged Juvenile Offenders: A Consultation Paper	Feb. 1991
Organising Supervision and Punishment in the Community: A Decision Document	Apr. 1991

[75] Home Office, *Partnership in Dealing with Offenders in the Community*, 1990.
[76] Cm. 434.
[77] *Parl. Debates*, HC, Standing Committee A, 1990–1, col. 12, 29 Nov. 1990.

IX

The final steps were to convert the policies so laboriously prepared into legislation, and to bid for the necessary resources in the 1990 Public Expenditure Survey.[78] Drafting legislation is one of the most highly specialist of the skills necessary in Government. It is performed only by a small cabal of lawyers dedicated to their arcane craft who usually have strong, and sometimes obsessive views, on how it should be done. Tension between the draftsmen and the officials who brief them is inescapable, particularly when, as in this instance, the briefing Department wishes to incorporate some declaratory statements of general principle. Such statements jar with a draftsman's tradition of precision and avoidance of doubt, leading to arguments that may not be resolved until the last moment before a Bill is due to be introduced into Parliament. In these circumstances, departmental legal advisers can find their role an awkward one.

Because some new and potentially controversial concepts were being attempted, Faulkner obtained ministerial sanction to take the previously unheard of step of showing a draft of the Bill to two or three judges in order to obtain their reactions. The Judicial Studies Board represented a suitable channel for the purpose, via its Chairman, Glidewell LJ, with the Deputy Chief Justice, Watkins LJ, and Lane also being kept informed. Due to the time factor, the drafts were early versions, incomplete and in some respects still crude, with little time available for detailed discussion. Already conditioned to accept the main thrust of the Bill, the judges were critical of certain provisions when they saw them in cold print.

Between the White Paper and the publication of the Bill, judicial scepticism was brought to bear mainly on the provisions relating to the sentencing of offenders who had been convicted of more than one offence, and the extent to which courts should be allowed to take account of previous convictions consistent with the principle of proportionality or just deserts whereby the punishment was to

[78] In a paper titled *Policy, Legislation and Practice*, presented at a conference organized by International Comparisons in Criminal Justice and the Dutch Association of the Judiciary at Breda in October 1990, David Faulkner gave a rare insight into the process of formulating legislation and the distribution of money and staff for the purposes of criminal justice in the United Kingdom, particularly in England and Wales. I have drawn on his account here.

be related to the seriousness of the offence. For example, previous convictions might show that housebreaking was unlikely to have been merely opportunistic, since the offender was a professional burglar; or they might negate a plea in mitigation that a business-man's latest offence of fraud was just an oversight. The treatment of previous convictions continued to be the subject of much debate when the Bill was before Parliament, and if the preliminary con-sultation with the judiciary was not wholly successful as a means of reaching agreement, the gesture at least demonstrated that the Home Office was prepared to act in the spirit of the proclaimed interdependence of the criminal justice system.

Getting the resources was, according to Faulkner, if anything, more difficult even than drafting the legislation.[79] Assumptions had to be made about the scale on which courts would use the various new forms of community sentence and the more intensive forms of supervision available under them. The future number and length of custodial sentences, taking into account the effects of the revised parole scheme, were also conjectural. Other uncertainties stemmed from the proposals to reduce certain maximum sentences, for the Crown Court to pass sentences of imprisonment for terms longer than commensurate with the seriousness of the offence in order to protect the public from serious harm; and the use made of powers to return prisoners to custody to complete their original sentences if they committed further offences soon after their release.

The calculations were overlaid by a further complication: the fact that the prison population had fallen from the total of over 50,000, including those in police cells, which was reached during the summer of 1987 and was maintained for most of the following year, to an average of 48,610 in 1989, marking the first fall in the average prison population since 1973. By the year end the popu-lation was about 2,100 lower than a year earlier,[80] and still falling. On 30 June 1990 the total was down to about 45,500, some 3,300 lower than a year previously.[81] When the Autumn Statement

[79] *Policy, Legislation and Practice*, para. 20.

[80] Home Office, *Prison Statistics England and Wales* (Cm. 1221), HMSO, London, 1990, p. 9.

[81] Home Office, *Statistical Bulletin* 33/90, para. 4. The population had fallen substantially since 1988 against a long-term upward trend, and this was at least in part due to changes in sentencing practice. The volatility of the prison population was stressed as a prelude to updating projections of long-term trends. It was pointed out that since 1946 there had been only three other periods when there was a

containing the outcome of the 1990 Public Expenditure Survey[82] was presented to Parliament by the Chancellor of the Exchequer it showed increased provision to divert offenders from custody, set off by a reduction resulting from the cancellation from the prison-building programme of three prisons on which work had not yet begun.

Once again, however, the unexpected had intervened, as additional provision had to be made to meet the high cost of restoration at Strangeways and other prisons in the wake of the riots and disturbances which had caused such extensive damage in April 1990.[83] After a review of the prison estate the Home Secretary announced the closure of four prison establishments: two in 1991 (Lowdham Grange and Campsfield House); and two more in 1992/3 (Eastwood Park and Northeye).[84] The enhancement of community penalties for less serious offenders led to provision being made for 360 more probation staff, including 180 probation officers, by the end of 1991/2. Further increases were planned for 480 additional probation staff by the end of 1993/4 to meet the demands of the Criminal Justice Act 1991.[85] Finally, late in the day, missing by a wide margin the surge in the prison population which took place in 1987 and 1988, the first major new prison in the building

reduction in the average population lasting more than a year, and that each of these falls had been followed by a substantial increase. Despite this volatility, there had been persistent increases in the prison population since the end of the Second World War, offset by reductions due to policy interventions. In accordance with this pattern, the Statistical Department expected the 1989/90 fall to bottom out and the long-standing trend increases to resume from the lower level before too long (paras. 14 and 15). Earlier in the same *Bulletin* the caveat had been entered that many factors affected the size of the prison population, and that considerable uncertainty attached to the projections. The impact of the forthcoming policy and legislative changes (under the Criminal Justice Act 1991) had not been incorporated into the projections. They could be expected to result in a significant reduction in the number of offenders in custody (para. 2).

[82] HM Treasury, *Autumn Statement* (Cm. 1311), HMSO, London, 1990, p. 18.

[83] The Home Office estimated that restoration of Strangeways alone would take three years and cost £68 million. The work would include integral sanitation in cells designed to contain about 1,000 inmates. At the time of the riot and extended roof-top protest, there were 1,647 prisoners at Strangeways compared with the certified normal accommodation of 970 inmates. Many inmates were sleeping three to a cell. *Prison Disturbances 1990*, Report of an Inquiry by Lord Justice Woolf and Judge Tumim (Cm. 1456), HMSO, London, 1991, pp. 45–7.

[84] Home Office, *The Government's Public Expenditure Plans 1991–2 to 1993–4 for the Home Office and the Charity Commission* (Cm. 1509), HMSO, London, 1991, p. 31.

[85] Ibid., p. 36.

programme launched in 1980 opened its doors to prisoners in April 1991. Located at Woolwich, HM Prison Belmarsh was designed as a local prison for 850 inmates drawn mainly from the London area. No new prison on this scale had been built in London for more than a century. The eventual cost amounted to £109 million.

Even when faced with the consequences of the unpredictable (and unpredicted) volatility of the prison population, the temptation must be resisted to portray the formulation of criminal policy in the late 1980s as being more orderly and rational than it was, or perhaps ever could be. To say this is not to deny the efforts and achievements of the small group of skilful and industrious people, essentially ministers, Home Office officials, and political advisers, at the centre of the decision-taking process. Some policy objectives, such as diversion from custody and proportionality in sentencing, without exaggeration could be looked on as guiding principles. But others, such as the twin-track approach, were calculated means to politically desirable ends. If the belief, which had obtained such a hold on the British mind, that imprisonment was the only real punishment for criminal offences and anything else was a soft option was to be loosened, arguments with the power of dynamite were called for. Yet the immediate aim, a reduction in the number of custodial sentences, with a resultant easing of prison overcrowding, could induce its own myopia.

Where was the other track leading? Did dangers lie in the progressive lengthening of custodial sentences for offenders convicted of the more serious crimes? What were the implications for the already burgeoning long-term prison population? Was there not something objectionable in the concept of 'topping up', that is of encouraging the Crown Court and the Magistrates' courts to impose custodial sentences longer than would otherwise be merited by the circumstances of the offence upon certain categories of violent and sexual offenders if it was considered necessary to protect the public? Was the insistence on maintaining the mandatory sentence of imprisonment for all murders justified, and what were the reasons for the tardiness in revising the administrative procedures which determined how long persons serving discretionary life sentences remained in custody in order to bring practice into line with the obligations incurred under the European Convention on Human Rights and a judgment by the Court of Human Rights? The reply given would be that these things were part of a package, and that all progress has its price. Evolutionary and pragmatic, its topmost branches swaying to the breezes of popular opinion made audible by Parliament and the press, the trunk of criminal justice policy in England and Wales is unyielding and especially resistant to ideas founded on principle. Familiar practices are abandoned only with reluctance, even when they have grown up piecemeal, often over long periods of time, never having been deliberately designed to work in the way they do. Two case histories which illustrate this proposition are pre-trial detention and sentences of life imprisonment.

6

Prisons, Prevention, and Privatization

I

When the Leeds Castle seminar was charting the future in September 1987, the remand population in England and Wales stood at 11,655 untried and unsentenced prisoners, including those held in police cells. Of these 11,227 were male and 428 female, with somewhat more than two-thirds (7,944) aged twenty-one or over, and 3,711 under twenty-one. If bail is refused, the case must come back before the court, normally at intervals of not less than eight days,[1] until it is disposed of by the Magistrates' court or committed for trial at the Crown Court. To reduce the often lengthy periods spent in custody awaiting trial, time limits were introduced in October 1991 of fifty-six days from first appearance to trial in the Magistrates' court, and seventy days from first appearance before the magistrates to committal to the Crown Court.[2] A limit of 112 days applies to the interval between committal and arraignment in the Crown

---

[1] Significant exceptions to the eight-day limit have been made by recent legislation. The Criminal Justice Act 1982 allowed a Magistrates' court to remand in custody an accused person aged eighteen or over in his absence for three successive periods of up to eight days if, on the last occasion when he appeared in court and was remanded, he was legally represented and agreed that he need not be brought up from prison on the next three occasions. Section 128A of the Magistrates' Courts Act 1980 (a provision inserted by Section 155 of the Criminal Justice Act 1988, and operative throughout England and Wales since 2 Dec. 1991) provides that if a defendant appears in court after a previous remand in custody and a date has been set for the next stage in the proceedings (i.e. something more than another remand hearing), magistrates may remand the defendant for up to twenty-eight days or for the interval until the next stage, whichever is the less.

[2] Statutory limitation on the period of time between committal and trial dates back to the Habeas Corpus Act 1679. Section 6 gave the prisoner the right either to be indicted within one term or session after his commitment, or bailed and to be either tried within two terms or sessions, or discharged. The provision endured for nearly three centuries, being repealed by the Courts Act 1971. For the use of habeas corpus as a device to secure the right of accused persons detained pending their trial to be either tried quickly or released, see R. J. Sharpe, *The Law of Habeas Corpus*, Clarendon Press, Oxford, 2nd edn., 1989, pp. 136–9.

Court. Time spent in custody on remand counts towards any sentence of imprisonment that may result,[3] although that is little consolation to those who are acquitted or sentenced to a non-custodial penalty. In the United States a defendant convicted of a crime has a similar entitlement to receive credit for time spent in detention before his term of imprisonment begins.[4]

The average number of days spent in custody by untried prisoners received into prison in 1987 was fifty-seven for males and forty-five for females. In the first half of 1987, the average remand population (including those in police cells) was 11,002. Rather under a half (44%) were involved with proceedings at the Magistrates' courts; two-fifths (38%) had been committed for trial at the Crown Court; and one in seven (14.3%) were convicted but unsentenced prisoners, including those remanded for a medical or social inquiry report to be prepared.

On a prison population that had been reduced by about 3,000 as a result of a decision in July 1987 to extend remission for shorter-sentenced prisoners up to and including twelve months from one-third to one-half of the sentence length,[5] the proportion of remand prisoners was 23.6% between August and December 1987. The comparative figures in Table 9 show that over a ten-year period 1981–90 an annual average of between 16.1% and 22.9% of the

[3] In 1987 the duration of a remand in custody also counted towards calculating the one-third point in the sentence when a prisoner became eligible for parole consideration, but not towards the minimum qualifying period of six months. The rule contributed to an anomaly in the relative periods of time served by shorter-sentenced prisoners, which was one of the reasons leading to the review of the parole system by a committee under Lord Carlisle's chairmanship in 1987/8. The recommendation of the Review Committee was that remand time should continue to count automatically towards the sentence and towards the proportion of the sentence which must be served in custody prior to conditional release. The minimum qualifying period should be abolished, and all prisoners serving four years or less should be released after they had served half of their sentence. The recommendations were accepted by the Government and incorporated in the Criminal Justice Act 1991, although short-term prisoners were defined as persons serving a sentence of imprisonment for a term of less than four years.

[4] The US Supreme Court has held that in the case of a defendant convicted of a federal crime it is for the Attorney General, acting through the Bureau of Prisons, to compute the amount of credit allowable after the defendant has begun to serve his sentence, and not for the District Court to do so when passing sentence. See *United States* v. *Wilson* 112 S. Ct. 1351 (1992).

[5] Half remission for prisoners serving sentences of twelve months or less was introduced on 13 August, 1987, having been announced by Hurd in the House of Commons the previous month. *Parl. Debates*, HC, 119 (6th ser.), cols. 1296–8, 16 July 1987.

total prison population was made up of untried criminal prisoners and convicted but unsentenced prisoners. The impact on the overall population of the faster rate of growth of the remand population, compared with the number of sentenced prisoners during the mid-1980s, stands out. National averages over the whole prison system mask significant variations. Whereas the dispersal prisons holding security A category prisoners in the Isle of Wight and elsewhere contain very few remand prisoners, local prisons may have up to 35% of their inmates on remand. At the time of the riot at Strangeways Prison in 1990, no less than 500 of the 1647 prisoners in accommodation certified to hold only 970 were adult or young prisoners waiting to appear at the Crown Court or the Magistrates' courts, with a further 193 who had been convicted and were awaiting sentence.[6]

The description 'remand prisoner' is undesirable as it appears to equate detention before trial to imprisonment after conviction. My contention in this chapter is that a fundamental distinction exists between the punishment of convicted offenders and the pre-trial detention of persons accused of a criminal offence; that the conditions in which persons on remand are confined are indistinguishable in most respects from the restrictions on liberty imposed in the name of punishment; and that entirely separate provision for as many as possible of those remanded in custody by the courts is not only the best way to recognize their special status, but is a practical method of easing the chronic pressure of numbers on the local prisons.

Freed from the burden of such a significant proportion of the prison population, the Prison Service would be enabled to concentrate on the vital task of improving standards, both of regimes and security, for the bulk of sentenced prisoners who have been deprived of their liberty as punishment.[7] Adequate provision

[6] *Prison Disturbances April 1990* (Cm. 1456), p. 45.

[7] This argument was first advanced in *Responses to Crime*, vol. 1, pp. 245–7. There I proposed the establishment of remand centres apart from the prison system, employing agency staff and licensed and supervised by the Home Office, to relieve the pressure on the prisons and signify the special status of the inmates. This was followed by an article in *The Times* on 8 July 1987 ('The Inappropriate Prisoners') and a more detailed study entitled: 'Punishment and Prevention: The Inappropriate Prisoners' [1988] Crim. L.R. 140. The present chapter reproduces, with some updating, the analysis contained in the early part of the *Criminal Law Review* article, relates it to the innovation of privatization, and brings the chronology of events to the end of 1991. It draws on the evidence on remand prisoners which I submitted

TABLE 9. *Remand population, 1981–90*

	1981	1982	1983	1984	1985	1986	1987	1988	1989	1990
Average population of prisoners[a] in all categories (sentenced and remand)	43,436	43,754	43,772	43,349	46,278	46,889	48,963	49,949	48,610	45,636
Untried criminal prisoners awaiting trial and convicted unsentenced prisoners, including those held in police cells	7,030	7,432	7,961	8,741	9,742	10,081	11,162	11,440	10,499	9,905
Average numbers held in police cells	125	47	310	54	45	119	537	978	103	465
Remand population as a proportion of all criminal prisoners (%)	16.18	16.99	18.19	20.16	21.05	21.50	22.80	22.90	21.60	21.70

[a] Including civil prisoners and immigration detainees.

Source: Home Office, *Prison Statistics England and Wales.*

in remand centres would also permit bringing to an end the pernicious practice of detaining large numbers of untried persons in wholly unsuitable accommodation in police stations. For over a decade the police have been required to manage an alternative prison system, which in 1991 contained a record population averaging 1,100 held in police cells.

II

Few would challenge the proposition that punishment is the touchstone which should distinguish sentenced prisoners from those who are awaiting trial on remand. Convicted offenders sentenced to a term of imprisonment for their crimes are being punished; untried persons are not. Yet remand prisoners are not only subjected to that loss of liberty which, in theory, is the sole justification for the punishment of offenders sentenced to imprisonment, but also to the same squalid and disagreeable way of life. Given the deplorable conditions that prevail in so many of the local prisons, there can be little argument that the punitive character of imprisonment is enhanced by the conditions in which sentences are served. Despite the fact that the rationale for detaining untried persons in custody is not penal, but precautionary, they suffer a similar penal surcharge. The reasons for pre-trial detention need to be clearly spelt out. They are: to prevent the possibility of offences being committed whilst awaiting trial; to prevent witnesses being tampered with; and to prevent accused persons from disappearing and failing to come to court to answer the charges against them.

A further ground for withholding bail is where the court considers that an offender needs to be held in custody for his own protection (reasons include the vengeance of injured parties or their friends, and suicide risks) or, if he is a child or young person, for his own

to the Inquiry by Lord Justice Woolf and Judge Tumim into the Prison Disturbances in April 1990, and a debate in the House of Lords on their report, *Parl. Debates*, HL, 531 (5th ser.), cols. 729–68, 23 July 1991. The nub of the argument, that individuals held on remand are different in kind from convicted prisoners, and deserve to be treated accordingly, remains unchanged.

welfare.[8] These are the long-established reasons, enshrined in the Bail Act since 1976, but going back much earlier, for empowering the courts to deprive of their liberty for a temporary period individuals accused of an imprisonable offence if the court is satisfied there are 'substantial grounds' why bail cannot be granted. Pre-trial detention, as Lord Hailsham has pointed out, is the solitary exception in peacetime to the Magna Carta.[9] The ever-present danger is that punishment may come to precede trial, rather than follow it in those cases where guilt has been established. The tests of whether the minimum restraints needed to achieve the purposes of prevention are being exceeded include the physical conditions, notably of accommodation, while detained; the restrictions to which the detainee is subjected; and the length of time spent in detention.

If we accept as a fundamental principle of the English system of criminal justice that anyone who is accused of a crime is entitled to be treated as innocent until he is proved guilty, it follows that only such limitations on normal rights and freedoms as are unavoidably necessary should be imposed.[10] The presumption of innocence does not sit comfortably with the denial of bail, and arguments for overriding it in the interests of greater effectiveness need to be scrutinized with particular rigour. Nevertheless, it is inescapably true that the administration of justice cannot function at all if the accused does not appear for his trial. The same applies if witnesses or jurors are intimidated or interfered with. Difficult as it is for magistrates or judges to reach decisions on such unpredictable grounds, lying in the future rather than the past, they must do the best they can to assess the risks on the basis of such information as is available to them.

The Bail Act 1976 gives some direction pointing to the nature and seriousness of the offence; the character, antecedents, associ-

[8] The Bail Act 1976 allows bail to be denied in more limited circumstances to defendants accused of non-imprisonable offences. In such a case the belief that, if released, the defendant would fail to surrender to custody is a sufficient reason for refusing bail only if he has previously been granted bail and failed to surrender. It is also a sufficient reason that the defendant needs to be held in custody for his own protection or, if a child or young person, for his own welfare.

[9] Speech to the Gloucestershire Branch of the Magistrates' Association on 11 Sept. 1971 published in *The Magistrate*, Feb. 1972, p. 21.

[10] In *Raymond* v. *Honey* [1983] 1 AC 1 at 10, an appeal to the House of Lords about prisoners' correspondence, Lord Wilberforce declared that 'under English law, a convicted prisoner, in spite of his imprisonment, retains all civil rights which are not taken away expressly or by necessary implication.'

ations, and community ties[11] of the defendant; and his record in fulfilling any previous bail obligations.[12] More recently bail information schemes under which verified information about the defendant is collected by the Probation Service and placed before the Court, have proved to be an effective means of improving the quality of decisions on bail. The Association of Chief Officers of Probation has estimated that one in five people are allowed bail as a result of bail information schemes who would otherwise have been remanded in custody.[13] Bail information schemes can also be used to help the courts to identify the bad risks more accurately. The point was made by Kenneth Baker as Home Secretary when replying to police inspired criticism of the large number of offences committed while on bail. Home Office estimates suggested that of nearly half a million people granted court bail, about 50,000 were convicted of an offence on bail. The trend was rising; five years earlier the comparable figure being about 35,000. The typical 'bail bandit' was likely to be male, aged between seventeen and twenty, and charged with a property offence, usually car crime or burglary.[14]

The controversy showed the knife-edge on which the Home Secretary had to balance. While respecting his duty to uphold the liberty of the subject, no politician can afford to ignore public attitudes towards the operation of criminal justice. Critical opinion, moreover, if widespread and seemingly reasonable, can be expected to spread to the Magistrates' courts and be reflected before long in

---

[11] 'Community ties' is the graceless term used in the Bail Act 1976 to describe a defendant's family circumstances, his home, and his livelihood.

[12] Bail Act 1976, Sch. 1, s. 9.

[13] S. Casale and J. Plotnikoff, *Regimes for Remand Prisoners*, Prison Reform Trust, London, 1990, p. 15. Bail information schemes were an initiative of the Association of Chief Officers of Probation, acting in collaboration with the Crown Prosecution Service. Eight pilot schemes were monitored and co-ordinated with the assistance of the Vera Institute of Justice which had done much of the preparatory work. A White Paper published in September 1991 in response to the findings and recommendations of the Woolf Inquiry declared Government support for the extension of bail information schemes in the Magistrates' courts. In 103 such courts in England and Wales the Probation Service was providing information to the Crown Prosecution Service. The intention was to extend schemes to all probation areas as resources allowed. The Government also supported bail information schemes in those prisons holding prisoners on remand. Schemes were available in eight prisons with plans to extend availability to eight more by the end of 1991/2, and subsequently to all local and remand prisons. Home Office, *Custody, Care and Justice: The Way Ahead for the Prison Service in England and Wales* (Cm. 1647), HMSO, London, pp. 100–1.

[14] *Parl. Debates*, HC, 204 (6th ser.), cols. 813–14, 25 Feb. 1992.

their decisions. Yet the Home Secretary is not simply a politician; he is also a senior departmental minister, acutely conscious of the cost and restricted availability of custodial resources, as well as the limited effectiveness of the remedies at his disposal. Declarations of intent to legislate sound bold and resolute, but Parliamentary time has to be found, often years rather than months ahead, and unless carefully thought out can have results different from what was intended. Baker's response was twofold: to announce some forthcoming changes in the criminal law, but to back them up by extensions of bail information schemes,[15] the provision of additional places in bail hostels, and a review by the Judicial Studies Board of the training of magistrates in the criteria set out in the Bail Act 1976. Magistrates' courts were being asked to ensure that the bail notices issued to all defendants made clear that if they failed to answer bail, or to comply with the conditions imposed, or if they committed an offence while on bail, they risked being remanded in custody.

Legislation would be introduced to require the courts to consider offending on bail as an aggravating factor when passing sentence, and to confer on the police a statutory power to arrest immediately those who breach police bail. These changes, the Home Secretary claimed, were substantial rather than modest ones, adding that the sentencing provision had been pressed on him by the police for some time. Front-bench Opposition speakers, and Sir John Wheeler from the Government benches, supported the commitment to bail information schemes and bail hostels, with the Parliamentary Adviser to the Police Federation confirming that the statement would be 'warmly welcomed' by the federated ranks of the police.[16]

Until the early part of the nineteenth century a general rule prevailed that a person committed for a misdemeanour was entitled to bail, although in the course of the seventeenth and eighteenth centuries a number of exceptions were made.[17] Parliament then

---

[15] Ibid., col. 813. By the time of Baker's statement schemes were operating in 113 Magistrates' courts and 13 prisons. It was intended to set up bail information projects in selected local areas, including the inner cities, to ensure that information from the police, Crown Prosecution Service, and the Probation Service was collated and made available to the courts.

[16] Michael Shersby MP had been adviser to the Police Federation since 1989. Ibid., col. 816.

[17] See F. W. Maitland, *The Constitutional History of England*, Cambridge University Press, 1908, p. 315.

took a hand, passing legislation affecting bail in 1826, 1835, and 1848. As to felonies, an Act in 1826 (7 Geo. IV c. 64) for 'improving the administration of criminal justice in England' provided that if there was a strong presumption of guilt the defendant should be committed to prison. Where the evidence given in support of the charge was not, in the opinion of the justices, such as to raise a strong presumption of his guilt, but there was nevertheless sufficient ground for judicial inquiry into the charge, the defendant should be admitted to bail. An Act of 1835 (5 and 6 William IV, c. 33) for extending the provisions of the earlier Act 'as to the taking of Bail in cases of Felony' allowed justices to grant bail even where there had been a confession of guilt, or where the evidence was strong enough to create a presumption of guilt. The Indictable Offences Act 1848 made the grant of bail entirely a matter for the justices' discretion.

For misdemeanours, the Act of 1826 and the Indictable Offences Act 1848 made the grant of bail discretionary in relation to various specified offences and any misdemeanour for which the cost of prosecution might be charged on the county. The Costs in Criminal Cases Act 1908, in providing for the cost of prosecuting any misdemeanour to be so charged, removed the last vestiges of an entitlement to bail on a charge of misdemeanour.[18] The discretion of justices to grant or refuse bail was open to review by the superior courts on an application for habeas corpus.

In the United States, where bail had been a positive right of the citizen (other than for capital offences) since the first Judiciary Act in 1789, legislators turned their attention to pre-trial detention in the Comprehensive Crime Control Act of 1984.[19] This legislation, which was part of a wider measure including sentencing reforms, went beyond the possibility that an accused person might seek to obstruct justice either by fleeing or by intimidating witnesses or jurors, hitherto the only grounds for refusing bail. The Act permitted, indeed required, the federal courts to detain an arrested person pending trial if the government demonstrated by 'clear and convincing evidence', after an adversary hearing, that no release

[18] The report which paved the way for the Bail Act 1976 contained a summary of the historical background, see Home Office, *Bail Procedures in Magistrates' Courts*, Report of the Working Party, HMSO, 1974, pp. 3–5.

[19] Ch. 1 of the Comprehensive Crime Control Act of 1984 is cited as the Bail Reform Act of 1984. Pub. L. No. 98–473, S. 203(*a*) *et seq*.

conditions would reasonably assure 'the safety of any other person and the community'.[20]

Thus for the first time in two centuries Congress enacted legislation allowing for pre-trial detention on the grounds of the dangerousness of those awaiting trial. In the absence of Parliamentary supremacy the Act had to surmount the hurdle of challenges to its constitutional validity in the courts. It was not long before cases began to reach the US Court of Appeals, with differing results, but none excelled the classic of modern American jurisprudence to be found in the leading judgment of the Court of Appeals for the Second Circuit in the *United States* v. *Melendez-Carrion* in 1986.[21] This case, and one that followed hard on its heels in the same court, the *United States* v. *Salerno*,[22] illustrated the absolute adherence to the spirit of the Constitution which still endures, even if it does not always prevail, in an age of international terrorism and organized crime that is so far removed from the world known by the framers of the Constitution. The fact that the Supreme Court later reached a different conclusion did nothing to diminish the elevated morality which the two highest courts in the land brought to their constitutional duty of reviewing the lawfulness of legislation passed by the Congress.

The circumstances could not have been more dramatic if the casting had been devised in Hollywood. In the first case the defendants belonged to a notorious paramilitary organization known as the Machete Wielders, dedicated to the use of force to advance the cause of Puerto Rican independence. They had claimed responsibility for an armed robbery in which $7.6 million had been taken, and had been detained in custody awaiting trial for more than eight months. Previous operations had included destroying by explosives nine aircraft of the Puerto Rican National Guard at an airbase. In a judgment ringing with the authentic tones of libertarian principle, Judge Newman held that the Bail Reform Act violated the Due Process clause of the Fifth Amendment, namely that 'no person shall ... be deprived of his life, liberty or property without due process of law'.[23] In his opinion, the total deprivation of liberty

---

[20] Bail Reform Act of 1984, S. 203, 18 USC, 3142 (*e*).

[21] *United States* v. *Melendez-Carrion* 790 F. 2d 948 (2nd Cir. 1986).

[22] *United States* v. *Salerno and Cafaro* 794 F. 2d 64 (2nd Cir. 1986).

[23] The protection against arbitrary power contained in the Fifth Amendment has long been regarded as one of the bulwarks of individual liberty. Both the Fifth and

exceeded the substantive limitations of the Due Process clause:

The liberty protected under that system is premised on the accountability of free men and women for what they have done, not for what they may do. The Due Process Clause reflects the constitutional imperative that incarceration to protect society from criminals may be accomplished only as punishment of those convicted for past crimes and not as regulation of those feared likely to commit future crimes.[24]

In the second case Anthony ('Fat Tony') Salerno was the boss of the Genovese family of La Cosa Nostra of which his co-defendant, Vincent ('Fish') Cafaro, was a captain. On the basis of court-authorized wiretaps and evidence from two well-placed informers, the Government alleged that both men were guilty of using violence to eliminate competition from their gambling operations, as well as extorting money in the course of a loan-sharking business and attempting to control labour unions. Were they to be released on bail pending trial, it was contended, their business would continue as usual. But in this instance since 'business as usual' embraced threats, beatings, and even murder, the danger to the community was self-evident. At the age of seventy-four, Salerno was unlikely to change the habits of a lifetime, while Cafaro was alleged to be conducting the activities of the enterprise and to have done so by directing others to commit violent acts. The District Court, after a hearing in which witnesses were called and cross-examined, found the Government had established by clear and convincing evidence that no condition of release, or combination of conditions, would ensure the safety of the community and of any person, and accordingly ordered the detention of the accused. The US Court of Appeals reversed this decision, again holding that pre-trial detention on the ground of future dangerousness was unconstitutional and violated the Due Process Clause of the Fifth Amendment, the majority relying on Judge Newman's reasoning in *Melendez-Carrion*.[25]

By the time the case reached the Supreme Court the constitutional issues had become detached from the fate of the two defendants,

Eighth Amendments formed part of the Bill of Rights in 1791. The Eighth Amendment, which states that excessive bail shall not be required, was deployed as a supporting argument for the defendants in *Melendez-Carrion* and *Salerno*, although silent on the question whether bail should be available at all.

[24] *United States* v. *Melendez-Carrion* 790 F. 2d 948 at 1001.
[25] *United States* v. *Salerno and Cafaro* 794 F. 2d 64.

Salerno having been convicted on unrelated charges after a jury trial and sentenced to a total of 100 years' imprisonment. Cafaro was more favourably placed, since in the interval he had become a co-operating witness assisting the Government's investigations and had been released on bail, with government consent, ostensibly for medical care and treatment. Neither man, therefore, whose potential dangerousness lay at the heart of the case for their pre-trial confinement, was directly affected by its outcome. No wonder one of the justices felt moved to quote Felix Frankfurter's laconic remark: 'It is a fair summary of history to say that the safeguards of liberty have frequently been forged in controversies involving not very nice people.'[26]

Like the court below, the Supreme Court was divided, by a majority of six to three holding that the Court of Appeals had erred in ruling that the Due Process Clause categorically prohibited pre-trial detention on the ground of community safety. In the majority opinion of Rehnquist CJ, the Government's regulatory interest in community safety could, and in the circumstances of Salerno's case did, outweigh an individual's right to liberty.[27]

III

We now enter uncertain and speculative territory, a borderland between the empires of law and social science. Legal distinctions between punishment and prevention have struck me, while reflecting on this subject, as being too narrowly focused upon the justifications for pre-trial detention. While admiring Judge Newman's constitutional purity, and applauding his legal scholarship, not many people engaged in the administration of English criminal justice, I suspect, would go so far as he did. Yet whenever lawyers have reviewed the conditions and restrictions imposed upon detainees and considered at what point such conditions and restrictions amount to punishment, they have become side-tracked by questions of intent to punish and measures that might be regarded as

[26] *US* v. *Salerno* 107 S. Ct. 2095 (1987) Marshall J. at 2111.
[27] Ibid., 2101.

being excessive in relation to available alternatives.[28] The scientific approach, on the other hand, as adopted by social scientists, is to proceed by way of observation or experiment. What is the actual experience of those remanded in custody awaiting trial or sentence, and how does it differ from the experience of convicted and sentenced prisoners?

With some exceptions the male adult is held in the same prison, although in a different part of it, guarded by the same prison officers, and subject to what in most essentials is the same system of regulation. True, he enjoys what are mistakenly called privileges: for example, the right to wear his own clothes if he wishes, to receive daily visits, to be attended by a doctor from outside the Prison Medical Service at his own expense, and to confer and correspond confidentially with his lawyer.[29] All of these have been curtailed by staff shortages and the managerial considerations which dominate the prison environment.

A revealing study published by the Prison Reform Trust in 1990 showed the extent to which remand prisoners' entitlements had been eroded.[30] In each establishment visited with a mixed population of remand and sentenced prisoners there had been a departure from the rule of separation by status. Organizational convenience and resources were found to exercise strong influence on local practice. Interpretation of the Prison Rules allowed latitude for limiting entitlements. Because the clothing of an unconvicted prisoner must be 'suitable, tidy and clean', the entitlement to wear his own clothes,

[28] In 1979 the US Supreme Court considered the extent to which the constitutional rights of pre-trial detainees might be infringed by the conditions and practices of their confinement. In reversing the Federal District Court in New York and the Court of Appeals, which had ruled against the practice of double-bunking (i.e. housing two prisoners in accommodation designed for one), the Supreme Court, by a majority, found there was no 'one man, one cell' principle lurking in the Due Process clause of the Fifth Amendment (*Bell* v. *Wolfish* 441 US 542). The Judge who had granted relief under numerous heads to respondents in the District Court was Marvin Frankel, one of the originators of the sentencing reforms which were enacted in the Comprehensive Crime Control Act 1984. See *United States ex rel. Wolfish* v. *United States* 428 F. Supp. 333 (1977) and *United States ex rel. Wolfish* v. *Levi* 439 F. Supp. 114 (1977).

[29] The right to have food and drink brought or sent into local prisons and remand centres for unconvicted prisoners was withdrawn with effect from 1 Mar. 1988 as part of a series of measures to counter the smuggling of drugs and other unauthorized articles (including escape equipment) into the prisons. *Parl. Debates*, HC, 123 (6th ser.), col. WA 689, 3 Dec. 1987.

[30] Casale and Plotnikoff, *Regimes for Remand Prisoners*, pp. 9–13.

the most conspicuous sign of a remand prisoner's separate status, existed more in theory rather than in general practice.[31] The ethos of one establishment was encapsulated devastatingly in its response to a survey: 'the wearing of issue rather than own clothing allows for easier supervision, reduces damage to own clothing, and opens up the way to full activities'.[32]

Prisoners who have been convicted, but remanded to await sentence, are treated in exactly the same way as the generality of sentenced prisoners, even though some of them will receive non-custodial sentences. Unenforceable entitlements apart, all remand prisoners, whether pre-trial or pre-sentence, share an identical way of life with convicted and sentenced prisoners. They get up at the same time, go to bed at the same time, take exercise (within an entitlement of one hour a day) in the same place, eat at the same time, are subject to the same discipline, the same disorientation and loss of privacy, enduring the same humiliating sanitation, the noise, and the overcrowded cells. In important respects their plight is even worse than that of prisoners being punished for the most serious offences, as a majority will be held in the local prisons where overcrowding is most acute. Since most unconvicted prisoners avail themselves of the right not to work, the opportunities for work and training have been reduced gradually in the interests of economy until they have become virtually non-existent. The Prison Reform Trust survey found that due to declining work opportunities in the prison system as a whole, remand prisoners, particularly unconvicted remands, were generally not given any choice.

Above all, remand prisoners are subject to uncertainty; they cannot plan ahead, or make friends, or settle down to serving a finite term of imprisonment with the prospect of progressing to conditions of lesser security, perhaps an open prison. The resulting state of tension and emotional instability pervades the whole establishment, spreading to the staff as well as the inmates. It is no surprise that three-quarters of all self-inflicted deaths between 1985 and 1990 occurred at local prisons or remand centres.[33] After the

---

[31] Women's prisons were an exception since in practice female prisoners of any status are permitted to wear their own clothes. Ibid., p. 11.
[32] Ibid.
[33] Out of a total of 232 self-inflicted deaths of people in prison custody between 1 Jan. 1985 and 31 Oct. 1990, 167 (74.89%) occurred in local prisons or remand centres. The total excluded persons held in police custody. See Home Office, *Report of a Review by Her Majesty's Chief Inspector of Prisons for England and Wales of*

death of an eighteen-year-old youth awaiting trial for burglary, who was found hanged in his cell at Feltham Young Offenders' Institution in West London, the governor was reported as saying that 59 of the 800 inmates (sentenced as well as on remand) had injured themselves deliberately in the months of October and November 1991.[34]

It may be argued that some or all of these features are the unavoidable consequences of managing an overburdened prison system, preserving order amongst the prisoners and preventing their escape. No one should underestimate the magnitude of the difficulties faced by prison administrators in attempting to perform their task in a decent and competent way. But would a scientist, studying and evaluating the empirical data, be confident enough to substantiate any significant difference between punishment and pre-trial detention in the interests of prevention? What began as a distinction upheld by legal formalism rather than by measurable differences has drifted perilously close to a legal fiction. Is it too fanciful to detect in recent years, on both sides of the Atlantic, a degenerative process accelerated by the passage of time and induced by the physical conditions of confinement, that has transformed legitimate detention in the cause of prevention into something barely distinguishable from illegitimate punishment?

The fact that the physical conditions are so similar raises a question whether compensation should be paid to an accused person who is acquitted after a lengthy period on remand.[35] Should

---

Suicide and Self-Harm in Prison Service Establishments (Cm. 1383), HMSO, London, 1990; Appendix 4(II). The report did not throw much light on the question of what type of prisoner was more prone than others to self-injury, for example remands or convicted prisoners, short term or long term. It noted that 'Researchers to date have given us limited guidance. The figures between remands and convicted for suicide 1980–88 . . . show a rapidly changing scene, but no clear pointer as to which group most suicides belong.' Ibid., p. 5. The statistics for 1991 marked a reduction in the number of self-inflicted deaths occurring in local prisons or remand centres compared with 1990. Self-inflicted deaths among life-sentence prisoners, however, rose sharply from an average of two in each of the years up to 1987, to eight in 1990 and nine in 1991. An information paper issued by the Prison Service in August 1992, *Caring for Prisoners at Risk of Suicide and Self-Injury: The Way Forward*, said that it was 'well established by research' that prisoners on remand, especially those experiencing custody for the first time and those with psychiatric problems, were at higher risk of suicide. Historically, most suicides had occurred in local prisons and remand centres, and the trend continued (p. 3).

[34] *The Times*, 1 Feb. 1992.

[35] Defendants who are convicted, but sentenced to a non-custodial penalty, are

he be entitled to some financial recompense, at any rate for loss of earnings or additional family expenditure directly incurred as a result of his incarceration?[36] In 1990, 7.2% of those charged with an indictable offence and remanded in custody for trial in the Crown Court were subsequently acquitted or not proceeded against. Of those finally dealt with in the Magistrates' courts, 13.5% of accused persons who had been remanded in custody were either acquitted or not proceeded against.[37]

Although the standard of proof required in a criminal trial ('beyond reasonable doubt')[38] means that a finding of not guilty does not necessarily demonstrate the innocence of the accused,[39] nevertheless the Crown Court might be empowered to use its discretion and decide on whether the circumstances of a case merited an order for compensation from public funds, in the same way as it does when making an order for costs. At present there are only two classes of case in which compensation can be claimed. The first is where there has been a miscarriage of justice within the terms of paragraph 6 of Article 14 of the International Covenant on Civil and Political Rights. This states:

When a person has by a final decision been convicted of a criminal offence and when subsequently his conviction has been reversed or he has been pardoned on the ground that a new or newly discovered fact shows

in a different situation. The preventive criteria for pre-trial detention may have been fulfilled although the offence itself, while carrying a liability to imprisonment, may in the outcome merit a lesser penalty.

[36] A case before the European Commission of Human Rights, *X, Y and Z* v. *Austria* (1982) 4 EHRR 270, established that under the European Convention on Human Rights there no inherent right to compensation for detention on remand in the absence of conviction.

[37] *Criminal Statistics England and Wales 1990* (Cm. 1935), HMSO, London, 1992. The figures for acquittals include cases which are not proceeded with, no case to answer, charge withdrawn, no evidence offered, unfit to plead, or died. See Tables 8.6 and 8.9, pp. 198–200.

[38] 'The time-honoured formula is that the jury must be satisfied beyond reasonable doubt ... attempts to substitute other expressions have never prospered. It is generally sufficient and safe to direct a jury that they must be satisfied beyond reasonable doubt so that they feel sure of the defendant's guilt. Nevertheless, other words will suffice, so long as the message is clear.' *Ferguson* v. *The Queen* [1979] 1 All ER 877 per Lord Scarman at 882 delivering the opinion of the Privy Council.

[39] Some jurisdictions overseas make a distinction between proof of innocence and absence of proof of guilt. In Holland and Japan innocence must be positively proved before the defendant can be compensated. For a full discussion of the practical issues arising in statutory compensation schemes, see C. Shelbourn, 'Compensation for Detention' [1978] Crim. L.R. 22.

conclusively that there has been a miscarriage of justice, the person who has suffered punishment as a result of such conviction shall be compensated according to law, unless it is proved that the non-disclosure of the unknown fact in time is wholly or partly attributable to him.

Until comparatively recently the obligation was met by the Home Secretary making *ex gratia* payments from public funds; but Section 133 of the Criminal Justice Act 1988 confers a statutory entitlement to compensation in cases where Article 14 of the Covenant applies. The decision on entitlement to compensation under the Act rests with the Home Secretary, although the amount is assessed by a legally qualified assessor.

The second class of case is dealt with by *ex gratia* payments. It comprises those in which the conviction resulted from serious default on the part of a member of the police force, or some other public authority.[40] Attempts to have compensation in cases of wrongful imprisonment settled by an independent review body were resisted by the Government during the passage of the 1988 legislation, and there was no discussion of acquittals resulting from the normal judicial process after long periods of remand in custody.

IV

Since I first argued the case for making separate provision for the pre-trial detention of individuals accused of a criminal offence who had been refused bail, a changing political climate seemed for a time to bring the objective closer. In this section I rehearse the arguments put forward in 1987/8, before moving on to give an account of subsequent developments. I did not pursue then, and I do not discuss now, the important issues that surround bail, such as the extent to which more bail hostels, or changes in court

---

[40] This class of case continues to be governed by the rules for *ex gratia* payments set out in a written answer by the Home Secretary given in November 1985. *Parl. Debates*, HC, 87 (6th ser.), cols. WA 689–90, 29 Nov. 1985.

procedures,[41] or time limits for bringing cases to trial, are capable of reducing pressures on the remand system. Desirable as they are in themselves, the cumulative effect of measures to divert accused persons who do not need the security of prisons to other accommodation, such as hostels for those who are of no fixed address, is unlikely to be more than marginal. The numbers are so large that radical structural reforms are required if there is to be any prospect of resolving the acute problems of overcrowded local prisons, while at the same time making a reality of the distinction between punishment and prevention.

The strongest of the original arguments related to the status of the prison officers who accompany remand prisoners at the courts. This work is a time-consuming disruption to prison routines which does not call for the special training or vocation of prison officers. Escort duties take officers away from their prisons, frequently unpredictably and at short notice, where their presence is needed to maintain the full range of services that a prison should provide. Thus while the court commitment could and did provide a welcome change of scene for prison staff, being also a useful source of overtime payments until changes in the pay structure were introduced[42] in 1987, it signally contributed to the impoverishment of regimes in the local prisons.

[41] An editorial in the *Criminal Law Review* in July, 1987 raised a number of pertinent questions about bail, calling for a clearer law and better information (including prediction data) as a guide to courts considering the possibility that a defendant may offend if released on bail; [1987] Crim. L.R. 437. The Inquiry by Lord Justice Woolf and Judge Tumim into the prison disturbances of 1990 recommended that magistrates should attach considerable significance to whether or not the offence which the defendant is alleged to have committed is one which, if proved, would justify a sentence of imprisonment. (*Prison Disturbances April 1990*, p. 440). Bail units located in the prisons can also assist the courts in providing relevant information for subsequent bail applications, as well as by making inquiries to ensure that bail conditions, such as the confirmation of sureties, are met. (See Casale and Plotnikoff, *Regimes for Remand Prisoners*, pp. 15–17).

[42] 'Fresh Start' was the name given to a Home Office initiative in 1986 with the aim of bringing about a fundamental reorganization of prison officers' working arrangements and of the management of Prison Service establishments. Its most significant elements were the unification of the governor grades and prison officer grades into a single grading structure; and a reduction in overtime worked by the prison officer grades, to be followed eventually by its complete elimination. This was to be reflected by a considerable improvement in salaries. The Woolf inquiry found that, although Fresh Start was much needed, it led to disillusionment which might have been avoided if its introduction had been less hurried and more sensitively implemented. (*Prison Disturbances April 1990*, pp. 347–8).

Court escorts were also a drain on police resources. Specially designated grades of escort officers, policemen as well as prison officers, might have eliminated some of the wasteful practices in the deployment of manpower that had grown up, but would do nothing to relieve the calls made on staff resulting from the multitude of remand prisoners, and convicted prisoners awaiting sentence, who had to be escorted to and from court. The solution lay not in the redistribution of functions within the existing boundaries, but in lifting altogether the crippling burden the court escort commitment imposed on the hard pressed police and prison officers.

The proposal also called for the diversion of part of the financial resources allocated to the building and refurbishing of high and medium-security prisons towards the provision of lower-security units designed exclusively for the containment of accused persons who had been remanded in custody. Reallocation within the building programme would allow for the conversion of some redundant Ministry of Defence properties and the construction of new accommodation, preferably making use of system-building methods. In the Prison Department of the Home Office official opinion was increasingly recognizing the advantages of camp-style layouts for lower-security establishments, in terms of manning levels and a more relaxed environment, as well as of cost.[43]

The degree of security in the new establishments would need to be related to the minimum restraints necessary to contain the bulk of the remand population, not many of whom posed an escape risk. More dangerous and higher-risk prisoners requiring the intensive security of the category A or B prisons should be remanded to prison when bail was opposed, and where the court was satisfied by the prosecution that the lower-security New Remand Unit (NRUs)[44] were inadequate to meet the obligations of secure deten-

[43] See a memorandum submitted by the Home Office to the Home Affairs Committee of the House of Commons (para. 25) in November 1986. This evidence was published with the Third Report of the Committee for the Session 1986/7 entitled *State and Use of Prisons*, Vol. 2, Minutes of Evidence and Appendices (HC 35-II), HMSO, London, 1987, pp. 1–17.

[44] The description New Remand Unit was used to distinguish separate pre-trial detention facilities from the existing remand centres in the prison system. In November 1987 the only distinct remand centres were six establishments (three of them for young people under twenty-one) used almost entirely to contain persons awaiting trial or sentence. Fourteen local prisons or youth custody centres had remand centres attached which were primarily used for young male offenders. At a further twenty-one (mainly local) prisons a variety of remand facilities existed for

tion before trial. To recap, these were that the accused should answer the charges against him; that he should be protected from the vengeance of others; that he should not interfere with witnesses or otherwise obstruct the course of justice; and that he should be denied the opportunity of committing offences during the remand period.

More unyielding than the functional problems of providing separate accommodation, and the process of allocating pre-trial detainees to NRUs or the prisons, were the questions of staffing and management. At this point in the argument I reached a junction which I feared would prove to be a parting of the ways with many of those who had assented in the reasoning so far. Overstretched as it was, and given its tenacity in preserving its interests, it was unthinkable that the Prison Service would welcome the advent of a rival service to manage the NRUs and provide escorts to and from court. Yet in formulating my proposal I could not accept that it was wise to perpetuate the existing monopoly in the supply of labour to the new units. They could, on one option, be manned exclusively by a newly created Crown Service, but that would take time to recruit, train, and get into post. There would be bureaucratic delays with the Home Office, disputes over funding with the Treasury, and determined resistance from the trade unions and staff associations.

The case for effective separation by status, as it seemed to me, did not rest solely on the necessity to reflect in practical administration the distinction of principle between punishment and prevention. A complete break with the past, and the deplorable standards that had come to be regarded, however reluctantly, as tolerable, offered a far better prospect of attaining a real improvement in standards.

The legislation appeared to leave the Home Secretary with a free hand. Section 4(1) of the Prison Act 1952 (as amended) provided that 'The Secretary of State shall have the general superintendence of prisons and shall make the contracts and do the other acts necessary for the maintenance of prisons and the maintenance of prisoners.'

A scheme of limited delegation, namely the appointment of

---

adults of both sexes, one of them for adult and young females who had been remanded in custody.

Home Office managers and the employment of private sector companies supplying operational staff under contract to attain and preserve laid down standards, had the advantage of conforming to the wording of a statute which neither specifically authorized nor debarred such a course. Contracts should be drawn in such a way as to lay down in detail the standards required and to provide for a system of monitoring. Personnel would have to be carefully selected and properly trained. The new units would be expected to demonstrate value for money and cost-effectiveness in the expenditure of public funds.

The emotive demon of privatization was bound to raise its head, and it did. It was not only the vested interests who opposed strenuously any abrogation of the state's duty, which they claimed should not be delegated other than to Government employees, to keep in safe custody those who had transgressed and were being punished for their wrongdoing. Some, although not all, penal reformers joined in a chorus of repudiation. 'No prisons for profit' was a compelling slogan, especially in its moral and political application to convicted prisoners. But I was not alone in regarding it as applying with less force to those who had been charged with a criminal offence, were innocent until proved guilty, and were awaiting trial or sentence in appalling conditions that equated with punishment.[45] The separateness of treatment to which their status entitled them was denied by current practice, and no one seemed unduly perturbed. The many thousands of remand prisoners were a constituency with neither spokesmen nor leverage.

V

There were some indications that the Government's mind was open as it searched for ways out of the severe and apparently intractable problems arising from the containment of what was seen as an ever-growing mass of untried or unsentenced inmates in the prison

---

[45] Unsolicited support from an influential quarter came in a letter dated 9 July 1987 from HM Chief Inspector of Prisons. Sir James Hennessy wrote: 'May I take this opportunity of congratulating you on your very interesting article in yesterday's *Times*? I have always thought that if there was a case for privatisation in the prison system, it lies in the field of remand prisoners. Certainly there must be scope for privatising their escorts—which play such havoc with prison regimes.'

population. Over the ten years 1979–88 the number had nearly doubled from 6,132 in 1979 to 11,440 in 1988. Greater private sector involvement in the staffing and operation, as well as the construction, of a new generation of remand units would be a profound change. Although not advanced on politically doctrinal grounds, the approach chimed with a powerful ideological current. While the extension of privatization to any part of the penal system would indubitably prove controversial, nevertheless it could be the means of correcting the shameful practice of treating accused persons worse than convicted offenders, while at the same time opening up the possibility of achieving the improvement that was so overdue in the physical conditions in the local prisons most afflicted by overcrowding.

It was acknowledged that not all of the remand population should be transferred from the prisons. Some would need to remain in higher-security establishments for the protection of the public. But a substantial majority, possibly amounting to between two-thirds and three-quarters of the eleven thousand inappropriate prisoners, could be detained more fittingly, and more humanely, in institutions geared specifically to their state of presumed innocence, rather than in appendages to prisons designed for convicted offenders. Was it too much to hope that a practical use could be found for the vast tracts of waste land, much of it in public ownership, which lay vacant year after year at the heart of so many inner city areas?[46]

The proposal arose from a reasoned analysis, concentrating on the principles rather than attempting to provide a detailed blueprint. Government Departments are skilled at preparing blueprints, but ministers periodically benefit from a reminder of the underlying principles. The motivation was to rectify a situation that was fundamentally wrong; not to promote the idea of privatization. There were clearly difficult administrative and cost issues to be resolved. In 1987 it was timely to join in a public debate that already had begun. But how best to bring the proposal to the notice

---

[46] An estimated half million acres in England, an area approximately the size of Nottinghamshire, was classified as vacant land in 1987. Much of it was concentrated in metropolitan areas, especially the inner parts of some cities. See M. Chisholm and P. Kivell, *Inner City Waste Land*, Institute of Economic Affairs, London, 1987, p. 14.

of ministers? After reflection, I decided to aim high and to approach the Prime Minister.

Ensuring that communications aimed at the Prime Minister reach their target calls for careful forethought. There are dense protective layers of officialdom to penetrate. When it is open, the recommended route is via an oral question followed up in writing. The opportunity to put a question to Margaret Thatcher directly came when she made her annual visit to address Conservative Peers in the House of Lords shortly before the summer recess in July 1987. On these occasions the Prime Minister was seen at her best; warmly thanking her Party supporters in the Upper House (under some of whom, notably the chairman of the meeting, Lord Boyd-Carpenter, she had served her ministerial apprenticeship);[47] exhorting the peers for what lay ahead in the next session, and demonstrating a remarkable command over a bewildering range of subjects with which she cannot have had any personal connection, and which were unlikely to have reached the Cabinet Room. The issue of remand prisoners fell into this category. While agreeing that all possibilities to reduce monopolies held by producers in the public sector should be explored, Mrs Thatcher sharply remarked that some remand prisoners were dangerous and needed to be held in secure conditions.

In a letter sent to the Prime Minister on 23 July I summarized the case for separate provision, enclosed the article on remand prisoners which I had written for *The Times*, and concluded:

your own response, together with the Home Secretary's willingness to look to the private sector to expedite the construction of new prisons, encourages me to think that the Government may now be in a position to make a determined effort to lift the burden of supervising remand prisoners off the shoulders of the police and the prison service in the way I have outlined.

My letter was copied to Douglas Hurd at the Home Office and to Lord Whitelaw, then Lord President of the Council and Leader of the House of Lords. On 12 August it elicited a detailed statement of Government policy from the Prime Minister, in the drafting of which the hand of the Home Office could be detected. The text is quoted verbatim:

[47] Mrs Thatcher's first ministerial appointment from 1961 to 1964 had been as Joint Parliamentary Secretary at the Ministry of Pensions and National Insurance when John Boyd-Carpenter was the minister. He then became Chief Secretary to the Treasury and Paymaster General, 1962–4, and Chairman of the Civil Aviation Authority, 1972–7. Created a life peer in 1972.

10 DOWNING STREET
LONDON SW1A 2AA

THE PRIME MINISTER   12 August 1987

Dear Lord Windlesham

Thank you for your letter of 23 July about the possibility of setting up new remand centres, distinct from the prison service, employing agency staff and licensed and supervised by the Home Office.

Both Douglas Hurd and I were very interested in your article in The Times and we were grateful for your kind words about our willingness to consider new and radical options. There are many aspects of the intractable remand problem on which you and we agree. In particular, we agree about the crippling burden that the court escort commitment at present imposes on the prison service; that more bail hostels and changes in bail procedures would be likely to reduce pressures on the remand system only at the margins; and we agree on the crucial importance in relieving overcrowding of the prison building programme on which the present Government has embarked. As you know, Douglas Hurd referred in his House of Commons statement on 16 July to the need for a substantial expansion and acceleration of the building programme, exploiting private sector techniques.

The Government is fully committed to making greater use of the private sector wherever this helps Departments like the Prison Department of the Home Office to get better value for money. We know that the private sector is involved in the day to day running of prisons as well as in constructing them for example in the United States, and we shall have a clearer picture of this after Malcolm Caithness has made his tour of American prisons in September. To that extent our minds remain open. But, as you yourself say, there would clearly be many problems to resolve before we could contemplate similar developments in this country. There is the security problem to which you allude: I was interested in your solution to this, though it would of course be difficult to ensure that the courts would remand a sufficiently high number of prisoners to the privately run centre to make it viable. There would also be legal problems, and problems to do with accountability, that have not yet been fully explored. At present the balance of the argument seems to be against moving in this direction, and that is why Douglas Hurd told the House of Commons on 16 July that he did not believe there was a case for handing over the business of keeping prisoners safe to anyone other than Government servants.

As to your specific suggestion that court escorting arrangements should be privatised, last year the Court Escort Scrutiny Report concluded that the use of private guards for escorting purposes would not be desirable since it would only further complicate an already complex system. It recommended instead that after implementation of the other recommendations, consideration should be given to the creation of a special grade of escort officer to assist the police with escort duties. We shall explore the scope for this once the other recommendations have been implemented. Meanwhile, with the introduction of group working under Fresh Start, court work is allocated to a particular team or teams of officers and the work will normally be contained by the group. The aim is to minimise the disruption which external duties now cause to the internal operations of establishments, because of their short-term unpredictability and inefficient use of manpower.

We are however grateful to you for putting the arguments for greater private sector involvement in prison affairs so cogently, particularly when the other side has had so much more exposure in the press. It is very helpful to see these arguments put forward by someone of your authority and background and we shall not lose sight of them.

Kind regards,

Yours sincerely
Margaret Thatcher

The letter went on record in Whitehall as an authoritative statement of policy from the highest level of government. Although not accepting the proposed scheme, the phraseology was more tentative than that customarily deployed by the sender: 'At present the balance of the argument seems to be against moving in this direction . . . ' Shortly before, Hurd had made a small but calculated move in the direction of privatization when he indicated that he would look to the 'skills and knowledge of the private sector' to supervise the prison-building programme and accelerate its delivery.[48] In doing so he was responding to pressures from two different quarters. One was the finding by the Comptroller and Auditor General, ventilated at hearings by the House of Commons Committee of Public Accounts, that delays, additional costs, inadequate supervision, and faulty designs made it improbable that the target of matching available places with the total prison population by the end of the decade would be met.[49] The Public Accounts Committee added the rider it was 'dismayed' that even when the objective of matching total places and prison population was achieved, there would still be overcrowding in some prisons and

[48] *Parl. Debates*, HC, 119 (6th ser.), col. 1297, 16 July 1987.
[49] National Audit Office, *Report by the Comptroller and Auditor General, Home Office and Property Services Agency: Programme for the Provision of Prison Places* (HC 135), HMSO, London, 1985, p. 6.

large amounts of substandard accommodation retained in use, especially at the local prisons.[50]

At the same time another, more political, current was stirring at Westminster. The Conservative members of the House of Commons Home Affairs Committee had recommended as an experiment that private sector companies should be enabled to bid for the construction and management of custodial institutions, initially tendering for a new establishment which was already planned, preferably a remand centre or youth custody institution.[51] Contracts should set standards and requirements, and failure to meet them would be grounds for termination by the Government. Standards should be made legally enforceable against the contractors. The Committee insisted that it was not contemplating privatization of prisons in the sense that the provider of a service was responsible only to his financial backers and subject to market competition. Contract provision, the term they used, allowed for regular inspection and strict supervision of facilities, leaving final responsibility with the public authority and the provider acting only as its agent.[52] Not surprisingly, Labour members on the Committee had been unable to support the proposal; the recommendations in the report being agreed by a vote of four to three, with the chairman not voting.

VI

The Conservative members had been 'profoundly impressed'[53] by what they had seen on a visit to the United States, a reaction endorsed by the Earl of Caithness, Minister of State at the Home Office with responsibility for prisons, when he reported 'very favour-

[50] House of Commons, Twenty-Fifth Report from the Committee of Public Accounts, Session 1985/6, *Prison Building Programme*, Home Office and Property Services Agency (HC 248), HMSO, London, 1986, p. xviii.

[51] House of Commons, Home Affairs Committee, Fourth Report, Session 1986/7, *Contract Provision of Prisons* (HC 291), HMSO, London, 1987, p. vi.

[52] Ibid., p. v.

[53] Press statement issued by John Wheeler MP, 31 Oct. 1986.

ably' after a tour of American prisons in the autumn of 1987.[54] There the provision of correctional or detention facilities by private interests under contract to public authorities, although still in its infancy, was gaining ground. Apart from a long-established network of secure facilities for juveniles operated by churches and private organizations, the contemporary movement towards contracting by public agencies had got under way only in the 1980s.[55] In the United States, as in Britain, the antecedents were pragmatic rather than doctrinaire. The ideological debates on both sides of the Atlantic over the proper size and scope of government had barely touched on criminal justice. The Adam Smith Institute, the fount of many Thatcherite ideas in Britain, had suggested an experiment in the contracting-out of prison management in 1984,[56] but the proposal was in advance of its time and regarded as 'rather outlandish'.[57]

Two factors conflated to start the movement towards privatization in the United States. The first was the dramatic increase in illegal immigration, particularly in the South-West of the country. By the late 1970s existing facilities were no longer adequate to handle the inflow of illegal entrants, sometimes accompanied by their families for whom there was no provision in local jails. Faced with these pressures, and lacking the funds to build sufficient new facilities, the United States Immigration and Naturalization Service (INS) set a precedent by signing a contract for a privately managed facility in 1980. A former convalescent home in Pasadena, California, was converted into a holding centre for 125 men, women, and children and was soon processing more than 3,000 aliens a year. Other INS contracted holding facilities followed in California,

[54] A critical account by Andrew Rutherford of these visits is contained in an essay on 'British Penal Policy and the Idea of Prison Privatization', published as part of a collection of papers commissioned by the Vera Institute of Justice and the Institute for Court Management of the National Center for State Courts in the United States. See Douglas C. McDonald (ed.), *Private Prisons and the Public Interest*, Rutgers University Press, New Brunswick and London, 1990. Andrew Rutherford is Reader in Law at the University of Southampton and Chairman of the Howard League for Penal Reform.

[55] See Charles H. Logan, *Private Prisons: Cons and Pros*, Oxford University Press, New York, 1990, pp. 7–37.

[56] Adam Smith Institute, *Omega Report: Justice Policy*, London, 1984. This was followed by a further report from the same stable in 1987, written by Peter Young, entitled *The Prison Cell: The Start of a Better Approach to Prison Management*. C. H. Logan contributed *Privatizing Prisons: The Moral Case* in the same year.

[57] Young, *The Prison Cell*, p. 3.

Colorado, and Texas. Two processing centres, both in Texas, were opened in 1984 and 1985. The newly constructed Houston Processing Center was a remarkable achievement. A 350-bed dual purpose facility for illegal aliens awaiting deportation by the INS and convicted alien offenders in the custody of the Federal Bureau of Prisons, it was planned, built, and financed in seven months.

Whereas the holding and processing centres, as their names implied, were places for the temporary confinement of illegal entrants and immigration offenders, whose unwanted presence in such numbers created a problem to which there was no other immediate solution, the maintenance of the prisons (or correctional facilities) had come to be regarded as part of the natural obligation of government.[58] That imprisonment lay on the outer rim of the debate on privatization did not mean it was thought of as peripheral to the argument. On the contrary:

> The privatization of corrections, or punishment, is an especially significant part of the broader privatization movement. By challenging the government's monopoly over one of its ostensibly 'core' functions, the idea directly threatens the assumption that certain activities are essentially and necessarily governmental.[59]

The consciences of those public officials who were troubled by such considerations were greatly eased by the principle of contracting, in its modern form a concept far more sophisticated and capable of protecting the public interest than anything known in the nineteenth and early twentieth centuries.[60] What was at issue, it was argued, was not the divestment of publicly owned assets to private interests, but the harnessing for public purposes of resources and skills that were more readily, and sometimes more cheaply,

---

[58] It had not always been so, since the assumption of overall responsibility by government for the provision and management of penal services was relatively modern. For much of the nineteenth and early twentieth centuries, numerous states and localities contracted for penal services. In Texas, Michigan, California, and Arkansas, for example, all or part of the prison system was at one time or another privately owned and operated. Standards were generally low, with abuses and corruption leading to demands for reform. (J. J. DiIulio, *Private Prisons*, National Institute of Justice Crime File, US Department of Justice, Washington, DC, 1987, p. 3).

[59] Logan, *Private Prisons: Cons and Pros*, p. 4.

[60] The constitutional and legal aspects of privatization, especially the ability of federal or state government to delegate functions that affect the liberty of the individual, were thoroughly reviewed by Professor I. P. Robbins in *The Legal Dimensions of Private Incarceration*, American Bar Association, New York, 1988.

available in the private sector. In the context of prisons, privatization means full operational management (and sometimes the design and construction) of penal establishments by private interests, subject to public control exercised through contractual obligations and regular monitoring.

A virtual moratorium on prison building in the 1970s had left the federal and state prisons chronically overcrowded. The inmate population grew by 179% between 1976 and 1986, not simply because of more offending, but because of mandatory sentencing laws and intermittently declared 'wars' on crime and drugs. As the physical conditions of confinement worsened, court orders called for immediate reforms and improvements. Budgets were overstrained, in some counties with as much as 65% of the total budget going on corrections. Bond issues to finance prison construction were tried, but proved unattractive to voters. As a result prison capacity, in the local jails as in the federal and state prisons, consistently failed to keep up with the rising population of sentenced offenders. By the end of 1986, 546,659 inmates were held in federal or state prisons, an all-time record. The increase of 43,000 additional prisoners from 1985 to 1986, as one commentator noted, called for seven new medium-sized (500-bed) prisons each month.[61] An overspill into the local jails was inevitable, and by 1987 it was estimated that over 12,000 state prisoners were held in local jails because of the inability of the state prisons to contain them.[62]

The original contract entered into by the Federal Bureau of Prisons resulted from the expiry of a federal law, the Youth Corrections Act in 1984, leaving a number of young adults, some of whom had been convicted of serious crimes, with part of their sentences still to serve. A private corporation was contracted to house about sixty of them in secure conditions. Other contracts followed for different categories of mainly lower-security prisoners, especially half-way houses for those nearing the end of their sentences. Throughout the period 1984–90, the Federal Bureau of Prisons maintained reservations about the ability of private contractors to operate medium to maximum-security facilities for adult male prisoners convicted of violent offences.

The first state prison to be entirely in private ownership, oper-

[61] US Department of Justice statistics cited in McDonald (ed.), *Private Prisons and the Public Interest*, p. 4.
[62] Logan, *Private Prisons: Cons and Pros*, p. 8.

ation, and management, the Marion Adjustment Center, was opened in a converted seminary in Kentucky in 1986. A minimum-security facility, it contained about 300 state prisoners within three years of parole eligibility. Other states contracted facilities for women in New Mexico, pre-parole in Texas, and return to custody in California. Counties also began to look to private operators for local jails. Two became well known, both operated by the largest of the new profit based corporations, Corrections Corporation of America (CCA). One was Bay County jail in Florida, for which CCA assumed full managerial responsibility in 1985, and the other Silverdale Detention Center in Hamilton County, Tennessee. Silverdale was a minimum to medium-security facility for a wide variety of about 400 state and county prisoners, male and female; pre-trial or sentenced. Some were convicted of felonies, others were serving terms of imprisonment for misdemeanours, or short mandatory sentences for driving under the influence of drink.[63] Many innovations were made in management style, staff training, and standards, with unarmed officers replacing the practice of trusty inmates being used to guard other inmates.

Silverdale and Bay County attracted wide interest, from overseas as well as elsewhere in the United States. Emboldened by their success, backed up by some admired programmes of education and training for juvenile offenders designed for the Juvenile Court of Memphis and Shelby County, CCA made a bid to take over the whole of Tennessee's prison system on a ninety-nine-year lease. The attempt was premature and was summarily rejected. By 1992, however, the Governor of Mississippi was giving consideration to a similar proposal, emanating from the Mississippi Economic Council acting through its Commission on Efficiency in Government which had reported on the state's Department of Corrections. Coincid-

---

[63] In the state of Tennessee driving while intoxicated attracted a mandatory penalty of forty-eight hours' imprisonment for the first offence, often served at weekends; a minimum of forty-five days on second offence; and a minimum of 120 days on third offence. As so often with mandatory penalties, unexpected problems resulted. The additional demand for prison places meant that, consequent on the intervention of the federal courts to curb overcrowding, some prisoners sentenced for violent or property crimes had to be released early, whereas those serving drink-driving sentences could not be. With a backlog of more than 2,000 drivers waiting to serve their sentences, long after the incident for which they had been convicted, the state legislature was debating in 1992 the substitution of community service (in the form of cleaning overnight government buildings or schools) for the less serious drink-driving offences.

entally, a bill was before the Mississippi legislature that would allow the private sector to manage local jails throughout the state.

The author of the scrupulously fair-minded book from which this commentary on the origins of private prisons in the United States is largely drawn, Charles Logan, ends his survey with the conclusion that the contracting of prisons and jails has been nowhere near as radical a departure from current practice as some of its opponents seem to believe: 'Contracting is a reform, not a revolution, and as such, it deserves at least to be given a try'.[64] His verdict was shared by the Conservative MPs in 1986/7. Later I was able to form my own broadly similar impressions on a private visit to some contract prisons and correctional facilities in Tennessee.

Politically, commercially, and even deriving encouragement from some scarce and unexpected fruits of academic study,[65] the strands of privatization began to come together into a similar pattern in Britain. Although not directly inspired by the American example, the emergence of the idea into the pre-legislative arena was helped by the way in which public authorities in several parts of the United States had turned to private contractors to supplement the inadequate facilities at their disposal. To many state corrections administrators, as well as elected officials, the ideological arguments had been overtaken by the urgent need to avoid the political pitfalls of early parole or the executive release of prisoners, some of whom inevitably would display their continued dangerousness by further crimes committed during the time they would otherwise have been in serving out their sentences in custody. Would the same apply in Britain? Or with the prisons coming directly under the control of central government, and with the necessity to gain sufficient Parliamentary consent to carry through any fundamental changes of policy, would the exclusive provision of penal services by the state prove more enduring?

[64] Logan, *Private Prisons: Cons and Pros*, p. 254.
[65] See Sean McConville and J. E. Hall Williams, *Crime and Punishment: A Radical Rethink*, Tawney Society, London, 1985, and M. Taylor and K. Pease, 'Private Prisons and Penal Purpose', in R. Matthews (ed.), *Privatizing Criminal Justice*, Sage Publications, London, 1989, pp. 179–93. Both Professor Hall Williams and Dr Pease had experience of penal administration having served as members of the Parole Board.

VII

By the spring of 1988 the traditional orthodoxy was beginning to weaken. Hurd's flat declaration, quoted in Mrs Thatcher's letter only seven months before, that he did not believe there was a case for handing over the business of keeping prisoners safe to anyone other than Government servants, was not repeated in a statement on 30 March to the House of Commons about measures to combat prison overcrowding. Indeed, faced with the need to find additional space for a prison population that had risen to 50,600 in mid-March and was forecast to reach 52,000 by the summer, the Home Secretary was forced to explore every avenue. In addition to announcing a series of measures to provide extra places, including the temporary use of two Army Camps staffed by military police, Hurd said:

We must be ready to think imaginatively to ensure that the prison service can meet its obligations. In that context, the possibility of involving the private sector more closely in aspects of the prison system should be urgently considered. I have already moved in this direction by establishing the Prison Building Board, which includes substantial private sector representation ... The board is inviting the private sector to make proposals for building remand or open facilities faster than has been done in the past. I propose in addition to publish a Green Paper on private sector involvement in all aspects of the remand system, and at the same time to engage consultants to help in working out the practical implications.[66]

Next came the long-delayed Government reply to the Fourth Report of the Home Affairs Committee on *Contract Provision of Prisons*, published over a year earlier. In a letter dated 15 April, the Home Secretary declined to follow the Conservative enthusiasts the whole way down the path that had so impressed them in the United States:

The scale of private sector involvement in America is still very limited and private sector establishments house only a very small percentage of the total number in custody. It offers no blueprint for practical application in this country nor an immediate panacea. The constitutional, legal and operational settings are very different.
I carefully considered the Committee's recommendation that the way

---

[66] *Parl. Debates*, HC, 130 (6th ser.), cols. 1084–5, 30 Mar. 1988.

ahead might be through an experiment. I concluded that this was not the best way to proceed at present . . .

Leaving aside the question of whether I have the power under existing legislation to mount such an experiment, I consider that because the change contemplated has substantial implications the Government should proceed to it only after full consultation and developing a workable scheme. There is also the issue of whether that scheme should be brought before Parliament for approval through the legislative process.[67]

On remand prisoners the tone of Hurd's letter was more forthcoming. The private sector might, he acknowledged, 'play a wider part in providing contracted out services, including staff or management ... especially in relation to remand prisoners'. Remand provision was under particular pressure of numbers and this was a possibility he wanted to explore. The promised Green Paper would cover not only contract provision and running of remand facilities, but also arrangements for escorting remand prisoners to and from court and for court manning.

Although the Home Secretary did not commit himself to bringing out his Green Paper until the autumn, the sense of urgency led to its appearance before Parliament rose for the long summer recess. Under the prosaic title *Private Sector Involvement in the Remand System,*[68] it spelt out the detail of a new strategy. The document recognized that the worst overcrowding was experienced by remand prisoners and that the remand population was rising the most rapidly. The options for private sector involvement were enumerated, including the provision and management of remand institutions, escorts, and court duties. Reactions to various options were sought, and management consultants had been engaged to examine questions of practical feasibility and cost.

During the time the consultants, Deloitte, Haskins, and Sells, worked on their brief the rolling stone continued to gather moss. Corrections Corporation of America, by now handling about 50% of all contracted facilities for county, state, and federal authorities in the United States, had formed a consortium with two substantial British building contractors, Sir Robert McAlpine and Sons and

[67] House of Commons, Home Affairs Committee, First Special Report, Session 1987/8, *Government Reply to the Fourth Report from the Home Affairs Committee, Session 1986–87* (HC 433), HMSO, London, 1988, pp. iii–iv.

[68] Cm. 434, HMSO, London, 1988.

John Mowlem, under the name UK Detention Services.[69] Contract Prisons, another company founded to exploit the new opportunities, recruited as its chairman Sir Edward Gardner QC, who had been chairman of the House of Commons Select Committee on Home Affairs until his retirement from Parliament at the 1987 General Election. Group 4 Securitas entered the field, setting up a subsidiary company for the purpose of examining how the remand system and court escort duties might be managed by the private sector. Two others were Securicor, claiming to be 'Europe's largest security provider', and the Detention Corporation. The latter was founded by a group of private individuals without any corporate financial backing, although when the tendering got under way in 1991 it linked up with BET (British Electric Traction). Each embarked on lobbying those who they saw as decision-takers, inside and outside Parliament.

The Home Office kept a record of all approaches from consortia and companies interested in the construction and operation of a prison. When the decision was made to invite tenders for the operation only of a remand prison, others made their interest known and were added to the list. Eventually a total of some thirty companies, groups, or individuals had expressed interest. All were invited to pre-qualify for the invitation to tender.

The overlap between Party political and commercial interests was exemplified by the attendance at a seminar held over dinner at the Carlton Club on 10 October 1988. The event was organized as one of a series by the Club's Political Committee, and a former Lord Chancellor, Lord Havers, agreed to preside. There were four main speakers: Gardner, John Hosking (Chairman of the Magistrates' Association), Jeremy Hanley MP (a member of the Home Affairs Committee who had visited private prisons in the United States), and the director of criminal justice planning for an American architectural practice. A ministerial contribution was made by Douglas Hogg, Parliamentary Under-Secretary at the Home Office. Several past and present Conservative MPs attended. Some were Carlton Club members and others invited guests. A member of the staff of the Prime Minister's Policy Unit, which was

---

[69] Submission to the Home Office by UK Detention Services in response to the Green Paper, *Private Sector Involvement in the Remand System*, Dec. 1988.

keeping a weather eye open and was later to intervene, was there with a watching brief.

The venue and auspices of the seminar had alerted civil servants that this was not the place for them, although Edward Bickham, and his successor as Hurd's special adviser, David Lidington, ensured representation from the Home Office. The ground was prepared by a discussion paper sent out in advance outlining ways of improving the quality of the Prison Service, with an emphasis on the private sector. The Adam Smith Institute and the Centre for Policy Studies both had staff members or advisers at the seminar, while a distinctively non-Tory flavour was added by the participation of a small, but vocal, group of academic criminologists.

The private sector was out in strength. As well as the new consortia, representatives of several other construction businesses were present, together with virtually all of the principal security firms. One of CCA's rivals from the United States also sent a representative. After the seminar, a detailed policy paper was drafted and circulated to all who had attended. Copies were sent to the relevant ministers and their special advisers, the Cabinet Office, and the Policy Unit at 10 Downing Street.

The discussion at the Carlton Club seminar ranged much wider than pre-trial containment of remand prisoners, one of the most startling moments coming when the speaker from the American architectural practice said that before long in the vicinity of 10,000 people would be housed in a single facility at Los Angeles. More than 7,600 inmates were already held at the Men's Central Jail, with another 2,400 places under construction making it one of the largest, if not the largest, concentration of persons deprived of their liberty in a single institution anywhere in the Western world.[70]

Despite the urging of enthusiasts for privatization to go further and faster, whether for commercial or ideological reasons, the Home Office was not prepared to raise the stakes beyond remand prisoners and court escorts. The way had been carefully prepared,

---

[70] In 1987/8 the total number of inmates at the Central Jail, predisposition and sentenced, averaged 7,681. The highest actual recorded figure was 9,016 on 3 Mar. 1986. Inmate numbers regularly exceeded the rated capacity for which the facility was planned, although restrained by a higher limit of the mandated capacity permitted under federal guide-lines. The expansion project, designed to add 2,408 places to the rated capacity, was due for completion in mid-1994 (letter from Robert Ciulik, Chief, Custody Division, Los Angeles County Sheriff's Department, 13 Aug. 1991).

and the new policy could after all, Hurd now decided, be presented as an experiment. In answering a supplementary question after making a statement on the Government's plans for private sector involvement in the remand system and court escorts when the consultant's report was made public on 1 March 1989, he said: 'We are doing many new things and we start them cautiously with experiments. I make no apology for that because new thinking and cautious experiments are what are required in the criminal justice system. This suggestion fits neatly and logically into that pattern.'[71] It was an impromptu remark entirely consistent with Hurd's character and methods. Neat and logical, he was at the same time open-minded and cautious, a good combination for a successful Home Secretary. The key to his move away from initial scepticism about 'handing over the business of keeping prisoners safe to anyone other than Government servants' was to be found in having persuaded himself, before he attempted to persuade others, that ministerial accountability, at any rate for remand prisoners, could be preserved adequately within a contractual framework of safeguards and controls.

In a lengthy Parliamentary statement Hurd said that, following the consultants' recommendations, he proposed that each contract should be subject to permanent on-site monitoring by a Government official (later named a controller) appointed by the Home Secretary. The official would have under his direct control the exercise of disciplinary sanctions over prisoners and the hearing of complaints. He agreed with the views expressed by most of the respondents to the Green Paper that contracted-out remand centres should have boards of visitors and be subject to inspection by Her Majesty's Inspectorate of Prisons. Depending on the result of further investigations, he intended to bring legislation forward when the Parliamentary programme allowed to provide a legal framework to permit contracting out to go ahead.[72] He ended resoundingly:

---

[71] *Parl. Debates*, HC, 148 (6th ser.), cols. 286–7, 1 Mar. 1989.

[72] Hurd had been reluctant to accept that legislation was necessary in view of the apparently wide terms of Section 4(1) of the Prison Act 1952. Adequate as the powers appeared to be for the purposes of the experiment, the Home Secretary received legal advice that devolving his responsibilities (even in respect of a single prison) to a contractor would be inconsistent with the scheme of the Act taken as a whole. For instance, Section 7(1) envisaged that every prison should have 'a governor ... and such other officers as may be necessary' appointed under Section 3(1) by the Secretary of State.

The introduction of the private sector into the management of the prison system in the way I have outlined would certainly represent a bold departure from previous thinking and practice. It offers the prospect of a new kind of partnership between the public and private sectors in this important, though often sadly neglected, aspect of our national life. We should not be scornful of new ideas which, if successful, will make an important contribution to the Government's programme of providing decent conditions for all prisoners at a reasonable cost.[73]

Hurd's statement, and his answers to a series of uniformly hostile questions from the Opposition benches, was the closest any ministerial endorsement got in the 1980s to the ideal of a separate system of detention for those charged with criminal offences who had been refused bail. While it fell short of the proposal outlined earlier in this chapter, and summarized in my letter to the Prime Minister, it was running with the grain. The exclusive management of all penal institutions by the state no longer stood as an insurmountable barrier. The switch in policy did not commend itself to the Opposition parties, being fiercely denounced by Labour and Liberal Democrats alike. Despite Hurd's conciliatory tone the Shadow Home Secretary, Roy Hattersley, was scathing in reply:

What the Home Secretary has announced today is as objectionable as it is absurd. It clearly has two intentions. The first is to create the illusion of activity—the Home Secretary's increasing preoccupation. The second is demonstrated by the tentative, apologetic and intellectually inadequate nature of his statement. This announcement is intended to prove that he is prepared to swallow any item of Conservative ideology no matter how distasteful. What he has announced today will damage the prison service and his reputation in equal measure.[74]

The theme of a proper obligation of the state being sacrificed in the interests of party dogma continued throughout the exchanges. It was countered by the Home Secretary's insistence on the importance of experimentation in trying out alternative arrangements which could result in an improvement in standards.

While no similar opportunity for a head-on national challenge to the adoption of contract provision existed in the more dispersed American penal system, with decisions being taken by federal, state,

[73] *Parl. Debates*, HC, 148, col. 278.
[74] Ibid., col. 279.

and county authorities across the nation, there was another, equally weighty, reason for the greater emphasis on experimentation and ideology. By the time Hurd made his announcement, the remand population had begun to fall. After the near doubling which took place between 1979 and 1988 the remand population had showed a small drop by 550 over the previous twelve months. Concurrently, the prison-building programme, launched by Whitelaw at the start of the decade, after many set-backs and delays, had begun to come on stream. The aptness, or indeed the deployment at all, of the pragmatic argument that some action had to be taken, however novel, to deal with the crisis of overcrowding, was consequently much reduced.

The unexpected vacuum in the political debate was filled by the Adam Smith Institute, which had brought out two further reports, the Centre for Policy Studies, the Selsdon Group, and the political advisers to ministers and at 10 Downing Street. The Adam Smith Institute, in particular, was enterprising in spreading the gospel of free enterprise. Working closely with John Wheeler and other Conservative MPs, it made representations to the Home Office and held seminars on the subject. The arguments typified the quintessential Thatcherite outlook which already had led to such far-reaching changes in other fields of policy. They deserve to be quoted *in extenso*:

The prison system has been subject to a phenomenon that commonly afflicts public sector institutions,—that of *producer dominance*. The assured income of a state monopoly service leads to complacency about existing practices and a failure to innovate. Political fears about strikes or unemployment lead to lax labour relations and overmanning. Political pressure from the employees diverts resources to current spending (on wages) and away from needed capital improvements. Those who work in such a state monopoly service represent a concentrated and united interest group and so have much more power in the political process than do ordinary members of the taxpaying public.

The prison system is just such a case of a state service being run to benefit the producers of the service, the employees, rather than the inmates and the taxpaying public. Yet despite a radical approach to other moribund areas of the public sector, the Thatcher administration has done little to reform the prison system.

This passive, unimaginative attitude to our disintegrating prison system need not and should not continue. Reformers need only look to the United States to see successful and fully functioning new approaches to prison management, pioneered by the private sector, which if adopted in Britain could do much to solve the problems of our prisons.[75]

This was not the language of the Home Secretary, still less of his civil servants or the penal reform movement. Yet it represented one of the most powerful of all political currents lapping the shores of criminal justice for the first time. Had the prison population not begun to decline, it is probable that the debate would have been less politicized. It would have been in character for Hurd to have acted as he did, but to justify his policy, as had happened in the United States, by reference to the urgent need to take any action to contain the pressure of a continuous upward trend on an already intolerably high population of sentenced and remand prisoners.

The pragmatic approach came through more strongly on the subsidiary, although important, issue of court escorts and custody in court. Hurd disclosed in the questioning which followed his 1 March statement that 1,000 policemen and 800–900 prison officers were engaged in escort duties every day.[76] The commitment was wasteful of manpower and did not call for the wide range of police and prison skills for which they had been trained. The consultants' report had indicated that whereas there was no marked saving to be achieved in the cost of detaining a remand prisoner, a daily figure of about £31 per prisoner per day being quoted, there was a good prospect that the private sector could provide a better service in escorting and court custody and at a lower cost. The existing system cost about £80 million annually.

VIII

Additional statements in the form of written answers to prearranged Parliamentary Questions put down in the name of Sir John Wheeler, Chairman of the Home Affairs Committee, were made by each of Hurd's successors as Home Secretary on 11 July 1990 and 2 May 1991. David Waddington's task was the harder. He had inherited from Hurd in October 1989 a clear commitment to reorganize court escorts and custody services, which would save money and redirect to better effect scarce resources of police and prison officer man-

---

[75] Young, *The Prison Cell*, p. 4.
[76] *Parl. Debates*, HC, 148, col. 280.

294 Prisons, Prevention, and Privatization

power, and a somewhat less firm one to pursue the possibility of contracting out to the private sector the design, construction, and operation of a small number of new remand centres (Hurd had mentioned a figure of two or three).[77] They would be treated as experiments and were not expected to result in material savings.

Both proposals were subject to the outcome of investigation into the practical and cost implications, and to Parliamentary approval when legislation was introduced. These qualifications, while on record, did not vitiate the political reality, of which Waddington as a former Chief Whip needed no reminder, that expectations had been raised on his own side of the House. Provoked by the vehement opposition of Labour and Liberal Democrat MPs towards what they saw as Tory dogma, Conservatives had rallied to the Government's support. An about turn was an unattractive political prospect.

The legislative moment also had arrived as the Criminal Justice Bill was imminent. Neither the Green Paper issued after the Leeds Castle meeting, nor the White Paper of February 1990 had anything to say on the still unresolved matters of competitive tendering by the private sector for court escorts and new remand centres. With the overall remand population continuing to fall as the Bill was in draft,[78] although the concentration of so many remand prisoners was still causing problems to the grossly overcrowded local prisons, Waddington's conundrum was unenviable. No visionary by nature, he lacked the inclination to go ahead with what was likely to prove a time-consuming and controversial policy in the absence of compelling practical reasons for doing so. Yet he could not afford to resile altogether from his predecessor's policy.

Following the omission of contracting out from the White Paper, I put down a Parliamentary Question for Written Answer in the House of Lords:

To ask Her Majesty's Government whether the legislation forecast in the

[77] Ibid., col. 286.

[78] The remand population in custody (including those held in police cells) had fallen from an average of 11,400 in 1988 to 10,500 in 1989. The annual average for 1990 was below 10,000 for the first time in five years (9,900), but rose again in 1991 to 10,200. The number in police cells (1,100) comprised about 7% of the average remand population in 1991, compared with 5% in 1990. The remand population was projected to increase to 14,600 by the year 2000. Home Office, *Statistical Bulletin*, 8/92 and 10/92.

White Paper, Crime, Justice and Protecting the Public (Cm 965), will include proposals to provide a legal framework to permit the contracting out of remand centres and escort services to and from court as indicated in the Home Secretary's statement of 1 March 1989 (HC Deb col. 277) on private sector involvement in the remand system.[79]

Learning that the submission had not yet reached the Home Secretary, being held up by the Minister of State, David Mellor, who had responsibility for the prisons, although not for the forthcoming legislation which lay with John Patten, I wrote to him. Having told the Home Office I would prefer to wait for a full reply, I received a letter from Mellor on 20 March which showed the indecision that prevailed:

> HOME OFFICE
> QUEEN ANNE'S GATE
> LONDON SW1H 6AT
> 20 March 1990

Dear David

Thank you for your letter of 14 February about private sector involvement in the remand system. The Question which you tabled on 12 February would have received the reply attached but for your indication that you would prefer to have a full Answer when we are ready to make an announcement rather than an interim one.

It may be a few weeks before we are ready to announce a decision. We have been advised by the relevant authorities in the House of Lords that it would not be in order to leave your Question on the Order Paper unanswered for that long. You may wish to withdraw your Question, or we could arrange for an interim reply to be made as drafted.

The position is that the Home Secretary and I are currently considering a report on the outcome of the further investigations which Douglas Hurd called for in his statement of 1 March. These included two parallel exercises to compare the costs of public and private provision of remand centres and of escorting and court custody services.

This information about costs has to be considered in the light of other relevant factors. I am grateful to you for including a copy of your article, a timely reminder of your own reasons for supporting the concept of privately-operated remand centres. Improving conditions for remand prisoners is at the forefront of our consideration also—the purpose of this initiative has been and continues to be to determine whether private sector involvement would contribute cost-effectively to the government's objective of reducing overcrowding and improving conditions for prisoners.

[79] *Parl. Debates*, HL, 517 (5th ser.), col. 1238, 2 Apr. 1990.

The decision is being made against a background in which the pressure of the prison population is rather less than it was in 1987 and 1988 when your article was written and Douglas Hurd launched the private sector initiative. The drop in the prison population of 2,100 between December 1988 and December 1989 included a fall of 900 in the remand population. On 2 February this year the total prison population was 46,950, which was 2,100 lower than the previous year and 3,438 lower than at the end of February 1988, when the remand population was 11,616 and there were 1,199 prisoners in police cells.

Another factor is that the prison building programme continues to make good progress. Out of the full programme of 28 new prisons, eight have already opened and 14 are at various stages of planning and construction, leaving only six on which construction work has not yet started. Construction is planned to begin on two of these in 1991/92 and 1992/93. Sites and planning permission are being sought for the four remaining prisons, but decisions on when and where to start building them have been deferred pending further analysis of the lower projected prison population.

The changes in the projections have allowed the emphasis of the prison building programme to be changed from building new prisons to speeding up improvements to the existing estate. Some of these developments include virtually rebuilding older prisons which are in such excellent locations that they need to be preserved. A major part of the expanded programme is a substantial reduction in slopping out.

If it were decided to go ahead to contract out either remand centres or court custody and escorting services, legislation would be needed. This would need to cover, among other things, the authority and status of private employees who supervised prisoners, and the necessary safeguards for the public interest and prisoners' rights. Detailed proposals would be published in advance.

It is helpful to know of your continued interest in and support for these proposals. We will make an announcement as soon as we can.

Yours, David
(David Mellor)

In reply, I accepted what was said about the welcome fall in the prison population and the desirability of taking a specific legislative power if there was any doubt about the adequacy of the Home Secretary's existing powers under the Prison Act 1952. Since legislation was pending, I argued that the opportunity should be grasped to secure such a power, whether or not it was likely to be implemented in the immediate future. This stimulated another letter from the minister:

HOME OFFICE
QUEEN ANNE'S GATE
LONDON SW1H 9AT
12 April 1990

Dear David

Thank you for your further letter, dated 26 March, about private sector involvement in the remand system. Your Question received an Answer as agreed on 2 April (col 1238).

We are still considering how the private sector initiative should be taken forward. As requested, I shall ensure that your support for the introduction of legislation to allow remand centres to be contracted out whether or not we intended to do so, is drawn to the attention of the Home Secretary. Legislation would certainly be required, not only to put it beyond doubt that it was open to the Secretary of State to contract out the operation of remand centres, but also to establish a framework within which private sector employees could be authorised to have the custody of prisoners and proper safeguards for prisoners' welfare and public safety could be put in place. Such legislation would undoubtedly attract considerable opposition, and I think we should need to be fairly sure that we would wish to implement it at some point in the future before we embarked on the difficult path of getting it through. We should certainly be pressed in Parliament to explain what use we planned to make of the powers being taken in the legislation. But I certainly take your point about the unpredictability of the prisons situation (recent events have brought this home all too firmly). This is why we are considering the way forward for this initiative with such care.

Yours, David
(David Mellor)

For some months the proposal hung in the balance. After being advised by the Department that a detailed study had confirmed that no substantial savings in cost could be anticipated, and swayed by the falling prison population, Waddington eventually came down against including a power to contract out certain remand prisons in the forthcoming legislation. Before proceeding, however, he took the precaution of enquiring whether the Prime Minister assented to the conclusion which he had reached so hesitantly. The answer was emphatic: she did not. Unlike Churchill's minute to Morrison quoted in Chapter 2, the communication of a decidedly contrary opinion from Number 10 was enough to induce a change of course. Shortly afterwards draftsmen were instructed by the Home Office to add the necessary provision to the Bill which was already taking shape.

The episode is enlightening on the methods of the Thatcher administration. The Prime Minister did not intervene in the sense of taking an initiative or issuing an instruction. Nor was the difference of opinion resolved in Cabinet Committee or other meeting of ministers. Whereas Waddington and Mellor, both of whom had been practising barristers, were thoroughly familiar with the contours of the system of criminal justice, and well informed about the implications of alternative policies, Mrs Thatcher was the ideologically convinced outsider, temperamentally opposed to vested interests, producer dominance, and the monopoly of labour in the public sector as in the private. Both were credible Tory viewpoints and it was by no means always the latter that carried the day.

Discordant as were the arguments advanced by the Adam Smith Institute and the other free market proselytizers with received opinion in most Whitehall Departments, nevertheless they were often a truer articulation of the political beliefs and objectives of the occupant of 10 Downing Street than the decisions of ministers in whom Mrs Thatcher not infrequently detected signs of having been brainwashed by the bureaucracy over which she expected them to take charge. It did not make for comfortable relationships, and some ministers handled it better than others. With much patience and skill, Hurd had succeeded in persuading the Prime Minister, as well as his Cabinet colleagues and back-bench supporters, of the merits of both punishment in the community and an experiment with privatized remand centres. Waddington fell at the initial fence even before he had the opportunity to put his proposal before his ministerial colleagues. It was not the end of the story, which is continued, with a different cast of ministers, in Chapter 9.[80]

When finally ready to announce the decision of the Government in July 1990, Waddington's statement differed noticeably in tone from Hurd's the previous year. On court escorts, he said that he had decided:

[80] An amendment to the Criminal Justice Bill at Report Stage in the House of Commons enabled the Secretary of State by order to extend the power to contract for the running of new establishments containing remand prisoners to new prisons holding sentenced offenders, or existing prisons, or both. The necessary statutory instrument would be subject to the affirmative resolution procedure in each House of Parliament. This provision was enacted as Section 84 of the Criminal Justice Act 1991.

to go ahead with preparations to reorganize arrangements for court escorts, custody and security services and to invite competitive tenders for the provision of these services. I am confident that the resulting rationalisation of the existing complex and overlapping arrangements will lead to a substantial improvement in the cost-effectiveness with which these services are provided. An important objective of the new arrangement will be to enable the police and prison services to concentrate their efforts on work which makes more effective use of the skills and training of their officers.

I am today issuing to interested parties a discussion document setting out the Government's proposals in greater detail, and describing the legislative framework which the Government proposes should support the reorganisation of these services.[81]

Value for money was the theme of the second part of the statement on privately operated remand centres. The aim of improving the conditions of pre-trial detainees was mentioned only in the context that competition should 'make a valuable contribution to the prison service's continuing and successful efforts to raise standards and improve efficiency'.[82] As the White Paper policies towards sentencing contained in *Crime, Justice and Protecting the Public* and the prison-building programme combined to produce an anticipated reduction in the overall numbers in custody, the future need for additional remand places provided by the private sector was now seen as being 'very limited'. The experiment forecast by Hurd, however, would go ahead at a new establishment which was already under development on Humberside by a private contractor and was due for completion in 1992. A trial would be mounted in which competitive tenders would be invited from the private sector for the operation of the facility. If one or more satisfactory tenders were received which offered better value for money than the Prison Service could offer, a contract would be awarded accordingly. The procedure for letting and supervising the contract would in the main follow the Deloitte, Haskins, and Sells recommendations. The staff would be prison custody officers with duties similar to the court escorts as described in the accompanying discussion paper.

As is often the case, the existing public service provider, the Prison Service, decided not to tender, although estimates of the cost of operating a comparable new establishment by the Prison Service were used as a benchmark against which the competitive

[81] *Parl. Debates*, HC, 176 (6th ser.), col. WA 205, 11 July 1990.
[82] Ibid., col. WA 206.

tenders could be assessed. This left the field open for the private sector, and in May 1991 Kenneth Baker, Home Secretary since the previous November,[83] announced that invitations to tender had been issued to nine potential contractors. In a press comment he described the move as 'an important new initiative offering the prospect of value for money and a desirable element of competition in the management of the prison system'.[84] Baker added that the 'system should be humane but challenging, designed to provide security for the public and a purposeful regime for prisoners'. The phrase echoed a previous comment when he had told *The Times* that he wanted a more humane, and hopefully therefore more stable, prison system.[85] The new establishment, described as Wolds Remand Prison, was to be located close to an existing Young Offender Institution near Hull. Its inmates would be some 300 remand prisoners awaiting trial or sentence, and classified up to and including security category B. In addition to maintaining security at all levels, potential contractors would be required to produce proposals for high standards of health, safety, food, and hygiene. A thorough induction process would inform prisoners of their rights, entitlements, and obligations. Facilities for exercise, work, and education would be provided with an emphasis on maximizing purposefully the time outside the cells. Inmates could expect to spend up to twelve hours each weekday out of their cells. Housing would be provided in single or double cells, all with integral sanitation.

Unlike the Prison Service which shared similar aspirations, but more often than not was unable to deliver regimes conforming to these standards, the requirements would be incorporated into the specification for contractually binding agreements. Although the inmates were still described as prisoners rather than as detainees, the specification document stated that conditions at Wolds must reflect the presumed innocence of its inmates. Would-be contractors were urged to draw up mission statements affirming their com-

---

[83] Minister of State with responsibility for Information Technology at the Department of Trade and Industry, 1981–4; Minister for Local Government, 1984–5; Secretary of State for the Environment, 1985–6; Secretary of State for Education and Science, 1986–9; Chairman of the Conservative Party, 1989–90; Home Secretary, 1990–2.

[84] HM Prison Service, *News Release*, 2 May 1991.

[85] See interview in *The Times* with Kenneth Baker, 8 Mar. 1991.

mitment to providing a constructive regime, the Home Office document stating that

The contracting out of the remand prison offers a unique opportunity to establish this fresh look and approach to the way in which prisoners on remand are treated. The Specification set out to point the way forward. Its main aim is to establish a set of general standards, expressed in terms of output or expected results. It is for Contractors themselves to decide how these outputs will be achieved.[86]

Doubts over the training and competence of the staff of private contractors, stemming from well-advertised criticisms of the short-comings of some employees of private sector security firms, led to a provision, included in the Criminal Justice Act, for contractors' custodial staff to be certified by the Home Secretary. As part of this process he must be satisfied that they have received training up to a standard which he has approved. Under the terms of the contract recruits would have to be tested to eliminate unsuitable candidates, and receive some 200 hours of basic training. On the key political issue of accountability to ministers for the operation of the remand prison, a Home Office controller would work alongside the director employed by the contractor to manage the centre. The controller's job would be to monitor contract performance, investigate allegations against staff, and adjudicate on disciplinary matters. As forecast earlier by Hurd, the remand prison would be subject to periodic inspection by Her Majesty's Inspectorate of Prisons and have its own Board of Visitors.

IX

The same mixture of self-interest and idealism which characterized the movement towards private management of prisons and jails in America[87] showed itself in Britain. Contractors, and their political supporters, genuinely did believe that a profitable business was not only consistent with, but would lead to, higher standards than the

[86] Home Office, *Tender Documents for the Operating Contract of Wolds Remand Prison*, p. 7.
[87] John J. DiIulio, 'The Duty to Govern: A Critical Perspective on the Private Management of Prisons and Jails' in McDonald (ed.), *Private Prisons and the Public Interest*, pp. 155–6.

existing public authorities were capable of providing. There was no other way of establishing whether or not this belief was justified than by experimentation. Limited though the trial project would be it was a beginning and, that most valuable of all tools in the slow uphill progress of British institutional reform, a precedent.

The ideological congruity of the opposition towards any transfer of authority from the state to private interests permitting the exercise of coercive power over individuals detained against their will was diluted by the examples of the immigration detention centres[88] and the weakness of the challenge to the Government's proposals for court escorts and custody services. While the latter seemed plain common sense, the former had already demonstrated at least one of the claimed virtues of privatization. When changes need to be made, but the existing management is deeply entrenched and resistant to any change, it is easier to replace one private contractor by another than to replace one governmental agency or operation by another which also forms part of the public service. Between 1970 and 1988 the operation of immigration detention centres at Harmondsworth, close to London Airport at Heathrow, and certain other airports, was contracted by the Home Office to Securicor. In 1988, following competitive tendering, the Home Office replaced Securicor by another contracted agency, Group 4 Total Security.[89]

The form of accountability devised for the contracted-out remand prison was far more comprehensive than anything previously seen. The presence of a full-time Home Office controller on the site, with powers and duties defined by statute, was an innovation. The result of failure to fulfil the terms of the contract, including the obligation to meet standards not generally set elsewhere in the penal system,

---

[88] In 1986 8,081 people were held overnight or for longer periods in detention accommodation for which the Immigration Service was responsible, with 1,473 held overnight or longer in police cells and 1,422 receptions to prison under Immigration Act powers. The total of 1,422 was the highest level of receptions under this Act for at least ten years, although there is believed to be an element of double-counting in all these figures. *Parl. Debates*, HC, 115 (6th ser.), cols. WA 437–8, 6 May 1987 and *Prison Statistics England and Wales 1986* (Cm. 210), HMSO, London, 1987, p. 88. In 1990 the total number of persons detained overnight or longer under the Immigration Act 1971 was 9,007. Of these 916 were received into prison.

[89] The contract was transferred with effect from 1 Jan. 1989. Group 4 Total Security is associated with Group 4 Remand Services which was awarded the contract to manage Wolds Remand Prison. The first inmates were received at Wolds in April 1992.

was a powerful sanction to maintain the public interest at the expense of profitability should there be a conflict. It was argued that in these circumstances, the Home Secretary was just as accountable as he was for the treatment of prisoners and the conditions in the establishments run by the Prison Service. In both instances his powers are delegated, but in both he remains answerable to Parliament for the way in which they are used.

In America, the source of so many penological trends, private prisons were no longer a novelty by the early 1990s. Faced with a federal prison system which in 1990/1 was operating at more than 160% of capacity,[90] the objections of federal agencies to utilizing privately managed facilities abated. While the policy of the Federal Bureau of Prisons was to move 'relatively slowly',[91] it extended its recourse to private sector correctional services. At Hinton, Oklahoma, a 500-bed privately operated prison was contracted to house primarily low or medium-security federal prisoners. In 1992 a contract was awarded to a private sector company for the construction and operation of a large 1,000-bed facility to be shared jointly by the Bureau of Prisons and the Immigration and Naturalization Service. According to the Bureau's Director, working with the private sector had not been trouble free:

We have continued to have operational problems with the private contractors we have used and have had to come to their assistance in a number of instances. The level of crowding is such, however, that we view the use of private prisons as a viable option for helping to relieve the situation. Although, as I have stated, we will move cautiously in this area.[92]

Another federal agency, the United States Marshal's Service, responded in a similar way to pressure of numbers. In 1990 it contracted for two newly constructed detention centres in West Tennessee and New Mexico. The facilities were designed to hold pre-trial detainees, as well as federal prisoners convicted and sen-

---

[90] On 1 Jan. 1990, the Federal Bureau of Prisons was housing a total of 53,360 inmates in institutions with a rated capacity for 32,494 inmates. This meant that the institutions were operating at 164% of capacity. On 1 Jan. 1991, 58,990 inmates were being housed in institutions with a rated capacity for 36,624, representing 161% of capacity. (Statistics provided by US Department of Justice, Federal Bureau of Prisons.)

[91] Letter from J. Michael Quinlan, Director, Federal Bureau of Prisons, 17 July 1992.

[92] Ibid.

tenced by the US District Courts pending their designation to a federal prison.[93]

By the year end 1991, the industry leader, CCA, had 5,134 beds under management in twenty-one facilities, mainly located in the Southern states and the South-West.[94] Nationwide, however, the number of inmates held in contract managed facilities amounted to no more than a very small proportion of the total number in prison or jail. The rated capacity of all private correctional facilities operational in November 1991 was estimated at 15,476.[95] This compared with an overall population in federal and state institutions which had risen from close on 550,000 at the end of 1986 to over 800,000 five years later.[96] When those held in local jails are added, estimated at 415,000 on average in 1991, it will be seen that the proportion of inmates held at private correctional facilities (assuming all capacity to be filled) was only about 1.2%.

In Britain, as in America, these are still early days. The distinction between the punishment of convicted and sentenced prisoners and pre-trial detention remains blurred, although the remand prison at Wolds is a step towards separate detention in better conditions for those who are denied bail in the interests of prevention. The future for contract provision is likely to depend as much on Party politics and market forces as on penal considerations. Once an ideological argument has been breached it is hard to recover its force. It is highly improbable that either of the opposing dogmas of unregulated

[93] An extension to the West Tennessee Detention Center at Mason provided additional capacity for felons convicted by the criminal courts in the District of Columbia and sentenced to more than three years' imprisonment. A considerable number had committed murder or other serious crimes of violence in Washington DC. The multi-security classification permitted the holding of prisoners requiring conditions of maximum security.

[94] Corrections Corporation of America, *1991 Annual Report*. Beds under management at the year end (5,134) represented a decrease on 1990 (5,410). This was due to the non-renewal of a three-year contract for the management of a 530-bed facility on grounds of a requested fee reduction (ibid., p. 1). The fact that CCA reported a loss for the year prompts the thought that, while contract provision offers an acceptable option to public authorities in a period of excess demand, the picture could change rapidly if the prison population and the public provision of places were to achieve equilibrium.

[95] C. W. Thomas and S. L. Foard, *Private Correctional Facility Census*, Nov. 1991. Professor Thomas is Director of the Private Corrections Project based at the Center for Studies in Criminology and Law of the University of Florida at Gainesville.

[96] US Department of Justice, Bureau of Justice Statistics, *Press Release*, 13 Oct. 1991.

privatization, or the absolute rejection of any delegation of public authority to private interests for the custody of persons deprived of their liberty by the courts, will prevail in their entirety. The rigidities and strongly vested interests of the Prison Service need to be appraised against the more adaptive style of the private sector. An open mind will be called for, inside and outside Government, as the evidence is assessed. In this spirit, we might dwell upon an eloquent passage written by one of the best informed American commentators on prison issues:

Despite a variety of claims to the contrary, there is absolutely nothing in either the scholarly or the nonscholarly literature on the subject—no journal article, no government report, no newspaper story, no conference proceedings, no book—that would enable one to speak confidently about how private corrections firms compare with public corrections agencies in terms of costs, protection of inmates' civil rights, reliance on particular management technologies, or any other significant dimension. The necessary comparative research simply has not been done, and reliable empirical data are still scarce. Sophisticated theoretical speculations, colourful anecdotes, impressionistic 'before and after' surveys, and raw statistics are in ample supply, but there is as yet little dependable information to tell us how, whether, or at what human and financial cost privatization will succeed or fail.[97]

Linked more directly to the starting-point of this chapter, the proposition that the physical conditions in which many untried and unsentenced prisoners are detained equate to punishment in most material respects, was a ministerial announcement in February 1991 of moves to end juvenile remands in custody. Although Waddington's 1990 White Paper had forecast the publication of a consultation paper aiming to relate custodial remands for juveniles more closely to the need to protect the public from serious harm or repeated offending, Baker went further. Responding to a wave of public criticism which followed the suicide by hanging of a fifteen-year-old boy awaiting trial in Swansea, one of several youths to have taken their lives in prison,[98] he decided to add provisions

[97] John J. DiIulio, *Private Prisons and the Public Interest*, p. 156. See also the same author's *No Escape: The Future of Corrections*, Basic Books, 1991, pp. 180–211.
[98] Between 1 Jan. 1971 and 31 Oct. 1991 the number of self-inflicted deaths of young persons under the age of seventeen, convicted as well as on remand, was eight. Four were aged fifteen, and four were sixteen. The deaths occurred at eight different establishments.

to the Criminal Justice Bill then passing through Parliament to end juvenile remands in prison altogether.

As in his comments on private sector involvement in the remand system, the Home Secretary, after only three months in office, showed a broader understanding than his predecessor in bringing out the underlying principles:

The Government is concerned that unconvicted people should only be remanded in custody when absolutely necessary, but our prime interest at all times is to ensure that the public is adequately protected against serious and dangerous offenders of whatever age.

It is now our intention to bring an end to juvenile remands in prison custody. Indeed, many 15 and 16 year old youths at present held in prison custody could remain in the community under close supervision, if they had better support and steps were taken to prevent them from committing further offences.

However, there are some juveniles from whom the public needs protecting and who need to be held in secure conditions. Some pose a danger to the public, especially those charged with very serious violent or sexual offences.

Prisons are clearly inappropriate places in which to keep juveniles on remand. They should instead be held in local authority secure accommodation, and courts will be given the power to require this. The Government's proposals will place a new duty on local authorities to provide secure accommodation. When enough places are available we can bring juvenile remands in prison to an end.[99]

Prisons are indeed 'inappropriate places' to keep juveniles on remand, as they are for all save the most dangerous adults, and it was heartening to hear it proclaimed from such a prominent quarter. Nevertheless, while welcoming the policy decision, the Howard League for Penal Reform was not alone in expressing discontent that it could take at least another four years to implement the new policy. In the meantime, there were stated to be 362 boys aged fifteen who had been remanded to prison establishments in 1990.[100]

Between 1987 and 1991 penal policy had progressed in fits and starts, answering to the rise and fall of the prison population and political pressures, and moving some way towards the ideal of

---

[99] Home Office, *News Office*, 4 Feb. 1991.

[100] After three suicides in 1990/1 the Howard League mounted a national campaign to bring to public notice the plight of fifteen-year-olds held in prison. The statistic is taken from one of its published leaflets.

separate treatment within the criminal justice process for those persons who had been charged with a criminal offence and detained pending trial or sentence, and those who had been convicted and sent to prison as punishment. Escorts and court security were to be contracted out. Within the existing organizational structure of the Prison Service specific responsibilities were recognized for remand prisoners and the upgrading of their regimes. A formal statement of purpose had been recommended by Lord Justice Woolf and Judge Tumim. This should 'reflect the principle that remand prisoners should normally be accommodated, treated and managed separately from convicted prisoners'.[101] When enough secure places became available in units run by local authority social services departments to contain fifteen or sixteen-year-old boys charged with having committed serious offences, or with a previous record of violence or absconding, the widely condemned practice of remanding juveniles to prison would be terminated.

Although for a time the objective of reforming imprisonment on remand coincided with the potent current of privatization, it had not been subsumed within it. At the start of a new decade, the legislative precedent of one new remand prison operated outside the Prison Service, but accountable to the Home Secretary, was a symbol as well as an experiment.

---

[101] *Prison Disturbances April 1990*, p. 26.

7

Life Imprisonment: A Sentence Nobody Can Understand?

I

The mandatory penalty of life imprisonment, denying the trial judge any sentencing discretion when an accused person is found guilty of murder, replaced the mandatory death penalty more than a quarter of a century ago.[1] Overshadowed by the great debate on the morality and expediency of capital punishment, the form of the alternative penalty for the crime of murder was not widely discussed.[2] It was, however, raised in the House of Lords, and the Lord Chief Justice of the day, Lord Parker of Waddington, although previously a supporter of capital punishment, argued against an inflexible penalty of life imprisonment which the sentencing court was bound to impose irrespective of the circumstances leading up to the crime.

When the abolition bill was in Committee in the Lords, Parker pressed the point and narrowly carried an amendment giving the trial judge discretion to mark the gravity of the offence and signify the public feeling of revulsion by passing whatever sentence, whether determinate or indeterminate, he believed to be necessary after having taken account of any mitigating or aggravating factors. The

---

[1] The death penalty was suspended by the Murder (Abolition of Death Penalty) Act 1965 with abolition made permanent in 1969. A young offender who is convicted of murder under the age of eighteen is sentenced to be detained during Her Majesty's pleasure in such place and under such conditions as the Secretary of State may direct by Section 53(1) of the Children and Young Persons Act 1933, as substituted by Section 1(5) of the Murder (Abolition of Death Penalty) Act 1965.

[2] Before abolition, life imprisonment was the penalty invariably substituted when a murderer under sentence of death was reprieved. The Royal Commission on Capital Punishment, which reported in 1953, followed an earlier House of Commons Select Committee (1929/30) in recommending that life imprisonment should be the mandatory sentence in cases where, under their proposals, the death penalty would no longer be applied.

object of the amendment, he said, 'which is very simple, is to abolish once and for all a fixed penalty for murder; in other words to prevent life imprisonment from being the only sentence which can be passed'.[3]

The effect would have been to bring sentencing practice in cases of murder into line with other serious crimes of violence including manslaughter, attempted murder, arson, rape, and robbery where the judge can pass a sentence of life imprisonment as the maximum penalty permitted by Parliament whenever he believes it is justified. The change was not acceptable to the Government, while the Bill's sponsors were also unenthusiastic, being apprehensive that it might jeopardize the chances of the abolition Bill becoming law.[4] To them, everything else was secondary to the ending of capital punishment. When the Bill was considered on Report two weeks later the moment had gone, and Parker proposed alternative amendments, this time with the support of the Home Secretary. The effect was to maintain the mandatory life sentence for murder, but at the same time to give the court an opportunity to recommend a minimum period which should, in its view, elapse before the Secretary of State ordered the release of the prisoner on life licence.

The amendments were agreed without a division in the Lords,[5] but after the Bill returned to the Commons the device of minimum judicial recommendations attracted considerable scepticism. The Home Secretary, Sir Frank Soskice, persuaded the House only with difficulty, his own support being notably muted: 'I do not want the House to think that I am wildly enthusiastic about the Amendment. The consideration I put before the House was that it would serve a moderate and limited purpose of utility and no more.'[6]

Later in the debate he was forced back onto one of the weakest of all ministerial arguments, namely that since the amendment did no more than to provide a statutory right for a judge to do something he was entitled to do already, it could not do any harm

---

[3] *Parl. Debates*, HL, 268 (5th ser.), cols. 1211–12, 27 July 1965. The amendment was carried by two votes. Eleven peers who held high judicial office took part in the division. All but one, the Lord Chancellor, who voted in accordance with Government policy, were in favour of the amendment.

[4] Although the Government was officially neutral, the Bill having been introduced by a private Member of Parliament (Sydney Silverman), the measure had nevertheless been included in the Queen's Speech for the 1964/5 session of Parliament.

[5] *Parl. Debates*, HL, 269 (5th ser.), cols. 418–25, 5 Aug. 1965.

[6] *Parl. Debates*, HC, 718 (5th ser.), col. 381, 28 Oct. 1965.

and might do some good. In the outcome, a reluctant House accepted the amendment without a vote, fearing that further delay might cause the Bill to be lost.[7] A second Lords amendment was more readily agreed. This incorporated a new clause providing that the Home Secretary could not release on licence any person convicted of murder unless he had first consulted the Lord Chief Justice, together with the trial judge if still available. The change represented a concession to opponents of abolition who wished to associate the judiciary more closely with the Home Secretary's power to release.[8] Can we detect here the planting of the first seeds of confusion of function: the legislature bringing in the judiciary to act as a brake on the powers of the executive, applied not through the courts but by way of private advice?

The judiciary already enjoyed a limited advisory role in that there was a long-established convention whereby the judge was encouraged to write privately to the Home Secretary at the conclusion of a murder trial, expressing an opinion about any special features of the case which he wished to draw to the attention of the minister and his officials at the Home Office. Unlike the minimum recommendation in open court, which is primarily a declaration directed towards the anticipated public response, the judge's letter was a private channel of communication and one that was crucially important during the era of capital punishment as it permitted the judge to say whether or not he saw any reasons why the death penalty should not be carried out. Such a confidential expression of judicial opinion was not the only, nor necessarily the dominant, factor in the Home Secretary's mind when deciding whether or not to commute the death penalty. There was always an ominous cloud of public opinion which loomed over these agonizing decisions, but it was almost unknown for the Home Secretary to allow a person convicted of murder to hang if the trial judge had recommended mercy. Whether or not such a recommendation was made, in every case where a convicted murderer was reprieved (and on average 45% of them were[9]) the advice of

---

[7] Ibid., col. 393.

[8] See Sir John Hobson, QC, MP, a former Attorney General, ibid., col. 395.

[9] The Royal Commission on Capital Punishment 1949–53, *Report* (Cmd. 8932), HMSO, London, 1953 found that 'during the past fifty years no fewer than 45 per cent of the persons sentenced to death for that crime [murder] have been reprieved', p. 10.

the judge who had sat throughout the trial, observing the accused and hearing the evidence and the witnesses, would have been a practical and influential way of informing the Home Secretary of the gravity of the crime.

This, then, is the terrain; the unyielding rock of statute law covered by the more workable top soil of convention, in which the foundations of post-abolition sentencing and administrative policies are rooted. Even before 1965 when capital punishment was ended for a five-year period, a reform made permanent by affirmative resolution of both Houses of Parliament four years later, judicial and executive functions coalesced in a way that diverged from the classical model. While the relationship hardly constituted a secure basis for what was to follow, it was just about defensible given the rigidities imposed by the mandatory sentence. Political compromise played a significant part in procedures which were evolved to determine how long a life-sentence prisoner should serve in custody, but on such an intensely emotional issue, cutting across party loyalties and sometimes in conflict with constituency pressures, how could it be otherwise?

II

A mandatory life sentence does not mean, and never has meant, that the convicted offender must be imprisoned for the remainder of his natural life. It means imprisonment for an indeterminate term of years, the duration of which is decided by the Home Secretary subject to two statutory fetters on his discretion. The first, already mentioned, is the obligation to consult the holder of the office of Lord Chief Justice and, if he is still available, the original trial judge before releasing a prisoner on life licence. The second requirement dates from the Criminal Justice Act 1967 which set up the Parole Board. Section 61 states that the Home Secretary may only release on licence a person serving a sentence of imprisonment for life if recommended to do so by the Parole Board,[10] although the important corollary that he need not accept a favourable recommendation is nowhere spelled out. Whenever the Parole

[10] This provision was re-enacted in Section 35(2) of the Criminal Justice Act 1991.

Board does not so recommend, the Home Secretary has no power to release a prisoner on licence.

In rare cases he may discharge a prisoner from custody by recourse to the Royal Prerogative of Mercy, in the form of a free pardon or special remission of the remainder of the sentence. Such action is irrevocable and does not carry liability to recall in the event of breaches of licence conditions, or behaviour indicating a risk that a serious offence might be committed. The distinction is an important one to grasp. It is not absolute liberty that the life prisoner regains on release; rather it is a status of conditional freedom. Although the conditions of the licence are usually lifted after a period of about four years of satisfactory behaviour under supervision, the liability to recall continues for the rest of his or her life.[11]

Once the court has pronounced the sentence required by Act of Parliament in cases of murder (a *mandatory* life sentence), or imposed a sentence of life imprisonment where it is available as a maximum penalty for manslaughter or other serious crimes apart from murder (a *discretionary* life sentence), it falls to the Home Secretary to decide how long a convicted offender should remain in custody. He must take certain advice before reaching his decision, but the ultimate responsibility is his alone. The later distinctions between tariff and risk should not divert attention from the fact that, if it is accepted that the degree of punishment is measured by the length of time spent in custody, the overall penalty for the crime is determined not by the judiciary, but by a minister.

The respective functions of the judiciary and the executive are further complicated by the intrusion of a third element, the Parole Board, a hybrid belonging to neither. The Parole Board for England and Wales is a statutory body, whose members are appointed by

---

[11] Between 1972 and 1986 a total of 194 persons who had been released on life licence were recalled to prison. The liability to recall was not affected by the judgment of the European Court of Human Rights in the case of *Weeks* (1988) 10 EHRR 293. In that case, the court held that the detention of an indeterminate life-sentence prisoner after he had been recalled did not breach Article 5(1) of the European Convention on Human Rights and Fundamental Freedoms, provided that there was a sufficient causal connection between the original conviction and the later deprivation of liberty. Both in *Weeks* and the later case of *Thynne, Wilson and Gunnell* (see Chapter 8) the Court of Human Rights held that the re-detention of persons who had been released from discretionary life sentences, without access to a court or an independent body with the characteristics of a court, was unlawful under Article 5(4).

the Home Secretary. Once appointed they are expected to use their own judgment and make such recommendations as they think fit in the circumstances of each individual case. During the 1980s six of the members were normally judges (three from the High Court and three from the Circuit bench), with the senior High Court Judge acting as Vice-Chairman of the Board.[12] They saw their loyalties, in common with the remainder of the membership, to the independent public body to which they had been appointed rather than as representing any vested interests of the judiciary.

At first sight Section 61 appears to give the Parole Board a more central part in determining the duration of life sentences than is in fact the case. As originally introduced, the legislation which became the Criminal Justice Act 1967 did not provide for a Board to advise the Home Secretary on the release of prisoners on licence.[13] This was added at Report Stage in the Commons, as was another new clause providing for the power of release under life licence to be exercisable only on the recommendation of the Board. The latter provision was a response by Roy Jenkins to pressure from MPs who wished to inhibit the freedom of action of any Home Secretary who might be disposed to take greater risks over the release of a life prisoner than an expert body considered advisable. Hence the absolute veto. If the Parole Board is not prepared to recommend release, then the Home Secretary is effectively prevented from releasing any prisoner, serving life or a determinate sentence. But, while the legislation gave determinate prisoners an absolute entitlement to have their cases reviewed after serving not less than one-third of their sentence (or a minimum qualifying period, whichever is the longer), it was silent on the crucial questions of timing and initiative in the review of life prisoners. When, and by whom, was the process to be set in motion?

In its Annual Report for 1969 the Parole Board explained that life cases were not normally considered by the Board until the prisoner had spent a number of years in prison. The number was

[12] Several members of the higher judiciary have served terms, usually of two years, on the Parole Board. They include Lord Lane CJ, Lords Griffiths and Roskill (the first Vice-Chairman, 1967–9), and in the Court of Appeal: O'Connor, May, Stephen Brown, Lloyd, Gibson, and McCowan, L JJ. It is likely that the number of judges will be increased after 1992 when new review procedures with judicial characteristics will be introduced for discretionary lifers in order to comply with a judgment of the European Court of Human Rights.

[13] See *Responses to Crime*, vol. 1, pp. 253–4.

not specified, although the Report disclosed distinct stages at four and seven years:

An initial scrutiny by the Home Office, following sentence and appeal, serves to identify a small number of cases in which very excellent mitigating circumstances might justify a review within the first four years. Normally, however, it is when the Home Office reviews all these cases again after four years that it is decided whether there are any exceptional ones that should be considered by Local Review Committees in advance of the customary time for first review, which is usually after seven years have been served.[14]

The seven-year point had been agreed between the Board and the Home Secretary as the time at which the cases of life prisoners would normally be referred to the Board for review, irrespective of whether or not there was any realistic prospect of release. Where it seemed to the Home Office that there was no prospect of release, the judiciary would not have been consulted before the case was referred; otherwise the views of the Lord Chief Justice and the trial judge, if available, would have been obtained and made known to the Board. In each case the prisoner would have been interviewed at the prison by a member of the Local Review Committee,[15] prior to that committee making a recommendation for or against release on licence, and if it favoured release, how far ahead. The Parole Board was mildly critical of the delay which the process of reporting and assessment entailed:

... often amounting to an interval of nine months, and occasionally even longer, between the Local Review Committee's deliberations and the presentation of the case to one of its panels, by which time information in the dossier is likely to be, in certain respects, out of date. If, because of this, the Board has to call for more up-to-date reports, this produces further delay. It is appreciated that during the period under review an unusually large number of cases have had to be considered as a consequence of an undertaking given by the Home Office to refer every life sentence case to a Local Review Committee after seven years of imprisonment.[16]

By 1972 it appeared that in roughly 60% of the cases seen at the

[14] *Report of the Parole Board 1969* (HC 48), HMSO, London, 1970, p. 16.
[15] Local Review Committees were composed of representatives of the Board of Visitors at the prison, the Probation Service, independent members, and the Governor of the prison or his representative. They will be abolished as a consequence of the changes in parole contained in the Criminal Justice Act 1991.
[16] *Report of the Parole Board 1969*, p. 16.

seven-year point the Board considered it too early to set a release date. Consequently much time was spent in reviewing cases prematurely, in the process often raising false hopes in the minds of the prisoner and his family. A more discriminating procedure was introduced in 1973 which aimed at identifying at an earlier stage in their sentence those cases where there was a reasonable chance of release. The mechanism was a Joint Committee composed of the Chairman and Vice-Chairman of the Parole Board (a High Court judge), together with a psychiatrist member of the Board, and two Home Office officials. This small group scrutinized one by one the cases of all life prisoners, initially after four years had been spent in custody (a period later reduced to three), with a view either to setting a date when the first full review should take place, or asking that the case should be brought back to the committee for further consideration in a certain number of years time. The function of the Committee was to recommend a date for review, not to make recommendations on release. The two were related nevertheless, since it would have been pointless to set an early date for review where there was no realistic prospect of release. The significance of a Joint Committee was that it represented a willingness to share with an independent body the power to initiate the cumbrous processes leading to review and ultimate release, which hitherto had been the sole prerogative of the Home Office.

These procedures, originating from a proposal by one of the judicial Board members, Waller J (later Lord Justice), and agreed personally between the Chairman of the Parole Board, Lord Hunt, and the then Home Secretary, Robert Carr, endured for a decade. Statistics were published annually in the Board's Report showing the number of cases considered by the Joint Committee and summarizing the recommendations made. The Reports also contained details of how many life cases had been formally reviewed by panels of the Board each year, having first undergone the preliminary scrutiny by the Joint Committee and being reviewed by the Local Review Committees. Tables recorded how many years' imprisonment had been served by those prisoners who were recommended for release; the number of cases in which the Home Secretary had not agreed to accept the recommendation of the Board; and the invariably larger totals of cases which had been considered, but not found suitable for release, or which had been deferred for further consideration.

III

On 11 October 1983, in a speech to the Conservative Party Conference at Blackpool, later amplified in a statement to the House
of Commons,[17] the Home Secretary, Leon Brittan, announced
important changes in the parole system including the handling of
life prisoners. In future, he explained, taking account of public
concern about the increase in violent crime, he intended to use his
discretion so that the murderers of police or prison officers, terrorist
murderers, sexual or sadistic murderers of children, and murderers
by firearm in the course of robbery could normally expect to serve
at least twenty years in prison. As to the decisions on release, he
would look to the judiciary for advice on the time to be spent by
lifers in custody to satisfy the requirements of retribution and
deterrence, and would seek advice from the Parole Board on risk.
At the three-year stage the judiciary would be asked to express an
initial view on the appropriate period to be served, after which the
Home Secretary would decide the date for the first review, often
many years ahead. The Joint Committee, then under my chairmanship, was disbanded.

Before long the lawfulness of this policy, together with the
introduction of a restricted category of determinate sentence
prisoners serving over five years for offences of violence or drug
trafficking,[18] was challenged in the courts by way of applications
for judicial review on behalf of four prisoners who had been
adversely affected. Although all life prisoners who had been notified
of a release date were exempted from the application of the new
policies, those who had embarked on a critical path (i.e. having
been moved to an open prison on the recommendation of the
Parole Board as a first step towards release), but who had not yet
received a definite release date, were less fortunate. In a move
reminiscent of snakes and ladders, two of the applicants for relief
had been transferred back to closed conditions in anticipation of
the statements.

[17] A detailed statement was made in the form of a Written answer to a Question.
Parl. Debates, HC, 49 (6th ser.), cols. WA 505–7, 30 Nov. 1983.
[18] The restricted policy was strongly criticized, at the time of its implementation
and later. The Report of the Review Committee on *The Parole System in England
and Wales* (Cm. 532), HMSO, London, 1988, p. 49, condemned it as 'flawed in
principle and harmful in practice', adding that it 'cut right across the normal criteria
for parole and ... operated in a particularly damaging way'.

The Divisional Court (Parker LJ and Forbes J) was divided on the lawfulness of the measures contained in the Home Secretary's statement. In the Court of Appeal, the Master of the Rolls accepted that the statutory framework permitted the Home Secretary to take the action he had, and that it was a matter within his discretion as to how many cases were referred to the Board. Sir John Donaldson MR (with Griffiths LJ concurring) held that the change in policy did not involve retrospective executive interference with the sentence of the courts, nor an interference with the judicial function of sentencing. He did not find that the Home Secretary had unlawfully fettered his own discretion by precluding himself from considering each case on its merits, although he did indicate that, in his view, if the operation of the new policy were in due course shown to depend upon such a rigid demarcation line as to cause unfairness in cases close to the margins of the categories, then the policy might be held to involve the giving of such unreasonable weight to the seriousness of the crime as to be unlawful.

Although these remarks, and those of Browne-Wilkinson LJ[19] in a powerful dissenting judgment, were principally directed towards the introduction of a new restricted category of determinate-sentence prisoners sentenced to more than five years' imprisonment, they applied equally to the new twenty-year category of life prisoners. In each instance the issue of principle was the same: the relative weight to be given to the gravity of the original offence and the deterrent effect of the sentence, as against the progress and circumstances of the prisoner subsequent to sentence. Browne-Wilkinson LJ argued that it was the Home Secretary's duty to consider all of the circumstances of each individual case and not to regard one particular factor, namely the nature and gravity of the offence, as paramount and to the exclusion of other relevant factors. According to this argument, the policy was unlawful because it prevented or inhibited the Home Secretary from performing his statutory duty.

The House of Lords disagreed, holding that although the nature and gravity of the offence in cases coming within the new policy would be the main or predominant factor, consideration of other factors was not precluded altogether. Lord Scarman accepted that

---

[19] Judge of the High Court, Chancery Division, 1977–83; Lord Justice of Appeal, 1983–5; Vice-Chancellor, 1985–91; Lord of Appeal in Ordinary, 1991– .

while the impact of the statement on the applicants, two of whom were serving life sentences, must have been shattering, nevertheless whatever hope or expectation they may have entertained of an early release could not in law be held to impose a fetter on the Home Secretary's discretion to formulate such a policy.[20]

IV

The justification for policies which steadily hardened throughout the 1980s[21] was that of retribution and deterrence. The prefix 'general' has been added more recently to deterrence since it is hard to see how the actual offender sentenced to life imprisonment can be said to be deterred by the process of determining the minimum term he must serve. The crude and ugly word 'tariff' was used to describe that portion of the sentence, fixed after consultation with the judiciary, which was intended as the appropriate punishment for the crime. If there are mitigating circumstances, for example some domestic murders or mercy killings with compassionate aspects which in the absence of a mandatory penalty would have led to a lighter sentence, these factors will be reflected in a lower tariff than, for example, a deliberate killing in the course of an armed robbery. There is room for a graduated scale between the two.

The idea of a scale or tariff was borrowed from determinate sentences where it had honourable antecedents, dating from the late nineteenth century as part of an attempt by James Fitzjames Stephen and others to achieve greater consistency, and so parity of treatment, in sentencing. In 1874 a judge, replying to a circular from the Home Secretary, referred to the opportunities available for judges to consult with each other 'forming a conventional tariff'.[22] In 1901, a memorandum sent by the Lord Chief Justice,

---

[20] *In re Findlay* [1985] AC 318, affirming *The Times*, 7 July 1984 (Court of Appeal), and *The Times*, 23 May 1984 (Divisional Court). The *Report of the Parole Board 1984* (HC 411), HMSO, London, 1985 contains a useful summary of the issues raised by the case at pp. 5–6.

[21] The statistics published in the annual *Reports* of the Parole Board showed an increase from 4% in 1973 to an average of 14% between 1981 and 1987 in the proportion of lifers who had served fifteen years or more by the time of their release.

[22] D. A. Thomas, 'Constraints on Judgment', *Institute of Criminology Occasional Series*, No. 4, Cambridge, 1979, p. 65.

Lord Alverstone, to the Home Secretary on behalf of the judges of the King's Bench Division enumerated a scale of 'normal punishments' for certain kinds of crime.[23] The application of the concept of a tariff to life sentences, however, led to a new connotation: a minimum term which must be served in all save the most exceptional cases before considerations of behaviour, motivation, and release plan, each with a bearing on the likelihood of reoffending, could be taken into account. These factors have become largely segregated from the element of punishment, being compartmentalized into a separate category of risk, and are not considered until the demands of punishment have been fulfilled.

The post-1983 practice endured only until 1987. In that year the Divisional Court, again on an application for judicial review, this time by a prisoner named Handscomb and three others, considered the review procedures where a life sentence had been awarded at the discretion of the sentencing judge (i.e. for offences other than murder with its unavoidable concomitant of a mandatory life sentence). In his judgment, Watkins LJ held that the initial consultation with the judiciary on the period necessary to meet the requirements of retribution and deterrence in an individual case should take place as soon as practicable after the imposition of the sentence, and should not be delayed for around three to four years. Furthermore the Secretary of State should not substitute his own views as to the requirements of retribution and deterrence for those expressed by the judiciary, which should take into account the notional equivalent determinate sentence less one-third remission.[24]

In a statement to Parliament on 23 July 1987, the Home Secretary, Douglas Hurd, said that after consulting the Lord Chief Justice it had been agreed the most satisfactory way of obtaining the judicial view was to ask the trial judge to write to him, via the Lord Chief Justice, in every case where a discretionary life sentence had been passed giving a view on the period necessary to meet the requirements of retribution and deterrence.

That view would be related to the determinate sentences that would have been passed, but for the element of mental instability

[23] The text of the Alverstone Memorandum was printed as an Appendix to a report of the Advisory Council on the Penal System on *Sentences of Imprisonment: A Review of Maximum Penalties*, HMSO, London, 1978, pp. 191–6.

[24] *R. v. Secretary of State for the Home Department ex parte Handscomb and others* (1988) 86 Cr. App. R. 59.

and/or public risk which led the judge to pass a life sentence.[25] It would also take account of the notional period of the sentence which a prisoner might expect to have been remitted for good behaviour had a determinate sentence been passed. The date for the first formal review by the Parole Board would be fixed in accordance with the judicial view and would take place normally about three years before the expiry of the tariff period. The new procedures would come into effect from 1 October 1987.[26]

Whereas the *Handscomb* judgment related only to discretionary life sentences, the Home Secretary evidently thought that so far as possible similar procedures should govern the review of prisoners serving mandatory sentences of life imprisonment. Here, too, the date of the first formal review would be fixed soon after conviction and sentence, once the views of the trial judge and the Lord Chief Justice had been obtained on the period of time necessary to meet the requirements of retribution and deterrence. This arrangement completed a gradual and almost imperceptible process of change in the true nature of the advice given to the Home Secretary by the judiciary. Between 1967 and 1983 the question put to the trial judge, several years after the sentence had been passed, was not how long the prisoner ought to be kept in custody, as whether sufficient time had elapsed to consider letting him out. In the wake of *Handscomb* the emphasis switched away from the possibilities of release on licence towards a recommendation made at the commencement of a life sentence on how long a convicted person should serve from the standpoint of punishing him and deterring others.

The Home Secretary's statement claimed that since the sentence was not at the discretion of the court in cases of murder no question of a notional equivalent determinate sentence could arise.[27] Thus

---

[25] The reasoning overlooks the fact that retribution and deterrence are concepts which are hard to reconcile with the situation of mentally disordered offenders who are sentenced to life imprisonment on grounds of risk or mental instability. It is unreal to talk of the determinate sentence which would have been passed had such a person not been unstable, since had he been stable he might never have committed the crime.

[26] *Parl. Debates*, HC, 120 (6th ser.), cols. WA 347–9, 23 July 1987.

[27] It does not necessarily follow that because a life sentence is mandatory in the case of murder no notional equivalent can be identified. Whether a life sentence is imposed in the exercise of the court's discretion, or pronounced because the law requires it, the ascertainment of the appropriate determinate sentence depends on the answer to the hypothetical question a trial judge must put to himself: 'what

he reserved the right in mandatory cases to take into account other factors, including the need to maintain public confidence in the system of justice, when determining the tariff. This reference illuminates for the first time a developing practice, virtually unknown until the mid-1980s, of ministers adjusting the judicially recommended tariff upwards if they felt it was not sufficient to reflect their own view of the gravity of the crime. By 1988 a situation had been reached in which no less than sixty-three out of a total of 106 murder cases which were considered in the six months between 1 April and 30 September had a tariff fixed which exceeded that recommended by the trial judge. In sixteen of these cases the Lord Chief Justice had made a higher recommendation.[28]

Judgments were given in the Queen's Bench Divisional Court by Appeal Court judges in four cases brought to test the procedures which the Home Office had devised for the release of life-sentence prisoners.[29] The Court of Appeal itself did not enter the tangled web until 1992. Then, on 6 May, a strong court constituted by Glidewell, Staughton, and Farquharson L JJ gave judgment in two cases: *R. v. Secretary of State for the Home Department, Ex parte Doody, Pierson, Smart and Pegg* and *R. v. Secretary of State for the Home Department, Ex parte Walsh.*[30] Each of the appellants in the first case was serving a mandatory life sentence for murder, and had been refused relief by the Divisional Court on application

determinate sentence would I have imposed if the special circumstances (i.e. mental instability and the risk to the public) or the law requiring a life sentence did not apply?' Judges already have to assess the needs of retribution and deterrence in cases of attempted murder and causing grievous bodily harm with intent where a conviction for murder may have been avoided only because the injuries did not lead to the death of the victim. In terms of culpability and dangerousness the offences are indistinguishable from murder. The only element missing from the equation is the fact of death.

[28] The judicial tariff had been increased by the Home Secretary in 80 out of 195 cases in the first six months of 1984, and in 25 out of 78 cases in the comparable period of 1986. House of Lords, *Report of the Select Committee on Murder and Life Imprisonment*, Session 1988/9 (HL Paper 78-I), HMSO, London, 1989, p. 43.

[29] Watkins LJ in *R v. Secretary of State for the Home Department, ex parte Handscomb* (1988); Lloyd LJ in *R. v. Secretary of State for the Home Department, ex parte Benson* (1988); Mann LJ in *R. v. Secretary of State for the Home Department, ex parte Doody and Others* (1991); and Nolan LJ in *R. v. Secretary of State for the Home Department, ex parte Walsh* (1991).

[30] Reported in *The Times*, 8 May 1992, and the *Independent*, 7 May 1992. The resumé which follows is based on a transcript of the judgments given in the Court of Appeal. Leave was granted to the Secretary of State to appeal to the House of Lords.

for judicial review of the decisions taken by the Home Secretary. The Court accepted that while they had been convicted of serious crimes, their appeals were not in a 'criminal cause or matter' within the meaning of Section 18(1) of the Supreme Court Act 1981. It was therefore the civil, and not the criminal, division of the Court of Appeal that had jurisdiction.

After a full review of the statutory background, the elaborate procedures, the tariffs which had been set, the relief sought, the general issues argued, and the principles of decision-making, Glidewell LJ turned to the question whether the Secretary of State was required by law to adopt the judicial view of the tariff. If the Court was bound by the decision in *Handscomb* he would see force in the argument that the same principle should apply equally to mandatory life sentences. In his opinion, however, the proposition that it was not lawful for the Secretary of State to adopt a tariff which differed from that of the judges was wrong. The ultimate decision on the period a life-sentence prisoner should serve for the purpose of retribution and deterrence was that of the Secretary of State. In making his decision the Home Secretary sought the advice of the judiciary, but provided he had good reason for doing so, as a matter of law he was entitled to set a tariff period which differed from the judges' recommendation. To that extent, *Handscomb* was wrongly decided.

Nevertheless, since Hurd's statement in July 1987 the Home Secretary had adopted a policy of accepting the judicial view on the tariff for discretionary life-sentence prisoners. In doing so he had probably created a legitimate expectation that the policy would continue to be applied. New procedures relating to discretionary life prisoners in the Criminal Justice Act 1991, Section 34, which would come into force in October 1992,[31] gave statutory expression to the post-*Handscomb* policy, and presumably the Home Secretary would not depart from it in the meantime.

The remaining questions were whether the prisoner had the right to make representations before the date for the first review was set, and whether he had a right to be informed of the judicial view on

_____

[31] Section 34 of the Criminal Justice Act 1991 was added at a late stage in the Parliamentary proceedings (Commons consideration of Lords Amendments) as a result of amendments carried against the Government in the House of Lords, and to comply with the judgment of the European Court of Human Rights in the case of *Thynne, Wilson and Gunnell*. See Chapter 9.

the tariff. Both issues came under the heading of procedural fairness. Since the right to be heard or to make representations was worth little unless the person making the representations knew, at least in general terms, the case he had to meet, a prisoner serving a mandatory life sentence should not only be given an opportunity to make representations in writing to the Secretary of State about the length of the tariff period before it was set, but should also be given such relevant information as he did not already have. This information should include the judicially recommended tariff as well as any comments made by the trial judge, for example in a case where there was more than one defendant his views on their respective culpability.

In Glidewell LJ's opinion, the present procedure was insufficient to achieve justice. There was, he said, nothing in the additional requirements to frustrate the apparent purpose of the legislation. From the judges' evidence to the House of Lords Select Committee on Murder and Life Imprisonment[32] it was clear that a majority favoured immediate disclosure of their recommendations on the tariff. In future, if prisoners were to be told the judicial recommendation on the tariff period, many judges might think it appropriate to announce their own recommendations in open court when passing sentence. If, after consideration of the judicially recommended tariff and the prisoner's representations upon it, the Home Secretary (or a Minister of State acting on his behalf) decided to set a tariff which exceeded the judicial tariff he was under no obligation to give his reasons for doing so. Nevertheless if the disparity was considerable, and no reasons were given, the decision would be open to challenge by way of judicial review as being irrational.

Staughton and Farquharson L JJ agreed that the appeals should be allowed and declarations granted (1) requiring the Home Secretary to afford to a prisoner serving a mandatory life sentence an opportunity to submit in writing representations as to the period he should serve for the purposes of retribution and deterrence before setting the date of the first review of the prisoner's sentence; and (2) before doing so, to inform the prisoner of the period

---

[32] A synopsis of the views of the judiciary had been prepared by Glidewell LJ on the basis of twenty-six replies to a letter from the Lord Chief Justice. *Report of the Select Committee on Murder and Life Imprisonment* (HL paper 78-III), pp. 564–6.

recommended by the judiciary as the period he should serve, and of any other relevant expression of judicial opinion.

In the second judgment, given on the same day by the same members of the Court, the Court of Appeal held that where a life sentence was not mandatory, but had been passed at the discretion of the court, the prisoner was entitled to be told what the Secretary of State had fixed as his tariff period.

Counsel in the *Doody* case included some well-known names at the Bar. Stephen Sedley QC and his junior, Edward Fitzgerald, had appeared in previous cases testing policies towards life-sentence prisoners. Soon after Sedley was appointed a High Court judge. Two more QCs, one of whom, Anthony Scrivener, had been Chairman of the Bar in 1991, with their juniors, appeared for the other appellants. Leading Counsel for the Home Secretary was David Pannick QC, who had argued life sentence cases in the domestic courts and at Strasbourg. A combination of legal aid and the willingness of some counsel to forgo part or all of their normal fees enables prisoners with no funds of their own to be represented by experienced and competent advocates. Certain firms of solicitors, notably B. M. Birnberg and Co. and Bindman and Partners, can also take credit for ensuring that test cases bearing on public policy are brought before the courts and properly argued.

V

The explanation of the tortuous development of policy towards life sentence prisoners can be found in ministerial attitudes towards public opinion. Public confidence in this branch of the system of justice was believed by ministers to be more assured in their hands than in those of the judiciary. Yet in reality public confidence is attuned to the degree of risk attached to the actual release of a life-sentence prisoner back into the community, and not to the inner workings of the Home Office. It is hard to accept without question the proposition that the setting of the tariff, an administrative act carried out in private, has any effect on the state of public confidence in the system of criminal justice. A minimum recommendation by the trial judge in the exercise of his power under the 1965 Act may have some effect because it is made in public, and in the expectation of being widely reported and received with a degree of satisfaction by some readers and viewers. This is quite distinct from the minister's function which consists in not releasing a lifer until it is safe to do so, and in recalling him (with the consent of the Parole Board) if it seems there is a real risk of serious offending while on licence.

It is only towards the end of the tariff period that the comprehensive range of factors which lie at the heart of an assessment of the risks of further offending are brought into play. The focus alters from what the prisoner did in the past, probably many years before, to what he may do in the future. There are no indisputable answers, and although the members of the Parole Board who consider the case on its way to the Home Secretary bring an impressive weight of experience to their task,[33] they must rely on reports which have been prepared by others. The reporting is more systematic and detailed than on prisoners serving long determinate sentences, and the information is generally well presented. Life prisoners are treated as a special group within the prisons, and a Grade 1 Governor is attached to the headquarters of the Prison Department at the Home Office with responsibility for their management.[34] Reports come not only from prison officers, but from probation officers who have visited the proposed home address and, where appropriate, from psychiatrists.

Throughout their sentence all life prisoners are subject to assessment by trained staff enabling them to follow a career plan moving from a lifer main centre (a maximum security prison such as Wormwood Scrubs, Wakefield, or Gartree) to prisons of progressively lower security where there are opportunities for greater trust and responsibility. Towards the end of his time in custody a life prisoner will typically move towards release on licence via an open prison and a period of several months in a pre-release employment scheme hostel.[35] In this way, targets can be set which fall outside the artificial confines of a closed institution enabling an assessment to be made as to how the prisoner is likely to react when eventually he attains a state of conditional liberty.

[33] Panels of the Parole Board reviewing life-sentence cases include a High Court Judge and a consultant psychiatrist with clinical experience of offenders.
[34] As Head of the Life Management Unit the Governor's responsibilities did not extend to life prisoners in the top security category, nor to women serving life sentences.
[35] The latter is only authorized once a provisional release date has been given.

Yet however thorough and well-informed the process of estimating the risk of future serious offending, the results are bound to be imperfect. It is clearly necessary that the task should be attempted at some stage, for the protection of the public demands it. Later in the sentence, when release has become a realistic possibility, is preferable to the early stages when there may be little more to go on than the information which was before the court at the point of sentence. As the years pass, the sad fact in many cases is that the experience of imprisonment will do more harm than good, pushing the goals of self-reliance and respect for others farther and farther into the distance. The idealism to be found amongst the ranks of probation officers, chaplains, governor grades, and prison officers should never be underrated, but the setting is inimical to the achievement of most of their objectives. Moreover there are the mental instability and personality disorders which are such a common feature in the prison population, besides being notoriously resistant to treatment. Despite the best efforts of the Prison Medical Service and outside consultants, such conditions may become more, rather than less, deeply engrained as a result of a lengthy term in prison.

The case for continued detention at this point shifts from punishment to prevention, the reasoning being that a life prisoner who has completed that part of his sentence which was deemed necessary to meet the requirements of retribution and general deterrence should be released whenever he is no longer considered to be dangerous. But dangerousness is an imprecise state, besides being a label which is much easier to attach than to remove.

Detention on grounds of prevention alone is an approach that bristles with practical and conceptual difficulties. Although it would be folly for the Parole Board to recommend, or for the Home Secretary to accept, the release on licence of a life prisoner if it was thought to be probable that he would commit a further serious offence, few instances are so clear-cut. Both the Prison and Probation Services contain people who are experienced in differentiating between those prisoners who will go on being dangerous and those who will not, and this is reflected in their reports. There are, none the less, numerous borderline cases in which the question is where to set the limits of acceptable risk. If there were more certain ways of foretelling human behaviour no doubt more lifers would be released earlier, and a few later, or not at all. But as it is, the estimation of risk is one of the most baffling of all forms of prophecy.

VI

The paradox posed by life imprisonment is that it is neither a sentence for life nor a genuinely indeterminate term. The importation of a stated tariff period means there is in effect a minimum fixed sentence contained within the indeterminate sentence. This must be fulfilled, irrespective of all save the most exceptional circumstances, before any other factors bearing on the prisoner's progress and future prospects can be considered. Although fixed by the Home Secretary, the quantum of the tariff is recommended by the trial judge and the Lord Chief Justice shortly after the conclusion of the trial. When making these crucially important recommendations the trial judge has no knowledge of what other judges may be recommending in the cases which come before them. There is consequently no body of precedent to which he may turn for guidance; no Criminal Appeal Reports, nor published commentaries. No wonder that Lane, when Lord Chief Justice, supported by trial judges, went on record as being unhappy about the role the judiciary was called upon to perform.[36]

In discretionary cases it is no longer the practice for the Home Secretary to vary the period recommended; whereas in mandatory cases he may add to it, or very occasionally reduce it.[37] Since *Doody*, the Home Secretary's right to determine the tariff (and to delegate the decision) has been upheld by the Court of Appeal. Before doing so, however, he must consider the prisoner's representations made with knowledge of the judicially recommended tariff. Once this becomes established practice there seems no reason why the judge's recommendation should not be stated publicly at the conclusion of the trial. It would be far from satisfactory if the Home Secretary's decision on the tariff was withheld from the

[36] See Chapter 9.
[37] In only one case between 1 Apr. and 30 Sept. 1988 did the Home Secretary set a tariff lower than that recommended to him by the judiciary. The significance of the Lord Chief Justice's function in aiming for a degree of consistency is demonstrated by the fact that in eight cases he recommended a lower, and in sixteen cases a higher, tariff than the trial judge.

prisoner leaving him to make approximate calculations on its length on the basis of the first review date.[38] From the perspective of the prisoner the setting of the tariff closely resembles a sentencing decision in that it is a measure of the punishment to be endured for the crime. While its determination owes much to the judges, it is now clear that they are regarded as advisers rather than sentencers, with a pattern having emerged whereby ministers may add to the judicially recommended tariff if they feel there are reasons of public confidence to suggest it is inadequately punitive.[39]

The creation of a specific tariff for lifers is a peculiarly English development, never designed as part of a rational scheme for deciding upon the amount of time to be spent in custody by offenders convicted of the most serious crimes. Born of uncertain parentage, it took on a life of its own in 1983,[40] being almost unnoticed at first, but before long coming to dominate the whole complex administrative structure of life imprisonment. A web of restrictions and distinctions has been spun around the Home Secretary's discretion to release a prisoner serving a life sentence. The system has become more and more complicated, and harder and harder to justify. Over-elaborate, piecemeal procedures have tended towards arbitrariness, attracting much critical attention from the well informed. The general public was aware that life did not mean life, but bewildered as to what it did mean. In a typically outspoken comment, made only a few months after leaving the Government, Lord Hailsham got to the nub of the matter: 'I do not believe that life imprisonment means anything at all at the

[38] A few weeks or months after being sentenced, life prisoners are told the date fixed for their first formal review. Except where the tariff exceeds twenty years (in which event the first formal review will take place after seventeen years in custody) it is possible to calculate the tariff by adding three years to the review date since the date set for the first review will generally be three years before the expiry of the tariff.
[39] On the ninety-one mandatory life sentence cases considered between 1 Apr. and 30 Sept. 1990, ministers set a longer period than that recommended by the trial judge in thirty-six cases; in twenty-five of these the Lord Chief Justice had made a higher recommendation than the trial judge. *Parl. Debates*, HL, 530 (5th ser.), col. WA 1, 17 June 1991.
[40] In deciding when a prisoner serving a life sentence should be released from custody, successive Home Secretaries (and those who have advised them) have always taken into account the relative gravity of the offence as well as the risk of the prisoner committing a further serious offence. But there seems no room for doubt that a process of crystallization has taken place since 1983.

present time. It is an indeterminate sentence which nobody can understand.'[41]

The problem, as so often, has been how to induce reforms which many knew were needed, but which Home Office ministers and officials were reluctant to contemplate. Nothing had changed since Radzinowicz and Hood's timeless description of attempts to reform the prisons before the First World War: 'Administrators may be willing to give way on small things but it is difficult to move them when it comes to more fundamental issues. The weight of the past and the fear of what the future may bring are powerful restraining factors.'[42]

Two avenues offered a potential for greater leverage than any other. The first was the House of Lords, where former ministers and Parole Board chairmen joined the higher judiciary and an articulate contingent of penal reformers in a chamber which had proved itself ready on occasion to subject the shortcomings of government policies to critical scrutiny from a non-party (or cross-party) viewpoint. The influence of the Lords was heightened whenever criminal justice legislation was before Parliament, since the consent of each House was necessary before the proposals contained in a Bill could be enacted, and in procuring that consent the Government Whips had fewer sanctions at their disposal than in the Commons. The fact that criminal justice legislation is normally widely drawn meant that there were invariably opportunities to debate new provisions by way of amendments. In this way, the Lords was able to perform its proper contemporary role of supplementing the effectiveness of Parliament when considering legislative proposals by bringing into play a range of interests different from those of the Commons.[43]

The second path, more recently laid but increasingly well trod, led to Strasbourg and the institutions set up to enforce the European Convention on Human Rights. Since their original applications to the European Commission of Human Rights in 1985[44] the case of three prisoners serving discretionary sentences of life imprisonment

[41] *Parl. Debates*, HL, 490 (5th ser.), col. 975, 1 Dec. 1989.
[42] Sir L. Radzinowicz and R. G. Hood, *A History of English Criminal Law and its Administration from 1750*, vol. 5, Stevens, London, 1986, p. 593.
[43] See Windlesham, 'The House of Lords: A Study of Influence Replacing Power' in *Politics in Practice*, Jonathan Cape, London, 1975, pp. 115–42.
[44] Report of the European Commission of Human Rights adopted 7 Sept. 1989. *Thynne, Wilson and Gunnell* v. *The United Kingdom* (1991) 13 EHRR 135.

for non-murder offences had been wending its way slowly through a sequence of intricate proceedings, finally reaching the Court of Human Rights in the early summer of 1990. The judgment, which went against the United Kingdom, was important not only because of the way in which the right to a judicial hearing of persons deprived of their liberty was affirmed and applied,[45] but because there was an obligation on the part of the Government to comply. The timing was fortuitous, as the necessity to make changes in the handling of discretionary life sentences in order to satisfy the requirements of the Court's judgment coincided with strong pressure from the House of Lords, culminating in a series of amendments to the Criminal Justice Bill in 1991 carried against the Government. A detailed resumé of the case of *Thynne, Wilson and Gunnell* forms the introduction to the next chapter on enforcing the Convention.

VII

The story in the House of Lords goes back to the previous legislation leading to the Criminal Justice Act 1988. At that time the implications of the *Handscomb* judgment and the administrative changes which flowed from it were only just becoming apparent. Several peers became interested in the subject through their dissatisfaction with the state of the law relating to murder, and the fine line distinguishing it from manslaughter. Lord Hailsham made the point that Parliament had 'never really grappled with the distinction between manslaughter and murder'. Referring to its historical origins as 'wholly illogical', he declared that there were only two options: to abolish the distinction altogether, creating a single offence of criminal homicide; or, as suggested by Lord Diplock in his dissenting judgment in the case of *Hyam*,[46] to limit murder to cases where there was a deliberate intention to kill.[47] Amongst others, he was supported by Lord Roskill: 'I say with

---

[45] For a discussion of procedural fairness in the context of life imprisonment, including the requirements of the European Convention on Human Rights, see Genevra Richardson, 'The Select Committee and the Sentencing Structure for Murder', (1990) 29 *Howard Journal of Criminal Justice* 300.

[46] *Hyam* v. *DPP* [1975] AC 55.

[47] *Parl. Debates*, HL, 489 (5th ser.), cols. 429–31, 27 Oct. 1987.

regret that the law of murder and manslaughter has got into a mess'.[48]

The mandatory sentence of life imprisonment for murder came in for more severe criticism than in the past, when it had been regarded by penal reformers such as Baroness Wootton as a price to be paid for the abolition of capital punishment. Two former chairmen of the Parole Board[49] and myself, as the chairman at the time, joined judicial and other peers in arguing that the court should have discretion to sentence up to a maximum of life imprisonment as in other cases of serious crime. But it was the way the life sentence was administered, in particular the device of the tariff, that was the target for the strongest censure. From every quarter of the House, save the isolation of the Woolsack where the newly appointed Lord Chancellor, Lord Mackay of Clashfern,[50] was left with the unenviable task of defending the indefensible, condemnation was voiced about the practice by which the trial judge was expected to make a private recommendation to the Home Secretary as to how long a life prisoner should spend in custody.

When fending off amendments at Report stage, the Lord Chancellor conceded there was a case for a thorough review of law and practice, while reserving the Government's position on the 'precise machinery for review'.[51] On Third Reading he agreed to a proposal, which I had put forward, that a Select Committee, including the higher judiciary among its membership, would be a form of inquiry with 'obvious advantages'.[52] The criminal justice legislation of 1987/8 was the first on which Mackay spoke for the Government as Lord Chancellor. Although well accustomed to the dispatch box[53] from his years as Lord Advocate of Scotland, he had made

---

[48] Ibid., col. 429.

[49] Lord Hunt was the first Chairman of the Parole Board for England and Wales, 1967–74. Lord Harris of Greenwich, a Minister of State at the Home Office in the Labour Government, 1974–9, was the Board's Chairman between 1979 and 1982.

[50] Throughout the Conservative administration, 1970–4, and again from 1979–87, Lord Hailsham was Lord Chancellor. He was succeeded for only four months by Lord Havers after the General Election in June of 1987. Lord Mackay of Clashfern was appointed as Lord Chancellor on 27 Oct. 1987. He had been Lord Advocate of Scotland, 1979–84; a Senator of the College of Justice in Scotland, 1984–5; and a Lord of Appeal in Ordinary, 1985–7.

[51] *Parl. Debates*, HL, 490 (5th ser.), col. 319, 19 Nov. 1987.

[52] *Parl. Debates*, HL, 490 (5th ser.), col. 972, 1 Dec. 1987.

[53] Although the Lord Chancellor normally speaks from the Woolsack, he moves to the dispatch box on the Government front bench for the Committee stage of any Bill on which he is speaking for the Government.

the transfer to his high office from the cross-benches where he had sat as a Lord of Appeal in Ordinary. Calm, rational, and always persuasive in debate, Mackay showed a readiness to take the first steps to cleanse the Augean stables. But the content of the criminal law and criminal justice policy, as Gardiner had found before him, was a jealously regarded preserve of the Home Office. It was the reaction of Hurd and his officials that was crucial to the prospects for a Select Committee.

Having taken preliminary soundings from one or two of the civil servants, I went to see Mackay first, and then Hurd, to press the case for an inquiry by a Select Committee. I also kept in close touch with one of my successors as Lord Privy Seal and Leader of the Lords, Lord Belstead.[54] While not opposed to a review that would run in parallel with Carlisle on parole, Pigot on children's evidence, and the working group on the right of silence, the Home Office had to accommodate the reservations of the Home Secretary's ministerial colleagues. Then, as later, any move that might be interpreted as diminishing the public opprobrium attached to the crime of murder was looked on with collective suspicion and apprehension. Ministers feared that to include in the remit of the proposed inquiry the demarcation between murder and man-slaughter might allow the door to be blown open by an unwelcome squall of protest if any recommendation were made to abandon murder as a separate crime.

After a pause, a letter arrived from the Home Secretary:

HOME SECRETARY   QUEEN ANNE'S GATE LONDON SW1H 9AT
                                                          27 June 1988

Dear David

MURDER AND LIFE IMPRISONMENT

I have now had some further discussions with colleagues about your proposal for a Lords Select Committee on murder and life imprisonment.

On reflection, we think it might be better to link the terms of reference more directly to the topics which exercised the House during the debates on the Criminal Justice Bill. Could I offer the enclosed draft for your consideration? As you will see, it still covers a very wide range.

---

[54] Parliamentary Under-Secretary of State: Department of Education and Science, 1970–3; Northern Ireland Office, 1973–4; Home Office, 1979–82. Minister of State: Foreign and Commonwealth Office, 1982–3; Ministry of Agriculture, Fisheries, and Food, 1983–7; Department of the Environment, 1987–8. Deputy-Leader of the House of Lords, 1983–7; Lord Privy Seal and Leader of the House of Lords, 1988–90; Paymaster-General and Minister of State for Northern Ireland, 1990–2.

I should be very glad to have another word if you would find it helpful to do so. Otherwise, might I suggest that you get in touch with John Belstead, with a view to setting in motion the necessary procedural steps towards establishing the Committee? Since we spoke, we have had some further thoughts about chairmanship, but John will be able to explore these with you.

Yours ever,
Douglas

DRAFT TERMS OF REFERENCE FOR A SELECT COMMITTEE
To consider

—the scope and definition of the crime of murder in England and Wales and in Scotland;
—the question whether imprisonment for life should remain a mandatory rather than a maximum penalty for murder; and
—the working of the arrangements for reaching decisions on the release of those serving life sentences for murder;

this consideration to include such matters as the sentencing judge's power to recommend a minimum period of detention and the means by which the Home Secretary and the Secretary of State for Scotland take judicial advice on individual cases where a life sentence has been imposed.

With the summer recess fast approaching, time was running out. Between 29 July and 10 October the House would not be sitting and the head of steam that had built up would be dissipated. There are times to settle for the bird in hand and this was one of them. I knew that the Opposition would support the proposal, as would some influential cross-benchers and Conservative peers. It is *ad hoc* coalitions of this sort which can present the most formidable challenges to the Government in the Upper House. I accepted the Home Secretary's suggested formulation.

VIII

On 21 July, after discussions with the Lord Chancellor, the Home Secretary and the Party Leaders in the Lords, the Lord Privy Seal moved to set up a Select Committee to consider the crime of murder and the penalty it should attract, as well as the arrangements for fixing the period to be spent in custody by those sentenced to life imprisonment.[55] The terms of reference did not depart from those offered in Hurd's letter. The motion was supported on all sides of the House. The Leader of the Opposition, Lord Cledwyn,[56] said:

We on these Benches warmly welcome the Motion. This is something to which Noble Lords throughout the House have been looking forward. We also approve the wording of the Motion, which we think is fully appropriate for the inquiry that is to follow.[57]

Cledwyn was followed by Lord Harris of Greenwich speaking for the Liberal Democrats, and two former Lord Chancellors, one Conservative and one Labour, Lords Hailsham and Elwyn-Jones. All were in favour. Elwyn-Jones, somewhat prematurely, congratulated the Government on setting up 'this committee to decide a matter which I know is causing great concern to the courts up and down the country. I hope that we may see the outcome of it sooner rather than later in view of its importance in the criminal law.'[58]

Although the House of Lords has a number of standing Select Committees, those on the European Communities and Science and Technology being the most important, a Select Committee to inquire into a specific subject is much rarer. Since 1971/2 no more than five had been established.[59] The business managers have to be convinced that the additional calls on public expenditure and on limited staff resources are justified. A larger obstacle to be surmounted is the attitude of the relevant government department. The greater the number of Select Committees of either House, with the power to call for persons and papers, the heavier the burden on civil servants in providing background information and formal evidence, orally and in writing. There is also the risk that a

[55] *Parl. Debates*, HL, 499 (5th ser.), col. 1491, 21 July 1988.

[56] As Cledwyn Hughes MP: Minister of State for Commonwealth Relations, 1964–6; Secretary of State for Wales, 1966–8; Minister of Agriculture, Fisheries, and Food, 1968–70. Created Lord Cledwyn of Penrhos, 1979; Leader of the Opposition in the House of Lords, 1982–92.

[57] *Parl. Debates*, HL, 499 (5th ser.), col. 1492.

[58] Ibid., col. 1493.

[59] Single-subject Select Committees were appointed on Sport and Leisure (1971/2), Commodity Prices (1975/6), a Bill of Rights (1976/7), Unemployment (1979/80), and Overseas Trade (1983/4). A brief history of the Committee work of the House, and the role of investigative committees, is contained in the *Report from the Select Committee on the Committee Work of the House*, Session 1991/2 (HL Paper 35-I), HMSO, London, 1992, pp. 10–13.

committee may embark on a course that is out of step with government policy, leading to recommendations that are politically embarrassing. For all these reasons, Select Committees are not lightly set up, and the House authorities will not act without consulting the ministers primarily concerned. Much care is taken over the terms of reference and the selection of a chairman and members, with the Party Whips on both sides of the House taking a keen interest in the preliminaries. It may surprise some readers to learn that ministers and Whips have such a central role in what is essentially Parliamentary rather than governmental business, but that is how it is.

As his letter implied, Hurd had raised the question of the chairmanship when we met. I had ruled myself out on two grounds at least: I was in my sixth year as Chairman of the Parole Board for England and Wales, a public appointment by the Home Secretary with the consent of the Prime Minister, and had accepted an extension until the end of September 1988. Over and above this impediment were the firm views I had already formed on what was wrong with the current law and practice, and what should be done to remedy the defects. A more open mind was called for. Various names had been discussed, including those of former Home Office ministers, but no conclusion was reached. The 'further thoughts' referred to in Hurd's letter stemmed from the House of Lords. There it was considered that an Independent peer, without party allegiance, but experienced in the committee work of the House, would be preferable.

When Lord Nathan's name[60] was suggested to chair the Committee it commanded universal support, which was fully vindicated by the assiduous and fair-minded way in which he conducted the proceedings. The all-party composition included several peers with special knowledge: a Lord of Appeal in Ordinary; Harris and myself from the Parole Board; an English Queen's Counsel; a Scottish judge; a former Lord Advocate of Scotland; and peers interested in penal reform. Three women, one with a particular interest in

---

[60] Solicitor. Senior Partner, Herbert Oppenheimer Nathan and Vandyk, 1978–86. Vice-Chairman, Committee on Charity Law and Practice (reported 1976); Member, Royal Commission on Environmental Pollution, 1979–89. Member, House of Lords Select Committee on the European Communities, 1983–8 and 1990– , and Chairman of its Sub-committee on the Environment, 1983–7 and 1990– .

disability, were included in the membership of eleven.[61] The fact that the Select Committee on Murder and Life Imprisonment contained lay people as well as experts, and sat in public when taking evidence, made it a genuine Parliamentary forum with a different character to other forms of specialist committee.

The remit included the scope and definition of murder in Scotland as well as in England and Wales (was this the hand of Mackay?), so encompassing the differences which exist between the two jurisdictions notably in the mental element in the crime of murder. The sentencing issues turned almost entirely on whether imprisonment for life should remain mandatory, rather than a maximum penalty. Capital punishment, the greatest of all political bogeys, was deliberately excluded by the wording of the terms of reference.

The first two heads, on which the arguments were fairly clearly marked out, and on which there was room for more than one view, were surpassed in complexity by the administrative and legal morass surrounding the procedures for reaching decisions on the release of prisoners serving life sentences for murder. Virtually everyone who got to grips with the subject, whether giving evidence to the Committee or as a member of it, sensed that the haphazard evolution of the procedures over the two decades since the abolition of the death penalty had led to the inadvertent creation of a system in which the intentions of Parliament, the powers of the courts, and the discretionary authority of the Secretary of State had become thoroughly confused.

The Committee held thirty-two meetings, at nineteen of which evidence was heard. A total of eighty-one witnesses submitted evidence to the Committee, of whom thirty-one gave oral evidence. Out of London the Committee sat in public at Parliament House in Edinburgh taking evidence from nine groups of Scottish witnesses, including the head of the Scottish Judiciary, the Lord Justice General. Five prisons were visited, and committee members attended meetings of Parole Board panels when life-sentence cases were being considered. The Select Committee had the benefit of two specialist advisers, Professor J. C. Smith QC and Professor

---

[61] The composition of the Select Committee was: Lords Ackner, Campbell of Alloway, Baroness Darcy de Knayth, Baroness Ewart-Biggs, Lords Harris of Greenwich, Morton of Shuna, Nathan (Chairman), Baroness Platt of Writtle, Lords Prys-Davies, Wilson of Langside and Windlesham.

A. K. Bottomley.[62] The report was agreed, with a single dissent to one of the recommendations, on 24 July and published on 18 October 1989.[63]

IX

The first matter to be tackled called for common sense as much as resort to the yardsticks of principle and practicality. It was whether uniformity in the law of murder on both sides of the border separating England from Scotland demanded an identical definition of the crime. With little difficulty the Committee agreed that the definition of murder in the common law of Scotland, which had survived virtually unchanged since 1797, should continue as at present. This conclusion arose out of the overwhelming weight of evidence that Scots lawyers and other witnesses were content with the functioning of the common law of murder in Scotland and would view any modification with reservation, if not with alarm. Whatever the desirability of uniformity as a goal, the Committee did not consider the aspiration sufficient to justify the imposition on Scotland of changes which would be so unwelcome. Murder, like other more frequent crimes such as theft and non-fatal offences against the person, had long been a distinct offence north of the border and should remain so until there was a stronger case for change.

Uniformity between the two jurisdictions could, of course, be arrived at via another route, namely by bringing the definition of murder in England and Wales into line with that in Scotland. To do so, however, would have meant finding a statutory definition for the elusive concept of 'wicked recklessness', which in Scotland is an objective test in the absence of a deliberate intent to perform a wilful act causing the destruction of life. Despite Lord Goff's

[62] John Smith, knighted in 1993, had been Professor of Law and Head of the Department of Law, at the University of Nottingham until his retirement in 1987. A past-President of the Society of Public Teachers of Law, he had also been a member of the Criminal Law Revision Committee. Professor Bottomley, one of the earliest graduates of the Cambridge Institute of Criminology, is Professor of Social Policy and Professional Studies at the University of Hull.

[63] House of Lords, Session 1988/9, *Report of the Select Committee on Murder and Life Imprisonment* (HL Paper 78), vol. 1: *Report and Appendices*; vol. 2; *Oral Evidence, Part 1*; vol. 3; *Oral Evidence, Part 2 and Written Evidence*; HMSO, London, 1989.

stylish arguments in a lecture on the law of murder, subsequently published in the *Law Quarterly Review*,[64] there was little support from witnesses for trying to graft the alien notion of wicked recklessness on to English law. In his evidence to the Lords Select Committee, Lane was especially scathing:

> I view with particular horror, the suggestion that the concept of 'reck-lessness' might be brought into the definition of murder. Recklessness, whatever it now means, is the trial judge's bugbear. The more experienced judge will, if he can, avoid raising the question at all—to the undoubted benefit of both the defendant and the jury—because he knows that he will be inviting a visit to the Court of Appeal (Criminal Division) if he does raise it. I beg of you not even to toy with the idea. It would be an unmitigated disaster.
>
> Robert Goff's article is delightfully readable. He does, I fear, fall into the same elephant trap which he warns others to avoid.[65]

In England and Wales, unlike Scotland where the law on murder has been settled for a long time, uncertainty has prevailed. Although the necessary intent to kill or cause grievous bodily harm sounded simple enough, difficulties arose where it was not the defendant's purpose to kill or cause serious harm, but he foresaw that such a result of his conduct would or might occur. For years the courts had struggled with the proposition that if at the material time the defendant recognized that death (or serious harm) was 'highly probable' or 'virtually certain', then the jury might infer that he intended to kill (or cause serious harm), even though he may not have desired that result. Lane conceded that the law of murder had gone 'off course' in some recent cases because of the confusion between intention and desire of the consequences, but he claimed that the uncertainties had been satisfactorily resolved by the Court of Appeal in 1986 in the case of *Nedrick*.[66] Some witnesses argued that the law was too broad, while others regarded it as too narrow. Several contended that notwithstanding the most recent decisions the common law still involved an unnecessary degree of uncertainty as to the meaning of intention. Continuing to rely on the common

---

[64] 'The Mental Element in the Crime of Murder', (1988) 104 LQR 30. For a reply by Professor Glanville Williams, see 'The *mens rea* for Murder: Leave it Alone', (1989) 105 LQR 387.

[65] *Report of the Select Committee on Murder and Life Imprisonment* (HL Paper 78-II), p. 254.

[66] Ibid., p. 262. *Nedrick* (1986) 83 Cr. App. R. 267.

law left open the possibility of future fluctuations as had been experienced over the past thirty years.

Those who wished to adopt a statutory definition, including the Law Commission and the Crown Prosecution Service, differed on how best to define the mental element. In making its recommendations the Committee agreed with those witnesses who argued that a person who intends only to cause serious personal harm and does not foresee even the possibility of death should not be liable to conviction of murder if death happens to result from his act. The report quoted the Criminal Law Revision Committee that a person is not generally liable to conviction of a serious crime where the prohibited result was not only unintended but also unforeseen, adding its own observation that this was a good rule of moral responsibility which should certainly apply to the most serious crime of all, murder. So long as the law continued to recognize two types of homicide, unforeseen but unlawful killings were properly left to the law of manslaughter. To this extent the Committee echoed the first imperative of the Howard League's submission to it: that the offence of murder called for as clear and narrow a definition as possible, and for the distinction in law between murder and manslaughter to reflect a clear moral distinction amongst offenders.[67]

On rational as well as pragmatic grounds the Committee came down in favour of the definition of murder already formulated in the Law Commission's draft Criminal Code, clause 54(1):

A person is guilty of murder if he causes the death of another—

(a) intending to cause death; or

(b) intending to cause serious personal harm and being aware that he may cause death ... [68]

As for the meaning of the word 'intend', for the purposes of the law of murder intention should be defined on the lines proposed in clause 18(*b*) of the draft Criminal Code: 'A person acts "intentionally" with respect to ... a result when he acts either in order to bring it about or being aware that it will occur in the ordinary course of events.'[69]

---

[67] *Report of the Select Committee on Murder and Life Imprisonment* (HL Paper 78-III), p. 353.
[68] *Report of the Select Committee on Murder and Life Imprisonment* (HL Paper 78-I), p. 25.
[69] Ibid.

The Select Committee stepped out onto thinner political ice when it came to the second and third of its terms of reference. To some politicians (and their constituents) the mandatory penalty of life imprisonment stands as a symbol of the total repugnance of Parliament towards the crime of murder. Yet much of the evidence indicated that it was the very inflexibility of the life sentence that had undermined progressively what should be regarded as the most severe of all penalties. Apart from a brief and unsuccessful interlude in 1957–65, the law did not recognize categories of murder. The only way of bringing about a relationship between the degree of punishment appropriate to the circumstances of the crime was to adjust the amount of time spent in custody. Yet the process of adjustment was demonstrably carried out not by the judge who had seen the defendant in court and heard the case against him, but by ministers of the Crown who might be influenced by other considerations. Murders vary as much, or more than, any other crime in heinousness, and the Select Committee concluded that life imprisonment should be reserved for the most heinous cases, or where there was a high degree of the risk of reoffending because of the defendant's mental state.

Of the evidence given to the Committee that which carried the greatest weight came from the Lord Chief Justice. Supported by twelve judges of the High Court and Court of Appeal, out of the nineteen who had expressed an opinion, Lane was unequivocally opposed to retaining the mandatory sentence for murder. The mandatory penalty had been part of the compromise which had enabled the death penalty to be ended nearly a quarter of a century ago, but had come to have a distorting effect which ran right through the procedural sequence following an unlawful killing: from the initial decisions on charging; the acceptance by the Crown of pleas of not guilty of murder, but guilty of manslaughter by virtue of diminished responsibility; the defence of provocation; the reluctance of juries to convict of murder in domestic cases or mercy killings with compassionate overtones; discrepancies in the amount of time spent in custody by life prisoners; and the release decisions. The Committee's recommendation to abolish the mandatory life sentence for murder was reflected in the evidence of a majority of witnesses who gave evidence in England, including the families of victims who believed that the existence of the mandatory penalty led to inappropriate verdicts of manslaughter.

With sentencing discretion in the hands of the court it would be likely that the life sentence would be reserved for two types of case; particularly outrageous murders, and those where there would be a degree of uncertainty about the risk, because of his or her mental condition, in releasing a prisoner at the end of a determinate sentence. Otherwise the trial judge should select the appropriate penalty to mark the gravity of the offence in the same way as for all other serious crimes. The Committee recognized that the courts had been faced by extremely grave crimes in recent years and that the public was entitled to demand firm and effective sanctions. The report pointed out that once implemented, the abolition of the mandatory penalty could be expected to result in a substantial increase in the average time actually served by those sentenced to life imprisonment, thus restoring the life sentence as the most severe sentence available to the courts.

X

Trying to unravel the intricacies of release decisions was a task which taxed the collective mind of the Committee to the full. Explanations by the Home Office and the Parole Board were unable to dispel the impression that the superimposition of successive procedural layers resulting from quite different pressures had led to an apparatus that commanded little or no support outside official circles. The Committee saw as the most objectionable feature the setting in private of a tariff which was disclosed neither to the defendant nor his legal adviser. The practice of ministers adding to the judicially recommended tariff became public when volunteered by a Home Office witness who appeared before the Committee.[70] The relevation came at the first meeting at which oral evidence was given,[71] and caused subsequent witnesses to express 'surprise and shock'[72] at the extent to which a junior minister could determine

[70] Douglas Hogg had instructed the officials who gave oral evidence that they were to offer the information freely if the Select Committee showed an interest in the subject.
[71] *Report of the Select Committee on Murder and Life Imprisonment* (HL Paper 78-II), p. 29.
[72] *Report of the Select Committee on Murder and Life Imprisonment* (HL Paper 78-I), p. 43.

the length of a prisoner's stay in custody in this way.

Looking to the *Handscomb* doctrine of 'notional equivalence' between a determinate sentence and the punitive part of a discretionary life sentence, the Committee recommended that whenever in future a judge decided it was appropriate to impose a life sentence for murder he should specify in open court the period which he considered necessary to satisfy the requirements of retribution and deterrence. This period, to be known as 'the penal sanction', would be open to appeal by either side, and not subject to revision by ministers. The penal sanction would attract remission and parole eligibility in the same way as a determinate sentence, and at its expiry the decision on whether to release or retain in custody would be taken by a tribunal with judicial characteristics composed of a High Court judge, a consultant psychiatrist and a chief probation officer. The prisoner would have the right to appear in person, to see all relevant documents, and to be legally represented. The decision of the tribunal would be final and beyond reach of ministerial intervention.

Reform, in the bald sense of removing an abuse, along the lines recommended by the Select Committee would mark the end of the Home Secretary's discretionary power to decide on the length of time served by life sentence prisoners. What had begun as a decent and humane way to ameliorate the finality and irreversibility of the death penalty, later being regarded as a device for preserving the protection of the public, had drifted into a situation in which ministers, rather than judges were deciding upon punishment.

Public opinion, and fear of public opinion, has seldom been far below the surface. Murder trials have always caught the public's imagination, not simply because of the sensational or sordid events that may come to light, but because of a consciousness of the profundities associated with the killing: what led up to it, and what came after. Law, morals, and public attitudes come together to fashion the way the trial is conducted and the culprit punished. Nearly a century ago, Maitland wrote:

if some fairy gave me the power of seeing a scene of one and the same kind in every age in the history of every race, the kind of scene I would choose would be a trial for murder, because I think that it would give me so many hints as to a multitude of matters of the first importance.[73]

[73] F. W. Maitland, 'The Body Politic' (1899), in H. D. Hazeltine, G. Lapsley,

What would the great historian of English law have thought had he been present at the conclusion of a murder trial in the late 1980s or early 1990s? Once found guilty the defendant automatically would be sentenced to life imprisonment, irrespective of the circumstances of the crime. No appeal would lie against sentence. Counsel might be invited to address the court in mitigation, although all the judge could mitigate, if moved by what he had heard, would be his entry on a printed form indicating the appropriate tariff period. No one in court would know what the suggested tariff was. When the form reached the Home Office, via a Lord Chief Justice who had publicly denounced the part he was called upon to play, it would be commented on by officials before being passed to a junior minister. At that stage, the tariff might be altered for reasons unknown either to the court or the convicted offender. Maitland would surely have been struck by the extent to which the death penalty, although abolished more than twenty years before, continued to be such a potent symbol in the minds of many of the public, and, through them, was transmitted to the elected holders of political office.

If he moved on across the Atlantic he would see, in wonderment, the extremes which characterize the administration of criminal justice in the United States. In thirty-five states (a fluctuating total) and the federal jurisdiction, capital punishment for murder was a legally valid sanction at the end of 1991. In none of them was there any uniform mandatory penalty. Separate sentencing hearings are generally required after a finding that capital murder has been committed. At such a hearing, if the state wishes to impose the death sentence, the jury must find the existence of one or more specified aggravating circumstances, for example that the murder was committed in the course of a felony. The jury must also consider mitigating circumstances, such as youth, co-operation with the police, and the defendant's emotional state at the time. Although only statutorily prescribed aggravating factors may be considered, the judge or jury must be free to consider any mitigating evidence that is presented.[74] Despite these constitutional safeguards, indeed because of them, the American experience has been far from a

and P. H. Winfield (eds.), *Maitland: Selected Essays*, Cambridge University Press, 1936, p. 253.

[74] See Lewis F. Powell, Jr, Associate Justice (Retired) of the United States Supreme Court, (1989) 102 *Harvard Law Review* 1035 at 1036–7.

paradigm for others.[75] Amnesty International, supported by empirical studies and legal analyses, has found much to criticize in
the uneven application of state statutes limiting and guiding the
sentencing discretion of the courts in cases of murder.[76] From
another quarter, legislators, state governors, and judges have concentrated their fire upon the intolerable delays, sometimes amounting to ten years or more,[77] which elapse between the passing of a
death sentence and execution.

The cause of the delays is the exhaustive pursuit of post-con-
viction remedies, primarily by way of habeas corpus, which are
available to the convicted offender, both in state and federal
courts. Pungent criticism has been directed at 'excessively repetitious
litigation'[78] which can lead to a conviction and sentence by a state
court being reviewed as many as four or five times in the state
courts, and three times in the federal courts up to and including
the Supreme Court.[79] The number held in custody, after having

---

[75] For a revealing account based on personal experience by a former Governor
of California (1959–67), see Edmund G. Brown, *Public Justice, Private Mercy*,
Weidenfeld and Nicolson, New York, 1989.

[76] *USA—The Death Penalty in the United States of America: Developments from
1 September 1989 to 31 December 1990*, AI Index: 51/13/91, Amnesty International,
London, 1991. The legal analyses, criminological investigations, and policy implications are summarized by Dr Roger Hood in *The Death Penalty: A World-wide
Perspective*, Clarendon Press, Oxford, 1989, pp. 91–116. Dr Hood's book is the
revised text of a report prepared for the tenth session of the United Nations
Committee on Crime Prevention and Control, which met in Vienna in August 1988.

[77] In 1988 the period of time between the date of the murder and the offender's
execution (if it occurs) averaged close on ten years in Georgia, nine years and nine
months in Florida, and seven years and eight months in Texas. Cited by Powell,
(1989) 102 *Harvard Law Review* 1035 at 1038.

[78] 'Our present system of multi-layered appeals has led to excessively repetitious
litigation and years of delay between sentencing and execution. This delay under-
mines the deterrent effect of capital punishment and reduces public confidence in
the criminal justice system'. Ibid., at 1035. The penological implications for capital
punishment of the attempts to curtail multiple appeals is brought out by Sir Leon
Radzinowicz in an article entitled 'Penal Regressions', [1991] *Cambridge Law Journal*
422 at 434–6.

[79] In its judgment in the case of *McCleskey* v. *Zant* 111 S. Ct. 1454 (1991), by a
majority of six votes to three, the US Supreme Court redefined the doctrine of
abuse of the writ which allows the federal courts to decline to entertain a claim
presented for the first time in a second or subsequent petition for a writ of habeas
corpus. The petitioner, McClesky, had been convicted of the murder of a police
officer in the course of an armed robbery in Georgia in 1978 and sentenced to death.
He had pursued various remedies in the state and federal courts between 1978 and
1991, the US Supreme Court considering applications from him on three separate
occasions. McCleskey was executed on 25 Sept. 1991.

been sentenced to death and awaiting execution (known as 'death row'), stood at 2,110 in August 1988. Three years later it had grown to 2,504.[80] No more than 152, about 4% of the total sentenced to death,[81] had been executed since the Supreme Court began to validate revised state capital punishment statutes in 1976.[82] Until April 1992 in nineteen of the thirty-seven jurisdictions (thirty-five states, the Federal Government, and the US Military) which had retained the death penalty, no prisoner had been executed since 1976. But in that month, after fourteen years on death row, Robert Alton Harris became the first person to be executed in California for twenty-five years after the Supreme Court rejected last minute applications that death by gassing amounted to cruel and unusual punishment. Harris had been convicted and sentenced to death for killing two teenage boys in 1978. His execution marked the ending of a lengthy moratorium on judicial execution in California, and if repeated could lead to the execution of more than 300 convicts in the state, some of whom had been on death row for almost two decades.

In Britain we are faced with the reverse. The ultimate penalty of death has gone, but its legacy is a flawed and discredited sentencing practice in which procedural fairness, the motor of American experience (if not always achieved), is spread very thinly indeed. By the end of the 1980s, over 1,000 more people were serving life sentences of imprisonment than when the decade began (see Table 10). The way the life sentence had evolved was as alien to the inheritance of the common law as it was inconsistent with the precepts of the European Convention on Human Rights. An escalating controversy was to lead to confrontation between the two Houses of Parliament in 1991. Before then, the action switched to Strasbourg.

---

[80] NAACP Legal Defense and Educational Fund, *Death Row, U.S.A. Summary*, 23 Aug. 1991. The race breakdown was: 1,273 white (50.83%), 979 black (39.09%), 179 hispanic (7.14%). 2,466 of the total (98.48%) were men, and 38 (1.51%) women.

[81] Twenty-three executions were carried out in 1990, an increase over the previous two years. The trend is expected to continue as appeals in many cases finally run out. Amnesty International, AI Index: 51/13/91, p. 1.

[82] The leading case is *Gregg* v. *Georgia* 428 US 153 (1976) in which the US Supreme Court upheld the validity of a new Georgia capital punishment statute incorporating sentencing provisions which were absent from an earlier statute struck down as unconstitutional in *Furman* v. *Georgia* 408 US 238 (1972) because of the arbitrary and capricious manner in which it had been applied. See Hood, *The Death Penalty*, p. 91 and Powell, (1989) 102 *Harvard Law Review* 1035 at 1036–8.

TABLE 10. *Life-sentence prisoners 1981–91*[a]

	Males	Females	Total	Mandatory	Mandatory % of total
1981	1,626	49	1,675	1,274	76.06
1982	1,735	53	1,788	1,346	75.28
1983	1,767	55	1,822	1,377	75.58
1984	1,856	61	1,917	1,462	76.26
1985	1,991	60	2,051	1,591	77.57
1986	2,126	68	2,194	1,706	77.76
1987	2,265	74	2,339	1,824	77.98
1988	2,427	76	2,503	1,973	78.83
1989	2,592	85	2,677	2,131	79.60
1990	2,704	91	2,795	2,237	80.04
1991	2,904	96	2,896	2,318	80.04

[a] Population on 30 June each year of persons serving a sentence of life imprisonment (including detention during Her Majesty's pleasure and custody for life) in England and Wales.

Source: Home Office Statistical Department.

8

Human Rights: Enforcing the Convention

I

On 25 June 1990 nineteen judges filed into the European Court of
Human Rights (the Court) at Strasbourg, taking their seats at a
table in the shape of a huge horseshoe. The full Court was meeting
in plenary session for a public hearing of the case of three United
Kingdom applicants, each of whom had been sentenced to life
imprisonment following convictions for serious sexual offences.[1]
These were discretionary, and not mandatory life sentences, bringing
into question the continued lawfulness of detention after the expiry
of the tariff period, determined by the UK authorities according to
the procedures described in the previous chapter. Two of the
applicants had been re-detained after conditional release on licence,
and recalled to custody.[2]

The case had been referred to the Court by the European
Commission of Human Rights (the Commission) on 12 October

[1] *Thynne, Wilson and Gunnell* v. *The United Kingdom* (1991) 13 EHRR 135.

[2] On the recommendation of the Parole Board, the Home Secretary had power
under Section 62 of the Criminal Justice Act 1967 to revoke the licence of any
prisoner who had been conditionally released, either from a determinate or a life
sentence, and to recall him to prison. In emergencies the Home Secretary might
revoke a licence and recall him to prison without consulting the Parole Board,
although the case would be referred to the Board as soon after the event as possible.
Any person so recalled was entitled to make representations in writing to the Parole
Board, being informed on his return to prison of the reasons for his recall and of
his right to make representations. If the Board recommended immediate release the
Home Secretary was required to give effect to its recommendation. The Crown
Court was also empowered to revoke a licence on conviction of a further indictable
offence. Under Section 39 of the Criminal Justice Act 1991 the Home Secretary's
powers to revoke a licence continue to apply to prisoners released on the recommendation of the Parole Board from life sentences or terms of four years' or
more imprisonment. The Crown Court's power of revocation was not continued,
but Section 40 contains a new provision on return to prison if a further offence is
committed by a long-term or short-term prisoner whilst on licence. See *Blackstone's
Guide to the Criminal Justice Act 1991*, Blackstone Press, London, 1991, pp. 110–
12.

1989; but its origins went back to 1985 when the applicants had complained to the Commission that Article 5(4) of the European Convention on Human Rights (the Convention) had been violated as no judicial procedure had been available to them to determine the continued lawfulness of their detention nor, in two of the cases, the lawfulness of their re-detention following release and recall. Article 5(4) states:

Everyone who is deprived of his liberty by arrest or detention shall be entitled to take proceedings by which the lawfulness of his detention shall be decided speedily by a court and his release ordered if the detention is not lawful.

One of the applicants submitted that since there was no right to enforceable compensation under United Kingdom law in respect of his complaints, there had also been a breach of Article 5(5). This states:

Everyone who has been the victim of arrest or detention in contravention of the provisions of this Article shall have an enforceable right to compensation.

Each of the three men was represented by civil liberties interest groups: one by JUSTICE, the British section of the International Commission of Jurists, and the other two by Liberty (the National Council for Civil Liberties). The first applicant, Michael Thynne, then aged twenty-four, had pleaded guilty at the Central Criminal Court in 1975 to charges of rape and buggery. He had a long criminal record and had previously served sentences of imprisonment for theft and burglary. Within thirty-six hours of his release from prison, having had little sleep, but having taken drugs and consumed some alcohol, Thynne gained entrance to a married woman's flat by pretending to be a police officer investigating a burglary. Telling the occupant that he had a knife and would kill her if she made a noise, he raped and buggered her, inflicting some minor puncture wounds with a pair of scissors in the course of the assault.[3] He was sentenced by the Recorder of London to life imprisonment on each count, the medical evidence having indicated that a hospital order was inappropriate since the personality disorder which had been diagnosed was not amenable to psychiatric

---

[3] The abstract of the facts of the three cases is drawn from the Report of the European Commission of Human Rights which was adopted on 7 Sept. 1989.

treatment. The life sentences were upheld on appeal.

Thynne had been in custody ever since, although he had twice absconded from prison. On the first occasion, after walking out of an open prison, he had stolen a gold bracelet from a jewellery shop, brandishing but not using a knife when pursued by the manager. Unlawfully at large for three months, he was arrested and returned to custody, subsequently being sentenced to six months' imprisonment for offences of theft, possession of drugs, and criminal damage. The sentence was to run concurrently with his existing life sentence.

A life-sentence panel of the Parole Board did not agree with the Local Review Committee that Thynne should be released in May 1989, recommending instead to the Home Secretary that he remain in custody with a further review one year after his transfer to an open prison. By the end of 1984, on the expiry of a nine-year tariff, the Home Office accepted that the punitive element of the sentence had been served, and that risk to the public remained the sole justification for his continued detention. At the Strasbourg hearing Thynne's counsel, the Legal Officer of JUSTICE, concentrated his argument on the fact that his client was now in the sixth year of post-tariff detention, solely because of risk factors, and that his continued detention was unlawful because it had not been decided by a body with the characteristics of a court.

The second applicant, Benjamin Wilson, born in 1916, was the oldest of the three. His record of sexual offending was of long standing, beginning as early as 1935, leading to a number of convictions and prison sentences. Because of the lasting detrimental effect on the psychological and emotional development of young persons, English law distinguishes buggery with children under the age of sixteen from offences with men over that age as an offence for which it is necessary to retain a maximum sentence of life imprisonment at the discretion of the court. In March 1973 he pleaded guilty to charges of buggery and indecent assault on boys under the age of sixteen and had been sentenced to life imprisonment for buggery, and seven years' imprisonment to be served concurrently for, *inter alia*, indecent assault. In passing sentence, the trial judge accepted that to a large extent Wilson could not help himself, but said that he had a duty to the public, and the young public in particular, to protect them from his lack of self-control. The Court of Appeal agreed with the trial judge that Wilson had better prospects of release under an indeterminate life sentence than a long fixed term if he used the opportunity it offered to build himself up and strengthen his character.

Reviewing Wilson's case three years into the sentence, the Joint Committee of the Parole Board and the Home Office recommended he should be considered for release on licence after serving seven years. In 1982, the Home Secretary accepted a recommendation from the Parole Board that Wilson should be released into a controlled environment with psychiatric supervision. Subsequently he was released to reside at a probation hostel, with conditions that he should co-operate with his probation officer; attend on an appointed medical practitioner and take any prescribed treatment; and refrain from any activity involving young boys without the permission of the probation officer. Wilson survived for five months at the hostel before being recalled to prison on the recommendation of the Parole Board, an adverse report having been received from the probation officer in charge of the hostel. The grounds for recall were that Wilson's conduct was giving cause for concern.

By means of judicial review Wilson successfully contested the adequacy of the reasons which he had been given.[4] The Divisional Court quashed the decision by the Parole Board to uphold his recall on the grounds that he had not been given sufficient reasons to enable him to make effective representations against recall in writing, as he was entitled to do under Section 62(3) of the Criminal Justice Act 1967. On the basis of the probation and medical reports a fuller statement of reasons was then prepared, although some of the factual details were contested by Wilson's solicitors when his further representations against recall were considered. At a second review the Board declined to change its assessment of the risks. Since the intervention of the court had been confined to the procedural impropriety that had occurred on the first occasion, Wilson remained in custody.

---

[4] Apart from the right to make representations to the Parole Board, a prisoner who is serving a life sentence may take proceedings in the High Court to obtain judicial review of any decision of the Parole Board or the Home Secretary on the ground that it is tainted by illegality, irrationality, or procedural impropriety.

II

In challenging the continued legality of detention without access to judicial procedure after the expiry of the tariff, and the lawfulness of the procedures leading to re-detention after release when no further offence had been committed, no one could accuse JUSTICE or Liberty of selecting cases that were designed to play upon the sympathy of the court or the wider public. The circumstances and gravity of the crimes that had been committed, combined with the records of the three men, were hardly calculated to distort the legal issues in question by any display of excess compassion.

Edward Gunnell, the third applicant, exemplified the truism that high principles may arise from the deeds of criminal or mentally disordered people. Aged thirty-five at the time he was convicted of four offences of rape and two of attempted rape, attracting four concurrent sentences of life imprisonment in 1965, he had a lengthy history dating back to his adolescence of detention in mental hospitals. He had incurred previous convictions, although none for offences of violence or of a sexual nature. In 1946 he had been committed to a hospital from which he had escaped eighteen times. In 1950, having again been admitted to another hospital he had absconded three times. He was transferred to the secure special hospital at Rampton in 1951, where he remained until 1959 when he was released on licence.

The four offences of rape, and two of attempted rape, were committed within a period of one month. All of the victims had been housewives in their own homes or gardens in the course of their everyday lives. The trial judge had described the offences as being 'amongst the worst cases of rape or attempted rape ever to come before a court in this country'.[5] Although the medical evidence, which was not contradicted, was that Gunnell was suffering from a psychopathic disorder within the meaning of the Mental Health Act 1959,[6] and that he needed treatment in a maximum security medical setting, the trial judge declined to make a hospital order, observing that because of the gravity of the offences: 'Pun-

---

[5] The trial judge was Roskill J who became a Lord Justice of Appeal, 1971–80, and a Lord of Appeal in Ordinary, 1980–6. He was the first Vice-Chairman of the Parole Board, 1967–9.

[6] *Responses to Crime*, vol. 1 discusses 'Mentally Disordered Offenders: Remedial or Penal Responses?' at pp. 102–43.

ishment must be an element in this case; and that punishment can only be achieved by imprisonment'. The Court of Appeal strongly endorsed 'every word' the learned judge had said, citing the earlier case of *Morris*.[7] The judgments in both courts recognized that the Home Secretary had power under Section 72 of the Mental Health Act, 1959 to transfer a prisoner to hospital if he was satisfied, by the report of at least two medical practitioners, that the prisoner's mental condition warranted removal to hospital for treatment.

In December 1980, fifteen years after Gunnell's conviction, the Parole Board recommended his release on licence, subject to the satisfactory completion of periods of time spent in open conditions and on a pre-release employment scheme. The Home Secretary agreed, and in March 1982 he was released. In February of the following year, information was received by the Home Office from the police that Gunnell had been seen watching a woman cleaning her car and had been found in her back garden. The police said there had been a similar incident in January 1983 when another woman had complained that he had been in her back garden looking through the rear window of the house. The police had arrested Gunnell on that occasion, but did not hold him. As a result of the second incident, the Minister of State, acting on behalf of the Home Secretary, had authorized the immediate revocation of his licence because of the similarities between his behaviour and the circumstances in which the original offences had been committed. Neither then nor later was Gunnell charged with any criminal offence in relation to these incidents.

On reception into custody Gunnell was told that his licence had been revoked because his behaviour was giving cause for concern. He was notified of his right under Section 62(3) of the Criminal Justice Act 1967 to make representations in writing against recall to the Parole Board, and did so. The Parole Board rejected his representations, thereby confirming the revocation of his licence, but recommended his release a month later subject to adequate arrangements being made for his housing and psychiatric supervision. After consultation with the trial judge and the Lord Chief Justice, the Home Secretary declined to accept the Board's recommendation. Gunnell then petitioned the Home Secretary, complaining that he had not been allowed to defend himself. The

[7] [1961] 2 QB 237.

petition was rejected, and he claimed it was only at that stage that he received an official account in any detail of the allegations made against him.

The next avenue explored was to move for judicial review of the decisions of the Parole Board and the Home Secretary in confirming the initial revocation of his licence. Gunnell was granted leave to move for judicial review in August 1983, but his application was dismissed by the Divisional Court in November. An appeal to the Court of Appeal, which included an application for discovery of the documents relating to the determination of his case by the Parole Board and the Home Secretary, was also dismissed.

This was not the end of the sequence of events unfolded before the Court of Human Rights. Another review by the Parole Board in 1984 was unfavourable, and it was not until September 1988 that Gunnell was released on licence for the second time. By then his case was already under consideration in Strasbourg, an application having been lodged in September 1985. On 6 September 1988, the Commission found the applications of Thynne, Wilson, and Gunnell admissible, and ordered their joinder.[8] For some months Gunnell lived at a probation hostel under the supervision of the Inner London Probation Service, but by the time his case was heard by the Court of Human Rights in June 1990 he was back in prison, his life licence revoked, awaiting trial at the Central Criminal Court. He had been charged with a series of sexual attacks on middle-aged or elderly women, sometimes involving robbery, carried out between November 1989 and February 1990.

On 24 September 1990 Gunnell pleaded guilty to one offence of attempted rape, five indecent assaults, and three robberies. He was sentenced to life imprisonment for the attempted rape, eight years' imprisonment for the indecent assaults and six years' imprisonment for the robberies, all sentences to run concurrently. It was reported in the press the court was told that Gunnell, by now aged fifty-nine, had asked to be castrated to destroy his sex drive.[9] Under such headlines as 'Once a rapist, always a rapist: Freed lifer's evil rampage' (*Daily Mail*) and 'Castrate me, sex "monster" urges judge' (*Daily Express*), the popular press gave extensive coverage to the sexual offences. Three of the victims were in court when he was

---

[8] The case of a fourth British applicant, Robert Weeks, was also declared admissible and joined, but was later resolved by friendly settlement.

[9] *Guardian*, 25 Sept. 1990

sentenced, and an MP was quoted as saying that he was appalled Gunnell had been released after receiving four earlier life sentences.[10]

One month later, on 25 October 1990, the plenary Court of Human Rights delivered its judgment in Strasbourg. In doing so, the Court was primarily concerned with the interpretation and application to the case before it of provisions of the Convention expressed in general terms, in this instance Article 5(4) of the Convention defining lawfulness of detention. By a majority of eighteen votes to one, the Court held that there had been a violation of Article 5(4) in the case of all three applicants; by the same majority holding that there had been a violation of Article 5(5) in the case of Wilson.[11] Under Article 50 of the Convention the United Kingdom Government was to pay Thynne legal costs and expenses amounting to £4,500, less an amount already paid by way of legal aid in respect of fees. Wilson and Gunnell jointly were awarded £18,000, less amounts already paid to Gunnell by way of legal aid in respect of fees, travel, and subsistence expenses. Both awards were to be increased by any value added tax that might be chargeable. The remainder of the claim for just satisfaction was dismissed unanimously. In the opinion of the Court, there was no evidence that the applicants would have regained their freedom had Article 5(4) not been violated. Even assuming that they had suffered certain feelings of helplessness and frustration, the Court shared the Government's view that in the circumstances the finding of violation constituted sufficient just satisfaction for the purposes of Article 50.

These findings illuminate the peculiarity and the underlying political sophistication of the Court's jurisdiction. The fact that the detention, or re-detention, of the three life-sentence prisoners had been found to be in breach of the requirements of the Convention, because each had been denied the opportunity to have the continued lawfulness of his detention decided at reasonable intervals by a court, or a tribunal with the characteristics of a court, did not mean that the applicants would have to be released from custody forthwith. It is central to our understanding of the way human rights are protected under the Convention to recognize that the Court has no power, and is careful not to be seen to be seeking

---

[10] *Daily Express*, 25 Sept. 1990.
[11] *Thynne, Wilson and Gunnell* v. *The United Kingdom* (1991) 13 EHRR 666.

any power, to quash decisions of national authorities, nor to order governments or public bodies in member states to take any particular course of action. Whenever the Court finds that an individual has been deprived of liberty in violation of the Convention, it has power to award compensation. In this instance it refrained from doing so, considering that its finding of a violation of Article 5 constituted just satisfaction. The consequence of an adverse ruling in such a case is that it is the procedures which have been pronounced incompatible with the Convention that must be changed, rather than the decision to retain an individual in custody.

All three men were in prison at the time of the Strasbourg judgment, Gunnell having only recently been convicted of further offences. The publicity given to his case underlines the outcry that would have occurred if Thynne or Wilson, similarly persistent offenders, had been released by order of what inevitably would have been portrayed as a foreign court. To appreciate the true nature of the enforceability of the Convention, and its impact on the workings of criminal justice in Britain, it is necessary to turn back to its origins.

III

Unlike other international declarations of human rights, the Convention for the Protection of Human Rights and Fundamental Freedoms, signed in Rome on 4 November 1950 by the member states of the newly-fledged Council of Europe, was more than declaratory in its effect. It had teeth, and was intended to have an enforceable quality from the start. In the immediate aftermath of the Second World War and the devastation it had caused, the focus was squarely upon civil rights. Many of the leading European statesmen had been imprisoned or fought in the resistance movements during the War and were determined to prevent any recrudescence of dictatorship in Western Europe:

They knew that as long as human rights are respected democracy is secure and the danger of dictatorship and war is remote; but that the first steps towards dictatorship are the gradual suppression of individual rights—infringement of the freedom of the press, prohibition of public meetings, trials behind closed doors, and so on—and that once this process has started it is increasingly difficult to bring it to a halt.[12]

The course adopted was to establish certain basic rights and freedoms which must be respected in the member states of the Council of Europe and to institute enforcement procedures to see that they were observed. By these means violations could be identified, the alarm sounded, and international machinery put in motion to restore the rule of law.[13] The mounting ideological conflict between Western Europe and the Soviet Union gave further impetus to the need to reinforce the values of democracy by laying 'foundations on which to base the defence of human personality against all tyrannies and against all forms of totalitarianism'.[14]

The Convention reproduced many of the civil and political rights which were contained in the Universal Declaration of Human Rights proclaimed by the General Assembly of the United Nations in December 1948, but with the all-important difference that they would be underpinned by machinery for enforcement. The wider economic, social, and cultural rights, so attractive to many members of the United Nations, were omitted. Only too conscious of the shortcomings of national sovereignty, which had allowed or even encouraged the excesses of a terrible and shameful era, the leaders of Western Europe, Winston Churchill being the most prominent of all, set out on the path of providing collective safeguards against tyranny and oppression at the hands of the state. There can have been little doubt in their minds about which were the most precious political rights calling for protection.

Security for life and limb, freedom from arbitrary arrest, freedom from slavery and compulsory labour, freedom of speech, freedom of religion, freedom of association, freedom of marriage, the sanctity of the family, equality before the law, and freedom from arbitrary confiscation of property, were the rights included in the original draft for the Convention.[15] The document had been prepared by an International Juridical Section, set up early in 1949 by the

[12] A. H. Robertson, *Human Rights in Europe*, Manchester University Press, 2nd edn., 1977, p. 3.

[13] Ibid.

[14] Robert Schuman at the signing of the Convention, cited by Robertson, *Human Rights in Europe*, p. 5.

[15] *Political Adventure: The Memoirs of the Earl of Kilmuir*, Weidenfeld and Nicolson, London, 1964, p. 176.

European Movement, with Sir David Maxwell Fyfe, previously a Law Officer and future Home Secretary and Lord Chancellor,[16] as joint rapporteur with a Belgian jurist, Professor Fernand Dehousse. The chairman was Pierre-Henri Teitgen, a former resistance leader and French Minister of Justice. In the early drafting, Maxwell Fyfe sought advice from two leading academic lawyers in Britain, Professors Goodhart and Lauterpacht.[17] The common law tradition, with its emphasis upon habeas corpus and procedural fairness was clearly reflected in the initial drafting.

The main difficulties in reaching agreement on the form of the Convention in 1949/50 centred on the rights of parents over their children's education, the right of property (to allow for nationalization but not to permit arbitrary confiscation), the right to free elections, and, what was to become the cornerstone of the whole edifice, the facility for private individuals to petition the proposed Commission. The Committee of Ministers of the Council of Europe set up a group of experts to advise them, the membership including a former Home Office official, Sir Oscar Dowson.[18]

In the Committee of Experts it fell to Dowson, on behalf of the British Government, to oppose both the right of individual petition and the creation of a Court of Human Rights. On the first point the United Kingdom was isolated:

his [Sir Oscar Dowson's] doubts of the wisdom of admitting petitions appear to have been shared by none of his colleagues. Although the two other general points which he made, namely the importance of defining both the rights and limitations thereto with the greatest possible precision and the undesirability of establishing a Court of Human Rights received a good measure of support, it appeared that we were, if not in a minority of one, at least in a very small minority in opposing petitions.[19]

---

[16] Solicitor General, 1942–5; Attorney General, 1945; Home Secretary, 1951–4. As Viscount Kilmuir, Lord Chancellor, 1954–62.

[17] Kilmuir, *Political Adventure*, p. 176. A. L. Goodhart was Professor of Jurisprudence at Oxford 1931–51, and editor of the *Law Quarterly Review*. He was Master of University College, Oxford, 1951–63. Sir Hersch Lauterpacht succeeded A. D. McNair (see n. 72) as Whewell Professor of International Law at Cambridge, 1938–55. From 1954 to 1959 he was a Judge of the International Court of Justice at the Hague, again following McNair. Both Goodhart and Lauterpacht had been born outside the United Kingdom and were internationalist in outlook.

[18] Legal Adviser at the Home Office, 1933–46.

[19] Letter dated 1 June 1950 from Miss B. Salt, United Nations (Economic and Social) Department, Foreign Office, to W. I. J. Wallace, Colonial Office. PRO reference HO 274/3.

Churchill's enthusiasm for a united Europe, to include Germany, and his immense prestige at the opening Assembly of the Council of Europe held in 1949, obscured the fact it was not he and his ex-ministers present at Strasbourg, Harold Macmillan and Maxwell Fyfe amongst them, who were briefing officials or representing the United Kingdom at the Council of Ministers, but the Labour Government at Westminster. With the single exception of Ernest Bevin, the ailing but still powerful Foreign Secretary, Attlee's Cabinet was indifferent towards the idea of the proposed Convention and totally opposed to the right of individuals to petition the Commission over alleged infractions by the United Kingdom and the jurisdiction of a Court in such cases.[20] Forcible critics were the Chancellor of the Exchequer (Sir Stafford Cripps), the Colonial Secretary (James Griffiths), and, most passionate of all, the Lord Chancellor (Lord Jowitt).

Not for the first, or last, time the Foreign Office incurred ministerial displeasure in going ahead notwithstanding their reservations. When the Cabinet met on 1 August 1950 it considered a paper, circulated in advance by Kenneth Younger, the Minister of State who was deputizing for Bevin.[21] Progress on the drafting of the Convention was reported and the approval of the Cabinet sought for its acceptance by the UK Government, with a proviso that an attempt should be made to try and secure the omission of the Article granting to individuals the right to petition. The memorandum remarked on a meeting between the Prime Minister and the Leader of the Opposition before the first session of the Consultative Assembly at which Churchill had stressed the importance he attached to the adoption by the Council of Europe of satisfactory arrangements for guaranteeing the enjoyment of human rights.

The timing was inauspicious. The Labour Government had been under strong domestic pressure in Parliament throughout the spring and summer. War in Korea had started in June when North Korean forces equipped with Soviet weapons crossed the 38th parallel into

---

[20] See A. Lester, 'Fundamental Rights: The United Kingdom Isolated?' [1984] *Public Law* 46. This informative article contains a historical review of British Government policy towards the Convention in 1950–1 and 1957–65. The account of the earlier period is especially valuable as it is based on contemporary state papers. I have drawn on some of the same sources, supplemented by others held in the Public Record Office.

[21] CP (50) 179.

South Korea. This had led to increased expenditure on defence, always a difficult issue for a Labour Government. According to Attlee's biographer 'The crisis in the Far East had burst upon ministers already fatigued and overworked.'[22] On 31 July, the night before the Cabinet meeting, Attlee broadcast to the nation supporting the military action taken by American forces on behalf of the United Nations. The Korean war, he said, was a war against aggression; Britain's security was as much in danger as that of any other country. His tone was sombre: 'The fire that has been started in distant Korea may burn down your house.'[23]

Against this background of events it is easy to see how Younger's memorandum was roughly treated at a meeting dominated by the situation in Korea, the representation of China on the Security Council of the United Nations, and an American request to increase armed forces and military production.[24] Ministers, tired and worried about an international situation the outcome of which was beyond their control, gave vent to their frustrations on something closer to hand. Cripps, like Bevin, a sick man near the end of his life, took the lead. He claimed that a Government committed to the policy of a planned economy could not ratify the Convention. He instanced Articles of the draft Convention, one affecting powers of entry into private premises, which were inconsistent with the powers of economic control essential to the operation of a planned economy. The draft Convention would be acceptable only to those who believed in a free economy and a minimum amount of state intervention in economic affairs.

From the Colonial Office, Griffiths also had circulated a paper[25] putting forward a second ground for opposition: that the right of petition by individuals and groups to the proposed Court of Human Rights was objectionable to British colonial territories overseas. In his opinion the introduction of such a system would lead to 'considerable misunderstanding and political unsettlement' by suggesting to colonial peoples who were still politically immature either that the ultimate authority in the affairs of their territory was not the Crown, or that there was more than one ultimate authority. The confusion would be prone to exploitation by extremists in

[22] Kenneth Harris, *Attlee*, Weidenfeld and Nicolson, London, 1982, p. 455.
[23] Ibid., pp. 455–6.
[24] CM (50) 52nd Conclusions.
[25] CP (50) 189.

order to undermine the authority of the Colonial Government. 'Loyalty would be shaken', Griffiths declared roundly, 'administration would be made more difficult and agitation more easy'.

In the course of further discussion, ministers agreed that the effect of the right to individual petition on our judicial system might be very serious. It was intolerable that the code of common law and statute law which had been built up in this country over many years should be made subject to review by an international court administering no defined system of law. It was noted that in the draft Covenant on Human Rights, which was under discussion by the United Nations, the right of petition against breaches was confined to states.

The conclusion of the Cabinet was that the Foreign Secretary should endeavour to secure that the Committee of Ministers remitted the draft Convention for further examination by governments. Younger, who was present for the discussion on this item, was asked to provide an explanation as to how a draft Convention which was not in accord with the Government's economic policy should have reached such an advanced stage of preparation before being submitted for consideration by ministers.[26]

Bevin was in Strasbourg when the Cabinet had met, but as soon as he was informed of the decision he sent a telegram to the Prime Minister saying he could not propose that the draft Convention should be remitted to governments for further consideration. His reasons were:

(i) The Assembly attaches considerable importance to its completion and if Ministers do not submit a draft to the Assembly all the latter's suspicions will be aroused that the Ministers are concerned chiefly to stifle its initiative. (ii) In any case if the Ministers do not put the question on the agenda the Assembly almost certainly will. (iii) As you know Maxwell Fyfe and the Conservative Members of the Assembly together with Layton and a

---

[26] A memorandum in reply was circulated to the Cabinet on 20 Sept. 1950. (CP (50) 211). Contemporary Foreign Office records reveal an intention to see the Convention completed during the next session of the Committee of Ministers and opened for signature. That objective was reflected in a dispatch to British Diplomatic Representatives in Europe dated 20 July 1950: 'It is ... the opinion of Her Majesty's Government that it is most desirable that the Committee of Ministers should complete the work on this Convention in the course of its next meeting so that it can be opened for signature forthwith. If this can be achieved it will ... constitute a significant achievement for the Council of Europe at the conclusion of the first year of its existence.' FO 371/88754.

number of Labour members favour the conclusion of such a convention. It would be unfortunate if my proposal were attacked by representatives of all three elements of the British Delegation.[27]

On 4 August Younger spoke to Attlee on the telephone to say that the Foreign Office was sending to Strasbourg suggested amendments to Article 8 (privacy of home and correspondence) and Article 23 (right of individual petition, later renumbered Article 25). The Cabinet had indicated that they had objections to other Articles as well, but as they had never been precisely formulated it had not been possible to deal with them. Treasury officials had been consulted about Article 8 but did not feel it conflicted with existing practices in this country. It had not been possible to consult the Chancellor himself. Attlee said he did not regard Article 8 as vital, and that the jurisdiction of the court and the right of individual petition were the main points. Younger reminded him that acceptance of the court's jurisdiction would be optional, even though the Cabinet had not felt that to be a completely adequate safeguard. Nevertheless, it might be possible to content ourselves with the optional clause provided we were able to obtain a modification of Article 23. The Prime Minister agreed, but said that if it was not possible to get the effect of the Article modified in any way, then he thought 'it would be the wish of the Cabinet that the Secretary of State should stand out against the adoption of the Convention even if it meant him being in a minority of one. He said if the Secretary of State felt this to be unacceptable he had better ring direct from Strasbourg to Chequers.'[28]

On 7 August the Committee of Ministers, having considered a report by senior officials, adopted a revised text of the draft Convention, accepting without difficulty the definition of the rights to be incorporated and the proposal to create a Court with optional jurisdiction. In the event it was at the insistence of the Consultative Assembly rather than the Committee of Ministers that the right of individual petition was included; the compromise being that the competence of the Commission to receive individual petitions should be established in the Convention, but that it should only apply to those member states which expressly accepted such com-

---

[27] Ibid.
[28] A full note of the telephone conversation between the Minister of State and Prime Minister is contained in FO 371/88754.

petence in a separate declaration. After further consideration by the Assembly, the three unresolved rights: the right of property, the right of parents to choose the kind of education to be given to their children, and the right to free elections, were held over to a later protocol. The Convention was then signed on 4 November 1950 by the Committee of Ministers, the United Kingdom included, during its sixth session held in Rome.

Although some British members of the Consultative Assembly at Strasbourg had been active in preparing the way for the signature of the Convention, Maxwell Fyfe especially in his capacity as chairman of the Assembly's Committee on Legal and Administrative Questions, no examination of the contemporary records bears out the claim that the United Kingdom made the running in establishing the most effective international system for the protection of human rights yet known. The Government at home was preoccupied with the less enduring demands of a planned economy and the effects on a colonial empire that was soon to dwindle into insignificance. Real and immediate as these concerns must have seemed at the time, they lacked vision. The legal profession was generally suspicious if not downright hostile, although one must hope that not all views were as intemperate as those held by the head of the judiciary, Lord Jowitt. His reaction to the August Cabinet meeting had been expressed vehemently in a letter sent two days later to Hugh Dalton: 'we were not prepared to encourage our European friends to jeopardise our whole system of law, which we have laboriously built up over the centuries, in favour of some half-baked scheme to be administered by some unknown court'.[29]

In a more considered but still caustic memorandum, circulated to Cabinet colleagues on 13 October after consultation with the Lord Chief Justice, the Master of the Rolls, the Law Lords, the Attorney General, and the Home Office,[30] Jowitt execrated the political necessity of accepting the Convention as 'an unqualified misfortune' from the point of view of the administration of the law. To the mind of the Lord Chancellor the Convention was

[29] LCO 2/5570.

[30] In commenting on the paper in draft, the Permanent Secretary at the Home Office, Sir F. Newsam, wrote: 'We share the Lord Chancellor's doubts about the usefulness of a Convention on this subject, and we have always felt that it would be preferable not to attempt ... to elaborate a Convention in addition to the Universal Declaration of Human Rights'. LCO 2/5570.

so vague and woolly that it may mean almost anything ... It completely passes the wit of man to guess what results would be arrived at by a tribunal composed of elected persons who need not even be lawyers, drawn from various European states possessing completely different systems of law, and whose deliberations take place behind closed doors ... Any student of our legal institutions ... must recoil from this document with a feeling of horror ... it is obvious that the whole document reeks of compromise. Vague and indefinite terms have been used because they were vague and indefinite ... so that all parties ... could be induced to sign them.[31]

Having already signed the Convention in November, the fact that the United Kingdom was the first state to ratify it on 8 March 1951 was more of a procedural accident than any whole-hearted demonstration of support for the new institution or the ideals upon which it was founded. In the other member states, where positive action by national parliaments was a prerequisite to ratification, the procedures were slower than at Westminster.[32] Constitutional practice in Britain is that the ratification of treaties is accomplished by the executive action of the Government of the day. Only when changes in domestic law are required to give effect to a treaty will legislation follow.[33] In 1951 the Convention on Human Rights was ratified on the assumption that United Kingdom law was already in accordance with its provisions. The normal procedure is simply for the text of a treaty to be laid before Parliament as a command paper. Nothing further is required, although the Government will not proceed with ratification until a period of twenty-one days has elapsed from the date on which it was tabled.[34]

[31] Ibid.

[32] Robertson, *Human Rights in Europe*, pp. 15–16.

[33] 'Within the British Empire there is a well-established rule that the making of a treaty is an executive act, while the performance of its obligations, if they entail alteration of the existing domestic law, requires legislative action.' *Attorney General for Canada* v. *Attorney General for Ontario* [1937] AC 326, per Lord Atkin delivering the opinion of the Privy Council at 347.

[34] This practice is known as the Ponsonby rule, originating from a departmental minute dated 1 Feb. 1924 signed by Arthur Ponsonby, then Under-Secretary of State for Foreign Affairs. Erskine May, *Parliamentary Practice*, 21st edn., ed. C. J. Boulton, Butterworths, London, 1989, p. 215.

IV

After signature the pace of progress slowed. Three further rati-
fications followed in 1952: Norway, Sweden, and the Federal
Republic of Germany, with the Convention coming into force on
3 September 1953 when the necessary ten instruments of ratification
had been deposited. The all-important ratification by France was
not deposited for a further twenty years, being received on 3 May
1974. By the end of 1974, the Convention had been ratified by
eighteen states, at that time constituting the total membership of
the Council of Europe.

In the intervening period, the most contentious issue continued
to be the willingness or reluctance of the contracting parties to
accept the optional provisions: the right of individual petition to
the Commission and the compulsory jurisdiction of the Court. Six
acceptances were needed before the right of individual petition
could become operational, while the Court could not be established
until eight contracting parties had accepted its jurisdiction as
compulsory. By September 1953 only three countries (Sweden,
Ireland, and Denmark) had accepted the right of individual petition;
and two of the smaller member states, Ireland and Denmark, the
compulsory jurisdiction of the Court. In an attempt to instil a
greater sense of urgency, the Consultative Assembly, at the instance
of Teitgen, adopted a recommendation to the Committee of Ministers urging all member states to ratify the Convention and the
First Protocol (containing the rights of property, education, and
free elections which had been omitted from the Convention but
added in March 1952), and to make the optional declarations.

It was now for the Conservative Government, which had come
into office in 1951, to decide how the United Kingdom should
respond. Advice on the question was proffered to the Home
Secretary in a departmental submission dated 20 October 1953. By
one of the quirks of fortune that party politics brings, the Home
Secretary of the day was the sole British politician with a genuine
claim to be counted amongst the Convention's pioneers: Sir David
Maxwell Fyfe. Addressing the Consultative Assembly on 25 August
1950, in the crucial period before the signing of the Convention,
Maxwell Fyfe had made a forceful speech contending that the
Convention stated human rights not as vague generalities, but in
terms that could be enforced by a court of law. As such it would

help to mobilize democratic opinion and might stop the progress of totalitarianism.[35]

In a covering minute, a senior Home Office official, Sir Samuel Hoare,[36] acknowledged 'the active part formerly taken by the present Home Secretary in advocating the right of individual petitions [*sic*] and the compulsory jurisdiction of the European Court'. This did not deter him, however, from deploying at length much the same negative arguments as had been expressed earlier by Dowson. The submission is so revealing of the prevailing climate of opinion in Whitehall, the Foreign Office apart, that it is quoted *in extenso*. On the right of individual petition, the submission argued:

The European Convention is in terms which we have been able to accept, and applies to a limited number of countries with a comparable democratic structure. Nevertheless the danger of the abuse of a right of petition for 'cold war' purposes is just as great [as under the draft United Nations Covenants then under discussion]. There are large and aggressive communist parties in many European countries which would not be slow to exploit the opportunity of individual or group petitions for making trouble. Moreover we are proposing to extend the Convention to practically all our dependent territories, and it is in regard to them that claims, specious or well-founded, of violation of human rights can most easily be made. There would be the strongest opposition by the Colonial Office to the UK's acceptance of the right of petition in respect of dependent territories, and acceptance only in respect of the metropolitan territory would be seized upon by anti-colonials, in the UN and elsewhere, as evidence that all was not well in the Colonies. Article 25 of the Convention provides that if the Commission accepts a petition, it may if need be, undertake 'an investigation, for the effective conduct of which the States concerned shall furnish all necessary facilities'. This seems to envisage the possibility of local investigation in the territory concerned. While the Report of the Commission (where a friendly settlement is not reached), may not be published by the States concerned until the Committee of Ministers has considered it, there is nothing to prevent any amount of publicity about the fact that a petition has been submitted to the Commission, and about the charges made.

---

[35] Kilmuir, *Political Adventure*, p. 183.
[36] Not to be confused with the Home Secretary (1937–9) of the same name, later Lord Templewood (see references in the text of Chapter 2 and in n. 51). Assistant Under-Secretary of State, Home Office, 1948–61; Head of International Division, 1950–61; member of Council of Europe Committee of Experts on Human Rights, 1961–73.

We do not yet know how the Commission will work: it has not yet been appointed. It may, on issues raised by individual petitions, behave sensibly; it may not. We have also, though this is a question of mechanics, always felt doubt about how arrangements for sifting petitions, which may well be in very great numbers, will work. There is provision in the Convention for the rejection of petitions which are manifestly ill-founded or an abuse of the right of petition, but the task of sorting these out will be a formidable one, and will probably involve a mass of correspondence with Governments concerned.

Consent by the UK to the admissibility of petitions under the Convention would undermine completely our policy of opposition to petitions under the UN Covenants. There are no satisfactory arguments we could adduce for refusing to admit the principle in the UN, while accepting it in the context of a European Covenant [*sic*].

So far Denmark, Sweden, and the Irish Republic have accepted the optional clause about petitions: 6 acceptances are required before the Commission can consider petitions relating to the States which have accepted. At the meeting of Ministers' Deputies which reviewed the position early this year, the UK representative said firmly that the UK Government did not intend to make declarations under Articles 25 and 46 and this is recorded in the Fourth Report of the Committee of Ministers. Norway said she had not made these declarations and was not at present contemplating a change of attitude on this point. Belgium said that 'certain doubts' had arisen with regard to the right of individual petition. The remainder reserved their position or said the matter was under consideration.

Jurisdiction of the Court

Our main objection to accepting compulsory jurisdiction of the Court is that our own code of common law and statute law, built up over so many years, would be brought under review by an international court administering no defined system of law. We took the view when the Convention was being framed, that enforcement should be obtained through the Committee of Ministers, and by eventual publicity for the decision of the Commission, and with the ultimate sanction of the application of Article 8 of the Statute of the Council—a request by the Committee of Ministers to an offending State to withdraw from the Council. An example of the far-reaching consequences which would result from acceptance of the Court's jurisdiction is Article 50 of the Convention, under which, if the Court finds that a decision or measure taken by a legal or other authority of a Party is completely or partially in conflict with obligations under the Convention, and if the internal law of the Party allows only partial reparation to be made, the Court's decision shall if necessary afford just satisfaction to the injured party. There is the further objection that the jurisdiction of the Court overlaps that of the International Court of Justice, and that a multiplicity of international tribunals is to be avoided. (The advocates of a European Court for this Convention have always had it in mind that once set up the Court would have other functions attributed to it, and would become one of a number of organs whose existence would accelerate progress towards European federation). The Court requires 8 declarations of acceptance under Article 46 to bring it into existence. So far only two states, Denmark and the Republic of Ireland, have made declarations. Sweden, Norway and the UK have indicated that they do not intend to make declarations.[37]

The Home Secretary's reply, terse and probably not unexpected, was conveyed in a minute dated 26 October 1953. It read:

I am in considerable difficulty and would like to discuss.

A discussion duly took place between Maxwell Fyfe, Sir Frank Newsam, the Permanent Under-Secretary of State, and Sir Samuel Hoare. The outcome was reported by Hoare in a letter to the Foreign Office:

I have consulted the Home Secretary and while he recognizes and accepts the force of the arguments against HMG's making either of these optional declarations at the present time, he feels that having regard to the support given to these proposals both by himself and by other members of the Consultative Assembly who are now members of the Government, it is desirable that HMG's refusal to make these declarations should be expressed in relation to world conditions at the present time rather than as an absolute and unqualified negative.[38]

With that evasion, British policy remained unchanged for a further twelve years. The Labour Party returned to office after the General Election in October 1964, but without any visible commitment towards the right of individual petition or the compulsory jurisdiction of the Court. Neither the Labour election manifesto, nor the seminal report of the Society of Labour Lawyers, *Law Reform NOW*, contained any mention of the Convention.[39] With the passage of time, however, one of the arguments that had counted for so much earlier, the possibility of abuse if the right of individual petition were to be extended to the dependent territories, carried

[37] HO 274/6.
[38] Letter of 9 Nov. 1953 to H. P. L. Attlee, Foreign Office. HO 274/6.
[39] [1984] *Public Law* 46 at 59.

less weight. While continuing to resist individual petitions and the compulsory jurisdiction of the Court, in October 1953 the Conservative Government had extended the general provisions of the Convention to forty-two overseas territories for whose international relations it was responsible. Their total population amounted to over ninety-seven million people.[40] By 1965 most of these territories had become independent, some with fundamental rights incorporated into their constitutions which had been modelled on the European Convention.

As in 1950 it was the Foreign Office rather than the Home Departments, or the Cabinet collectively, which took the lead. Since any decision to accept the right of individual petition or the compulsory jurisdiction of the Court would require the exercise of options available to member states under an international treaty, the Foreign Secretary was the minister responsible for bringing forward proposals as to whether the Government should exercise either or both of these options. Before the matter reached ministers there would have been interdepartmental consultation embracing the Lord Chancellor's Department, the Law Officers' Department, and the Home Office as the three offices of state most affected by a positive decision. Had there been reservations on the part of the Lord Chancellor or the Attorney General it is unlikely that proposals would have been pursued.

The Convention is contained within the setting of the Council of Europe, whose Parliamentary Assembly[41] was considerably more vigorous in the 1960s than later when the focus shifted to the institutions of the European Community, including a European Parliament. In the 1950s and 1960s the Assembly had an interest in persuading member states to accept the optional provisions and it is probable that at least some British Parliamentarians in the Assembly would have lobbied the Government at home in the same sense.

Then there was the characteristic Foreign Office interest that the UK Government, in the context of our general relations with other Western European countries, should be seen to be prepared to accept international supervision of the performance of the sub-

[40] Ibid at 55.
[41] The Consultative Assembly of the Council of Europe was renamed the Parliamentary Assembly in July 1974 on the grounds that the new title reflected more accurately the role and composition of the Assembly.

stantive obligations which had been accepted under the Convention. By 1965, a number of other Western European governments had already accepted the right of individual petition and the compulsory jurisdiction of the Court, and the Foreign Office did not like the idea of the United Kingdom being exposed to nagging criticism in Strasbourg and elsewhere for being unprepared to accept the two options. Their discomfort was heightened by the feeling that British censure of the human rights record of the Soviet Union and other Eastern European states 'was being somewhat undermined by our failure to accept the right of individual petition and the compulsory jurisdiction of the Court'.[42]

Viewed in retrospect, the mid-1960s was the optimum moment for a positive move by the UK Government. The early hostility had abated, the suspicions had not been borne out by events, and a new generation of ministers, with Roy Jenkins at the Home Office from December 1965, looked on Europe with very different eyes to their more insular predecessors. Nor had the forces which were to explode in Northern Ireland in 1969 yet gathered sufficient strength for the prospect of emergency legislation to be envisaged.

The Foreign Secretary between January 1965 and August 1966 was Michael Stewart.[43] Having secured the agreement of the Law Officers and the Lord Chancellor, Gardiner, a libertarian whose values were far removed from those of the crusty Jowitt, the Foreign Secretary proceeded by the classic route favoured by civil servants whenever a subject does not call for reference to the Cabinet or a Cabinet Committee.[44] Letters were exchanged between the Foreign Secretary and ministers having a departmental responsibility, namely the Home Secretary, the Secretary of State for Scotland and the Colonial Secretary; other Departments being consulted at official level. No more was heard of incompatibilities with the

[42] Letter to the author dated 31 Jan. 1991 from Sir Ian Sinclair QC, Legal Adviser at the Foreign and Commonwealth Office, 1976–84.

[43] Secretary of State for Education and Science, 1964–5; First Secretary of State, 1966–8; Secretary of State 1966–8; Secretary of State for Economic Affairs, 1966–7; Secretary of State for Foreign and Commonwealth Affairs, 1968–70. Created a life peer as Lord Stewart of Fulham in 1979. There is no mention of the Convention, or of the right of individual petition and the compulsory jurisdiction of the Court, in Lord Stewart's memoirs (*Life and Labour*, Sidgwick and Jackson, London, 1980), nor in those of Harold Wilson (*The Labour Government 1964–70: A Personal Record*, Weidenfeld and Nicolson, London, 1971).

[44] Sinclair is quoted by Lester as confirming that the matter was not discussed by Cabinet or a Cabinet Committee. [1984] *Public Law* 46 at 60.

planned economy, the only impediment being seen in the situation of the remaining dependent territories. They too were consulted over some months in 1965, resulting in a decision not to extend to them the right of individual petition.[45]

Parliamentary interest was not confined to MPs who attended the Assembly in Strasbourg. In the House of Commons a newly elected Conservative back-bencher, Terence Higgins,[46] put four consecutive Questions to the Prime Minister pressing the Government to recognize the competence of the Commission to receive applications by persons, non-governmental organizations, or groups of individuals, within the terms of Article 25 of the Convention, and to declare, under Article 46, that it recognized as compulsory *ipso facto* and without special agreement the jurisdiction of the Court. The Prime Minister, Harold Wilson, answered each Question orally, saying in reply to the first one on 22 December 1964 that the Government was looking into the whole matter.[47] Higgins persisted with further Questions on 9 February,[48] 6 May[49], and 7 December 1965.[50] Although married to the international lawyer, Dr Rosalyn Higgins,[51] with whom he had discussed the matter, Higgins was not acting for, or briefed by, any interest group. Nor was he aware of any widespread support in Parliament. He believed that Sir Elwyn Jones, the Attorney General, was sympathetic,[52] but received no encouragement from either front bench.

In reply to the fourth and final Question on 7 December, the Prime Minister said that the Government had decided to accept, in

---

[45] See letter from Sinclair to Lester, ibid. at p. 60.

[46] Minister of State, Treasury, 1970–2; Financial Secretary to the Treasury, 1972–4. Chairman of House of Commons Select Committees, 1980–91. Knighted, 1993.

[47] *Parl. Debates*, HC, 704 (5th ser.), col. 1052.

[48] *Parl. Debates*, HC, 706 (5th ser.), col. 194.

[49] *Parl. Debates*, HC, 711 (5th ser.), cols. 1556–7.

[50] *Parl. Debates*, HC, 722 (5th ser.), col. 235.

[51] Staff specialist in international law, Royal Institute of International Affairs, 1963–74; Professor of International Law, the University of Kent at Canterbury, 1978–81; Professor of International Law at the London School of Economics since 1981. QC, 1986.

[52] Attorney General, 1964–70; Lord Chancellor (as Lord Elwyn-Jones), 1974–9. In his autobiography, Elwyn Jones recalled that although he did not believe the Convention should be incorporated into our law he had, in a Commons debate in 1959, urged recognition of the right of the individual British subject to petition the European Commission and Court of Human Rights if his or her rights under the Convention were being infringed. *In My Time*, Weidenfeld and Nicolson, London, 1983, p. 150.

respect of the United Kingdom and for an initial period of three years, the right of individual petition[53] to the European Commission of Human Rights and the compulsory jurisdiction of the European Court of Human Rights. Formal acceptance followed early in 1966. As the persistent back-bencher, gratified to have elicited such a favourable answer, sank back in his seat after thanking the Prime Minister 'very much indeed' for a reply that would give great satisfaction to all those who had the cause of human rights at heart, he heard a veteran Tory voice beside him growl, 'Never thank the other side'.

V

Although the jurisprudence of the Commission since 1955, and the Court since 1959, has been developed largely on the basis of individual applications, complaints may also be made by one member state against another.[54] This happened in 1971/2 when the Republic of Ireland pursued claims against the United Kingdom arising in particular out of the interrogation techniques used by the security forces in Northern Ireland. By the time the Court had found that these techniques amounted to inhuman and degrading treatment rather than torture as alleged, they had been discontinued and no further action was taken by the Committee of Ministers. Interstate applications, fertile ground for diplomatic and political embarrassment, as the Irish case proved, have been rare. Very few disputes have come before the Commission or the Court in this way, the most prominent being the case brought in 1967 by Denmark, Norway, Sweden, and the Netherlands against Greece, alleging torture and ill-treatment by the security police of persons

---

[53] The term 'petition', which is used in the English version of the text of the Convention, has been largely replaced in the practice of the Commission by 'application', as being closer to the French 'requête'. That it is more than a petition in the strict sense is indicated by the fact that an application institutes a procedure requiring an initial decision to be taken on its admissibility by the Commission, and failing a friendly settlement a binding decision on its merits by the Court. J. E. S. Fawcett, *The Application of the European Convention on Human Rights*, Clarendon Press, Oxford, 2nd edn., 1987, p 346.

[54] Article 24 of the Convention allows any state party to refer a case against another state party to the Commission.

who had been arrested for political reasons.[55] In December 1969 the military government in Greece denounced the Convention and withdrew from membership of the Council of Europe. With the restoration of democratic government in 1974, Greece resumed its membership and again ratified the Convention.[56]

Applications by private persons, non-governmental organizations, or groups of individuals claiming to be victims of a violation by a member state ('a High Contracting Party') of a right recognized in the Convention, have swollen from a trickle to a flood over a period of three and a half decades. Between 1955 and 1991 19,216 applications were registered by the Commission, from a total of 57,190 provisional files.[57] Only a relatively small minority surmounted the first hurdle; that of admissibility.[58] For a petition to be found admissible the applicant has to fulfil four conditions. He must show (*a*) that he has been a victim[59] of a violation of a right or rights set forth in the Convention; (*b*) that the alleged violation was committed by the Government or a public authority in a state which has recognized the right of individual petition; (*c*) that he has exhausted all domestic remedies available to him; and (*d*) that not more than six months has elapsed since the final domestic decision was taken. There is some confusion over the domestic remedies which the Commission will consider are available and therefore must be exhausted before it can declare an application admissible.[60]

More general criteria are that the applicant must not be anonymous; that the complaint must not be the same as one already examined by the Commission or previously submitted to another international body; and that it must be covered by the scope of the

[55] For a summary of the Greek case, see Robertson, *Human Rights in Europe*, pp. 39–42.

[56] Ibid., p. 50.

[57] European Commission of Human Rights, *Survey of Activities and Statistics 1991*, Strasbourg, 1991, p. 21.

[58] A total of 1,038 applications was declared admissible over the period 1955–91. The number of applications (217) declared admissible in 1991 comfortably exceeded the total of 127 declared admissible between 1955 and 1974.

[59] For a discussion of the status and definition of the victim of a violation of rights recognized in the Convention, see Human Rights file No. 2 entitled *The Presentation of an Application before the European Commission of Human Rights*, Council of Europe, Strasbourg, 1978.

[60] A. Lester et al., *A British Bill of Rights*, Constitution Paper No. 1, Institute for Public Policy Research, London, 1990, p. 14.

Convention.[61] After preliminary scrutiny by the Secretariat,[62] the Commission makes a decision on admissibility. In 1991 the number of applications declared admissible was 217; 1,441 were declared inadmissible, including 70 struck off the list.[63] There is no appeal against rejection. In the same year the Commission disposed of 1,619 applications, leaving a backlog of 2,332 applications pending, of which 1,563 were awaiting first examination.[64] The Commission's decisions on the admissibility of individual applications in the years 1989, 1990, and 1991 are analysed in Table 11 by reference to the government which was a party to the case.

Once the Commission has accepted an application (Article 29), and before it decides on its admissibility, it proceeds to a more thorough review of the case. At this stage the Commission may ask both parties for their observations, although in a large majority of cases the decision to reject an application as inadmissible is taken without the respondent government being called on to give its comments. When the Commission does invite a government to comment it normally goes on to deal with the question of admissibility and the merits of the application together.[65] This may lead to an oral hearing. Having admitted a petition referred to it, the Commission is bound to 'place itself at the disposal of the parties concerned with a view to securing a friendly settlement of the matter on the basis of respect for Human Rights as defined in this Convention'.[66]

Since an individual applicant may incur costs in pursuing his case before the Commission, discretionary legal aid for applicants of modest means was authorized in 1963. Although the facility was originally meant to last for two years, it has been extended at

[61] Council of Europe, *The Protection of Human Rights in Europe*, H (90) 6, Strasbourg, 1990, p. 9.

[62] At the end of 1991 the Secretariat consisted of thirty-two lawyers, twenty-one administrative staff, and a translator. The Commission was composed of twenty-two members, one from each member state (except San Marino), each elected for a period of six years by the Committee of Ministers of the Council of Europe. The Commission does not sit on a permanent basis. Eight sessions were held in 1991, amounting altogether to sixteen session weeks. *Survey of Activities and Statistics, 1991*, pp. 1–2.

[63] Ibid., p. 6.

[64] Ibid., p. 2.

[65] During 1991 the Commission held forty oral hearings on individual applications. Thirty-seven were on admissibility and merits, and three on merits only. Ibid., p. 6.

[66] Article 28(*b*). Thirty-two applications were settled on this basis in 1991.

TABLE 11. *Individual applications to the European Commission of Human Rights: decisions on admissibility, 1989–91*

Government	Applications admissible			Applications inadmissible or struck off		
	1989	1990	1991	1989	1990	1991
Austria	11	9	24	104	79	129
Belgium	4	5	4	77	60	90
Cyprus	—	1	—	1	1	5
Denmark	—	—	—	18	14	24
Finland	—	—	—	—	2	14
France	17	16	25	187	135	247
Germany	3	4	5	215	124	154
Greece	2	5	5	7	17	24
Iceland	1	1	1	—	—	1
Ireland	1	2	—	8	8	12
Italy	21	62	64	46	72	74
Liechtenstein	—	—	—	—	—	1
Luxembourg	—	—	—	2	3	2
Malta	1	—	—	3	1	5
Netherlands	4	3	20	80	58	116
Norway	—	—	—	5	5	12
Portugal	3	23	—	16	11	3
Spain	1	1	1	40	70	80
Sweden	12	6	13	115	85	143
Switzerland	3	6	5	91	97	103
Turkey	2	—	12	10	18	23
United Kingdom	9	7	38	218	205	178
Others	—	—	—	—	—	1
TOTAL	95	151	217	1,243	1,065	1,441

Source: European Commission of Human Rights, *Survey of Activities and Statistics.*

regular intervals since. Member states are obliged not to hinder in any way the effective exercise of the right of individual petition.[67] This provision is of particular importance to prisoners who have

[67] Article 25 (1).

consistently been one of the largest groups of petitioners.[68] That so many applicants should write from behind bars is not surprising. In the words of a Vice-President of the Commission, 'They are naturally tempted to try anything to regain freedom particularly if procedures are devoid of any additional risk, including that of costs'.[69]

If the endeavour to promote a friendly settlement fails, the Commission draws up a report on the facts and expresses an opinion as to whether the facts found disclose a breach of obligations under the Convention. This report is sent to the Committee of Ministers and to the state concerned. The Commission's report, which need not be unanimous, is not published at this stage. As the executive arm of the Council of Europe, the Committee of Ministers comprises the Foreign Ministers of the member states or their appointed deputies. Within three months of its receiving the Commission's report, either the Commission or any of the states involved can refer the case to the Court. Provided that the member state has accepted the jurisdiction of the Court, the Commission will normally refer the case to the Court for a judicial hearing.

The right to bring cases before the Court will cease to be reserved to the Commission and member states when the Ninth Protocol comes into force. This will enable individuals, once their applications have been declared admissible, to refer their case direct to the Court after it has been accepted by the Commission.[70] The procedure would eliminate the need for the Commission's report to be sent to the Committee of Ministers which would have no function to perform while the case was before the Court.

The United Kingdom did not sign the Ninth Protocol, and in answer to a Parliamentary Question in February 1992 the Minister of State at the Foreign and Commonwealth Office confirmed that the Government had no plans to ratify it. His answer continued:

The UK considers that the interests of an individual complaining about a

---

[68] *Survey of Activities and Statistics, 1991*, p. 19. As the total number of applicants has increased, the percentages of applicants detained or interned have fallen in the 1980s from 21% to 11%; in the 1970s from 49% to 24%; and in the 1960s from 56% to 23%.

[69] Professor S. Trechsel, 'The Right to Liberty and Security of the Person: Article 5 of the European Convention of Human Rights in the Strasbourg case-law', (1980) *Human Rights Law Journal* Nos. 1–4, 88.

[70] European Court of Human Rights, *Survey of Activities 1959–1990*, Registry of the Court, Council of Europe, Strasbourg, 1991, p. 2.

breach of the Convention are adequately taken care of by the European Commission of Human Rights. Under the present system the Commission refers cases to the European Court of Human Rights on behalf of individual complainants in appropriate cases. The UK considers that the delicate balance of the supervisory organs would be upset if individuals had the right to seize the Court. The implementation of this Protocol would increase the already heavy workload of the Convention organs.[71]

That these reservations were not universally shared was shown by the fact that seventeen member states had signed the Ninth Protocol. Since, however, few had ratified it by February 1992 there was little prospect of it coming into force at any early date.

Initially cautious, being aware of the need to earn the confidence of the governments by which it had been set up, the Court gradually earned a reputation as an international judicial tribunal of high standing. Lord Jowitt's doom-laden forebodings did not come to pass. The Court is composed of as many judges as there are member states of the Council of Europe. They are not underqualified. In the same way as members of the Commission, judges must either possess qualifications for appointment to high judicial office, or be jurists of recognized competence (Article 39). They are elected by the Parliamentary Assembly on the recommendation of member states. Each state submits the names of three candidates, two of whom must be its own nationals. The Assembly may not choose two or more judges from any one state (Article 38), although in the interests of the smallest member states appointments from countries outside the Council of Europe are not precluded. Thus a Canadian judge sat on the plenary Court hearing the case of *Thynne, Wilson and Gunnell*, having been nominated by Liechtenstein. Once appointed, a judge serves for a nine-year term (Article 40), and is expected to act independently of the government of the state from which he comes. Two of the Presidents of the Court have come from the United Kingdom: Lord McNair (1959–65) and Sir Humphrey Waldock (1971–4).[72]

[71] Earl of Caithness, *Parl. Debates*, HL, 535 (5th ser.), col. WA 23, 10 Feb. 1992.
[72] Both had been university teachers of law. McNair had practised as a solicitor before returning to Cambridge where he held the Whewell chair in International Law (1935–7) and was Professor of Comparative Law in 1945–6. In the intervening years, he had been Vice-Chancellor of Liverpool University. He was elected a judge of the International Court of Justice at the Hague in 1946, and was its President, 1952–5. He became the first President of the Court of Human Rights in 1959. Waldock was an academic lawyer, the holder of the Chichele chair in Public

Except when the full Court meets in plenary session to consider a major issue of interpretation, a Chamber of nine judges will be empanelled to consider the report from the Commission and detailed written submissions, known as memorials, from the applicant and the government of the member state. These are then supplemented by an oral hearing in public at which a delegate for the Commission[73] and legal representatives of the applicant and the state address the Court. There are no witnesses and no testing of evidence. The judges may question counsel in the course of the hearing, but interjections are less frequent than those made in the highest British judicial tribunals. At the conclusion of the hearing the judges deliberate in private and vote on whether or not they consider there has been a violation of the Convention. The view of the majority forms the decision of the Court, with any dissenting opinions annexed to the judgment. In due course, the judgment is delivered in open Court, usually by means of the President or Vice-President reading out that part containing the legal findings, the full text being made available afterwards and published in the series of Publications of the Court. The judgment of the Court is final and there is no appeal.[74]

Few cases reached the Court in the early years. There were two reasons why on average no more than one case per year was brought before it in the fifteen years following its establishment in 1959. The first was the slow rate at which member states, and not only the United Kingdom, accepted the compulsory jurisdiction of the Court and the right of individual petition. But there was also an initial reluctance, shared by the Commission as well as the states concerned, to refer admitted cases to the Court. In time the reluctance evaporated, with both the Commission and a growing number of governments coming to consider it 'appropriate or even necessary that the final decision should be given by the Court'.[75]

International Law at Oxford, 1947–72, which he combined with practice as an advocate before various international tribunals. Before his appointment to the Court, Waldock had been President of the European Commission of Human Rights, 1955–61. He was Vice-President of the Court, 1968–71.

[73] The Commission itself is not a party to the case before the Court. The delegate's function is to assist and enlighten the Court as 'defender of the public interest'. European Court of Human Rights, *Survey of Activities 1959–1990*, p. 2.

[74] Council of Europe, *The Protection of Human Rights in Europe*, p. 12.

[75] 'The Future of the European Court of Human Rights', lecture given by R. Ryssdal at King's College London, 22 Mar. 1990. Publication of the European

Subsequently the road to Strasbourg became so well trod during the 1980s, that by 1990 the number of cases referred to the Court in the first ten months of that year (fifty-seven up to 23 November 1990) exceeded the total number which had been referred during the first twenty-four years of its existence (fifty-six).

VI

The final step is an unusual interaction of law, politics, and custom. If the applicant fails to convince the court that a violation has taken place, he will have to meet his own costs, mitigated by whatever sum may have been allowed as legal aid. He will not be required to contribute to the costs of the government of the member state against whom the breach of the Convention was alleged. If successful, the applicant may claim financial compensation and will be entitled to his costs before the domestic courts as well as the Strasbourg Commission and Court. Justice is done not only in providing the individual applicant with some remedy or 'just satisfaction' for the wrong done to him, although its implementation may be delayed, but more profoundly in requiring general changes to be made in law or practice.

How and when to introduce the necessary changes are decisions for the government of the member state. Political and diplomatic pressure play their part, but there is more to it than that. The Convention is a solemn undertaking incorporated in the form of a public international law text which, having been signed and ratified by the governments of member states of the Council of Europe in their capacity as high contracting parties, becomes a binding legal obligation on those member states. The status of the judgments of the Court as final and binding has been accepted by the contracting parties. The Convention itself does not oblige member states to make its provisions justiciable in their own courts,[76] although many

Court of Human Rights, Strasbourg, 1990, p. 3. Rolv Ryssdal (Norway) is President of the Court.

[76] See the observations of Sir Robert Megarry, Vice-Chancellor, in *Malone* v. *Commissioner of Police of the Metropolis (No. 2)* [1979] 2 All ER 620 at 647: 'The United Kingdom, as a High Contracting Party which ratified the convention on 8th March 1951, has ... long been under an obligation to secure these rights and freedoms to everyone. That obligation, however, is an obligation under a treaty which is not justiciable in the courts of this country.'

have done so. In some signatory states, for example France and the Netherlands, treaties automatically form part of domestic law. A majority of the remainder, with the exception of the United Kingdom, Denmark, Iceland, Ireland, Norway, and Sweden, have passed legislation expressly incorporating the provisions of the Convention into domestic law. But every member state shares an unavoidable duty to comply with the Court's judgments.

Supervision of the measures necessary to ensure compliance lies not in the hands of the Court, but of the Committee of Ministers, which in this capacity forms the third limb of the elaborate structure which has been developed for the protection of human rights in Europe. The Committee will expect to receive a report from the government of the state found to be in violation of the Convention explaining what action has been taken to alter national law or administrative practice to bring it into line with the obligations which by international treaty the contracting party has undertaken to observe.

The ultimate sanction of the Committee of Ministers in the event of a member state refusing or failing to take action to implement a judgment is to institute proceedings against it under the Statute of the Council of Europe for its suspension, or exclusion, from the organization. This has never happened since there is an escape route which enables a member state to denounce the Convention, as the Greek government did in 1969 when it withdrew from the Council of Europe.[77]

Less drastic action is open to member states by virtue of Article 15 of the Convention. This Article was based upon a draft amendment proposed by the United Kingdom to the original Consultative Assembly recommendations.[78] It permits a High Contracting Party in time of war, or other public emergency threatening the life of the nation, to take measures derogating from its obligations under the Convention to the extent strictly required by the exigencies of the situation, provided that such measures are not inconsistent with its other obligations under international law. An example was when Turkey derogated from Articles 5, 6, 8, 10, 11, and 13 of the Convention because of their incompatibility with decrees prom-

---

[77] Under Article 65 a High Contracting Party may denounce the Convention only after the expiry of five years from the date on which it became a party to it, and after six months' prior notification.

[78] Fawcett, *The Application of the European Convention on Human Rights*, p. 308.

ulgated to counter terrorist activities in South East Anatolia. In
a declaration of derogation dated 6 August 1990 the Turkish
Government informed the Secretary General of the Council of
Europe that:

The Republic of Turkey is exposed to threats to its national security in
South East Anatolia which have steadily grown in scope and intensity over
the last months so as to amounting [*sic*] to a threat to the life of the nation
in the meaning of Article 15 of the Convention.

During 1989, 136 civilians and 153 members of the security forces have
been killed by acts of terrorists, acting partly out of foreign bases. Since
the beginning of 1990 only, the numbers are 125 civilians and 96 members
of the security forces.[79]

Laborious and slow moving as the process undoubtedly is, partly
as a consequence of the intricacy of the procedures and partly
because of the volume of business, the Convention has come to
have a growing influence on the framing of legislation and the
execution of public policy in the United Kingdom as elsewhere. It
is a strength of the Convention that its organs do not examine
national legislation *in abstracto*. An example from Northern Ireland
was furnished in the case of *Fox, Campbell and Hartley*.[80] Two of
the applicants, a separated husband and wife, were arrested by the
Royal Ulster Constabulary in Belfast on 5 February 1986 and
taken to a police station. There they were informed that they were
being arrested under the powers contained in Section 11(1) of the
Northern Ireland (Emergency Provisions) Act 1978 on the grounds
that they were suspected of being terrorists. They were also told
they could be detained for up to seventy-two hours. Later the same
day they were questioned about their suspected involvement in
intelligence gathering and courier work for the Provisional IRA,
and their suspected membership of that organization. No charges
were brought, and they were released the following day, having
been detained for some forty-four hours. The man had been
sentenced in 1979 to twelve years' imprisonment for explosives
offences and for belonging to the IRA. In the same year, the woman
had received an eighteen months' suspended sentence after being
convicted of involvement in explosives offences.

The third applicant in the case, who was unconnected with the

---

[79] Council of Europe, *Information Sheet No. 27*, H/INF (91) 1.
[80] *Fox, Campbell and Hartley* v. *The United Kingdom* (1991) 13 EHRR 157.

other two, was arrested at his home in County Antrim six months later, under the same powers, on the grounds that he was suspected of having been involved in a kidnapping connected with the Provisional IRA. After questioning, he was released without charges being brought against him after some thirty hours in police detention. The case turned on the distinction between suspicion and 'reasonable suspicion of having committed an offence', being the words used in Article 5(1)(c) of the Convention. By a majority of four votes to three, the Court held there had been a breach of the Convention, in that the minimum standards of reasonableness of suspicion for the arrest of an individual had not been met. But since all three applicants had been released speedily before any judicial control of the lawfulness of their detention had taken place, it was not for the Court to rule *in abstracto* as to whether, had this not been so, the scope of the remedies available would or would not have satisfied the requirements of Article 5(4).

The powers of the Commission and the Court are thus directed towards specific applications. Within the institutional framework which exists to interpret the written Convention thrives a living body of case law whose development has sometimes led the Court in unexpected directions. Unpredictable and inconvenient as Strasbourg rulings may be to ministers and public officials in member states, their great virtue is that at the end of the day it is the member state itself that takes the remedial action. There is no compulsion by a supra-national body. British law or practice has been altered as a consequence of each adverse judgment of the Court,[81] save only the power to detain for up to seven days a person suspected of involvement in terrorism connected with the affairs of Northern Ireland.[82]

Voluntary action in accordance with obligations undertaken by treaty is crucial to the continued observance and political tolerance of the Convention. In the *Third Periodic Report by the United*

[81] The European Court of Human Rights' *Survey of Activities 1959–1990* lists the action taken by respondent states to comply with the Court's judgments at pp. 43–50.
[82] In *Brogan and others* v. *The United Kingdom* (1989) 11 EHRR 117 the Court held by twelve votes to seven that detention under Section 12 of the Prevention of Terrorism (Temporary Provisions) Act 1984, now Section 14 of the 1989 Act, constituted a violation of Article 5(3) of the Convention because none of the applicants after their arrest had been brought 'promptly' before a judge or other judicial authority.

Kingdom of Great Britain and Northern Ireland to the Human Rights Committee under Article 40, International Covenant on Civil and Political Rights the Government stated unequivocally to the United Nations Human Rights Committee that the United Kingdom 'must abide' by the judgments of the Court in cases to which it was party. The Report added a comment that 'The rulings of the Court have had a considerable impact on United Kingdom law and practice, often giving increased priority or urgency to changes which were already under consideration.'[83]

<h2 style="text-align:center">VII</h2>

The element of unpredictability in the application of the provisions of the Convention to new kinds of cases, previously not foreseen, can make life difficult for lawyers or public officials in member states who have to assess, when preparing legislation or responding to an individual citizen's claim against the government, the chances of a proposed statutory provision or a particular administrative act surviving eventual challenge at Strasbourg. The difficulties are felt all the more keenly in Whitehall, because the Court's dynamic and evolutionary method of interpretation is alien to British traditions. Consequently on issues not yet covered by Strasbourg judgments, the Convention is generally perceived more as a constraint than as a guide to good practice. Politically, the general mood has been one of unenthusiastic acquiescence as the superimposition of an international code on our unwritten constitution has begun to bite.

Behind this somewhat uneasy relationship can be detected two natural human responses: lack of trust in what is unfamiliar, and reluctance by national governments and legislatures to accept external limitations on their freedom of action. The fact that the Court's way of interpreting the Convention is not always in tune with our own legal system, either in law or in methodology, does not mean that irreconcilable incompatibility is inevitable. The important point is that the Convention should never be seen as a substitute or replacement for the national protection of the human rights of its citizens. It is supplementary to the safeguards provided by the legal systems in member states and essentially subsidiary to

[83] Published report dated October 1989, pp. 2–3.

them. The President of the Court elaborated this doctrine in a public lecture given in London in 1990:

as the Court has said on several occasions, the Convention system is of a subsidiary nature. The primary responsibility for the effective safeguarding of human rights and freedoms lies with the Contracting States, in particular with their judiciary. This is reflected in the rule that no State has to answer before the Convention bodies for its acts before it has had an opportunity to redress the alleged wrong within the context of its own legal order.[84]

For three centuries the constitution of Britain has adhered to the ideal of a general state of freedom, subject only to limitations imposed by a sovereign Parliament. Particular remedies have been related to particular wrongs, instead of looking to the courts to interpret and enforce abstract principles or declarations of civil rights. Unlike the United States, where the Supreme Court can set aside legislation as unlawful if it fails to conform to the requirements of the American Constitution, British courts are bound by the terms of Acts of Parliament. It is a well-established constitutional convention that the courts are not entitled to disregard the terms of any statute. This is the rock upon which Parliamentary supremacy has been built.

The mounting waves of judicial review which have swirled around the rock in recent years have not eroded Parliamentary supremacy, bearing instead on the way ministers and officialdom use the powers conferred upon them by statute. Yet Lord Denning was right to perceive the high tide sweeping in from Europe: 'when we come to matters with a European element, the Treaty [of Rome] is like an incoming tide. It flows into the estuaries and up the rivers. It cannot be held back.'[85]

United Kingdom statutes are open to challenge in domestic courts for inconsistency with European Community law, and doubtful issues are referred to the European Court of Justice. But where the law of this country alone is in question, judicial review is not a device for questioning the validity of legislation. It will provide a remedy only if the action of a minister or other public body is tainted by illegality, irrationality, or procedural impropriety.[86]

[84] Ryssdal, 'The Future of the European Court of Human Rights' p. 3.

[85] *Bulmer Ltd* v. *Bollinger SA* [1974] Ch 401 at 418.

[86] This threefold, but not exclusive, classification of grounds for a successful application for judicial review derives from Lord Diplock's speech in *Council of Civil Service Unions* v. *Minister for the Civil Service* [1985] AC 374 at 410.

In plain terms, this means that the minister or body, in the opinion of the Divisional Court, has exceeded his or its legal powers, or come to a decision such as no reasonable person or body could have reached,[87] or denied someone the right to a fair hearing.

It was not the commitment to human rights in Europe, but the accession of Britain to the European Communities, sanctioned by Parliament after much public debate in 1972 and strengthened by the Single European Act in 1987, that marked the historic departure. Unlike the earlier and looser association of the Council of Europe, membership of the Communities was accompanied by a formal obligation to recognize the primacy of Community law. To ensure the equal and consistent application of Community law in all member states, whenever a national rule and a community rule come into conflict, the Community rule must prevail.

The Court of Justice of the European Communities, which sits at Luxembourg, is an entirely distinct body from the European Court of Human Rights at Strasbourg, with which it is often confused. Its status, its powers, and origins are all dissimilar. Constituted under the founding treaties of the three original European Communities (the European Coal and Steel Community, the European Economic Community, and Euratom), the European Court of Justice exists to ensure that in the interpretation and application of each treaty the law is observed. So long as the issues remained relatively obscure, the primacy of Community law attracted little controversy. The main complaint of business and other interests was that their competitors in other member states of the European Community were not being required to conform to agreed Community rules. Certainly much still remains to be done in improving the consistency of implementation and enforcement of Community law. Contrary to the experience with the Convention on Human Rights, Denmark alone was referred to the European Court of Justice on fewer occasions than Britain during the 1980s.

---

[87] The degree of unreasonableness, amounting to what Lord Diplock called irrationality, is often described as '*Wednesbury* unreasonableness' after the case of *Associated Provincial Picture Houses Ltd* v. *Wednesbury Corporation* [1948] 1 KB 223. The phrase is hardly fair to Wednesbury, the case being one in which the Court of Appeal refused to set aside as unreasonable a prohibition imposed by the Corporation on the admission of children aged under fifteen to Sunday cinema performances.

At the end of 1989 eighty judgments of that Court were outstanding, to only one of which was the United Kingdom a party.

This one case,[88] however, was enough for national hackles to be raised. In the course of a dispute over the fishing rights of some Spanish-owned but British-registered boats, the European Court of Justice ruled that the English courts had the power to suspend the provisions of an Act of Parliament if they were thought to conflict with the requirements of Community law. Denning did not remain silent, fulminating against 'a French court dominated by French thinking',[89] and there was a predictable outcry against loss of sovereignty in the House of Commons.

Yet as Lord Bridge of Harwich pointed out in his speech in the House of Lords, the suggestion that the decision of the European Court of Justice was 'a novel and dangerous invasion by a Community institution of the sovereignty of the United Kingdom Parliament' was based on a misconception. He went on to say:

If the supremacy within the European Community of Community law over the national law of member states was not always inherent in the EEC Treaty (Cmnd. 5179-II) it was certainly well established in the jurisprudence of the European Court of Justice long before the United Kingdom joined the Community. Thus, whatever limitation of its sovereignty Parliament accepted when it enacted the European Communities Act 1972 was entirely voluntary. Under the terms of the Act of 1972 it has always been clear that it was the duty of a United Kingdom court, when delivering final judgment, to override any rule of national law found to be in conflict with any directly enforceable rule of Community law. Similarly, when decisions of the European Court of Justice have exposed areas of United Kingdom statute law which failed to implement Council directives, Parliament has always loyally accepted the obligation to make appropriate and prompt

[88] *R.* v. *Secretary of State for Transport, Ex parte Factortame Ltd and others (No. 2)* [1990] 2 AC 85; [1991] 1 AC 603. In this case, concerning the qualifications of residence and domicile required by Part II of the Merchant Shipping Act 1988 for registration of a vessel as British, the House of Lords originally held that the courts had no power to grant the applicants' request for an interim injunction restraining the Secretary of State from enforcing the Act. Subsequently the House referred the case to the European Court of Justice, which ruled that the courts of member countries were required to consider granting interim relief to applicants challenging provisions of national law as inconsistent with Community Law, even if the court's own domestic law would not permit such relief to be granted. When the case returned to the House of Lords the applicants were granted an injunction requiring the Secretary of State not to implement the legislation.
[89] *The Times*, 17 July 1990.

amendments. Thus there is nothing in any way novel in according supremacy to rules of Community law in those areas to which they apply . . .[90]

The processes for the implementation of the Convention on Human Rights have avoided this kind of political controversy, principally by upholding the distinction between the application of the Articles of the Convention by the Commission and the Court, and their enforcement by national governments at the bidding of the Committee of Ministers. The objections to the Strasbourg institutions are more mundane. The complexity of the bureaucracy, the overlapping responsibilities of the Commission and the Court, the resulting duplication of work, and above all else the length of time taken to pass through the successive stages, are all open to criticism. Five years passed between the first applications on behalf of *Thynne, Wilson and Gunnell* and the judgment of the Court in their case. Such lapse of time was not unusual.[91]

Institutional reforms range from eliminating or combining some of the stages by merging the Commission and the Court into one organ, to less radical changes. An alternative would be to replace the present system with a two-tier procedure, whereby the Commission would function as a court of first instance, and the Court as a Court of Appeal. But it is questionable whether the maintenance of successive stages is justified when an applicant in the course of exhausting domestic remedies has already had his case argued in at least one national court, and often more than one. The better solution would be to put the Court on to a permanent basis, making it responsible for determining both the admissibility and the merits of applications submitted under the Convention.

In 1990 the Committee of Ministers asked a group of experts to draw up proposals for reform. By June 1992 two proposals were before the Commission and the Court for an opinion. The first was the establishment of a full-time Court responsible for the duties currently divided between the Commission and the Court. The second proposal, a Dutch and Swedish initiative, favoured a two-tier procedure. Despite the difference of opinion, the President of the Court made it abundantly clear in a series of speeches that

[90] [1991] 1 AC 603 at 658–9.
[91] In *Granger* v. *The United Kingdom* (1990) 12 EHRR 469, a case arising out of a refusal of legal aid in Scotland, the application had first been lodged with the Commission in December 1985.

his personal belief was that converting the Convention control mechanism into two separate courts would be a mistake.[92]

Less threatening to the status quo was the Eighth Protocol which allowed the Commission to sit in Chambers for certain purposes. Additional resources granted by member states were intended to enable the part-time Commission and Court to meet more frequently, although in the event the Commission was in session for sixteen weeks in 1991, the same period as the previous year.[93] For the Court, the judges were occupied for an average of 135 days a year in dealing with their Strasbourg work.[94]

Applications submitted under Article 25 can go to a Chamber where they can be dealt with on the basis of established case law, or where they raise no serious questions affecting the interpretation or application of the Convention. A Chamber is able to take any action that the full Commission can take, save for referring a case to the Court. Committees of three members of the Commission have also been set up under Article 20(3) of the Convention, as amended by Article 1 of the Eighth Protocol, to declare inadmissible or strike from its list of cases individual applications where such decisions, which must be unanimous, can be taken without further examination. Whether these procedural reforms, designed to clear the bottleneck at the initial stages, will do more than keep up with the rapid increase in the volume of applications, seems improbable.

In Britain there has been consistent pressure for the incorporation of the provisions of the Convention into domestic law, it being argued that implementation would be transferred thereby to the jurisdiction of the United Kingdom courts. The Commission's handling of racial discrimination and minorities cases has not satisfied the relevant interest groups, whilst the quasi-judicial role of the Committee of Ministers has been criticized by purists as inappropriate for a political body, and superfluous since all of

[92] Addresses by R. Ryssdal to: International Commission of Jurists, Conference of European National Sections on *Human Rights Problems in an Enlarged Europe*, Strasbourg, 23–5 Apr. 1992 (Cour (92) 126); Conference of Presidents and Attorney Generals of the Supreme Courts of the European Communities, Brussels, 19–22 May 1992 (Cour (92) 135); *The Protection of Human Rights in Europe*, Potsdam University Law Faculty Conference, Potsdam-Babelsberg, 3–5 June 1992 (Cour (92) 173). All published by the European Court of Human Rights, Strasbourg.

[93] Commissioners are expected to work an equivalent number of weeks at home.

[94] R. Ryssdal, *Forty years of the European Convention on Human Rights: Past Achievements and Future Prospects*, European Court of Human Rights, Cour (91) 61, Strasbourg, 1991, p. 14.

the member states have already bound themselves to accept the jurisdiction of the Court. Another proposal for change came at the end of 1990 when the President of the European Commission in Brussels, Jacques Delors, sought a mandate to open negotiations to enable the European Community to accede to the Convention. Although accession would have symbolic value as a reflection of the importance of safeguarding human rights in the eyes of the Community, a Parliamentary inquiry concluded that it would bring about no practical improvements to the protection of the rights of individuals resident in its member states.[95]

VIII

Incorporation of the Convention into domestic law seems to be an attractive prospect at first sight. It is asserted that the United Kingdom is now the only member of the Council of Europe with no written constitution or enforceable Bill of Rights, and that other countries in Europe are providing remedies for their citizens which are not available to UK citizens through the British courts.[96] Those who advocate this course would like to see the substantive rights conferred by the Convention entrenched in a Bill of Rights with a special constitutional status, which would prevail over any inconsistent provisions of future as well as past legislation. The problems of entrenchment should not be underestimated, however, being regarded as formidable, even insurmountable, in the opinion of some authorities.[97]

[95] See House of Lords Select Committee on the European Communities, Session 1992/3, 3rd Report, *Human Rights Re-examined* (HL Paper 10), HMSO, London, 1992, p. 41.

[96] Lester *et al.*, *A British Bill of Rights*, p. 6.

[97] A House of Lords Select Committee on a Bill of Rights published with their minutes of evidence a memorandum in which their Specialist Adviser (Derek Rippengal QC, Counsel to the Chairman of Committees) concluded that 'the principle of Parliamentary sovereignty as traditionally understood in the United Kingdom is a bar to the effectiveness of any purported form of entrenchment that a Bill of Rights might adopt'. (Sessions 1976/7 and 1977/8, HL Paper 81, HMSO, London, pp. 1–10.) In his evidence (Ibid., Q.1) Lord Hailsham agreed that the question whether entrenchment was possible at all presented a crux of British constitutional law. He thought the issue was more open than had been suggested, although the Committee's Report none the less stated that the Specialist Adviser's memorandum had received general support from three of the Law Lords. (Session 1977/8, HL Paper 176, HMSO, London, p. 22.)

Throughout the 1980s there was articulate although minority support for the idea of incorporation, whether by means of a single comprehensive enactment or by introducing the Convention rights piecemeal into domestic law by the amendment of existing statutes and automatic inclusion in new ones. Among the judiciary, the most prominent advocate of enacting the Convention was Lord Scarman. Speaking in the House of Lords in support of a Private Member's Bill to provide protection in the Courts of the United Kingdom for the human rights and fundamental freedoms specified in the Convention, he said:

under this Bill any individual person present within the jurisdiction of the United Kingdom will have immediate access—I emphasise the word 'immediate'—within the United Kingdom to a British court if he claims that a public authority has violated a right guaranteed to him by the European convention.

The Bill, by providing the aggrieved citizen with a remedy in a national court, will at the same time ensure that the United Kingdom meets its international obligations.[98]

The House of Lords debated Private Member's Bills on four occasions between 1976 and 1985/6. A Bill of Rights Bill introduced by Lord Wade received a Second Reading on 25 March 1976, but was not proceeded with until a Select Committee had taken evidence and reported to the House. The Committee set up in the following year under the chairmanship of Lord Allen of Abbeydale was instructed to consider two questions: whether such a Bill was desirable, and if so, what form it should take. On the first question there was no agreement, the Committee dividing six to five in favour, but on the second question there was unanimity that if there were to be such legislation, it should be based on the Convention.[99] Similar Bills, again introduced by Wade, were debated in the Lords in the sessions 1979/80 and 1980/1. Each progressed to Third Reading, but failed in the Commons. In 1985, the Human Rights and Fundamental Freedoms Bill, introduced by Lord Broxbourne also passed through the House of Lords, although opinion in debate was still divided. The Bill was opposed by the Government, and fared no better than the earlier attempts in the Commons.

---

[98] *Parl. Debates*, HL 467 (5th ser.), cols. 161–2, 10 Dec. 1985.
[99] House of Lords, *Report of the Select Committee on a Bill of Rights* (HL 176), HMSO, London, 1978.

There is a certain sensitivity shared by people of all parties and none, inside and outside Parliament, that the number of judgments against the United Kingdom in the Court of Human Rights is something of a national embarrassment. Nevertheless, it does not follow that Britain's record would necessarily be improved by incorporation. The statistical evidence of the number of cases in which the Court has held there had been a violation expressed as a percentage of the total number of cases brought against a government indicates that incorporation provides no safeguard against being arraigned before the Court at Strasbourg, nor being found to have violated an Article of the Convention which domestic courts have failed to remedy. On this basis, the following states where the Convention is enforceable in domestic law have a higher violation rate over the period 1959–92 than the United Kingdom (72.5%): Austria (76.9%), Belgium (81.8%), France (81.8%), Italy (91.6%), and the Netherlands (82.3%).[100] As the figures under each heading for France are exactly double those for Belgium, the percentage is the same.

Between its creation in January 1959 and the end of February 1992, the Court has had referred to it a total of 352 cases, of which the United Kingdom accounted for 46. With one of the earlier dates of acceptance of the right of individual application and the recognition of the compulsory jurisdiction of the Court (1966) the United Kingdom had, up to the end of 1990, more cases against it referred to the Court than any other signatory state. It has since been overtaken by Italy, which from the later starting date of 1973 took the lead with a total of ninety-five by the end of February 1992. The cause of the increase was a large number of cases alleging excessive delay in the Italian legal system which by 1991 had matured to the stage when they were ready to be brought before the Court. Next come Austria and France, each with thirty-two, Belgium with thirty, Sweden with twenty-seven, and Germany with twenty-four.[101] All had different starting dates. France, exceptionally, had accepted the right of individual application in 1974, but the compulsory jurisdiction of the Court only in 1981.

Of the forty-six cases, the United Kingdom was found to be in breach of the Convention in twenty-nine. In eleven cases the Court

[100] Extracted from information provided by the Foreign and Commonwealth Office, 30 Mar. 1992.
[101] Ibid.

found no violation, and six cases were pending. Of the eleven cases where the finding was that there had been no breach, the Commission had expressed an opinion at the preliminary stages that there had been a violation of the Convention in six cases. The Court, however, had taken a different view. Table 12 lists each of the cases by name, and shows into which category it fell. The year indicated in brackets is the date of the Court's judgment.[102]

Bearing in mind the extended sequence of ever narrower gates through which the applicant has to pass on his long trail to the Court, it is to be expected that it will be those with the strongest cases who complete the journey. At each stage the number of survivors dwindles: the first approach, registration, the decision on admissibility, the preparation of the Commission's report, the opinion of the Commission as to whether there has been a violation, and the reference to the Court. At the end of February 1992, out of the 352 cases referred to the Court judgment had been delivered in 267. Of these 267, the Court found a failure on the merits to comply with the Convention or an additional protocol in 207 cases. In 60 cases it found that no violation had occurred. Thus the overall proportion of adverse findings works out at 77.5%, or just over three to one—slightly higher than the British record which stands at 72.5%. On these figures there is no cause for embarrassment.

Throughout the debate on incorporation, each of the main political parties has adhered to the proposition that our traditional style of government differs from that which prevails on the continent of Europe. Whereas the experiences of the 1930s and after left most European countries wary about giving unfettered power to the executive, in Britain it is ministers answerable to Parliament, rather than judges, who are accustomed to have the final say on what the public interest requires. The general state of freedom, already referred to, is neither expressly enacted nor protected. The private citizen believes that he is entitled to do anything he likes which is not forbidden by law. The restrictions on his conduct, and the rights he has in respect of those restrictions, are set out in explicit statutes. The courts apply the statutes, but they can neither subject them to the style of interpretation allowed by the Court of Human

---

[102] Information provided by Directorate of Human Rights, Secretariat General, Council of Europe, 7 June 1991 and 8 Apr. 1992.

TABLE 12. *United Kingdom cases decided by the European Court of Human Rights: 1966–92*

Cases where the Court found no violation

1. Handyside (1976)
2. Ashingdane (1985)
3. James and others (1986)
4. Lithgow and others (1986)
5. Rees (1986)[a]
6. AGOSI (1986)[a]
7. Monnell and Morris (1987)[a]
8. Chappell (1989)
9. Powell and Rayner (1990)[a]
10. Cossey (1990)[a]
11. Vilvarajah and others (1991)[a]

Cases where the Court found a violation

1. Golder (1975)
2. Ireland *v.* the United Kingdom (interstate) (1978)
3. Tyrer (1978)
4. *Sunday Times* (1979)
5. Young, James and Webster (1981)
6. Dudgeon (1981)
7. X. *v.* United Kingdom (1981)
8. Campbell and Cosans (1982)
9. Silver and others (1983)
10. Campbell and Fell (1984)
11. Malone (1984)
12. Abdulaziz, Cabales and Balkandali (1985)
13. Gillow (1986)
14. Weeks (1987)
15. O. *v.* United Kingdom (1987)
16. H. *v.* United Kingdom (1987)
17. W. *v.* United Kingdom (1987)
18. B. *v.* United Kingdom (1987)
19. R. *v.* United Kingdom (1987)
20. Boyle and Rice (1988)
21. Brogan and others (1988)
22. Gaskin (1989)
23. Soering (1989)
24. Granger (1990)
25. McCallum (1990)
26. Thynne, Wilson and Gunnell (1990)
27. Fox, Campbell and Hartley (1991)
28. *Sunday Times* (No. 2) (1991)
29. *Observer* and *Guardian* (1991)

[a] Cases where the Commission expressed the preliminary opinion that a violation had occurred.

Rights, nor disregard the intentions of Parliament as stated in statutory form.

No shift towards entrenching general rights could be accomplished without limiting the powers of Parliament, substituting judicial for political decisions on matters of public policy. In opposing another Private Member's Bill, the Human Rights Bill introduced by Sir Edward Gardner in the House of Commons in 1987, the Solicitor General, Sir Patrick Mayhew, outlined the constitutional implications:

The judiciary must be seen to be impartial. More especially, as far as practicable it must be kept free from political controversy. We must take great care not to propel judges into the political arena. However, that is what we would do if we asked them to take policy decisions of a nature that we ought properly to take ourselves and which under our present constitution we do take. We would increase that danger if we required or permitted them to alter or even reverse decisions taken by Parliament. For a long time I have felt that herein lies the key to the general issue that we are debating ... Our constitutional history rather strongly shows that over the centuries the British people have preferred that these matters should be decided by people whom they can elect and sack rather than people immune from either process—wiser, less opportunist or even less venal than [sic] such people might well be considered to be.[103]

The danger of politicizing the judiciary can be taken a step further. There is a real possibility that incorporating the Convention into domestic law would put the judges onto a collision course with ministers and Parliament. Envisage a court finding that an action taken by a government department, in the proper exercise of statutory powers, was inconsistent with its interpretation of the requirements of an Article of the Convention. Consequently it concludes that a violation had occurred. The ability to grant redress to the applicant would be as limited as that of the Strasbourg Court. But whereas the Court of Human Rights can look to the Council of Ministers to ensure that the Treaty obligations of the member states are honoured in their capacity as contracting parties, how would an English court be able to get its way? If the necessary changes in policy or practice did not call for the repeal or amendment of a statute, they might be accepted voluntarily by ministers and those who advise them, although that could not be taken for

[103] *Parl. Debates*, HC, 109 (6th ser.), cols. 1267–70, 6 Feb. 1987.

granted. But where legislation was needed, and the Government was confident it could count on a majority in the House of Commons to support its view against that of the court, then the result could be the fate of so many endeavours to protect human rights: stalemate and non-implementation.

The doctrine of dynamic or 'evolutive' interpretation, as practised by the Court of Human Rights, permits a latitude not open to the English courts and has its rightful home in Strasbourg. Treating the Convention as a living instrument which should respond to society's changing needs is a notion more familiar in the United States with its different historic tradition. There it is the Supreme Court, and not the federal or state legislatures, which has concerned itself with capital punishment, abortion, telephone tapping, and compulsory sterilization for the subnormal, all of them issues to be settled by Parliament in Britain.

The indefensible outcome of conflicting, even contradictory, policies towards the death penalty in America was recounted in the previous chapter. In the case of *Soering*,[104] the Court of Human Rights held that if a young German national were to be extradited from the United Kingdom to the United States, and convicted of capital murder and sentenced to death, his detention probably for six to eight years while state and federal courts heard a series of appeals, designed to safeguard his constitutional rights, would amount to inhuman and degrading treatment contrary to Article 3 of the Convention. Thus the constitutional rights afforded to a person accused of a criminal offence carrying the death penalty in one jurisdiction clashed with the protection of human rights in another. The rationale for the Court's decision was that under certain conditions extradition by a member state might involve the responsibility of that state for the foreseeable ill-treatment which the extradited person was likely to suffer in the receiving non-member state. Whereas the primary purpose of Article 3 was to proscribe inhuman and degrading treatment by the agents of the member state, the obligation was so fundamental that it extended to the sending of an individual to a non-European destination where he faced a probable fate of prohibited ill-treatment. The very long period likely to be spent on 'death row', in conditions of extreme stress and mounting anguish awaiting execution, would

---

[104] *Soering* v. *United Kingdom* (1989) 11 EHRR 439.

expose him to a risk of ill-treatment going beyond the threshold set by Article 3.[105]

Following this judgment, the Government of the United Kingdom informed the United States authorities that Soering's extradition on a charge of capital murder, or any other offence the penalty for which might include the imposition of the death penalty, was refused. He would be surrendered only if there was an assurance that he would not be proceeded against on such a charge. The USA confirmed by diplomatic note that in the light of the applicable provisions of the Extradition Treaty 1972 US law would prohibit his prosecution in the State of Virginia for the offence of capital murder. Soering was subsequently extradited to the United States and the ruling of the Court of Human Rights implemented.

IX

The observance of the Human Rights Convention, by deed as well as by word, has been the most significant accomplishment of the Council of Europe to date. The rights and freedoms recognized by the Convention and protected by its institutions are listed in Table 13 at the end of this chapter. With a few later additions they reflect the priorities of national governments still recoiling from the horrors of Nazism and Fascism in the immediate post-war years. The primary objective, to curtail the arbitrary power of the state over the individual, has been faithfully reproduced in the judgments of the Court. The physical liberty and security of the individual citizen has been paramount throughout: the right not to be arrested without just cause, the right to a fair trial, and constraints on detention. Freedom of expression includes a free press and freedom of assembly. Some wider social rights were later included in a European Social Charter,[106] covering such matters as the right to work, the right to bargain collectively and to take strike action, the

[105] Ibid., at 478.

[106] The European Social Charter was signed at Turin in October 1961 and came into force in 1965. It is a Council of Europe instrument, and distinct from later proposals for a social charter which have emanated from the European Community. The text of the 1961 Charter is published as an Appendix to Robertson, *Human Rights in Europe*. With its additional protocol, the Charter sets out twenty-three fundamental social rights and principles which states can accept as aims of their social policy.

right to social security and medical assistance, and rights for migrant workers. But here the enforcement machinery was weak; depending upon appeals to member states to assume commitments to comply with the aims of the Charter, backed up by supervision and monitoring, *inter alia* by independent groups of experts.

Human rights are not a fixed quantity. The range is indefinite and the value placed on them varies according to who is seen as the oppressor, and the proximity of the danger. Campaigners for social and environmental rights today are not so concerned with the power of the state, arguing that the exercise of the rights that bear most directly on the daily lives of millions of people depend less on state interference with personal autonomy than with corporate invasions of personal liberties.[107] Yet watchful curtailment of governmental power is still an indispensable safeguard in any society. Litigation based and court-oriented as the Convention may seem, its inherent strength lies in the way a written code inherited from an earlier era has been interpreted and applied. As a direct result of the non-static jurisprudence of the Court, the content of such quintessentially latter-day policies as pre-trial detention, immigration, and extradition have been altered throughout the member states. The scale of the achievement has been masked by the undemonstrative proclivity of the Commission and Court to persuade the governments of member states to change their domestic legislation or administrative practice, rather than beat a drum loudly for the supremacy of the Convention and its institutions.

Genuine as the success is, and it has not been matched let alone surpassed anywhere else, the Convention is not beyond criticism; nor is it deeply rooted enough to be regarded as a permanency. Whether the current level of applications to the Commission, or judgments given by the Court, will be maintained or increased in the future, or whether a decline in authority and respect will set in, is likely to depend on three factors. First, the institutions of the Convention, lacking the connections which bind national systems of law to their constituent publics, must take care not to get out of touch with what is generally regarded as fair and reasonable in member states. This is a matter for instinct, experience, and good sense rather than formal rules. However distinguished the quality of its judgments, a Court that became isolated from public opinion

---

[107] See Stephen Sedley QC, *London Review of Books*, 19 Dec. 1991, pp. 3–5.

prevailing in the member states before long would lose its legitimacy and cease to see them implemented. That the Commission and Court are not blind to the danger was shown in the rejection of an ingenious attempt by two British applicants living near London Airport at Heathrow to have aircraft noise brought within the ambit of Article 8: the right to respect for private and family life, home, and correspondence.[108]

Next come certain unavoidable activities in which the modern state is engaged that do not sit easily with the public view of the Convention. Action to counter terrorism is the only sphere in which the British Government has entered derogations.[109] On the introduction of internment in Northern Ireland in 1971 notices of derogation were entered relating to the Emergency Provisions legislation as a whole. The notices were withdrawn in 1984. In 1987 the amended Emergency Provisions legislation[110] contained changes which were intended to bring the right of suspects into line with the Convention. These were:

1. a requirement introduced into the main Army arrest power, as well as for police and Army powers under the Acts to enter and search dwelling houses, so that they should be exercised only on the basis of 'reasonable suspicion', as Article 5(1)(c) of the Convention requires;

2. the grounds on which confessions in scheduled cases may be ruled inadmissible, which previously replicated Article 3 of the Convention, were expanded so that confessions are inadmissible where prima-facie evidence is adduced that the accused was subjected to torture, to inhuman or degrading treatment, or to any violence or threat of violence (whether or not amounting to torture), in order to induce him to make a statement;

---

[108] In its report adopted in January 1989 the Commission expressed the opinion that there had been a violation of Article 13 (the right to an effective domestic remedy) in relation to the claims under Article 8, but no violation of substantive rights. *Powell and Rayner* v. *The United Kingdom* (1990) 12 EHRR 288. In September 1989 the Court held that there had been no violation of Article 13 in respect of either applicant (ibid., at 355). The legal liability of aircraft operators for damage caused to third parties on the ground is limited by the Civil Aviation Act 1982, S. 76(1) which has the effect of conferring exemption from liability in nuisance for noise emanating from aircraft flying at a reasonable height and observing the relevant air navigation regulations, including those on noise certification.

[109] Permitted under Article 15 of the Convention.

[110] The Northern Ireland (Emergency Provisions) Act 1987 amended the Northern Ireland (Emergency Provisions) Act of 1978.

3. statutory rights were introduced for terrorist suspects to have access to a solicitor, and for a friend or relative to be informed of the suspect's arrest. The legislation also made provision for free legal aid for applicants for bail, as Article 6(3)(c) of the Convention specifies.[111]

The only current derogation by the UK Government arose out of the case of *Brogan* in 1988. This was defended by the Home Secretary in the House of Commons on the grounds that detention up to seven days was necessary to deal with those suspected of involvement in the commission, preparation, or instigation of acts of terrorism connected with the affairs of Northern Ireland. After the Court of Human Rights had delivered its judgment on 29 November 1988, the Government investigated the possibilities of adding a judicial element to the procedure for authorizing extensions to the initial period of forty-eight hours during which a person arrested on reasonable suspicion of being involved in acts of terrorism might be detained by the police. The attempt failed to find a way of reconciling the provisions of the Convention with the imperative of not weakening the effectiveness of the measures to contain terrorism. The Government pointed to the scale of the threat to the United Kingdom posed by organized terrorism connected with the affairs of Northern Ireland, which was not matched elsewhere in Europe. It also referred to the continued necessity for the power to hold suspected terrorists for up to seven days before being released, or charged, or excluded from part or all of the United Kingdom, to be reviewed annually by both Houses of Parliament.[112] The derogation is of indefinite duration for as long as circumstances require the continuation of the emergency provisions.

Controls on immigration,[113] exclusion orders,[114] and the rigorous

---

[111] Legislative changes summarized in a letter dated 10 Jan. 1991 from Lord Belstead, Paymaster General and Minister of State for Northern Ireland.

[112] *Parl. Debates*, HC, 160 (6th ser), cols. WA 209–10, 14 Nov. 1989.

[113] See *Abdulaziz, Cabales and Balkandali* v. *The United Kingdom* (1985) 7 EHRR 471 at 495. Although the right of a foreigner to enter or remain in a country was not as such guaranteed by the Convention, immigration controls had to be exercised consistently with Convention obligations.

[114] Since 1974 there has been power to exclude from the United Kingdom, Great Britain, or Northern Ireland named persons in order to prevent terrorist acts aimed at influencing policy or opinion concerning Northern Ireland. The current statute is

investigative procedures associated with them, sometimes leading to temporary detention or other restraints on liberty, are current manifestations of the power of the state over the individual which would have been unlikely to be in the minds of those visionaries who met at Strasbourg to draft the Convention in the late 1940s. Yet anti-terrorist legislation and restrictions on immigration are foreseeably two of the tests which will determine the future standing of the mechanism that has been so laboriously constructed for the legal protection of human rights in Europe.

The third factor is jurisdictional expansion and the possibility that it may bring dilution in its train. Freed from their dictatorial regimes, the states of Central and Eastern Europe, with Hungary, Czechoslovakia, and Poland in the vanguard, displayed an early enthusiasm to join what they saw as one of the most efficacious instances of European co-operation outside the economic sphere. The Convention is potentially open to those European states which have accepted, or are on the way to accepting, democratic principles and the rule of law.[115] The organs of the Convention stand ready to assist, if necessary within the framework of transitional arrangements, in bringing national institutions, laws, and practices into line with the contemporaneous, but by no means immutable, standards of the Convention. Hungary acceded to the Council of Europe on 6 November 1990; on the same day signing the Convention and its nine protocols. Ratification and acceptance of the right of individual petition (Article 25) and the Court's compulsory

---

the Prevention of Terrorism (Temporary Provisions) Act 1989. In 1989/90 sixteen exclusion orders were made in Great Britain against persons not previously excluded, a total comparable to that in each of the two previous years. There are no powers under the Act to exclude in connection with international terrorism, although persons detained on these grounds may be deported or removed from the United Kingdom under the Immigration Act 1971.

[115] These criteria are not defined, although Article 3 of the First Protocol requires the holding of free elections at reasonable intervals, conducted by secret ballot in conditions which will ensure the free expression of the opinion of the people in the choice of the legislature. As understood by the member states of the Council of Europe, the references to democracy and democratic societies which occur in the preamble to the Convention and its articles and protocols are taken to mean pluralist parliamentary democracies characterized by respect for those human rights and fundamental freedoms which are spelt out in the Convention. See H. Klebes, 'Human Rights and Parliamentary Democracy in the Parliamentary Assembly', in *Protecting Human Rights: The European Dimension—Studies in Honour of G. J. Wiarda*, ed. F. Matscher and H. Petzold, Carl Heymanns Verlag, Cologne, 1988, pp. 307–16.

jurisdiction (Article 46) followed two years later on 5 November 1992.

The Czech and Slovak Federated Republic came next, signing the Convention on 21 February 1991 and becoming a full member state of the Council of Europe. The Parliamentary Assembly had debated the question of admission in advance of the ministers' decision,[116] holding a session at which the Czechoslovak Prime Minister was questioned. A question, put twice, was whether the Republic would accept the optional Articles 25 and 46. This was side-stepped twice on the grounds that the Federal Assembly had not yet had an opportunity to debate the ratification of the Convention. On 18 March 1992 Czechoslovakia was the first of the ex-Communist states to ratify the Convention and accept the right of individual petition and the compulsory jurisdiction of the Court. Its membership terminated at the end of the year, when the Czech lands and Slovakia split into two separate republics[117]. Poland and Bulgaria have each joined the Council of Europe; Bulgaria ratifying and accepting the optional clauses on 7 September 1992, with Poland due to do the same in the course of 1993. Yugoslavia too had expressed keen interest before its statehood was destroyed by civil war.

The initial euphoria which accompanied the overthrow of communist rule in Central and Eastern Europe stimulated an aspiration towards participation in those political institutions of the West which had combined economic prosperity with a far higher degree of individual liberty and freedom than anything known in the Eastern bloc. Constitutional and economic reforms, based on the principles of free elections to representative assemblies and the development of market economies, were put in hand without delay. The democratic processes which have been established are fragile, while age-old conflicts over boundaries and minorities are already

---

[116] The power of decision to admit new members to the Council of Europe lies in the hands of the Committee of Ministers, having first sought the opinion of the Assembly. In the instances of Portugal after the overthrow of the military dictatorship in 1974, and Spain after the death of Franco in 1975, the Assembly was well aware that the emerging democracies were not yet 'perfect'. (Klebes, ibid., p. 311). Nevertheless, in the interests of 'benevolent encouragement', Portugal was admitted in 1976 and Spain in 1977. In the latter instance, it was the Assembly which took the initiative in recommending the Committee of Ministers to invite Spain forthwith to join the Council of Europe. Amongst existing members, political upheavals in Greece, Turkey, and Cyprus have given rise to periodic problems.

[117] Both the Czech and Slovak Republics applied for membership on 1 Jan. 1993.

re-emergent. The countries of the region lack strong democratic traditions[118] and it would be implausible to expect too much too soon. When reporting on an inquiry into *Central and Eastern Europe: Problems of the Post-Communist Era*, the House of Commons Foreign Affairs Committee warned:

It is far from certain that the people and new politicians of the region have truly understood the nature of a properly functioning democracy, and there is evidence that the attitudes of communism persist in the minds of many. There has been a tendency on the one hand to expect an automatic solution to the difficulties of creating a fully-functioning democratic system, and a failure to recognize that such systems are not so much created as grown over years. Political parties are often fragmenting as bigger groups split endlessly into smaller factions ... there has in many quarters been a failure to recognize that democracy is not simply a question of fighting through parliament for control of power, a struggle in which the winner takes all, but rather a method of discussion and debate through which problems can be attended to and resolved, and in which the needs and desires of different groups can be balanced and met.[119]

The same point was made by one of the most articulate of the new political leaders. Addressing the Heads of Government at Helsinki in one of his last international appearances as President of Czechoslovakia, Vaclav Havel said that the citizens of the new democratic regimes were not used to freedom and were confused:

They find it difficult to get used to being fully fledged citizens and to get rid of the bad habits which communism planted in them ... All the ancient conflicts, wrongs, injustices and animosities are suddenly coming back to life and back to mind.

There was an awareness of national identities repeatedly suppressed. It was understandable that this should breed fanaticism, xenophobia, and intolerance, as well as all kinds of demagogues, authoritarians, and populists to whom people, overcome by a deep feeling of uncertainty, were turning for salvation.[120]

In a prophetic passage of his final speech before the signature of

---

[118] The chequered history of their democratic traditions is outlined in a lively survey by Dr R. J. Crampton, printed as an Annex to the House of Commons Foreign Affairs Committee, *First Report*, Session 1991/2, (HC Paper 21-I), HMSO, London, 1992, pp. xlix–liv.

[119] Ibid., pp. ix–x.

[120] *The Times*, 10 July 1992.

TABLE 13. *Articles of the European Convention on Human Rights and Protocols Nos. 1 and 4*

Convention

Article 2	Right to life
Article 3	Freedom from torture or inhuman or degrading treatment or punishment
Article 4	Freedom from slavery, servitude, and forced labour
Article 5	Right to liberty and security of person
Article 6	Right to a fair hearing within a reasonable time by an independent and impartial tribunal established by law
Article 7	Freedom from retroactive criminal law
Article 8	Right to respect for private and family life, home, and correspondence
Article 9	Freedom of thought, conscience, and religion
Article 10	Freedom of expression
Article 11	Freedom of assembly and association
Article 12	Right to marry and found a family
Article 13	Right to an effective remedy before a national authority
Article 14	Freedom from discrimination
Article 15	Derogation
Article 25	Applications by persons, non-governmental organizations, or groups of individuals
Article 30	Report of the Commission in case of friendly settlement
Article 31	Report of the Commission 'if a solution is not reached'
Articles 38–41	Composition of the Court
Article 46	Compulsory jurisdiction of the Court

Protocol No. 1

Article 1	Protection of property
Article 2	Right to education
Article 3	Free elections

Protocol No. 4

Article 1	Freedom from imprisonment for debt
Article 2	Freedom of movement of persons
Article 3	Right to enter and remain in one's own country
Article 4	Freedom from collective expulsion

Source: European Commission of Human Rights, 1990.

the Convention in 1950, delivered to the Consultative Assembly of the Council of Europe, Maxwell Fyfe had described the Convention as 'a beacon to the peoples behind the Iron Curtain, and a passport for their return to the midst of the free countries'.[121] Forty years on, with the vision on the verge of becoming reality, some troublesome questions arise. If we accept that no functioning legal system worth the name can flourish without effective means of implementation, it follows that in the absence of any powers of coercion the maintenance of the Convention as a potent stimulus to improving conduct by governments and their servants will depend on the capacity of member states to enforce it. Will an enlarged membership lead to a diminution in enforceability, so altering the topography of a relatively confined judicial domain over which the existing institutions hold sway?

Will the desire to be good Europeans and good democrats in the Western liberal tradition survive when the going gets rough and what are perceived as the needs of the state collide with the rights of minorities or individuals? Would the newly liberated citizens of Eastern and Central Europe be better served in aiming at the creation of indigenous political cultures centred upon that ultimate sovereignty of the individual which has been constricted by governmental action in many Western states? Should such considerations modify or preclude the 'benevolent encouragement' of the proliferating applications[122] to subscribe to the Convention and join its institutions? Or does the West once again face a great historic challenge which demands a positive and idealistic response?

[121] Kilmuir, *Political Adventure*, p. 183.
[122] At 1 Jan. 1993 eleven applications were pending from: Albania, Croatia, Czech Rep., Estonia, Latvia, Lithuania, Romania, Russian Fedn., Slovak Rep., Slovenia, and Ukraine. Information from Directorate of Human Rights, Council of Europe, Strasbourg.

9

Culmination and Retreat: The Criminal Justice Act 1991

I

The Criminal Justice Bill published on 9 November 1990 held out greater promise than any of its predecessors in the cycle of criminal justice legislation since 1948. For the first time, after a long and painstaking period of gestation, Parliament was presented with what was intended to be a coherent statutory framework for sentencing, relating the severity of punishment to the seriousness of the offence. The opening clauses contained restrictions on the imposition of custodial sentences on adults and young offenders (Clause 1), and criteria for determining the length of custodial sentences (Clause 2). Although at the heart of the Bill, these provisions attracted relatively little Parliamentary debate, ministers being fearful that the legislation might be branded as an attempt to empty the prisons. As a result, more time and emphasis was devoted to explaining and amending the exceptions to the restrictions on custodial sentences than to the positive arguments for limiting the use of custody as a punishment. Much less was heard of the still nebulous concept of punishment in the community than when it had been first unveiled in the Green Paper in July 1988 and refined eighteen months later in the White Paper of February 1990.

Both the judicial and political omens were favourable. Despite some reservations about the way the sentencing provisions were expressed, there was no attempt by the higher judiciary to oppose or reject them on the grounds that their independence or prerogatives were being encroached. The discreet consultation with the judges, dating back to the first tentative approach by Whitelaw a decade earlier, paid the hoped for dividend. Politically, the Opposition parties, and the criminologists and penal practitioners to whom they looked for specialist advice, were generally well disposed. Speaking at Crime Concern's Annual Conference in London on 18 October, Roy Hattersley, the shadow Home Secretary, had welcomed the approach to increased non-custodial sentencing:

Whilst the rhetoric of punishment continues—for a variety of political reasons—the Government finally recognizes that sentencing policy must change. Therefore, although I anticipate a variety of differences of opinion over the detail, I am confident that the Labour Party will support the broad thrust of the forthcoming Criminal Justice Bill.[1]

The only substantial difference on sentencing between the main parties was the Government's unwillingness to accept the argument for a sentencing council or commission. The idea of a standing body wider in membership than the higher judiciary, although including senior judges, which would subject sentencing policy to review and from time to time issue guide-lines, had originated from academic study. Because of his consistent advocacy, directed at policy-makers as much as scholarly audiences, the proposal had come to be associated particularly with the name of Professor Andrew Ashworth.[2] As a platform speaker at a Labour Party conference on an alternative strategy for criminal justice on 12 December 1990,[3] and the author of a publication by the free market oriented Centre for Policy Studies,[4] Ashworth actively sought to influence opinion leaders in both the main parties inside and outside Parliament. Noting the paradox whereby prison was increasingly deplored and increasingly used, he argued that sentencing, the 'sheet anchor' of the criminal justice system, should be made more intelligible, clearer, and more consistent. His main conclusion was that

a small Sentencing Commission should be set up, with the principal

[1] *Safer Communities: Making Them Happen*, Report of a one-day conference organized by Crime Concern, London, 1990, pp. 48–9.
[2] See *Sentencing and Penal Policy*, Weidenfeld and Nicolson, London, 1983, pp. 447–51. A revised version, taking account of developments since the early 1980s, was published in 1992 under the title of *Sentencing and Criminal Justice*, Weidenfeld and Nicolson, London. The sentencing council proposal is reiterated at pp. 319–28.
[3] The conference was held at Church House, Westminster, and was opened by Roy Hattersley. Other speakers included Helen Reeves of Victim Support, Stephen Shaw of the Prison Reform Trust, and representatives of the National Association of Probation Officers and the Society of Black Lawyers.
[4] *Custody Reconsidered: Clarity and Consistency in Sentencing*, Centre for Policy Studies (Policy Study No. 104), London, 1989.

duties of defining sentencing aims and policies; and establishing sentencing guidelines for all categories of crime.

These guidelines might follow the example already set down by the Lord Chief Justice from time to time—but with the important difference that they would be systematic, designed to form a corpus to be consulted by every court in the land.

The Commission, which would be responsible to the Lord Chancellor, would include not only members of the judiciary but representatives from all parts of the criminal justice administration.[5]

As had happened before, with criminal injuries compensation in the 1960s and community service orders in the 1970s, the imminent prospect of legislation or governmental action focused attention on certain ideas which, although current for some time in the 'surrounding world of penal thought', were taken up by a broader spectrum of political opinion as being innovative and timely. The proposal for a sentencing council was the clearest example in 1990. A committee established by JUSTICE under the chairmanship of Lady Ralphs, a former chairman of the Magistrates' Association, added authoritative reinforcement, recommending

the creation of a Sentencing Commission with the task of drawing up these guidelines and then monitoring, evaluating and updating them. The composition of the Sentencing Commission should be broadly based and include senior members of the judiciary, other representatives from judges and magistrates (including some with experience of Juvenile Court work), the Probation Service, the Prison Service and other groups or individuals. These should include not only those involved in work with offenders but also members of the public. The Chairman of the Commission should be a senior member of the judiciary on secondment. The Commission should have a permanent secretariat which would be responsible for monitoring the operation of the guidelines, gathering statistical information, providing information to, and monitoring the opinions of, the public and educating sentencers to operate the guidelines system.[6]

The depth of support was shown when the organizations forming the Penal Affairs Consortium,[7] ranging from the Prison Governors' Association, the Prison Officers' Association, and the Association

[5] Ibid., p. 5.

[6] *Sentencing: A Way Ahead*, a Report by JUSTICE, London, 1989, p. 15.

[7] Thirteen organizations combined in February 1989 to issue a *Manifesto for Penal Reform*. The number grew and by the time the Consortium published a revised version of the Manifesto in March 1992 it had the support of twenty-four organizations.

of Chief Officers of Probation to the main reform groups: NACRO, the Howard League, the Prison Reform Trust, and JUSTICE, endorsed the projected sentencing commission or council, as did most of the informed press. The Labour Party's unqualified adoption of the proposal in its policy document on criminal justice[8] guaranteed that it would be pressed in Parliamentary debate on the Bill, but at the cost of politicizing the idea by diverting it into adversarial channels.

David Waddington moved the Second Reading of the Bill on the afternoon of Tuesday, 20 November. The House was thinly attended and increasingly restive as the debate went on. The reason lay not in the business under discussion, but in dramatic events outside the Chamber. Throughout the afternoon Conservative MPs were voting in the fateful first ballot for the leadership of the Conservative Party. The result, announced in the early evening, was that Margaret Thatcher had received 204 votes to Michael Heseltine's 152, with sixteen spoilt papers. The Prime Minister's majority was insufficient by only four votes to avoid a second ballot a week later. Yet the reality was that the number voting against was too large to enable her to remain as an effective leader, even if she were to win on the second ballot.

Two days later Mrs Thatcher withdrew, leaving the field open to John Major, Michael Heseltine, and Douglas Hurd. On 27 November the Conservative Party had a new leader and, when the Queen sent for Major the next day, Britain had a new Prime Minister. The immediate effect on the handling of the Criminal Justice Bill was more significant than the depleted attendance at its Parliamentary début. In constructing his administration, the Prime Minister translated Waddington to the Lords as Leader of the House, and switched Kenneth Baker from the chairmanship of the Party to the Home Office. Heseltine, back in the Cabinet for the first time since his resignation in January 1986, had been the Prime Minister's first choice as Home Secretary. He had no hesitation in refusing the offer, preferring a return to the Department of the Environment. Waddington's speech on Second Reading was thus not only his first, but his last, words on the Bill in the

---

[8] 'The Labour Party will establish a Sentencing Council to produce sentencing guidelines for a range of cases in an inter-related structure.' *A Safer Britain: Labour's White Paper on Criminal Justice*, The Labour Party, London, 1990, p. 14.

Commons. It was not a farewell as he was to play an active part in getting the Bill through the Lords.

The twenty-five ministerial appointments made to the Home Office during the Conservative administrations between 1979 and 1992 are listed in Table 14. It does not include the changes made by John Major following the General Election in April 1992.[9]

Baker brought to the Home Office a contrasting style to Waddington. Whereas Waddington, like so many lawyers before him, lacked the creative imagination and intuition to be a successful Home Secretary, Baker was nimble and skilled at presentation. He was departmentally experienced, having been Secretary of State for the Environment and for Education and Science, and a member of the Cabinet for five years. His tenure at the Department of the Environment and as Party Chairman at Conservative Central Office had been relatively brief earning him the reputation, perhaps unfairly since it is the Prime Minister who instigates Cabinet changes, of moving on and leaving problems behind for his successors to resolve.

The pattern of frequent ministerial moves, often for reasons unconnected with departmental performance, does nothing to foster the qualities of vision which are needed to develop policies and see them through to completion. It is more likely to breed short-sightedness, promoting agility at the cost of persistence. Unlike each of his three immediate predecessors: Brittan, Hurd, and Waddington, Baker had never served in the Home Office as a junior minister, and so was deprived of first-hand knowledge of the inveterate problems and sometimes idiosyncratic ways of one of the least fathomable of all Whitehall Departments. The combination of factors was to deny him a declared ambition to assume the mantle of a progressive penal reformer,[10] or indeed to prolong his stay at the Home Office beyond the General Election which followed less than nine months after the Criminal Justice Act reached the statute book on 25 July 1991.

---

[9] The new team was: Home Secretary, Kenneth Clarke; Ministers of State: Peter Lloyd (previously Parliamentary Under-Secretary), Michael Jack and Earl Ferrers; Parliamentary Under-Secretary: Charles Wardle.

[10] See an interview with the Home Affairs Correspondent of *The Times*, 8 Mar. 1991, and a Home Office *News Release* headed 'Baker Commits Government to penal reform', 18 July 1991.

TABLE 14. *Home Office: ministerial appointments, 1979–92*

Ministers	Dates
Secretaries of State	
William Whitelaw	May 1979–June 1983
Leon Brittan	June 1983–September 1985
Douglas Hurd	September 1985–October 1989
David Waddington	October 1989–November 1990
Kenneth Baker	November 1990–April 1992
Ministers of State	
Timothy Raison	May 1979–January 1983
Leon Brittan	May 1979–January 1981
Patrick Mayhew	January 1981–June 1983
David Waddington	June 1983–June 1987
Douglas Hurd	June 1983–September 1984
Lord Elton	September 1984–March 1985
Giles Shaw	September 1984–September 1986
Earl of Caithness	September 1986–January 1988
David Mellor	September 1986–June 1987
John Patten	June 1987–April 1992
Timothy Renton	June 1987–October 1989
Earl Ferrers	January 1988–
David Mellor	October 1989–July 1990
Angela Rumbold	July 1990–April 1992
Parliamentary Under-Secretaries	
Lord Belstead	May 1979–April 1982
Lord Elton	April 1982–September 1984
David Mellor	January 1983–September 1986
Lord Glenarthur	March 1985–September 1986
Douglas Hogg	September 1986–July 1989
Peter Lloyd	July 1989–April 1992

II

The concentration on sentencing made the Bill narrower than previous omnibus legislation on criminal justice. There were important changes apart from the sentencing powers of the courts: the reorganization of parole, children's evidence, the responsibilities of parents or guardians, the putting out to tender of court escorts and security, youth courts, and private sector management of remand prisons. On the powers of the courts, maximum penalties were to be reduced for certain offences when tried on indictment, from ten years to seven for theft, and from fourteen years to ten for non-domestic burglary. The maximum sentence for domestic burglary was to remain at fourteen years, reflecting the greater impact of intrusion on victims in their own homes.[11] Means-related fines, calculated in units, were to be introduced enabling magistrates to take account of the varying ability of offenders to pay, and to impose fines at levels which made equal demands on offenders with different means.[12]

Ministers insisted that community penalties should be 'rigorous and demanding',[13] with national standards of supervision being set for the Probation Service. For the first time, community service and probation could be combined in a single order. New curfew orders would be introduced, which could be enforced by electronic monitoring during curfew periods in appropriate cases. The Probation Service was to have an extended responsibility in implementing the requirement to prepare written pre-sentence reports for the courts,[14] as well as providing post-custody supervision of offenders released on licence and overseeing community penalties.

Most of these proposals had been well ventilated in advance via the series of Government publications listed in Chapter 5. Two

[11] M. Wasik and R. D. Taylor comment that the reduction in the maximum penalty for burglary, as for theft, is of symbolic rather than practical importance since very few sentences approach the maxima. They add that splitting the offence of burglary into two for sentencing purposes is an interesting example of the legislature endorsing what had already become well established as a 'two-tier' sentencing practice of the courts, with separate guide-lines for burglary of a dwelling house and of non-domestic premises. *Blackstone's Guide to the Criminal Justice Act 1991*, Blackstone Press, London, 1991, pp. 10–11.

[12] Under Section 18 of the Criminal Justice Act 1991 the system of unit fines applies only to the Magistrates' courts. It does not apply to fines imposed by the Crown Court following a conviction on indictment. Under Section 19 the Crown Court is bound to take into account the means of the offender 'so far as they appear or are known to the court'.

[13] See David Waddington's speech on Second Reading, *Parl. Debates*, HC, 181 (6th ser.), col. 141, 20 Nov. 1990.

[14] Section 3 of the Criminal Justice Act 1991 requires a court to obtain and consider a pre-sentence report when contemplating a custodial sentence under Section 1, unless the offence (or any other offence associated with it) is triable only on indictment. The reason for the exception is to avoid the need to call for a report in cases where, given the nature of the offence, custody is inevitable. See *Blackstone's Guide to the Criminal Justice Act 1991*, p. 22.

subjects in particular had been subjected to detailed scrutiny. The first was the operation of the parole system which had become overloaded with well over 20,000 cases each year being considered at two levels, local and national. Originally intended as a selective process, with recommendations being made to the Home Secretary on an individual case-by-case basis, various special categories had been created over the years which left the system vulnerable to simultaneous criticism from the judiciary and penal reformers, although seldom acting in concert. In 1983 a restricted policy had been brought in by Leon Brittan which meant that prisoners sentenced to more than five years for offences involving violence, sex, arson, or drug trafficking would be granted parole only when release under supervision for a few months before the end of their sentence was likely to reduce the long-term risk to the public, or in circumstances which were genuinely exceptional.

Coincidentally, a reduction in the minimum qualifying period, seen as a liberalizing measure, led to a parole rate averaging 75–80% for prisoners serving sentences of less than two years. What had been conceived as a privilege to be conferred selectively had become, in the eyes of the judiciary at least, a device dangerously close to automatic release in order to clear space in the prisons. Anomalies in the amount of time actually spent in custody by prisoners who had been sentenced to between nine and eighteen months further undermined the confidence of the judiciary in the operation of the parole system. A review committee under the chairmanship of Lord Carlisle of Bucklow was set up in 1987 and produced an impressive report in the following year.[15] The bulk of its recommendations were accepted and, with some modifications, formed the basis of the parole changes in the 1991 Act.

The second topic was the work of the advisory group under the chairmanship of Judge Pigot on the vexed issues raised by children's evidence in criminal proceedings, especially the implications of video recording, which had been left over from the 1988 Act.[16] The aim was to make it easier to bring prosecutions in cases of child abuse and to reduce stress on children as witnesses, whilst avoiding putting the defendants in such cases at an unfair disadvantage.[17]

[15] *The Parole System in England and Wales*, Report of the Review Committee (Cm. 532), HMSO, London, 1988.

[16] Home Office, *Report of the Advisory Group on Video Evidence*, 1989.

[17] *Blackstone's Guide to the Criminal Justice Act 1991*, pp. 4–5 and 121–36.

Other provisions emanated from within the Home Office, often after discussion, not always ending in agreement, with interested parties. Some policies had political overtones, most notably parental responsibility, the 'beefing up' of community penalties, and the contracting out of court escorts and prison establishments, each of which has been discussed in earlier chapters. Although the origins indicated should not be regarded as exclusive, Table 15 attributes the sources of the main sections of the Criminal Justice Act 1991. In several places, amendments made in the course of the Bill's passage through Parliament altered the original provisions.

TABLE 15. *Criminal Justice Act 1991: origins*

Section	Subject	Origin
1–4	Restrictions on custodial sentences	*Crime, Justice and Protecting the Public* (Cm. 965), ch. 3
5	Suspended and extended sentences	Carlisle Report; Cm. 965, paras. 3.17–3.22
6–16	Community sentences	Cm. 965, ch. 4
17	Increase of maximum fines	Departmental
18–22	Unit fines	Cm. 965, ch. 5
23	Periods of imprisonment for fine defaulters	Departmental
24	Deduction of fines from income support	Ministerial/departmental
25	Committals for sentence	Cm. 965, para. 3.15
26	Reduction of maximum penalties for theft and burglary; increase in others	As to theft and burglary, Cm. 965, para. 3.14; otherwise ministerial/departmental
27	Amendment of Mental Health Act 1983	Departmental
28	Mitigation and mentally disordered offenders	Departmental response to representations from judiciary
29	Effect of previous convictions	Departmental response to representations from judiciary
30–1	Supplemental	
32–51	Parole	Carlisle Report (with modifications)

TABLE 15. *Criminal Justice Act 1991: origins—continued*

Section	Subject	Origin
34	Duty to release life-sentence prisoners	European Court of Human Rights/House of Lords Select Committee
52–5	Children's evidence	Pigot Report (with modifications)
56–8	Responsibilities of parent or guardian	Ministerial/political
59–62	Detention of juveniles pending trial	Consultation paper on remand of alleged juvenile offenders (February 1991) in response to public opinion
63–5	Custodial sentences on young offenders	Cm. 965, paras. 8.28–8.29 (modified)
65–7	Supervision orders and attendance centre orders	Departmental
68–70	Juvenile courts (renamed youth courts) to have jurisdiction over 17-year-olds	Cm. 965, paras. 8.14–8.19 and 8.30
71–2	Miscellaneous	Departmental
73	Probation Inspectorate	*Supervision and Punishment in the Community: A Framework for Action* (Cm. 966), para. 6.4
74	Probation service: default power	Cm. 966, paras. 6.7–6.9
75	Inner London Probation Area	Amalgamation of City of London probation area with Inner London hinted at in Cm. 966, para. 5.11
76–83	Court security and prisoner escorts	Discussion paper on court escorts, custody, and security (July 1990)
84–8	Contracted-out prisons	Ministerial/political
89–92	Supplemental	
93	Cash limits for magistrates' courts	Ministerial/departmental

TABLE 15. *Criminal Justice Act 1991: origins—continued*

Section	Subject	Origin
94	Cash limits for the probation service	Cm. 966, para. 7.2
95	Secretary of State to publish information relevant to (*a*) financial implications of court decisions;	(*a*) Cm. 965, para. 2.21;
	(*b*) avoidance of racial or sex discrimination	(*b*) added in response to amendments seeking to impose an obligation not to discriminate on grounds of race or sex
96–102	Supplemental	

Only the item listed under Section 95, a statutory reminder to persons engaged in the administration of criminal justice of their duty to avoid discriminating on grounds of race or sex or on any other improper ground, could be attributed directly to the Labour Opposition, and even here the soil had been prepared as a result of Home Office contacts with representatives of ethnic minority communities. In the form enacted, the provision was a pale reflection of Labour's stated policy to tackle racism and discrimination against women offenders throughout the criminal justice system.[18] Drawing attention to this feature is not intended to belittle the diligent scrutiny and amendment of the Bill by Opposition MPs and peers during its passage through Parliament, but to contrast the gulf in the policy-making process that lies between Whitehall and Westminster. Similarly on the Conservative side, with the important exception of privatization, back-benchers in the Commons contributed more to fine-tuning than to nourishing the springs of policy.

By 1990 the Labour Party was making a conscious effort to change its image of being on the defensive on law and order issues, with the Tories making the running and gaining electoral advantage at Labour's expense. Barry Sheerman, a front-bench spokesman on

---

[18] 'We will ... take steps to eradicate the discrimination in sentencing policy which particularly affects women and ethnic minority offenders': *It's Time to Get Britain Working Again*, Labour's election manifesto, Apr. 1992, p. 20.

Home Affairs, had taken the lead in recruiting expert advisers in sympathy with the Party, as well as consulting widely with practitioners working in various parts of the criminal justice system. Ideas were voraciously sought and consumed; existing policies were systematically appraised by topic groups; a comprehensive crime prevention programme was drawn up; and greater priority urged for assisting victims of crime. A recurring theme was the economic and environmental conditions which can foster criminality, especially amongst younger and disaffected people. The result was a detailed policy document, titled *A Safer Britain: Labour's White Paper on Criminal Justice*, published by the Labour Party in January 1990. The sections dealing with sentencing reform, juvenile and young adult offenders, and prison reforms were summarized in a submission in September 1990 to Lord Justice Woolf's Inquiry into prison disturbances.

Party politics were never far from the surface. 'We are on the attack', Sheerman told an interviewer from the Prison Service:

... and getting opinion polls that suggest that we are ahead of the Conservative Party. In relation to 'Law and Order' there is a background which the Tories will find difficult to defend: crime has doubled since they have been in office. More importantly they have overseen a change in the country's value system, which affects crime. Mrs Thatcher said there was no such thing as society, no such thing as community, only individuals pursuing their own selfish self-interest. Now I think an increasing number of people would say that if we don't have a society, if we don't have a community, we won't control crime at all.[19]

A further publication in 1991[20] reprinted *A Safer Britain* and brought together a collection of papers on the causes of crime, youth crime, policing, reform of the Police and Criminal Evidence Act 1984, tackling racism in criminal justice, and drugs. When the time came the preparatory work, probably the most intense to be carried out by any political party for a decade, was the mainspring for Opposition speeches on the Bill. Briefing was carried out mainly by the Labour Campaign for Criminal Justice, supplanting in that role the longer established but more legalistically inclined Society of Labour Lawyers.

Many of Labour's proposals for legislation, such as statutory

[19] (1991) 84 *Prison Service Journal* 46.
[20] *Seven Steps to Justice: Proposals for Reforming the Criminal System.*

restrictions on the use of imprisonment for adults, means-related fines, some readjustment of maximum penalties, and ending the remand of juveniles to Prison Department establishments, were already either included in the Bill or consistent with Government policy. Hence the well-worn tactic, pressed into service for the debate on Second Reading, to concentrate hostile fire on the Bill's omissions rather than dwelling on the common ground between the parties. Despite Hattersley's earlier declaration of support the decision of Labour's business managers in the Commons was to vote against the motion to give the Bill a Second Reading.

A reasoned amendment was tabled declining to give a Second Reading to a Bill which failed to include measures to encourage crime prevention or to reduce the use of imprisonment for minor offenders; which ignored the scandal of remand prisoners; which contained neither a sentencing council nor a code of prison standards; and which made no provision for adequate examination of alleged miscarriages of justice. For these reasons, trenchantly deployed by Hattersley at the start of the debate, the Opposition front bench contended that the Bill would have little impact either on the efficiency of the courts or the unacceptably high prison population. After six and a half hours, punctuated by interruptions calling for the Leader of the House to come to the Chamber and make a statement about the Conservative leadership, the amendment was defeated by 350 votes to 190. The Liberal Democrats voted with the Government. Having been agreed without a further division, the Bill was then committed to a Standing Committee.[21]

Once away from the excitable atmosphere on the floor of the House the proceedings in the more intimate setting of Standing Committee A were generally harmonious. On all save the clauses on prisons and parole, John Patten was in charge for the Government, with Sheerman leading for the Opposition. The Committee had its first sitting on 29 November, and met twenty-four times with the final sitting on 7 February 1991; 208 amendments and 86 new clauses were proposed. Fifteen amendments were withdrawn after ministerial assurances had been given to consider the points raised in the hope of meeting them in whole or in part. Apart from the Government's own amendments, ministers accepted seven amendments, five of which were moved by the Government back-benchers.[22] Even when Patten could not go as far as committing the Government to further action, he was forthcoming in his response to points raised with the result that the Committee was usually conducted in a mood of good-natured debate and compromise. In addition to the proposal for a sentencing council, matters pressed by the Opposition included youth courts and hearings in them, local authority accommodation for juvenile remand prisoners, and ending the mandatory sentence for murder. Periodic frustration was vented by Opposition members who would have liked to raise other matters precluded by the scope of the Bill.

On 17 December the Bill was recommitted to the floor of the House to allow a number of new clauses on capital punishment to be debated. It was the fifteenth time the Commons had debated, and voted upon, the death penalty since its suspension in 1965. On each occasion the outcome had been the same: on a free vote the rejection by substantial majorities of attempts to reintroduce capital punishment as the penalty for murder or for particular categories of murder.[23] 'Why are we having another debate on capital punishment?' asked one of its proponents. His answer was:

We are having another debate because Parliament is the sounding board of the nation and because, if the public opinion polls are right, the nation is overwhelmingly in favour of the restoration of capital punishment. Those whom we represent are entitled to hear us discussing and debating the issue, giving our reasons for and against and taking the matter seriously because it goes to the heart of our fundamental security and stability that law and order should be preserved. We are taking the opportunity presented to us by the Criminal Justice Bill to suggest new provisions. That is why we are here.[24]

According to *British Social Attitudes* there had been no diminution, indeed a slight hardening, of public support for capital punishment between 1983 and 1989. While the straightforward question 'Are you in favour or against the death penalty for ... ' did not raise directly the prospect of its restoration, nevertheless the overall

---

[22] I am indebted to Dr M. R. Jack, Clerk to the Standing Committee, for these statistics. Letter dated 7 June 1991.

[23] Table 8 of *Responses to Crime*, vol. 1 (pp. 158–9) gives the results of all votes in the House of Commons on capital punishment between 1955 and 1987. Three more debates took place between 1987 and 1991; see Chapter 2 above, n. 158.

[24] Ivan Lawrence QC, *Parl. Debates*, HC, 183 (6th ser.), col. 58, 17 Dec. 1990.

picture was clear enough. In 1983, 74.2% of respondents were in favour and 21.0% against the death penalty for murder in the course of a terrorist act; 70.5% were in favour and 23.1% against the death penalty for the murder of a police officer, and 63.1% in favour and 32.9% against for other murders. In 1989 the comparable statistics were: for murder in the course of a terrorist act, 76.3% were in favour of the death penalty and 19.2% against; for murder of a police officer, 71.4% in favour and 23.4% against; and for other murders, 70.3% in favour and 25.8% against.[25]

The Commons debate started after Questions at 3.30 p.m. and continued until 10.00 p.m. when the House divided on four of the new clauses. These were: to restore the death penalty for the murder of a police officer acting in the execution of his duty (*defeated* 215 : 350); to restore the death penalty for murder when the offender was aged eighteen or above, subject to a power of the Court of Appeal to substitute life imprisonment if the circumstances warranted (*defeated* 182 : 367); the substitution of life imprisonment in place of the death penalty for offences under the Treason Acts of 1790 and 1814 and the Piracy Act 1837 (*defeated* 257 : 289), and to restore the death penalty for persons aged eighteen or above for murder committed by means of firearms, explosives, or an offensive weapon, or the murder of a police or prison officer, unless the court determines that the circumstances of the case make the penalty of life imprisonment more appropriate (*defeated* 186 : 349).

Baker survived his first test as Home Secretary well. In a long speech lasting for nearly an hour he reviewed the incidence of homicide before and after abolition, drawing on the experience of other jurisdictions in advising the Commons that the evidence on capital punishment as a deterrent was 'far from conclusive'.[26] He referred to the lengthy time spent awaiting reprieve or execution by convicted offenders sentenced to death for murder in the United States, quoting an average of close to eight years, and the possibility of a miscarriage of justice resulting in an innocent person being hanged. Hattersley followed from the Opposition front bench, congratulating Baker on a persuasive and lucid speech. At the end of the debate, released from adversarial politics by the free vote, the Home Secretary and his Shadow voted against the clauses

[25] Social and Community Planning Research, *British Social Attitudes Cumulative Sourcebook*, Gower, Aldershot, 1992, Table B-2.
[26] Op. cit. n. 24 above, col. 46.

which would have reintroduced capital punishment as a penalty for murder. The Prime Minister, Hurd, and Heseltine did the same. Waddington had gone to the Lords, but Mrs Thatcher was present, voting for the restorationist clauses in company with Norman Tebbit, Michael Howard, Angela Rumbold, and a largely Conservative minority.[27]

It is the disproportionate party balance within the total numbers voting for and against restoration, as well as their own experience in the constituencies, that makes Conservative ministers so uneasy in their approach towards any aspect of policy relating to murder. Having had to undergo the unavoidable set-piece debate on the death penalty, albeit a replay of those that had gone before, ministers showed a marked reluctance to consider the merits of any other amendments, notably those on the mandatory penalty of life imprisonment, which might stoke the fires once again. But that obstacle lay ahead.

III

Unlike capital punishment, the next controversy was resolved on party lines. The hesitant first steps towards the contracting of certain court services and experimentation with a privately operated remand centre have been related in Chapter 6. As published, the Bill contained powers to enable the contracting out of court security and prisoner escorts as well as of the operation of remand centres. Clauses 65–8 were clearly headed 'Remand Centres', and the power to contract out was limited to any prison which was established after the commencement of the resulting Act 'for the confinement of remand prisoners' (clause 65). The remaining clauses dealt with staffing. Instead of a governor, each contracted out prison would have a director, who would be a 'prisoner custody officer' specially approved by the Secretary of State, and a controller, who would be a Crown Servant directly appointed by and answerable to the Secretary of State. The powers and duties of the staff, to be known as prisoner custody officers, were defined, and the necessary modifications made to the Prison Act 1952. There was no mention of prisons for sentenced offenders, nor of existing remand centres.

[27] Ibid., cols. 112–28.

Before long it became apparent that not all of the reins of policy were in the hands of the officials charged by the Home Secretary to brief the draftsman and see the legislation through. On the privatization issue a sub-plot existed, to which at least one Home Office junior minister was sympathetic, and which only came to light as the Bill progressed.

The first of the privatization clauses, dealing with court security officers, was reached in Standing Committee on the morning of the seventeenth sitting on 29 January 1991. From then until the conclusion of the twenty-first sitting on 5 February, the Committee was preoccupied with contracting out. The crucial moment came on 31 January when Angela Rumbold, the Minister of State with responsibility for the Prison Department, replied to a series of amendments tabled by a Conservative back-bencher and former policeman, John Greenway, who had visited the United States with the Select Committee. The effect of Greenway's amendments was to extend the power to contract out to any prison, existing as well as new, whether holding remand or sentenced prisoners. Mrs Rumbold seemed ill at ease with her departmental brief, rehearsing arguments against the amendments, but with little conviction. In the course of the debate she agreed to consider their implication before the next stage. Her next undertaking was reported differently in Hansard and *The Times*. The *Official Report*, which is corrected by ministers' Private Secretaries, read:

I do not want to reject out of hand the possibility at some time in the future of considering contracting some prison services to the private sector.[28]

The Times version, omitting any reference to the possibility of consideration 'at some time in the future', was:

I do not wish to reject out of hand the concept that it could be possible . . . to consider contracting out some of the services of existing prisons.[29]

Later, when pressed by Greenway to say whether she accepted that the private sector could be involved in the prison service and not just the remand prison service, Mrs Rumbold replied:

I said that I was willing to think about it further. It would be unreasonable

[28] *Parl. Debates*, (HC), SC (1990–1), 19, col. 578, 31 Jan. 1991.
[29] *The Times*, 1 Feb. 1991.

to do otherwise. I am happy to give my hon. Friend an assurance to that extent.[30]

Facing allegations from Opposition members of collusion with the Government, Greenway insisted that he was acting on his own account. His amendments nevertheless carried unusual authority, being signed by Sir John Wheeler, the Conservative Chairman of the Select Committee on Home Affairs, even though he was not a member of the Standing Committee on the Bill. In the light of the ministerial assurance of further consideration, the amendments were not pressed to a division and were withdrawn.

A Minister of State at the Home Office since David Mellor's move to the Office of Arts and Libraries in July 1990, Angela Rumbold was a member of the No Turning Back group of Conservative MPs who believed unquestioningly in Margaret Thatcher and all that she stood for. In the account of one well-informed insider[31] this group alone had campaigned energetically for Mrs Thatcher in the days before the fatal ballot on 20 November. There was no doubt that Mrs Rumbold was a 'true believer' in the cast of those who had been placed strategically in the key departments to prevent backsliding. Ideologically she was more Thatcherite in outlook than Patten or either of her predecessors, David Mellor and Douglas Hogg.[32] It was the departmental responsibilities for the prisons which she inherited from Mellor, however, rather than any differences of opinion in the ministerial team, that led to Mrs Rumbold answering for the Government on the one part of the Bill in which party dogma was conspicuously evident.

The interest of the Prime Minister's Policy Unit at 10 Downing Street was mentioned in Chapter 6. As the preparatory work on the Bill progressed, the Unit kept a close eye on the proposals for contracting out prisons, on which it believed the Home Office blew hot or cold depending on functional considerations, principally the fluctuating size of the prison population. When Mrs Thatcher took a hand in the summer of 1990 to reinstate in the draft Bill a power to allow privately operated remand centres she did so because of her conviction of the need for radical reform outside the prevailing

[30] *Parl. Debates*, (HC), SC (1990–1), 19, col. 579, 31 Jan. 1991.
[31] Nicholas Ridley, *'My Style of Government': The Thatcher Years*, Hutchinson, London, 1991, p. 242.
[32] Both Mellor and Hogg had voted in the same lobby as Baker against the amendments to reintroduce capital punishment on 17 Dec. 1990.

consensus; not for any reasons of penological principle or administrative practice.

The Bill returned at Report stage to the floor of the Commons later in the month for further debate. On the evening of 25 February, the same day as the Home Secretary had made a statement on the publication of the report by Lord Justice Woolf and Judge Tumim on their inquiry into the causes of the disturbances at Strangeways and other prisons in April 1990, a new set of amendments on privatization was reached. Once again moved by Greenway from the back benches, the amendments were almost certain to become part of the Act with the Whips taking their lead from the Government. This fact, as well as the technically convoluted approach, pointed unmistakably to the amendments having been drafted by Parliamentary counsel and handed to Greenway by the minister to put down in his own name. The practice is quite common, but in this instance the suspicions of the Opposition were aroused and their spokesmen were determined to 'flush out the Government's true intentions'[33] because of what they regarded as the minister's equivocation in Committee.

The draftsman's device was to retain the wording of the original clause (with some rearrangement), but to enable the Secretary of State to make an order by statutory instrument giving effect to the power to contract out, omitting either the limitation to prisons established after the commencement of the Section, or the restriction to establishments for remand prisoners, or both. Any such order would be subject to the affirmative resolution procedure in each House of Parliament. For the Opposition, Sheerman condemned privatization as the part of the Bill to which it objected most strongly, adding:

'I am sure that no hon. Member fails to understand the reasons for our objection. We believe that pressure is being exerted by certain elements in the Conservative Party to push the Bill in an even more radically rightward direction.'[34]

A Labour back-bencher said that he was appalled by the idea of prisons as an industry, with the state delegating its responsibility for punishment to the private sector and prisons being run for profit. He feared that a private prison system would be largely

[33] *Parl. Debates*, HC, 186 (6th ser.), col. 713, 25 Feb. 1991.
[34] Ibid., col. 708.

unaccountable and would fail to deliver the benefits held out by its proponents. The private sector was ill-equipped to manage and staff prisons. Bidding for contracts would mean good companies being driven down to the lower levels of their competitors. Staff salaries and staff training would suffer.[35] His vehement speech encapsulated the reasons why privatization was anathema to the Labour Opposition.

A Liberal Democrat spokesman argued that both the clause and the amendments were inconsistent with the purposes of the Woolf Report, and that their acceptance by the Government would be seen as pre-empting the Woolf recommendations, indeed 'thumbing their nose' at them.[36] At the end of the debate, Mrs Rumbold replied.[37] She rejected any incompatibility with the Woolf recommendations, saying that she did not see why private remand centres, which might use different methods but would have the same aims, could not operate successfully. The minister interpreted the amendments as meaning no more than if it was proved that remand prisons could be effectively managed by the private sector, the Government, having carefully considered the implications and ramifications, might extend the proposal to, for example, a young offenders' institution. It was, she said, a reasonable proposition. In advising the House to accept the amendment, Mrs Rumbold ended her speech with this statement of intent:

The Government are taking the first step in considering contracting out a remand prison. We believe that this opportunity will not arise easily again ... If, and only if, the contracted out remand centre proves a success might we move towards privatization of other parts of the prison service.[38]

The Opposition divided against the first amendment which was carried by 258 votes to 174. Three consequential amendments were accepted without further divisions.

Hurd was in the chamber for part of the debate, and voted with Baker and the other Home Office ministers in the Aye lobby. As he did so memories of a speech he had made from the same Dispatch Box two and a half years before may have been in his mind:

[35] Bruce George, ibid., col. 716–17.
[36] Robert Maclennan, ibid., cols. 717–18.
[37] Ibid., cols. 718–20.
[38] Ibid., col. 720.

I do not think that there is a case, and I do not believe that the House would accept a case, for auctioning or privatising the prisons or handing over the business of keeping prisoners safe to anyone other than Government servants.[39]

Mrs Rumbold's words were overtaken by events even more rapidly than Hurd's had been. In December of the same year, by way of a low-key reply to a prearranged Parliamentary Question for Written Answer in the name of Sir John Wheeler, Baker unexpectedly announced that tenders would be invited for the management of a new establishment which was under construction near Redditch in Hereford and Worcester.[40] HM Prison Blakenhurst had been designed as a large local prison holding both remand and convicted prisoners, not including high-security prisoners. Invitations to tender were expected to be issued in February 1992. The contracting out of the management of the prison would require the consent of Parliament since, although new, it would not be confined to remand prisoners.

Commenting on the proposal for Blakenhurst, Baker said:

The recent experiment to involve the private sector in the prison system has demonstrated that they have much to offer.

Although Group 4 won the contract, a number of exciting proposals were submitted which revealed a clear understanding of the problems to be addressed and some imaginative solutions.

They also showed that tenderers had fully appreciated the difficult task of operating a prison establishment securely, efficiently and humanely. In the light of this experience I am sure we should extend the involvement of the private sector by inviting tenders for the management of a prison holding convicted prisoners.

Work has therefore been put in hand to prepare for contracting out the management of Blakenhurst prison, subject to satisfactory tenders and the agreement of Parliament.

The tender documents will again set very high standards in terms of security and the regime at the prison. But I am confident that the private sector will rise to the challenge.[41]

On 10 December I wrote to the Home Secretary saying that in view of the statements made by Government spokesmen during the passage of the Criminal Justice Bill, it was surprising for such a

---

[39] *Parl. Debates*, HC, 119 (6th ser.), col. 1303, 16 July 1987.
[40] *Parl. Debates*, HC, 200 (6th ser.), cols. WA 219–20, 5 Dec. 1991.
[41] HM Prison Service, *News Release*, 5 Dec. 1991.

development to come so soon. As recently as 1990 I had been urging on Waddington and Mellor the case for the private management of remand centres to make a clearer distinction between pre-trial detention and the punishment of convicted offenders. At that time there had been considerable scepticism in the Home Office, although in the event, as described in Chapter 6, a power to contract out new remand prisons had been included in the original Bill. I questioned the wisdom of going ahead immediately with contracting out a local prison designed to hold convicted as well as remand prisoners. One consequence would surely be to perpetuate on a new site the current policy of holding remand and convicted prisoners in the same establishment, and subject to many of the same restrictions.

On 16 January 1992 Baker replied:

HOME SECRETARY   QUEEN ANNE'S GATE LONDON SW1H 9AT
Dear David,

Thank you for your letter of 10 December 1991 about my intention to extend contracting out to prison establishments other than those holding only remand prisoners.

As you are aware, I have decided to seek the agreement of Parliament to the contracting out of the management of HM Prison Blakenhurst, a local prison, currently under construction near Redditch in Hereford and Worcester. I hope to lay an order before the House in the Spring. The capacity of the prison, due to open early in 1993, will be 649. It will provide a further opportunity for private sector companies to offer high quality, secure regimes at a price which offers value for money.

Blakenhurst was designed as a local prison to provide relief to Birmingham, Gloucester and Shrewsbury prisons, which are all overcrowded. Our aim, as the recent White Paper, Custody, Care and Justice, explained is to create separate units for remand prisoners, but this will be a long term programme. It would of course have been possible to give Blakenhurst in its entirety a remand function, but in order to use all its accommodation the establishment's catchment area would have had to be very large indeed involving long journey times to and from court.

I believe that it is right to extend contracting out to another type of prison. The successful tendering exercise for Wolds remand prison showed that it is not too early to plan for the next development in contracting out. The exercise suggested that the private sector had much to offer and a number of the tenderers' submissions showed that they were capable of undertaking the task of operating a prison establishment securely, efficiently and humanely.

As I have already said, whilst the long term aim of separate accommodation for remand prisoners is one to which the Government subscribes, I cannot agree that it would be appropriate to limit private sector involvement to remand prisoners. The Wolds tendering exercise has demonstrated how much the private sector has to offer, and I believe that contracting out is an important initiative which will allow the Prison Service to work alongside the private sector and gain experience in new ways of tackling this important task. Restricting this initiative to prison establishments holding only remand prisoners would restrict what the Prison service can learn from it.

I hope that what I have said will help to reassure you that it is not too soon to press ahead with the contracting out initiative in order to maintain its momentum.

Yours ever
Kenneth

Maintaining the momentum was hardly an adequate explanation for what was in effect a significant change in policy, and one which seemed to have been launched in advance of the necessary Parliamentary approval to extend the power to contract out. In agreeing to the enlargement of the Bill by adding such a potentially wide power to what was initially a clause with limited scope, Parliament had been left with the clear impression that ministers would not be returning with proposals for its extension until the experiment with the first contracted out remand prison at Wolds had been thoroughly assessed. To claim that the tendering exercise had been a success in showing how much the private sector had to offer fell well short of fulfilling the undertaking to evaluate the actual experience of private sector management in practice. Home Secretaries should know, from another part of their domain at the time, the allocation of broadcasting franchises, the gap that can open between promise and performance.

Because of the uncertainties created by the anticipation of a General Election, invitations to tender were delayed until after the election had taken place in April 1992. Had Labour won, there would have been no question of any extension of privatization, and the future of Wolds would have been in the balance. As it was, the new Home Secretary, Kenneth Clarke, announced on 15 June that work on the operational specification for Blakenhurst had been completed and issued to potential contractors an invitation to tender. The necessary Parliamentary authority was obtained, after sharply critical debates in both Houses, on 6–7 July.[42]

As in the earlier stages of privatization, pragmatism reigned supreme. Since a newly constructed prison nearing completion was too large for remand purposes only, a decision was taken to fill up the rest of the space with sentenced prisoners. Little weight seems to have been given to the distinction of principle between the two categories, and it was frankly admitted by ministers in private that the relationship between the Prison Service and the contract prisons had not yet been thought out. Carried away by the heady new wine, the Home Office, typically so cautious and thorough in the assessment of any radical departures, had laid itself open to the charge of acting first and thinking afterwards.

IV

The peculiarity of the composition of the House of Lords permits the independent judiciary at its highest level: the Lords of Appeal, the Lord Chief Justice and the Master of the Rolls, to participate in the legislative process. Owing to their judicial commitments the Law Lords are unable to speak in general debates with any regularity, indeed it would be unwise for them to do so too freely. By convention, they sit on the cross-benches and take no party whip. Yet they are not in any sense supernumerary. On the contrary, the Palace of Westminster is the working habitat of the Lords of Appeal in Ordinary. The Appellate Committee sits in public in a Committee Room at the Lords; judgments are given in the Chamber at times when there is no Parliamentary business; the legal Library is a key resource; as are the rooms occupied by the Law Lords and their staff. Like the Bishops, they are full and valued members of the Upper House, standing apart from party politics, but contributing from their expertise to the business of law-making.

[42] The Commons approved the Criminal Justice Act 1991 (Contracted Out Prisons) Order 1992 by 251 votes to 200 in a division shortly before midnight on 6 July. *Parl. Debates*, HC, 211 (6th ser.), cols. 141–4, 6 July 1992. Following its normal practice of not opposing statutory instruments, the Lords approved the Order the following day, even though all speakers save the Minister of State, Earl Ferrers, were critical of the Government's handling of the issue. *Parl. Debates*, HL, 538 (5th ser.), cols. 1094–1109, 7 July 1992.

Whenever criminal justice legislation comes before the House, one or two of the Law Lords, and sometimes the Lord Chief Justice (who is based at the Law Courts in the Strand), will attend and speak, especially on matters of sentencing and the powers of the courts to deal with offenders. Their presence may appear to be a constitutional anachronism, but it adds greatly to the authority and independence from government of a Parliamentary assembly whose legitimacy does not depend on the method of its composition.

Several of the most important of the Criminal Justice Bill's provisions broke no new ground in the Lords. The restrictions on imposing custodial sentences contained in the first clause, for instance, were in direct line of descent from the statutory criteria limiting the use of imprisonment for young offenders under the age of twenty-one which stemmed from an amendment carried against the Government's wishes in the Lords in the course of the legislation enacted as the Criminal Justice Act 1982. The Lords had also debated at length the endorsement and extension of the criteria needed to justify imposing a sentence of imprisonment on young offenders, and the other sentencing provisions contained in the 1987/8 legislation. The idea of a sentencing council had been advanced then, but had not found favour. In the 1987 debates the outright opposition of Lord Lane CJ had been put on record:

I would suggest it is quite wrong that matters of sentencing should be taken out of the hands of Parliament which sets out the basis in law of sentencing and of the judges whose task it is to interpret those laws. It is quite wrong that such matters should be given to this sort of hybrid body [a Sentencing Council] to determine. It is neither a parliamentary body nor a judicial body. The members are apparently answerable to no-one. The fact that I am apparently to have the doubtful privilege of presiding over the body's deliberations does not seem to me a sufficient attraction. It is introducing a concept into the law which creates a very dangerous precedent for the future. It is removing a large portion of the independence of the judiciary and putting in its place something of which it is very difficult to see the end.[43]

Leading for the Opposition when the 1991 Bill reached the Lords

---

[43] *Parl. Debates*, HL, 489 (5th ser.) col. 327, 26 Oct. 1987.

at Second Reading on 12 March, Lord Richard,[44] while welcoming much of its content and aims, said that his party none the less regarded it as a missed opportunity. The criteria for sentencing were to be reformed, but without a sentencing council to help promulgate and guide them. The parole provisions were to be changed, but in a way that might increase the prison population. Proposals which he could only describe as doctrinaire—curfews and tagging, parental responsibility, and prison privatization— marred what could have been 'a good, and indeed, admirable Bill'.[45] A few others spoke up for a sentencing council, amongst them the veteran penal reformer, Lord Longford, who contended that it was the only way to encourage judges to pass less severe sentences.[46] But it was not strongly argued, perhaps because its advocates were saving their powder for an amendment at Committee Stage. The most vigorous statement came from a Lord of Appeal in Ordinary, Lord Ackner, who rejected the proposal out of hand. His dismissiveness was echoed by the Minister of State, Earl Ferrers,[47] when winding up for the Government:

As the noble and learned Lord, Lord Ackner, blasts out of the water everyone who has a contrary view to him, I do not think it necessary to reply to that business about the sentencing council. We take the view that sentencing councils would not be a proper way to do this, not least because it would involve a regimented system of sentencing; whereas what we propose under the Bill is a continuation of a system whereby the Court of Appeal gives guidance.[48]

With this unpromising prelude, the first amendment to be debated in Committee on 26 March was a new clause providing for a sentencing council 'to consider and review sentencing policy and from time to time to issue guidelines in respect thereof'. Its membership would be essentially judicial, comprising the Lord Chief Justice and not less than four judges of the Court of Appeal,

---

[44] As Ivor Richard MP, Parliamentary Under-Secretary of State (Army), Ministry of Defence, 1969–70. QC, 1971; UK Permanent Representative to the United Nations, 1974–9; Member of the Commission of the EEC, 1981–4. Life peer, 1990. Leader of the Opposition, House of Lords, 1992– .

[45] *Parl. Debates*, HL, 527 (5th ser.), cols. 79–80, 12 Mar. 1991.

[46] Ibid., col. 115.

[47] Parliamentary Secretary, 1974, Minister of State, 1979–83: Ministry of Agriculture, Fisheries, and Food. Deputy Leader of the House of Lords, 1979–83, and 1988– . Minister of State, Home Office, 1988– .

[48] *Parl. Debates*, HL, 527, col. 167.

supplemented by specialist advisers with experience of the prison
and probation services, the after-care of discharged prisoners, and
the study of the causes of delinquency or the treatment of offenders.
The amendment attracted cross-party, but not all-party, support,
being tabled in the names of Lords Richard and Mishcon for the
Labour Opposition and Lords Hunt and Hutchinson of Lullington
for the Liberal Democrats. Each of them spoke in the debate,
pointing out the inadequacies of the current situation and arguing
in favour of a mechanism to bring about greater consistency in
sentencing. Neither Lane nor any current Lord of Appeal took
part in the debate or voted. From the Government benches, Lord
Hailsham added his weight against creating what he believed would
be a new quango: 'It will provide not the fifth wheel of the coach
but probably the sixth or seventh, and will create greater confusion
than the status quo.'[49] Despite the keen interest of the penal
reform groups and much of the quality press, reinforced by the
Parliamentary support of the two main Opposition parties, the
amendment never took fire and was defeated with a comfortable
majority for the Government of 91 votes for and 152 against. An
analysis of the voting shows that only one Conservative peer
supported the amendment, with the cross-benchers divided for and
against.

V

The failure of the sentencing council to make any headway in either
House reflected its lack of all-party appeal, especially on the
Conservative side, and the hostility of the higher judiciary. Neither
of these factors were present in what was to become the major
confrontation with the Government on the Bill, one that had been
rehearsed, although without success, in the Commons before the
Bill arrived in the Lords.

The mandatory penalty of life imprisonment for murder, and the
defects of the procedures which had grown up around it, had been
raised in the Lords during the 1987–8 legislation. Chapter 7 traced
the tortuous way in which the life sentence had evolved and the
setting up of the Select Committee on Murder and Life Impris-

---

[49] Ibid., col. 968.

onment by the House of Lords in 1988. When the Select Committee's report was published Home Office officials working on the
preparation of the Bill were ready to look into the implication of
its recommendations, especially in the light of the possible outcome
of the cases before the European Court of Human Rights, and to
advise ministers accordingly. Before starting to put pen to paper
they found there was no leeway at all. Alternative policies for life-
sentence prisoners were never given serious consideration since
ministers were convinced that public opinion was not willing to
accept any change, and that was that. As a consequence of political
decisions, therefore, two of the most important criminal justice
issues, the penalty for murder and the privatization of the prisons,
were never subjected to the full pre-legislative process of assessment
and consultation that characterized the remainder of the Bill.

The omission of any provisions relating to the penalty for murder
and life imprisonment was strongly criticized by peers who had
served on the Select Committee, and by the most influential of all
the witnesses who had appeared before them, the Lord Chief Justice.
On Second Reading, Lane expressed his 'great disappointment' that
all the work put in by the Select Committee seemed not to have
been reflected in any way in the Bill before the House. He went on
to state unequivocally that the mandatory life sentence for murder
was no longer necessary. It was in this speech that Lane made the
remarkable confession that he had only himself to blame for
accepting an invitation from the then Home Secretary, Leon Brittan,
to take part in the tariff-setting exercise 'not realizing the full
import and implications of what it was that I was agreeing to do'.[50]

The plan for the attempt to force the Government to change its
unyielding stance was carefully drawn up. The membership of the
Select Committee constituted an all-party nucleus, with Ackner as
the link with the higher judiciary in England and Wales, and Lord
Morton of Shuna, a Senator of the College of Justice in Scotland,
performing a similar function North of the Border. Close contact
was maintained with the Parliamentary All Party Penal Affairs
Group (PAPPAG) and, through its clerk, Paul Cavadino, with

---

[50] Ibid., cols. 99–100. During the Committee Stage, Lane disclosed that his
task of reviewing mandatory and discretionary life-sentence cases involved the
consideration of between three and four hundred cases a year. He knew that many
judges agreed with him in feeling 'most unhappy' about the way the system operated
behind closed doors. Col. 1596.

NACRO. The two organizations worked together in supplying a comprehensive service of briefing and draft amendments for interested MPs and peers on all aspects of the Bill throughout its passage in both Houses. They also made sure that the press and broadcast media were kept abreast of developments and aware of their significance. By agreement with PAPPAG, the drafting and briefing on the life-sentence amendments was done by JUSTICE, which had the advantage of direct experience in the representation of cases before the European Court of Human Rights. Moreover JUSTICE was able to draw on the services of one of its Council Members, Sir Denis Dobson QC,[51] to work on the draft amendments. A Law Commissioner was consulted informally, and Professor J. C. Smith, one of the Select Committee's Advisers, remained on hand as a source of unfailingly wise counsel.

The first decision to be taken called for political judgment rather than legal expertise. The Select Committee had recommended the mandatory life sentence for murder should be abolished, in England and Wales, and in Scotland.[52] Yet when it came to projecting the case to non-specialist audiences, in Parliament as in the wider public, the word 'abolition' had too close an association for comfort with the controversy over capital punishment. Abolition of the mandatory sentence also assumed that the dubious and complex distinctions between mandatory and discretionary life sentences were fully understood. The Select Committee had considered, but rejected, the abolition of life imprisonment as the maximum sentence for murder, and it would have been politically maladroit to have jeopardized the support of those who wanted to ensure the continuation of life imprisonment, with its concomitant power of recall to custody after release on life licence should the circumstances justify it. Reform by way of repeal of the provisions of the Murder (Abolition of Death Penalty) Act 1965 was not favoured for similar reasons.

The solution was a succinct new clause, plainly stating that 'No court shall be required to sentence a person convicted of murder to imprisonment for life.' This wording was tabled for consideration

---

[51] Clerk of the Crown in Chancery and Permanent Secretary to the Lord Chancellor, 1968–77.

[52] *Report of the Select Committee on Murder and Life Imprisonment*, HL Paper 78-I, para. 201, p. 50.

in Committee.[53] Some manœuvring was necessary to ensure that its placing in the Bill would be such as to result in the amendment coming on early enough in the day when there would be a full House. Another tactical device was the demonstration of all-party support. No more than four names are allowed to be printed on the marshalled list as the sponsors of an amendment. The art is to indicate within this confined compass the range and quality of its support. Lord Nathan, the Independent peer who had been Chairman of the Select Committee and was to move the amendment, was the first name. Mine was the second from the Conservative side of the House, with Richard, the Labour Opposition front-bench spokesman, as the fourth. In between came Lane, a great prize in signifying judicial support.

The Select Committee report dominated the debate on 18 April. In his opening speech Nathan enunciated three fundamental reasons for objecting to the mandatory life sentence.[54] First, it vested in the Executive an effective power of sentencing, exercised in secrecy. Second, punishment must fit the crime and be seen to do so. The application of one uniform sentence to all those who are convicted of murder, in a wide variety of circumstances, was patently unjust and brought the law into disrepute. Third, the existence of the mandatory life sentence had resulted in distortions in the administration of the law. Lane followed, reminding the House that the arguments in favour of abolishing the mandatory life sentence had been rehearsed time and again, in the Lords Chamber and elsewhere.[55] There was, he claimed, no greater difficulty for judges in assessing the proper length of a determinate sentence for murder than for any other form of serious crime. In the great majority of cases it would be a matter of applying the same sentencing principles as in cases of rape, manslaughter, and other crimes where the maximum sentence was life imprisonment. The advantage of the amendment, and those that went with it, was that what was currently decided 'no doubt by some admirable but anonymous person in the Home Office', after considering advice from a variety of sources including the trial judge and the Lord Chief Justice, all of it tendered in private, would be done openly in court and subject to appeal. If it was argued that it would be a sign of weakness to

[53] *Parl. Debates*, HL, 527, col. 1559, 18 Apr. 1991.'
[54] Ibid., cols. 1560–2.
[55] Ibid., col. 1562.

depart from the mandatory life sentence, that was surely a serious miscalculation. He ended: 'It is no weakness to replace what I suggest is a flawed system with one which at the very least offers an opportunity to achieve greater fairness and so greater justice.'[56]

Three Law Lords: Bridge of Harwich, Ackner, and Griffiths, spoke similarly, as did Lord Alexander of Weedon, Chairman of the Council of JUSTICE.[57] Four members of the Select Committee, in addition to Nathan and Ackner, took part in the debate, all save the single dissentient to the recommendation[58] speaking for the amendment. From the Opposition front bench, Richard noted that as a result of the mandatory life sentence the United Kingdom had accumulated more life sentence prisoners than all the other countries of Western Europe put together.[59] By the time Waddington rose to reply for the Government it was clear that a strong tide of support for the amendment was sweeping the House. His defence of the status quo rested on the proposition that confidence in the system of criminal justice would be eroded if the penalty for murder became discretionary:

I believe that if we abandoned the mandatory life sentence for murder, it would greatly damage public confidence in the criminal justice system and its ability properly to punish the most grave of crimes ... all the wrong signals would go out to the public.[60]

Even with a Government Whip to fall back on, the Leader of the House was unwise to declare he could not agree that the report of the Select Committee, 'however illustrious' the Members who composed it, should be accepted rather than the view of the House as a whole: 'It is now for the whole House to decide whether the Members of the Select Committee, who tried hard, at the end of the day came out with the right result. I happen to believe that

---

[56] Ibid., col. 1564.

[57] Robert Alexander QC; Chairman of the Bar Council 1985–6; Chairman of the Panel on Takeovers and Mergers, 1987–9; Chairman, National Westminster Bank, 1989– . Life peer, 1988.

[58] Baroness Platt of Writtle had dissented from the Select Committee's recommendation that the mandatory life sentence for murder should be abolished.

[59] *Parl. Debates*, HL, 527, col. 1566. In 1990 a total of 3,503 prisoners were serving life sentences in UK prisons, 3,050 in Great Britain and the rest in Northern Ireland. (The statistics on the life-sentence population in Table 10 relate to England and Wales only.) For the other member states of the Council of Europe the aggregate of all life-sentence prisoners was 2,688.

[60] Ibid., col. 1582.

they did not.'[61] Within minutes the House gave its answer. By a majority of nearly one hundred the amendment was carried, the voting being 177 Content and 79 Not Content. Analysis of the division by party allegiance showed that those voting for the amendment were: Labour, sixty-five; Independent, forty-three; Conservative, thirty-four; Liberal Democrat, twenty-six; and Social Democrat, eight. One bishop (unclassified by party allegiance) also voted with the Contents. The list included the only surviving former Lord Chancellors (Hailsham and Havers), the Lord Chief Justice and Master of the Rolls (Donaldson of Lymington), and five Law Lords. Joined by no more than a single Independent, all of the remaining Not Contents took the Conservative Whip. Later, when giving evidence before another Lords inquiry, Waddington conceded that he had been 'discomfited' by the Select Committee's conclusions and the amendments to the Bill which had stemmed from its recommendations. Ruefully, he added: 'Nobody could doubt that was a very important and very influential Committee which excited the interest of the whole of the House when its proposals were before the House by means of amendments to the Criminal Justice Bill.'[62]

Nathan then moved the first of a series of amendments specifying judicial procedures to govern setting the length of the penal term contained within an indeterminate sentence of life imprisonment, and for the release or continued detention of life prisoners on the expiry of the penal term. New provisions would apply whenever a court passed a life sentence, whether for murder or for any other serious offence for which life imprisonment was the maximum sentence. The judge would be required to give reasons in open court for imposing a life sentence, in preference to a determinate sentence, and for the quantum of punishment. This would be expressed in the form of a penal term based upon the requirements of retribution and deterrence. It would not be open to revision by ministers, but would be subject to appeal by either side.

At the expiration of the penal term the decision whether the prisoner should be released or further detained would be considered by a judicial tribunal constituted to conform to the case law of

---

[61] Ibid., col. 1583.
[62] House of Lords, *Report from the Select Committee on the Committee Work of the House*, Session 1991/2 (HL Paper 35-II), HMSO, London, 1992, p. 116.

the European Convention on Human Rights.[63] Any life-sentence prisoner convicted of murder would be released only on life licence, with the Home Secretary retaining a power to revoke the licence. Recall to custody would be subject to the consent of the tribunal. If the tribunal determined not to direct the release of a life prisoner, usually because of the risk to the public of further serious offences being committed, his case would have to be referred back to the tribunal for fresh consideration within a maximum period of three years. The tribunal would be subject to procedural rules enabling the prisoner to make his own representations or to be legally represented; to know what was said about him; and to have an opportunity to challenge reports and other information before the tribunal.

After further debate, in which Waddington argued that it would not be right to rush into hasty measures at a time when the Government was considering the implications of the judgment of the European Court of Human Rights in the case of *Thynne, Wilson and Gunnell*, the first of the series of amendments was put to the vote. Once again it was carried by a large majority, the result of the division being 120 voting in favour and 68 against. The subsequent amendments were accepted without divisions being called.

VI

Faced by such overwhelming defeats, ministers did not try to reverse the decisions during the later stages of the Bill in the Lords. What would be the reaction of the Commons? Given the size of the Government's overall majority, the probability was that it would turn on decisions taken in Cabinet. Baker made no pretence of concealing his irritation and displeasure, heightened by the Lords' action on 30 April in rejecting the War Crimes Bill for the second time.[64] To his mind popular opinion would not stand for

[63] The composition of the tribunal recommended by the Select Committee was a High Court judge, a consultant psychiatrist, and a chief probation officer.
[64] The War Crimes Bill was rejected for a second time by the House of Lords by 131 votes to 109. It had been reintroduced in the Commons after its rejection by the Lords in the previous session, and again completed all its stages there. One year having passed between the Second Reading in the Commons in the first session and the Third Reading in the Commons in the second session, the Bill was presented

the abolition of the mandatory life sentence for murder and, as a non-elected chamber, the Lords should refrain from amending legislation on potentially controversial matters when its members did not have to face the electorate.

As a result of a chance meeting shortly afterwards, I followed up by writing to the Home Secretary about the political implications which in his mind evidently counted for more than the merits of the argument. My contention was that the House of Lords, as a non-elected but expert assembly, should do its duty in the scrutiny of legislation in the way it thinks best. Many of its most active members had served in the Commons; a considerable number of those who voted against the War Crimes Bill and for the amendment on the sentence for murder having held ministerial office in Conservative administrations. It was a strength of our legislative institutions that the Lords did not have to look over its shoulder at the likely reception of its actions by the electorate. To that extent it was insulated from the dangers of populism which had been expounded so eloquently by Lord Hailsham in a memorable speech on the War Crimes Bill on 30 April.[65] In return, the Lords did not have the last word which rested, very properly, with the elected House.

I suggested that a change in presentation was a way out of the difficulty. Nobody wanted to see further conflict between the two Houses. More could be made of the fact that the Select Committee had recommended the retention of the life sentence for murder in appropriate cases. Various other alternatives had been considered, but rejected. The mandatory life sentence for murder was undermined by the fact that it had become firmly lodged in the public mind that life imprisonment 'only' meant something of the order of between ten and twelve years. The Select Committee's proposal, that it should be reserved for the gravest cases, or where there was a high risk of future offending, would restore the life sentence to

for Royal Assent without the approval of the Lords under the terms of Section 2 of the Parliament Act 1949.

[65] 'Populism is the enemy of justice, the enemy of freedom and, ultimately, the enemy of democracy. There is nothing in common between populism and democracy and those things in which we believe. Populism destroyed the life of Socrates and forever left an indelible stain ... upon the reputation of Athenian justice. It was populism which led a Roman ruler to give in to rent-a-mob when he [*sic*] said: "If [thou] let this man go, thou art not Caesar's friend".' *Parl. Debates*, HL, 528 (5th ser.), col. 639, 30 Apr. 1991.

what it should be: the heaviest penalty permitted by law. Thus the average time served in custody by life prisoners could be expected to go up. I ended with a reminder of the careful way in which Douglas Hurd and John Patten had handled the sentencing reforms contained in Part I of the Criminal Justice Bill, without incurring public or party political opposition.

The Home Secretary's reply, no doubt drafted by civil servants, did not elaborate on what he referred to as the 'important political considerations to be taken into account over the future of the mandatory life sentence'. A concession was offered in the shape of government amendments to give effect to the judgment of the European Court of Human Rights on discretionary life sentences. Initially, despite the passage of time since the judgment in the case of *Thynne* and others, the intention had been to postpone any action until after the Criminal Justice Bill had been completed. Now there was the prospect of new provisions being added when the Bill returned to the Commons for consideration of Lords amendments. However reluctantly taken, it was a useful step forward.

HOME SECRETARY

QUEEN ANNE'S GATE
LONDON SW1H 9AT
17 MAY 1991

Dear David,

Thank you for your letter of 3 May about the amendments passed in Lords Committee on 18 April to abolish the mandatory life sentence for murder, and to introduce new procedures for determining how long life sentence prisoners should serve.

David Waddington will be setting out the Government's response to the votes and explaining how we intend to proceed in the light of them, when Lord Nathan's further amendments are debated on Monday. But, as he has already indicated to Lord Nathan, the Government remains of the view that a life sentence must remain the mandatory sentence for the offence of murder, and that the existing arrangements should remain in place for determining how long such offenders should serve. We recognise, however, that there is a need to amend the procedures governing discretionary life sentences in the light of the recent ECHR judgment, and the Government amendments will be tabled at Commons consideration of Lords amendments for this purpose. I hope these will be seen as a positive response to the concerns expressed in the House of Lords, though I recognise of course that they do not deal with what many would feel to be the most critical issue, that of the mandatory life sentence.

There are, as you say in your letter, important political considerations to be taken into account over the future of the mandatory life sentence. But I would not want you to think that this is the only reason for the Government's taking the position that it has. On the contrary, I believe that there are important grounds of principle for retaining the mandatory life sentence and the existing procedures for determining when prisoners given such sentences should be released. As David Waddington says in his letter, the question of the penalty for murder concerns the public's right to be assured that offenders who have shown themselves capable of intentionally taking another person's life will receive a punishment which marks the unique nature of that offence. I accept that not everyone would agree about this, but I have to say that in my view there is indeed something particularly abhorrent about the crime of murder—even where there are extenuating circumstances—which should continue to be reflected in a unique penalty. I believe that it should also be reflected in the procedures for deciding when a convicted murderer should be released. As you know, the European Court drew in its reasoning a clear distinction between mandatory and discretionary life sentences, and I believe, with respect, that they were right to do so.

I would not, incidentally, necessarily accept the implication in your letter that domestic murders are any less serious than non-domestic murders or are viewed as such by the public. Domestic murders can be horrific crimes, and it is not of course unknown for domestic murderers to kill again after they have been released from a previous life sentence.

I am sorry that it does not look as if we shall be able to find common ground on the mandatory life sentence question. I fear that it is simply a genuine difference of view on a point of principle where substantial argument can be advanced on both sides of the case.

I am sending a copy of this letter to David Waddington and John MacGregor.

Yours ever,
Kenneth

The most important consequence of the set-back to the Government's legislative programme was to bring the issue before the Cabinet as a whole. At every Cabinet meeting when Parliament is sitting, the Government Chief Whip in the Commons reports on Parliamentary business. The Leaders of either House add their comments to what he has to say. Waddington, as he had made plain in the Lords' debates, was personally unsympathetic to the change of policy contained in the amendments and had been Home Secretary when the Bill was in draft. In receiving a deputation from the Select Committee at that stage he had been firmly opposed to any departure from the mandatory life sentence for murder, and seemed indifferent to arguments for reforming the much criticized procedures for deciding the term a life prisoner should serve and when he should be released on licence. Baker was similarly committed to preserving the status quo for as long as possible.

A clash between the two Houses opens the way for other ministers, without a direct departmental interest, to join in collective decision-taking. Apart from the Prime Minister, the two most powerful members of the Cabinet were Hurd and Heseltine. The former had been Home Secretary at the time the legislation was first planned and had a hand in the setting up of the Lords Select Committee. After his triumphant return, the latter was even less inhibited by bureaucratic boundaries than he had been before his resignation. I wrote to both of them, as well as to John MacGregor, the Leader of the House of Commons. All three replied personally. MacGregor acknowledged courteously, and Heseltine said, 'This is an important issue and it is very helpful to have the arguments set out so clearly and forcibly. I will give the matter the most serious consideration.'[66]

The Foreign Secretary's letter, broad-minded and thoughtful, showed that, despite the heavy burden of his office, he had not lost interest in penal matters. Although its contents offered little encouragement, it made clear that Hurd's support for the Home Secretary's view was no automatic reflex, but resulted from his own experience and political judgment. It is quoted in full, with the writer's permission:

PERSONAL   Foreign and Commonwealth Office
                                                        London SW1 2AH
14 May 1991
                                               From The Secretary of State
Dear David,

Many thanks for your letter of 22 April. My apologies for not having replied more swiftly. I have been giving the matter of mandatory life sentences for murder a fair bit of thought. I see a good deal of force in the arguments which you set out in the full version of the article you wrote for 'The Times'.

The view which I held when I was Home Secretary, and to which I still

---

[66] Letter dated 13 May 1991. Quoted with permission.

incline, is that in this highly emotive area it is almost uniquely difficult to divorce the politics (in the widest sense) of the issue from the rest of the argument. We have just come through a decade in which capital punishment continued to be a very raw issue. Parliament rightly and repeatedly rejected by decisive majorities all the models for restoration put before it, but, as we all recognise, rather against the strongly held instincts of a significant proportion of the population. I believe the tide has turned on the capital punishment issue. But whilst the issue remains potentially so raw I am far from convinced that opinion in the House of Commons or the country is ready to move away from the mandatory life sentence as a means of distinguishing between murder and all other forms of violent crime. The importance of the symbolism should not be under-estimated.

I do not have a closed mind on the issue and I shall seek to have a word with Kenneth Baker about it in the coming weeks. Perhaps we shall then have an opportunity for a further exchange on the matter?

Yours,
Douglas

VII

Public, as well as private, channels for communication were exploited in the crucial interval before the Bill returned to the Commons. The quality daily and Sunday press was consistently favourable, providing opportunities for articles, interviews, and quotations. The broadcast media, and BBC Radio 4 in particular, reported on the controversy fully, not shirking the daunting task of explaining the intricacies of mandatory and discretionary sentences and the tariff setting and release procedures. The penal reform groups activated their existing networks. As a result the topic remained in the news while the Lords completed the remaining stages of the Bill.

Parliamentary and special interest channels merged with the publication of a lengthy letter in *The Times* from Lord Alexander of Weedon on behalf of JUSTICE, by prior arrangement with the editor and after consultation with Nathan and myself, in the week before the Commons consideration of the Lords amendments. It argued that since 1965, when the mandatory life sentence replaced capital punishment as the penalty for murder, it had become increasingly apparent that the administration of justice, as it bore on murder and life imprisonment, was open to grave criticism. The letter ended:

JUSTICE hopes that, when the amendments come before the Commons, they will be regarded as issues of conscience and not appropriate for recourse to party whips. This is surely an area in which the views of individual members should be taken without any pressure being applied to them.[67]

The plea fell on deaf ears in the Whips' Office in the Commons. It was the Government's political judgment that was being challenged, and this was not thought to be a fit matter for a free vote. In opening the debate on 25 June, the Home Secretary invited the House to disagree with the Lords amendment to abolish the mandatory life sentence for murder. Later the Government would propose substitute amendments to those made in the Lords, but only so far as they affected discretionary life sentences. Baker, like other speakers on the Government side of the House, made no attempt to meet the arguments that had been put forward, simply reiterating the assertion that retaining the mandatory sentence was essential to mark the uniquely heinous nature of the crime of murder. The public, whose views on capital punishment were clearly known, 'would feel very let down if there were a weakening in the mandatory sentence for murder ... '[68]

Opposition speakers, led by Hattersley, rehearsed once again the principal objections to the mandatory life sentence. Sentencing should be the responsibility of the courts, not of ministers or civil servants. In the case of men and women convicted of murder and receiving a mandatory sentence the custodial period was being determined by the Executive. This fact in itself, Hattersley said, was enough to justify support for the Lords' amendment, but there were additional reasons why the mandatory sentence was wrong in principle as well as in practice. The prisoner left the court not knowing how long he or she was to serve. There was no appeal against the sentence. A sentence imposed by ministers in secret and allowing no appeal was a denial of justice. It was not surprising that the amendment should have been sponsored by the Lord Chief Justice and supported by so many Law Lords and other lawyers. On the evidence there was no doubt that the mandatory sentence,

[67] *The Times*, 17 June 1991.
[68] *Parl. Debates*, HC, 193 (6th ser.), col. 868, 25 June 1991.

as it was applied, distorted the system of criminal justice in a way that was deeply damaging. The Home Secretary had not begun to refute the criticisms on their merits. The Government was resisting change because of what they believed to be public opinion, and because they feared incurring a reputation of being soft on murder and murderers.[69]

After more than two hours of debate the Question was put and the Commons accepted the Government motion to disagree with the Lords' amendment by 236 votes to 158. Voting was strictly on party lines. On an issue of this sort, the adversarial nature of the Commons, heightened by party loyalties and party discipline, points up the disparity between the two Houses. In the first division to take place in the Commons on 25 June, for example, it was notable that even the Conservative officers of PAPPAG, which had been briefing MPs and peers with arguments to support the Lords' amendment, voted with the whipped majority. Inconvenient as it is for the business managers when the two Houses conflict, especially when time is short as the summer recess approaches, such incidents nevertheless demonstrate the elemental working of the component parts of the Parliamentary whole. The injection of expert opinion and the representation of special interests are the province of the Lords, while a majority in the democratically elected assembly rallies to support the Government when it is attacked by the Opposition, reacting also, fitfully and sometimes unpredictably, to what MPs sense to be the beliefs and instincts of their constituents.

Mrs Rumbold then moved a group of amendments in lieu of the Lords' proposals for judicial procedures to determine when and by whom life-sentence prisoners should be released from custody.[70] Since the recent judgment of the European Court of Human Rights the Government accepted there was a need to alter the current procedures as they affected non-murder convictions, i.e. prisoners serving so-called discretionary life sentences. In the opinion of the Government, it did not follow that mandatory life-sentence prisoners, who had not been applicants before the Court of Human Rights, were entitled to have their cases reviewed by an independent judicial body after the expiry of the penal term, because the lawfulness of their detention for life had been determined by the

[69] Ibid., cols. 869–74.
[70] Ibid., cols. 902–4.

trial judge at the outset. The Home Secretary would have preferred more time to digest the implications of the judgment in the case of *Thynne and Others*, but as a result of the pressures in both Houses he was bringing forward amendments at this stage.

The Government's proposal was to require the trial judge to announce in open court the term within a discretionary life sentence which was commensurate with the seriousness of the offence. That term would be open to appeal in the same way as a determinate sentence. Once the term set by the trial judge had been served, the prisoner's continued detention would depend on an assessment of the risk that he posed to the public if released, rather than the seriousness of the offence. In exceptional cases it would be open to the trial judge not to set a term. Such an action would be an indication that, in the eyes of the court, the crime was so wicked that detention for life was justified according to the seriousness of the offence alone, irrespective of the risk to the public. A life prisoner falling within this special category would be treated in the same way as a mandatory life prisoner with the question of his eventual release being decided by the Secretary of State.

For the generality of discretionary life cases the prisoner would be entitled to have his continued detention after the expiry of the term set by the trial judge reviewed by an independent body having the status of a court for the purposes of the European Convention on Human Rights. Rather than accepting the Select Committee's preference for a tribunal modelled on the Mental Health Review Tribunal, which since 1983 had handled without any loss of public confidence the onerous decisions on the discharge of restricted patients, the Government proposed that special panels of the Parole Board chaired by a judge should be adapted for the purpose. When considering cases of discretionary life prisoners the panel would be subject to separate procedures, including the right of the prisoner to appear in person and be legally represented, and would be empowered to direct the Secretary of State to release the prisoner where it was satisfied that his continued detention was no longer necessary for the protection of the public. The Secretary of State would then be obliged to release the prisoner, although he could delay release for up to six months if he judged it to be in the public interest to do so.

The Opposition spokesman, Barry Sheerman, noted the transformation that had occurred in the Government's speed of reaction to the Court of Human Rights judgment as a result of its defeat in the Lords.[71] The incompatibility of release procedures with the European Convention had been clear since the earlier case of *Weeks* in 1987,[72] and the judgment in the *Thynne* case in October 1990. The Opposition was not persuaded that the procedures now put forward by the Government fully met the requirements of the European Convention and regarded the Lords proposals as superior. For the Liberal Democrats, Robert Maclennan shared Sheerman's anxieties and was not satisfied that the new provisions, which had been produced at such a late stage in the Bill's passage, would rectify the wrong to which the Court of Human Rights had drawn attention.[73] After further debate, the motion rejecting the Lords' amendments, and substituting the Government's alternative provision for discretionary life prisoners only, was agreed by 219 votes to 147.

In the remaining weeks before the Recess the Bill went back to the Lords and returned to the Commons a second time with further changes. On 3 July the Lords bowed to the inevitable, accepting that the Commons should have the last word, for the time being at least, on the mandatory life sentence. In moving that the House did not insist on its amendment, to which the Commons had disagreed, Waddington was conciliatory and pragmatic:

I am certainly not saying baldly to your Lordships that another place has spoken and your Lordships must agree. I am well aware of how often your Lordships have helped shape public opinion and attitudes, and I would not be surprised if at some future date policy on this matter changes as a result of a change in public opinion which this House influenced. I

[71] Ibid., cols. 904–7.

[72] In *Weeks* v. *The United Kingdom* (1988) 10 EHRR 293, the Court of Human Rights found there had been a violation of Article 5(4) on the lawfulness of detention. For the purpose of determining the application of the Article to detention under a sentence of life imprisonment, including detention after recall to prison following release on licence, the Court drew a distinction between a life sentence imposed by reason of the gravity of the offence and one imposed not so much as punishment but primarily as an indeterminate sentence enabling the offender's progress to be monitored to permit his release when it is safe to do so. The Court found that the stated purpose for which Weeks's sentence was imposed, taken together with the particular facts of the offence, placed him in the second category in which the lawfulness both of the continuing detention and the recall of a prisoner following his release on licence must be subject to review by a body with the powers of a court. The Parole Board and its procedures did not, in the Court's opinion, meet the requirements of the Convention in that respect.

[73] *Parl. Debates*, HC, 193, col. 907.

am simply saying that I wonder whether the time for change is now.[74]

More outspoken was Hailsham who directed his fire towards the reason given for disagreeing with the Lords' amendment, namely 'because the mandatory life sentence is necessary to mark the uniquely heinous crime of murder':

The reason given by the Commons is frankly, and intellectually, ridiculous ... Murder is not the most heinous offence in the calendar. It is an offence ... carried out for quite a variety of different motives ... One day people will see sense, even in another place, and the hairy heel of populism which they have followed will ultimately disappear.[75]

The House was less accommodating when it turned to the procedures now proposed by the Government for the review and release of discretionary prisoners. It was unwilling to accept the establishment of two distinct procedures running in parallel, one with judicial characteristics for persons sentenced to life imprisonment for any offence other than murder, and an entirely separate one, still subject to the arbitrariness attaching to the reliance on the Secretary of State's discretion, where the offence was murder. The Government's sole justification, that because murder was the most heinous crime it demanded different administrative process, did not survive the battery of authoritative opinion to the contrary. An amendment moved by Nathan to extend the procedure proposed for discretionary life prisoners to all life-sentence prisoners[76] was carried by a comfortable majority of 134 votes to 83.[77] Ackner's speech contained a passage which went to the heart of the matter:

There is now to be a new regime, not because the Government have seen the light, which necessitates according little more than the principles of natural justice to a prisoner, but because the Court of Human Rights has said so ... The new regime will give the discretionary life sentence prisoner the right to hear how long the penal element is and, I imagine, a right to appeal ... It will also give him the right to make an application to be released when that period has ended, to be represented and to have legal aid. All those aspects are most sensible. However, that regime is not to be accorded to the subject of a mandatory life sentence. Why on earth not? It is a sound, sensible, straightforward process that takes the art of

[74] *Parl. Debates*, HL, 530 (5th ser.), col. 991, 3 July 1991.
[75] Ibid., col. 993.
[76] Ibid., col. 1013.
[77] Ibid., cols. 1035–6.

sentencing away from the Executive where it should never be and entrusts it, together with all other sentences, to the judiciary.[78]

Strongly argued as it was, a gloss could be added to Ackner's point. If the Government accepted, with whatever degree of reluctance, the need to implement a judicial procedure for those prisoners whom the sentencing court had specifically selected as requiring a sentence of life imprisonment because of the exceptional gravity of their offence or the risk to the public that might result from their release at the end of a determinate sentence, how could a similar procedure be denied to those life prisoners caught by an inflexible mandatory sentence to whom neither the criteria of exceptional gravity nor risk to the public might apply?

Forecasting that the Government would again use its majority to overturn the uniform procedure in the Commons, the Lords made two changes to the judicial procedure which would still be relevant were it to be confined to discretionary life prisoners only. The first was to eliminate the power of the trial judge not to make an order setting a penal term, which would have the effect of barring the release procedures from coming into effect on the expiry of the specified term. The second was the power of the Secretary of State to defer a prisoner's release on licence for up to six months after the Parole Board had directed his release. Waddington had justified the need for a limited power enabling the Home Secretary to delay a life prisoner's release for a short period on the grounds that release at a particular time might 'cause public outrage and public danger'.[79] As an example, he cited the release of a terrorist coinciding with the anniversary of the tragedy caused by his actions being marked by a public meeting which might turn a peaceful demonstration into a public riot. Peers were unimpressed by his argument, pointing out that it applied just as much to the release of offenders serving fixed terms of imprisonment. Doubts were also voiced about the compatibility of such a power with the jurisprudence of the Court of Human Rights, although Waddington maintained that in its judgment in the *Thynne* case the Court had said release could be delayed on grounds of expediency. What constituted expediency, and who should have the power of defer-

[78] Ibid., col. 1019.
[79] Ibid., col. 1011.

ment, were unanswered questions. Both amendments were carried against the Government on a division.

On 16 July the Commons disagreed that the procedure for discretionary life prisoners, as modified by the Lords, should be extended to apply to all life-sentence prisoners giving as their reason that

the considerations applicable to the release of persons serving mandatory life sentences are not the same as those applicable to prisoners whose cases will be dealt with under the new clause (Duty to release discretionary life prisoners).[80]

The Government's original amendment was reinserted into the Bill, but with one important concession. The power to delay a life-sentence prisoner's release for up to six months after it had been ordered by the Parole Board was deleted. Having reflected on what had been said in the previous debate, Waddington told the Lords when the Bill returned on 23 July that the Government had concluded it was not essential to have this power after all, and that the Lords' views had prevailed.[81]

With the summer Recess only two days away, the opportunity for further dialogue between the two Houses was exhausted. The Lords had had its say, important changes had been incorporated in the Bill, notably in the provision of the new procedures governing discretionary life prisoners, but at the cost of inconsistency with the handling of mandatory life prisoners, many of whom presented less potential risk on release. Informed public opinion had been influenced by the exchanges. Even the Government's own spokesman seemed resigned to accept that in time the mandatory life sentence for murder would be replaced by a discretionary power for the courts to sentence up to life imprisonment, so ending the unwarranted distinction between mandatory and discretionary life prisoners which had been used to justify maintaining such inequitable practices.

The outcome was a compromise satisfactory to none of the parties to the controversy. The Lords' attempt to end the mandatory penalty for murder had been frustrated. The Government had been forced to abandon the exclusive control over all life-sentence prisoners that was implicit in the previous arrangements. The

---

[80] *Parl. Debates*, HL, 531 (5th ser.), col. 648, 23 July 1991.
[81] Ibid., col. 649.

judiciary had been alienated from the role they were called upon
to play in recommending tariffs in mandatory cases which would
still be open to adjustment by ministers in private. There were
formidable difficulties to be faced in devising practical arrangements
to give effect to the Government's plans for the release of discretionary prisoners on licence; nor was it by any means certain
that the provisions of the Act would be accepted without question
by the Committee of Ministers of the Council of Europe as adequate
implementation in domestic law of the judgment of the Court of
Human Rights against the United Kingdom in *Thynne, Wilson and
Gunnell*.[82] In this instance, as elsewhere in the Act, the inheritance
of the policy of toughening up its contents for presentational
purposes was to leave behind a residue of dubious special categories
for the future.

The power of the trial judge not to make an order specifying the
term of years to be served as punishment by a discretionary life
prisoner sentenced for a violent or sexual offence, which would
have been eliminated under the amendment carried by the Lords
on 3 July, meant that a special category of non-murder discretionary
life prisoners would be treated as if they were mandatory life
prisoners. Yet it is a requirement in mandatory cases that the Home
Secretary receives a recommendation from the trial judge on the
appropriate period to be served in the interests of retribution and
deterrence, and it is this which ultimately triggers the release
procedures. If no term is specified for the special category of
discretionary life prisoners, unless it is really intended that life
imprisonment should mean custody for the remainder of the
prisoner's natural life without any possibility of release on licence
at any time in the future, a crucial element would seem to have
been omitted from the detailed provisions of the Act setting out
the release procedures for life prisoners.[83]

The sentencing provisions of the Act were not due to come into
effect until October 1992, and in the intervening period procedures
for the release of discretionary life prisoners would have to be
devised to withstand challenge in the domestic courts, as well as at
Strasbourg. Ministers gave the impression of being resigned to
make the best of a bad job by doing as little as possible, as late as

[82] The Council's Directorate of Human Rights had raised a query about the
legislation proposed to give effect to the judgment.
[83] See *Blackstone's Guide to the Criminal Justice Act 1991*, p. 106.

possible. It was a poor way to approach the reform of an acknowledged abuse, and it would have been better had the nettle been
grasped two years earlier.

VIII

The same timidity towards public opinion lay behind the Government's gradual retreat from the sentencing objectives enshrined in
the opening clauses of the Bill. The original intention had been
straightforward enough: to extend to adults aged twenty-one and
over similar restraints on the use of custody to those which had
been enacted for young offenders in 1982 and 1988, so reducing
the reliance on imprisonment as a penalty for those offenders who
could be punished in the community without exposing the public
to undue risk. The scale of punishment for the offence, whether
custodial or non-custodial, would in future be directly related to
the gravity of the crime. Where the seriousness of the offence was
such that imprisonment was justified, the length of the sentence
was to be commensurate with the harm done. The Government
would prescribe a legislative framework for the use of custodial,
community, and financial penalties, but would not bind the courts
to strict sentencing guide-lines. The discretion required to deal
justly with the great variety of cases coming before them would
remain in the hands of the courts, subject to the correct application
of the statutory principles. As time went on, it was expected that
the provisions of the Act would be interpreted by the Court of
Appeal, as had happened with the sentencing of young offenders
under the 1982 and 1988 Acts. Case law and statute law, it was
hoped, would fuse in the creation of a new order.

The principles of proportionality and just deserts survived into
the Act. But on the journey from the first publication of the
Government's proposals in February 1990, to enactment eighteen
months later, accretions formed around the nucleus. The first, and
most important, was added when the White Paper was in draft.
Waddington, newly appointed as Home Secretary, was apprehensive
about the reception likely to be accorded to the undiluted doctrine
of proportionality in sentencing and punishment in the community.
Whilst undoubtedly aligned with much penal thinking, what would
be the reaction of the judiciary? Awkward questions loomed: how

would previous convictions be reconciled with sentencing based on the seriousness of the actual offence charged? What would happen when multiple offences were before the court?[84] How would mentally disordered offenders be fitted into the scheme of things? More pressing was the risk of an erosion in the support of the Conservative MPs so assiduously canvassed by Patten in the formative stages of the policy. A sterner touch was needed, he felt, if the legislation was to be presented convincingly as being a 'tough', as well as a reformist, measure.

The chosen vehicle for this message was a proposal to empower the Crown Court to give custodial sentences longer than would be justified by the seriousness of the offence (i.e. the just desert) to persistent violent and sexual offenders if it was necessary to protect the public from serious harm. The policy of 'topping up' a sentence differed from the discredited and little used extended sentence, which was to be abolished by the legislation, only in that the enhanced term would have to be contained within the maximum penalty for the offence allowed by law.

So a subtle process of toughening up the Bill began: here the addition of some new wording; there an increase in emphasis on the punitive aspects at the expense of the aim of diverting offenders from custody. Taken on their own, few of the retreats seemed to be of major significance, but cumulatively they amounted to a drawing back from the coherence of the strategy drawn up after the Leeds Castle meeting. That some advance took place cannot be denied, but the objectives were diffused and a rare opportunity to change the direction of public opinion, as Hurd had begun to do, was allowed to pass by.

When the Act comes to be implemented the lack of public

---

[84] In the statute as enacted, Section 29 provides that for the purpose of deciding between a custodial and a non-custodial sentence, or on the length of a custodial sentence, an offence is not to be regarded as more serious by reason of the offender having previous convictions or having failed to respond to previous sentences. The court may, however, take account of the circumstances of previous offences which disclose factors aggravating the seriousness of the instant offence. Where an offender is convicted of more than one offence, then for the purpose of deciding between a custodial and a non-custodial sentence, account is to be taken of the seriousness of a combination of no more than two offences (Section 1(2)(a)). In deciding on the length of a custodial sentence, all the offences may be taken into account (Section 2(2)(a)), subject to the totality principle (Section 28(2)(b)). The juxtaposition of the seriousness of the offence and the defendant's previous record was always likely to lead to difficulties in practice which duly emerged as soon as the Act came into force.

preparedness may have far-reaching consequences. To acknowledge that punishment in the community for certain crimes is a true penalty, not to be regarded as a 'let-off' with the offender 'walking free' from the court, will call for a change in public attitudes. Unless public attitudes change, and are positively encouraged to change, sentencers will be less inclined to depart from the existing pattern of custodial sentencing to the extent necessary to achieve the original objectives of the legislation.

The success of the strategy did not depend simply on sending fewer offenders to prison. A crucial element in the new system of parole, which had been generally welcomed when the Bill was before Parliament, was that there should be reductions in sentence length to compensate for the fact that in future many prisoners would serve one-half, rather than one-third, of their sentence in custody before release. Remission, previously up to one-third of the sentence would be abolished, being replaced by a period of conditional freedom on licence in the community. The Act provided for the automatic release of short-term offenders sentenced to terms of less than four years' imprisonment when they had served half their sentence. Release would be on licence and subject to recall for all prisoners sentenced to twelve months' or more imprisonment. A word of warning may not be out of place here. Non-selective parole, although less costly and fairer in its application, does not call for consent on the part of the prisoner to co-operate with the Probation Service during the period of the licence. It may well lead to problems when, and if, it comes to be seen as mandatory supervision.

Once long-term prisoners sentenced to terms of four years or more have served half of their sentence (rather than one-third as before) they would be eligible for release on licence if the Parole Board was satisfied that certain published criteria were fulfilled. For those serving very long determinate sentences of seven years or more a favourable decision by the Parole Board would not be sufficient; the Board's recommendation would have to be endorsed by the Home Secretary (or more likely a junior minister on his behalf advised by officials). Supervision by the Probation Service was to be compulsory for all offenders from the date of their release on licence up to the three-quarters point in the original sentence. If another offence punishable with imprisonment was committed at any time until the expiry of the full term of the original sentence, the offender would be liable to be recalled to custody to serve the full amount of that sentence in addition to any further sentence.

Automatic release for prisoners serving sentences of less than four years was estimated as likely to reduce the total of some 24,000 cases reviewed for selective parole each year, either by the Parole Board or the Local Review Committees (with approximately 7,500 being reviewed by both), to about 4,500 cases annually. The new procedures were intended to be more open, the White Paper declaring an aim of 'moving towards disclosing reports made to the Board and the Board giving reasons for its decisions'.[85] Formal hearings, with the prisoner present, and legally represented if he wished, were not in prospect; nor was there to be any right of appeal. Under a new power, the Board could expect to be given directions by the Home Secretary on those matters which it should take into account in reaching its decisions.[86]

Less predictable than the reduction in work-load is the effect the parole changes will have on the size of the prison population. The Carlisle report made clear that a reduction in the use of imprisonment as a penalty, and in the length of custodial sentences, should accompany the implementation of its proposals to give greater meaning to the sentence of the court. Prudently prefacing its calculations with the remark that it was difficult to predict the impact of the proposed new scheme on the prison population with any confidence, the report stated that its 'best guess' (not really Command Paper phraseology) was that it was likely to be broadly neutral.[87] Following an example contained in the report, the White Paper referred to a conjectural reduction of 5% in the length of sentences up to four years.[88] Whether or not the hoped for reductions will occur, no one can foretell. While it is true that the parole reforms will bring the amount of time spent in custody closer to the sentence passed by the courts, the probability is that the prison population will rise unless set off by more lenient

[85] *Crime, Justice and Protecting the Public: The Government's Proposals for Legislation* (Cm. 965), HMSO, London, 1990, p. 34.

[86] Section 32(6) of the Criminal Justice Act 1991 states that in giving such directions the Secretary of State shall in particular have regard to (*a*) the need to protect the public from serious harm from offenders; and (*b*) the desirability of preventing the commission by them of further offences and of securing their rehabilitation.

[87] *The Parole System in England and Wales*, p. 103.

[88] *Crime, Justice and Protecting the Public*, p. 48.

sentencing and the wider use of community penalties. Yet ministerial emphasis on 'tough' sentencing for offenders convicted of violent or sexual crimes can hardly fail to influence the courts in a contrary direction.

The Government itself forecast an increase in the prison population of 400 if 10% of released prisoners were returned to custody after reconviction for another imprisonable offence to serve the new sentence consecutively to the remainder of their original sentence. If 20% of released prisoners were to be returned with consecutive sentences, the prison population would be likely to increase by 1,400. This would cost an extra £22 million a year.[89] But predictions of the size of the prison population, as we have seen earlier in the narrative, are notoriously unreliable. There are too many imponderables: the number of crimes committed and their gravity; the success of the police in bringing offenders before the courts; prosecution policies; rates of conviction; sentencing practice (the use of custody and length of custodial sentences); breaches of suspended sentences; and re-offending by those who have been released on licence or are subject to supervision.

IX

The clauses empowering the court to pass a custodial sentence more severe than the offence would otherwise deserve on certain types of offender were amongst the most hotly contested. Although the policy was carried through into the Act, its formulation was unsettled and the drafting twice amended by the Government as a result of second (and further) thoughts while the Bill was before Parliament. As published, the provision excluded the most serious offences triable only on indictment from clause 2 which governed the length of custodial sentences. The sentence was to be commensurate with the seriousness of the offence, or the combination of the offence and other offences associated with it, except in the case of a violent or sexual offence when the Crown Court could pass a sentence of imprisonment for such longer term (not exceeding the maximum) as in the opinion of the court was necessary to protect the public from serious harm from the offender. In the

---

[89] *Crime, Justice and Protecting the Public.*

Commons the Bill was amended to include violent or sexual offences triable summarily in the Magistrates' court as well as either way in the Crown Court or Magistrates' courts. The most serious offences triable only on indictment in the Crown Court remained outside the scope of the clause at that stage. An amendment to leave out the power to impose disproportionate sentences altogether was promoted by the Parliamentary All-Party Penal Affairs Group and moved in the House of Lords by the author. It was narrowly defeated on a division by sixty-nine votes to fifty-two.[90]

The Lords returned to the 'topping-up' provision at each stage of the Bill. Although the Government could not be shifted from its conviction that the protection of the public from serious harm was sufficient justification for a custodial sentence in circumstances where one would not otherwise have been imposed, or for a longer term than was commensurate with the offence, it agreed on Report to amend the Bill so as to include indictable-only offences. Ministers still insisted, however, on the retention of offences triable summarily in the Magistrates' court, even though they could result in a sentence of no more than six months' imprisonment.

On Third Reading I moved another amendment to relate the objectives of the clause, questionable though they might be, to the sentencing powers of the courts. Since the Bill defined serious harm as 'protecting members of the public from death or serious personal injury, whether physical or psychological'[91] it was clear that any violent or sexual offence that would imperil the public to such an extent would be tried, or at the very least sentenced, in the Crown Court. The phrasing of the Bill made it quite inappropriate for the Magistrates' courts to have this power and the amendment would have confined it to the Crown Court only. All-party support came from Richard on the Opposition front bench, Hutchinson of Lullington for the Liberal Democrats, and Roskill, a former Lord of Appeal, speaking from the cross-benches. For procedural reasons, the amendment, which was stubbornly opposed by the Government, was voted on after a messy debate which covered

[90] *Parl. Debates*, HL, 527 (5th ser.), cols. 1008–21, 26 Mar. 1991.
[91] The wording in Section 31(3) of the Criminal Justice Act 1991 was added during the passage of the Bill. Section 31(1) defines sexual and violent offences, the latter meaning an offence which leads, or is intended or likely to lead, to a person's death or to physical injury to a person. Arson is specifically covered by the definition.

another unrelated amendment as well, and was lost on a division by 104 votes to 121.[92]

Given the Government's determination to exempt offenders convicted of violent or sexual offences from the restrictions on the imposition of custodial sentences, and from the principles of proportionality in setting their length, the amendments made in each House to what became Part 1 of the Act were only limited improvements.[93] The criteria for the use (Section 1) and length (Section 2) of custodial sentences were extended to the most serious offences triable only on indictment in the Crown Court. The power to pass a custodial sentence in order to protect the public from future serious harm (Section 1(2)(*b*)), or to increase the length of a custodial sentence for the same purpose (Section 2(2)(*b*)), was made exercisable only on conviction for a violent or sexual offence. The effect was to narrow the power in Section 1, which originally had included any offence.

A new Section 4 was added, requiring a medical report to be obtained before a custodial sentence was passed on a mentally disordered offender. The classification of violent and sexual offences was amended by the exclusion of some homosexual offences from the interpretation of a sexual offence in Section 31(1), and by adding a definition of serious harm in Section 31(3). More restrictive treatment for sexual offenders, however, recurred in another Government amendment which became Section 44 of the Act. This section provided for a longer period of supervision after release, up to the end of the full sentence rather than the three-quarters point, in the case of sexual offenders where the court so ordered.

X

For some policies the 1991 Act was a culmination. The restrictions on the use of imprisonment, the criteria for the length of custodial sentences, the extended range of community sentences, the rationalization of fines, the reform of parole, an improvement in the rules governing the giving of evidence by children in criminal proceedings,

---

[92] *Parl. Debates*, HL, 529 (5th ser.), cols. 560–1, 4 June 1991.
[93] Government amendments were also influenced by representations made direct to Home Office officials, including proposals for the redrafting of clauses 1 and 2 by Dr D. A. Thomas, a leading authority on sentencing practice (see n. 109 below).

and the contentious issue of the responsibilities of parents or guardians, had been long in the making. Others had come to the boil over the months while the legislation was going through Parliament. The mandatory life sentence and the release procedures for life prisoners were hardly new issues, but they had been given fresh impetus by the judgment of the European Court of Human Rights and the Lords' Select Committee. Contracting out was essentially a political rather than a penal policy, and one that caught a late tide. The remanding of juveniles to prison, acknowledged in the White Paper as being unsatisfactory, was ended in principle as a result of the publicity surrounding the tragic suicides of three fifteen-year-old boys, as well as other incidents of self-injury, although it would be some years before the local authorities could provide enough secure accommodation to contain all juveniles on remand.

Continued resistance by the Probation Service towards curfew orders monitored by electronic tagging, seen by some probation officers as the last punitive straw, combined with high costs and technological unreliability meant that this part of the Act was not brought into effect at the same time as the other community orders.[94] Of far wider application was a novel provision tucked away under the heading 'Miscellaneous' in Part V of the Act. Although camouflaged by the description 'Information for financial and other purposes' Section 95 was the result of concern which had been expressed about the alleged discrimination against ethnic minorities in the criminal justice system. In future the Secretary of State will be required to publish information annually, to the courts and others engaged in the administration of criminal justice, for the purpose of helping them to discharge their duty to avoid discrimination on racial or other improper grounds.

The Section had a curious provenance. During the summer of 1990, Home Office officials were beginning to hear criticism that

---

[94] Sections 12 and 13 were excluded from the Commencement Order which brought most of the sentencing provisions of the Act into force on 1 Oct. 1992. Less resolute than his predecessors while the Bill was before Parliament, the Minister of State, Michael Jack, later informed the House of Commons that current spending priorities did not permit any early introduction of the arrangement for monitoring curfew orders under the Criminal Justice Act 1991. Before determining the way forward, he intended to 'review and assess the operation of existing community penalties as a whole in the new context created by the Act'. *Parl. Debates*, HC, 215 (6th ser.), col. WA 814, 11 Dec. 1992.

the proposals in the White Paper, which had been published in February, would be discriminatory in their effect on members of ethnic minorities. It was contended that black people in particular would be excluded from the benefits of the shift towards community sentences by a systematic discrimination against them which existed at the early stages of the process: arrest, bail, and pre-sentence reports, each of which, especially the last, would be more relevant than ever under the Act.[95] To tease out these criticisms one of Faulkner's last acts as Head of the Criminal Division was to hold a three-day conference with members of the ethnic minority communities. The main conclusion to emerge was the desirability of some kind of statutory provision, the actual form of which would have to be worked out. Officials reported accordingly. Their report caused consternation in the Department, both to ministers, who shied away from action on political grounds, and to the Legal Advisers, including the draftsman, who were alarmed at the implication that discrimination could exist in the legal process or that the courts be capable of it. Intensive external lobbying followed. The Commission for Racial Equality had a meeting with Patten, and the Labour Party pressed hard for the inclusion of a new clause. There was still no agreement on any wording.

In the meantime, arguments had been gathering speed on a separate but familiar track, indeed a main line of Government policy, to the effect that the courts, as well as the operational services, should have more regard to the cost of the decisions taken in their own and other parts of the system. The outcome was an interdepartmental decision to include in the Bill a provision requiring the Secretary of State to disseminate information enabling 'persons engaged in the administration of criminal justice' to become aware of the financial implications of what they were doing. With considerable ingenuity, it was to this opaque clause that the anti-discrimination provision was joined by way of amendments in the Commons.

Racial discrimination is always a sensitive Parliamentary issue,

---

[95] Home Office research on sentencing in the Crown Court had shown that black defendants plead not guilty more frequently than white defendants. As a result, if they were found guilty and sentenced to custody disproportionately fewer of them had the benefit of having a pre-sentence report considered by the court before being sentenced. P. Drew, (1992) 86 *Prison Service Journal* 3. For a fuller treatment, see Roger Hood (with G. Cordovil), *Race and Sentencing*, A Study in the Crown Court, Clarendon Press, Oxford, 1992, pp. 150–60.

with the views of some assertive Conservative members diametri-
cally opposed to Labour's inclination to legislate. Patten handled
it skilfully, both in Standing Committee and again on the floor of
the House on Report. He argued that, while allegations of racial
bias by police officers or any others in the criminal justice system
certainly called for investigation, the best way forward was to
commission detailed surveys of the problem, since the data already
collected did not uniformly support the claims of bias.[96] As a
Parliamentary solution the resulting provision was adroit, if inel-
egant. But as a legislative response to an embryonic challenge,
pregnant with significance for the future, to the legitimacy and
integrity of the institutions of criminal justice it was pitiably
deficient.

XI

How will all this zeal in law-making bear upon the steady rise in
law-breaking as indicated by the consistently upward trend of
recorded crime? By the end of 1991, a total of 5.3 million notifiable
offences were recorded by the police, 16% more than the previous
year.[97] A large upward jump of 17% was similarly experienced in
1990. These increases compared with an average annual percentage
rate of increase throughout the 1980s of 5.4%.[98] There was widespread disquiet about offending by young people, especially when
offences were committed on bail, and by what had all the features
of an epidemic of motor crime. New and disturbing evidence was
coming to light about the extent of violence in the home.[99] Domestic

[96] Section 95(1). See *Blackstone's Guide to the Criminal Justice Act 1991*, p. 7.
[97] Home Office, *Statistical Bulletin*, 2/92.
[98] The average concealed some marked variations from year to year. See Home
Office, *Criminal Statistics, England and Wales, 1990* (Cm. 1935), HMSO, London,
1992, Table 2.1, p. 40.
[99] Information recorded by the police indicated that domestic violence as a
proportion of all offences of violence against the person rose from 10% in 1985 to
15% in 1989 (ibid., Table 2F, p. 36). Domestic violence against women accounted
for 32% of such offences in 1990. British Crime Survey findings likewise suggested
that domestic assaults increased significantly between 1981 and 1987. Both statistics
are affected by a greater willingness on the part of victims to admit to such incidents,
and to report them to the police. In 1981 about a fifth of women who suffered
domestic assaults said they had reported them to the police, whereas by 1987 half
of them said they had. See L. Davidoff and L. Dowds, 'Recent Trends in Crimes of
Violence against the Person in England and Wales', Home Office Research and
Planning Unit, *Research Bulletin*, 1989, pp. 11–17.

burglary, and the fear of intruders, blighted the lives of large
numbers of people.

The Permanent Secretary at the Home Office was right to point
out:

The history of public administration in this country over much of the last
thirty years has often been one of disappointment that the energy and
imagination which have under successive governments been put into
drafting new legislation or designing new structures and new administrative
systems have not seemed to have produced the results expected from
them.[100]

Such disappointment can arise from several causes. An unfounded
belief in the ability of legislation to change attitudes and behaviour
leading to crime can mean that expectations are pitched too high.
There is a growing belief on the part of criminologists, although
not yet widespread amongst legislators, that laws as they are
enforced by the criminal justice system are unlikely to change
offending behaviour to any great extent. In this context the emphasis
on penal policies designed to 'control' crime is misplaced. Only
when there is a convergence between informal mores and formal
policies will the pattern change.[101]

That said, public officials, and those who work alongside them,
have to do their best to make legislation work in the way intended
by government. There are many impediments in their way.
Insufficiently thorough preparation, too many changes of direction,
and faulty management information systems, are the main factors
which combine to hamper the sustained effort and commitment
that is needed to make a reality of new policies. Neither the effort
nor the commitment can be taken for granted. They have to be
worked at, by government and by the leadership of the institutions
and services which make up the system of criminal justice. The
process is weasrisome and services which are independent of each
other, sometimes fiercely so: the judiciary, the magistracy, the

[100] *Developing Policies and Practice*, address by Sir Clive Whitmore to a Criminal
Justice Conference held at Shrigley Hall, Cheshire, 12–17 Jan. 1992.
[101] H. L. A. Hart's felicitous description of how accepted social morality and
wider moral ideals permeate the legal system has not been bettered: 'The law of
every modern state shows at a thousand points the influence of both the accepted
social morality and wider moral ideals. These influences enter into law either
abruptly and avowedly through legislation or silently and piecemeal through the
judicial process.' *The Concept of Law*, Clarendon Press, Oxford, 1961, p. 119.

police, the Crown Prosecution Service, the Prisòn and Probation Services may not all be pulling in the same direction. Although central government does not share its functions of promoting legislation and authorizing public expenditure with the criminal justice services, it is vital that the policies approved by Parliament are not seen as being solely vested in government. Some sharing of a sense of ownership is necessary if the objectives are to be accomplished.

Yet it is not always possible to discern exactly what the Government of the day actually does intend to achieve by criminal justice legislation. Objectives are not static; they change according to the differing styles of successive ministers and how they react to the political climate around them. Events beyond their control can affect policies while legislation is in preparation, as was evident with the fluctuations in the prison and remand populations. Ministers come and ministers go, and it is understandable that they should proclaim their intentions differently when addressing audiences with such markedly different interests and viewpoints as party supporters, the judiciary, or penal reform groups. Nevertheless the practice of adjusting the message too readily to the presumed outlook of the audience does nothing to facilitate that single-minded projection which is the precursor of changing public opinion.

The origins of the 1991 Act are mapped in the frontispiece. The objectives between 1987 and 1989 were clearly enough stated. Hurd took pains to communicate a consistent message to a variety of audiences, including the most difficult of all for a Tory Home Secretary. When addressing the Conservative Party Conference in October 1989 he made few, if any, compromises in a speech that was well received.[102] Looking back, his policy aims can be abridged like this:

- to resolve the muddles (his word) obscuring the principles and aims of sentencing;

[102] 'Our sentencing system has become muddled, and many of our fellow citizens lack the confidence which they should have in the decisions of our criminal courts. It is not the fault of the courts. They administer the system which Parliament has given them. A system added to and amended piecemeal over the years. We need to make better sense of sentencing. I shall be publishing detailed proposals soon, and the guiding principle is plain. Every convicted criminal should receive his just deserts in the severity and length of his sentence.' Conservative Party, *Conference News*, 191/89, p. 7.

- to remove some of the anomalies which had grown up in the parole system, and to update it more generally;
- to provide the courts with a wider and more demanding range of community-based sentences, convincingly administered, which held out the promise of reducing offending more effectively than the often pointless, and sometimes corrupting, experience of imprisonment;
- to reduce the prison population, and its underlying rate of growth, in order to achieve greater stability in the prison system, and to limit the costly public expenditure on its expansion.

After the arrival of Waddington, other objectives began to emerge from ministerial decisions on the shape and content of the Bill, most obviously the addition of the provisions enabling, even encouraging, the courts to deal more severely with offenders convicted of crimes of sex or violence. This objective had then to be harmonized with the clarity and consistency aimed for in the first item of Hurd's catalogue. As the Bill progressed, there was a gradual toning down of the last of the original aims, although the reasoning of the Leeds Castle meeting in 1987 still remained as topical as ever.

Fulfilling the original intentions underlying the 1991 Act will be made more doubtful because of the neutralization that has occurred. A sufficiently recognizable structure endures, however, to identify the steps which must be taken. First of all, it is clear that any material diversion from custody towards community sentences will depend in large measure on the professional reorientation of the Probation Service. On it will fall the burden of providing the mandatory pre-sentence reports and the supervision of most community sentences.[103] Reconciling the twin roles of the probation officer as the friend of the pathologically weak and as the instrument of punishment will be an uphill task. It will not be done unless adequate resources of manpower, money, and training are forthcoming.[104] Professional leadership, too, will be decisive, and here

---

[103] It was estimated that an extra 20,000 pre-sentence reports each year will be required for the purposes of assisting the courts to decide on the most suitable method of dealing with offenders. In July 1991 over 150,000 offenders were under supervision by fifty-five probation services in England and Wales. Information from M. J. Ward, Association of Chief Officers of Probation, letter of 8 May 1992.

[104] Central government support for Probation Service expenditure in 1992/3 was estimated at £290 million, an increase of nearly 26% over the 1990/1 out-turn figures. The provision allowed for 560 more staff in 1992/3, the majority of whom were intended to provide for the implementation of the Criminal Justice Act. *Parl.*

the appointment of one of the most respected chief probation officers in the country as HM Chief Inspector of Probation is a good omen.[105] Properly supervised community-based programmes, accepted by the courts, the police, and the public are the foundation stones for the policy of punishment in the community.

Equally important is the need for the sentencing principles and detailed provisions of the Act to be grasped and accepted by the courts and the legal profession, including the Crown Prosecution Service. As soon as the Act reached the Statute Book training for sentencers and court staff became a priority. Once it has come into effect the Court of Appeal can be expected to begin to develop a jurisprudence arising from its judgments on individual cases. The youth court, and the principles it should apply, will need special attention, as will the relationship between the court, the Probation Service, and the Social Services.

Contemporaneously, the closer identification and working of the agencies of criminal justice which had been the first recommendation of Lord Justice Woolf's report, was beginning to take shape. A Criminal Justice Consultative Council, at first under the chairmanship of the Permanent Secretary at Home Office, was set up in late 1991. It consisted of eighteen members, including the Permanent Secretaries of the Department of Health and the Lord Chancellor's Department, the Metropolitan Police Commissioner, the Director General of the Prison Service, a Lord Justice of Appeal,[106] and the Acting Director of the Crown Prosecution Service. At the inaugural meeting on 15 January 1992, the intention was affirmed to provide a forum in which issues affecting the collective operation of the

Debates, HL, 537 (5th ser.), col. WA 26, 19 May 1992. Of the additional numbers, 378 would be in probation officer grades, with forty-four ancillary staff and 138 others. While the settlement was generally welcomed by the Chief Officers of Probation, they believed that the demand would be greater because of the intensity of supervision called for when the more serious offenders were dealt with by way of community sentences. Extra posts were also needed for co-ordinators working at the courts and with other agencies to assist in diverting mentally disordered offenders from the criminal justice process. Letter from the Association of Chief Officers of Probation, 15 May 1992.

[105] Graham Smith, Chief Probation Officer of the Inner London Probation Service since 1981, the largest in the country, assumed his duties on 1 June 1992. He was Chairman of the Association of Chief Officers of Probation in 1989/90.

[106] Lord Justice Farquharson, who succeeded Lord Justice Glidewell as Chairman of the Judicial Studies Board on 1 Apr. 1992. A Judge of the High Court of Justice, Queen's Bench Division, 1981–9; Lord Justice of Appeal, 1989– .

system of criminal justice could be discussed by senior representatives of the operational services.[107] The status of those attending is crucial, since any council lacking the power to make decisions will be unable to alter the course of events and will soon degenerate into a talking shop. It is only if its members have authority to take decisions in their own hierarchical services that the Council will be effectual.

The preliminaries were inhibited by Lane's objections to judicial involvement. Despite Woolf's recommendation that 'a very senior judge' representing the Lord Chief Justice should chair the Council,[108] and that a resident or senior judge of a large Crown Court complex should do the same at each of the area committees, Lane vetoed the participation of judges (including the circuit bench) in the work of the area committees. He was not willing to go any further than agreeing to the inclusion of a Lord Justice of Appeal as a member, but not as chairman, of the Council. His successor took a different view, and shortly after his appointment Lord Taylor informed the Permanent Secretary at the Home Office that he was in favour of judicial chairmanship both of the Council and of the twenty-four area committees. Whitmore agreed with alacrity, and new arrangements with Farquharson as chairman were formally approved by the Home Secretary, the Lord Chancellor, and the Attorney General in June 1992.

XII

Intense activity was under way during the early months of the year to prepare the courts for the new sentencing regime. The Criminal Committee of the Judicial Studies Board organized a comprehensive series of seminars for circuit judges and Recorders at which the rationale and requirements of the Act were expounded by the

[107] The terms of reference of the Criminal Justice Consultative Council are: to promote better understanding, co-operation, and co-ordination in the administration of the criminal justice system; in particular by (1) considering reports about developments in and affecting criminal justice; (2) considering other information about the operation of the system; and (3) overseeing the arrangements for Special Conferences; but excluding consideration of individual cases.
[108] *Prison Disturbances April 1990* (Cm. 1456), HMSO, London, 1991, pp. 21, 262 and 264.

Board's studies consultant, Dr David Thomas,[109] and other speakers. Newly appointed judges, Recorders, and Assistant Recorders attended induction courses with a similar scope, and explanatory seminars on the Act were organized for every circuit. Publications were circulated and a computer programme devised by Dr Thomas was prepared for the technologically minded.

The judiciary and the magistracy, advised by their clerks, must be ready from 1 October 1992 to sentence every convicted offender appearing before every criminal court in England and Wales in accordance with the provisions of the 1991 Act. It is a huge and demanding commitment, calling for familiarity with the contents of a strange and complex statute, and an awareness of the discipline which it imposes on sentencing decisions. Many of the criteria are familiar, although some are entirely novel.[110] It is not good enough for sentencers to claim that, in the exercise of their present discretion, the same ground is traversed and the same questions asked and answered in their own minds. Often they will be, but it would be surprising if there was uniformity in the approach adopted by the large number of sentencers who are not required to explain the reasoning lying behind their conclusions.

With the *Bulletin* of the Judicial Studies Board[111] and other instructional material to hand, sentencers are reminded that no longer is there one regime for the sentencing of young offenders and another for adults. All custodial sentences are to be subject to the same statutory restrictions. In brief, a custodial sentence may only be passed if one of three conditions is satisfied. These are: that the offender has refused to give his consent to a community sentence; that he has committed a violent or sexual offence, irre-

[109] A Fellow of Trinity Hall and Reader in Criminal Justice at Cambridge, Dr D. A. Thomas is a Main Board member of the Judicial Studies Board and sits on its Criminal Committee. He is author of the indispensable compendium, *Current Sentencing Practice*, Sweet and Maxwell, London, 1982, and editor of the *Criminal Appeal Reports (Sentencing)*.

[110] The most important innovations are the restriction to two offences only in considering if their seriousness justifies either a custodial or a community sentence, and the power to 'top up' the length of a custodial sentence in cases of violent or sexual offences.

[111] *Bulletin* No. 3 of the Judicial Studies Board, Lord Chancellor's Department, 1991, was a special edition devoted to the sentencing changes brought about by the Criminal Justice Act 1991. The factual details in the summary which follows are drawn from this source. The Home Office has also printed a general guide to the Act and some further guidance on specific aspects. For a critical analysis, see a special issue of the *Criminal Law Review* [1992] 229–87.

spective of its seriousness, and only a custodial sentence would be
adequate to protect the public from serious harm from him; and
that the offence, or the combination of the offence and one other
offence associated with it, is so serious that only a custodial sentence
can be justified. Pre-sentence reports in writing replace the existing
social inquiry reports prepared by the Probation Service, and must
be obtained and considered before the court decides that either of
the criteria for imprisonment are satisfied.

If the offender is, or appears to be, mentally disordered, the court
must obtain and consider a medical report before passing a custodial
sentence, with the exception of one fixed by law. Here, once again,
we see the consequences of the inflexibility of the mandatory
sentence of life imprisonment for murder; in this instance, the
inability of the court to make a hospital order where it would be
justified on medical evidence for any other offence. Whenever a
court decides that a custodial sentence is required it must state in
open court which of the conditions justifying custody is satisfied.
The only exception is where the offender has refused his consent to
a community order. It must also explain to the offender in ordinary
language why it is passing a custodial sentence on him.

The Act sets out specific criteria governing the length of custodial
sentences and the imposition of any form of community penalty.
Two of these, the combination order and the curfew order (if
implemented), are new. No community sentence may be passed
unless the offence, or the combination of the offence and one other
offence associated with it, is serious enough to warrant such a
sentence. Although the Act contains definitions of sexual and
violent offences and serious harm in the context of protecting the
public from an offender convicted of a violent or sexual offence,
many of the interpretations of the degree of seriousness necessary
to warrant either a custodial or a community sentence, and its
length, or the restrictions on liberty inherent in a community order,
will remain a matter for the individual judgment of the sentencer.

Neither the judge nor the bench need to have any reason to fear
that they will be relegated to the status of a technician, simply
fitting a pre-ordained penalty, designed by government and adapted
and approved by Parliament, to the circumstances of the individual
before the court. Reconciling persistent offending behaviour with
the proper sentence for the offence (or offences) before the court
calls for a balance between statutory guidance and judicial dis-

cretion. The borderline will never be static, but consistency to a set of principles embodied in a publicly accessible and reasoned legal framework, applicable to all sentencers and all offenders, must be an aim worth pursuing in any system of criminal justice deserving the name.

Proportionality in sentencing is essentially about fairness. Levels of penalty can be adjusted either downwards (as most desert theorists favour)[112] or upwards. Variations result from political decisions, and are always prone to be influenced by the intensity of public opinion. Fairness, of course, has all manner of meanings depending on the standpoint of the observer. Apart from those directly affected by the consequences of a crime: the offender and his associates; the victim, his friends, and his family; the police; the courts; and the Probation Service; there is the wider question, raised by representatives of racial minorities in 1990/1, of how punishment can be fair in a society that is not itself equitable. A study of the origins and passage of a particular statute is not the place to pursue these large and disturbing questions. But one assertion can be made. It is that the notion of fairness, whether in the sentencing of an individual offender or in the functioning of the various institutions which make up the penal system, is fundamental to the way we regard criminal justice. As faith in deterrence, incapacitation, and rehabilitation has waxed and waned we are left with one lifebelt to clutch. The name it carries is fairness.

Important as the implementation of a statute is, and however resolute the effort and commitment to see it through, it can only build on what Parliament has enacted. Even making every allowance for what Hurd's successors saw as the political inhibitions on their freedom of action, it is hard to avoid the conclusion that the cutting edge of what could have been a bolder and less confusing advance in penal policy was blunted. In the event, neither Waddington nor Baker survived in the Government after the General Election of April 1992. The Act for which they had shared ministerial responsibility, although not for its original conception, deserves support as a move in the right direction. But the tactic has been that of grandmother's footsteps, two steps forward and one back. It need not have been so.

---

[112] See Andrew von Hirsch's chapter on 'The Politics of Just Deserts' in his forthcoming book *Censure and Sanctions*, Clarendon Press, Oxford.

Index

NOTE: All references are to England and Wales unless otherwise stated.

Evans, Timothy 82 and n
evidence
  children, of 205–6, 411
  fraud trials, in 205
  unfairly obtained 191
executive: judiciary, boundary with 26
extradition
  definition of 196
  European Convention on 196–7
  law, changes in 196–7
  procedure 196
  reform of law 195

Faithfull, Baroness 169–70
Farquharson, Lord Justice 321, 323, 463n, 464
Faulkner, David ix–x, 8, 14n, 212–13, 215, 224 and n, 231, 243–4, 250–1, 458
Ferrers, Earl 408n, 409, 427n, 429
films: obscene publications 130–1
Financial Management Initiative 210 and n
fines
  means-related 410
  parents' responsibility to pay 235
firearms offences: penalties for 122
Fisher, Sir Henry 126
Fitzgerald, Edward 324
Forbes, Mr Justice 317
Fox, Sir Lionel 76
Franks, Sir Oliver (Lord Franks) 34 and n, 35
Fraud Trials Committee 195
Fry, Margery 63, 71 and n, 107, 110

Gardiner, Gerald (Lord Gardiner) 36–7, 86n, 95–7, 97n, 98, 102, 123n, 131, 332, 369
Gardner, Sir Edward 6n, 114, 288, 393
Garel-Jones, Tristan 137
general elections: manifestos 19
Gibbens, Dr T. C. N. 100n, 102
Glenarthur, Lord 409
Glidewell, Lord Justice 250, 321–3, 463n
Goddard, Lord 68 and n
Goodhart, Professor A. L. 125n, 357 and n
Gowers, Sir Ernest 67n
Green, Sir Allan 42n
Greenway, John 420–2

Griffiths, James 358–60
Griffiths, Lord 317, 434
gross indecency: private prosecution for 25
Group 4 Securitas 288, 302 and n
Gunnell, Edward 351–4

Hailsham of St Marylebone, Lord 15 and n, 33 and n, 37n, 111 and n, 112 and n, 119–20, 178, 260, 328, 330, 331n, 334, 435, 437, 446
Hall Williams, J. E. 86n, 285n
Hanley, Jeremy 288
hard labour: abolition 64
Harris of Greenwich, Lord 7n, 331n, 334, 335
Hart, H. L. A. 460n
Hattersley, Roy 188, 190, 291, 405, 416, 418, 442
Havel, Vaclav 401
Havers, Sir Michael (Lord Havers) 183, 288, 331n, 435
Hawser, Lewis 127
Head, Michael 212
Heath, Edward 103, 113 and n, 114–17, 119
Heathcoat-Amory, Derick (Viscount Amory) 48n, 101 and n
Hennessy, Sir James 156, 275n
Herrnstein, R. J. 161 and n
Heseltine, Michael 407, 419, 440
Hetherington, Sir Thomas 206
Heuston, R. F. V 95n
Higgins, Dr Rosalyn 370
Higgins, Terence 370
Hindley, Myra 25–6
Hoare, Sir Samuel (civil servant) 365 and n, 367
Hoare, Sir Samuel (minister) *see* Templewood, Viscount
Hogg, Douglas 201, 215, 220, 288, 341n, 409, 421
Hogg, Quintin *see* Hailsham of St Marylebone, Lord
Hollis, Christopher 6n, 48n, 85n
Home Office
  advice, sources of 93
  cautious nature of 12–13
  Criminal Justice Act 1991, publications linked to 249
  criminal law, responsibility for 39
  day-to-day routine of 12
  financial restraints 13

Royal Commissions (*Cont.*)
  Capital Punishment, on 36, 67 and n,
    68n, 83, 87
  Criminal Procedure, on 13, 126–7,
    185–6, 204–5
  legislation stemming from 3
  Penal System, on the 93, 100–3, 146
  police, on the 125
  table of 128–9
  Thatcher's premiership, none
    during 130
Royal Prerogative of Mercy 312
Ruggles-Brise, Sir Evelyn 75, 77
Rumbold, Angela 79, 409, 419–21, 423–
  4, 443
Rutherford, Andrew 281n
Ryssdal, Rolv 377n, 383n, 387n

Safer Cities *see* crime prevention
Salisbury, Marquess of 62n
St Johnston, Colonel Eric 116 and n
Scarman, Sir Leslie (Lord Scarman) 23,
  97 and n, 187, 191, 193, 270n, 317,
  389
Scotland: murder, definition of 337
Scrivener, Anthony 324
Securicor 288, 302
Sedley, Stephen 324, 396n
Select Committee on Murder and Life
  Imprisonment
  all party support for 334
  chairman 335
  meetings 336
  members 335
  murder, consideration of
    definition 337–9
  proposal for 332–3
  release decisions, consideration
    of 341–5
  remit 336
  report 337, 431–3
  support for 334
Sellers, Lord Justice 71n, 98
Senior Liaison Committee 41–2
sentences
  appeal against 27
  burglary, for 410
  community penalties 246, 410
  Court of Appeal, increase by 222
  custodial
    length, criteria for 466
    regime for 465–6
    restrictions on 428

sentences (*Cont.*)
  custodial (*Cont.*)
    policies 242
    pre-sentence reports, need for 242,
      410, 466
    scheme for 241
    use of 456
  fixed 27, 54–5
    see also life imprisonment
  lenient
    controversy over 178
    criticism of 26–7
  life imprisonment *see* life
    imprisonment
  maximum 140
  partly suspended 130, 132–5,
    172–3
  suspended
    introduction of 109, 121
    mandatory 110 and n
    use of 110
  topping-up 253, 451, 454–5
  toughness, call for 237
sentencing
  appellate review 174
  Conservative approach to 221
  council or commission, proposal
    for 28, 405–7, 416, 428–30
  Criminal Justice Bill 1990, framework
    in 404, 409
  guide-line judgments 174, 175 and n,
    176
  judiciary, consultation with 250–1
  just deserts, principle of 165n, 241,
    450–1
  more severe sentences, power to
    pass 451, 454–5
  magistrates' court, powers of 455
  new regime, preparation for 464–5
  previous convictions, handling of 251
  proportionality, principle of 165n,
    450, 467
  resources for 251
  training 174, 463–5
  twin track policy 221–3
  White Paper (1990) 243, 245–6
  young offenders 240
sentencing policy
  Labour Party 28, 414–16
  territory of 27
serious arrestable offence:
  definition 189
Serious Fraud Office: setting up 29